AF228209

NIGHTSTALKERS

NIGHTSTALKERS

The Wright Project and the 868th Bomb Squadron
in World War II

RICHARD PHILLIP LAWLESS

CASEMATE

Philadelphia & Oxford

Published in the United States of America and Great Britain in 2023 by
CASEMATE PUBLISHERS
1950 Lawrence Road, Havertown, PA 19083, USA
and
The Old Music Hall, 106–108 Cowley Road, Oxford OX4 1JE, UK

Hardback Edition: ISBN 978-1-63624-205-7
Digital Edition: ISBN 978-1-63624-206-4

A CIP record for this book is available from the British Library

Printed and bound in the Czech Republic by FINIDR s.r.o.

Typeset in India by Lapiz Digital Services.

For a complete list of Casemate titles, please contact:

Casemate Publishers (US)
Telephone (610) 853-9131
Fax (610) 853-9146
Email: casemate@casematepublishers.com
www.casematepublishers.com

Casemate Publishers (UK)
Telephone (0)1226 734350
Email: casemate-uk@casematepublishers.co.uk
www.casematepublishers.co.uk

Front cover: "868th Squadron B-24J *Lady June II* leads strike against Batavia, Dutch East
Indies" by Shigeo Koike whose work can be found at http://www.shigeokoike.com.

Contents

Prologue

A few minutes after 2200 on the night of 7 August 1945, an all-black U.S. Army Air Force (USAAF) B-24 Liberator bomber brought its four engines to maximum power, released its brakes and rumbled down the runway of Yontan Airfield on the recently captured island of Okinawa. The aircraft that broke its bonds with earth and lifted into the night sky was a very special airplane with a special crew undertaking a unique mission. Aboard were 11 young Americans under the command of Lieutenant Edward Mills Jr., and *Lady Luck II* was headed north toward Korea, then part of the Empire of Japan, to search for and confront Japanese forces. The United States and its allies had been at war with Japan since December 1941 and although this struggle was nearing its end, that end was still in doubt, and the fight still had to be taken to the enemy.

The day before, on 6 August, another U.S. warplane, the *Enola Gay*, had made a similar journey to Japan from Tinian Island and dropped an atomic weapon on the city of Hiroshima. The President of the United States, Harry S. Truman, had decided to do so to hasten the surrender of Japan, hoping to avoid the invasion of those Home Islands, an invasion that portended the deaths of hundreds of thousands on both sides.

Yet as the B-24 began its hunt that dark night, the Mills crew had no illusions that the end of the war might be at hand. Rather they, like all others similarly committed to seeing the conflict through to its end, assumed the war in the Pacific would last months longer, if not a year or more. All assumed that the final struggle would involve multiple invasions of the Japanese Home Islands and witness intense fighting like that so recently experienced in the capture of Okinawa. Forever unknown to the crew of this plane, the Japanese decision to surrender was only eight days away. But Lieutenant Mills and his crew would have their rendezvous with destiny that very night. And with that rendezvous, a multi-decade journey into the history of two nations—the United States of America and the Republic of Korea—would begin.

As the Mills crew reached its assigned search and attack area off the southern coast of Japanese-occupied Korea, their focus was on their mission—hunting and sinking Japanese shipping moving between Japan and Korea. A second special B-24 from the same unit—the 868th Bomb Squadron of the Thirteenth Air Force—flew a similar mission profile that night, also alone on its stealthy search for enemy shipping. A bit past one in the morning, the Mills's aircraft radar identified targets off the island of Namhae, near a major Japanese base at Yŏsu, and locked on to a ship to press home its attack. The enemy harbor came alive with searchlights and anti-aircraft guns that reached out to find and destroy the intruder as Mills banked and descended to attack altitude. His radar operator and bombardier armed the bombs tucked into the plane's belly and turned the delivery of those weapons over to their on-board computer. Bomb bay doors opened and prepared to deliver a lethal spread of ordnance on the enemy shipping below.

This was the 868th's first mission to this part of the Japanese empire and the fiftieth mission for this well-worn 868th "Snooper" bomber; its veteran crew had only seconds to live. The Mills crew simply disappeared, at least to the men of the 868th Squadron who were waiting for their return to base on Okinawa.

The squadron B-24 which flew a similar mission profile that evening, captained by Ed Mills's close friend Lieutenant Bob Ellingson, had radioed the Mills crew to wish his squadron mates "good hunting and best luck" just after midnight. An hour later, in the early morning, Ellingson waited at the pre-arranged meeting spot over the Sea of Japan, circling as long as his fuel allowed. He then turned back toward Okinawa to recover at Yontan Airfield at first light. In the war against Japan, the 868th had lost its last plane and crew in combat. The squadron would head home within weeks as the war ended, and America demobilized much of its military in its rush to embrace peace. The men of the 868th would not learn the fate of the 11 men of the Mills crew for 30 long years. But that same night, others would know their fate and embrace that crew to build their own history around them.

★ ★ ★

The night of 7 August 1945 began as a typical humid summer evening for the farmers and villagers of Namhae Island, but signs of monumental change were in the air. The Americans were coming. There had been rumors in the past months that Korea's Japanese colonial masters were being beaten and pushed back across the Pacific to the Imperial homeland. A liberation radio station from Free China, broadcasting the voice of Chinese leader Chiang Kai-shek and those of Korean government leaders in exile, promised that the end of Japanese rule was near. These broadcasts were monitored in back rooms in the village by Koreans who had one eye on the door as the Japanese military police and colonial constabulary sought out disloyal subjects. Although semi-isolated from the mainland, Namhae Island was near the city of Yŏsu, an important industrial and military port with a military airfield at Sacheon. The island and its inhabitants were subjects of Imperial Japan and had lived as such since the nation was forcibly annexed by Japan in 1910.

But now it all seemed true. In recent days, strange aircraft bearing unfamiliar insignia had ranged over Korea, seemingly attacking Japanese military installations and sinking shipping at will. These same vessels that the Americans were now striking and sinking had supplied the Japanese Home Islands with the farm and mineral wealth of Korea and Manchuria under the rubric of the Greater East Asia Co-Prosperity Sphere. And as the Allies sought to seal Japan off from its raw materials coming from southern Asia, the Korea–Japan sea link was still active, providing Japan proper with one of its last remaining economic and military lifelines. Even more importantly, Tokyo was calling home its Army units from Manchuria to prepare to meet the expected invasion of the Home Islands. Those critical men and materials were flowing through Korea, embarking in Yŏsu and other ports on the southern coast, for the short trip to Japan. Thus, on this night, the American aircraft which had come to Namhae was one of several efforts being made to cut the seaborne supply line that was reinforcing Japan.

It was now certain that the Americans were indeed coming, and it was finally possible for Koreans to silently hope that their 3000-year-old nation would again be free. America had pledged to Korea its liberation and freedom and it seemed that the 40-year colonial subjugation might end with Japan's defeat.

About an hour after midnight the sky around Namhae came alive. Japanese defenders surrounding Yŏsu opened a deafening barrage from their anti-aircraft weapons, tracers arcing through the night sky, seeking an aircraft that the villagers could hear but not see. They knew the plane was flying low across Yŏsu Bay and they assumed that it was seeking out the vessels that lay at anchor there to take on the war cargos that were destined for the Home Islands. Moments later, the ground shook and a crash of metal on rock resonated from the top of Mangun Mountain, a soaring peak that dominates the island. When explosions continued to rumble down from the mountain for several minutes, it was natural to assume that the attacking plane had either been shot down or collided with its peak.

Hours later, with the guns silent and the Japanese fighters returned to their airbase, the mountain could be seen emitting a dull glow, backlit by a fire that was spreading on the reverse slope of its peak. With all of the 500-pound bombs scattered from the B-24's shattered belly having detonated, the village gathered around one man to consider what it should do. A young pharmacist who had seen his older brother go to war two years before and die in Japanese Army service in Burma was certain of his obligation. He explained to the people of his village that an American plane had probably crashed at the mountain top, with men on board who had come to liberate Korea from Japan. The villagers of Namhae should climb to the location and see what could be done. In the pre-dawn hour, they began the trek up the mountain.

The villagers arrived at the crash scene shortly before the Japanese search party dispatched from the nearby Japanese Army base at Yŏsu made its appearance. The villagers found the scattered remnants of the plane still smoldering and the bodies of 11 868th airmen scattered about the crash area. The villagers carefully collected the human remains, dug shallow graves and covered them with rocks, planning to return the next day to conduct a proper Christian burial. Soon after, a Japanese Army party arrived and scoured the scene; they collected every scrap of the shattered aircraft and its equipment and carted these down the mountain. The remains of the aircraft were displayed as a trophy on the Japanese base on the mainland. Later that day, in the absence of the Japanese, the villagers returned to the crash site.

The village leader, Kim Duk-hung, was determined to create graves that would better protect the bodies of the dead, as he would later explain to the Japanese. On their first day at the crash site, Kim and others had removed and hidden personal identification from the bodies, an act which the Japanese belatedly discovered. The personal effects of the American crew were confiscated, and the villagers were marched off to the Yŏsu military base for interrogation, with Kim identified as the disloyal ringleader of the group. The other villagers were released but Kim was held and subjected to a prolonged interrogation by the military police. His fingers broken and his body exhausted, he was released weeks later when word of Japan's surrender rippled through the now-liberated Korea.

When Kim returned home to the village, he began a decades-long personal commitment to honor the sacrifice of the 11 airmen who rested at the top of Mount Mangun, or "Man Gun San" in Korean. The balance of the story of the dedication of the people of Namhae to the memory of the Mills crew is fittingly recounted in more detail in the Epilogue of this book for the reason that it completes the narrative of the Wright Project and the 868th Squadron. When they learned the details of that night on Namhae Island and its aftermath some three decades later, the veterans of the 868th Squadron were finally able to reconnect with their last missing crew. This closure allowed the veterans to extend their appreciation to the people of that village who had continued to honor the Mills crew at the very location where the 11 young Americans had died that humid August night in 1945.

Author's note

The narrative begins by tracing the evolution of the classified "Wright Project" as it was developed by the Massachusetts Institute of Technology's Radiation Laboratory for the Douglas B-18 Bolo bombers of the 1st Sea-Search Attack Group at Langley Field, Virginia, in 1942. The development of the low-altitude bombing concept and the pioneer electronic systems involved are described, as is the formation of the original 10-aircraft Wright Project as the first of three LAB-equipped units dispatched to combat in the Pacific. The arrival on Guadalcanal and the first combat missions of the unit in August 1943 are provided along with first-person accounts of these early missions and the fates of the aircrews and planes that flew them. The combat history of the squadron is traced as the unit, commissioned as the 868th Bombardment Squadron in January 1944, moved forward toward Japan and took on targets at Rabaul, Truk, Palau, the Dutch East Indies, Indochina and finally Korea and the Japanese Home Islands in August 1945. The storyline highlights the fates of individual crews and aircraft.

The manuscript is organized chronologically on a chapter-by-chapter basis. Several chapters contain a historical preface which places the individual missions described in the context of the broader Pacific war. Primacy is given to detailed descriptions of individual missions and the successes and losses of the squadron as it took on specific targets. The size of the unit (usually no more than 10 aircraft and crews) and the volume of the primary source material available have allowed the assembly of a comprehensive account in which several interesting missions are featured in detail. Appendices are provided which cross-reference individual aircraft and aircrews. The text is annotated, and an index is included as a reference aid.

The source material for this history comes predominantly from: U.S. Army Air Force official records including squadron monthly operational summaries; individual mission reports; unit and personnel orders; correspondence exchanged with individual squadron members, air and ground crew, during the period 1978–82; oral histories (tape recorded) at squadron reunion meetings; and photographs provided by the 868th Squadron Association and individual correspondents.

Beyond acknowledging the immense contribution of the more than 20 officers and men of the Dolan Group, the Wright Project, and the 868th Squadron who shared their experiences with me, I wish to express my gratitude to the fine individuals at Casemate Publishers who worked so hard to make this book possible. To Ruth Sheppard who championed *Nightstalkers* from the outset, and to Felicity Goldsack, who polished the text to its completion, I say "well done indeed!" On this side of the Atlantic, U.S. Army Colonel Barbara Springer (retired) was the essential organizer of my thoughts and applied her firm hand to every chapter.

Finally, to my wife, Mimi Janian Lawless, I will be ever grateful for your insights, encouragement, and devotion.

Introduction

The story of the "Wright Project" and the 868th Bomb Squadron in World War II deserves to be told. In one sense, it is the straightforward saga of young men fighting and often dying in the skies above the Pacific Ocean. In another sense, it is the narrative tale of technological innovation—microwave radar—further perfected to perform a specific mission and be successfully carried into combat. Through the men and aircraft of the 868th, one can follow the evolution of tactical airborne radar, from its humble beginning under the pressures of war that came to America's homeland in the immediate aftermath of Pearl Harbor, to its commitment to combat, and chart its success. The electronics systems of the 868th "Snoopers" not only contributed to America's victory in the Pacific but helped to elevate the United States Air Force to a position of postwar dominance with the advanced military technology that sustained the U.S. during the Cold War.

The 868th was a unique unit when it was dispatched from Langley Field, Virginia, as the Wright Project and first committed to combat in the Pacific Theater at Guadalcanal in August 1943. It could then boast America's newest suite of electronic equipment mated to 10 B-24 Liberator heavy bombers, each crewed by carefully selected and trained young airmen. The unit had been built by a dedicated group of innovative leaders, led by Lieutenant Colonel William "Bid" Dolan, initially organized into the 1st Sea-Search Attack Group to combat the German U-Boat threat ravaging the East Coast of the United States. The classified radar workshops of the Radiation Laboratory (Rad Lab) of the Massachusetts Institute of Technology (MIT) were enlisted to design and commission, on an expedited "crash project" basis, a special application of the electronic technologies that were only then in their infancy. The capability created by Rad Lab, working in cooperation with Dolan's specialized search and attack group, equipped men to hunt and fight in the dead of night in the Pacific.

In its two years of combat, the specially equipped B-24 unit served as an independent attack squadron of the Thirteenth Air Force, claiming its own place in history. In these actions, the 868th would experience the loss of many good men as the United States fought its way westward across the Pacific, to conclude that march only when Japan agreed to surrender terms in August 1945. Because the 868th was a unique unit that worked to perfect its night-stalking equipment in company with the tactics adapted to these special systems, the project and its successor squadron drew to its ranks men who were both leaders and innovators—pilots, aircrew, service personnel and technicians. Each of these individuals viewed the war through the eyes of men who had come of age during the Great Depression and were now embarked on what would be for many the most daunting and rewarding experiences of their lives.

The following chapters present a thread of aerospace history that begins soon after the attack on Pearl Harbor and extends through those early battles against the U-boats, the involvement of Rad Lab, the perfection of microwave airborne radar and the conceptualization of a system that would mate Air-to-Surface Vessel (ASV) radar to the B-24 airframe to create the Low Altitude Bombing system. The formation of the Wright Project that carried this new capability to war and the combat history of the successor 868th Squadron is charted here.

In discussing the technology, the aircraft, the tactics and the surrounding conflict that came together over the three-year period of 1942–45, one cannot ignore the human element. Wherever possible in this narrative, that aspect is highlighted as the essence of the tale, in part because many of these men who climbed into their aircraft to fly into the night sky to hunt the enemy did not survive the ordeal of the Pacific War. Those who were fortunate enough to return and build their lives anew, while enjoying all of the advantages that America provided, did not forget the sacrifice of those with whom they flew—men who perished when their aircraft went down and were consumed by the ocean. A good deal of this book is presented in the words of these survivors and that presentation is often quite personal and rich with emotion.

This book is possible, in large part, because those who were graced to return to their families and hometowns at the conclusion of the war recalled their experiences so well. Some 30 years after Victory over Japan Day, I was honored to be invited to a gathering of 868th Squadron veterans. By a quirk of chance, I had discovered, and I was able to convey, the fate of the last missing aircrew of this unit. I sought out the men who had waited in vain that August night in 1945 for the return of their friends and fellow warriors. I was asked to speak at their fourth reunion and helped to organize an outreach to a very different and very special group of people who inhabited a small island off the southern coast of Korea. These were humble villagers who had honored, in their own very special way over these many years, this last missing aircrew of 11 young Americans.

At the reunion, I was asked to compile a history of the Wright Project and the 868th, an undertaking I accepted and embarked upon with enthusiasm and with the best of intentions. Over the following years, I worked on this endeavor as I was able, but I was too often compelled by career and circumstance to put this assignment to the side. A full 75 years after the 868th flew its last combat mission and lost its last crew in combat, that task has been completed with this book. I hope I have done justice to these fine men and their wonderful machines and to the times in which these airmen served their nation so well.

To the degree possible, this book is a testimony to the efforts and sacrifices these men made so many decades ago. Almost all the men of the 868th have now gone to their final resting place. This book is therefore dedicated to all the American men and women who answered the call of their nation in World War II and came together to serve with pride and without complaint. Their efforts served to protect and advance the position of their great nation and to allow their children, my generation, to prosper in a free and dynamic society. To each I would say, "Well done and we thank you."

It is necessary to state what this narrative is not. I make no attempt to discuss or describe the vast panorama of the Pacific War, its themes and strategies, or even its defining personalities and events. These grander subjects are covered in great detail by authors whose works are referenced and recommended in this book. In a similar vein, this book does not portend to describe the B-24 Liberator in its many variations and deployments throughout all combat theaters in the great span of World War II. Dozens of publications devote themselves to this fine and storied aircraft and while this incredible airplane plays a central role in this book as the instrument mated to technology and forged in war, it is a supporting actor to the men involved.

Lastly, while the technology developed and deployed by the scientists and technicians at Rad Lab is central to this story, the full account of the contribution made by the men of these organizations is well told elsewhere in the detail these accomplishments deserve. I have tried to make this a tale about a wonderful collection of young men, courageous in their war and in their generation, and, in doing so, capture the essence of their experiences and sacrifices.

Richard Phillip Lawless
Great Falls, Virginia
October 2022

CHAPTER I

World War Comes to America and to "Bid" Dolan

January–May 1942

Pearl Harbor lights a fire

On Sunday morning 7 December 1941, a Japanese Navy air attack shattered a sleeping U.S. Pacific Fleet as it lay at rest in Pearl Harbor, Hawaii. Within hours, Germany joined Imperial Japan with a formal declaration of war against the United States of America and President Franklin Roosevelt and the U.S. Congress took America to war. Hitler's decision to declare war on the United States and begin active combat with submarine attacks on the U.S. East Coast presented a double blow to U.S. Army and U.S. Navy forces which were still in the early stages of organizing and expanding themselves for war.

Although Roosevelt and his military leaders had planned for the strong possibility of a U.S. entry into this war for more than two years, the suddenness of the Japanese onslaught and the precision of its execution caught American military leaders and planners ill-prepared and dazed. Preparations begun years before would not reach fruition for another year or more. Millions of men and women had to be enlisted and mobilized, scores of Army divisions had to be formed and trained, and badly needed ships were still on the building ways. Equally important, America's embryonic armaments industry had barely begun to retool its factories for the production of the tanks, ships and airplanes that would be required to carry the war and defeat the Axis enemies. These were desperate times and everywhere in the world, from Europe to North Africa to the Eastern Front in Russia and now in the Western Pacific, the allies of America were on the defensive. The outcome was very much in doubt and it would remain so for many long months to come.

In this turbulent period, one of the great leaders of the American military, Army Air Force General Henry "Hap" Arnold, had the foresight to recognize that mere numbers of men and planes would not be enough to win the war. He saw that the evolving technology of war would have to be mastered and deployed to counter the quality of the men, equipment and tactics that America and its allies faced in combat. The United Kingdom, well before Pearl Harbor and under secret agreements reached at the highest levels, had agreed to share its advances in new systems with America. This closely held transfer of technology included the critical components that made microwave radar possible. Once in hand, the challenge was to refine that capability and build around it systems that could be optimized for battle. Once optimized, these systems had to be adapted and deployed in fighting machines manned by crews who could employ the new capabilities to maximum advantage.

How microwave radar technology came to the United States and the incredible success America was able to build around this technology will be properly addressed in later chapters. The fact was that its potential was fully understood by Arnold and the team with which he surrounded himself. And while these men could not predict how this technology would evolve, they were determined to find a way to adapt and deploy it in combat, and to do so as quickly as possible. The Arnold "brain trust" was innovative and decisive and did not hesitate to utilize the imprimatur Arnold gave them to advance their priorities. Arnold also made it a point to replenish this group as the war moved forward. In these early months of war, several men stand out and we will meet many of them.

Lieutenant Colonel "Bid" Dolan gets the call

As the tide of war swept over America in the opening weeks of 1942, a low-profile but respected career U.S. Army Air Corps (USAAC)[1] lieutenant colonel named William C. Dolan was selected by Arnold's staff to organize and lead a special project that was still being defined. It was hoped that Dolan would find a path to utilize the new technologies that America was developing in its laboratories. The focus was on one technology above all others—radar. Known to all as "Bid," in February 1942, Dolan was plucked overnight from his command, ordered to proceed across the country on an unspecified mission and instructed not to ask questions until things were explained to him at his destination.

Wisconsin-born Dolan was not an engineer or a scientist and he could not claim a completed university education; he was a pilot's pilot, a man who was recognized as a premier "instrument man" who was able to master any aircraft he flew and get the best performance out of it. In every assignment to date, Dolan had approached each innovation brought into the Army Air Corps (AAC) as a tool of war, be that a new bombsight, an improved machine gun or a new bomber like the Martin B-26 Marauder he flew. In the months ahead in Boston, he would come to embrace radar as another tool of war, yet one which he realized held incredible potential. He understood that his job was to master this new technology and incorporate it into the airplanes that would win the war.

The weeks after Pearl Harbor found Bid Dolan assigned to the Fourth Air Force defending the U.S. West Coast where the USAAF was engaged in deploying additional units to defend against the anticipated Japanese attack on facilities there. One of these units was the 42nd Bombardment Group, a former Douglas B-18 Bolo unit that had been moved from its home base at Gowen Field in Boise, Idaho, to McChord Field in Seattle, Washington. This latter location, with the nearby factories of Boeing Aircraft Company, was considered a prime target for Japanese attacks. The men expected to deploy shortly to the Pacific or Alaska for immediate combat. But for some, combat would have to wait. The 42nd was then training with some of the first production versions of the B-26 Marauder medium bomber. This was a "hot ship" with unforgiving aerodynamic qualities and its early version would kill many a pilot. Dolan's squadron was up to the challenge and had begun to master the aircraft, and Dolan was eager to get his squadron into the fight.

Fate intervened on 16 February 1942 when the Fourth Air Force, reacting to a telex from USAAF Headquarters in Washington, D.C., published Special Order (SO) Number 22. The message ordered Dolan to select a seven-man group from the unit for a temporary duty assignment that would last no longer than 45 days. The SO further instructed Dolan to:

> Pick up one B-18A airplane of the 6th Reconnaissance Squadron at Municipal Airport, Sacramento and proceed in that airplane to San Antonio Air Depot, Duncan Field, Texas … for the necessary alterations, then to Municipal Airport, Boston, Massachusetts, reporting thereat to the Liaison Officer, Radiation Laboratory, Massachusetts Institute of Technology, Boston, for instruction.[2]

Apart from being told that the orders directing these movements had originated from the AAC Assistant Chief of the Materials Division and that unnecessary delays in transit would not be tolerated, the men involved did not have a clue as to what they were heading into. The five additional B-18s dispatched by Fourth Air Force Headquarters in San Francisco involved a total of 43 officers and men from 10 different squadrons. From the 6th Reconnaissance Squadron came Adam Breckenridge, Frank Reynolds and Leroy Tempest. The 16th Reconnaissance Squadron and the 48th Bomb Squadron sent Leo Foster and Francis Carlson respectively. John Scanlon, James Pope and Travis Boykin were dispatched from the 76th Bomb Squadron, while the 38th Squadron's Bill Foley, Robert Lehti and Crowell "Butch" Werner also made their way east, in company with John Zinn and Bill Walker of the 2nd Reconnaissance Squadron. These men, among others, were the original "Dolan Boys" and we will encounter many of them in the months and years ahead. This collection of 50 or so men and six aircraft would be among the first American airmen to advance the development and deployment of airborne radar for many of the tactical and strategic bombing applications used operationally in combat during World War II.[3]

At MIT's Radiation Laboratory (Rad Lab), the scientists were waiting for Dolan and his men. In many ways, the Rad Lab researchers had been working toward this day for two years and, in their own way, Rad Lab's time had come to join the war. What they had to offer the B-18 crews was a capability they explained as airborne ASV, in a version that Rad Lab had dramatically improved as an instrument of war. The story of how this system had come to be in a Rad Lab fast-track development program will be more fully told, but when it was first described to the Dolan crews, who were "all from Missouri" and conventional daylight bombers, they had their serious doubts.

A waiting engagement at Rad Lab

In Boston, the Dolan crews were immediately plunged into an intensive training course designed to familiarize them with the new world of radar and its capabilities, real or, as then, imagined. Crews were trained on mock-up systems as other Rad Lab technicians worked to install the first sets of equipment in the B-18s. As soon as the systems were ground tested and declared operational, the six crews began daily flights from Logan Field. Most of these crews were experienced night flyers. As "instrument men," they had been selected by Dolan because, in part, the equipment was new and crude and unpredictable. Night and instrument flying was a challenge for the best of pilots and asking them to rely on a new and unproven technology while maneuvering in the dark required a leap of faith that challenged several. But they were in the game with Dolan and had confidence in their abilities and Dolan's judgment that the prize was worth the risks undertaken.

In mid-March, while the Dolan group spent days in the classroom to learn the basics of radar and sat before a mock-up radar trainer, Rad Lab researchers assembled the first sets for installation in the B-18s that Dolan's group had flown into Boston. They worked in an unheated worse-for-wear National Guard hangar at Logan Field, bolted down the ASV boxes and antennas and prayed for the best. Bid Dolan took the first fully equipped B-18 ASV aircraft aloft, pronounced to his satisfaction that there might just be something to this project and then pushed for daily flights to test and refine the system. Beyond the performance of the ASV itself, Dolan focused on defining tactics for its operational use. In a test flight a few days later, with Rad Lab technicians on board to operate the ASV equipment, Dolan found a U.S. Navy aircraft that had been forced down at sea some 60 miles off the coast. Once pinpointed with the ASV system, Dolan's airplane was able to plot coordinates and direct a ship to rescue the downed airmen.

These training flights off the Massachusetts coast during March–April 1942 were unarmed and typically used U.S. Navy and merchant ships as their search and identification targets. The early days of still-imperfect operational skills and unreliable equipment produced a situation which one of the Dolan men, Lieutenant Jim Pope, recalled, "We only knew that we had found a target. It could have been a carrier, a destroyer or a whale." Weather was also recognized as a huge problem for the existing ASV system as storm-reflected signals cluttered the radar screens. However, once the ASV operators gained experience in reading the weather on their scopes, overall performance improved and, to the delight of pilots, the operators' growing mastery allowed the pilots to fly around adverse weather rather than through it. It was a time of learning, of sharing ideas and experiences and trusting "radar."

As his men trained, Dolan became a convert to the new religion of airborne radar and embraced its application in ASV for sub hunting as his mission. He realized that airborne radar stood conventional daylight, fair-weather bombing on its head. He saw that ASV and airborne radar generally opened opportunities for precise night and foul-weather bombing that few of his colleagues realized existed or could even imagine. He sought time in the air with the equipment, making it a point to fly the first mission with each B-18 that was declared ready for testing with its installed ASV to satisfy himself that each aircraft had fine-tuned its new equipment. He knew these first systems were crude and were prone to in-flight failure but became convinced that the underlying concept was a winner. His crews also recognized that once the technical bugs were worked out, and the crews became comfortable with these delicate early systems, ASV would allow hunter/killer search aircraft to cover a much greater area in a typical mission, find surfaced U-boats in the dead of night, and attack and sink them.

During an April nighttime training mission, Dolan's aircraft identified a target which he assumed would be a U.S. Navy destroyer on patrol. Instead, as his aircraft passed low over the contact, he was shocked to discover a surfaced U-boat refueling from a "milch cow" supply submarine. He was that night, as was the case in all missions flown from Boston, on an unarmed training flight, but this brush with the enemy brought home the efficacy of the ASV-equipped bomber. Had his trusty B-18 been armed, the U-boat and its companion submarine would have been dead meat for a rack of bombs or depth charges.

These early weeks at Boston and with Rad Lab also demonstrated that once the armed ASV-enabled patrols began, the U-boats would be denied the haven of night. The certainty of detection and attack while cruising on the surface to recharge their batteries and hunt for targets at higher speed, permitted by surface running under diesel power, would drive the U-boats underwater and keep them there. German submarine commanders would be forced to seek less-contested waters as losses grew and calculations of self-preservation encouraged wise commanders to hunt where the ASV predators were not overhead.

Dolan, as the project manager responsible to Army Air Corps headquarters in Washington, D.C., reported regularly to Hap Arnold's staff there, with Arnold continuing to take a personal interest in the progress of the Rad Lab efforts. Arnold's brain trust of planners and managers saw the Dolan ASV project as but one element, albeit the first, that promised a far broader use of airborne radar in the strategic bombing campaigns that were then only being conceptualized at the headquarters level.

Rad Lab and its parent organization were suggesting with confidence that they could develop and deploy more advanced radar systems in the coming months; many of these confident assertions were influencing decisions being made on aircraft production and force planning. Arnold's experts wanted to be certain that these claims were founded in reality and were not, in the doubting lexicon of the day, mere "science projects" advocated by researchers who were incapable of applying their theories or test systems to machines of war.

During these weeks, Dolan managed to fly the test missions and still maintain a steady flow of reporting from Boston to his senior levels. As his commentary flowed into Arnold's team, respect for the project manager continued to grow. In overseeing the initial four months of the ASV project, Bid Dolan would earn himself a well-deserved promotion to the rank of full colonel and solidify his position as the USAAF's "go-to" man to manage the broad range of radar projects that were then in the Rad Lab pipeline.

Support for the Dolan Initiative

Crucial to Bid Dolan's ability to advocate and sell his confidence in the ASV system then being tested in Boston, and the potential offered by radar to Army Air Force bombing in future systems, was the support he received from three men in whom Arnold had absolute confidence. Working against Dolan were in-bred Air Corps' pressures to satisfy the various commands and individual geographic Air Force authorities by breaking up the unit once it finished its proof-of-concept work in Boston. Under this proposal, the original six aircraft and crews would be instructed to return to their original units, or at least to their parent Air Force. Dolan fought this. The obvious next move was to retain the integrity of the unit and deploy it to a priority location on the East Coast to hunt U-boats, all while making the aircraft and the crews available for follow-on work with Rad Lab in Boston. This would not be the only threat to the autonomy of the Dolan group, but it would set the stage for the fights yet to come.

Important support for Dolan came from Colonel Edwin E. Aldrin, a World War I veteran who had left the air service after the war to pursue a business career where he worked in the aviation products field for Standard Oil while earning a PhD in engineering from MIT. While with Standard Oil, he had managed relationships in Europe, spent time monitoring the growth of Germany's air arm, the *Luftwaffe* and established direct relationships with its leaders, including Hermann Göring. He shared his assessment with U.S. military leaders and predicted war, sooner rather than later, and the probable dominance of German air power based on its technology and ground-attack approach. The Germans had recently demonstrated the latter in its Stuka attacks in the Spanish Civil War. Aldrin saw radar as a critical technology that had to be mastered and applied to the U.S. air warfare doctrine. In his role on Arnold's staff, he understood what was underway at Boston's Rad Lab and appears to have had a hand in the selection of Bid Dolan for the task assigned there.

Returning to active service soon after war broke out in Europe in 1939, Aldrin was assigned to the Army Air Corps General Headquarters in Washington, D.C., and would be assigned to direct operations at Wright Field where the Air Corps Materials Division managed the weapons and technology projects that put systems into aircraft, sent them off to war and supported the evolution of those systems as the war progressed. Aldrin acted as a special technical advisor to Arnold and became his service-wide troubleshooter, dispatched as Arnold's personal representative to resolve conflicts and impose, often with a heavy hand, top-down solutions to get a given project moving forward at maximum speed.

Aldrin was a sharp-elbowed engineer who, as one of Dolan's men described him, did not suffer fools gladly. The colonel was often known to arrive at a given airfield without notice to take charge and force a solution on the spot, rank and authority be damned. From the outset of the Dolan effort at Rad Lab and over the months to come, Aldrin injected himself and supported Dolan's every decision and proposal, visiting Rad Lab every few weeks for briefings on the various systems then under development or proposed for research. The same Dolan man who knew Aldrin, then Lieutenant Butch Werner, described the approach: "He sized up a situation quickly, advocated his position with absolute certainty, and accepted only one point of view—his. We were fortunate that Aldrin agreed with and championed everything Bid Dolan did in those early months." Although Aldrin's initial interest was ASV, he soon expanded his mandate to every radar-related project, including the application of radar operating in the X-Band for strategic blind-bombing operations. The latter, in which Dolan would become intimately involved, saw the perfection and deployment of the H2X system within two years, followed by the Eagle program, an ultimate manifestation of Rad Lab's contribution to the war effort.

Another advocate and Dolan protector was Colonel Stuart B. Wright, a career Air Force officer who had been assigned by Arnold to Rad Lab at about the same time as Dolan's arrival. Wright was the resident Air Force liaison officer and was the perfect counterpart for Aldrin and Dolan. "Stud" Wright was an airman's airman and, as a career bomber pilot, he was determined to get as much out of the technology of radar as possible, as quickly as possible, cutting all corners and red tape to get systems tested and accepted for production. It is perhaps no coincidence of wartime America that brought Wright and Dolan together at Rad Lab, men with sequential Air Corps serial numbers; one man to found and build the system that would become Low Altitude Bombing, or "LAB," and the other to lead that capability into combat in the Pacific.

Support from a third individual came from Major General Barney M. Giles who served at Air Force Headquarters at Arnold's right hand. When Dolan made the pilgrimage to Washington, D.C., for meetings in the War Office, and later in the Pentagon, Giles typically hosted meetings in which Dolan made his case to maintain unit cohesion and transition the technology to a combat unit for overseas deployment. These sessions had

Colonels Aldrin and Wright standing with Dolan to add their support and, when Dolan was not present, both supporters pressed Giles and Arnold to continue to support the project. These four men—Dolan, Wright, Aldrin and Giles—guaranteed that ASV and its next generation of combat technology, LAB, would get its chance to prove itself in the South Pacific in the form of a dedicated unit—the highly-classified special night attack squadron to be known as the "Wright Project."[4]

Bid Dolan's contribution to the entirety of the Army Air Forces' airborne radar effort cannot be overstated. His untimely death in 1945, as he rushed back across the Atlantic to deploy the above-mentioned Eagle system in Europe, exacted a heavy toll on Arnold's team and cut short a career that would have seen him play a premier role in the postwar creation of the U.S. Air Force. It is instructive that, in the dark days of February 1942, his superiors judged that this man would be the right leader for the job at Rad Lab, both for the initial efforts in Boston and to carry radar to every aspect of war in the air, and to do so in every combat theater over the next three years. In early 1942, Dolan's ASV may not have been the only "crash project" designed to enter this fight but it was at that moment the premier undertaking of the Army Air Force. In Boston, the pressure was on him, his crews and the Rad Lab researchers to get ASV right and working as soon as possible.

ASV pioneer—The B-18 Bolo

The aircraft which the original Dolan group flew to Boston in March 1942, the Douglas B-18A Bolo, had seen better days and was already regarded as obsolete. But this aircraft would serve its purpose within the ASV program and remain a radar mainstay for more than a year. The B-18, essentially a bomber development of the DC-2 airliners (the predecessor of the famous DC-3), had been designed in the early 1930s and first flown in 1935. Working from the same basic design as its commercial sister, the B-18 had a deeper belly to accommodate a bomb bay which gave it a pregnant look compared to the sleek DC-2. The Bolo had been ordered in quantity by the USAAC in part because it was then the only aircraft on offer for delivery and its components were proven, an expedient solution until medium bombers then under development arrived in service.

Yet for a brief time, the B-18 had been the pride of Army Air Corps attack aviation. However, its mediocre performance (220 knots top speed with a cruising speed of 180 knots or so) and limited range and bomb load made it a second-tier airplane well before the attack on Pearl Harbor. Most of the men who flew with Dolan to Boston had turned in their B-18s for early examples of the sleek and dangerous B-26 only weeks or months before or were expected to do so. What the B-18 did have to recommend itself to Dolan and the ASV anti-submarine project was its dependability. With a reduced cruising speed of 145 knots, its two engines allowed it to carry a ton of bombs for a thousand miles on just 400 gallons of fuel.

What the Bolo lacked in speed, and speed was hardly essential for the ASV sub hunters, it made up for in durability. It gave Dolan's men and the Rad Lab technicians a warplane that was sturdy, with sufficient capacity for the onboard ASV systems. Rad Lab was reassured by the B-18 as it was easy to bolt in and swap out the various systems for test and refinement and, as a bonus, it seemed to always come home safely with minimal losses of valuable equipment and men.

Most of the B-18s flown by the Dolan unit were the B-18A version, a slightly improved version of the original B-18. From various active and reserve squadrons, the aircraft were flown first to San Antonio Air Depot for modification, typically installing new internal equipment racks and cabling for the anticipated ASV equipment. These aircraft flew on to their destinations along the East Coast as "B-18Bs." As the Dolan effort expanded in the summer and fall of 1942, his aircrews turned their original B-18s over to other units and alternated their anti-submarine patrols with ferry missions that delivered newly assigned B-18As from their squadrons, first to San Antonio and then to Boston for the installation of the ASV systems. By late 1942, most of the active ASV B-18s were routinely designated B-18Bs and these trusty veterans continued to serve their missions well into mid-1943 and beyond.[5]

Further attesting to the Bolo having been the right aircraft at the right time was the fact that, in early and mid-1942, the Army Air Forces needed experienced, high-quality aircrews capable of night and instrument flying, both to deliver the routine ASV sub-hunting patrols and to fly and evaluate the next iteration of onboard systems in a combat environment. The B-18 was the perfect test-bed aircraft in this role, having served as the medium bombing squadron mainstay aircraft for several years. Without the Bolo, the Rad Lab teams of engineers would have been hard-pressed to find suitable platforms with the combination of dependability and supply of airframes required for their efforts. Over the first two years of America's response in the war, this simple airplane, whose combat time had come and gone, allowed the Army Air Forces and Rad Lab to perfect a range of radar and electronic systems that would, over the ensuing years, find their way as proven systems into the B-17, B-24 and B-29. These three heavy bombers would become America's mainstays in the coming air wars over the Atlantic Ocean, in the European Theater and the Mediterranean and in the Pacific, and all would owe a heavy debt to the ungainly but ever-reliable B-18 Bolo.[6]

The ASV version of the B-18 Bolo would continue to serve in its anti-submarine search and attack role until replaced by the B-24 in early 1943, with a total of 122 of the B-models deployed in that configuration. In USAAF service, the ASV Bolo was credited with two U-Boat kills, U-654 on 22 August 1942 and U-512 on 2 October 1942. As this story unfolds, however, the true measure of the aircraft was the level of the threat it brought to U-boat operations wherever it patrolled, particularly in its nighttime role. Time and again it would detect U-boats, attack them, then bring surface warships to the action and continue to direct and coordinate the kill from overhead.[7]

In service with the Royal Canadian Air Force (RCAF), 20 B-18A models were assigned to No. 10 Squadron (coded "BR") to operate from RCAF Station Gander in Newfoundland. From this base it provided cover for the outbound and inbound convoys transiting this area of the Atlantic. The Douglas Digby Mark I, as it was known in RCAF, would carry out a dozen attacks on U-boats and score one confirmed sinking, that of U-520 on 30 October 1942.[8]

CHAPTER 2

Rad Lab and Microwave Radar

1940–43

War in the Pacific—The Japanese drive

When Bid Dolan and his men began their work with Rad Lab in Boston in March 1942, General MacArthur was in full retreat in the Philippines. The USAAF contingent there, caught on the ground, had been shattered by Japanese airstrikes in the opening days of the war and would not recover. In many ways, the disaster in the Philippines was abetted by gross mismanagement on the part of the American leadership there which was responsible for the defense of the American protectorate. The Japanese had landed fresh divisions and had pressed the American and Philippine forces down the Bataan Peninsula and would push them onto Corregidor Island, where a last stand would be mounted until General Wainwright surrendered the island and the Philippines on 6 May.

In Malaya, the Japanese 25th Army of Lieutenant General Tomoyuki Yamashita had swept down the 500-mile length of the peninsula in just 54 days. Singapore Island, with its 85,000 British, Australian and Indian defenders, vastly outnumbering the Japanese, surrendered on 15 February, a defeat that imposed on Britain, as Winston Churchill would lament, "the worst disaster and largest capitulation" in the history of that nation. Two of the Royal Navy's finest capital ships, the battleship HMS *Prince of Wales* and the battlecruiser HMS *Repulse*, lay on the ocean floor off Malaya, victims of a Japanese naval air force torpedo and bomb attack delivered two days after Pearl Harbor. In the mid-Pacific, Wake Island had fallen after a spirited defense and Guam would soon follow as the Japanese offensive rolled through the mid-Pacific and ranged out from their naval and air bases in the Gilberts, centered on Truk. In the Southwest Pacific, Japanese forces moved into the Bismarcks and the Solomon Islands, capturing Rabaul, from where they planned to move directly against Australia.

From Malaya and the Philippines, the Japanese were driving north into Burma, south into the Dutch East Indies and east into the middle Pacific. In a series of surface ship engagements, including the battle of the Java Sea in late February, Japanese cruiser and destroyer forces decimated the remnants of a combined Australian, British, American and Dutch naval force and drove the survivors from the region. The heavy cruiser USS *Houston*, flagship of the once-proud U.S. Asiatic Fleet, in company with HMS *Exeter* (Royal Navy) and HMAS *Perth* (Royal Australian Navy), were soon thereafter pounded under by Japanese naval forces, ably supported by a naval air arm that had fine-tuned its bombing and torpedo skills.

The old USS *Langley*, America's first aircraft carrier, by then relegated to serving as an aircraft transport, plus a dozen Allied destroyers, would also be gunned, torpedoed and bombed under by the Japanese during this six-month period of sustained defeats. One of Britain's aircraft carriers, HMS *Hermes*, and its escorting destroyer and two heavy cruisers would also meet the same fate in the Indian Ocean at the hands of the *Kido Butai* carrier strike force that had pivoted to mount an offensive there after slamming Pearl Harbor.

Stalemate in Europe, the Mediterranean and the Atlantic

In Russia, the Soviet winter counteroffensive to save Moscow had run its course. Hitler was preparing to launch a massive late-spring offensive into the Caucasian oil fields and toward Stalingrad. In North Africa, General Rommel executed a slashing counterattack with a reinforced tank spearhead that smashed three British armored regiments. The groundwork was laid for the pending British defeat at Gazala and the continuing eastward advance of the *Afrika Korps* toward Cairo and the Suez Canal.

England, having prevailed in the Battle of Britain by exhausting the German *Luftwaffe* in the skies above London the previous year and, in so doing, staving off the invasion of the United Kingdom proper, had turned to plan how to best carry the war back onto the continent. London and Churchill were "rebooted and re-spurred," reinforced and inspired by the U.S. entry into the war and the flow of men and machines across the Atlantic. Inclined to action, British planners would mount the ill-fated raid on the French port of Dieppe in August, where the mostly Canadian landing force would be decimated by the German defenders.

In the Atlantic Ocean, the German submarine campaign against Allied shipping routes sought, with building success, to sever the commercial and military lifeline between the United Kingdom and North America. For German Admiral Karl Dönitz, the first months of 1942 provided some of the best hunting his submarines would ever experience. He could count more than 30 U-boats constantly at sea with 20 new boats joining the fleet from the shipyards each month. He had accurately predicted his U-boats' ability to destroy more Allied merchant tonnage than could be built as replacements. By March 1942, his commanders were sinking some 16,000 tons of Allied ships each day. Countermeasures by the hard-pressed Royal Navy and the Royal Air

Force (RAF) Coastal Command succeeded in driving German submarines further into the Atlantic, but the U-boats adjusted and deployed new technology and tactics, further complicating Allied efforts to get the convoys through.

Operation Paukenschlag

America's immediate focus in this world at war was to mobilize and organize itself to best prepare to go to battle on many fronts, accelerating the preparations that had been underway for three years. This had been an attempt to buy time based on America's distance from the fields of combat. But war with Germany made such sanctity from direct conflict no longer an option. The war was brought to the United States by a Germany determined that America would begin to pay the price of its admission to the conflict from day one. This long-planned and well-executed German onslaught would bring death to America's shores and shake the country's confidence in its ability to prevail. The German weapon of choice was the ubiquitous U-boat.

In March 1942, the U-boat offensive off America's East Coast was in its second month and these early weeks would find the United States disorganized, ill-prepared and chancing defeat. In an incredibly naive approach to the protection of America's shores during this early period of the war, the U.S. Navy abysmally failed in its charge to protect its merchant ships and seamen. Commercial shipping of all flags was allowed and often instructed to sail independently, with the result that Hitler's submarine commanders had a field day torpedoing and deck-gunning their quarry, often on the surface and at will.

The formal name of this German U-boat offensive was Operation *Paukenschlag* (Drumbeat), a strategy that saw U-boats shifted from the North Atlantic hunting grounds to the virgin areas of the U.S. East Coast. The U-boat commanders who had been redirected to the new hunting ground by Dönitz referred to the period as the "Second Happy Time," and with good reason. In the three-month period of Dolan's temporary assignment in Boston and movement to Langley Field, German submarines would claim 87 merchantmen and tankers off U.S. shores for the loss of only four U-boats.

This tragedy occurred as the U.S. scrambled to address the U-boat threat amid disagreements between the U.S. Navy and the USAAF over the disposition of air and sea assets and areas of responsibility and operational control. Admiral Ernest J. King of the U.S. Navy was slow to grasp the seriousness of the German onslaught and reluctant to ask the USAAF to operate in the sea frontier area where he was determined to assert and preserve U.S. Navy responsibility and control. The Germans had little knowledge of this disorganization on the U.S. side of the battle but were quick to take maximum advantage of the situation.

Even as the bloody months of spring 1942 moved into summer and the U.S. anti-submarine effort improved with inter-service compromises and greater cooperation, the U-boats would shift their main area of attack to the Caribbean to continue the wholesale slaughter of the tankers attempting to deliver crude oil to East-Coast refineries. Here again, the U.S. Navy response was inadequate and ineffectual until escorted convoys were organized by the Navy, and USAAF resources were redeployed to mitigate the threat. Bid Dolan and his aircraft would join this fight as well, but in February 1942, that experience and the ability to contribute to the U-boat fight lay in the future.

In these early days of the American anti-submarine effort in the air, most of the weight was carried by an odd assortment of U.S. Navy patrol aircraft, blimps and the U.S. Army's I Bomber Command. The anti-submarine component of the latter was a hodgepodge force—soon to become the Army Air Forces Antisubmarine Command—made up of units flying B-17s, B-25s and B-18s, some of them equipped with the long-wave SCR-521 ASV radar. The reality was that, in the waters off the U.S. East Coast, the situation was so desperate that just about anything that could fly or float was pressed into the war against the U-boats, including Navy dirigibles. But in these months, the U-boats ruled the nights and bested the U.S. Navy and other American defenders, including the USAAF. America was losing this battle and the tankers blazing offshore at night were a testament to a nation ill-prepared to go to war against the U-boat.

A reorganization of the U.S. Army Air Corps

As America prepared to enter the war, there was broad recognition, from President Roosevelt on down, that the U.S. defense establishment would have to reorganize itself along more functional lines. One result was the creation of the Army Air Forces (AAF) on 20 June 1941, under the command of then Lieutenant General Henry H. Arnold. Secretary of War Henry Stimson and Army Chief of Staff George C. Marshall accepted that a much more robust air component would be needed for the conflict ahead. After the United States entered the war, in March 1942 the AAF attained an important level of autonomy when, as part of an overall reorganization of the War Department, the AAF and the Army Ground Forces were made co-equal commands. Importantly, the Commanding General of the AAF, Hap Arnold, became a member of the World War II Joint Chiefs of Staff, in company with Army Chief of Staff General Marshall, Chief of Naval Operations Admiral King and Presidential Advisor Admiral William D. Leahy.

Initially, the AAF had two subordinate elements, the Air Corps and Air Force Combat Command. The former was responsible for training and equipment and the latter replaced the General Headquarters Air Force. The March 1942 reorganization set the stage for a future evolution as the Air Corps ceased to be an operating organization when the Army Air Forces assumed all responsibilities for Army aviation. This was in spite of the fact that the Air Corps continued to legally exist as an Army branch. By 1943, the Army Air Forces was an autonomous service with all aviation training and operational units under its authority. These transitions did introduce some levels of confusion, particularly in the early months of the war, and some records continued to refer to AAF units and activity as that of the "Army Air Corps."

Notably, the title used in the official correspondence of the man who guided these changes and managed every aspect of the U.S. Army air war throughout the war's duration was unambiguous—H. H. Arnold, General U.S. Army, Commanding General, Army Air Forces. As such, he reported directly to Secretary of War Stimson and elevated the stature of the AAF to the level that would allow it to become a fully independent service in 1947 as the United States Air Force.

The birth of Radiation Laboratory

The story of the people waiting in Boston for Bid Dolan's arrival begins well before Pearl Harbor. It begins, in fact, in June 1940 when German tanks were completing their slashing *blitzkrieg* drive through France and the Low Countries to Europe's Atlantic coast. A group of American scientist planners, among them Vannevar Bush, J. B. Conant, K. T. Compton and F. B. Jewett, determined men with a genius for foresight, decided to start the ball rolling for "scientific collaboration" in the American defense effort. They knew that war would very likely come to America and that, if the United States was to prevail, it had to have the advantage of the best technology available. In June 1940, Bush committed his ideas to paper and met with President Franklin D. Roosevelt for 15 minutes. He emerged from the meeting with an "OK, FDR," which authorized establishing the National Defense Research Committee (NDRC).

This organization, probably the single most important entity contributing to America's victory in World War II and its postwar position of world supremacy, was originally viewed as a broadly based, civilian-run and staffed military research agency. Within weeks, Bush organized the NDRC into five "divisions" and placed Dr. K. T. Compton in charge of the division concerned with "detection." Detection meant radar and the radar effort quickly focused on microwave detection. Dr. A. L. Loomis was chosen to head a brain trust of America's finest scientists working on the far frontier of the then poorly understood field of radar. This group became the "Microwave Committee." Its survey of available technology during the summer of 1940 discovered that America did not have the answers at hand that would allow the country the quality of radar equipment it needed.

At this time, the military potential of radar was only beginning to be realized, but it was clear that, if the technology could be mastered, a range of opportunities were there. This was particularly so in the field of airborne application of radar in the air-to-air, air-to-ground and air-to-surface vessel missions. The early British ASV set, the Mark I, had been installed in a few U-boat-hunting Lockheed Hudsons and Short Sunderlands in 1940. In early 1941, the Mark I was followed by the improved long-wave Mark II, which claimed its first U-boat in March. During 1941, the RAF Coastal Command successfully employed the Mark II as a U-boat hunter-killer. The ASV radar made night aircraft patrols possible in the areas where RAF Coastal Command aircraft flew, making U-boat transits of waters such as the Bay of Biscay hazardous.

When the U-boats switched to mid-Atlantic "Wolf Pack" tactics in mid-1941 to operate in areas not covered by shore-based aircraft, the British counterpunched with a combination of long-range ASV-equipped aircraft and escort carriers. But the Mark II radar was limited in its capability by its relatively short range and its imprecision at the point of attack. The Germans were also able to deploy a radar search receiver that allowed U-boats to detect the Mark II long-wave signals and submerge before the air attack could be pressed home. These radar limitations, when combined with the jumbled mixture of aircraft available to carry the systems, lessened the effectiveness of the ASV anti-submarine weapon.

At the time the NDRC's Microwave Committee was organized in 1940, many of the ASV Mark II-related events lay in the future, but the inherent limitations of the long-wave Mark II were recognized, and the Committee realized that it had to develop an improved ASV instrument and then mate it to a long-range patrol aircraft to create a viable weapons system. Microwave radar seemed to be the answer. The Committee soon identified the key challenge facing the American effort—the absence of a vacuum tube that could supply power at the 10cm wavelength which such a system required.

In September 1940, the American radar research effort received a momentous injection of technology and enthusiasm with the arrival of the super-secret British team of scientists, to be known forever after as the famous Tizard Mission. The visit to America had been arranged as a by-product of a recent agreement between Roosevelt and Churchill to share military technology and brought with it a wealth of knowledge about the operational British long-wave radar systems. That was not a great surprise, but the 10cm cavity magnetron that was delivered was. It was one of a few delicate prototypes crafted in utmost secrecy by some of Britain's finest engineers. This palm-sized magnetron provided the foundational core component for all microwave radars and gave the NDRC Microwave Committee a point of departure for its microwave radar development program.

The exchange with the British scientists also convinced the Americans that they must establish a central laboratory dedicated to both fundamental research and system development staffed by the best minds in the country. In October 1940, the NDRC established the Radiation Laboratory (Rad Lab) at MIT in room 4-133. Dr. L. A. Dubridge was selected as Rad Lab director and an intensive recruitment campaign began to staff the center. The NDRC's Microwave Committee oversaw the expansion of Rad Lab and identified research priorities. Rad Lab "Project One" was the mastery of microwave airborne radar.

During this period, the Rad Lab scientists and the U.S. Army Air Corps were learning the inherent limitations of the Mark II sets firsthand. Samples of production Mark IIs were delivered to the U.S. as early as July 1941, installed in B-17 test aircraft and assigned the American military nomenclature "SCR-521." In this designation, in absence of any better system, it would continue to serve on a limited basis in the U.S. inventory and much more broadly in the aircraft flown by the RAF Coastal Command that were then hunting U-boats in the Atlantic.

Rad Lab at flank speed

By the end of 1940, the Rad Lab was beginning to hum. As Roosevelt asked Congress for arms, planes and ships for England, the U-boat war raged and the British fitted their first Mark II ASV sets to aircraft. The lab took delivery of its first magnetrons (fabrication having been contracted to Bell Laboratories), expanded its research quarters and began to assemble and test its first bench-scale systems. America was not yet legally at war, but through the spring of 1941 and into that summer Rad Lab continued to expand, experiment and produce and, in the case of every system to which its engineers applied themselves, the timetable its management had set was met or bettered.

The original focus of Project One, microwave airborne intercept (AI) radar, soon diffused into a broad microwave radar program that included, in addition to AI radar and an ASV project that seemed to have great promise, the first sets of Navy "SG," or surface detection radars. New research groups were created almost overnight and took on the development of radar-related electronics to allow the production of dozens of other air defense and navigational systems. Taken together, over the 1942–45 period, the scope and quality of these varied systems would provide America with an almost unimaginable technological edge in the war.

The ASV microwave program was in the air by July 1941, and additional test sets were provided to the U.S. Navy and the British. During the same time, the U.S. military and civilian contractors were also gaining experience by adopting, manufacturing and installing the long-wave British Mark II set on a limited basis. The Mark II set received the U.S. designations SCR-521A and B. Apparently, only a few sets of these systems found their way into American aircraft due to a combination of factors; among those were limitations on the availability of systems, the bulk of the equipment and its limited operational capabilities. In any event, it would soon be replaced by a much better system.[1]

In the second half of 1941, as the specter of war approached America, Rad Lab shifted all its research programs into high gear, its staff growing to 500 by year end. The expansion of its air activities focused on the nearby East Boston Airport, where a National Guard hangar was appropriated to support Rad Lab's Air Force B-18 "Flying Laboratory," and in the weeks and months ahead the sturdy Bolo would be a flying test platform mainstay. The attack on Pearl Harbor found *Dumbo I*, a B-24 Liberator equipped with a microwave ASG/ASV prototype system, the DMS-1000, preparing for its first test flight. Projects with follow-on airborne systems, including the SCR-582, SCR-584, GCA (Ground Control Approach) and ASD (Airborne Search and Detection) development projects were well underway, but all had yet to demonstrate they would perform as promised. Beyond design, testing at bench scale in the labs and hardening the original sets for test in the air to confirm they would operate as advertised, the systems had to then be adapted to commercial production.

But Rad Lab's development schedules were met, systems were perfected and qualified and contracts for the commercial production of the initial sets were signed. Critical to the success of Rad Lab, indeed to the entire NDRC collection of advanced projects, was the ready availability of private sector companies skilled in the manufacture of electronics. These firms were eager to participate in the production of the state-of-the-art components and systems generated by the designers at Rad Lab. While profit was an obvious incentive for these firms, each having just pulled themselves through the depths of the Great Depression, the opportunity to participate in the design and production of new products was a huge draw. As a result, these companies assigned their best technicians to the "classified equipment" production lines, with fierce competition among the companies for contracts. The useful by-product of this was that, with very few exceptions, the quality of components delivered was exceptional.[2]

Additionally, individual engineers from these same firms were eager to work alongside Rad Lab researchers in Boston and willingly accepted relocation to Langley Field and other Air Force installations, such as Wright Field in Ohio, to maintain the new systems. Also, as we will see with the Wright Project, individual engineers, who considered themselves as "owning" a given system that was untested in combat, often volunteered for overseas deployment to accompany the systems they had built to war.

Once war did come to America, the NDRC overseers and the War Department insisted that Rad Lab further accelerate its work by making "quick-fix crash installations" that would provide U.S. aircraft with an ASV capability that could be committed to war immediately. It was no secret that the U.S. anti-submarine effort was disorganized, poorly led and ill-equipped to meet the coming German onslaught. Responsible parties, namely the leadership of the U.S. Navy, and to a lesser degree the Army Air Force, who should have absorbed the lessons delivered by Britain's U-boat struggles notwithstanding, had wasted critical time in preparing for the war that approached. Immediately following the Pearl Harbor attack, Rad Lab began converting a number of AI radar sets to ASV capability for installation in Army aircraft. Many of the early microwave radars were reworked from AI-10 night fighter sets, which had been hand-built to use in Douglas A-20 aircraft. The microwave ASV radar would later receive the British designation ASV-10 and the U.S. military designation SCR-517 once they entered full-scale production, but, in early 1942, only a few pre-production SCR-517 sets were available. Rad Lab engineers supervised the hand assembly of these microwave sets and declared its staff ready to begin their ASV contribution to the war once the aircraft and the men to fly them were found. Bid Dolan and his six crews had just arrived at Rad Lab, so Rad Lab technology had finally met the men and their aircraft who would prove that ASV in its new incarnation would work.[3]

The early Rad Lab ASV sets

As noted, the ASV radar sets field tested by Dolan's team were pre-production SCR-517s, reworked from the AI sets intended for use in night fighter aircraft. The early focus on the application of airborne microwave radar had been on airborne interception—the detection by radar-enabled fighter aircraft, typically at night, to track, intercept and destroy targets such as bombers—but this emphasis would quickly change. The critical need was for a higher-performing radar for long-duration patrol aircraft expected to cover wide swathes of sea in the hunt for U-boats. In converting the microwave AI to the ASV configuration used in Dolan's B-18 patrol bombers, the Rad Lab team simply eliminated the vertical sweep motion of the AI antenna to allow the radar beam to sweep a 180-degree horizontal arc forward of the aircraft. The addition of a B-scope tube allowed the system to display the position of all surface targets in range of the radar system (a B-scope is a secondary or repeater scope with less detail than the main radar operator scope).

Although the original ASV tests conducted during 1941 using a U.S. Navy Lockheed Lodestar had successfully detected surface vessels at 30 nautical miles and surfaced submarines at five miles, these ranges had been increased by the time Dolan's B-18B aircraft received their rebuilt ASV sets. The radar–bomber combination, as demonstrated by Dolan's small unit in weeks after it arrived in Boston, held such promise that, in April 1942, the Signal Corps was asked to assign procurement priority to the ASV-10 "over any other radio equipment now being procured" for USAAF units deployed or preparing to deploy for overseas duty.

This same period also witnessed the head of the NDRC, Dr. Vannevar Bush, lobby at the highest levels for his microwave radar projects. Frustrated with the embedded resistance from many of the old guard military leadership, Bush did battle at the level of President Roosevelt and Secretary of War Stimson. His comment on the Navy's Ernie King resonates: "Admiral King had a terrible blind spot for new things—and about as rugged a case of stubbornness as has been cultivated by a human being." As Bush watched the torpedoed tankers burn off America's coast and the British fight the battle of the Atlantic with older, less precise radar systems, the USAAF was blessed to have Hap Arnold and his circle of advisors embrace NDRC, MIT's Rad Lab and its own circle of private sector electronics companies gearing up to produce new systems and solutions for the U.S. war effort.

In the months ahead, Rad Lab and its contractor firms, led by Bell Telephone Laboratories, would continue to refine the first edition of the SCR-517 to standardize it as the SCR-517A, evolve it into the 517B version and finally deploy the system by early 1943 as the further-improved SCR-717 A and B series. In each variant, the system components were rearranged, strengthened and made more compact and operator friendly. Such modifications were intuitive and made the systems more convenient to troubleshoot and maintain. This improvement would create a true state-of-the-art production-scale ASV radar that would serve throughout the war in U.S. as well as Allied aircraft.[4]

As the Dolan aircraft were testing their first systems from Boston, other initiatives were afoot that would reinforce the value of the microwave technology being perfected. The value of military cooperation between the United States and the United Kingdom was also on full display when Rad Lab began paying its dues to the cousins who had mounted the Tizard Mission to share critical technologies more than a year before. In March 1942, the ASV-equipped B-24 *Dumbo I* departed Boston and flew to Northern Ireland, where testing validated the substantial improvement in radar detection provided by microwave systems.

A sister B-24, *Dumbo II*, was demonstrated the following month to Secretary of War Henry Stimson and other high-ranking military officers, thereby securing the status and the priority of the project. A crash program managed by Rad Lab and executed by the Research Construction Company produced 14 sets for delivery to RAF Coastal Command B-24s, where they were deployed under the British designation of DME-1000 during the August–December 1942 period. These sets and the ones to follow had arrived just in time to join RAF Coastal Command's struggle with the U-boats as they transited the Bay of Biscay.[5]

Meanwhile, back in Boston, Dolan's B-18s were completing their equipment training program with a six-man crew of three officers and three enlisted men. In addition to the pilot, co-pilot and radio operator who occupied their normal positions in the B-18, the aircraft carried a radar operator perched at a new station on the flight deck. The navigator doubled as the bombardier in the nose where, in some B-18 ASV versions, he had a position plot indicator (PPI) type of repeater radar scope installed to give him the benefit of the master scope view being fine-tuned by the radar operator. A crew chief rounded out the aircraft complement.

Commentary by one of the original "Dolan Boys," Lieutenant Crowell "Butch" Werner, who flew as a navigator with the crew of Lieutenant William Foley, provides a flavor of these early experiences:

> Our ASV radar was in its infancy but it worked to a degree and anyway, we were all radar amateurs. We were often able to detect targets in the black of night at 20 miles or more but we lost them on the final attack run about a mile out when the screen cluttered up, and the needle indicator only reacted when we passed directly over the target. The result was that any bomb or depth charge released at that point would result in an "over" and a miss. This meant that we had to calculate a bomb release point based on solving a time and distance problem, working from the location of the target we had run over the first time, then returning for a second run on a reciprocal heading with

our radar. But with this, we were really releasing depth charges blindly and hoping for a hit or near-miss. In those early days in Boston, the "blind bombing" capability that we would later develop and take to war in the Pacific was still in the future. But the above defines the core problem—not the detection or the tracking of the target but the lack of precision in the attack phase.[6]

Dolan ASV missions

Beyond equipment familiarization and flight testing of the ASV systems, the Dolan group began sub-hunting missions from Boston. The results of this first effort by a small group were impressive. U-boats were detected by Dolan's ASV-equipped B-18Bs on the night of 1 April and again on 1 May, and in both cases, the submarines were detected, tracked, attacked and driven under, with near-miss damage claims made.

On one occasion when Dolan was piloting a night-search training mission with a newly configured B-18B, his ASV detected a target and he ran a straight-in attack approach, with an aircraft that carried no ordnance. His run at the "target" assumed that the detected ship moving at speed close to the shoreline was friendly. As the aircraft passed low over the ship, the U-boat opened up with all it had and anti-aircraft fire laced around the plane. Dolan's only comment was that if he had bombs on board, he could have walked them across the submarine. It was a missed opportunity for sure, but also a very close call.

Other opportunities presented themselves that allowed Dolan and his crews on the flying side, and the Rad Lab technicians working to perfect the equipment, to "prove the system works." On 12 April 1942, a B-18B, with Dolan at the controls, was contacted by the Navy and asked to assist in a search for one of its observation aircraft believed down in the Atlantic some 50 miles offshore. Dolan was given a heading, made his own course correction for the drift he expected had occurred since the plane disappeared, and the Rad Lab technicians bent over their scopes to probe the night. At three in the morning, a radar return from a target some 20 miles distant was received but as the B-18 bore in and over the estimated target, nothing was seen. At that point a star shell appeared, arcing over the survivors, and Dolan radioed the position to a destroyer that was then searching many miles to the south. The downed crew was rescued before dawn, but because the project remained highly classified there was no official, let alone public, mention of this early ASV success. Dolan and his plane with its Rad Lab radar had been at the right place in the air and all involved embraced this as a solid validation of what they had undertaken together.

By mid-April, the basic training of the original six crews had been completed with no major problems. The only aircraft incident to mar the training program occurred when a B-18B flown by two later Wright Project leaders—then Captains Leo Foster and Francis Carlson—retracted its landing gear before becoming airborne on take-off at Logan Field. The crushed coal cinder surface of the runway was forgiving and cushioned the impact of the airplane as it belly flopped and skidded to a stop. Some time was required to shovel out the several hundred pounds of cinders which the plane's bomb bay had scooped up as it slid down the field. Cleared for a mission the following day, the same two pilots lifted off in the same plane and, once airborne with the landing gear tucked away, the Bolo headed into the Atlantic. Unlike the "hot and deadly" B-26 Marauders that many of Dolan's pilots had been pulled from, and the massive B-24 Liberators that lay ahead, the B-18 Bolo was both very dependable and almost always forgiving.

Holding the Dolan team together

Because written orders had not caught up with Dolan and his men, the first weeks at Boston were considered to be a deployment based on "temporary duty" assignments, the crews having been individually released for a specified duration by their original units. At some point in April, the decision was made that these first crews and their aircraft, as they were acknowledged to be successfully fulfilling an important "proof of concept" mission, would not return to their original units on the West Coast. Some senior officers in the former bomber groups had assumed that they would be able to reclaim these ASV crews and aircraft, while the First Air Force planners on the East Coast considered a plan to seize and scatter-deploy Dolan's six planes to anti-submarine units assembling themselves to patrol the Atlantic seaboard.

The "Sea Search Attack Group Command History," compiled as a SECRET document in 1944, provides some flavor for the political and bureaucratic campaign that was being waged by Dolan in early April 1942 to hold his unit together:

> In a room in the Nanger Hotel at North Station in Boston, Colonel Dolan outlined for Dr. Bowles and his associates Dolan's ideas for the creation of an outfit that would develop tactics and explore the potentialities of airborne radar. He reasoned that by concentrating the planes at one point the special servicing necessary to the equipment could be more effectively rendered, while the planes could be from time to time detached to strategic points to afford vital protection to shipping.

Finding receptive ears on the technical side, Dolan then took his argument to the most senior levels of the USAAF to drive home his case for an independent and cohesive unit. As he made his approaches, he was supported behind the scenes by Colonels Aldrin (then working at Wright Field) and Colonel Wright (the Rad Lab liaison head) as well as others within General Arnold's inner circle. The "Command History" continues:

> On April 15, 1942, the Colonel was in Washington D.C. A conference was held in General Arnold's office attended by General McClennan and Colonel R.G. Breene, then Director of Technical Services. Colonel Dolan submitted his proposals and it was agreed that ten planes should operate as a unit. Langley Field was selected as the base partly because of its strategic situation in regard to enemy submarine activity and partly because of excellent facilities there for experimentation. Basic plans were laid for the Sea Search Attack Development Unit and Colonel Dolan was authorized to leave immediately for San Antonio to pick up ten bombsights.[7]

Dolan worked hard to protect his flock and soon found his collection of B-18Bs and their crews, onward and provisionally assigned, as directed by the highest-level authorities at USAAF Headquarters, to join the 20th Bombardment Squadron of the 2nd Bombardment Group at Langley Field, Virginia. Dolan would dash to San Antonio and return with his bombsights on 27 April, and the move to Langley for the 10 crews would then begin within a week. In addition to Dolan's original six crews and aircraft, a further four crews already assigned to Langley would be transferred to his unit. The new crews would be sent to collect additional aircraft for conversion and fly to Boston where the Rad Lab technicians would complete radar installation and training. The original six crews and their B-18B Bolos bid Rad Lab and Boston farewell in late April and headed south to Virginia's Tidewater, to be joined a few weeks later by the four additional crews and their ASV B-18Bs. Langley Field would be their new home and, in the coming weeks, additional unit identities would be bestowed on this embryonic collection of Bid Dolan's ASV Bolos and flyers.

First Sea Search Attack Group 1942–43

Colonel William "Bid" Dolan, Commander First Sea Search Attack Group. (MIT/ Radiation Laboratory and MIT/Rad Lab Radar *magazine, 1944)*

Three leaders of the LAB project, Colonel Edwin Aldrin, Lieutenant General Barney Giles and Colonel Bid Dolan, at Langley Field, 1943. (MIT/Radiation Laboratory and MIT/ Rad Lab Radar *magazine, 1944)*

B-18A Bolo bomber, 1942. (MIT/Radiation Laboratory and MIT/Rad Lab Radar *magazine, 1944)*

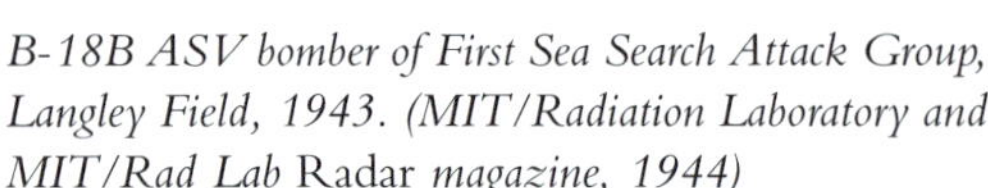

B-18B ASV bomber of First Sea Search Attack Group, Langley Field, 1943. (MIT/Radiation Laboratory and MIT/Rad Lab Radar *magazine, 1944)*

B-18B anti-submarine test equipment, Langley Field, 1942. (MIT/Radiation Laboratory and MIT/Rad Lab Radar magazine, 1944)

SB-24D LAB test installation, bombardier position, 1943. (MIT/Radiation Laboratory and MIT/Rad Lab Radar magazine, 1944)

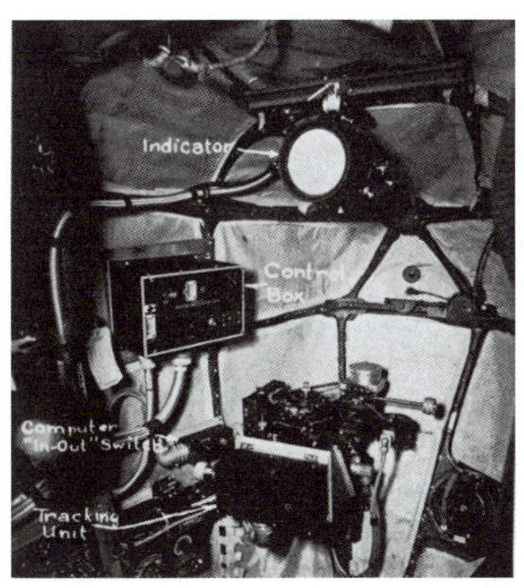

SB-24 LAB training rig, bombardier position, 1943. (MIT/Radiation Laboratory and MIT/Rad Lab Radar magazine, 1944)

B-18B emergency beach landing, near Langley Field, 1942. (MIT/Radiation Laboratory and MIT/Rad Lab Radar magazine, 1944)

CHAPTER 3

Langley Field and the 1st Sea-Search Attack Group

June–December 1942

Operations from Langley Field

By early May 1942, the 10 aircraft and crews of Dolan's unit had settled into Langley Field and had begun launching into the night for their operational patrols. On 4 May, the first all-microwave ASV search-and-attack bomber unit was officially consolidated into the 20th Bombardment Squadron (H) of the 2nd Bombardment Group, of the First Air Force's I Bomber Command. Lieutenant Colonel Dolan was designated the officer-in-charge. At the same time, the various West Coast units, which then still technically controlled the men and planes of Dolan's unit, were instructed to relinquish their ownership. They did so and ordered the crews and aircraft released for duty to the First Air Force and its bomber command.[1]

Langley Field was the natural choice for the Dolan unit given its proximity to the Atlantic sea lanes where the war was being fought against the U-boats. Its relatively close distance to both Washington, D.C., and headquarters there, and to the Rad Lab researchers in Boston, made this basing location an easy decision. Moreover, Langley was the home of the Langley Memorial Aeronautical Laboratory, the nation's first, and then premier, aviation research facility. Although the base at Wright Field in Ohio would grow to become the center of AAF system development and installation, the facilities at Langley Field were ideal for Dolan's purposes in 1942. No shirker in its own right, the Langley operation would grow from the staff of a few hundred that Dolan and his men found there in May 1942, to nearly six thousand by the end of the war three years later. It was, therefore, appropriate that the testing of Army Air Force radar systems and advanced electronics would take place at a location that offered both proximity to the war in the Atlantic, where combat missions could be flown to perfect the new systems, and that personnel with the right attitude were available to support these high-priority programs.[2]

The 1st Sea-Search Attack Group

During that same May–June 1942 period, as Dolan's ASV B-18Bs were patrolling over the Atlantic, his supporters at Army Air Force Headquarters worked their magic to ensure that this special group received its own designation, an action that would give it increased independence and elevated status. The effort bore fruit on 17 June 1942 when six combat crews of Dolan's original team were transferred to a new organization, the 1st Sea-Search Attack Group (Medium). These six crews formed the group's 2nd Squadron. In the following weeks, five more planes and additional crews joined this new organization. Although the group initially remained subordinate to I Bomber Command, the 1st Sea-Search effectively answered to the direct command and control of the Commanding General, AAF. In Washington at AAF Headquarters, the 1st Sea-Search Attack Group was also known as the "Sea-Search Attack Development Unit," or simply "SADU."[3]

By the summer of 1942, Bid Dolan had 11 ASV-equipped B-18Bs working full time and could count on the assignment for test purposes of a variety of aircraft sporting a mix of improved old and exotic new electronic equipment. During July, more personnel, including the aircraft maintenance, radar and electronics specialists, plus the support officers and men that were needed to make the 1st Sea-Search a self-sustaining organization, were added. The group was given the twin missions of developing new tactics and equipment for anti-submarine warfare and, when time allowed and the enemy demanded, war patrols into the Atlantic. In the latter role, it most often operated under Navy tactical command. In the former mission, it continued to work hand-in-hand with Rad Lab and the equipment manufacturers, such as Bell Laboratories, which were now playing an increasingly active role in the military electronics field. As Rad Lab systems were combat tested and certified, the pre-production versions were tested by Dolan's group and qualified for standard-issue production by the manufacturers.

On the active patrolling side, the group's first armed anti-submarine patrols were often dangerous and usually frustrating. Each night patrol carried the crews out from Langley and into the shipping corridors of the Atlantic coast for five- to seven-hour searches. The ASV sets provided the bombers with many contacts and these radar contacts frequently developed into attacks on surfaced submarines. More often, a surfaced submarine radar contact would be flashed by the B-18 crew to the nearest destroyer team, which would rush to the contact point to begin a sonar search for the U-boat. The presence of the B-18s overhead ensured that the U-boat would not be able to outdistance the destroyers rushing in to make contact. If the submarine resurfaced to maximize its speed using its diesels, the ASV aircraft would detect it and attack, forcing it to crash dive. Held below the surface, the U-boat's speed was limited by its electric motors and battery capacity. The Germans had been playing this hide-and-seek game with RAF Coastal Command airborne hunters for two years at this point, but the advent of microwave ASV added a new and deadlier dimension to the game of death.

A typical 1st Sea-Search crew averaged 15 ASV night missions a month with three planes up every night to work their assigned patrol areas. Irrespective of any damaging attacks or sinking of U-boats, the mere presence of the ASV patrol bombers over shipping lanes and their ability to communicate their radar "contacts" to U.S. Navy surface ships helped drive the U-boats underwater. This persistent patrolling coverage compelled the U-boat commanders to find a more distant, less threatening environment in which to operate; the U-boat offensive adapted and shifted to emphasize attacks on the oil tankers and other shipping in the southern sea lanes off Florida and into the Caribbean.

By early summer, this all-hands combined and coordinated services effort was finding and killing U-boats. Following a first sinking of U-656 by a Navy Lockheed Hudson from VP-82 (patrol squadron) on 1 March, a PBY Catalina from the same squadron sank U-503 mid-month, followed by the flush-deck destroyer USS *Roper* attacking and sinking U-85 with gunfire and depth charges in early April off Nags Head, North Carolina. On 9 May, the U.S. Coast Guard got its first U-boat kill when the U.S. Coast Guard cutter *Icarus* depth-charged U-352 to its grave off Cape Lookout, North Carolina. In the southern area, where Dolan's team was operating as part of a Miami-based task-force approach, the U.S. Coast Guard Cutter *Thetis* sank the U-157 in the Gulf in mid-June, while a U.S. Navy Martin PBM Mariner of VP-74 claimed U-158 south of Bermuda two weeks later. Throughout the summer of 1942, during this aggressive counter-offensive, the U.S. Navy, Coast Guard and AAF squadrons would continue to rack up victories: by mid-July, U-701, U-153 and U-576 would die at the hands of aircraft and ships working together. The so-called "Second Happy Time" for the U-boat fleet off American shores would end that month, never to return.

Although the Dolan unit was too small to act as a day-to-day operational patrol unit while also continuing to serve as a dedicated test squadron for the field evaluation of new electronic equipment, the U-boat threat meant that it was often drafted and redeployed as a fast-response unit. Higher-level command viewed the group's 10 ASV B-18Bs as a well-trained and aggressively led squadron capable of rapidly deploying to another operating base to meet a U-boat surge. In late May, the 10 aircraft and crews of the 20th Bombardment Squadron (soon to become the Sea-Search Attack Group) were injected into the fight by orders that instructed Dolan to take five aircraft to Key West, Florida, and to send his remaining five aircraft to Miami to operate there in the ASV search and attack mode. Here they would remain until mid-June, flying night missions over their assigned patrol areas.[4]

The Dolan crews received a brief reprieve from this deployed and distributed situation in late June when the unit returned to Langley Field. Here it resumed patrols, with three to five planes up each night, while its aircraft shuttled between the San Antonio Air Depot in Texas, Wright Field in Ohio and Boston to collect the redesigned electronics systems for field testing at Langley Field.

By August, 70-plus men were assigned to the unit on a permanent basis, allowing additional aircraft and crews to join the expanding group. In mid-September, the 2nd Squadron of the 1st Sea-Search Attack Group, the single functional unit of that command, was comprised of no fewer than 15 combat crews, as follows, identified by the command pilots of each crew: Flight A: Hartbrodt, Herrick, Biddison, McIntosh; Flight B: Foley, Reynolds, Coleman, Easterling; Flight C: Zinn, Lehti, Rockwood, Harris; and Flight D: Walker, McKay, Wood. Other more senior officers, such as Captains Foster and Carlson, men who would soon be selected to play leading roles in the Wright Project, remained with Dolan's group as part of its operational and planning leadership.

Each combat-rated crew comprised seven men—pilot, co-pilot, navigator, bombardier, radio operator, radar operator and flight engineer. Over the next few weeks these crews would be reorganized as Dolan rebalanced his organization. The addition of the bombardier as the seventh crewman set the stage for the migration to the aircraft that the unit had been promised—the Consolidated B-24 Liberator.

A typical mission

Years later, a Dolan B-18B navigator recalled a typical Atlantic patrol mission in the mid-summer of 1942:

> We entered our patrol area off the Florida coast. In the distance we could see one or two tankers burning and exploding, lighting up the night sky. They had been hit by U-boats earlier in the evening. Our ASV equipment was up, and the hunt was on. Sometime after midnight our radar operator picked up a contact and at 20 miles or so we confirmed it as a solid U-boat signal. The radar operator guided our attack run to the target. Jammed in the nose of the plane with me sat our bombardier, Henry "Parson" Wise, an ordained Baptist minister. A mile or more distance from the target, the ASV operator turned over the control of the attack to the "Parson."
>
> As we ran into the target, we maintained an attack altitude of 1,000 feet, but we dropped still lower as we used the radar to bring us right up to the U-boat. The most serious limitation of the radar—its inability to return a decent scope image due to ground clutter once your aircraft got within a mile or so of the target—was partly compensated for by our MAD [magnetic anomaly detection] gear. The tail stinger fed a needle indicator, which jumped on the panel when we passed over the target. Thus, we had to make a dry run directly over the target, watch the scope and MAD needle interplay and pray that the noise of the sub's diesel engines and our height combined to hide us from the U-boat's deck watch. Passing over the submarine, we then quickly ran a time and distance calculation, made a tight 180-degree turn, armed our bomb load and made our attack run on a reciprocal heading.
>
> Our bomb release was keyed to our radar, MAD equipment when we had it, hand calculations and gut feelings; but somehow the bombs normally came down damn close to our target. On this night, our bombs were right on target and in the second they exploded next to the sub, we saw men—our enemy—caught on the exposed deck, seemingly frozen in place by the bomb flash. We banked and made a second attack run, but the sub was gone, probably damaged, or maybe even sunk. When "Parson" looked up from the handheld bombsight, I saw tears in his eyes. In the cramped nose of that old B-18, I asked him what was wrong. He answered quietly, "I prayed to God to guide my bombs, but I said a prayer for their souls." Such emotion is hard to explain and comprehend. But such is war.[5]

Trinidad—Operation Torch

"Special assignment" missions continued to inject themselves into Dolan's radar and crew development program. In late September, the 1st Sea-Search was ordered to Trinidad, British West Indies, to temporarily base itself there and operate search patrols into the Atlantic. Operating there from October, Dolan's unit provided anti-submarine air coverage for the invasion convoy that was being assembled for the North Africa landings. America was coming into the war on the ground in the broader European Theater by launching an offensive in North Africa that would press the *Afrika Korps* from the west, as the British-led Commonwealth forces fought Rommel on the eastern front of that extended desert conflict.

The Sea-Search B-18s flew daylight and night missions over the Operation *Torch* invasion fleet as it assembled and flew ahead and above the convoy as far into the Atlantic as the aircraft's range would allow. In a scene to be repeated time and again in the coming months, one Rad Lab hand washed the other when the ASV radars protected ships headed for North Africa that carried five sets of the brand new, Rad Lab-developed SCR-582 harbor defense radar.

Toward the end of the deployment, a U-boat was caught running on the surface at night and repeatedly attacked by several B-18s rushing in for the kill. Although it was not confirmed as a sinking, the fact that Dolan's planes detected the sub, drove it under and kept it there provided yet more confirmation that the unit was in the right place at the right time. Months later, higher command, after sorting through intelligence that strongly suggested the U-boat had been sunk, credited the 1st Sea-Search with a confirmed kill. Dolan pocketed this and used this recognition to promote his group, requesting attention to a project that one of his officers had suggested as both essential and technically possible—a low altitude, radar-enabled, computer-assisted blind-bombing system.[6]

This deployment, the first and only assignment outside the United States for the SADU, was uneventful in the combat context, but there were those special moments. During the flight south, a B-18B piloted by Lieutenant Pohan lost an engine over the Dominican Republic and made a controlled emergency landing in a sugar cane field. Soon after the Bolo bounced to a stop, an aging U.S. Marine, white-haired and bearded, sitting tall on a donkey, appeared through the eight-foot-tall sugar cane. The Marine, a veteran of the U.S. intervention that would later be dubbed the "Banana Wars," had gone local when the Marines departed the island in 1924. After dismounting, he approached the plane and stood to attention, snapped a salute and offered to coordinate the local assistance. The following day he was back, shaved and in uniform, "strack" as a U.S. Marine could be, reporting for duty. Accompanying him was his "woman" and their children, plus a large collection of villagers ready to lend a hand. Negotiations began immediately for their services.

A plan came together. The distressed aircrew sent word to Dolan that they were down and safe but needed a replacement engine. Dolan had, in fact, circled the area when the B-18 reported its engine problems but needed to know the status of the aircraft. With help on the way from Puerto Rico, but still a few days out because the engine had to be flown in and then trucked to the field, the town council met and decided that its mission as a proper host was to get the visiting airmen drunk each night. The mayor took charge, and the festivities began with dinner each night accompanied by lots of singing, dancing and even more drinking. Booked into the local establishment, the El Hotel Colon, the "El Capitan Pohan and Tiente Marcus" crew was happy to oblige. As the replacement engine arrived and was installed, a crew of locals cut the cane and foot-stomped a crude runway that baked for two days in the sun to a rock-hard surface. The new "runway" allowed the lightened Bolo to lift off the mud strip to join its squadron-mates in Trinidad.[7]

The missions from Trinidad were deeply appreciated by the U.S. Navy leadership who monitored each flight and came to understand how ASV worked at the tactical level. This created another threat to Dolan when he learned, via the Navy grapevine, that the regional command had submitted a special request that the 1st Sea-Search be permanently assigned to the U.S. Navy and kept in place in Trinidad for an unspecified time. Dolan called his crews together in the early morning hours and announced, "Guys, we head home TODAY. Pack your stuff and fuel your planes. We fly in three hours for Miami and then home to Langley." One of his pilots, Rockwood, approached him to ask if they had orders and Dolan only replied, "Rocky, the damn Navy is trying to take us over. I have no orders but today we are gone from here, period." The aircraft made a stop in Puerto Rico to stock up on rum, an ostensible "emergency refueling stop," flew to Miami, and then straight home to Langley Field. Only then did Dolan contact Arnold's office in Air Force Headquarters to explain what had happened. As he expected, he received immediate post-escape approvals for his unannounced departure from the claws of the U.S. Navy.[8]

One important aspect of the Dolan group operations in Trinidad was that it demonstrated the capability of the SCR-517A ASV system while educating the group on the quantities and types of spare components required to accompany the aircraft in any away-from-base deployment. At the conclusion of the Dolan group deployment several of the eight deployed aircraft were turned over to the 9th Bomb Group stationed there and were replaced at Langley by the same number of newly converted B-18Bs, all equipped with the improved SCR-517C ASV. Again, the 1st Sea-Search became the test bed for the improved system—its detection range had been increased to 100 miles—and it was Dolan's group which then identified its shortcomings for Rad Lab revisions.

These same crews would soon test the successor ASV system, the SCR-717 series, and work with Rad Lab to perfect new features, such as the PPI, which would become a standard component. As each iteration of the ASV radars was developed, tested and standardized for commercial production, the aircraft into which they were placed improved the quality of detection and attack. Importantly, apart from the sea-search and attack aspects, the ASV radars allowed dramatic improvements in navigation, adverse weather avoidance and higher-quality mission planning and routing.

A most-classified project

The Sea-Search unit's excursion also brought some limited public attention in the October 1942 edition of *Airview* magazine, an in-house publication of the Douglas Aircraft Corporation. Entitled "Caribbean Sub Patrol" and subtitled "Rugged Douglas B-18, America's oldest type of combat airplane, is still in the fight. From scores of Caribbean bases the big bombers hunt and sink submarines." The article is careful to make no mention of the classified word "RADAR" or the fact that ASV technology was the defining aspect of the B-18 deployment, nor does it identify the 1st Sea-Search Attack Group as a unit.

The article intentionally misleads by suggesting daylight patrols, with a "dawn to dusk" operations theme, and also notes the aircraft were operating subordinate to General George Brett's Caribbean Defense Command in Panama. The article also promotes the company's product by stating that the "backbone of the anti-submarine air force is a ship that admittedly would not stand up in today's fast-moving air war"—the Douglas B-18—and remarks on the Bolo's endurance by stressing that "they can stay in the air from dawn to dusk, as long as a submarine can be seen."[9]

The ASV radar equipment itself, and its installation and use in the B-18s, was considered a most sensitive and highly classified activity. In these early days, radar was a "secret" technology and each advance, particularly in the airborne context, was protected from any accidental compromise which might alert the enemy to the presence or application of the technology. The members of Dolan's group were regularly briefed on the high classification of their project, the possibility of radar compromise and warned against even using the word "radar" in the presence of uncleared military or civilian personnel. One early Dolan veteran, Frank Reynolds, recalls rolling out of Langley Field in his car on a weekend pass, fresh from yet another "loose lips sink ships" briefing, only to encounter a huge billboard a few miles down the road promoting "Radar" brand gasoline. The fact was, in mid-1942, the word "radar" was out there but few knew it was flying in the ASV B-18B Bolos at Langley Field.[10]

By late 1942, the B-18s had worked their way through a number of minor and major equipment conversions and additions. The unit continued to evaluate new systems and test production versions of SCR-517 units. The B-18s also tested, and were later equipped with, the aforementioned MAD, a tail-mounted magnetic anomaly detector that registered changes in the earth's magnetic field caused by a metal object in the water. It had a very limited range and, like the other electronic equipment the Sea-Search unit used, it was crude, but it did help narrow the distance. Other systems would be sent to Dolan's unit at Langley Field from Boston's Rad Lab and from Wright Field for test and evaluation, including the H2X blind-bombing system that would be deployed in strategic bombing offensives in Europe and later against the Home Islands of Japan.

The "Sea Search Attack Group Command History," compiled by I Bomber Command of the First Air Force in 1944, observed that Dolan's unit really was asked to perform three functions: direct support for the testing and validation of new airborne electronic systems; training of operators for onward deployment to combat areas where those systems were being introduced and would be operated; and, when directed and as available, active patrol and search for submarines. The history records that during the group's first year, its aircraft flew 1,500 hours of patrol and search, and was credited with sinking two submarines and badly damaging or destroying three more during the course of 43 U-boat sightings. The latter score included 22 instances of the activation of the MAD equipment and the balance by ASV. The narrative goes on to note that each B–18B was equipped with ASV, MAD and a radar altimeter, with the ASV in the nose and the MAD housed in an appendage to the tail, or "stinger," and that the Dolan unit was the first to utilize the microwave ASV which was confirmed to be "incomparably better than the Mark II then in general use for submarine search."[11]

One of the ASV-enabled attacks, on 21 August 1942, mounted by the B–18Bs during their deployment to Key West, where they were under the control of the Gulf Sea Frontier command, is recounted in detail as follows:

> At 0505, airplane #7602 took off from Meacham Field on a sea search flight … piloted by Lt. Franklin T.E. Reynolds … the operator noticed a signal on the ASV screen at 28 miles dead ahead, the signal then disappeared … was picked up again at 19 miles. Operator continued to direct the pilot by ASV until the contact became visible at 7 miles … aircraft dropped to 200 feet altitude at a distance of one mile from the target with a heading of 133 degrees and the bombardier prepared to release the bombs (325-pound Mark IV depth charges) and at 0952 released two bombs in train on the port stern of the submarine. One detonated 25 feet off the port side abeam of the conning tower and 25 feet off the starboard bow, two more depth charges were dropped in train at 0953.
>
> On the second run the submarine was visible at a depth of 15 feet, with the MAD detector registering a "Direct" over on both runs. After the first attack air bubbles and an oil slick 30 feet wide and 150 feet long appeared in the wake of the submarine. The pilot climbed to 500 feet altitude and circled the oil slick as that slick continued to widen, and the aircraft turned away to head to Key West to reload depth charges. "S-41" command instructed the aircraft to return to the area until replaced by a relief plane that was being sent. At 1118 an ASV signal was picked up at 8 miles, aircraft #7602 descended to 300 feet and a periscope was sighted at three miles, moving in the direction of 30 degrees true at a speed of three knots. The periscope submerged when the plane was two miles distant, but the MAD produced a strong off-side signal, indicating that the submarine was moving abreast of the plane's course.
>
> Other "off-side" signals were obtained, with more oil slicks appearing to mark the submarine location. At 1240 a destroyer, an SC boat and patrol boat were sighted and at 1247 the submarine was located again by the MAD equipment and smoke flares were dropped to complete the normal MAD tactical operation and completely bracketing the position of the submarine with smoke flares.

> The destroyer was bearing down on the position of the smoke flares and at 1306 the destroyer and other ships began releasing depth charges. At 1309 the aircraft flew over a pattern of just released depth charges and detected the submarine, with huge oil bubbles then surfacing, and the destroyer releasing more depth charges on the position. The depth of water was charted at 400 fathoms. Aircraft #7602 departed the area at 1324 having its relief plane in sight.

The "Command History" narrative also captures the full range of anti-submarine hunt and attack devices under development, including project reports on items as diverse as advanced MAD systems, low-altitude optical bombsights, retro-flares, sonic radio buoys, radio altimeters, wingtip MAD and marker slicks. Dolan's crews were operating from Langley and other bases to test such new equipment. Mention here is also made of the use of the recommissioned Navy submarine S-15 as a detection target for MAD and ASV search missions run out of Key West. These test runs to validate new equipment moving from the experimental to the limited production phase would continue through the balance of 1942 and well into 1943. B-24s would begin to replace the B-18Bs as the desired air testing platform as those aircraft became more readily available late in 1942.

Dolan lobbies for the B-24

During the fall of 1942, after the return to Langley from the Trinidad operation, Dolan continued to advance his overlapping goals. He needed to continue building the unit to a minimum of 20 combat crews and train them on the ASV while securing the best patrol bomber the AAF had to offer. His immediate objective was to build out an entire group of ASV-equipped aircraft and crew, a minimum of three combat squadrons, and to prime two or more for assignment overseas. His eye was on the growing demands of the war in the Pacific and in this, he and others—Colonels Wright and Aldrin in particular—saw a great opportunity to take the next iteration of ASV radar to the front lines of the battle.

During this same period, the earlier production variant of the B-24 supplied to the RAF Coastal Command, the LB-30 in U.S. Lend-Lease nomenclature, and the Liberator Mk.I as equipped for the maritime patrol role, was establishing its reputation as a U-boat killer par excellence. The history of one such aircraft, Liberator AM 929, and crew is useful; the aircraft crossed the Atlantic in August 1942 to join No. 120 Squadron as that unit's "H/120." Over the next 15 months, it would fly 60 combat missions, find and attack U-boats 20 times, sink four and share credit for a fifth. Dolan and Wright took note.[12]

Into the early winter months of 1942, the recently promoted Colonel Dolan was able to make regular trips to AAF Headquarters in Washington for SADU updates. In doing so, he was able to best protect his group's equities and lobby for the asset he most prized—the top-down commitment that his unit would receive the B-24 as the successor to his aging B-18s. The B-24s coming off the Consolidated Aircraft production lines were in short supply, however, and Army Air Corps and the Navy were competing for them, with each service demanding priority in delivery for onward assignments to combat squadrons in the European, Mediterranean, Pacific and China–Burma–India theaters.

In making his case to his leadership for an allotment of this aircraft, Dolan was now confident that his Sea-Search Unit, the SADU, had established a solid track record of operational performance and demonstrated its ability to interact with Rad Lab, as well as the managers and technicians at Wright Field, to define requirements for improved systems and to team with Rad Lab to test them in the field at Langley.

During the initial year at Langley Field, into the spring of 1943, Bid Dolan ruled the ASV program with an iron hand and a determination that his project would succeed. He fully expected that he would lead the first B-24 ASV contingent overseas to combat in the Pacific and was heartbroken when told by headquarters that he was too valuable to perform in that front-line combat role. It is probable that General Arnold and his staff, knowing Dolan's personality and his inclination to lead from the front, assumed that he would fly combat missions and lead in the most demanding ones, placing his life on the line. Many Air Force group-level commanders had done so, often against direct orders to refrain from such risk-seeking, and more than a few had been lost in combat. AAF leadership was not going to give Dolan that opportunity. Besides, this was a man who knew all the Air Force radar secrets, both the existing classified programs as well as next-generation systems still in the concept or experimental stage. Lost in combat was one thing, but to be declared "missing in action and fate unknown" was yet another level of risk that could not be entertained by the men who admired him.

Instead, Dolan would lead many of the critical Rad Lab projects supporting the AAF, a position enhanced by the steady improvements in radar and bombing technology being made by Rad Lab engineers and their private-sector manufacturers. In early 1943, he would find himself stewarding a related project that would greatly advance U.S. Air Force's strategic bombing efforts in the European Theater and later come to define the operations of the B-29 Superfortress over Japan. That project was the H2X blind-bombing system and Dolan, recognizing its importance from day one, would soon throw himself into this program with passion. In delivering the Eagle, the successor to the H2X, to the Eighth Air Force in Europe, shuttling between B-24 and B-17 bases in England, Wright Field and other U.S. installations, Dolan would exhaust himself and those around him.

Dolan the man, the leader and the friend

Because of the critical role he played in shepherding the entire ASV program, his foundational position in the creation of the Wright Project that he would send off to war and the success he would have with other high-priority electronic projects, some personal observations by the men who served under Dolan are in order.

Lieutenant Jim Pope, navigator:

I had been flying the first production versions of the B-26 but I was culled out for assignment to the "Dolan project," whatever that was. I was with Dolan from day one back in early February 1942 at McChord Field when he selected me, by a coin toss, to join his journey to Boston and Rad Lab, then on to Langley Field with the Sea Search. When we did the coin toss he was selecting his own crew to head to Sacramento to get a plane, then to San Antonio with the first B-18A to be converted there and then on to Boston. He had selected two navigators out of twenty or so, pulled us aside and asked me to call a coin toss. I won and we left the next day, the seven of us covered by Special Order Number 22, and I would be with him until I shipped out for the Pacific with the Wright Project in August 1943.

Dolan and I did not always get along and sometimes we actually fought, and I mean physically. One time we had to take it into the boxing ring to settle an issue and let the emotion burn off. Shortly after arriving at Langley Field in May 1942, although a rated navigator, I had tried to put in for pilot training but Dolan blocked me. He called me into his office and said that I was "too young (age 21) and too ambitious" and, in any event, I was badly needed in his unit, citing the needs of the service and all that. I called him out on that lame explanation and he stood from his desk and said, "let's head to the gym."

When we put on the gloves, I stood a full head taller than him and he complained that my height was another reason I would not make a good pilot. Dolan stepped on an ammunition box and looked me in the eyes. When I yelled "what the hell does height have to do with it?" he punched me and the fight was on. My anger did not wear off for a long time, but he had his priorities and my leaving him and his unit, my abandoning him and Sea Searchers to become a pilot, was not one of them. I stayed the course at Langley and many months later went out to the Pacific as a member of the Wright Project. But Dolan was the main reason I stayed until then.

I flew as his navigator many times, the early ASV test missions in Boston, at Langley Field and the Florida and Jamaica deployments, and we bantered a lot, he by then a full Colonel and I only a just-promoted First Lieutenant. I was one of the few who had the guts to tell him the truth to his face—that he was a "lousy pilot" who was too often distracted or tended to drift off course. The truth was that his flying usually scared his co-pilots sitting in the right-hand seat half to death. But I respected him, as did all the other officers and enlisted men. He had a vision and a determination, and he was very savvy politically and he had managed to collect several important supporters along the way.

Lieutenant (later Colonel) Crowell "Butch" Werner:

I was with Dolan from the first days, detached from the 38th Bomb Squadron at Muroc Field, to fly to San Antonio for aircraft modification and then on to join Dolan and his crew at Boston's Rad Lab. I flew with Lt. Bill Foley as his rated 1034 bombardier, or "aircraft observer-bombardier" as we were sometimes identified in our orders. I ended up eighteen months later as part of the Wright Project Crew 5 of Lieutenant Bob Lehti when we headed for Guadalcanal. Initially we had no navigator assigned to a B-18 crew—that would come later—so I had a dual-function and a lot to do as we crisscrossed the U.S. on our B-18 flights moving aircraft among the San Antonio Air Depot, Boston, Wright Field, Langley Field and other bases.

For some reason (perhaps because he had no son) from early on Dolan sort of adopted me as one of his "boys," as he did a few other very young officers and men who he thought had promise but needed some close attention. That we needed attention came to Dolan's attention in Boston—we were ten single guys in a brownstone townhouse on the Commons, officers and enlisted men in residence together, which was against all Air Corps protocol. We partied every night, with two liquor stores on call to deliver the goods and Dolan kept an eye on us.

At Langley Field, Dolan joined our poker games, in fact, he promoted them, and he delighted in cleaning us out. At Langley, once every few weeks, he would host a "Spanish dinner" for seven or more younger officers, provide lots of drinks and turn it into a poker game. At that time, I was paid $150 a month plus $75 flight pay and we could easily lose a month's pay in one night. I held my own against Dolan and at one time he owed me $200, which he paid back the next month. I expected him to hold my win against me, but he never did. But he did not shy away from fleecing other less-skilled officers and men of their cash either! He did take a special liking to me, perhaps because I was not a boot-licker and sometimes talked back to him.

Dolan was a great operational type and I often was selected to accompany him on his flights up to Washington to Air Corps Headquarters. He would make his report every six weeks or so to General Giles and his staff, and Colonel Aldrin would always be present. I became close to Colonel Aldrin who would usually seek me out for a private conversation, a "how are things going at Langley" debriefing. The purpose of the Giles–Aldrin meetings, at least for Dolan, was to secure approval for Dolan to organize, dispatch and lead a B-24 ASV unit into combat in the Pacific.

When Dolan was told that Colonel "Stud" Wright would take the first squadron into combat and that he (Dolan) had to remain at Langley to organize, qualify and dispatch the two LAB subsequent squadrons—the Scott and Hopson projects—and also finish the development of another blind bombing high-priority system, his ego was badly damaged. He was determined to gain a combat command, both to get into the fight and because he sought promotion, and he saw others being rapidly promoted while he was left behind. He got his combat assignment wish but he died in a B-24 on the way back to England to take up that command.[13]

Another member of the original Rad Lab group of "Dolan's Boys," Charles Rockwood, recalled Dolan's consideration for his men. On a Saturday morning in early November, Dolan called together 20 or so of his men and told them to prepare two B-18s for a "special mission" that morning, a non-scheduled "off the record" flight for special consultations in New York City. Upon landing at Mitchell Field on Long Island, Dolan produced front-section tickets for the Army–Notre Dame football game that same day. The Army–Notre Dame rivalry was in its heyday and the previous week the number six-ranked "Fighting Irish" had beaten the Army's other traditional rival, Navy. The Army was nationally ranked 19 and Dolan thought that an upset was in the offing, but the Irish beat the Army 13–0 in front of 75,000 fans at Yankee Stadium. The Dolan men spent the night at the premier Roosevelt Hotel, all courtesy of their commander.

Colonel Bid Dolan did perish on Valentine's Day 1945 in the company of nine other AAF airmen in the crash of a B-24M on approach to Gander, Newfoundland. Dolan's aircraft was making a refueling stop at Gander en route to rejoin the Eighth Air Force in the United Kingdom. His cargo included an upgraded version of the APQ-7 blind-bombing system—the Eagle—and other sensitive materials. Dolan was responsible for introducing this system to operations and was eager to bring the capability to the front. The weather that day, as Dolan's B-24 (44-42169) made an instrument approach, was described as "atrocious," with skies snow-blocked with zero visibility. His aircraft crashed some 20 miles northeast of Gander in a remote location. Despite a desperate air and ground search, the wreckage was not found for more than a month, the plane, Colonel Dolan and crew meanwhile having been reported "missing and presumed lost."[14]

Dolan's death was keenly felt in many locations by the diverse groups of men whom his leadership had impacted. In Washington, D.C., his death was mourned by the AAF leadership that respected him and called him a friend, including General Hap Arnold, Major General Giles, Colonels Aldrin and Wright and their colleagues. The men of the Eighth Air Force, to whom he was hurrying with the latest version of the Eagle radar bombing system, would not have the benefit of his energy, while the officers and men at Langley Field, where he had left an indelible impression in his two years there, found themselves shaken. The hardest hit may have been those of the three units he had personally crafted by selecting the crews and overseeing their training at Langley Field, and then sending them into combat in the Pacific. As the aircraft had been declared missing and was not found for some time, confirmation of Dolan's death did not reach the men in the Pacific or those who had already returned home after completing their combat assignments for several months.

Rad Lab's *Radar* magazine published a full-page profile of Dolan. The edition only mentioned in the last sentence that he had "encountered storms over Newfoundland and disappeared" while returning to England with the most recent version of his latest project, the APQ-7 radar system. It was a fitting obituary within the radar community for a man who had done so much to realize the technology developed by the Rad Lab scientists and engineers. The profile is provided at Appendix A.[15]

Other AAF commands wrote glowing obituaries at the time of Dolan's death. Prominent among them was a classified version compiled, it appears, by the headquarters staff at the request of Generals Giles and Arnold. This document, "Notes on Colonel William C. Dolan," SECRET, is provided at Appendix B. It is noteworthy for its comprehensiveness as well as the compassion it expresses over the nation's loss of an AAF leader and its most prominent "airborne radar pioneer."

CHAPTER 4

Low Altitude Bombing

January–July 1943

The world at war

The Allies entered 1943 hopeful but with the future course of the war still very much in doubt. The battle of the Atlantic was in its darkest hours. In November 1942 alone, the U-boats had sunk more than 100 ships totaling over 700,000 tons. This would drive their year-end scorecard to more than 1,100 Allied ships and six million tons. Operational U-boat strength had increased to over 200 vessels and the U-boat menace showed every sign of choking the Allied war effort. Unless the U-boat was beaten in the Atlantic, there could be no invasion for a second front in Europe. In North Africa, Operation *Torch* had placed a British–American force on the continent to press Rommel's *Afrika Korps* from the west while Montgomery's Eighth Army drove toward Tunisia from the east. But here the battle would rage for months and not be resolved until mid-May. In Russia, although the Germans were encircled and about to be defeated at Stalingrad, they were preparing a strategic withdrawal that would shorten their lines by spring and position their forces to go back onto the offensive.

In the Pacific, the Japanese eastward advance had been stopped with the battles of the Coral Sea and Midway in May and June 1942, and the Americans had begun their counteroffensive at Guadalcanal in the Solomon Islands in August. Here, a land, air and surface battle had raged for seven months. Although Japanese air and naval power was being ground down by mounting losses in the Guadalcanal battles to the point that the Japanese High Command was about to order a withdrawal from the island, the Japanese were continuing to exact a heavy toll on the U.S. Navy. U.S. naval victories around Guadalcanal were still being offset by Japanese counterstrikes that would claim a number of ships and thousands of sailors even as 1943 approached. In January 1943, the final conquest of Guadalcanal and the battle up "The Slot" toward Rabaul still lay in the future.

ASV and the U-boats

New Year 1943 found the 1st Sea-Search Attack Group facing new priorities as the U-boat war directly off the U.S. eastern seaboard ebbed. By this time the focus of the battle of the Atlantic had shifted back to mid-ocean where events on both sides were building up to the "death struggle" that would begin in March 1943 and rage for many months. The U.S. Army Air Forces' (USAAF) Antisubmarine Command found most of its patrol bomber units positioned on the wrong side of the Atlantic to participate in the new U-boat battles, and as a result, the anti-submarine patrols flown by U.S. based units, like Dolan's at Langley Field, became more routine, less hectic and often just plain boring.

The U-boat struggle in the Atlantic during the spring and summer of 1943 also included the large-scale operational introduction of related microwave radar equipment, including the U.S. Navy's AN/APS-2 System and the British Mark III airborne unit. This technology, when combined with the Allied intelligence message interception and the wholesale breaking of German codes, the improved organization of anti-submarine assets, new convoying techniques and the deployment of escort carriers, would tip the balance once and for all against the U-boat. The U-boat wolf packs did succeed in pressing home vicious attacks on Allied convoys over the summer of 1943, but the price the Germans were forced to pay in experienced crews and U-boats was appalling. The war in the Atlantic would continue for two more long years with millions of tons of Allied merchant shipping sunk and hundreds more U-boats destroyed, but by late summer 1943, the writing was on the wall. The Allies knew that with enough men, escorts, patrol aircraft, new merchant ships and radar, they would prevail.

The AAF had moved quickly to place its patrol bomber units in the field in Europe at the turn of the new year. The 1st Antisubmarine Group (Provisional) was transferred into the combat zone and was operating 20 B-24s equipped with SCR-517 sets from English soil by January. This small but eager microwave radar-equipped long-range patrol bomber unit received its baptism by fire over the Bay of Biscay with the RAF Coastal Command. It was later shifted to Morocco from where it patrolled north into the Mediterranean Sea off the North African coast and west into the Atlantic where it would find heavy action against Axis submarines. The Liberator units, using an aircraft that possessed the range, durability, armament and bomb capacity, and fitted with second-generation ASV radar systems, demonstrated the excellent potential of the microwave ASV long-range bomber concept.

The two forward-deployed AAF units, the 480th and 479th Antisubmarine Groups, would sink no fewer than eight German submarines during the six-month period from February–August 1943. In RAF Coastal Command hands during the duration of the war, the B-24 would prove to be spectacularly successful, tallying no less than 66 confirmed submarine kills between October 1942 and May 1945. The Liberator's reputation as the finest U-boat hunter-killer aircraft of the war was established, due in large measure to the systems developed at Rad Lab and the operational tactics perfected at Langley by Dolan's 1st Sea-Search Attack Group.

The United Kingdom was also keen to share its sub-hunting experiences and tactics with its American counterparts. In July 1943, under arrangements made by AAF Director of Technical Services, the 1st Sea-Search hosted a detachment of two RAF Coastal Command LB-30s and crews (led by Flight Lieutenant Peter Cundy) to "obtain first-hand knowledge from an experienced ASW crew." Flying from Langley with Rad Lab's latest ASV radars installed, the two LB-30s conducted 25 patrol missions, made two submarine sightings and one attack to damage a U-boat.[1]

The U.S. Navy, confident that it now had a firm handle on the U-boat war, indicated that it desired to assume responsibility for the entire American anti-submarine war by late 1943, including all airborne operations. This move saw the U.S. Navy accomplish the complete takeover of USAAF's anti-submarine assets, namely the B-24 squadrons then operating against U-boats in the Atlantic. An intra-service agreement allowed the U.S. Navy to assume ownership of all 77 B-24s then being operated by the USAAF in the anti-submarine role, and by October 1943, this transition had been completed. The Liberator, designated the PB4Y, would continue to render excellent service to the U.S. Navy in all theaters, both in anti-submarine roles in the Atlantic and as patrol bombers with U.S. Navy and Marine units in the Pacific.

With the service boundaries of the anti-submarine war being redrawn to remove the Army Air Force from the responsibility of frontline anti-submarine fighting, mid-1943 saw the AAF shift its interest. While sub-hunting would continue to be important to the United States and its allies, the technology and aircraft required to sustain the counter-offensive had now come together for the U.S. Navy and the RAF Coastal Command. It was time for the Air Force to focus on applying radar developments to other pressing wartime mission requirements. New technologies, better-defined requirements and the availability of new aircraft in ever greater numbers would combine to deliver these capabilities to the front lines.

The B-24 comes to the 1st Sea-Search

By October 1942, it was apparent that the tried and trusted B-18B needed to be replaced by a larger front-line platform capable of longer-distance missions and with the capability to defend itself in contested airspace. The systems that were under development testing by the group at Langley Field needed to be installed and validated in an aircraft that could take such improved patrol bomber capabilities into combat deployment. The B-24, already deployed and proved successful in its anti-submarine ASV role in the Atlantic, was an obvious choice to replace the B-18s at Langley Field.

The first to be assigned to the 1st Sea-Search were flown to Langley Field by Dolan's men in late October, fresh from the factory after a stop at Wright Field for some equipment installation. But with this long-awaited and welcomed infusion of new aircraft came a tragedy—the first loss of a Dolan crew and aircraft. Captain William Foley, who had been part of the Dolan team from its first days in Boston, crashed 10 miles from Langley Field during his flight from Wright Field, killing the entire crew, on 27 October. Up to this point, the group had been incredibly fortunate to not lose an aircraft and crew in the many night missions they had flown over their 10 months in operation. Foley's loss was attributed to "fuel exhaustion" but it was clear that the B-18 pilots, many of whom had mastered the B-26 "Widow Maker" medium bomber before joining the Dolan B-18 effort, now had to master every aspect of the B-24.[2]

Activation of the 3rd Sea-Search Attack Squadron

On 9 December 1942, the group activated the 3rd Sea-Search Attack Squadron, with Dolan assigning Major Leo J. Foster from his staff to lead the unit, effective 1 January 1943. A cadre of eight officers and 30 enlisted men drawn from the group's 2nd Squadron was initially assigned and within a month the new squadron would include 37 officers and more than 200 enlisted men in its ranks. On New Year's Day 1943, in Hangar 532-A at Langley Field, the squadron declared itself operational, with three B-18Bs transferred to the unit. The only other operational squadron of the group, the 2nd, would retain several of the original Dolan crews and add additional personnel to bring itself up to a full complement of men and aircraft. The 3rd Squadron, as it accepted delivery of B-24D aircraft, would form the basis of the Wright Project. This would be the first LAB unit to be dispatched to combat, while the 2nd Squadron would allow the formation of the second combat unit to be raised by the group for deployment to the Pacific—the Scott Project.

Innovation explodes at Rad Lab

As a direct consequence of the reduced level of U-boat hostilities in the patrol areas assigned to the 1st Sea-Search Attack Group, Dolan's men spent more of their hours working with new electronic equipment provided by Rad Lab and its civilian contractors. Under the watchful care of civilian scientists and technicians, Dolan's men mated a variety of new equipment to more modern aircraft such as the B-24, which had been selected for air combat service.

By the spring of 1943, Rad Lab had over 50 projects going full swing, six different types of radar already in service in the field, hundreds of production sets that had arrived at, or were on the way to, front-line units, and thousands more on order. In addition to airborne radar systems, the laboratory was working on anti-aircraft fire control radar, air defense early-warning radar, air and navigation radar and improved naval "SG" surface systems radar. The work was also moving forward on a project called H2X, an effort that would turn into a "crash program" by June at the insistence of the Eighth Air Force. It would become one of Rad Lab's great success stories just six months later when it rode into combat over Wilhelmshaven, mounted in a crude housing in place of the chin turret on a Pathfinder B-17.

By early 1943, Rad Lab had been joined by a host of powerful firms from America's private sector in an all-out wartime effort of electronic systems development and production. Some of the firms included Western Electric Company, Bell Laboratories, Philco, Raytheon, Bendix, Gilfillan Westinghouse and Rad Lab's own Research Construction Company. These firms provided Rad Lab, the Committee and the American war planners with the depth and breadth of research and production talent. This industrial-scale capacity allowed a wide variety of systems to reach American fighting men, often within months of the system's conception. In some cases, Rad Lab proper would wisely balance its own priorities and capabilities and opt to assign major responsibility for a given project to a civilian firm better positioned to turn a concept into a weapon. Such a project was Low Altitude Bombing or, as it would soon become known, "LAB."

LAB: The concept

The idea for a low altitude blind-bombing system based on radar was apparently first suggested by a member of the 1st Sea-Search Attack Group in May 1942. The need for such a system was not only obvious, it was also glaring. Microwave ASV radar allowed aircraft such as the B-18 and B-24 to patrol vast areas of ocean with a very high probability for target detection. The system permitted the patrol bomber to strip away the protective cloak of darkness used by enemy submarines and surface vessels with target detection at ranges of 50 or more miles in the dead of night or in inclement weather. The frustration came when the ASV radar brought the aircraft to within less than a mile of the target with pinpoint accuracy but then lost it on the center of its scope due to ground clutter.[3]

The British were the first to find a partial solution to this ASV point-of-attack problem when they deployed the five-million candlepower Leigh Light on ASV Mark II-equipped patrol bombers by mid-1942. The radar brought the aircraft up to the contact and held the aircraft on a correct heading until ground clutter on the scope obscured the target. The wing-mounted light was then switched on within a few hundred yards of the target to permit the visual sighting which enabled the final attack run. A human-triggered bombing by the sight of the submarine was then possible, often delivered with impressive results. This technique, while quite successful for a time, had inherent limitations, not the least of which was its reliance on a two-element system that required the attack aircraft to ride its searchlight beam down the gun barrels of a submarine target. The latter was often alert to the possibility of attack, sometimes utilizing radar-warning receivers to alert gun crews to the approach of a patrolling aircraft. Obviously, the approach by an attacker that had to illuminate itself as it closed with the surface-running submarine made the aircraft a hard-to-miss target for the U-boat gunners. The Germans adjusted quickly to the ASV–Leigh Light and crammed their U-boats with more anti-aircraft guns. This was not an acceptable longer-term solution and a technology development scramble was underway to find an improved approach that kept the attack initiative in the hands of the Allied aircraft crews.

What was truly needed was an all-electronic, blind-bombing system that would allow a patrol bomber to detect, home in on and attack a surface target with great accuracy, relying completely on instruments with no requirement for visual contact. Such a concept required American designers in 1942 to modify several state-of-the-art electronics systems, create from scratch at least one new component and interface these components to produce an effective and reliable weapons system.

Rad Lab worked from the concept paper that developed a design in mid-summer 1942 to create crude versions on a laboratory scale. It was then shared with Dolan's team at Langley. Suggestions from the 1st Sea-Search on the location of components, the character of the scopes and the requirements of the system operator and aircraft crew were incorporated and the Rad Lab basic design was completed. Field tests were conducted at Elgin Field in the panhandle area of western Florida, then home to the AAF's Proving Ground Command, with aircrews for these tests provided by Dolan's group.

Once the LAB concept was validated, Rad Lab turned to secure the able assistance of Bell Telephone Laboratories to begin constructing experimental units. By October 1942, the Rad Lab and Bell Laboratories Group pronounced the concept sound and reported the first successful test runs with the experimental sets. Bell Laboratories (Bell Labs) received a production contract for the low altitude blind-bombing attachment, later to receive the official designation AN/APQ-5, and was responsible for mating this component with the other elements of the new weapons system. Essentially a small but functional "black box" computer, the AN/APQ-5 served as the system interface and was the heart, if not the brains, of the LAB system.

During late 1942, Bell Labs worked to perfect the black box and build into the design the rugged construction and dependability the system would require in the field. Bell Laboratories, and its sister production firm Western Electric Company, also had to balance the men and equipment devoted to the LAB project against other armed forces radar projects, but the potential that this system offered immediately caught the attention of Dolan, Aldrin, Wright and Miles and they assigned this project a high priority. By the spring of 1943, the LAB black box computer had been married to other components, tested at Rad Lab and in the air and was ready for a trial installation at Langley Field in combat aircraft capable of carrying the system into war.

The Low Altitude Bombing weapons system

The LAB system, as it was evolved by Rad Lab and in testing with Dolan's unit during the spring and into the early summer of 1943, included the following elements:

A. The SCR-717-B airborne search radar unit (and aid to navigation). This system was an improved and repackaged model of the earlier SCR-517 microwave ASV radar system which had been in use with Dolan's unit since the spring of 1942. The SCR-717-B entered operational use in the spring of 1943, and shortly thereafter was mated to the LAB, representing, as it did then, the state-of-the-art ASV system. This radar, when mounted in a B-24, permitted sea search at a rate of 7,500 to 10,000 square miles an hour, coupled with detection rages up to 100 miles.

B. The SCR-729 Interrogator-Responder was an instrument that allowed the radar operator, once his scope had identified a target blip and guided the aircraft to an attack position, to electronically interrogate the target to determine (identify) if it were friend or foe (IFF). If friend, compatible IFF equipment on the contact under interrogation would receive the aircraft's signal and respond with its own signal. If foe, there would be no response.

C. The AN/APN-1 Radio Altimeter (Absolute Altimeter) was an instrument that allowed for a precise altitude measurement using radio waves to establish an exact distance between the ground level (water surface) and the aircraft, doing so on a real-time basis to feed this information into the computing attachment.

D. The AN/APQ-5 low altitude precision-bombing attachment was a small computer that collected the data on aircraft speed, height and distance to target as provided by the other system components. This information, constantly updated by the radar system and adjusted by the bombardier, allowed the bombardier to select the appropriate bomb intervals and number of weapons and then activate the attachment. The device functioned on an automatic basis during the attack, even taking over the bomb release mechanism which toggled the pre-selected bomb pattern at the split second that the optimum release point was reached.

In recounting the development of this core component of the LAB system—the AN/APQ-5—a full measure of credit must be given to the engineers at Bell Labs. A reconstruction of that effort is offered in a publication that covers the full scope of Bell Labs during World War II. Noting the possibilities offered by the SCR-517 and 717 radars as they were being modified for sea search and the possibility of further modifying them for bomb sighting, Bell Labs worked with Rad Lab to push the concept as a priority, and in field testing the system, was mated with the Dolan Group and its testbed B-18s and B-24s.

The Bell Labs account related that these radars:

> ... accurately gave the slant distance to the target, and this data, together with altitude above ground and flight speed, could be used to compute the ground range and bomb release point. These were not simple calculations, and since this was long before the days of miniature solid-state devices, the computer size and complexity threatened to become unreasonable. In this predicament, the former "television people" proposed an ingenious idea in late 1942. If one bombs at low altitude, they pointed out, the ground range is almost the same as the slant range, in which case some computations become much simpler. Thus, a radar bombsight could be devised with operating characteristics similar to those of the Norden optical sight on which bomber crews had been trained.[4]

The Bell Lab narrative continues:

> Some months and considerable cooperation among many technical groups were required to develop and construct a flight test model of what was then coded as the RC-217 Auxiliary Siting Unit. In the meantime, small-package development had progressed rapidly and the X-band and 700-series radars could be adopted for use with the bombsight. A two-month test in Florida ending in April 1943, showed the new equipment was as simple to operate as the Norden bombsight and produced high bombing accuracy. The (Army) Air Force requested the immediate outfitting of a wing of B-24 bombers with this equipment. Twenty pre-production models were quickly constructed for this purpose in Bell Laboratories shops but a further simplification was made combining three units into one control unit. The equipment was now coded AN/APQ-5.[5]

In March 1943, the first compete LAB prototype system came to Langley Field for the group to test more rigorously. A B-24D, serial number 42-123708, was the first to receive the production version, allowing equipment calibration testing and mission familiarization for the bombardiers to validate the performance of the overall system. In mid-April 1943, a second B-24D, 42-123878, arrived with Model Number 1 of the further-refined pre-production LAB RD-217-T-1 system. From June forward, a number of tests were completed by the group to determine system accuracy at higher altitudes (10,000 feet) and slant ranges of up to 15,000 feet.

With the system design standardized, more of the group's crews were trained on the system with records indicating some 90 flights and 260 hours committed to this introduction phase. Rad Lab engineers were there to instruct and fine-tune the system, some 400 man hours were involved in installing and testing the LAB equipment. During this same period, beyond the validation of the AN/APQ-5 attachment as the computer-like heart of the system, other elements were being improved and standardized for incorporation. For example, the SCR-729 IFF interrogator was tested by the 1st Sea-Search and declared operational, both with regard to aircraft and surface ship interrogations. If the B-24 LAB aircraft were to fly in the contested waters of the South and Southwest Pacific, any risk of a LAB attack on a friendly ship had to be mitigated, not to mention situations where surface ships failed to interrogate and identify aircraft overhead as "friendlies" and, in so doing, holding their fire.

The combat advantages offered by the LAB system were manifold. For the first time in the history of air warfare, a patrol bomber could be sent into combat in the dead of night with the capability to electronically search vast expanses of enemy water, detect and home in on a target and, most importantly, deliver a precision low-level attack without any requirements for visual contact. A complete non-visual mission, from take-off, through search and tactical attack, to recovery to home base and landing, was possible on a routine basis. Such a capability would deny enemy surface ships the protection provided by darkness and inclement weather and force them to reckon with the high probability of detection and attack in contested waters, not only during the day but also at night.

LAB to the Pacific

At the time the LAB system was being mated to the B-24 and that hardware tested for deployment into combat, there was more than a routine need for such capability on the front lines of the war in the Pacific. As the naval and air conflict raged in the Solomon Islands and shifted from that island chain to the Bismarck Archipelago and more distant targets, the United States remained engaged in its own death struggle with the battleships, cruisers and destroyers of the Imperial Japanese Navy. The latter were brilliant tacticians, highly skilled at night surface combat and operations. When the Americans gradually won command of the air over the southern Solomons, the Japanese Navy switched almost exclusively to night operations, a medium that preserved many of their advantages and reduced the edge provided by the American air power.

At this same time, the Japanese submarine fleet was committed in greater numbers to run supply missions among these islands to sustain land garrisons, some of which had been bypassed, and others which were still fighting invading U.S. forces. These same Japanese submarines were also on patrol to disrupt invading fleets, threaten supply convoy routes into the battle zones and attack U.S. Navy warships. In the spring of 1943, when LAB equipment was being installed and tested, the requirement in the South Pacific to field attack aircraft which could deny the Japanese Navy their night shelter was strong indeed. Once again, Rad Lab, Bell Labs and Western Electric had developed, tested, refined and commissioned an electronic weapons system badly needed in combat. The aircrews at Langley Field who knew how to use ASV, and were adept at testing, validating and accepting new technology, were the natural partners to take LAB to war in the Pacific.

Dolan mission at Langley

At the time Colonel Wright was preparing his crews to depart for the Pacific, work at Langley Field transitioned further. The reduced threat of the U-boats along the Atlantic coast (the former patrol area of the group's B-18B ASV aircraft), and the ongoing assumption of all airborne anti-submarine activity by the U.S. Navy, permitted Dolan to focus on two high-priority training efforts—the preparation of additional B-24 LAB units for dispatch overseas and bombardier training related to the H2X high-altitude bombing system that would soon be deployed by the Eighth Air Force in Europe. The 1st Sea-Search Attack Group swapped out the "Group" identifier for "Unit" effective 7 September 1943, reflecting the fact that its mission was, from that point forward, a training effort. Concurrently, the AAF's Antisubmarine Command was disbanded, effective 30 September 1943, and Dolan's entire operation, at his recommendation, was then subordinated to the East Coast's First Air Force. A direct channel between the Dolan unit at Langley Field and AAF Headquarters was no longer necessary.

From this point forward, Dolan and his executive team dedicated themselves to organizing and training the next two LAB units destined for the Pacific, and Dolan increasingly involved himself in the system development and operational elements of the H2X program. The organization eventually partitioned itself into three squadrons, with the 2nd Sea-Search retaining responsibility for the training of LAB crews, the 3rd Squadron training B-24 H2X crews and the 4th Squadron training B-17 H2X crews. The Dolan team was further reorganized in late 1943, and in April 1944, as part of the overall AAF Base Unit Plan, was inactivated and its personnel transitioned into the 111th Air Base Unit. This organization continued the mission of training and the staging of aircrews and aircraft for forward deployment to the combat theaters. In the fast-moving pace established by Hap Arnold to build capacity, deploy technology and evolve AAF units to support ongoing initiatives, the Dolan Sea-Search Attack Group had served its purpose and had its day.

In this period of transition, Dolan, ever restless for a combat assignment, pressed Arnold and all his contacts at AAF Headquarters for transfer to the Eighth Air Force in the United Kingdom. He would get his wish, be welcomed as an established technology innovator and find his niche, albeit not as a combat commander leading missions over Europe. Rather, he would be held back from flights over enemy-occupied territory as a man who had too many secrets and limited to senior-level support roles. Still, he found ways to fly those combat missions. He became the lead for the assessment of the H2X system and took responsibility for expediting the qualification and deployment of a subsequent radar-based precision bombing and navigation system—the Eagle. As previously noted, Colonel William Dolan would perish in a B-24 hurrying back to England with one of the first Eagle sets.

Wright Project Aircraft and Crews 1943

Wright Project group photo, Langley Field, August 1943. (Author's collection)

Wright Project Crew One, Major Foster and crew. (Author's collection)

Wright Project B-24D Madame Libby the Sea Ducer *with Rockwood crew, Guadalcanal, 1943. (Author's collection)*

Wright Project B-24D Uncle's Fury *with Zinn crew, Guadalcanal, 1943. (Author's collection)*

Wright Project B-24D Miss Cuddles *with Carlson crew, Guadalcanal, 1943. (Author's collection)*

Wright Project B-24D Devil's Delight, *Langley Field, August 1943. (Author's collection)*

Wright Project B-24D Bums Away, *Guadalcanal, August 1943. (Author's collection)*

The Wright Project

July–August 1943

Taking radar to war

Colonel Aldrin, Major General Giles and Army Air Force Commanding General Hap Arnold in Washington, D.C., carefully charted the progress made by Rad Lab's researchers in perfecting the LAB system and its validation at Langley Field in the hands of Bid Dolan's 1st Sea-Search Attack Group. Dolan had a number of radar and electronic test programs underway but was most excited by the opportunities offered to tactical aviation by LAB and enthusiastically advocated the near-term commitment of LAB-equipped bombers to combat in the Pacific. The Rad Lab liaison officer, Colonel Wright, had also championed the potential LAB offered, and in company with Colonel Aldrin, lobbied for this at AAF Headquarters. Wright had supervised the development and testing of the system, and by early 1943, he was convinced that the system should be deployed into combat immediately. Moreover, the battles then being fought in the Pacific demanded that such a capability, if it existed, should be committed as soon as possible. The Japanese were reeling but were striking back, and in many instances still contested the night as their own.

The powers at AAF Headquarters agreed and, in early 1943, authorized the formation of a test LAB program, which would be based with the 1st Sea-Search Attack Group at Langley Field, for a summer 1943 combat assignment in the Pacific. Colonels Dolan, Aldrin and Wright all very badly wanted to command this deployed combat unit and argued for it. Drive, ability, experience and leadership qualified them all, but Stud Wright received the nod and the "Wright Project" was born. Anticipating that AAF Headquarters would eventually bless this proposal, Dolan had reorganized the group and created the 3rd Squadron in December 1942, drawing most of the personnel from the group's operational unit, the 2nd Squadron. Dolan placed his Group Operations Officer, Captain Leo Foster, in charge and by January 1943, the new squadron comprised 29 officers, 180 enlisted men and three B-18Bs.

During this same January–June period, additional crews were brought into the group and assigned to the 2nd Squadron to bring it up to full staffing. It was then obvious that at least two LAB combat squadrons would be sent to the Pacific and that this would happen as expeditiously as possible. Dolan's group would therefore be expected to certify, train, equip and dispatch these units as well, and time was of the essence. By June 1943, Dolan had nominated, and Wright finalized, the 10 combat crews of the 3rd Squadron that would go to the Pacific. This decision was made official within the group by the 2 June 1943 General Orders Number 2.

This order relieved 70 officers and enlisted men from service in the 3rd Sea-Search Attack Squadron, assigned them to duty with the Wright Project and made the 3rd Sea-Search responsible for the maintenance of aircraft and operational facilities required for this project. This core group was told to prepare for movement overseas as they continued training with the B-24 LAB systems then being delivered by Bell Labs and Western Electric. To this initial group of pilots, navigators, bombardiers, flight engineers, assistant flight engineers, radio operators and aircraft armorers were added co-pilots, radar operators and gunners to round out the 10 crews of 10 men each that would leave Langley Field for the Pacific some eight weeks later.[1]

Colonel Wright was fortunate in that Dolan had already assigned the cream of the pilots, airmen and technicians who had served with him from the outset. Many were from Boston Rad Lab days and the rest had months of experience in the 1st Sea-Search Attack Group. Some, like squadron navigator Jim Pope, had flown with Dolan since Special Order Number 22 directed their temporary assignment back in February 1942. Most of Dolan's original group came from West-Coast squadrons to join him at Boston and Langley Field in the spring of 1942 and participated in the B-18B ASV sub hunts and radar system development activity. All were experienced men, were proficient in their B-24 aircraft, knew the radar and trusted the technology. They were also very eager to enter combat under the leadership of Colonel Wright.

Colonel Stuart "Stud" Wright

For AAF Headquarters and AAF Commanding General Hap Arnold, the choice of Wright was obvious—he knew Dolan's people, the LAB system and was a natural combat leader. Moreover, Colonel Dolan was judged to be too valuable where he was at Langley Field, involved in the flight testing of new radar systems, and could not be spared for a front-line assignment. The same was also true of Colonel Aldrin who continued to work his classified projects at Wright Field and served as part of the Hap Arnold "brain trust" planning other elements of the war. Wright was a taskmaster with the B-24s. He made it a point to fly multiple times with each crew, eventually satisfying himself that they were ready; this dedication impressed the men he would take into combat.

All of the men who went to the Pacific with Wright recalled him with respect and saw him as a perfectionist, not the same persona of Bid Dolan who tended to "father" his men while he drove them. Wright was seen as a man who was determined to prove that the LAB that he had overseen added a whole new dimension to airborne attack. A squadron lead pilot, Bob Lehti, recalled that, on his first B-24 checkout flight with Wright, with Lehti in the right-hand co-pilot seat and Wright in the left seat—which Lehti normally occupied as the command pilot—Lehti made the mistake of reducing the throttles too soon after take-off. Wright reached across from the left seat to chop the side of his fist into Lehti's left forearm, stunning him. Wright poured on the power and climbed out to gain altitude. When the plane reached level flight, Wright turned to Lehti and spoke evenly, "Don't ever retard the throttle on take-off. Ever!" Lehti was certain that Wright had broken his arm, as it blackened and hurt for days, but he never forgot the message, nor did any of the other project pilots or aircrew to whom Lehti told the story.

As his command pilots, Wright chose Majors Leo Foster and Francis Carlson; Captains Bob Lehti, John Zinn and Frank Reynolds; and First Lieutenants Bob Easterling, Charles Rockwood, Ken Brown, Fred Martus and George Tillinghast.

In May 1943, Colonel Wright began an intensive training program to qualify his handpicked crews on the LAB-equipped Liberators. Although many of the men had experience in the B-24, either as LB-30 or B-24 ferry crews or in radar-configured B-24s flown in Rad Lab test projects, this "nodding acquaintance" did not even begin to satisfy Wright. He was a perfectionist who insisted on by-the-book excellence in flying and crew coordination. Wright began his pilots and aircrews with the basics of B-24 flying and pushed them into demanding instrument-only, long-duration cross-country and over-water flights designed to test and qualify each man. Wright flew with each crew, repeatedly, until he was personally satisfied that each man measured up. He was demanding and tough. It was well-known throughout the project that Wright had pressed hard to take the unit overseas and that the decision to go with Wright and not Dolan or Aldrin was made by Arnold personally.

Another of Wright's pilots recalled that nobody ever called their project officer "Stud" to his face and were even careful to use this name behind his back. Stud was a name of reverence and respect and, by the time July 1943 rolled around, Wright's 10 crews had nothing but admiration for their leader.

Later in June, with the 10 crews confirmed, Colonel Wright called the men of his new unit together in one of the old balloon hangars at Langley Field and laid the mission out in front of them. He promised that they would train hard for combat, but warned that, as night attack pioneers, he expected the unit to live dangerously. Combat and operational losses would be heavy and he expected many of the men standing before him in the hangar to lose their lives in the Pacific. Any man who did not feel he could make the sacrifice could walk away from the project then and there with no questions asked. No one walked away that June day.

The plane for the LAB mission—the B-24 Liberator

As already mentioned, the aircraft selected for the Wright Project was the four-engine B-24 Liberator heavy bomber designed and manufactured by the Consolidated Aircraft Corporation. Although the B-24 had not, at the time that it was selected for the Wright Project, received the heavy press play lavished on its sister heavy bomber, the Boeing B-17 Flying Fortress, the Liberator would prove to be every bit the fighting machine as the B-17. The Liberator was not as photogenic as the B-17, but it could fly faster, higher and farther with a comparable bomb load. With its boxcar-like fuselage, slab sides and distinctive, high-aspect ratio Davis wing spanning some 110 feet, the Liberator was as graceful in flight as it was gangly looking on the ground. Its two bomb bays were almost 18 feet long and allowed the B-24 to haul thousands of pounds of bombs to distant targets.

Compared to the aging B-18 and B-17, the B-24 was the new kid on the block, the XB-24 prototype having made its first flight in December 1939. However, once contracts were awarded, Consolidated tooled up quickly and within a year was rolling out its initial production batch of Liberators. Many of these early B-24s were produced for immediate handover to England as LB-30s, and, of course, some of these aircraft found their way to Rad Lab and Langley Field where radar systems such as the DMS-1000 were tested.

The first Liberator model mass-produced for combat use, the B-24D, began to come off production lines in large numbers in early 1943 for assignment to bomber units preparing for movement to the European and Pacific combat theaters. In April 1943, 10 B-24Ds had been selected for assignment to the Wright Project. Dolan's men picked them up almost factory fresh at Wright Field where they had been modified for the LAB equipment and brought them "home" to Langley Field for pre-deployment familiarization with the 3rd Squadron. Here, the men of the project, no longer distracted by the B-18Bs and B-24 test and evaluation missions with other equipment, learned the capabilities, shortcomings and idiosyncrasies of the airplanes on which their survival in combat would depend.

The typical B-24D weighed in at 56,000 pounds (combat load) and had a war maximum gross takeoff weight of 71,000 pounds. At combat weight, the D-model Liberator could hit a top speed of just over 300 miles per hour at 25,000 feet. It could carry a 5,000-pound payload to a range of 1,800 miles, and with no payload could stretch its ferry range to 3,500 miles. The B-24 was powered by four of the famous and dependable Pratt & Whitney R-1830 series engines, each of which could deliver 1,200 horsepower at sea level to an 11½-foot diameter Hamilton Standard three-blade propeller. For armament, the earlier D-models carried twin 0.50-caliber machine guns in the top and tail turrets, a single tunnel gun firing aft from the belly, single waist guns on each side and one, two or three individual, socket-mounted nose guns.

Although the later model B-24s would add a twin-gun power nose turret, the D-model assigned to the Wright Project had a greenhouse-type nose of plexiglass and metal frame construction that allowed the bombardier an excellent view but provided a minimum of defensive firepower for the vulnerable nose area. An "ownership chit" signed by one of the pilots when he accepted the handover of his aircraft from the pilots who had ferried it from the factory to Wright Field confirmed the price that the U.S. taxpayer had shelled out for the airplane. As delivered, guns and radar systems not included, the amount was $287,251.00.

The space provided within the B-24 was cramped, particularly with the addition of more guns and electronic equipment, but it was adequate to the mission and, according to one crewman who was upgrading from the Bolo, "she was a Cadillac when compared to the Ford that was the B-18 Bolo." The bombardier and navigator lived in the nose, while the flight deck provided space for the pilot, co-pilot and radio operator. The flight engineer occupied a station on the half-deck behind the flight deck when he was not busy with his top turret. Two waist gunners and the tail turret gunner occupied the aircraft area aft of the twin bomb-bay compartment.

The radar operator, the only non-standard B-24 aircraft crewman included on the Wright Project aircraft, sat with his tuning equipment and scope on the half-deck, directly behind the co-pilot, in the D-model. The radar dome, which was lowered into place from the belly of the aircraft once the B-24 was airborne, took the position occupied by the lower turret and, as a consequence, no gunner was required for this station. As the LAB Liberators would be attacking at altitudes of no more than 1,500 feet, and more often at 1,000 feet or less, the trade-off of the radar dome for the displaced belly turret was deemed acceptable, at least for the combat anticipated by the Wright Project.[2]

Training for combat

During July, Wright put the finishing touches on his aircraft and crews. He scheduled them for longer overwater and overland missions and more LAB bombing runs off the Atlantic coast against half-submerged wrecks. For moving target practice, the aircrews used Navy ships and merchant vessels. Using small 100-pound practice bombs, Wright's bombardiers established an average circular error of only 230 feet. Each aircraft made dozens of simulated LAB attack missions and each bombardier experienced over 100 trial bomb releases. In the last month of the intensive training program, a typical crew went up into the night sky two out of every three days and Wright's LAB bombardiers were making direct hits on one out of every three attack runs.

Just as importantly, the radar operators were perfecting their individual abilities with the scope, and the pilots, all night flying experts by this time, had gained great respect for the B-24. In late July, as the unit's departure date drew near, Wright led his men on a simulated full combat test mission from Langley to Wichita, Kansas, and back. When everyone came through with flying colors, he pronounced his unit ready and eager to go to war.

Wright and Dolan also arranged for three civilian radar technicians to be seconded by Rad Lab and two private firms, including Western Electric, as members of the project team, each volunteering to go to war in the Pacific. As the reliability of the LAB system in each aircraft would define the ability of the aircraft and crews to perform in combat, the technicians were essential, particularly given that Wright's goal was to establish a mission-capable threshold of no less than 90 percent.

Orders for movement

On 3 August 1943, Headquarters, 1st Sea-Search Attack Group issued its Special Order 155 assigning Project Number 96131R with its 10 Liberators, 40 officers and 60 enlisted men, followed by Movement Order Number One of the same date. Interestingly this movement instruction referenced a Pacific Air Command order of 31 July 1943 for "ten (10) replacement Combat Crews, comprising forty (40) Officers and sixty (60) Enlisted Men, assigned Shipment Number FP-617-AD, One (1) Flight Leader assigned Shipment Number FP-617-AD, one Technical Officer, and two Technical Enlisted Men … from Langley Field to an overseas destination … this being a permanent change of station." The text of this order would create some issues along the way and threaten to divert and dismantle the Wright Project before it even reached its combat destination, but that incident still lay in the future. In any event, Colonel Wright had anticipated such and had a plan in hand to resolve it.[3]

As noted, the movement orders also authorized Captain E. R. Barriere, the project Technical Officer, and three civilian technical representatives to travel with the 10 aircraft and 100-odd aircrew of the Wright Project deployment flight. The civilian representatives were more than technicians along as observers; rather, they were the conceptual and engineering "brains" assigned to the project from American private industry to ensure that the complex electronics systems worked in combat and stayed in service. Amid the limited personal effects and extra passengers packed into each B-24 were crammed hundreds of pounds of spare electronic parts and test equipment. Because there were no field facilities capable of even understanding, let alone servicing, the new electronic systems carried by the aircraft of the Wright Project, the unit was responsible for the repair, maintenance and rebuilding of all its own equipment. The long, uncertain supply lines between East-Coast labs and the South Pacific island combat airfields meant that, technically speaking, the Wright Project would have to live for months off the equipment and talent it carried with it when it departed Langley Field for the 5,000-mile journey west.

Interestingly, this same Movement Order Number One, in Paragraph 8, includes the statement, "The Commanding General of the theater of destination will: On or about six months after the acceptance of these replacement crews, return the flight leader to an air transshipment point for transfer to his home station in the United States." Hap Arnold had spoken. Stud Wright would have six months and no more to demonstrate that his LAB program could produce results. He would then go home to walk the walk at AAF Headquarters and make his report to Arnold and his staff. The pressure to produce results with the assets one was provided was ever-present, and so it was just as well that it would be with Dolan and Wright's project.

In this series of orders, Colonel Wright, as the provisional flight commander and special project leader, would fly with Major Foster in his aircraft. The 10 original Wright Project crews, by pilot-in-command, squadron aircraft number, its full serial number and name, were as follows:

> Crew One: Major Leo J. Foster (FP-617-AD-1), aircraft 832 (42-40832), *Devil's Delight*, with flight commander Colonel Stuart P. Wright embarked.
> Crew Two: Major Francis B. Carlson (FP-617-AD-2), aircraft 836 (42-40836), *Miss Cuddles*
> Crew Three: Captain John F. Zinn, Jr. (AD-3), aircraft 854 (42-40854), *Uncle's Fury*
> Crew Four: Captain Franklin T. E. Reynolds (AD-4), aircraft 833 (42-40833), *Coral Princess*
> Crew Five: Captain Robert W. Lehti (AD-5), aircraft 822 (42-40822), *Bum's Away*
> Crew Six: First Lieutenant Robert E. Easterling (AD-6), aircraft 839 (42-40839), *Princess Slip*
> Crew Seven: First Lieutenant Charles L. Rockwood (AD-7), aircraft 838 (42-40838), *Madame Libby the Sea Ducer*
> Crew Eight: First Lieutenant Kenneth E. Brown (AD-8), aircraft 651 (42-40651), *Ramp Tramp*
> Crew Nine: First Lieutenant Fredrick A. Martus (AD-9), aircraft 653 (42-40653), *Gremlins' Haven*
> Crew Ten: First Lieutenant George A. Tillinghast (AD-10), aircraft 639 (42-40639), *The Lady Margaret* (639)[4]

Amid this serious preparation for war, there was also the occasion for humor. The day before the project's departure, each of its 10 aircraft was towed, one at a time, into an old balloon hangar at Langley and rolled onto a precision weighing/balancing table. This system allowed the mission planners to identify the exact center of gravity for each plane and scientifically load each aircraft for the flight time and maximum fuel efficiency over the upcoming long-distance ferry flights. The following morning, when the 10 crews of the Wright Project walked onto the field to man their planes, they were greeted by the strange sight of *Coral Princess*. Its precision balancing job notwithstanding, the *Princess* sat poised for takeoff almost tipped on its tail, the nose pointed at the sky, completely out of balance. The only man not surprised by this sight was the aircraft's command pilot, Frank Reynolds.

It happened that, with Frank's wife headed back to reside in California to await his return from the South Pacific, some personal accommodations had to be made. The issue was their household effects, and it seemed only reasonable for Frank to take advantage of the government flight to ferry a ton of furniture to San Francisco in the *Coral Princess*.

Because Frank Reynolds could "fly a grand piano if you spotted him wings and an engine," no one doubted his ability to get *Coral Princess* airborne and keep it that way. Wright knew his men and did not object. The furniture arrived on the West Coast without a scratch and Mrs. Reynolds was quite pleased. Thirty years later, Frank Reynolds would still be alive and still living dangerously in the left seat of a maneuvering aircraft, flying for the Central Intelligence Agency's proprietary operation, Air America, over and through the jungles of Laos.

Although more than 100 of the project men would fly to the combat zone, two of Wright's men were destined to take a more convoluted route. Sergeant John Purvis and Corporal Vince Hoover were responsible for the final assembly, packing, shipment and safe arrival of the project's two beacon systems. These first-generation ground-based units had been designed to provide a beacon signal which the airborne B-24 could use to determine bearing and distance for navigational purposes. Both men had recently graduated from the AAF's new electronics school at Boca Raton, Florida, and were assigned temporary duty at Rad Lab, where they participated in the assembly and testing of prototype beacon units. As their movement date approached, the two men worked around the clock with Rad Lab technicians in an old horse barn at MIT to assemble the handmade units.

The Lab's technicians gave Wright's two men a drunken send-off and poured them on the train with six tons of crated electronics headed to New Hebrides in the South Pacific. The men and their equipment first traveled by train to San Francisco where the shipment was split into two identical packages for onward movement. Then, Pervis and Hoover each traveled aboard different vessels, and each ship joined separate convoys in moving to the war zone, thereby guaranteeing the best chance that at least one shipment would survive to catch up with the Wright Project on Guadalcanal. Both of the men and their equipment arrived a few weeks behind the aircraft, all cargo safe and sound. Once again, hand-fabricated Rad Lab systems were coming out of Boston, heading directly to war where they were needed and being tested in the field, in this case in a combat environment.

Forward to Guadalcanal

The Wright Project departed Langley Field on 5 August 1943 and arrived at Fairfield-Suisun Army Air Base, California, some seven days later. The flight across the United States, interspersed as it was with overnight stops at Patterson, March and McClellan Fields, had been carefully plotted by Wright to give each man under his command one last opportunity to meet with his family. Stud Wright, the hard-driving operator was all too aware that some of these men, many of them barely into their twenties, would not be coming home from the Pacific. Wright apparently felt that America owed them a final chance to say goodbye and he made sure his boys got it.

Wright assembled his 10 aircraft and crews at Fairfield-Suisun and departed the continental United States from there on 12 August, flying west into the Pacific for 13 hours before arriving at Hickam Field, Hawaii. From Hickam, on the 16th, the project flew southwest to Canton Island, a tiny flyspeck of a rock in the vast open area south of Hawaii. For the navigators of the project, this 11-hour flight was the most anxious leg of the deployment. The flight required pinpoint navigation and close attention by the pilots for optimum throttle settings to reduce fuel burn. Many other U.S. military aircraft and crews had simply disappeared on this leg. The previous year, an aircraft containing American World War I ace Eddie Rickenbacker, on a special war zone inspection trip for Secretary of War Henry Stimson, had gone down over this lonely stretch of sea. Rickenbacker and seven companions were found and rescued after drifting on rubber rafts for 24 days. The Wright Project navigators were accurate, however, and all aircraft arrived at Canton as planned and with near-perfect fuel burn.

After overnighting at Canton Island, the 10 B-24s continued southwest and arrived at Espiritu Santo Island in the New Hebrides group where Colonel Wright reported, as his orders instructed, to the Commanding General, Thirteenth Air Force Service Command. The ultimate destination—Guadalcanal and the combat zone—was still several hours by air to the northwest, but Wright found himself fighting his first battle for the survival of his unit in the Thirteenth Air Force rear area headquarters huts at Espiritu Santo. The problem arose when Thirteenth Air Force staff officers, desperate to locate, dragoon and dispatch new combat crews and aircraft to beef up understrength front-line squadrons, made known their desire to disband and parcel out Stud Wright's 10 brand-new aircraft and crews among these units. The project's official orders identified the movement as "ten replacement crews and aircraft" and under the standing rules of the day, this made Wright's aircraft and men open game for any authority of higher rank.

The situation in the Pacific was desperate and combat attrition was high. Wright had already faced a similar crisis when his ownership of the 10 crews was tested in Hawaii and he had rebuffed attempts by the Seventh Air Force there to grab his aircraft and crews. In the coming weeks on Guadalcanal, he would have to defeat more takeover attempts by the Thirteenth Air Force's Bomber Command where there was a strong inclination to either convert the Wright Project's crews and aircraft to a daylight attack role, by folding the entire squadron into an existing bomb group, or break them up and disperse the aircraft and crews among the Thirteenth's other B-24 squadrons.

On Espiritu Santo, when he faced off with those attempting to "kidnap and reassign" his planes and crews, Wright patiently explained that the orders were written so as to not draw attention, basically providing "cover," for the movement of his specialized and therefore classified project group. But Wright's real trump card was a personal letter addressed to any command authority between Langley Field and Guadalcanal.

The letter briefly described the special nature of Wright's project and ordered that nothing should be permitted to interfere in the execution of the project. It was signed by AAF Commanding General Hap Arnold. When Colonel Wright placed this document on the table it resolved the issue every time.

The Jungle Air Force

For five days on Espiritu Santo, Wright's men stretched their legs, serviced their aircraft and listened to the tales of men who had fought in skies above Guadalcanal. Many were back at "ES" to collect new aircraft, repair shot-up airplanes that they had flown back from the "Canal" or were recovering on temporary medical leave from front-line action. In its movement into combat, the Wright Project was joining a relatively new organization, the Army Air Force's Thirteenth Air Force or, as its men would come to call themselves, "The Jungle Air Force." When the Wright Project arrived at Espiritu Santo in late August 1943, the Thirteenth was all of eight months old, having been created from elements of the Hawaii-based Seventh Air Force to support the drive in the South Pacific toward Rabaul. Established in mid-December 1942 in New Caledonia, the new organization did not activate until January and picked up momentum when additional units were assigned in the following months. The headquarters of this Air Force would soon relocate to Espiritu Santo, but the Thirteenth was all Guadalcanal and the Solomons and the Bismarcks, all the time.

Operating from the Guadalcanal's Carney Field—Allied code name "Cactus"—and later an expanded Henderson Field, plus the fighter strips that were built there, XIII Bomber Command and its companion XIII Fighter Command had two missions: defend Guadalcanal and the islands to the northwest, as they were invaded by the Allies, while taking the fight to the enemy. The latter task involved both the Japanese ships that plied these same waters by day and night and the airbases and harbor facilities that underpinned the Japanese advance into these areas. The Thirteenth Air Force was one of three such air forces which operated in the Central, Southwest and South Pacific areas at this time: the Seventh was based in Hawaii and ranged into the Central Pacific; the Fifth worked with MacArthur's Southwest Pacific forces to push northwest from New Guinea on its march back to the Philippines, slamming the important Japanese base of Rabaul as a primary target along its way, while the Thirteenth was pushing itself up the Solomon–Bismarck chain.[5]

Two other U.S. Army Air Forces were then present in the greater Asia-Pacific Theater. In the North Pacific, the Eleventh Air Force was engaged in battles in Alaska and out along the Aleutian Island chain toward Japan. In the China–Burma–India Theater, the Fourteenth Air Force was flying from bases in India and China to press the Japanese from the west. The Thirteenth, the Fifth and the Eleventh Air Forces would come to overlap one another as their respective advances across the Pacific developed and converged on Japan. The heavy bomber groups from the three would often fly complementary and even conjoined missions against important targets as this geographic convergence occurred, and their advanced bases were shared and new targets selected.

In all five of the numbered air forces, the B-24 Liberator would become, by mid-1943, the heavy bomber of choice, present in every major operation. Until the arrival of the B-29 Superfortress as a strategic bomber, the Liberator in its various guises would dominate the Pacific. In addition to the Army Air Forces, the U.S. Navy and Marines would adopt the B-24 in their own special configuration for the long-range patrol bombing mission, as well as deep-penetration reconnaissance. It was also the heavy/long-range patrol bomber chosen by the Royal Australian Air Force (eventually equipping no fewer than nine squadrons) and was used extensively in those roles, and for agent/supply dropping behind the lines, by the RAF in the Mediterranean and over Burma and the Far East).

As we will learn, three of the five U.S. Army Air Forces in the Pacific would deploy LAB-equipped B-24s in combat but, in late August 1943, when the 10 aircraft of the Wright Project were inbound to Guadalcanal's Carney Field, they were all that there was to prove the worth of the LAB experiment. When the decision was made in early 1943 to dispatch the first LAB squadron to Guadalcanal the issue in the Central Solomons was very much in doubt. While the Japanese had been bloodied at Guadalcanal and had been forced to recoil, they had plenty of fight left and were determined to stand fast in the islands above. The Japanese Navy managed to inflict serious blows on the U.S. Navy in sea battles, almost all-night actions, that devastated U.S. cruiser forces attempting to establish control of the waters north of Guadalcanal.

In the early months of 1943, the Thirteenth Air Force, initially under the command of Major General Nathan F. Twining, fielded a hodge-podge of bomber and fighter aircraft with war-worn B-17s of the 5th Bomb Group holding the line, waiting to be replaced by B-24s at year's end. B-24 squadrons of the sister 307th Bomb Group were dispatched by the Seventh Air Force in Hawaii, beginning in February, to join the Thirteenth Air Force, and by June all four squadrons of that group were operational at "Buttons," the Allied code name for the island. This bomber buildup allowed the Thirteenth to send the 11th Bomb Group, which it had borrowed with its B-17s, back to their home with the Eleventh Air Force in May 1943. When the Wright planes set down at Carney, the Thirteenth was just hitting its stride in the B-24 bomber department and things were finally coming into place.

The Thirteenth Air Force's two fighter groups—the 347th and the 18th—initially had to make do with a combination of tired Curtiss P-40 Warhawks and Bell P-39 Airacobras until their replacements, Lockheed P-38 Lightnings, arrived, a process that began slowly in early 1943 and was not completed until the end of the year. A medium bomb group, the 42nd, with four squadrons of Martin B-26 Marauders and North American B-25 Mitchells, complemented the two-group heavy bomber attack component, while night fighter, photo recon and transport squadrons completed the Air Force's table of organization.

Operational control over the squadrons at Guadalcanal was exercised by a joint service organization, Commander, Aircraft, Solomons, or COMAIRSOLS, which was itself subordinate to Command Air South Pacific. The mix of U.S. Army Air Force units and U.S. Navy and Marine units sharing and operating from the growing collection of airfields on Guadalcanal, plus the promise of more of the same as the advance up the Solomons and the Bismarcks continued, made such an arrangement both essential and efficient. COMAIRSOLS would be the operational command that directed the daily operations of the B-24 groups, including the Wright Project once it arrived and was declared ready for action. XIII Bomber Command would provide administrative and logistical support to its subordinate B-24 units, with the Wright Project at the end of the line as the interloping newcomer.

The Thirteenth had been in combat from Guadalcanal since mid-January, in the thick of the fight for the island itself, with a strong and determined Japanese ground force continuing to do battle in the jungles. The Japanese high command would soon decide to throw in the towel and withdraw the 10,000 or so troops that remained but even this event was misjudged by U.S. intelligence and operations types with the Japanese preparations mistaken as portending a new attack on the American presence on the island. While the issue on the island was not in doubt at that point in the six-month struggle and became a moot point after the Japanese withdrawal in February 1943, the Japanese Army, including its air arm, and the Imperial Navy remained determined to contest the waters around the island.[6]

The new Air Force was in action from 17 January, its fighters tangling with Japanese Navy A6M "Zeros" and Army Ki-43 "Oscars" some 100 miles up The Slot (the body of water that, more or less, runs through the middle of the Solomon Islands chain and was heavily contested by both sides), and on 13 February, as a Valentine's Day eve event, the first B-24s launched from Carney as part of a strike on the shipping in the Shortland–Buin area. The six B-24s of the 424th Squadron that were escorted by P-38 and P-40 fighters had a mixed day, with only three Liberators and six fighters reaching the target area. They were greeted by 45 enemy fighters and strong anti-aircraft fire over the target vessels. Two of the B-24s were shot down, with one disintegrating over a target with a direct hit, and the third, hit hard, was forced to ditch in the water off the north coast of Choiseul Island. The losses for the day were three B-24s, two P-40s and four of the precious P-38 Lightnings. Other "Cactus" units were equally challenged and on the following day a strike by nine U.S. Navy PB4Y Liberators, escorted by 10 P-38s and 12 F4U Corsairs, attacked the same target area. The cost, in exchange for three Zeros downed and a cargo ship hit, was two PB4Ys, four P-38s and two Corsairs. It would be a long war.

As the Wright Project prepared to fly into Guadalcanal, the Thirteenth Air Force and its 5th Bomb Group (Heavy) was in the final stages of re-equipping with the B-24 bomber, and with that action, yielding some of the last of the war-weary B-17s still in use in the South Pacific. The other heavy bomber group of the Thirteenth Air Force, the 307th, had completed its transfer to Guadalcanal, arriving with its transition to the B-24 already completed at its home base in Hawaii. All four of the 307th's squadrons were in action with its new Liberators over the Solomon and Bismarck Islands. These two daylight heavy bomber groups, each allocated four operational squadrons, were part of XIII Bomber Command.

When the Wright Project arrived, it was officially designated the 394th Bomb Squadron (H) of the 5th Bomb Group, under the control of XIII Bomber Command of the Thirteenth Air Force. This designation was provisional, mainly because the arrival of Wright's men and planes happened to coincide with a period of aircraft and unit reorganization and aircraft transition within the 5th Bomb Group. The 394th position on the 5th Bomb Group organization chart was available and someone along the way had presumed that Wright's 10 aircraft would provide the core component for the build-out of that daylight bombardment squadron. But the staff officers who had made this very reasonable assumption had not seen the Hap Arnold letter and did not understand the special mission that had been assigned to the Wright Project. They would soon learn and turn to rebuilding the 394th as a straight B-24 daylight unit. It would take a few weeks for this issue to sort out. In the interim, the Wright Project aircraft and crews would administratively accept the 394th identity, albeit with some discomfort in both the group and the new arrivals.

Irrespective of the project's subordination within the Thirteenth Air Force and its XIII Bomber Command, Wright's 10 aircraft would fly under the operational control of COMAIRSOLS, the tactical command for all Navy, Army and Marine air units active in the Solomons. On 23 August, the 10 airplanes of the 394th Bomb Squadron lifted off from the quiet of Espiritu Santo and flew toward Guadalcanal, to the Japanese and into the war.

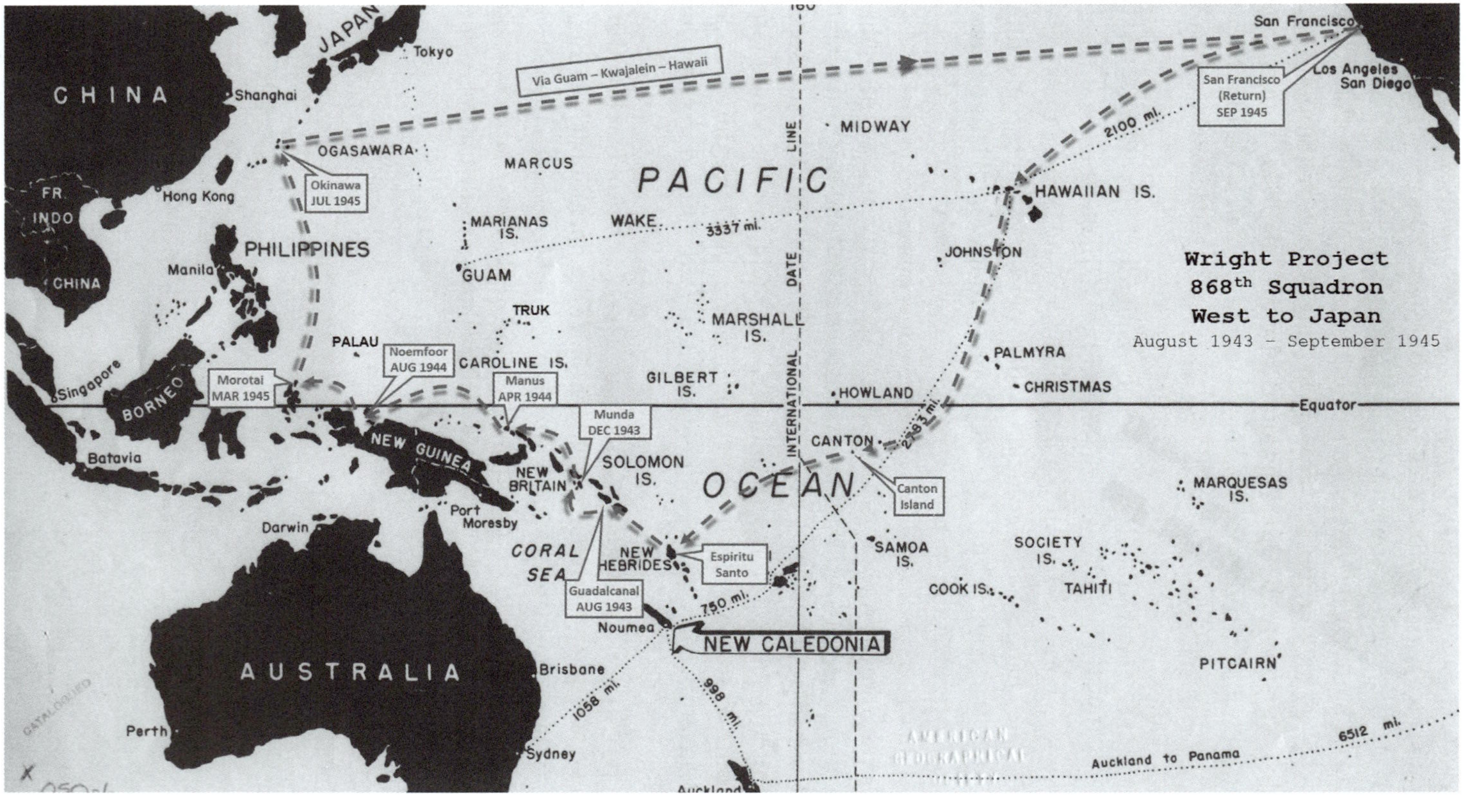

Wright Project/868th Squadron West to Japan, August 1943–September 1945, tracking Wright Project and 868th Squadron movement across the Pacific Ocean, with six bases identified with dates the squadron operated from those six bases, namely Guadalcanal, Munda, Manus, Noemfoor, Morotai, and Okinawa, plus movement home to United States in September–October 1945. (Author data overlay of U.S. Government map, 1946)

CHAPTER 6

Guadalcanal

August–September 1943

The Canal

Colonel Stuart Wright led his B-24s into Guadalcanal's Carney Field on 23 August 1943. The 10 B-24Ds flew up from Espiritu Santo with a half-dozen P-38 Lightning fighters as company and arrived in the middle of a blinding rainstorm. Many of the Wright veterans vividly recall their first impression of Guadalcanal, impressions formed the second their planes touched down. They were greeted by an ear-shattering racket and vibration that shook each aircraft as the rubber tires of its landing gear contacted the "Marston Mat" steel runway at Carney Field. When each plane found the steel and rolled down the runway, water and mud shot through the perforations in the matting and sprayed against the belly and sides of the Liberators. The only incident marring the project's arrival occurred when Bob Lehti's *Bums Away* slid to one side of the gray clay and mud-packed taxiway as it was making its way to its revetment. Three feet of the wingtip was peeled back by a coconut tree and the pilot was forced to endure Wright's wrath. Repairs were quickly made and Wright's 10 planes certified for LAB night missions within a day.

First missions

On the afternoon of 27 August, the 5th Bomb Group headquarters ordered Wright's unit, by then designated the 394th Squadron, to put up a night anti-shipping patrol mission of three aircraft. *The Lady Margaret* (Tillinghast crew), *Gremlins' Haven* (Martus crew) and *Bums Away* (Lehti crew) were given the nod for this first LAB patrol. Because interest in the Wright Project ran high within the 5th Bomb Group and XIII Bomber Command, many senior bomber officers were eager to see the LAB aircraft in operation. On this first mission, 5th Bomb Group Commander, Colonel Unruh, rode as an observer with the Tillinghast crew while Lehti's B-24 carried his adjutant, Lieutenant

Colonel Burnham. Colonel Wright flew with Martus and invited the Thirteenth Air Force XIII Bomber Command's Colonel Matheney along for the ride. The guests that night observed that the LAB systems of the three aircraft operated flawlessly and that the interaction within the crews was textbook perfect.

The three aircraft were ordered to patrol independently in their respective assigned mission areas. George Tillinghast in *The Lady Margaret* (639), designated Flight One of the 5th Bomb Group's Mission 73, flew a patrol route to cover the shipping areas northeast of the coast of the Choiseul, Bougainville and Buka islands to a point 20 miles beyond the end of the islands. Bob Lehti and his crew, Flight Two in *Gremlins' Haven* (822), flew directly up St. George's Channel to within contact range of shipping suspected to be operating out of the Japanese harbors there. Fred Martus as Flight Three in *Bums Away* (653), patrolled south of New Georgia and along the southwestern coast of Bougainville and Buka to a point 40 miles beyond the tip of Buka Island. The mission profiles that followed would thereafter become a typical three-aircraft nightly mission set. The three Wright "ships" took off from Carney at 2238 hours for the anticipated eight-hour missions. Each plane carried six 500-pound bombs, each with a 0.10-second delay nose fuse and a 0.45-second delay tail fuse. Recovery at Carney was scheduled to take place at about 0600 hours the following morning.

Tillinghast completed his anti-shipping search, making no radar contact and attacked Suavanau Port at Rekata, dropping his bombs on Japanese positions there from 5,000 feet at four in the morning. Lehti's aircraft established radar contact with what it thought was a ship and attacked. After bombs away the contact was discovered to be a group of small islands and Lehti turned home leaving small fires burning among the trees.

Fred Martus in *Gremlins' Haven* had drawn the hottest patrol area. He made radar contact with a moving enemy ship near the Shortland area shortly after midnight. Martus's bombardier Bob McLeod made his first LAB run from 1,000 feet, set his bomb spread at 75 feet and toggled three bombs onto his target. At least one hit squarely, the heavy concussion from the hit tossing the plane, leaving behind a dull red glow and spitting sparks, indicating that the steel ship was on fire.

After the first attack, the enemy below was alert and laced the night sky with heavy and accurate pom-pom machine gun fire. Martus backed off for a second run and attacked again, this time using the glow of the burning ship to set up his LAB run. *Bums Away* took several anti-aircraft hits but returned home safely to report that the first LAB attack against the Imperial Japanese Navy had drawn blood.[1]

On the following night, three more Wright Project aircraft went into the night sky, flying Mission 74 on patrol patterns similar to the previous evening. The northwestern aircraft found maneuvering ships, picked out what it believed to be a light cruiser and attacked down the length of the ships with six bombs. Two bombs fell alongside for near hits and four bombs hit in a walking-away bomb pattern. More impressively, the LAB radar approach and low-level precision of the initial LAB attack did not provide the

Japanese time to man and fire their anti-aircraft guns, let alone maneuver their ships to evade the falling bombs. Less impressively, the two other Wright Project aircraft hunting that night were forced to abort their missions when their radar systems malfunctioned; they recovered from their patrols early.

Once the three night hunters were on the ground at dawn at Carney Field, three more of Wright's aircraft were scrambled for a daylight mission to chase down a "Tokyo Express" run that had been spotted—a cruiser-destroyer group that was reported to be making a dash to run back up "The Slot." The ships were not found and the three crews recovered to Carney and were immediately refueled for night anti-ship patrols. That night, 29 August, Colonel Wright took *The Lady Margaret* up The Slot for a long radar patrol. North of Choiseul Island, he turned 90 degrees to run into the shipping area favored by Japanese destroyers and convoys off Shortland Island. He then turned his plane to search the Buka area. At 0130 hours his radar operator picked up a five-ship convoy. Selecting the largest target, Wright made a three-bomb LAB attack, running broadside to the largest steaming vessel to deliver one starboard and one port side straddle, and a center bomb direct hit on deck. The ship erupted in flashes that turned to a dull red glow.

The attack was a perfect LAB run and, again, the enemy did not even suspect the presence of an attacking bomber until it toggled its bomb load. At this point in the Pacific War, with very few exceptions, the Japanese warships and auxiliaries did not have radar to warn them of the LAB bomber approach. In this important respect, the night attack advantage laid completely with the B-24, and it would remain so for many months. The Japanese came to understand that a new element had been introduced into the war in the South Pacific and they no longer would enjoy the protection from attack that the dark of night had allowed for so long.

First loss

The Pacific War claimed the first Wright Project crew in the early morning hours of 31 August. Three planes had sortied at dusk as Mission 78, and two of them had found and attacked targets. One of the crews that found and attacked Japanese shipping was that of Lieutenant Robert Easterling and the men of *Princess Slip*, working the northern sector patrol that night. Although they did not radio in that they had been hit and were in trouble, contact at the time of the aircraft's return was lost and many on the ground suspected that the plane's radio had been knocked out. It was assumed that the plane had come home with Easterling and his co-pilot, Lieutenant Eugene White, dead or dying at the controls, victims of Japanese anti-aircraft fire. On the final leg of its landing approach at Carney Field, aircraft 839, *Princess Slip*, plunged into the ground and exploded. The entire crew of 10 men died instantly.

The men of the Wright Project took their first loss hard. Because the 10 crews had formed a tight-knit fraternity over several months, living and training together under Dolan and Wright at Langley Field, the deaths cut each man deeply. Wright had promised them that, given the nature of their missions and the single plane, long-duration night patrols, combined with the low-level attack profile of LAB, the group should be prepared to incur heavy losses. Bringing a damaged aircraft home to land safely at night or by the early light of dawn demanded extraordinary skill and courage. Bob Easterling was regarded as one of the unit's best and most experienced instrument pilots. A fellow Wright Project pilot noted that if Easterling could not bring home a crippled B-24, no man could. The exploding fireball of *Princess Slip* drove home the fears inside each man that the next plane to fall and explode in a ball of fire might be his own. Lieutenant Crowell "Butch" Werner, who was among the Wright Project officers who rushed to the Easterling crash site, was shocked by the destruction of the aircraft and the condition of the remains of his close friends. "The medics were picking up pieces of bodies and placing them in bags for burial. The Bob Easterling crash brought home the fact that we all had entered into a fight to the death with the Japanese. The LAB runs were now personal and pay-back for our losses. In future years, even in my own command when I lost two aircraft and several fine airmen, I made it a policy to not visit a crash site unless I absolutely had to do so. That night I sat in my tent and wrote a letter to my girlfriend from Texas Tech, trying to share with her the impact these deaths had on me. I have a copy of that letter to this day. It's absolutely heartbreaking."

Into September

The following night Stud Wright sent men back into the skies to fly three patrols. On 2 September, a Wright B-24 found two large barges off the southwestern tip of Choiseul, mounted a LAB attack and bombed one under. A few nights later, Fred Martus and crew (Mission 86), when pressing an approach against surface contacts in the Shortland area, picked up a dozen fighter blips on the SCR-717 scope. An unequal game of cat and mouse ensued as the pilot used his radar to track and avoid the prowling fighters. Two got close and tried to stay tight, lining up for an attack. The pilot banked hard and dove his 30-ton Liberator from 1,000 to 400 feet. He then asked his radar operator to find heavy weather and was guided into it, allowing their aircraft to make an escape. The blind Japanese fighters never had a chance.

The bank-and-dive evasive action allowed the LAB aircraft to avoid enemy fighter patrols and, on those occasions when the fighters found a night-stalking B-24, coordination between the radar operator and the pilots allowed the bomber to ditch them, often by seeking weather that provided an escape route. When the LAB B-24s did later encounter the initial versions of ground-based Japanese radar, and interceptors attempting to find the bombers in the dark of night, the tracking precision of the SCR-717 usually provided the edge needed by the B-24s to make their escape; this would not always be the case, however, and the Japanese hunting at night were also learning from their encounters with the LAB aircraft.

On the night of 8/9 September 1943, Charles Rockwood took *Madame Libby the Sea Ducer* (838) into the Shortland area. His radar operator promptly found a fat blip on his scope. Five miles off Fauro Island, Rockwood made three LAB runs against a large merchantman (or "AK" in U.S. Navy vessel designation system) escorted by a destroyer. His first run was "free" with both the target and its escort caught completely off guard. But his first bombs went wild, the intervalometer sticking and scattering two of his three bombs 300 feet over the target. By the time he lined up for his second run, both ships were alert and had begun to maneuver wildly. They both threw up medium and light anti-aircraft fire mixed with brilliant tracers. Rockwood's second bomb drop was perfect and placed a 500 pounder squarely on the AK's deck. A series of detonations followed on the ship to confirm that the bomb had hit home and all anti-aircraft fire from the target ceased. Japanese fighters attempted to find Rockwood's aircraft but were ditched as *Madame Libby* dove away and started home.

On 10 September, Captain Zinn in *Uncle Fury* jumped a three-ship convoy off Bougainville and delivered four LAB attacks. The following night, Major Carlson and his crew, flying in their standard mount, *Miss Cuddles*, hit a five-vessel convoy in St. George's Channel while Martus discovered, attacked and scattered a five-destroyer group at Buka Passage. On the night of 12 September, Colonel Wright, flying 639, and Captains Zinn and Foster were up and active (Mission 94), pressing LAB attacks on convoys off New Ireland and Bougainville. Zinn's attack on a four-ship convoy shortly after midnight claimed near misses and scattered the ships, while Foster found a three-ship convoy off New Ireland and delivered several LAB attacks.

An after-action report noted that in the attacks delivered some 15 miles off Kieta, Bougainville, on four cargo ships and two destroyers, the LAB radar found the convoy at a considerable distance and guided the aircraft to a perfect attack position, with the ships visually sighted at three miles under clear skies and bright moonlight. The destroyers were alert, maneuvered in a circle to protect the cargo ships and threw up an impressive amount of anti-aircraft fire. The B-24 deferred its initial approach, went out some distance and came in at a different angle of attack, lining up on one of the destroyers.

Toggling the bomb load set at a 40-foot spread, the crew saw the first and second as "short near-misses," the third a square hit on the bridge area, and the balance of three as "near miss overs." The report noted that the concussion from the solid hit at 1,500 feet threw the aircraft up violently and, while that ship ceased return fire, its companions continued an accurate barrage. At that point, radar detected seven inbound fighters and, in maneuvering to avoid these planes, Foster managed to lose all but one. This fighter pressed home an attack but, after a 15-minute pursuit, trailed away when the B-24 found a heavy cloud area that obscured it, allowing the plane to return to Carney Field safely.

The Wright Project becomes the "Snoopers"

At some point in late August, the Wright Project, officially but "provisionally" designated the 394th Bombardment Squadron (Heavy) of the 5th Bomb Group, gained the appellation of "Snooper." Around this same time, the LAB aircraft received the informal but accepted designation SB-24, the "S" denoting either "Special" or "Snooper," depending on which account is accepted. Also in this period, XIII Bomber Command and its 5th Bomb Group stalled in attempts to convert the Wright Project to a daylight unit that would complete the group's table of organization of four identically configured squadrons. As a consequence, XIII Bomber Command elected to detach the 10 Wright Project crews, their aircraft and their support components and build out the 394th Squadron with new standard-configuration daylight B-24D aircraft and crews as quickly as possible.

These changes resulted in the Wright Project being designated the "5th Bomb Group Provisional Squadron (Heavy),"[2] effective the last day of the month. Although this designation technically allowed the 5th Bomb Group to retain some level of control over the Wright Project, the de facto reality was that the project would operate directly under XIII Bomber Command from this point forward. This arrangement was fine with Colonel Wright as it protected the aircrews and aircraft from being "poached" by other groups, while permitting his unit to perform as a quasi-independent entity within the Thirteenth Air Force. This luck would hold for the balance of the war, with all future iterations of the Wright Project avoiding any capture by a group-level organization and any direct "bomb group" affiliation.

This evolution in the Wright Project's identity continued to play out in late September and would not fully resolve itself until late December when an entirely new unit designation would be assigned. As noted above, the notional nickname or *nom de guerre* that surfaced during September, "Snooper," began to stick within the Thirteenth Air Force. The men of the Wright Project thought it appropriate and adopted it for themselves. Moreover, "Snooper" was an improvement on some of the appellations assigned to the unit by senior XIII Bomber Command leaders who were not necessarily pleased to be dealing with, and required to support, a rogue unit that slept through the day and flew only at night. The "Jungle Air Force" would adapt, had a war to fight. In any event, the Wright Project, whatever they were called or called themselves, were climbing into their LAB B-24s every night and going out to hunt and sink ships.

The September hunt

The heady days of September 1943, the loss of the Easterling crew notwithstanding, were a target-rich period for the Wright Project. Enemy ships were found on most patrols, LAB attacks made and the losses incurred by the attacking aircraft seemed manageable. In the next 10 days, the crews of Foster, Carlson, Brown, Rockwood and Reynolds all found and attacked convoys in the Buka and Shortlands area. On 15 September, an eight-ship convoy off Shortland was attacked and on the same night a second Wright aircraft found a six-ship convoy and made several LAB runs. Japanese fighters were up again that night trying to protect their ships, found the LAB SB-24 and made several runs, damaging the aircraft. Again, the Wright aircraft were fortunate as they made it home with no casualties. On 21 September, a small convoy was detected and attacked in the Buka area with near-miss results. The following night, Major Carlson in *Miss Cuddles* (836) and Lieutenant Brown in *Ramp Tramp* (651) each found convoys to attack in the Buka area (Mission 105), while on the following night the Rockwood crew detected a group of warships and delivered a LAB attack just off Buka on what they determined to be a light cruiser. The Buka area stayed hot in the following days and Captains Carlson and Sumner found targets there on 26 September.

Sub hunters supreme

That same night a single LAB patrol bomber (Mission 94) caught two Japanese submarines on the surface. The first attack developed just before midnight when a submarine surfaced and suddenly appeared on the radar screen of the LAB bomber. Reacting quickly, the operator vectored the pilot into an attack run and the bombardier scrambled to set the APQ-5 for weapons delivery, releasing three 500-pound bombs on the submarine. Two near misses were observed as well as a direct hit on the stern of the vessel. The aircraft lined up for a second attack run but discovered the submarine was gone and a large oil slick remained on the surface. Two hours later, some distance away, another surface-running submarine was detected and bombed. This one was quite large, estimated to be 350 feet in length, and the attacker's three near misses were not claimed as more than a damaged sub.

The next morning, Colonel Wright was handed the following message from COMAIRSOLS:

> To 21V26 and 23V26 of Wright's Snoopers, COMAIRSOLS send well done for an excellent Performance night of Sept 12 and 13.

The dusk-to-dawn patrol routine continued through the end of the month with the SB-24s staging through the forward air base at Munda to increase their patrol range. On the night of 27/28 September, Captain Brown in *Ramp Tramp* jumped a target with a LAB attack which appeared to be a surfaced submarine. Spacing the bombs at 30-foot intervals, his crew obtained a direct hit that broke the target in two. *Ramp Tramp* circled the area to watch its target drift and sink, and then flew home to claim a probable submarine.

On the same night, Frank Reynolds and his men in *Coral Princess* detected a Japanese submarine running on the surface with the radar operator's scope finding its target at 30 miles. Reynolds attacked on the I-boat's port beam and exploded three bombs directly alongside. The sub was damaged by the attack and unable to submerge. *Coral Princess* followed up with another bomb attack and no fewer than eight strafing attacks, the latter pressed home as the *Princess* roared in at 50 feet. The submarine attempted to regain headway, continued to drift in the St. George's Channel, but refused to sink. With its deck awash and conning tower protruding from the water at a crazy angle, the sub left its life-blood trail of oil streaming behind as it drifted out of control. Reynolds returned home at dawn, with all his bombs and ammunition expended. He had tracked his prey with his radar for four hours and delivered ten separate attacks.

The following day the commander, Third Fleet, sent a message to Reynolds's crew expressing his appreciation. It read:

> A pat on the back for the pilots and crew of Plane Eleven, Flight 21, who left that Nip sub and his stern sheets hanging out. Halsey

During this period the Japanese were running every submarine they could bring to the war to convey supplies to the bypassed island garrisons or to shuttle air crews and troops between positions that they assumed would be targeted next for invasion. Although records for this period are incomplete and postwar assessments as to which Allied service or unit sank which submarine are unreliable, it seems clear that the Wright Project made Japanese submarine duty in the contested area a very dangerous undertaking. Sometime after 28 August, submarine I-182 disappeared as it moved from Truk naval base to its mission area in the New Hebrides, its chosen course crossing SB-24 mission zones. In late August, I-25 checked in as it approached these same areas where the Wright Project LAB aircraft patrolled and was never heard from again after early September. Other Japanese submarines met unknown fates in these waters as well during the September period, thus it was highly likely that one or more of the submarine kills claimed were made by Wright's SB-24 LAB men.

"Tokyo Express"

The biggest single battle to that date between the Wright Project SB-24 Snoopers and the Japanese Navy occurred on the night of 28/29 September. American naval intelligence was, by this stage of the Pacific War, breaking Japanese naval codes and cyphers on a regular basis. The U.S. Naval Intelligence Group was able to intercept, break and read Japanese tactical instructions on a real-time basis, and on this date alerted COMAIRSOLS to the probability that a convoy led by eight destroyers planned to run down the coast of Bougainville to the Kieta area. The COMAIRSOL alert for Mission 115 was cryptic:

ONE SB-24 AP 854 AND ALL OTHER AVAIL A/C OF 394 SQ OF 5TH BOMB GROUP
WILL SEARCH AND STRIKE TASK FORCE REPORTED TO CONTAIN 8 DDS COMING
DOWN NE SHORE OF BOUGAINVILLE IN KIETA AREA.

Wright selected the crew of Frank Reynolds to lead the hunt and got them off to an early start. Reynolds's aircraft made radar contact in the area suggested by intelligence at 1920 hours and flashed the word to other patrolling Snoopers and to Carney Field.

The LAB hunt that night was for the infamous "Tokyo Express" that the Japanese routinely ran down The Slot. It was a group of destroyers dispatched at high speed to replenish ground forces while contesting the waters where the U.S. Navy was establishing a dominant position. The destroyers were aggressive and looking for an opportunity to loose their deadly "Long Lance" Type 93 torpedoes at U.S. cruiser-destroyer forces active in the St. George's Channel that defined The Slot. But, on this night, the LAB bombers found the Express first. These same Japanese destroyer groups had been at this work for a year and at this point knew the territory, had established themselves as exceptional night fighters and were alert for combat with U.S. Navy surface forces. What they were not prepared for was detection from above and precision attack by radar-equipped heavy bombers pressing home their bomb runs at 1,000 feet or less.

Reynolds's radar operator found the fast convoy, located at position 6°33'S 156°17'E, and Reynolds visually confirmed that it comprised 11 vessels traveling in-train down The Slot toward Vella Lavella. *Coral Princess* reported the contact and selected a large target toward the rear of the convoy which Reynolds assessed to be a high-speed cargo vessel. He elected to make a beam-on run in hazy weather at 1,000 feet and a reduced airspeed of 135 miles per hour. With bombs spaced at 75-foot intervals, Reynolds's bombardier LAB toggled all six bombs on this first pass, achieving a near miss and two direct hits amidships.

Aboard the ship, the fires raged out of control and were visible for over 20 miles. The inferno provided the other Snoopers with a beacon for their own attacks. Striking first, Reynolds had caught the convoy with its defenses down and he drew no anti-aircraft fire. As he turned the *Coral Princess* toward home, his crew watched the night sky light up with tracers and explosions as the Japanese greeted the other planes of the Wright Project that were arriving to pile into the fight. They also called all available aircraft to the fight that seemed to present a set-piece opportunity for the LAB strikers.

At this point in the battle, the Snoopers had five of their nine surviving aircraft in the air. With Reynolds headed home, the four others covering other nearby patrol areas diverted to attack the convoy. The Zinn crew, flying *Uncle's Fury*, picked up radar contact soon after Reynolds called out the convoy and attacked immediately after Reynolds set his target ablaze. Meeting heavy anti-aircraft fire, Zinn's bomb runs achieved near misses, but failed to make direct hits. Major Foster, flying *Devil's Delight*, arrived within 20 minutes, attacked repeatedly, but also failed to hit any of the wildly maneuvering destroyers. *Bums Away*, flown by Lehti, arrived next over the convoy but elected not to attack when his IFF equipment failed to confirm that the twisting ships below were not U.S. Navy destroyers. Brown, flying *Ramp Tramp* arrived to attack, but when he received the same confusing IFF signals on his equipment that turned Lehti away, he also decided to abort.

Martus down

Back at Carney Field, the initial alert flashed by Reynolds sparked activity as Wright and his staff scrambled to get the remaining three aircraft into the air for a maximum effort against the convoy. Some crewmen were not in the immediate area and one plane was down on maintenance, but by 2144 hours Martus and Tillinghast, both flying with incomplete or pick-up crews, were bombed up and lifted off from Carney Field to join the fight. Reaching the convoy, Tillinghast and Martus attacked, the latter lining up first and signing off to Tillinghast with "This is Martus. Have them in sight. We're going in." Tillinghast rolled in to attack the convoy, which was by then a scattered group of maneuvering ships, approaching the fight a mile behind Martus. Tillinghast selected another target, completed his bomb run at 800 feet, near-missing a destroyer. Other crews circling at a distance saw the bomb explosions and heavy tracers lacing through the night sky. In those seconds, Martus and his crew disappeared without a trace. The Wright Project had lost its second crew.

When the crews relived the night battle at daybreak the next morning at Carney Field the loss of their second crew resonated, in part because Fred Martus and his men were well-liked. Each Martus crewman had "best friend" relationships with counterparts in other crews that were developed over a year or more back with Dolan at Langley Field. Doubling the pain was the fact that, in the scramble to get the Martus airplane into the fight, other crews had contributed men. When the alert had gone out for reinforcements, the Martus crew was in a stand-down mode, having just finished a mission the previous night. As *Gremlins' Haven* was being hurriedly bombed up, three of its crew were not available—one was in sick bay and two others had joined a U.S. Army patrol that was hunting Japanese stragglers reported to be near the airfield. Other Wright crewmen rushed to complete the Martus crew, filling in for their missing mates, thereby allowing Martus to lift off with a full complement.

Martus's radar operator, Technical Sergeant Leroy Rubin, radar mechanic Staff Sergeant Harold Shirey and aircraft armorer/tail gunner Staff Sergeant Augustus Sayko avoided death that night when Martus and his crew went down as they pressed their attack on the convoy. The three replacement men that joined Fred Martus that night were members of three other crews and thus their loss directly struck not one but four different crew families.

The unit's second loss in four weeks resonated throughout the entire Wright Project aircraft mechanics, radar technicians, operations officers and men. The unit's aircraft mechanics had come to "adopt and own" individual planes and serviced their engines, flight controls and hydraulic systems with loving care. Intelligence officers prepared the mission briefings, sat with crews before take-off to confirm routing and targets and waited for each aircraft to return at dawn to debrief each man. After-mission reports had to be drafted and assessments completed of the equipment performance. The radar technicians, at work on their "radar shack" test benches and alongside aircraft with their jerry-rigged "portable" test set, prepared for the next outbound mission by testing and retesting the LAB system, swapping out any troublesome components.

This was a very close-knit group of about 200 officers and men at this point and would remain so even as others joined the Wright Project. Twenty of their members were dead or missing and every man knew this number would grow in the months ahead. It was a long way to Tokyo and the journey for the Wright Project was just beginning. Barely six weeks into its combat debut, the project had lost 20 percent of its crews and was down to eight operational aircraft. One pilot noted that, if the current pace of operation and attrition continued, the Wright Project would find itself exhausted and extinct by Christmas.

But the squadron was fulfilling the role for which it was envisioned and had been dispatched to Guadalcanal—to fly into the night and take that darkness away from the enemy. Night after night, with three or more aircraft patrolling the assigned "hot sectors" up The Slot and beyond, the LAB SB-24s were finding Japanese destroyers, cargo ships, lighters and submarines and homing in on them to deliver pinpoint bombing attacks. Jim Pope recalled "we were doing exactly what Dolan, Wright, Aldrin and others thought we could do. And although we lost both the Easterling and Martus crews in those early weeks, we thought of this time as being 'almost a cakewalk'. We expected to take losses, we had real confidence in ourselves, our planes and our radar, and we came to Guadalcanal to rule the night. And we did."[3]

Liberator brothers-in-arms

The nightly excursions of the Wright Project during these initial few weeks of "combat testing in knife fights with the Tokyo Express destroyers," as one crewman described the action, were complimented by the daily sorties mounted by XIII Bomber Command's two groups of daylight B-24s. The 5th and 307th Bomb Groups, with four squadrons assigned to each, could routinely put 20–30 bombers in the air for a single mission or send multiple missions of a dozen or more aircraft, each chaperoned to the target and covered by "Cactus"-based fighter escorts eager for a fight with Zeros and Oscars.

Back on 15 August 1943, as Wright and his men were winging their way across the Pacific, American forces had invaded Vella Lavella Island, up the Solomon chain from Guadalcanal, and in that "island-hopping" process had bypassed Kolombangara Island and the Japanese forces stationed there. By early October, Vella Lavella's Barakoma airfield was operational and the stage was set for a much bigger undertaking—the invasion of Bougainville further up the Solomon chain. Japanese air units at Rabaul, Kahili and other airdromes dispatched waves of medium and dive bombers and fighters to contest these advances, directing attacks at both the new beachheads and at U.S. bases on Guadalcanal.

On 27 August, as Wright's LAB aircrews were flying their first combat missions, 27 B-24s struck Kahili on the southern tip of Bougainville as other formations bombed nearby Buin and Ballale airdromes. During September, COMAIRSOLS directed XIII Bomber Command to launch 14 B-24 missions, most of them targeting the Bougainville airfields and supply points that had to be neutralized before any attempt was mounted to seize the island. Based on a planning decision to conquer Bougainville proper, the September–October period would see Guadalcanal and the Thirteenth Air Force continue to throw its full weight against Bougainville itself, along with all nearby airfields that could mount aircraft to dispute the landings that would soon occur at Cape Torokina on the island's Empress Augusta Bay. These airfields included Rabaul, with its sprawling complex of airdromes, Buka, Ballale and Bougainville itself.

When this offensive was set to unroll in October, XIII Bomber Command had some 52 B-24s on strength (inclusive of Wright's eight), an equal number of B-25 Mitchell medium attack bombers, and its sister XIII Fighter Command had 300-odd fighters of various types available. Other COMAIRSOLS-managed aircraft included U.S. Navy Liberators, Marine bombers and Royal New Zealand Air Force assets which had arrived the past summer to join the team. In all this planning and ongoing operations there was one primary target—Rabaul—a harbor, airbase complex and headquarters second only in importance to Truk, the Japanese Central Pacific stronghold.

Rabaul—or "Fortress Rabaul" to many—represented to Admiral Nimitz and his South Pacific commanders, and equally to General MacArthur and his Southwest Pacific Command, the essential target for neutralization and destruction. The Wright Project, now operating with the transitional designation of the "5th Bomb Group Project (Provisional)" would find itself deeply engaged in this all-out effort to neutralize Rabaul, stepping up to take on this tasking with gusto. Too many of its men would find themselves paying a price for this commitment.

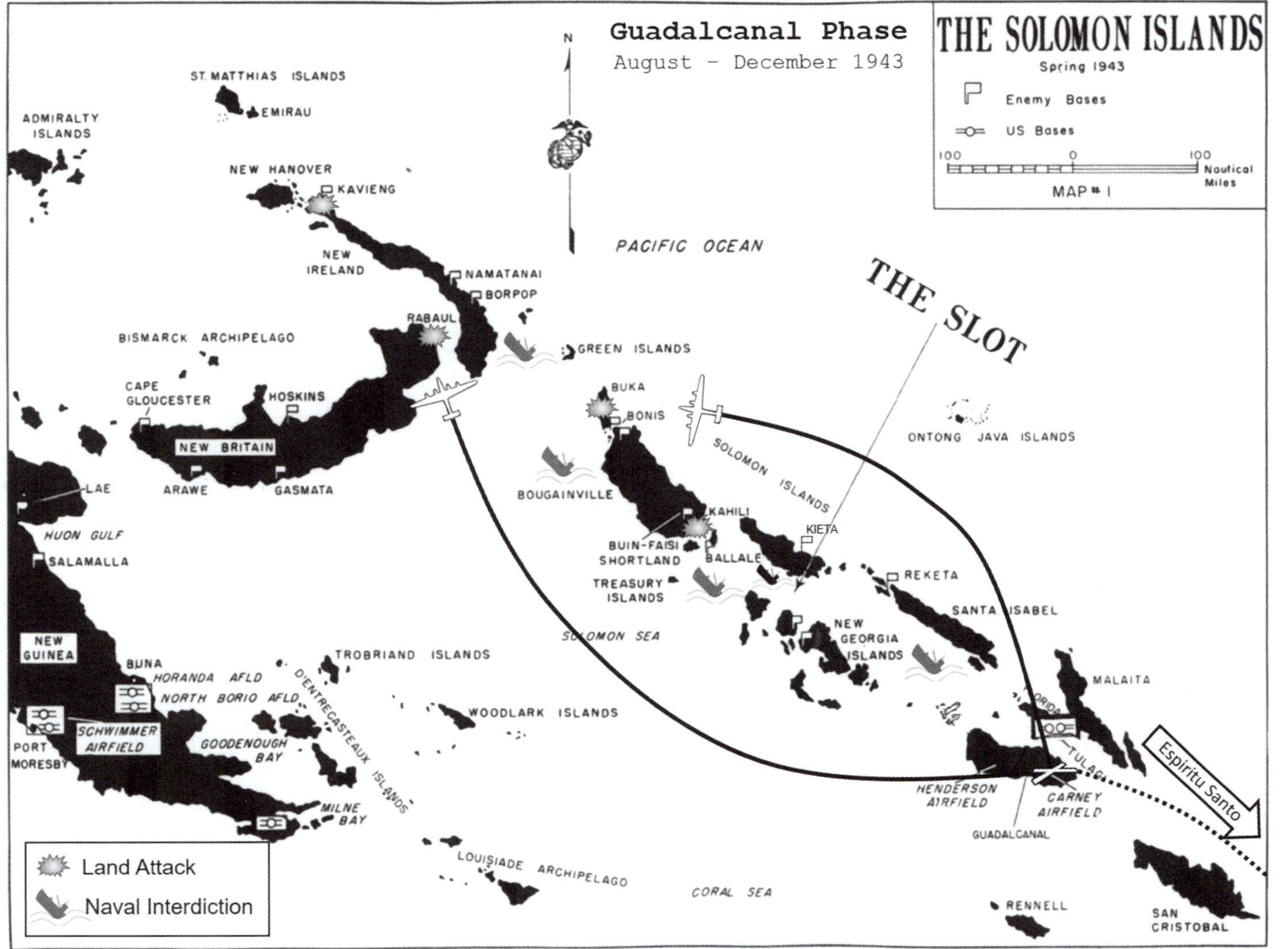

Guadalcanal phase August–December 1943, indicating Wright Project sea-search attacks and land target strikes to the northwest in Solomon and Bismarck Islands. (Author data overlay on U.S. Marine Corps Historical Center map, "Marines in the Central Solomons," 1947)

CHAPTER 7

Battles in The Slot

October–December 1943

Arrivals and departures

Colonel Stud Wright packed his bags and technical reports, went home from Guadalcanal in early October 1943, and placed his LAB squadron in the capable hands of Major Leo Foster. Army Air Force Commanding General Hap Arnold had allowed Wright two months to fly and prove the LAB concept in combat and Wright was under instructions to return to Washington, D.C., and report its progress no later than mid-October. Wright drafted his report during his transit back to the United States and delivered it in mid-October at Army Air Force (AAF) Headquarters. Wright detailed the events on Guadalcanal to the AAF leaders and planning staff, flew to Boston to meet with the Rad Lab leadership and technicians and moved on to Ohio to confer with Colonel Aldrin and his engineering and logistics experts at Wright Field. Wright also made the pilgrimage to visit with Dolan and his team at Langley Field. There was much to share at Langley as, although the second LAB squadron had already departed for the war in the Pacific, a third was forming and would benefit from Wright's briefings. Hap Arnold recognized Wright's contribution with the award of a Distinguished Flying Cross.

Dolan and Langley Field were responsible for training additional LAB crews that would be dispatched over the next many months to replace Wright Project combat and operational losses, as well as the new crews required to replace the men who had completed their combat tours. In the case of combat missions flown, it was then becoming clear that the "relief, replacement and return to the States" point for a given crew would occur after about one year in combat and somewhere between the 40–50 missions point. At Langley Field, new LAB crews had to be trained, mated to more advanced models of the B-24 and dispatched to combat squadrons to ensure that these units maintained their edge and operational effectiveness. Wright also gave presentations and interviews in a classified format on the LAB combat experience, bringing further attention to the possibilities of radar technology. Beyond sharing the LAB experience, Wright's combat role provided a firsthand endorsement of airborne radar in all its permutations, prototyped or imagined.[1]

Back on Guadalcanal, new Wright Project leader Foster had been with Dolan from the first days in Boston, had flown with the 1st Sea-Search against the U-boats and tested ASV systems from day one. He had been selected by both Dolan and Wright to captain the lead plane of the Wright formation—*Devil's Delight* (832)—when it headed to Guadalcanal. He was also designated to replace Wright when the latter departed the unit, assuming Foster survived the first weeks of combat. With Wright gone, Foster held eight surviving aircrew and aircraft and managed to send three LAB SB-24Ds into the night most evenings. He would need to rebuild the unit by inducting additional pilots from other XIII Bomber Command squadrons as they were released to him, and he was careful to scout out the best. He was also awaiting the arrival of replacement crews and aircraft then preparing to depart from Langley Field. Foster and his staff endeavored to field a full squadron of at least 12 aircraft with at least 16 crews to be certain those aircraft could be fully manned and ready. His ground crews, both mechanics and radar technicians, had given the Wright Project's initial 10 aircraft a "mission available" rate of over 90 percent during the first month of combat. However, this impressive performance would be a challenge to sustain as the aircraft and equipment wore themselves down and aircrews were depleted by operational losses, injuries and health issues ever-present in the tropical environs of the South Pacific islands. Living conditions were primitive and the men burned away body weight as they swatted away malarial mosquitos under netting that seemed to invite the nighttime invaders through the mesh.

On the key personnel side, Wright Project veteran John Zinn, who had commanded *Uncle's Fury* (854) in its flight across the Pacific and into combat as a captain, was promoted to major and in late October was transferred out to take command of his own B-24 squadron, a daylight unit then completing its build-up to join the 5th Bomb Group. The earlier loss by transfer of another command pilot (Bob Lehti) to lead a new Thirteenth Air Force C-47 transport squadron brought the Wright team down to five lead pilots for the remaining eight aircraft and their crews.

These departures were offset by promotions within the unit and the transfer into the squadron of three veteran pilots—Lieutenants Vince Splane, Duward Sumner and Art Enger—which brought the unit up to full crew strength for its October patrol missions. Lieutenant Charles Conrad, originally John Zinn's co-pilot with crew AD-3 in aircraft 854, took command of the *Uncle's Fury* crew and aircraft upon Zinn's departure and Art Enger became his co-pilot. Splane and Sumner, both veterans of two months of daylight bomber combat over the Solomons, with most of those missions in B-17s, checked out as B-24 pilots and assumed command of the original Foster and Tillinghast crews. In doing so, they accepted responsibility for *Devil's Delight* and *The Lady Margaret*, respectively. Squadron commander Foster took over the Lehti lead pilot position (AD-5) and flew those missions while that aircraft (*Bums Away*) and crew awaited its new command pilot.[2]

The change in the unit's designation from the 394th Bomb Squadron to the 5th Bomb Group Provisional Squadron (Heavy) as of 1 October 1943, meant little to the men flying missions but it had freed up the 394th to establish itself with regular daylight crews and replacements. The 5th Bomb Group now had its full complement of four daylight B-24 squadrons and attempts to pull the remaining eight Wright Project aircraft and crews into that group abated. But those eight aircraft remained subordinate to XIII Bomber Command, essentially operating as an orphan unit with no support cadre for maintenance, armament and messing. These confusing weeks of October and November, when the senior bomber command management debated what to do with the remnants of the Wright Project, were a blur to its pilots and aircrew, and the abiding attitude was "Let's just do what we came here to do and not worry about the politics of command."

Denied many of the basic support materials available to other "line" daylight squadrons, the 200-odd men of the unit continued to borrow, barter and steal their equipment and maintenance services from the better-supported elements of the 5th Bomb Group and other units based at Carney and Henderson Fields. Amid the confusion and the mixing of aircraft and aircrew assignments, there was plenty of opportunity to do this and Wright Project veterans proved adept. Their special status also allowed them to "game" the Thirteenth Air Force supply system to the maximum degree. When caught poaching, they simply explained that they had no choice but to provide for themselves if COMAIRSOLS expected them to continue to send aircraft into the sky night after night.[3]

Success in October

The month started with a bang when five aircraft made a midnight attack on a convoy in the Buka area on 1/2 October. LAB strikes were made on several ships and confirmed bomb hits were obtained on a cargo ship and on a large escort, probably a destroyer, that Carlson and crew watched as it continued to explode and burn after the attack. The following night the squadron sent off six SB-24s (Mission 119) in anticipation of another Tokyo Express run. Foster, Carlson, Zinn, Reynolds, Sumner and Rockwood found their convoy off Buka and struck multiple vessels hard with every LAB system performing with perfection. Sumner's attack on a destroyer or fast cargo ship lit up the night and he circled the target after the attack to watch it continue to explode and burn, finally breaking in half to sink. Radar also saw the target separate into two contacts, drift apart and then disappear beneath the waves.

On the night of 8/9 October, Carlson was again in action, this time in *Coral Princess*, making an attack on a convoy in the ever target-rich Buka area. Carlson's after-action report described a classic attack from the point the radar contact turned to visual:

> … a 400-foot vessel was seen from two miles at 0135 hours following a LAB radar contact and run
> that began from eight miles out at 1,300 feet altitude. Six bombs were released in train and walked
> up the ship's wake, two exploding in the wake and four exploding on the front side of the ship.
> Japanese air cover did not see the attacker and anti-aircraft did not react until after the bomb release.

With the fighters now active and detected on the radar scope, Carlson banked and dove from 1,300 to 400 feet to evade the air cover.

At this point in the LAB night-stalking effort, it was apparent that the Japanese were attempting to deploy countermeasures and had a plan. When Captain Zinn attacked a three-ship convoy in the early hours of 4 October, soon after his first pass to near-miss the largest target his radar could find, that ship launched three yellow flares that brightened the sky. Within minutes, Japanese fighters appeared on the scene and seemed to detect and close with *Uncle's Fury*. Zinn had by then climbed to 2,800 feet to expand his radar coverage but when the fighters began to close on his plane, he dove 2,000 feet at 190 knots airspeed to elude the fighters and race away for home.

Not all missions went smoothly, however. It was obvious that the aircraft and the LAB systems were getting tired given the mission pace that had been set for the eight remaining SB-24s. When Major Carlson, on Mission 117, taxied out in 836 he discovered a failing hydraulic system that forced *Miss Cuddles* to return to the staging area. The backup alert crew, Brown in 651, rolled out to replace Carlson only to discover, as they taxied for take-off, a fuel leak spraying a fine mist in the bomb bay. This forced a mission abort for *Ramp Tramp*. A second alert aircraft, 854, was then alerted for dispatch but, during its system checkout, it was determined that the IFF of *Uncle's Fury* was down. All attention then turned to 822, but in the pre-flight engine run-up *Bums Away* experienced a ruptured hydraulic line, sidelining it. Finally, 838, respected as a very dependable machine, proved itself to be fully mission ready. Ordnance was transferred, it was gassed up and *Madame Libby the Sea Ducer* went off into the night, two hours late but still out there hunting.

In many cases such determination to "get the mission done" required extraordinary efforts on the part of a given crew. On 7 October, during Mission 123, Reynolds caught yet another Tokyo Express convoy just as its eight ships assembled off Buka. In a nearby patrol area, Rockwood pivoted to the scene to join the attack, but his aircraft suffered a radar failure. With the SB-24 now flying blind and Japanese fighters known to be out and hunting that night, Rockwood made a full-throttle run back to Carney Field and landed to refuel and swap out the set. He had radioed ahead and the "radar shack" team was waiting next to the runway with the replacement system. The two units were exchanged, the new set was tested with the radar cart connected alongside the airplane and the LAB system was declared "mission ready." The Rockwood crew and *Madame Libby* went back out at 0300 to complete the mission. Rockwood found no ships but immediately picked up the fighters on the radar, one of which locked on to the bomber and attempted to close. Turning off his IFF, Rockwood evaded the fighter, completed his search and came home. In other squadrons, such a mid-mission equipment failure, a return to base for an equipment switch-out and a relaunch to complete a mission, would have been unthinkable. With the Wright Project, it was a case of "do the mission."

As related above, by mid-October Japanese fighter aircraft had become much more active against the LAB aircraft. The experiences of several crews were evaluated and patterns emerged. The series of air-to-air contacts that began in October would continue for months and it was assessed that Japanese fighters were possibly using the SB-24s' IFF systems to home in on the bombers. Repeated IFF "triggers" were experienced in combat over the Shortland and Buka area and, not coincidental with these electronic triggers which automatically generated an IFF rapid code response from the SB-24s' own IFF equipment, the fighters would suddenly home in on the SB-24 for a firing pass. Once a Japanese Zero or Oscar found the SB-24, it became a game of bank, dive and evade. The Liberators made it standard procedure to preemptively counter this activity by simply shutting off their IFF system once they entered enemy airspace. It was important to turn it back on when entering more friendly territory, of course, but when and where was always a judgment call.[4]

This situation was also a dangerous game for the SB-24s given that American night fighters also roamed from dusk to dawn with an open mandate to intercept and shoot anything out of the sky that did not respond with the proper IFF signal. Of the four components of the LAB system, the SRC-717 radar did the detecting, the radio altimeter made sure the pilot knew exactly how many feet separated his plane from the ground or the surface of the water, the AN/APQ-5 device computed bomb release in an ASV attack phase and the IFF told the crew whether a target aircraft or vessel that appeared on their radar scope was friend or foe. Just as importantly, it told patrolling American night fighters, and there were now many more of these on hand in the South Pacific, if a target detected by their AI radars was "friendly." A bad IFF on a combat patrol of a SB-24 was reason enough to abort a mission and go home, and this occasionally did happen.

The radar hut

As Colonel Wright would note in his technical report, the overall performance and availability of the LAB system in the field was exceptional, particularly for a first-generation system that had been hastily developed and only briefly field tested before deployment to a forward combat area. This outstanding performance record for a state-of-the-art weapons system during its first combat deployment was due to the design and construction of the equipment and to the maintenance support that the equipment received in the field. The latter reflected the high quality of the men the Wright Project had brought with it. The project's team of 12 AAF radar mechanics was led by Project Radar Officer Captain E. R. Barriere and they were supported by two civilian electronic experts from American private industry who had volunteered to deploy overseas with the Wright Project. Edward H. Sharkey, a Bell Laboratories technical representative specializing in the AN/APQ-5 blind bombing equipment, and Horace L. "Pappy" Clark, a Western Electric Company technical representative who specialized in radar systems, were considered the secret ingredient that permitted the Wright Project to identify and fix equipment problems on a same-day basis.

With the assistance of its two civilian "wizards," the project's radar team wasted no time setting up facilities at Carney to service the delicate radar equipment. Wright's 10 aircraft had carried a large number of spare parts and test equipment when they went overseas. Upon arrival at Carney, two Quonset huts were requisitioned by Colonel Wright and quickly refitted to house the project's radar workshops. A former Wright Project radar operator, Horace Sullivan, recalled the early weeks at Carney and some of the challenges facing the technical team:

- The Quonset Hut radar shops were crowded with a variety of test equipment and ready-to-go replacement components, not to mention entire systems. The "substitution system" developed by the technicians allowed the radar crews to unplug and remove a troublesome unit in a given aircraft and replace it with a fresh unit straight off the test bench. This was the system that provided the project with a very high equipment availability rate.
- The radar shop was unorthodox and creative to the point that it developed and assembled its own portable test and service sets. A complete AN/APQ-5 unit, for example, was mounted on a salvaged Jeep and served as an "on-call" field service unit. When APQ-5 failure in an aircraft was reported, the portable unit was rushed to the aircraft's side on the field and plugged into the SB-24's power system. The bad component was quickly identified, a substitution made and the entire electronics system declared back online.
- Other innovations initiated by the "radar wizards" followed as these men adapted to the tempo of LAB missions and the inclinations of the various components of the LAB system. The combination of the load of spares that the Wright Project brought with it from Langley Field, the presence of the two civilian volunteers and the hands-on leadership and energy provided by radar chief Captain Barriere allowed the Wright Project to survive with practically no material or expert assistance from the homeland for more than a year.

The squadron's radar team received a lot of attention from its counterparts back home at MIT's Rad Lab and Langley Field, particularly given the more primitive conditions in which the Wright team worked. These were in stark contrast to the hospitality of the English countryside where their fellow radar technicians soldiered to support the bombers of the Eighth Air Force. MIT's *Radar* magazine profiled the Wright Project team in one article that described the improvisations being made with the SRC-717-B radar and the AN/APQ-5 computer to keep the aircraft in a high rate of commission.[5]

During the balance of October, the low-altitude attacks by the crews of Foster, Carlson, Rockwood, Reynolds, Brown, Conrad, Splane and Sumner continued with many hits and convoy-disrupting near hits. If the Japanese ships were at sea, sailing individually or in convoy groupings, the LAB radar found them, even as these targets became more inclined to hug shorelines in an attempt to blend into the clutter offered by a landmass. On 28 October (Mission 151), several SB-24s found and attacked a convoy with multiple direct hits registered, claiming two vessels hit and one sunk. Hours later a message came into the 5th Bomb Group headquarters and was shared with the SB-24 crews as they sat down for a back-from-mission breakfast of green (powdered) scrambled eggs and canned New Zealand mystery meat:

BCF NR38 V TSC OCT 28 43
260016 ROUTINE SECRET RELAYED BY 1330MCOM
FROM: COMSCPAC TO: COMAIRSOLS INFO: COMAIRSOLPAC – ALL TPFC'S
MY HAT IS OFF TO THAT BAKER 24 SNOOPER ON SUCCESSFULLY BOMBING ANOTHER JAP SHIP FROM A BRIGHT RED GLOW TO BIZZLING WHITE SMOKE X HALSEY COMSOPAC

November missions

On the night of 1/2 November, the Vince Splane and Duward Sumner SB-24 crews found themselves involved in one of the biggest cruiser-destroyer night battles of the Northern Solomons campaign, the battle of Empress Augusta Bay. This running gun and torpedo battle pitted Rear Admiral "Tip" Merrill's Task Force 39 against Rear Admiral Ōmori's powerful cruiser-destroyer force. Ōmori flew his command pennant in the heavy cruiser *Haguro*, leading an impressive, battle-tested force comprising sister heavy cruiser and Division Five Flagship *Myōkō*, light cruisers *Sendai* and *Agano*, plus a complement of six destroyers.

Earlier on 1 November, an American amphibious force had landed 14,000 Marines at Cape Torokina, Bougainville. The Japanese, determined to throw the Marines off their beachhead, counterattacked with a well-coordinated air assault and dispatched Ōmori's surface force. The latter would attempt to repeat the Japanese Navy's one-sided victory at Savo Island in August 1942 when a similar cruiser-destroyer force decimated the U.S. Navy's surface fleet that was assigned to protect the Guadalcanal beachhead. Ōmori hoped to do one better at the Torokina beachhead by destroying the U.S. covering force and then slaughtering the transport group. The Japanese assumed that the latter was still standing off the landing area and, once past the defending U.S. Navy combatants, the Japanese strike force would have easy pickings. American command anticipated a Japanese night surface attack and Allied code breaking confirmed that a strong Japanese surface action force had departed Simpson Harbor at Rabaul that afternoon. It was on the way and headed at high speed toward the U.S. beachhead, but the critical questions were what direction would Ōmori approach from and when would he and his cruiser-destroyer force arrive to begin the slugfest?

COMAIRSOLS directed two SB-24s to patrol the optimal Japanese approach routes and ordered them to detect, report contact, track and only then attack the advancing ships. Although Merrill's Task Force 39, comprising four light cruisers and eight destroyers, was outgunned by the Japanese, he enjoyed two distinct advantages—the early warning and tracking provided by the two SB-24s and the radar-controlled gunfire his cruisers would be capable of delivering against an enemy who had yet to master this important technology.

As Ōmori prepared to depart Rabaul, Sumner and Splane flew to Munda in the late afternoon to prepare for their night-stalking missions. They sortied at dusk into low clouds and light rain with instructions to patrol the entrance of St. George's Channel. Sumner, flying *Ramp Tramp*, found Ōmori's force at 2100 hours at a radar range of 35 miles. This first alert, complete with the number of ships and their position, course and speed was flashed to Admiral Merrill, allowing him to deploy his forces accordingly and anticipate the time of battle. Sumner continued to track Ōmori with his radar and, during a two-hour period, delivered six different bomb and strafing attacks on *Sendai* and several destroyers of the Ōmori Force.

Shortly before midnight, Splane and his crew, having confirmed the absence of any Japanese strike force moving through their assigned search area, departed to join and relieve Sumner. Having established radar contact, *Devil's Delight* bid farewell to the Sumner crew as the latter headed home. Splane reported in to COMAIRSOLS to confirm that he was taking over the watch and continued to report the Japanese striking group's position, track and speed. He also updated Merrill's force on the fast-approaching Ōmori.

Splane then began his own LAB attack, based on his radar operator identifying the largest warship target. Splane closed on the target and dropped to 800 feet to deliver a six-bomb closely spaced attack against Ōmori's flagship, the heavy cruiser *Haguro*, at 0130 hours. In attacking the *Haguro*, the men of the *Devil's Delight* had selected a real veteran for their bombs and it was luck that the target selected was the flagship and not the cruiser division leader *Myōkō*. *Haguro* was among the most powerful of Japan's 18 heavy cruisers that had paced the string of Japanese Navy victories over the first year of the war. During Japan's "First Stage Operations" from December 1941 to April 1942, *Haguro* participated in the invasion of the Philippines, followed in short order by invasions of the Celebes, Ambon, Makassar and Timor Islands in the Dutch East Indies, capped off by the taking of Java proper.

During actions in the Java Sea, *Haguro*, in company with sister ship *Nachi*, led the battle line that defeated and destroyed the combined Allied fleet. During the "Second Stage Operations" of May through June 1942, *Haguro* was part of Operation *Mo*, the planned invasion of Midway Island, and as such, was a member of the invasion force's "Main Body" group slated to cover the actual landings on Midway scheduled to occur on 7 June 1942. The U.S. defeat of the Japanese carrier force, which resulted in the loss of four fleet carriers, checked any invasion of Midway, and *Haguro* and Cruiser Division Five dashed north to cover the Japanese landings on Attu and Kiska Islands in the Aleutians. *Haguro* had been dispatched to Rabaul to join the Solomons Campaign shortly after the U.S. invasion of Guadalcanal, but the first surface battle the ship actually participated in would be the fight it faced in Empress Augusta Bay.

The *Devil's Delight* attack on Ōmori's flagship was on target. One of the 500 pounders toggled drew first blood by scoring a close alongside near miss, catching *Haguro* and Admiral Ōmori by complete surprise and drenching the bridge and the midship's deck with a column of water. The explosion damaged *Haguro* in the bridge area, its chart room and the hull amidships. The bridge crew scrambled to clean up the damage as the ship reduced speed from 32 to 26 knots and then still further to 18 knots to assess the damage and regain composure.

Aboard *Haguro* some confusion and indecision ensued, abetted by various sighting reports, plus the reality of the obvious fail—they had been spotted, tracked and attacked. It was now certain that they were going into a dark-of-night surface engagement stripped of the element of surprise that had served them so well in the past. That advantage had now passed into the hands of the Americans. As Ōmori's strike force again increased speed to race toward the U.S. transports they assumed were anchored in the bay, Rear Admiral Merrill's Task Force 39, with four light cruisers and eight destroyers, were able to plot the Japanese approach based on the updates provided by the SB-24 trackers.[6]

Tip Merrill deployed his ships for an optimum interception and his destroyers locked on to the approaching Japanese ships with their SG surface radar. In the confused gun and torpedo night action that followed, Merrill used radar-controlled gunfire and turned his destroyers loose for free-for-all torpedo attacks that bloodied the Japanese by sinking the light cruiser *Sendai* and the destroyer *Hatsukaze*. Confusion and collisions among the Japanese ships denied them any ability to organize a collective response and the intensity of the U.S. task group's gunfire and torpedo attacks unnerved the Japanese. Ōmori overestimated the damage his own ships had done to Merrill's ships and he retired with *Myōkō* and *Haguro*, with two of his destroyers limping away separately after having damaged themselves in a collision.

While the U.S. force took its hits as well, the Ōmori strike force withdrew and headed home, licking its many wounds, and yielded the battleground to the defenders. Merrill had successfully protected the Cape Torokina beachhead by turning the Japanese back and, in doing so, had prevented a repeat of the Savo Island disaster that Ōmori had hoped to accomplish. Captain Tamaichi Hara of the destroyer *Shigure*, which accompanied Ōmori that night, would later reflect on the advantages held by the Americans with their "all seeing radar." After watching Splane's attack on *Haguro*, he noted that the "enemy was keeping close track of where we were and where we were going."[7]

The following morning, with Empress Augusta Bay clear of any Japanese ships, the beachhead protected and more Marines, Seabees and equipment pouring in, Admiral Kinkaid sent the Wright Project a "well done" for their crucial contribution to the U.S. Navy's victory:

FROM CASP
TO COMAIRSOLS
INFO COSOPAC COMAIRGUADAL GUADAL BOMBER COMM
COMAIRSOPAC SIGNALS A WELL DONE TO ONE AND TWO VZ3 FOR SPLENDID
NIGHT
TRACKING MISSION COMPLETED NIGHT 1-2 NOVEMBER X.

But the Japanese high command was not done with Bougainville just yet, the smack-down Ōmori's force received from Merrill's task force notwithstanding. Even as Ōmori's damaged ships were pulling back into Simpson Harbor, Allied code breakers picked up strong indications that Truk had dispatched an even more powerful surface striking force to do evil to the U.S. operation. On 4 November, Vice Admiral Kurita Takeo led the seven heavy cruisers and half-dozen destroyers of his Second Fleet from Truk with the intent of refueling at Rabaul. He planned to then sail south at flank speed to smash the Bougainville beachhead, completing the invasion-ending strike that Ōmori had failed to deliver. But Admiral Halsey and the U.S. South Pacific Command were watching and the carriers and aircrews of Task Force 38 positioned themselves for an ambush.

The Thirteenth and Fifth Air Forces were ordered to join them as they were able, but the brutal onslaught that was to be delivered the next day was an all-U.S. Navy event. Almost 100 aircraft rose from the decks of the USS *Saratoga* and USS *Princeton*. F6F Hellcat fighters, SBD Dauntless dive bombers and TBF Avenger torpedo bombers formed up and headed up the St. George's Channel. Arriving over Simpson Harbor at midday, they caught the Rabaul garrison poorly prepared, brushed aside the Zeros that rose to intercept them and proceeded to bomb every warship in the harbor. When the Task Force 38 air groups headed back to their carriers, they left a dozen crippled ships in their wake. Kurita had no choice but to retire to Truk with his damaged ships to lay up there, sending many back to Japan for repairs. The Task Force 38 strike was brilliantly conceived and executed and convinced the Japanese leadership that Rabaul was fast becoming more of a liability than an asset. But Rabaul remained Rabaul and it would necessarily continue to be the focus of the Thirteenth Air Force for some time.[8]

More ship hunting and sub busting

Beyond the attacks on Rabaul, the SB-24s still had their missions and the primary one remained to deny the night to the enemy. On 6 November, Major Carlson surprised a surfaced submarine and delivered a three-bomb near-miss attack. A few minutes later, his radar found a large cargo ship and he improved his LAB bombing technique by planting direct hits on the ship's deck. Violent explosions continued throughout the vessel and it burned and remained visible as the Snooper turned for home. Rockwood and crew staged through the improved Munda airstrip on the night of 7 November to patrol over Buka. His radar found a light cruiser and destroyer escorting a score of large troop barges moving toward Buka at one in the morning. From an initial detection range of 35 miles, two nine-mile LAB runs were made against the light cruiser with close and near misses both times. Rockwood then took full advantage of a full moon emerging through the clouds to make several close strafing runs at 400 feet. His gunners raked the crew with 600 rounds as the cruiser responded with heavy but wildly inaccurate anti-aircraft fire. Immediately after the first attack, the light cruiser shot up three white flares and Japanese fighters poured into the area. Rockwood's IFF was immediately triggered and a particularly aggressive fighter closed. Rockwood switched off his IFF and dove to the deck to lose the fighter.

November 1943 was also the month the squadron intensified its battles with the Japanese submarine fleet. With Japanese Army, Navy and Air Force garrisons in the Solomons and in nearby New Georgia bypassed and isolated by the Allied advance, Japanese fleet class I-boats and smaller coastal submarines were pressed into service to supply garrisons and recover crucial personnel who had been stranded with the bypassed garrisons. Beginning with Carlson's described attack of 6 November, the squadron began to find many submarines on their radar scopes, most running on the surface at maximum speed. All seemed to be counting on the blanket of night to cover their movement and it was clear to the LAB patrol bombers that none had been briefed by their destroyer counterparts on the menace of airborne radar. The submarines headed down The Slot were packed with supplies and those on return runs were carrying high-value personnel, most often aircraft technicians being redeployed to still-active airfields.

On 14 November, Rockwood jumped a submarine headed south and drove him under with a LAB attack. Using the SCR-717 radar to its best advantage, Rockwood patrolled the area over several hours waiting for the submarine to reappear and pounced each time it surfaced, repeatedly driving it under. In the early morning hours of the 27th, Colonel Edwin Aldrin, on an inspection visit to assess XIII Bomber Command performance, flew as a second pilot with Sumner's crew. That night the LAB mission tracked a large submarine running south and delivered two LAB near-miss attacks. With Colonel Wright back in the U.S. by then to make his report, Aldrin, as his fellow LAB birth father, was "in the field" with the unit. He had logged his first LAB combat mission and attack, satisfying his real priority with this visit to the front.[9]

The following night, Ken Brown searched in the same area, found another submarine and made three LAB attacks at midnight from different quarters to get two hits. Secondary explosions flashed to outline a confirmed kill as the crew watched their target break in two and sink. Additional submarine attacks were made during the balance of November with Brown and squadron leader Foster claiming probable damage on surface-running submarines. The SB-24s were now the established nemesis of the Japanese Navy's night-running submarines and they continued to harass and disrupt the supply line, sinking or damaging several more in the anti-submarine effort over the final weeks of November.[10]

A ringside seat

On the night of 24/25 November, Ken Brown and his SB-24 crew were in the front row for the battle of Cape St. George, a brilliant U.S. Navy destroyer night action in which Captain Arleigh "31-knot" Burke taught the Japanese how to execute with tactical precision night torpedo and gun attacks. U.S. code breakers had provided advance knowledge of the probable Japanese Tokyo Express destroyer supply run to Buka Airdrome, and Burke led his five destroyers of Destroyer Divisions 45 and 46 to patrol the western entrance to St. George's Channel.[11]

Brown and crew in *Ramp Tramp* were positioned several miles to the north to patrol the Buka to New Ireland stretch. The SCR-717 equipment found the approaching Japanese five-destroyer force under heavy cloud cover an hour before midnight, heading at speed toward Buka Passage. The U.S. destroyer group was alerted as Brown continued to monitor the movement of the Japanese with his radar as the supply mission landed 900 army troops and recovered personnel from the now useless Buka airstrip. Brown's crew watched the Japanese ships depart and shortly after midnight tracked them as they came into radar range of Burke's waiting destroyers. Ordered not to attack, Brown dashed north as the surface action began to scout for any possible Japanese reinforcements. Finding none, he returned to circle the battle and watch the U.S. destroyers as they torpedoed and gunned veteran destroyers *Ōnami*, *Makinami* and *Yūgiri* under, with *Uzuki* hit but headed home along with the undamaged *Amagiri*.

Commander Burke's after-action message flashed from his flagship, destroyer USS *Charles Ausburne*, reporting on the just-concluded battle, directed some praise at the SB-24 contribution to his victory:

> ON THIS THANKSGIVING DAY WE ARE TO BE THANKFUL TO COMAIRSOLS FOR COVER X AT ZERO FOUR TEN LOVE IN LATITUDE ZERO FOUR DASH FIFTY-FIVE AND LONGITUDE FIVE THREE DASH THIRTY-EIGHT HAVE COME TO COURSE ONE FIVE ZERO SPEED THIRTY-ONE KNOTS OUR MAXIMUM X LOW ON AMMUNITION FEW TORPEDOS X HAVE ENOUGH FUEL X SOME SHIPS GETTING LOW ON FEED WATER X FOUR ENEMY SHIPS SUNK SEEN VISUALLY X ONE DAMAGED AND ONE UNDAMAGED ESCAPED WEST XX

So ended the last run of the infamous Tokyo Express and the last surface battle in the Solomons. Brown's Snooper SB-24 was there, making its contribution in yet another Army Air Force/U.S. Navy joint effort. This teaming was working well, proving that the combined-service COMAIRSOL operational approach to the war in the South Pacific had been perfected. The tables on the Japanese had been turned, and they certainly no longer dominated the night.

The Jungle Air Force and Rabaul

November 1943 had also been a busy month for XIII Bomber Command writ large. Beyond its daily raids against targets in the Solomons and Bismarcks in support of the surge of Allied ground forces up the chain, COMAIRSOLS had finally turned its heavy and medium bombers loose on the big target—Rabaul. This bastion had been a primary target for months and a regular destination for the Thirteenth's sister Fifth Air Force operating in the Southwest Pacific area. In late October, that air force had intensified its air war against Rabaul with a maximum effort, sending its B-24s to bomb shipping in Simpson Harbor from a high level with companion strikes by waves of B-25s mounting wave-skimming attacks.

Notwithstanding this onslaught and expecting a major U.S. move to invade Bougainville, Japan was determined to stay on the playing field. By early November, some 200 Japanese Navy carrier aircraft had been dispatched from Truk to reinforce a similar number of land-based Eleventh Air Fleet aircraft stationed there. As previously mentioned, a U.S. Navy carrier strike hit Rabaul on 5 November as the Japanese Navy reinforced itself in the wake of the battle of Empress Bay and caught the fleet preparing for another surface action attack on the U.S. beachhead. The strike waves dispatched from the U.S. carrier fleet caught the attack force in the harbor and damaged six cruisers. The damage inflicted was serious enough to compel the Japanese to cancel another surface attack and send their ships limping back to Truk for repairs.

On 11 November, during a three-phased effort, the Fifth Air Force hit Rabaul, followed by a larger U.S. carrier strike, and complemented by the first Thirteenth Air Force attack on Rabaul. Two dozen Liberators of the 5th and 307th Bomb Groups hammered Rabaul with high-altitude bombing and were told that, from this point forward, they would have the lead role in suppressing this target. The 11 November strike was notable when the 5th Bomb Group commander, Colonel Unruh, not satisfied to bomb through the overcast, led his 23rd Squadron B-24s beneath the clouds to attack individual ships in the harbor. The 31-year-old Unruh was an inspirational leader who made it a point to fly the toughest missions undertaken by his group. He had flown combat patrols with the Wright Project since the day of its arrival on Guadalcanal and continued to provide his enthusiastic support.

The pounding of Rabaul would continue through November and the toll taken on the Japanese aircraft based there was dramatic, to the extent that some 200 were lost in defending the port and attempting to blunt the mounting attacks on their airfields. By mid-month, these losses forced the Japanese Navy to withdraw to Truk what was left of the carrier air groups that had been on loan. The Japanese high command had not yet decided to abandon Rabaul to its fate, but the Combined Fleet would never again risk high-value surface ships in Simpson Harbor, and its elite naval air units, or what was left of them, would not return to Rabaul's airfields.

Yet the threat of Rabaul remained. It was a fortress-in-being with a dominating position in the theater, capable of being reinforced from Truk and the Home Islands on short notice. Its excellent harbor, multiple airfields, expanded base structure and division-level Army garrison required constant Thirteenth and Fifth Air Force attention. Even after a U.S. decision had been made to bypass it entirely, the *sine qua non* for such an Allied isolate and leap-around strategy required that Rabaul be neutralized and be made to remain neutralized. The Snooper crews would soon get their assignments in this effort and, in company with their daylight brethren of XIII Bomber Command, would pay a price for taking on Rabaul.

The Wright Project aircraft continued to put two to four aircraft up every night to patrol and hunt. Ken Brown finished the month by getting back to LAB business on 27 November with a shuttle run that took *Ramp Tramp* from Guadalcanal's Koli Field to Munda for mission staging. Launched from Munda, Brown delivered double beam attacks over a two-hour period on a surface-running submarine that he had detected and bombed. *Ramp Tramp* proceeded to track it for over two hours as the crippled sub limped along, bombed it again and claimed a kill. Brown and crew recovered to Munda at dawn, had a great breakfast with the U.S. Navy at its "Munda Canteen," caught some sleep and came home to Koli the next day. It was a good close to a great month for the squadron.

Pathfinder missions

One of the first "radar pathfinder" missions of the air war in the South Pacific occurred on 4 November when an SB-24 accompanied a 5th Bomb Group strike against an escorted convoy that had been reported in the Green Island area. Mission 189, comprising 21 daylight Liberators from the 23rd and 72nd Bomb Squadrons, departed Munda Field mid-morning and flew into inclement or "instrument weather." The weather cleared to allow the strike force to assemble but the entire force looked to the SB-24 to detect the convoy and lead the Liberators to their target. The Mission Report gives full credit to the Wright Project crew: "Despite adverse weather conditions this formation found its moving target immediately. This was largely due to the use of the SB-24 to guide them into the target, which was picked up by radar. [the SB-24 then] … took the flight to the point of visual contact."

On this escort and guide assignment, the SB-24 shifted its position in the overall formation once the targets were acquired visually and bombed from altitude that day as part of the 23rd Squadron, targeting the three large vessels. There was no fighter escort on this daylight mission and the B-24s were jumped soon after bomb release when they turned away from the target and the heavy and accurate anti-aircraft fire from the escort vessels abated. Forty Japanese fighters pressed their attacks over an hour and two B-24s were hit hard by the fighters, one ditching on the return home with only half the crew surviving. The second aircraft crash-landed at Munda with its flight controls shot away and several wounded on board.

The overall results of this mission were judged to be no better than "fair," in part because the aircraft bombed from 8,000 feet, releasing their bombs in sections, dropping on the release by the lead aircraft. Damage to a large cargo ship that was caught transferring materials to the beach by cables was claimed, but for these daylight B-24 crews this was not a typical mission. It was an eight-hour flight that bounced its way through inclement weather with no fighter escort, to attack a maneuvering convoy and was met by intense fighter opposition. This was more an SB-24 mission which a strike by the LAB crews could have delivered much better results with one-seventh of the aircraft that were sent against this convoy. But there were only eight SB-24s available at the time. As a consequence, the daylight crews would get more of these "bombing from formation assignments" in the future.[12]

On 21 November, the unit was again tapped for a radar lead on a daylight mission, this time on a strike against Nauru Island organized by the 307th Bomber Group. Some 26 B-24s from that group and its sister 5th Bomb Group would depend again on the single SB-24 involved. The SCR-717 radar would lead the bomber formation to target through inclement weather for a late-morning bombing run that would continue the neutralization program directed at this once active Japanese outpost. While low-level blind bombing was the Snooper game, the navigation capability which its systems provided, particularly in the unpredictable and often rough weather conditions routinely encountered in the South Pacific, made the SB-24s a double threat.

A Snooper pilot, Lieutenant Don Thomson, who made several of these pathfinder runs to accompany and guide the longer-range daylight missions noted that, "On every one of these missions we flew alongside the lead B-24 command aircraft, often picked up and homed in our target from 80 to 100 miles away, and only dropped back in the flight when the leading bomber radioed to us that their bombardier had the target on his Norden bombsight." And while LAB patrol and attack would remain the main task assigned to the unit, these same aircraft and men were also proving that the vision that Bid Dolan and his supporters had formed around the potential of airborne radar was inspired and valid.

December round out from "Cactus"

November had ended well for the Wright Project, with many missions dispatched, targets hit and no operational losses. Most assumed that this tempo had set the stage for an active December. By this point, the Wright Project, still designated the 5th Bomb Group (Provisional) Squadron, had relocated to the recently completed Koli Airfield on Guadalcanal. As noted with the Brown mission in late November, the SB-24s were also increasingly able to make use of Munda Airfield on the island of New Georgia, which had been captured on 5 August by U.S. Army forces. The airfield was declared secure in September and improvements on the Japanese work began immediately, creating an operating base for tactical aircraft covering this area of the Northern Solomons. By November, Munda was available to heavy bombers as a staging base, a launch point for deeper-ranging missions to the northwest.

A typical mission from Koli on Guadalcanal had one SB-24, or more typically three, a night depart home base in the early afternoon and fly an hour-and-a-half to Munda to prepare for a late-night dispatch. Post-mission recovery could be either to Munda or back to Koli, depending on the mission length and fuel consumption, but at Munda, the U.S. Navy took good care of the visiting Snoopers. The Navy food was exceptional, warm blankets plentiful and closed sleeping quarters with flooring available, all of which put Guadalcanal's primitive accommodations to shame. Given the choice, the Liberator crews always tried to get in two nights at what they came to call the "Munda Hotel," and it helped that the sailors at Munda were impressed with the SB-24 men they were hosting. One SB-24 aircraft commander recalled being pulled aside by a senior Navy officer when he heard an SB-24 warming up at midnight to launch for a mission. A tropical rainstorm was raging outside the tent, and he asked, "Are you guys seriously planning on flying into this mess tonight?" The answer was, "Of course, Captain. It's what we do every night at about this time."

While some SB-24 missions had been run through Munda in the preceding weeks, the field came into its own as a routine mission launch point for the Snoopers in December. On 2 December, Sumner took *Uncle's Fury* through Munda to penetrate up the coast of New Ireland to hunt the waters near the Admiralty Islands. A few days later, Rockwood took his crew on a similar routing for what the project was now calling "prowling missions," with no targets assigned but with the crew cleared to hit anything that moved in the night.

More subs and other things

On the night of 17/18 December, Major Foster and *Uncle's Fury* tracked and attacked another submarine at midnight with unknown results. At four in the morning, his radar found another target, this one initially judged to be a very fast-moving surface contact. The radar line up was made and the bomb run turned over to the LAB system and the bombardier. At the second of "bombs away," the target was visually sighted and immediately identified as a Japanese four-engine "Mavis" flying boat skimming the surface of the water. The bombs missed and Brown began a radar-assisted air-to-air gun battle—the squadron's first with a flying boat—that yielded a claim for one seaplane probably destroyed. One SB-24 aircraft commander, Frank Reynolds, recalled, "You never know what that radar is going to find for you out there in the night, but find it, it will."

On 20 December, Vince Splane in *Devil's Delight* discovered and hit the biggest express target of the month, an eight-vessel convoy northeast of and headed toward Rabane. Splane hit a large AK with several bombs which quickly caught fire and burned for hours. A second AK was also attacked and damaged. The flames from the first victim were visible for over 30 miles as *Devil's Delight* and crew returned home. Three nights later, Major Foster's radar operator found a large barge convoy at 25 miles distance in St. George's Channel and set up bombing and strafing attacks that took three large barges packed with soldiers and supplies off the Japanese rolls. By this time, the Japanese Army and Navy had many bypassed garrisons to provision—with food, fuel and ammunition in short supply—and they needed to move personnel to and from these isolated outposts on the chance that a bypassed base would be attacked in the future. At the same time, the Japanese Navy was tasked with evacuating stranded personnel who were deemed to be essential to the next line of defense. The submarines, which were hunted with success by the Snoopers, could only haul so much, and the destroyers that had been the Tokyo Express were exhausted and by this time had been mostly withdrawn.[13]

The result of this drawdown of destroyers and submarines was that large self-propelled barges were now carrying the bulk of the cargo. These boxy shallow-draft vessels were detectable, highly vulnerable and very sinkable, and the USAAF and U.S. Navy and Marine air units feasted on them. While not high-value warships or cargo vessels, the barges represented a Japanese lifeline that had to be interdicted. Unable to move during the day given the near total dawn-to-dusk dominance of Allied air power over the Solomon chain, the barge traffic concealed itself until dusk and then cast off to make as much speed as it could at night. The SB-24s knew where they gathered, how they moved at night and sought them out for bomb and strafing attacks. It was bloody business, but it had to be done, night after night. On Christmas Eve 1943, Frank Reynolds took off for his last patrol of the year, searched for the barges, but instead found a slow-moving destroyer. He attacked it three times for three near misses alongside. The heavy and accurate anti-aircraft holed his wings and chewed up his tail, but he made it home for a Christmas morning landing and breakfast with no casualties.

Up to Munda

The SB-24s took a break on Christmas Day and for several after to prepare for and complete their move to Munda, a new location that they were familiar with and eager to relocate to. Compared to Carney and Koli, they thought the U.S. Navy-built and managed Munda Field to be a double step-up in the world, and their routine targets would be an hour or more closer, thereby making new targets available at the SB-24's full range.

Over 26–29 December, the relocation of aircraft and their support structure to Munda was completed. Rumor had it that the unit had survived its experimental phase and, by acquitting itself in combat, had earned a more permanent billet on the Thirteenth Air Force roster. A few replacement crews were drifting in and a long-awaited squadron designation seemed likely.

The movement to Munda notwithstanding, the month and year ended on a depressing note for the men of the Wright Project due to the loss in combat over Rabaul of 5th Bomb Group Commander Colonel Unruh. On 18 December, the 5th had begun its missions against New Britain and Rabaul, focusing daylight attacks on the "Big Five" airfields that were part of the Rabaul complex. The weather was often lousy to impossible, mechanical problems plentiful and the fighter opposition vicious. The anti-aircraft fire at Rabaul was always heavy and accurate over the target. On a 30 December mission, Unruh led 20 of his group's B-24s through heavy anti-aircraft fire and attacks by 60 interceptors. Unruh's aircraft was hit over Rabaul by heavy anti-aircraft fire, pursued by tenacious fighters and was seen going down. The Wright Project closed out the year with Major Carlson flying the length of the New Ireland coast in a determined search for any survivors from Unruh's ill-fated *Pretty Prairie*, but this and other search efforts mounted by the 5th Bomb Group for its commander were in vain.

Unruh was one of the most dynamic personalities of the Thirteenth Air Force, a man who routinely took on the 5th Bomb Group's toughest missions and often flew the lead aircraft, and now he was gone. Unruh had flown with the Wright Project on its first mission and had consistently supported the unit, understanding its combat potential. Colonel Stud Wright and Unruh had bonded and at the time of the former's departure from Guadalcanal to brief Hap Arnold, Unruh had assured Wright that he would protect the integrity of the special unit. Wright Project pilots, returning Unruh's respect, had flown with Unruh on a number of daylight missions on an unofficial basis. Within his group and within the Wright Project, his leadership and strong persona would be missed.[14]

No targets

The most visible development in the final weeks of 1943 was the evaporation of surface vessel targets in the areas where the Wright Project was poised to patrol. The surface and air battles of the previous months had exacted a heavy toll on the Japanese and had seen them pull critical resources back to Truk, initiating the collapse of their so-called "outer defense perimeter."

One result of Japan's fighting retreat from the front of the battle was the suspension of destroyer-led convoying within the range of the SB-24s, the reduction in submarine shuttle supply runs (in large part due to the losses inflicted) and a reduced level of large barge activity. During December, the eight aircraft and 11 crews flew 32 night patrols to discover targets only 18 times. With few exceptions, the targets were small craft or barge convoys rather than the fat cargo ships or warship targets with which the unit had regularly done battle. The Japanese Navy and Army were licking their wounds, counting their mounting losses in ships and planes and regrouping away from the Solomons, the Bismarcks and the Admiralties for the next series of battles. As the SB-24 squadron built up its strength, relocated to its new base at Munda and prepared to begin operations in the new year of 1944, the unit would find its mission set shifted to accommodate new targets which reflected new priorities for the Thirteenth Air Force and the Central Pacific Theater.

Year-end 1943 accounting

Over the past 17 months, since the U.S. mounted its counteroffensive at Guadalcanal in August 1942, the Japanese had won many of the dozen or so night actions in which they had participated, but, in a net calculation, these were Pyrrhic victories for Japan and the extended Solomons campaign had resulted in a resounding defeat for its forces. The Japanese Navy and its air arm had paid a crippling price in valuable ships, aircraft and crews that could not be replaced as the U.S. injected more ships into the fight and gained experience and confidence. At the same time, the Allied forces were learning to make the best use of the technologies the United States brought to the fight.

The United States Strategic Bombing Survey in its postwar accounting "Campaigns of the Pacific War" noted that, in the Solomons, Japan had lost 50 combat vessels, 2,900 aircraft and tens of thousands of soldiers, aircrews and sailors. Other ships sat in shipyards back in the Home Islands where battle damage was being repaired and the training of replacement aircrews for combat strained a system which found itself ill-equipped to generate more capabilities. Slowly but surely, it was dawning on the Japanese leadership that their nation was not able to compete in an extended conflict with America, particularly one dominated by mass production, quality aircraft and ships, dedicated men and deployed technology that Japan often could not understand, let alone match in combat.

The Wright Project had not been present that dark night off Savo Island some 15 months earlier in August 1942 when the Japanese delivered a resounding defeat to America in Guadalcanal's "Iron Bottom Sound," but one year later in August 1943, the LAB SB-24s were all over The Slot, hunting the Japanese at night and scouting for the enemy in support of the U.S. Navy's cruiser-destroyer forces. Night stalking had altered the dynamics of this slugfest close-quarter war by finding and busting Tokyo Express convoys, joining the mix at the battle of Empress Augusta Bay, pounding submarines off New Britain and scouting overhead at Cape St. George. During five months of combat, the Wright Project had made tangible contributions and had inserted itself as an important component of the increase in tempo that America brought to the war in the Pacific. In this relatively brief period of combat, the 10 aircraft and crews demonstrated a powerful new military capability that denied the night to Japan, manifesting the growing American material and technological strength that was turning the tide in the Pacific.

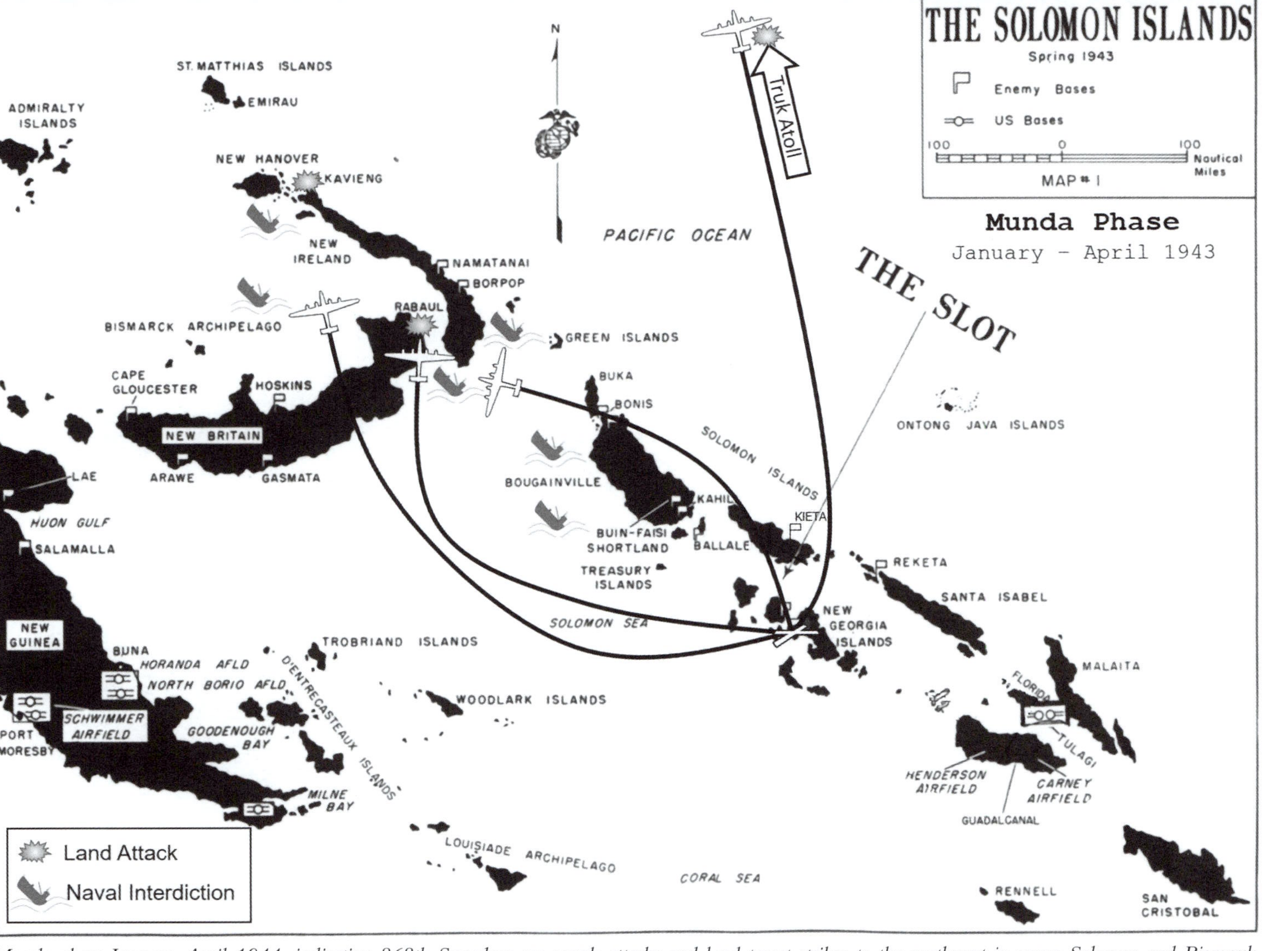

Munda phase January–April 1944, indicating 868th Squadron sea-search attacks and land target strikes to the northwest in upper Solomon and Bismarck Islands and to Truk to the north. (Chris Chen/Telemus)

CHAPTER 8

Munda and Rabaul

December 1943–March 1944

Welcome to Munda Airstrip

Although strike aircraft of the Wright Project had staged through Munda on New Georgia from their bases on Guadalcanal in the November period, the airfield did not become "home" for the unit until it relocated there in late December. The invasion of New Georgia, a combined U.S. Army and U.S. Marines undertaking, code-named "Toenails," was an important milestone in the Allied advance in the Central Solomons toward the overall objective, the destruction of Japan's "Fortress Rabaul." Initial landings on New Georgia had taken place in late June 1943, a few weeks before the Wright Project's arrival on Guadalcanal. A key objective of the operation was the capture of the partly completed airfield that the Japanese were building at Munda Point on the northwestern tip of the island.

Back in late 1942, as their ground force counterattacks continued on Guadalcanal and the issue there remained in doubt, the Japanese had selected Munda to construct a main air base to support ongoing operations over Guadalcanal. The 550 miles between Guadalcanal and Japan's main air and sea hub at Rabaul was simply too far for Japan to project its air power effectively. Munda, only 150 miles from Guadalcanal, offered a solution, and construction on the new airfield there was undertaken in early 1943. Earlier in the campaign, the Japanese had recognized the requirement to base air operations closer to Guadalcanal given the extreme range involved in missions mounted from Rabaul, but they had poorly managed the process. In October 1942, they had also begun a new airfield at Buka Island, off the northern tip of Bougainville, located about one-third the distance to Guadalcanal, and added airfields at Buin and Kahili at the southern end of Bougainville. Too little, too late, but Munda would be the SB-24s' new home.

The Buin and Kahili airfields, some 120 miles closer to "Cactus" (Guadalcanal), but still 300-plus miles away from the targets they needed to strike, figured prominently in the Solomons air battles in the second half of 1943 and into 1944. The flight paths from Rabaul or Buka to the south carried Japanese aircraft over Empress Augusta Bay, the site of the later U.S. landing on Bougainville, and passed close to Munda. Also, the Buin–Kahili complex was proximate to the Shortland Islands from where the Japanese Navy, particularly the Tokyo Express high-speed destroyers, staged for their runs to the south. But Munda, given its one-hour flight time to "Cactus," should have been the Japanese construction priority. The fact that they were very slow to do this was a major tactical, if not strategic, mistake.

By summer 1943, Munda was a "must take" objective for the Allied forces, both to deny it to the Japanese and to provide a base that would extend Allied air operations to Rabaul, to New Ireland to the north of Rabaul and to the Admiralty Islands to the northwest. The Allied landings on New Georgia in late June 1943 had been challenged by the Imperial Japanese Navy surface fleet, as well as its air force and that of the Army. American Marines and the U.S. Army's 43rd Infantry Division, later joined by the 37th Infantry Division, battled determined Japanese counterattacks for weeks before pushing through the jungles to secure those parts of the island deemed essential. Munda itself was not captured until 6 August.

By October 1943, the U.S. engineers had the airfield operational. Munda hosted fighters and dive bombers and served as an emergency field for B-24s returning damaged or short on fuel from raids to the north. The Wright Project SB-24s staged through Munda from early November, thereby extending their patrol range by 100 miles or more. With the original Japanese airstrip of crushed coral expanded and air defense units in place, Munda became operational just in time to press the air offensive against Rabaul, support the invasion of Bougainville and contest the air above the other remaining Japanese air and naval bases in the northern Solomons and the Bismarcks. Soon thereafter the Munda Point area, in company with nearby Rendova Island, underwent a vast expansion by U.S. forces to support the next phase of the Solomons–Bismarcks operation.

As these developments occurred at Munda, the ground fight occasioned by the Allied invasion of Bougainville to the north on 1 November 1943 continued apace. Here at Cape Torokina on Empress Augusta Bay, the 3rd and 9th U.S. Marine Regiments had stormed ashore and were holding a beachhead perimeter against Japanese troops. The U.S. Navy's 71st Naval Construction Battalion, better known as the "Seabees," had joined at D+3 day and immediately begun work to build a fighter strip there. Soon joined by the 36th, 77th and 75th Construction Battalions, as the perimeter was expanded against strong Japanese resistance, the Seabees carved two additional airfields out of the jungle landscape, commissioning both Piva Uncle and Piva Yoke by January 1944. These three airfields would host U.S. Marine air wings, mainly the fighters that could now visit Rabaul and stay overhead to beat down any remaining Japanese air assets. These same three airbases would also provide staging airfields for bomber aircraft based at Munda and Vella Lavella, but the Japanese counteroffensive to push the Marines off

Bougainville initially made it impossible to permanently locate heavy squadrons at this point in the Allied offensive. A Japanese counterattack in late March 1944 pressed within a few miles of the two inland airfields and, while the Allies prevailing on Bougainville was hardly in doubt, the land campaign would drag on for many months.

Short of a direct attack on Rabaul, an Allied seizure of Bougainville was the Japanese command's nightmare scenario, suggesting a plan to outflank Rabaul and push beyond into the west and north with a move that would bypass the fortress. With the invasion of Bougainville underway and the mandate to neutralize Rabaul still the order of the day, Munda was the natural next stop for basing the Wright Project SB-24s. The Allies would continue their westward march across the Pacific to Tokyo and eventually bypass Rabaul, but it would first have to be bombed into submission and eliminated as a base from which the Japanese could mount any counteroffensive. This was the assignment to which the Wright Project would be committed, in company with all of the daylight B-24 and B-25 medium bomber formations available to the Thirteenth Air Force in the early months of 1944.[1]

Birth of the 868th Bomb Squadron

As mentioned in a previous chapter, at the time of the arrival of the Wright Project at Guadalcanal's Carney Field in late August 1943, the 5th Bomb Group of the Thirteenth Air Force was completing its reorganization by transitioning from the B-17 to the B-24. The latter aircraft would become its standard heavy bomber for the balance of the Pacific War. The conversion of the fourth squadron of the 5th Bomb Group had been complicated by the presence of the 10 aircraft and 100 men of the special LAB unit just in from Langley Field. The two bombardment groups (Heavy) of the Thirteenth Air Force, under the operational authority of XIII Bomber Command, comprised two heavy bombing groups—the 307th, which identified itself as the "Long Rangers," and the 5th, the "Bomber Barons."

Each bombardment group's table of organization was assigned four heavy bomber squadrons, and the 5th Bomb Group saw its fourth squadron, the 394th, temporarily occupied by the Wright Project. But the LAB project was not a standard daylight bombing unit and, although it appeared to be a part of the 5th Bomb Group administratively, the Wright Project operated independently. As such, when the 10 aircraft and crews arrived at Carney Field in late August 1943, the unit commander, Colonel Stud Wright, had resisted attempts to transfer the aircraft and crews of his project to the 5th Bomb Group's roster of daylight B-24 aircraft. His resistance, supported by 5th Bomb Group commander Colonel Unruh, produced a temporary or transitional solution for the identity of the unit, as well as a separate place on XIII Bomber Command's table of organization—the "5th Bomb Group Provisional Squadron." At this point, the Thirteenth Air Force was retiring the last of its battered fleet of B-17s but was retaining some of those former B-17 aircrews to man the new B-24s as they arrived. As earlier related, several of the veteran B-17 pilots and some crew members, who had recently converted to B-24 aircraft and had begun flying combat missions, found themselves assigned in the September–October period to fill vacancies that opened in the Wright Project's ranks.

This provisional arrangement for the Wright Project allowed the 5th Bomb Group to reclaim its fourth squadron as a standard daylight unit and build it up to full operational strength with incoming B-24s and crews fresh from the United States. Yet, amid this reorganization of units and aircraft within the Thirteenth Air Force, the original Wright Project still needed to find its own place and establish its own squadron-level support organization. Hence, effective 1 January 1944, the 868th Bombardment Squadron (Heavy) was activated as a subordinate unit of the Thirteenth Air Force and XIII Bomber Command. It would retain this identity for the balance of the Pacific War, take its direction from XIII Bomber Command and other higher authorities and remain operationally and organizationally independent of either the 5th or 307th Bomb Groups.[2]

Reinforcements arrive and more on the way

The formal activation of the 868th at Munda involved the assignment of personnel from the 5th and 307th Bomb Groups, with additional support cadre drawn from the 6th Replacement Depot in New Caledonia, and officers and men reassigned from the disbanded 18th Combat Mapping Squadron. The latter would be sent forward from Espiritu Santos, New Hebrides. The Wright Project's capture of many of the veteran personnel of the last-mentioned unit when it was dis-established was a real bonus as many of these individuals would staff the 868th in critical support roles for the duration of the war. On the date of its activation, the 868th comprised 49 officers and 100 enlisted men, and personnel added over the next three months would see the squadron manifest grow to 86 officers and 349 enlisted men by 1 April.

In this same period of movement to Munda and the transition of the unit into a numbered squadron, more aircraft crews were reporting for duty and others were on the way from Langley Field with their aircraft. In late December, three new crews had reported in, those of Lieutenants Fred Bryan, Don Thomson and Dick Gay, but all without bringing new aircraft with them. Fred Bryan and crew flew their first combat mission (868-224) on 27 December. Pete Colt and crew were on the way as well, as were Phil Hoffman and Art DeLand, both of whom were checking out their new J-model B-24s at Langley Field as they prepared to move to the Pacific for assignment with the 868th. By mid-March, the squadron would have 13 aircraft on its roster, including eight of the original D-models and five of the more advanced Js. Unfortunately, late-month losses would soon impact the crew and aircraft roster.

January LAB hunting parties

New Year's Day 1944 saw Deward Sumner and his crew launch from Munda on a LAB search and attack mission in aircraft 639, to track, attack and damage a surfaced Japanese submarine. Sumner had inherited his crew and assigned aircraft from project veteran Captain Tillinghast when the latter was promoted out to take command of a daylight B-24 squadron. On 4 January, Vince Splane and his crew in *Devil's Delight* worked their LAB search area to find and attack a warship, identified as a light cruiser, with three bomb straddles and near-miss damage claimed.

The next day, Don Thomson and crew, after failing to find any shipping target worthy of their bombs during their LAB mission, elected to hit a secondary land target, Kavieng Airfield. They delivered an early morning wake-up strike on one of the most active Japanese airfields in the area. This was one of the first land target night strikes conducted by a solo mission aircraft of the 868th since the squadron's inception. The attack was mounted at the initiative of the Thomson crew in that they did not have a mandate or instructions to divert to a specific land target. Thomson recalled that, after five hours of "no contact, not even a damn barge," he had polled the crew with "Guys, we have a solid airfield target that is giving our daylight boys a lot of trouble. Do any of you have an objection to hitting Kavieng?" The response was "Let's do it and stop talking about it." Thomson had an "intercom consensus" to deliver the attack.

The airfield, located at an important juncture on the northwestern tip of New Ireland, was known to be a well-provisioned Japanese aircraft base and had regularly launched fighters against daylight crews operating against the base and the area in general. The attack by the Thomson crew was successful and generated fires that could be seen from 20 miles away.[3]

Upon their return to Manus, and immediately after the mission debriefing with squadron intelligence officers, Thomson was summoned for a "dressing down" by XIII Bomber Command. By taking the initiative of hitting a land target, and having actually prepared to do so in the pre-mission work-up without senior-level blessing, Thomson had "risked the compromise of highly-sensitive equipment that would fall into the enemy's hands if your aircraft was shot down over the target." Thomson and his bombardier and navigator explained that they had selected a possible land target that could be attacked at the conclusion of their sea search because it seemed impractical to either bring home their bomb load or dump it into the ocean upon their return. Also, these airfield and port targets inherently lent themselves to the SCR-717-B-equipped aircraft where a strong radar signature could be acquired and subjected to a LAB attack. This was particularly so when the airfields were sited on a coastline, as almost all were.

After considerable discussion between XIII Bomber Command and squadron leadership, the former reversed its stance and instructed the Snoopers to thereafter include, in all future mission planning, the option to divert to a "designated secondary target, including active enemy airfields" in the event sea-search patrols failed to detect shipping targets. The cut-over point to divert to the "secondary" was generally at the four-hour point in the sea-search mission. But the pilots soon learned to plan well ahead for the diversion by making sure that they were in range for a run to their land target at the three-hour point. This decision was critical for the 868th's ability to retain its relevance and was a logical recognition of the new reality—surface vessel targets were becoming scarce in the patrol areas being assigned. The new norm became the crew selecting, at the time of mission briefing, a possible land target that could be attacked at the conclusion of its sea search, ideally one that would lend itself to a radar signature and a LAB attack.

On 11 January, Reynolds and his crew in their B-24D 836 searched the Cape St. George area with no results. This was a 10-hour mission that turned up no activity in an area that had until recently teemed with Japanese shipping running The Slot to support Japanese bases north of New Georgia. Following the path blazed by Don Thomson's crew, Reynolds diverted to a pre-selected target of interest, a location of new construction at the tip of Cape St. George and delivered what became known as an "early morning piss-call attack" to the Japanese working at the site. On a 17 January mission, Vince Splane found a large transport that had been set on fire, probably during a daylight attack, but was still limping along and making headway. It was an easy target and *Devil's Delight* put several LAB-directed bombs into the target and left it burning throughout its length.

Three days later, on 20 January, a LAB mission by Richard Gay and his crew found a large barge hugging the coastline and destroyed it with bombs and gunfire. On 23 January, Lieutenant Bryan and crew hunted in a location where the large sea-going barges were now known to collect after loading with cargo. He hit this group hard and claimed at least one destroyed. The following night, returning to this same area, Sumner and crew found a Japanese Navy gunboat escorting barge traffic and attacked, bombs near-missing to damage it. In the early morning hours of the 25th, the Splane crew hit a group of cargo-heavy barges and claimed to have damaged and scattered the lot.

This pattern of discovering the barge convoy assembly locations and returning night after night to hit these points denied the Japanese the ability to organize, load and transport cargoes at night, even by the coast-hugging self-propelled barges. Bypassed Japanese units dependent on these fragile supply lines would be starved of food, munitions and reinforcement with fresh troops, negating their ability to disrupt the Allied advance. Allied daylight raids were of limited effect as the large barges and their escorts utilized hiding points along the coasts and were heavily camouflaged with trees, netting and blankets of palm fronds. They moved only at night, and thus the SB-24s were tasked to hunt and destroy them when they moved from their hide locations. This disruption of the supply network was important work for the 868th and such attacks would become a priority.

On the night of 25/26 January, Fred Bryan and Frank Reynolds patrolled near one another in 838 and 832 respectively. They hit a jackpot when Bryan's LAB radar peeled back the night to discover a six-ship convoy at 2°15S 150°30E making its way to the northwest. The LAB radar operator picked up this group of ships from 20 miles away early in the mission. Bryan then stalked the convoy from several miles for over an hour, reporting the contact and summoning Reynolds from his patrol area to join for a two-aircraft coordinated attack. To confirm that they were not lining up on a U.S. or Allied convoy, Bryan contacted COMAIRSOLS to receive clearance to attack. Once the target was validated as not Allied, Bryan began his LAB run from 10 miles, selected the largest target on the scope and put three 500-pound bombs alongside the ship.

Clearing the immediate area, with a heavy volume of anti-aircraft fire filling the night sky above the scattering convoy, Bryan came back in again to unload his second salvo of three 500-pound bombs on an escort, striking it hard and seeing it separate into two parts to sink. When Reynolds joined the wolf-pack ambush from the sky, the two aircraft coordinated a series of attacks that spanned two hours, during which repeated bombing and strafing runs hit the two other cargo ships and damaged a destroyer. Reynolds saved his last two bombs for a large merchantman that he originally identified as a hospital ship. In so identifying it, he opted to pass on an attack but ran in close to be sure. When the ship's anti-aircraft guns reached out for his plane, Reynolds went out several miles, came back to make his bomb run and hit the target, claiming "one large confirmed non-hospital ship damaged."

The Bryan mission report provides a running narrative of the action:

> … on the run on the gunboat-type escort, bombs fell and hit the target directly, a violent explosion, followed by a burst of flame, and the target appeared to break into several pieces, some disappearing and some still floating. An attack on a destroyer followed with a hit squarely on its stern, ship stopped, then resumed movement, attacked again. On all three runs accurate, steady, intense, medium-caliber anti-aircraft fire was thrown up from all the vessels in the convoy.

The Bryan aircraft was hit in several places but none of the crew were wounded and the plane recovered safely to Munda.

During the last three days of the month, Sumner and crew found a small cargo ship, attacked it and set it afire. His crew reported seeing it ablaze from 30 miles away. Lieutenant Brown discovered a surfaced submarine and attacked to drive it under, claiming near-misses for damage delivered. The 868th scorecard for the month showed 52 LAB missions flown, 20 of which produced targets and bomb runs on the same, with four ships claimed sunk and a further 10 damaged with hits or near-misses.

But the quantity and quality of enemy shipping targets that had been routinely discovered and attacked at sea in the first months of the Wright Project deployment in combat were no longer out there in the night waiting to be found. The end-of-month squadron report reflected this disappointment by noting, "As the primary mission continues to be to search out and destroy enemy shipping it has become necessary to change patrol areas; we now have the mission of preventing enemy ships from entering the great naval base offered by Simpson Harbor at Rabaul from either the Bismarck Sea or from the south through the St. George Channel." In other words, the 868th, finding fewer targets at sea, was evolving its basic strategy from one of search-to-find interdiction over a broad patrol area to one of "access denial" at the approach choke points of selected Japanese bases. The two entry routes mentioned in the monthly report suggested the 868th should be assigned to establish a LAB-enforced nighttime blockade of Rabaul's once-mighty, now reduced but still functioning, harbor and airfield complexes. This would be done by aggressively patrolling the western and eastern approaches to Simpson Harbor, and only diverting to pre-approved "secondaries" if no suitable surface ship targets had been detected on those access routes.

February with the 868th Snoopers

The squadron's operations from Munda in February 1944 began with renewed success in its primary anti-shipping role. Fred Bryan was out in the early hours of 6 February and his radar found a three-ship convoy at 4°02S 162°10E. He selected the largest target, a medium-sized cargo ship, and attacked to place several bombs on and alongside the ship. The ship exploded and was left on fire and settling into the water. A few days later, on 11 February, Rockwood and crew found their own three-ship convoy, a merchantman with two small escorts. They rolled in to strike at the cargo ship and near missed for a damaged claim. Over the next week, the Carlson, Brown and Conrad crews would have luck finding groupings of large barges hugging the coastline on their supply runs headed south from Rabaul, each crew attacking with bombs and strafing to claim damage delivered.

During February, the squadron would fly a total of 62 missions but only find and attack its designated "primary target," shipping, on 14 occasions, making some 29 "runs over target" in those attacks. Four ships were claimed as either sunk or extensively damaged, with the now routine attacks on barge traffic not included in the shipping totals. The unit record shows that in no case did inclement weather turn back a squadron patrol, establishing the unit's claim that it provided the Thirteenth Air Force with a sustained and dependable true "all-weather" attack capability. During this same period, in part due to the dearth of shipping targets, the 868th was assigned to perform nine "heckle" missions over Rabaul, plus four missions in support of U.S. naval task forces operating in the area. To this mix was added two missions to attack and disable a Japanese radar station that had been detected at Adler Bay.

Wright Project command pilots, still serving with their original crews and assigned aircraft, included Major Foster, the squadron commander, Major Carlson (833), Captain Rockwood (838), Captain Brown (651) and Captain Reynolds (822). Departed Wright Project command pilots included Captain Zinn, who had been reassigned the previous October to assume command of the 394th Bomb Squadron, and Lieutenants Lehti and Tillinghast who had requested to move on to other units. Several months before,

First Lieutenants Vince Splane and Charles Conrad had been inducted as experienced B-17 and B-24 pilots from other Thirteenth Air Force units to lead the Lehti (832) and Tillinghast (639) crews respectively, and were now well settled into the unit's mission routine.[4]

December saw the arrival of two new crews fresh out from Langley Field, well-trained on B-18s and B-24Ds. Both crews would fly in with brand-new B-24Js, the first addition of such aircraft to the squadron roster. First in was Lieutenant Arthur DeLand and crew, with *Ready, Willing and Able* (42-73396), arriving at Munda on 15 February 1944. A few days later, DeLand's close friend Phil Hoffman and his crew touched down in *Long Distance* (42-73410), finally returning the squadron to a full complement of 10 aircraft. Pilots Thomas Arthur, Peter Colt, Robert Robins, Robert Alsop and their crews would complete a 17-crew roster compiled on 21 March 1944.[5]

The DeLand and Hoffman crews and their aircraft, the first J-models to join the remaining D-models of the Wright Project now based at Munda, were flown on the routing: Langley Field, Virginia; Mitchell Field, New York; Memphis Municipal, Tennessee; Davis-Monthan, Arizona; Fairfield-Suisun, California; Hickam Field, Hawaii; Canton Island; Nadi, Fiji; and Espiritu Santos in the New Hebrides. The two aircraft and crews overnighted at Carney Field on Guadalcanal and flew the next day to reach their combat base at Munda Field. This movement across the U.S. and out to the South Pacific over the 19-day period, from 26 January to 15 February 1944, emphasized the ability of the B-24s to deploy combat-ready, with spare parts included, from a standing start at Langley Field into the front line, teed-up for combat operations.

Three days after arriving, DeLand and company flew their first strike mission, an 11-hour shipping search of the St. George's Channel and Bismarck Sea area. Flying in a veteran B-24D and not his preferred 396, DeLand came up short with no shipping contacts and returned to base with his bombs still on board. Joining the squadron's normal rotation schedule, DeLand was back out on the 18th in the aircraft he "owned," the J-model he had brought over, for a 12-hour LAB search in the same area where he again came up with no targets. The month would have the DeLand crew flying three more times, these being their Strike Missions 3, 4 and 5, and hitting the designated or "secondary" land target at the end of each unsuccessful sea-search effort. The recipient of 396's attention in each of these was Kavieng at the far tip of New Ireland, by now a much-visited (by the Snoopers) location that was still active in daylight hours with its fighters sent against the daylight B-24s and medium bombers of XIII Bomber Command.

At this time, the 868th had more fully embraced the name Snoopers for its aircraft and crews, to the extent that signboards at the squadron's operational center and in its officers' club carried the name proudly. This unofficial unit name would remain with it for the balance of the war and in years thereafter in both official and unofficial histories of the unit.

March madness and Rabaul

Missions during March 1944 reflected the change in emphasis from sea-search and attack to dedicated dark-of-night harassment runs over selected Japanese airfields and ports. With the crew numbers and aircraft available, the squadron attempted to maintain a tempo of three missions a night, with two dedicated to sea search and one to harassment. The harassment missions, more colloquially known as "heckling runs," typically lasted 10 hours and had the SB-24s overhead a target for four hours or more, flying a random in-and-out pattern at altitudes of 10,000 to 20,000 feet for repeated bomb drops. Smaller capacity 100-pound bombs were delivered incrementally with the goal of disrupting port and airfield operations from midnight through dawn.

A typical harassment mission was that of Lieutenant Arthur and crew on 2 March over the Rabaul base area, in which his aircraft made five bomb runs at 14,000 feet over several hours, hitting the town of Rabaul and two primary airfields at Lakunai and Tobera. The anti-aircraft response was heavy on each bomb run and at one point the garrison searchlight team caught and held Arthur's aircraft for over 10 minutes. During the first two weeks of the month, DeLand, Rockwood, Colt, Sumner, Carlson, Conrad and Hoffman would harass Japanese airfields at Rabaul, Rapopo and Keravat on seven occasions, while other crews flew the standard sea-search missions.

In the harassment missions, the LAB system was used to navigate to the target, guide the bombardier to his final run and release point and search for the Japanese night fighters that could have been scrambled to intercept the harassing bomber. Art DeLand opted to harass Rabaul on 17 March after a fruitless sea-search mission, for the last attack on that target of the month. Other options were coming into focus and the squadron was directed to look at more attractive, but more distant and far more dangerous targets.

The 868th sea-searching Snoopers found the balance of March to be slim pickings in terms of the availability of Japanese Navy and cargo ships for LAB detection and attack. The destroyers which had once raced south from Rabaul or the Shortlands for surface action or to escort ships throughout the Northern Solomon and Bismarck area had seemingly disappeared. In fact, a progressive Japanese pullback to Truk and beyond was underway with higher command much less inclined to risk precious surface combatants, even in night runs into and out of Rabaul. During the entire month, only two ship targets were sighted and attacked. The sea search aircraft on such empty-handed missions then opted to hit their assigned secondary land targets. Typical airfield targets included Namatanai, Kavieng and Panapai airdromes, with these being particularly attractive given the radar signal performance of the LAB equipment.

Reflecting this steady increase in the tempo of 868th Squadron operations, March included 78 strike missions, 13 of which were harassment runs to Rabaul. A typical bomb load to disrupt that base included a mix of 100-pound general-purpose and M-4 incendiary bombs disbursed over a dozen runs at random times over a four-hour period.

The squadron's monthly report identified five mission areas: routine search and attacks directed at shipping, with diversions to secondary targets; dedicated harassment missions against primary airfields and ports; search missions dedicated to locating and attacking Japanese radar sites; accompanying and supporting daylight strikes by the 307th Bomb Group by providing navigation assistance; and, finally, LAB night missions in support of U.S. Navy destroyer divisions engaged in the nighttime bombardment of shore targets.

Painful losses

The operational tempo mentioned above—with three aircraft scheduled to fly missions each night—saw the squadron experience losses in aircraft and men that it had somehow managed to avoid over several months of combat. On 10 March, Lieutenant King and crew flew in 805 to harass Rabaul and failed to return at daybreak, their fate unknown. The squadron assumed they had begun their harassment runs over the target on schedule at 0200 hours and were either shot down by the highly-competent anti-aircraft gunners or by a night fighter. The following day, the squadron dispatched several aircraft on daylight runs on the course flown by the newly arrived King crew hoping that, had King been hit over Rabaul and managed to limp away, the plane had ditched along the return leg. No trace of this crew was ever found.

On 20 March, the aircraft of command pilot Lieutenant Richard Gay took off east-to-west from Munda Field to begin a harassment mission against Rabaul. His aircraft (468) experienced a severe engine malfunction at about 800 feet during its climb out. When engine number one's (port outer) supercharger would not reduce power and ran away, Gay feathered the engine and called to the crew to prepare for a water landing. The fully loaded plane could not gain altitude and began its descent. The flight was doomed and hit the water about 15 miles off Munda Point, breaking its back and separating into two pieces that sank quickly.

A squadron accident investigation board assessed that it was likely that the fully laden bomber had suffered an engine cut-out shortly after take-off and that the oil pressure at that engine was lost so quickly that the crew was not able to properly feather the propeller. The runaway prop would have then wind-milled, creating enormous drag and reducing the effective power of the aircraft by at least another half an engine. The aircraft, still attempting to climb with full fuel and bomb load, would have essentially been attempting to stay in the air on two and a half engines. This would have presented Dick Gay with an unrecoverable situation, making the crash unavoidable.

In other situations like this, where power was lost on an engine, and propeller windmilling continued, the disabled engine would typically catch fire after four minutes or so. An unattended engine fire could eat through the engine firewall to enter the wing tanks, resulting in an explosion. In the case of the Gay crash, it was judged that the loss of the engine and the windmilling prop simply pulled the heavy Liberator into the ocean.[6]

The survival of three men from the Gay crew cast into the waters off Munda was nothing less than a miracle. Co-pilot John Toole had been ejected through the front windscreen of the cockpit on impact, smashing the plexiglass with his head and shoulders and was left floating in the fuel-covered water near the plane. Technical Sergeant Isadore La Mica, the flight engineer, was badly injured and stunned, but composed himself and sought out any other survivors, calling into the night and circling the sinking plane. He found the radar operator, Odell Dyer, and pulled him forward, then found Lieutenant Toole, semi-conscious and face down in the water.

The three men managed to survive in the water until they were picked up by a crash boat in the early hours of 21 March, but the rest of the crew was lost. La Mica would later be awarded the Air Medal for holding both his injured and semi-conscious crewmates above the water for nearly three hours. This same man, a hero within his squadron, would return to duty a few days after this experience, fly many more missions and be lost in another squadron tragedy that would play out a few months later.

868th Bomb Squadron Aircraft and Activity 1943–44

Three 868th Squadron B-24Ds at Munda Field, March 1944, back to front: Madame Libby, Devil's Delight *and* Ramp Tramp. *(Author's collection assembled/restored from 868th Squadron veterans and Colonel Werner, MIT Museum and MIT/Rad Lab* Radar *magazine)*

B-24D Devil's Delight *returning from 50th mission. (Author's collection assembled/restored from 868th Squadron veterans and Colonel Werner, MIT Museum and MIT/ Rad Lab* Radar *magazine)*

B-24J Long Distance *with Hoffman crew, Munda, 1944. (Author's collection assembled/restored from 868th Squadron veterans and Colonel Werner, MIT Museum and MIT/Rad Lab* Radar *magazine)*

Japanese heavy cruiser Haguro. *(Kaigun, Imperial Japanese Navy at http://www.combinedfleet.com)*

B-24J Ready, Willing and Able *with Deland crew, Munda, 1944. (Author's collection assembled/restored from 868th Squadron veterans and Colonel Werner, MIT Museum and MIT/Rad Lab* Radar *magazine)*

B-24J Lady June *with Thomson crew, Noemfoor, 1944. (Author's collection assembled/restored from 868th Squadron veterans and Colonel Werner, MIT Museum and MIT/Rad Lab* Radar *magazine)*

Radar system test bench, Guadalcanal, 1943. (Author's collection assembled/restored from 868th Squadron veterans and Colonel Werner, MIT Museum and MIT/Rad Lab Radar *magazine)*

Wright Project radar section "the shack," Guadalcanal, 1943. (Author's collection assembled/ restored from 868th Squadron veterans and Colonel Werner, MIT Museum and MIT/Rad Lab Radar *magazine)*

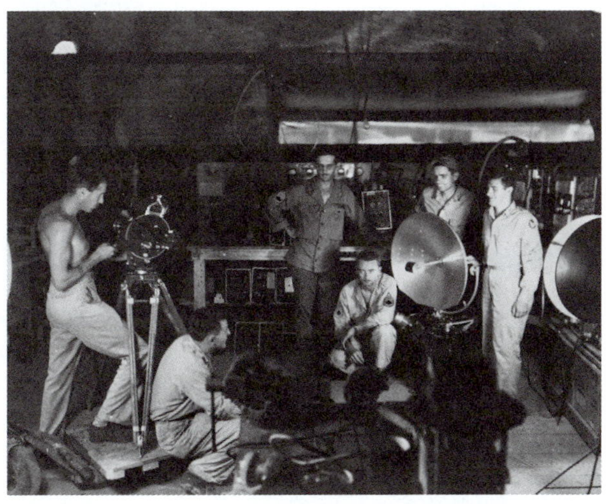

CHAPTER 9

Mighty Truk, Deadly Truk

March–June 1944

Next up—the Central Pacific bastion of Truk

A new addition to the 868th target list in March was Truk, probably Japan's most important outpost in the entire Pacific Ocean. This base had routinely been referred to as the "Gibraltar of the Pacific" since before the start of the Pacific War, and for good reason. The Caroline Islands, of which the atoll of Truk was a part, had been in Japanese hands since 1914, essentially as a by-product of Japan associating itself with the Allies against Germany in World War I. In the mid-to-late 1930s, Japan, recognizing the importance of Truk and the fine harbor it offered to its Navy in the context of Pacific War planning, began a fortification program that would establish the atoll as its Central Pacific military bastion. By the time of the Solomons Campaign in 1942, Truk sustained the forces that supported the Japanese push into the Solomons, the offensive in New Guinea and actions designed to cut Australia off from the United States. The Combined Fleet, including its flagship battleship divisions and carrier forces, forward-based at Truk, as did the various cruiser-destroyer divisions which shuttled between Truk Lagoon and Rabaul to press into the fights around Guadalcanal. As a supply point and air base, it was formidable as well, serving as it did to back up Rabaul with aircraft, supply ships, fueling and fleet repair facilities.

Recognizing the centrality of Truk, American planners responsible for mounting the drive through the Central Pacific toward Japan proper placed a high priority on neutralizing the collection of islands that constituted the complex. The proverbial U.S. hammer fell in February 1944 when the U.S. Navy launched Operation *Hailstone*, with massive carrier aircraft strikes on Truk's main islands and its harbor, combined with surface ship attacks on the atoll. The former sought to sink the ships in place and the latter was designed to intercept and destroy Imperial Navy vessels attempting to flee the aerial onslaught. On 17–18 February 1944, the U.S. Navy's Task Force 58 dispatched some 500 sorties in waves of attacks against shore facilities and the ships caught in the harbor. Although the bulk of the Japanese Navy heavy units, anticipating such a raid, had left the atoll days earlier for temporary refuge in the Palau Islands further to the west, the carrier air raids were devastating. The merchant ships and Imperial Navy auxiliaries caught at anchor were bombed, torpedoed and strafed under—nearly 30 in all—along with two light cruisers and four destroyers. Nearly 250 Truk-based aircraft were destroyed in the air or on the ground and thousands of tons of fuel oil, an increasingly scarce commodity for the Japanese fleet, went up in fire and smoke.[1]

Yet, as the nine fleet and light fast carriers and their escorts of Admiral Marc Mitscher's Task Force 58 departed the scene, the smashing of Truk had to be sustained and the Japanese denied any opportunity to reconstitute the forces based there. This second-third punch mission fell to the land-based aircraft of the Thirteenth Air Force and U.S. Navy patrol squadrons, B-24 units all, making repeated blows that had to be delivered both day and night to ensure maximum pressure was maintained on Japan's "Gibraltar." The hammer had to continue to fall on Truk.

Although the Thirteenth Air Force was continuing to support MacArthur's drive in the south, as his forces moved up the coast of New Guinea, by striking Rabaul, the focus of the overall fight was falling increasingly on the Central Pacific. That drive toward Japan had begun in late November 1943 when, as the Wright Project was staging through Munda to hit Rabaul, Pacific Ocean Area Command, managed by Admiral Nimitz from Pearl Harbor, invaded the Gilbert Islands. Located northeast of the Solomons, a third of the distance to Hawaii, the Gilberts represented the furthest eastern penetration of the Japanese Empire toward America, save for the action in the Alaskan Theater. The invasion of Tarawa was bloody and the U.S. Second Marine Division paid a high price to secure that island.

The drive through the Central Pacific was favored by the Joint Chiefs over MacArthur's parallel drive to the northwest from New Guinea in the Southwest Pacific, and the former was reasonably perceived as a more direct, more efficient and possibly less costly, route to bring the fight to Japan's Home Islands. As this dual-approach strategy evolved, there were strong disagreements among the commands, with MacArthur determined to take the war through the Philippines by way of western New Guinea, Halmahera and the Celebes. Alternative approaches to Japan, advanced at the highest command levels in Washington, D.C. (Admiral King), involved the invasion of Formosa (Taiwan) and a bypassing of the Philippines, or at least the main island of Luzon. Although the Thirteenth Air Force, and thus the 868th Squadron, would find itself supporting both drives, it would soon find itself subordinated to MacArthur's command.

But the occupation of the Gilberts laid the groundwork for the relentless Central Pacific push to the west, into the Marshall Island chain, and beyond to the Carolines. The latter were anchored by the atoll of Truk and if Truk were to be bypassed, as was desired, it had to be beaten into submission. Truk was located directly north of Rabaul and Kavieng, and therefore north of recently secured Allied airfields in the Solomons, including those at Bougainville. Truk was a long haul for the B-24s, but the Thirteenth was the obvious choice for missions there, and thus the 868th found itself playing a key role in that commitment.

The unit participated in the sustained suppression of Truk in several ways. In daylight, given the distance to the target and the configuration of the low-lying islands that formed the circular atoll, XIII Bomber Command assigned individual Snooper aircraft to guide larger B-24 formations to the target. On a typical "escort" mission, the SB-24 guide aircraft remained on the wing of the lead aircraft to guide the formation until a visual sighting was made and then turned the attack over the daylight aircraft. At that point, the crews of the 5th and 307th Bomb Groups locked on with their Norden bombsights and collectively released when the lead aircraft dropped on target. These missions were flown at 10,000 feet or more, thereby avoiding a high percentage of the anti-aircraft guns that guarded the islands. These were not the low-level, strike-in-the-night LAB missions for which the 868th crews had trained, but they did allow multiple squadrons of XIII Bomber Command Liberator groups to navigate to the target with pinpoint accuracy, including through inclement weather, to bomb in formation, vastly improving the chances for a successful mission.

This SB-24 pathfinding role was critical to the success of daylight missions in maximizing fuel management, target acquisition and weather avoidance. The latter was a common problem that too often caused missions to be aborted en route. During the April–July period, the Pearl Harbor-based planners for the Allied drive through the Central Pacific would depend on the Thirteenth Air Force, supplemented by the U.S. Navy Liberator squadrons, to continue to neutralize Truk, even as fast carrier task forces swept in from time-to-time to slam the base for good measure.

First to Truk

Yet the initial 868th strikes against Truk had actually begun on 29 March when two SB-24s departed Munda and staged through Piva Airfield on Bougainville to hit installations there at night. Don Thomson and Art DeLand shared the honors of delivering the "first land-based attack on Truk" with Thomson off Piva Airfield 10 minutes before DeLand and therefore arriving over Truk to bomb first. Don Thomson recalled that the pre-mission briefing at Piva was excellent and the approach to the target well mapped out. The U.S. Navy strikes 10 days before had wreaked havoc on the shipping caught there, had knocked out about half the Japanese aircraft based on the atoll, but had failed to do heavy damage to the petroleum, oil and lubricant (POL) storage tanks, a priority target. Thomson and DeLand were to hit these with a combination of high explosive and incendiary bombs.

The first aircraft over target made a LAB approach and delivered its ordnance on the storage tanks, causing fires that lit up the entire area, before exiting with no damage. DeLand's aircraft lost its SCR-717-B radar system about 10 miles out and bombed visually on the fires set by Thomson and his crew. This was a near 14-hour mission on the Piva–Truk–Munda routing and was the "Lucky Thirteenth" mission for both crews and the now-vintage B-24Ds that they flew that night. The Thirteenth Air Force, more than willing to claim credit for this event, allowed press coverage, albeit with some acknowledged "delays" built into the release. An Associated Press (AP) story carried worldwide was breathlessly headlined "M'Arthur Fliers Ran Race To Truk" and managed to spread the news of the long-range strike while containing several errors in fact and implication.

The flyers were not those of MacArthur's command per se but rather were elements of the Thirteenth Air Force, which MacArthur and his Fifth Air Force did not then (yet) control. There was not a "race" between Don Thomson and Art DeLand, and Thomson's name was repeatedly misspelled in the communique that provided the information for the AP story. Many of 868th assumed this media release was yet another of MacArthur's many attempts to claim credit under his "General Headquarters" banner for another command's success, but the notoriety given to the crews was welcome, particularly when their respective hometown papers picked up the AP story and highlighted this story of their sons in combat over Truk.[2]

The Thomson–DeLand initial attack did establish a precedent for the balance of the 868th and the unit rose to the occasion with a steady tempo of night missions to Truk, typically dispatching single aircraft to harass the base. This effort was complemented by XIII Bomber Command's daylight missions. These usually comprised a force of 20 or more bombers put up by either or both of the command's two bomb groups. On those occasions where inclement weather was expected or daylight mission leadership wanted added insurance that the target could be found most directly, individual SB-24s were included on the mission to guide the sister B-24 crews to the target.

No milk runs to the atoll

On 30 March, the crew of Lieutenant Arthur followed that first strike, flying alone to Dublon Town on Truk's main island, where the Japanese headquarters was located and, as had been the case in the first attack, was not intercepted. On 1 April, DeLand and crew were back for another Munda–Piva–Truk–Munda midnight bombing run, and on the following night, Bryan and crew struck Dublon Town with six 500-pound incendiaries from 14,000 feet, starting immense fires visible from 50 miles. Vince Splane and crew visited Truk on the 4th and, for the first time, his radarman picked up night fighters attempting to locate the SB-24 as it made its bomb run. The Japanese failed to find the bomber, but the fighters were now out there and searching, aided by some combinations of massed searchlights, sound detectors and perhaps radar.

On the 7th, Squadron Commander Major Leo Foster led a flight of daylight B-24s from the 307th Bomb Group on the first squadron-led formation night attack on Truk. Foster's radarman picked up Truk at a distance of 190 miles and the formation bombed from 11,000 feet to start fires in and around Dublon Town. On this mission there was heavy but inaccurate anti-aircraft fire, but no night fighter opposition. The fellow 868th Liberators of Rockwood and Thomson flew with the formation in the A-2 and A-3 positions on Foster's wing. On the 11th, it was the turn of Lieutenant Alsop and crew to raid Truk in a LAB run and, once again, the scores of searchlights were scanning the night, anticipating the aircraft as it arrived overhead.[3]

On 12 April, DeLand and crew returned to Truk, this time staging through the newly acquired Green Island, recovering there for a mission debriefing before returning to home base on Munda. Other 868th Snooper crews would fly a similar routine of single-aircraft night harassment missions and alternate with daylight pathfinder assignments. Three days later, Don Thomson was directed to lead a formation of daylight B-24s on a nighttime raid on Truk by arriving 10 minutes ahead of the group and attacking Moen airbase by dropping incendiaries on which the following B-24s could then deposit their ordnance. Thomson was caught and held by six searchlights for several minutes while on his bomb run, then jumped by several fighters over and beyond the target who apparently saw and closed on him to make firing passes. Thomson dove away after his tail gunner had engaged the fighters, put his plane "on the deck" and ran for home. This and the Splane encounter a few days before were the first instances of night fighters rising to engage the SB-24s. It was a portent of things to come and did not bode well for the night stalkers over Truk.

Truk the killer

Truk was bad luck for the SB-24 Snoopers of the 868th. It was a tough target that bedeviled the crews sent against it, both in terms of active combat over the atoll and in operational accidents related to missions mounted against it. After the initial attacks, the Truk garrison developed countermeasures for both the day and night missions, making do with what resources they had, and they reinforced it with aircraft and systems from the Home Islands. Japan desired to keep Truk viable, available as a logistics base for its submarine fleet and as a possible launching point for air raids against the invasions of the Marshalls and the Carolines.

On 1 April, the squadron experienced its first Truk-related loss when Lieutenant Robert Robbins staged from Munda through Piva to attack Truk. Aborting that mission, he returned directly to Munda, possibly with his aircraft in mechanical distress. Shortly after midnight, his Liberator (805) overflew Munda and continued 20 miles to the southeast where it slammed into the hills of Rendova Island. All 10 of the Robbins crew, plus the 5th Bomb Group Weapons Officer, Major James Conway, died. Search crews found the wrecked aircraft two days later some two miles from the island's shoreline. The remains of the crew were recovered and it was concluded that the aircraft's engines and navigational systems had malfunctioned, resulting in the pilots' loss of situational awareness.

The second Truk-related loss followed a few days later when Lieutenant Thomas Arthur, another recent arrival with the 868th, departed Munda with a refueling stop at Green Island. The Arthur crew, with a U.S. Navy observer on board, disappeared without a trace, the only sign being a weak distress signal which could not be triangulated. Arthur was flying aircraft 446, another of the recently joined J-model SB-24s.

Having lost no crews or aircraft for the first two months of the year, over three weeks spanning mid-March through early April, the 868th lost four crews and their aircraft, two to Rabaul and two to Truk. All of these losses involved either recently arrived crews on their first or second mission, or experienced daylight crews who had come to the squadron with limited experience in night flying. While each loss had its own distinctive character, the suspicion was that Truk had become a tough target from the perspective of adverse weather and sheer distance to the growing proficiency of anti-aircraft and night fighters that defended the atoll.

The Thirteenth Air Force would continue to send the 868th Snoopers against Truk in the coming weeks and there would be more losses. During May, a dozen missions were mounted and several aircraft returned with flak damage or tales of close calls with the night fighters, but the following month, June 1944, would be doubly deadly.

On 10 June, Lieutenant Irving Booth departed Morotai for Truk, was shot up and ditched into the ocean in 831. In a night crash landing, the aircraft bounced in well, but the impact with the sea broke its back and it sank quickly. Three of the 10-man crew escaped the aircraft, found a life raft and were soon rescued by a Catalina *Dumbo*[4] search aircraft assigned to patrol the bomber routes to Truk. Seven good men were lost to the sea.

An after-action mission report included the following information and conclusions:

> The strike aircraft hit Dublon Town on schedule at 0322 hours, explosions were noted in the town area, and the plane began its return with no significant damage. At 0620 a signal was sent by the aircraft noting an expected ETA of 0745 at Mokerang home base and at 0732, with the aircraft some fifteen minutes out, an emergency beacon message was received by the airfield. The aircraft ran out of fuel— engines quit in sequence Number 1, Number 4, Numbers 2 and 3, with the pilot executing a water landing. Nine hours later a PBY found and rescued the three survivors, all badly injured.

On the 11th of the month, Lieutenant Donald Dyer and crew departed Morotai for Truk in aircraft 273, found their target, but were shot up as they bombed. Dyer managed to limp his plane away from the target and crash-landed on or near Falieu Island, with the 10 men of that crew lost. Out that same night on separate Truk strikes, two other squadron crews saw what appeared to be a bomber burst into flames and watched as what was probably Dyer's damaged aircraft descended, crashed into the island and burned there as they made their bomb runs on Truk.

Also on the 11th, Lieutenant Haynes and crew struck Truk but were heavily damaged coming off the target. The aircraft limped back to Mokerang Airfield and crash-landed there. It was salvaged and the crew returned to their squadron to receive further orders. Those would come almost immediately with tragic consequences.

On 13 June, in a mission over Truk described in more detail below, Lieutenant Jack Wagner and crew were hit hard by anti-aircraft fire and departed the atoll with two engines shot out and controls damaged. They were forced to ditch a hundred miles south of the atoll and all but two of the crew scrambled out of the plane before it sank. They were rescued 19 days later as they drifted on their life rafts.

On 24 June, Lieutenant Haynes, returned to duty after his crash landing on the 11th, flew again to Truk. For this mission he had assembled a crew that included volunteers from other crews and made a single-aircraft strike run to Truk. The Liberator was last seen as it approached the target by Lieutenant Hickson who was there that night with his crew to follow Haynes in. As Hickson closed in on Truk, his radar detected a "blip" and tracked an aircraft that was headed into the target area but still 40 miles out; it was assumed to Haynes's bomber. Haynes and his crew disappeared after their bombing run, with all 10 men later declared "missing in action and presumed lost." Their fate was that of another crew of young American airmen that seemingly vanished in the Pacific.[5]

When the crews launched to strike Truk and failed to return, often lost without a trace or even a fellow crew member there to record their demise, there was grim work to be done at home. In addition to the letters of condolence that had to be written by squadron commander Leo Foster to the parents and wives of the lost aviators, the effects left behind had to be inventoried, carefully packaged and sent home. One such task was assigned on 26 June 1944 to Lieutenants Werner and Mishkin, appointed as Summary Court Officers, to "inventory and dispose of the effects" of the 10 men of the Haynes crew, declared as missing in action on 25 June.

Werner, a member of a crew flying every third night and reasonably assuming that another officer might soon be inventorying his personal effects for shipment home to his parents, was careful to keep his things in order. It was fatalistic—just being realistic—particularly given the losses being incurred over Truk. As he sorted through the personal items of the Haynes crew and drew in Art DeLand to package the effects of DeLand's navigator, Gerald Westerland, who had volunteered to join the Haynes crew for this mission, they carefully selected what would go to Westerland's wife Ginny who had returned to Chicago to await her husband's return.[6]

The Wagner crew endures

The travails of the SB-24 crew led by Lieutenant Jack Wagner, further to the above-mentioned loss of the aircraft, only began with the crash-landing just south of Truk in the early hours of 12 June. The broader story is more a tale of survival over the forces of nature than of combat. With two engines torn apart over their target soon after bomb release, Wagner's plane was destined to ditch in the sea, a situation complicated by the loss of electrical power and its LAB systems. In his attempt to put distance between his plane and Truk and prepare the crew for a water landing, Wagner ordered everything possible to be jettisoned from the plane. The struggling SB-24 re-entered a tropical storm front and was buffeted far off course. At the ditching, two men were lost in the aircraft, either killed on impact or injured in the crash and trapped as the Liberator broke apart and sank. The men who managed to scramble from the broken plane knew that they had somehow survived but had no idea that they had just begun a 19-day ordeal that would carry into July and bring them repeatedly to the edge of death.

The Wagner crew had first formed in Clovis, New Mexico, then moved on to Blyth, California, where it was introduced to the B-24. The men next went to Harrington, Kansas, where Wagner signed for and picked up a new B-24J. Here the crew was joined by its radioman Jerome Rokos. The next stop was Langley Field, where they were assigned to the 1st Sea-Search Attack Group for LAB training. At Langley, the crew's new B-24J was handed over to another crew and the Wagner team was joined by its radar operator, Merle Musey. A new B-24J with the latest LAB system was assigned to the Wagner crew and promptly named *The Joker*. Both the airplane and crew proceeded overseas, some of the crew with *The Joker* and others by Air Transport Command passenger aircraft. The crew reunited at Carney Field in Guadalcanal in early May 1944, and, beginning on 23 May, flew a half dozen combat missions with the B-24 daylight formations based there, hitting the Rabaul airfields several times from 18,000 feet.

On 1 June, the Wagner crew moved forward in *The Joker* to join the 868th Squadron at Momote. The initial couple of missions saw the members of the crew distributed among other crews to gain combat experience, but by 11 June, the original crew was ready to fly together. Their first (and only) mission as a complete crew with the 868th was to Truk. The debrief from the Splane mission the previous night noted the increased aggressiveness of the night fighters and the heavy flak that was expected over the target. Wagner and his crew took careful notes but entered their assigned aircraft with confidence in the mission.

The after-action report related:

> ... at least fifteen searchlights picked up the Wagner plane and held it in their beams from the beginning to the end of the bomb run ... after bomb release the plane was put into a spiraling dive from 12,000 feet but number three engine was knocked out ... once again in level flight the aircraft was hit in the bomb bay area with all controls damaged ... this damage was followed by a series of heavy hits that walked from the tip of the right wing, down that wing and through the fuselage, continuing across the left wing ... all the oil in number one engine was lost and the propeller ran up to 3000 RPM ... the gas tanks were shot up as well. In the water landing Wagner attempted a "back stick stall" at which time the two remaining engines were pulling 35 inches of mercury at 2300 RPMs indicated.

The tail gunner, Charles Whitmore, picks up the narrative:

The weather was horrible that night with severe storms at all altitudes. We thought this would be good over Truk as we would have no trouble centering in on the target with our radar and could bomb through the weather. But our luck ran out about an hour from the target when it suddenly cleared and a bright moon came out. Over Truk, the searchlights caught and held us and we caught a lot of accurate flak. We were badly damaged coming off Truk, with the two engines out, the hydraulics gone, the radar and other systems inoperable, and we all knew we could not make it home. Lieutenant Wagner was in total control when he announced over the intercom that we had to prepare for a water landing, and he then came back to [the] waist gunner area where several of us collected whatever could be dumped from the aircraft to lighten it. Every mile we could get from Truk was important.

Lieutenant Wagner and Lieutenant Russell Pickering, our co-pilot, descended the plane slowly and the six of us who were not in the cockpit area sat on the deck behind the bomb bay bulkhead, wrapped our legs around one another, held tight and prayed. When we hit there was one bounce and we slammed down right at the section just aft of the bomb bay, the water blew in and everything went dark for me. I was underwater for a long time and when I surfaced Lieutenant Wagner was standing on the wing, deploying the two life rafts and trying to account for members of the crew. Once in the two rafts, he made a roll call and tried to square us away in the two rafts. Our plane and two men were missing—our co-pilot Lieutenant Pickering and Sergeant Wolfsberger, our assistant engineer/gunner. The plane was gone but wreckage was floating around our rafts and we had to move as far away as possible before daybreak.

I was not a good swimmer and was the smallest guy among the survivors so I was not sure I was going to make it, even on day one in the raft. The next nineteen days were very tough but Jack Wagner kept us focused, with a lot of positive talk mixed with discipline. We occupied the two small rafts, tied them together, which was not easy given the heavy seas, and tried to conceal ourselves during the day by laying under the dark side of the sail we pulled up. The aircraft flying over our rafts were Japanese given how close we were to Truk when we went down. One of the first things we did when the sun came out was check one another for injuries.

All eight of us had flak cuts, some severe with embedded pieces and with others random slices on our bodies where smaller pieces had sliced through the plane. We applied sulfur powder and bandaged as best we could, examined these wounds every morning and treated them. We watched our planes overhead at night as they passed from the south to the north on their way to bomb Truk and again as they came off their targets and headed home.

We eight survivors had one good compass, two boxes of K-rations, a single canteen of water, two boxes of chocolate bars and gum and a small sail with a pole. The sharks stayed with us from the first day, circling and probing and while they would rub up against us with their dorsal fins, they did not attack the rafts. We caught small sharks and ate them, including one of 15 pounds, captured rainwater in our Mae West vests and found ways to store it. One huge shark, which we named "ol' Man Moe," stayed with us for five days, waiting for a meal, and when he was around, the other sharks were nowhere to be seen.

The sun was unbearable but a lot worse for some than others—Lieutenant Bonney had very fair skin and he burned badly. Every night we peeled more skin off him, and the next day he would burn more in spite of everything done to protect him. Water was scarce so we thirsted for rain, and when we got it on day four, we used our Mae Wests to collect it as it fell and drank quarts. On the tenth day we got rain again but this time it was an incredible storm that lasted a day and a half. We had to fight the rain, bailing our rafts nonstop for hours to keep them afloat, tightening the connecting ropes as we rode 25-foot waves to stay together, always fearing separation in the middle of the night.

We managed our food but it ran out and we ate fish, mainly tuna and small sharks we could catch. At one point we spotted a single coconut in the distance and rowed madly to grab it. We cut it into eight equal parts and it was delicious.

Lieutenant Wagner and our navigator Lieutenant Bonney did some calculating and we decided to sail home. We manned the sail and a crude rudder in shifts, slept in shifts and had assigned tasks among us, including non-stop fishing. By the second week we knew we had probably missed the Admiralties but assumed that we could still make it to somewhere on the coast of New Guinea in a week or two. We had sighted U.S. Navy PBY "Black Cats" twice in our third week on the rafts but when we put out distress panels in the water and waved wildly, they did not see us.

The third PBY did spot us, and when he dipped his wing and came around us in a circle we had hope for the first time that we might be rescued. He circled for two hours to burn off gas to make a better landing, and as they came in to land its waist gunner fired several bursts, which we thought was their way to put us on notice in the case where we might be Japanese. Convinced we were Americans, the PBY taxied up to us and helped us on aboard, slowly and gently. We settled into the belly of the PBY, devouring the crew's sandwiches, water, candy bars, cigarettes and whatever. Our Black Cat circled our two empty rafts one more time and the PBY gunners sank them both. But we had survived on those two rafts for 19 days, and while we were a sunburned, wasted-away crew of castaways, we were joyful as we flew to the Admiralties.

The PBY landed us at Los Negros and when they took us onto the pier, several of us were too weak to stand. General Street was there to meet us, told us our families and our squadron had been informed as we headed home on that PBY that we had been found and were alive. We went into the 58th Evacuation Hospital where a U.S. Navy nurse, a Lieutenant Donahue led a team who cared for us and we slept for a week. We would go back to the squadron two weeks later and the XIII Bomber Command sent us home. But for us eight who had survived, the war was over.[7]

Command pilot Vince Splane was the 868th Squadron's Accident Investigating Officer and years later he shared impressions gained in his debriefing of the Wagner crew survivors, observations that were not contained in the official report:

When informed by a call from the U.S. Navy that they had found the Wagner crew we were all flabbergasted. The Wagner crew had been gone almost twenty days and nights. They were "Missing In Action." We had all assumed they were just another 868th crew that had gone to Truk, run into the atoll's flak and night fighter buzz saw, been shot down and disappeared.

I was very impressed by the way Jack Wagner handled the damaged aircraft and the crash landing. He had the presence of mind to engage the autopilot to compensate for the damaged controls, allowing a smooth descent and impact. His shoulder was dislocated by the crash and he managed to pop it back into place when he slid into the life raft. He was a solid pilot and a real leader who kept his head and held his men together for almost three weeks.

The radar operator (Musey) broke his right arm in the crash but continued to knead it with his left hand for the entire period in the raft, with the result that medical exam X-rays showed a perfect healing of the bone. Some of the deeply embedded shrapnel could not be pulled out and emerged later when their bodies forced it out months later. The four who were more seriously wounded were lucky to survive the time they spent in the rafts.

The pilot of the U.S. Navy PBY Catalina patrol plane that found them adrift was not looking for them or any other downed crew. Rather, they were hunting for Japanese submarines that our intel had said were in that area. The pilot had departed his left seat position to move to the middle of the aircraft to relieve himself out the bay window. As he did so, he happened to see a random glint in the distance. He grabbed a set of binoculars and spotted the two small rafts. He then checked his position and discovered that his plane was 15 miles off course. Had he been on course and where he should have been, or not taken that relief break, he would never have passed near the Wagner crew and certainly not spotted that glint in the distance.

Examining the track of the two life rafts, they had made good progress over the water but were off by ten degrees or more on their basic course. If they had continued on that 510-mile run, they would have ended up on the north shore of Biak, then still occupied by the Japanese. We all knew that the Japanese, particularly when they were in a bypassed or active combat area, routinely executed captured aircrew on the spot. So, there was a very strong chance that, had the Wagner crew not been spotted by the Black Cat, they would have made landfall on Biak, been captured and killed.

The Wagner crew were fortunate that some of their life raft equipment failed to function. On night sixteen they spotted some faint and moving surface lights that appeared to be headed toward them. They decided to give it a chance, hoping that it might be a U.S. Navy ship. The "Gibson Girl" signaling light failed to work and the ship passed them close by. It was a Japanese submarine running on the surface for Truk. Rokos told me some years later that he never won a card game, craps or even a football bet during the balance of his life and he is sure that he used up all the luck that God gave him during those 19 days adrift in the Pacific.[8]

The opposition

Beyond the anti-aircraft guns emplaced on Truk's islands in the hundreds, the many searchlights, the sound detectors that directed the lights and guns and radar systems that detected the approach of Allied aircraft, there were the fighters that climbed into the night to greet the arrival of the 868th aircraft. Some were standard-issue single-seat A6M Mitsubishi Zeros. As the SB-24 bomb runs began, they hoped to catch sight of an aircraft caught in a searchlight's beam and then move in for a firing pass. Yet other interceptor aircraft were out there in a more dedicated role and with a much greater capacity for destruction.

By this stage of the war, mid-1944, it had simply been too great a challenge for Japan to combine a functional AI radar system with an aircraft capable of tracking high-altitude bombers and bringing them down. This said, Japan did manage to modify an existing aircraft, the twin-engine Nakajima J1N land-based reconnaissance aircraft. Originally designed as a long-range fighter to escort bombers, the J1N had been converted to the recon role because of its high speed and long range and, in this role, it flew from Rabaul in 1942–43. A decision was made to modify the aircraft with cannons mounted at a 45-degree inclination, braced in the fuselage behind the pilot to fire at upward and downward angles. The modification proved successful and the night fighter variant was dubbed "Gekkō" or "Moonlight" by the Japanese. The Allies had assigned the name "Irving" to earlier variants and this was retained for the night fighters.

In the South Pacific, the advent of Allied night attacks over Rabaul in early 1943 was the catalyst that drove the design and the deployment of the initial versions of the Gekkō. The first four prototypes operated with Japanese Navy Air Group 251 and claimed success against the B-17s and B-24s that were raiding Rabaul during spring 1943. In each case, the night fighter would close with a bomber that had been captured by a searchlight and then attack its adversary with 20-mm cannon fire delivered to the underside or topside of the bomber. These first Gekkō aircraft were expended, destroyed in the air and on the ground at Rabaul. But the next deployment of the deadly Gekkōs shifted to Truk, among other front-line locations. Other Navy Air Groups would operate the Gekkō, including the 153 Group, which absorbed surviving Gekkōs of the 251st when the night combat against roaming Allied bombers moved further to the west.

Several Gekkōs were based at Truk in early summer 1944, by which time the 868th had arrived on the scene and was sending its night-stalking SB-24s to that target. This interceptor also operated in defense of other targets struck by XIII Bomber Command's B-24s over the balance of the Pacific War. These Gekkōs could well have opposed and downed other SB-24s in a number of locations, including Palau, Guam and Tinian in the Marianas, Peleliu, the Biak area and throughout the Philippines. The extent of the losses suffered by the Japanese units, and the manner in which the Gekkōs were shuffled among the islands that were being targeted by the Allies, defeat any reasonable attempt to assign specific Snooper losses to Gekkō pilots or even units. But in the black skies above the targets against which the SB-24s flew, this interceptor was the premier night predator.[9]

An accumulation of painful losses

An additional squadron loss in May on a mission to Palau, a Central Pacific target similar in many ways to Truk, delivered a Grim Reaper accounting of nine 868th aircraft and crews down, with almost 100 men dead, missing, or survived but injured; all in the space of 50 days. These April–June 1944 losses, averaging one aircraft and crew lost every six days, were collectively more than the squadron had experienced during its entire existence, even if one counted from the Wright Project's formation at Langley Field in the summer of 1943. By one accounting, missions related to Truk and its sister islands in the Caroline Islands claimed seven of the 14 aircraft and crews that the 868th would lose in its first year of combat in the Pacific.[10]

With the bloody June tally of four crews lost in 10 days of action against Truk, the question of the day became, "Is Truk simply too tough for this type of Snooper one-aircraft night mission?" A better question was, "Is the price being paid by the 868th in attacking Truk worth the effort, particularly as that atoll's importance to the overall war continues to decline?" By July 1944 the answer to the latter question was probably "No." This was increasingly so as the war moved westward, and the squadron with it, to embrace missions that targeted enemy locations more important to the larger war effort than the increasingly isolated Truk.

In the ensuing months of the war, a neutralized Truk would be bypassed by the Allied advance but it could not be ignored, even as U.S. B-29s based in the Marianas and the U.S. Navy fast carrier task forces closed on and pounded Japan's Home Islands. As the 868th shifted its attention further to the west, other bomber groups would continue to hit Truk periodically to keep it suppressed. But as June drifted into July 1944, the 868th was pleased to see Truk in its rearview mirror. The men who had watched their names appear on the squadron blackboard with assignments for the next day's mission, too often with "Truk" underlined, and then climbed into their aircraft to fly against it, would never forget the toll this island bastion had exacted on the squadron and their friends.

CHAPTER 10

Vince Splane and *Devil's Delight*

September 1943–March 1944

As previously recounted, back in early September 1943 the Wright Project had found itself reduced to eight aircraft and only six crews with lead or command pilots. At that point suggestions resurfaced within the Thirteenth Air Force's XIII Bomber Command to simply inject those crews and their LAB aircraft into the daylight squadron to which the unit was then provisionally assigned. The 394th Squadron was then still in the process of building itself out as a full-complement daylight B-24 unit, swapping out what remained of its tired and beat-up B-17Es for inbound B-24s. The 394th and its B-24Ds would complete the 5th Bomb Group's four squadron organization. It therefore seemed reasonable to permanently graft the remaining eight Wright Project aircraft into that squadron, assuming its numbers would be worn down by daylight combat and operational attrition within a matter of weeks.

But Stud Wright strongly disagreed, as did 5th Bomb Group Commander Colonel Unruh. The latter's position was crucial—he insisted that the Wright Project remain an independent activity and that his fourth daylight squadron be just that, 12 to 16 B-24s dedicated to daylight missions. This would allow the reformed 394th to blend its new aircraft and missions with his other daylight B-24 squadrons. Wright and Unruh carried the day, the complaints of XIII Bomber Commander Metheny and his staff notwithstanding.

But Wright needed replacement pilots for two of his eight remaining crews, not to mention additional aircraft and more crews to man them. He also needed dedicated maintenance, servicing and support personnel drawn from other Thirteenth Air Force units to create a self-sustaining organization. Unruh agreed to help and together they lobbied during that fateful September 1943 to pull together some semblance of a stand-alone unit. Unruh's first action was to select three pilots from his cadre of experienced B-17 flyers, who were by now flying B-24s, for transfer to the Wright Project. Those men were Lieutenants Vince Splane, Duward Sumner and Arthur Enger.

Some years later, Vince Splane recalled these events:

<u>Before Combat</u>
It was curious that the three of us selected by Unruh for transfer to the Wright Project had all left
Fort Worth together on 14 May 1943 for the Pacific. I had logged several hours on B-24s there plus
five hours in a trainer, had qualified as a co-pilot and by September on Guadalcanal found myself
flying as Unruh's second or right-seat pilot in B-24s. There were 25 of us on those orders to go to
the Pacific back in May 1943 and we went to San Francisco by train, loaded it down with beer and
booze and partied all the way. After all, we were going to war! A couple of weeks later we found
ourselves at La Tontouta airfield in New Caledonia, assigned to the Thirteenth Air Force. Enger and
I were assigned to the 5th Bomb Group to fly B-17s, he went to the 394th and I went to the 23rd
Squadron. Sumner drew the 307th with its new B-24s. We had to wait for ours.[1]

When we arrived in the South Pacific, we were incredibly naïve. We assumed that we had the best
of everything and the Japanese only poor-quality equipment, so we accepted the characterization
that our enemy was "building everything from scrap metal." We would soon learn that this was not
the case. My co-pilot at the time was Robert Little and he had many classmates flying P-40s who
had been in combat over Guadalcanal. They set us straight about the Zero fighter and explained
how they flew those P-40s to survive the Zero's superior performance. By the time we reached
"Cactus," we were no longer so confident nor so eager to meet the Japanese in combat.

<u>Up to "Cactus"</u>
The 5th Bomb Group was then based at Bomber Strip Number two on "Buttons" (Espiritu Santo
Island in the New Hebrides) and flying reconnaissance missions to the north and west to patrol pie-
shaped sectors approaching "Cactus" or Guadalcanal. The routine of the 5th was to rotate two of its
four squadrons up to "the Canal" for six weeks of combat and then return what remained of those
two squadrons to Espiritu for rest, replenishment and replacements. The 23rd went up for its time
in the barrel on 15 July and I had "Kahili" on my mind. While Rabaul was obviously the big show,
it seemed that Kahili Airdrome, on southern Bougainville, was the Group's main target.[2]

<u>Combat Missions</u>
I flew my first mission on 16 July, took off from Henderson (Carney was still under some construction)
at dusk and our formation hit Kahili. We used only our formation lights atop the B-17s and homed
in on a radio transmission that we knew broadcast from a site at the base of a mountain near the
airdrome. That night they were playing Tommy Dorsey and would frequently intersperse the songs
with a station identifier two-character code. On that night it was "VD," my initials, calling us in on
my first mission. Hard to forget. We were at 19,000 feet and, with my oxygen on, my feet were
dancing with anticipation and fear.

At the target, we went inland to the radio signal, turned around to start the bomb run and came
back out over the island to cross the airfield. The searchlights caught us as we approached and held
us for what seemed like five minutes, with lots of anti-aircraft fire falling short well below us. We
cleared the target and my tail gunner called on the intercom to report that one aircraft was being
attacked, was on fire and was headed down. This B-17 was piloted by Rex Engles and his co-pilot
was one of my best friends, Lieutenant David Jones. This was David's first combat mission. He
and I had trained on bombers and roomed together at Fort Worth and we had spent a lot of time
together. I even went with him to visit his mother in Dallas. The plane was shot down by a Japanese
fighter aircraft that had, we suspected, homed in from below on the engine exhaust flames that we
emitted on the underside of these B-17s. Unlike the B-24s that I would fly with Wright Project,
those B-17s had no flame dampeners on their superchargers.

The next night we went right back to Kahili, with no losses this time. These first missions told a man if he could take it and after that second Kahili mission one of my friends, maybe David's closest friend, simply quit, with an, "I cannot do this again" statement. He was a very good pilot, and to our surprise, he did not end up being court-martialed. He became a co-pilot on the B-17 of Thirteenth Air Force Commanding General Nathan Twining and served out his tour in the Pacific. We then realized that we needed every pilot we could find and keep.

During July I flew nine more B-17 combat missions, all except two were night missions to Kahili, with no other losses that I can recall. The first outlier mission was an attack on a convoy that we bombed from 8,000 feet and all missed every ship by a mile. On the 31st we were part of a big show to hit Munda at the time of the invasion there, and we were up there from dawn with a hundred airplanes in the air—Navy SBDs and TBFs, B-17s and B-25s, all supporting that pre-landing bombardment. As we bombed, we watched seven U.S. Navy destroyers pounding the beachhead. And it was an impressive sight, to see the United States on the offensive.

This same pace continued into early August where we were still striking Kahili in night missions. At mid-month I went on leave to New Zealand, flew a B-17 down and back, stayed at a beautiful rest place run by the Red Cross that overlooked Auckland Bay. My roommate was a XIII Fighter Command fighter pilot named Bob Westbrook. When I returned to Espiritu our entire bomb group was converting to B-24s, with the 31st and 72nd Squadrons flush with new airplanes. The 23rd was still pending, waiting on additional B-24s to come in. When we went back into combat at "Cactus," the aircraft transition was still not complete and our squadron flew back to the 'Canal with some B-17s. I may well have flown the last B-17 mission in the South Pacific, on September 8th. As I recall, they took that plane away for a flight to somewhere in the rear area the next day and I think that, when she flew away, it was the only combat B-17 left on the 'Canal.[3]

<u>Transition to the B-24</u>
I first flew the B-17 on 9 June 1943 at Espiritu and it was absolute heaven, with great visibility from the cockpit. In the air, she was a stable aircraft that did not require constant attention and trimming—with that big vertical stabilizer working to reduce rudder control to the point that a pilot could just prop his feet up on top of the rudder bar and, "steer her like an auto." Its broad chord wing allowed us to fly on one engine if we had to and, although a B-17E could not carry as much a bomb load as the B-24 and was about 10 miles-per-hour slower, depending on the configuration, that airplane was a pilot's dream.

The B-24 was an entirely different breed of cat. The B-17 had its disadvantages when compared to the B-24 and while many were minor, some were the kind that could get a crew killed. On the brakes side, the B-17E we flew had only one expander tube that operated hydraulically for each wheel where the B-24 had two per wheel. We watched the B-24s of the 307th as they taxied for takeoff and moved at recovery like bats out of hell while we B-17 pilots had to nurse our aircraft along with care—too fast or too much braking caused the expander tubes to rupture and spray hot hydra[ulic] fluid over the red-hot brake bands. Fire on a fueled and bomb-laden B-17 taxing down a runway was a recipe for a disaster.

The B-17's Wright Cyclone engines were noticeably louder than the Pratt and Whitney's of the B-24 and both types were dependable. The B-17 could fly on one engine unless there was a lot of battle damage and the latter could fly on just two, and then only if you dumped everything expendable from the aircraft. With the B-24, "one engine was no way" and with only one left, you needed to find a place to put your aircraft down. Visibility from the B-24 cockpit was more restricted and the plane required near-constant hands-on management, with more attention to the instruments, eyes on the needle and ball, artificial horizon and other gauges. When I took over Foster's crew with the project, after my first flight with that crew, our flight engineer, Sam Pona, pulled me aside as we climbed out of the aircraft and said, "Thank God we have a big strong guy to haul this damn airplane around. Because that is what she needs—hauling."

<u>With Unruh and the B-24s</u>
On Guadalcanal and now transitioned to B-24s, I was assigned to 5th Bomb Group Headquarters and flew often with Colonel Unruh as his co-pilot, more often than not on daylight missions. The colonel was creative to the point that he devised a bullet-proof (good for the Zero's 7.7-mm rounds anyway) Plexiglas-like screen that he dragged on the plane and positioned on top of the control pedestal. Behind that, as the mission developed, he would watch the Zeros make their head-on firing passes at us, as was their norm. I had no such panel and just sat there as the Zeros came at us, calling off the bogeys on the intercom to our gunners, watching the fighters roll in and come at us frontally with their wing guns twinkling fire and tracers. We were then hitting Kahili and Buka almost daily, with fighter escort protection to Kahili but not to Buka, so Buka and Kahili each had its own dangers. But my fate seemed to be tied to Kahili, both with Unruh and later with the Wright Project folks.

From mid-to-late September I flew six B-24 missions, mostly to Buka, and we were able to pick up a fighter escort on the way back, often P-40s still trying their best to protect us. On one mission that I vividly recall we were jumped by about thirty Zeros after bomb release over Buka. They stuck with us for a good period intermittently making firing passes, eventually peeling away to head to Kahili. On that day we were treated to an aerobatic performance of sorts—the Zeros would pace us at our level at three or nine o'clock, perform elaborate loops and rolls, seemingly working themselves up for their attacks. They would then collect in a line-abreast formation at one o'clock, pitch up and over into level flight and roll in individually for a stream of head-on passes. The attacks pressed to within 100 and often to 50 yards of our plane with closing speeds at 400 miles an hour or so. It seemed impossible that they could miss, but they mostly did.

One pilot I still see clearly 30-plus years later. He came at us head-on and broke down at our nose and dove away so close that I could see his face, with a red bandana he had wrapped around his forehead. He did a split-S right under our nose. Incredible. These were real airmen, but any respect for those abilities did not stop us from trying our best to shoot them out of the sky. It seemed important to them that they could demonstrate their airmanship as they took on the B-17s and B-24s. Our planes took the punishment and dished it back at them in spades.

<u>Introduction to the Wright Project</u>
The Wright crews had arrived in late August and I first met a few of these guys at the craps table in the officers' club. They looked and talked like new guys, wore issue Oxford shoes, regulation caps and so forth while we were standing around the table in our standard G.I. brogans, cut-off khaki shorts, T-shirts and baseball caps with rank pinned on. We had no idea what they were doing, only knew that it was "secret and special" and we did not ask. One Wright crew we met that night would all be dead within a few days and another a few weeks later, so it is difficult to recall who was standing there with us that first evening.

A few weeks later, I was sitting next to Colonel Unruh over breakfast as we prepared for another daylight mission. He turned to me and said, "Splane, I have been looking for you all morning and here you are sitting next to me. I am sending you to Stud Wright. He needs a new command pilot!" It was that simple. Zinn, who had just been promoted to captain and assigned to take over the 394th Squadron, and Wright's designated successor, Major Leo Foster, checked me out and I was cleared as an SB-24 command pilot. I was transferred over on the 29th and flew on 3 October in the left seat with Zinn's crew. He flew in the right seat to confirm my abilities I guess, and he seemed satisfied when we landed eight hours later.

Colonel Unruh also pulled Sumner from the 307th Bomb Group and he took over the Tillinghast crew and their plane, the *Lady Margaret*. His co-pilot was Beck, a solid flyer, and Beck later checked out as a first pilot. He flew me from the Admiralties to Port Moresby when I rotated home at my end of tour. Conrad was checked out at the same time and took Zinn's original crew and airplane, with my close friend Art Enger who now became Conrad's co-pilot. Rounding out those changes, Foster took over Lehti's crew and *Bums Away*, at least until the unit could be fleshed out with more pilots, crew and planes.

Devil's Delight and Her Crew

At this time the pilots and crew pretty much stuck with the planes to which they were assigned and I was eager to claim ownership of *Devil's Delight*. On the first five missions in early October, in a "making sure we knew what we doing" approach at confidence building, Conrad and I flew together with our respective crews, swapping out left and right seats. I was happy with my crew (inherited from Foster), my co-pilot John Thompson and our airplane. But Thompson was an issue—a good pilot but very frustrated as he did not want to be in bombers, and he was not happy with his co-pilot role in the B-24. He had graduated from single-engine advanced training, thought he was headed for a fighter assignment and he was lost in the cockpit of our B-24. He was quite short—about five foot six—and flew with a pillow at his back so he could reach the rudder pedals. He obsessed with flying fighters and sometimes tried to mimic fighter maneuvering with our *Devil's Delight*. This managed to scare the living hell out of the crew and me, and he had to be restrained from doing so.

As I mentioned, as a command pilot replacement, I drew the crew of Leo Foster and this meant that my, or rather "our" aircraft, was Wright Project veteran B-24D serial number 42-40832, or just plain "832" as she was carried on the mission reports. The crew was great: my aforementioned co-pilot Thompson; my navigator Cecil Cothran; bombardier Vince Zdanzukas; Tech Sergeants Sam Pona, Bernie Nachbe, Al Smith, Leon Armstrong; and Staff Sergeants Howard Estabrooks and John Dohan. When I got her, *Devil's Delight* was worn down a bit but still solid mechanically and dependable. We seldom aborted a mission due to equipment failure. As a crew, we flew her almost exclusively and we always had first claim on her when we were designated to fly a mission, normally every third night.

The airplane was special, to me and to our crew, to the point that we sort of got superstitious about it. It was almost a love affair because *Devil's Delight* took us to so many places and always brought us home. We were in her the night we hit Palau and she was again our "security blanket." The airplane was probably the best of the original 10 B-24Ds and had great flight characteristics, particularly when compared to the J-models when they came into the squadron. That nose turret made the J-models at least 10 miles per hour slower and we said the Ds were like "spirited thoroughbreds compared to a J plow horse," which was of course an exaggeration, but that's how some pilots thought. We were very sorry when we heard that *Devil's Delight* was lost.

Flying From Carney Field

When I was in B-17s and after converting to B-24s and then with the Wright SB-24s, I flew from Carney and it was a real challenge. The Marsden steel mating was a mixed blessing. I thought it presented problems on take-off in that it took longer to get up to flying (rotation) speed and this was no good in a full-load B-24 trying to get into the air, even in good weather, let alone in a rainstorm. The deafening metal rattle was one thing but the mud, sloshing up through the holes in the matting, bathed the plane in cruddy water and oily slime. One of the original Wright Project pilots who asked to be transferred to daylight bombing was unnerved one night when the matting and the rain made his take-off problematic. He went long on a take-off run, clipped a palm tree at the end of the runway and came home after an eight-hour mission with a big chunk of that palm sticking out of his engine nacelle. He asked for a reassignment to a daylight unit the next day.

I learned on Carney to use every inch of runway on takeoff. I would set the parking brake, put down 20 degrees of flap, run the throttles to the full forward position, let *Devil's Delight* just sit there until she was shaking all over, release the brakes and let her run to get that nose wheel off the ground as soon as possible. I would get her up to the flying speed quickly, then pull her off the metal at 120 mph and stagger out, get the gear up, keep her at 135 climbing out, reduce the power setting to 35 inches at 2,300 rpm, milk up the flaps, close the cowling flaps, all while flying on instruments only from the second of lift-off. We did this into heavy weather time after time, but it was always a very close thing and any mistake would crash you on take-off, including the loss of an engine.

On landing, the steel mat could mess you up. A man who came over with me was the co-pilot on a 31st Squadron (5th Bomb Group) B-24 that blew a tire on landing and veered right across the slimy metal surface, hitting a pile of stacked steel matting, knocking off the number three prop. That prop came into the side of the cockpit and sheared off both of Lieutenant Ken Haines's legs just above the knees. He bled to death in that airplane before the medics could get him out. The mission had apparently been a rough one but the airplane had come home without a scratch, until it landed, blew a tire, hit that matting and killed Haines.

Battle of Empress Augusta Bay
We all thought that our SCR-717-B radar set was a great piece of equipment. On the night of 1/2 November, our crew was second into the air behind Sumner and he found a fast-moving Japanese task force just as it cleared St. George's Channel coming from Rabaul. We responded to the Sumner position report and as we, in *Devil's Delight*, flew to the scene of the action, Sumner radioed that he was having a problem with his LAB equipment. His bombardier, Bob Tressel, had dropped his bombs short on several runs on a maneuvering warship, and Sumner had no hits. This Japanese task force was headed to Empress Augusta Bay where our Marines had landed the previous morning, steaming hard to tear up the beach and destroy the transports.

My radarman, Al Smith, detected the targets from 75 miles away, and because he had his scope set on its 100-mile range, he initially saw only one big blob. At 25 miles that blob became 10 individual blips when "Smitty" gradually ranged the radar down as we closed on the target. We picked the largest ship at 10 miles range to set up our bomb run and went back out a ways, descended to attack level and made the approach. We had already radioed in a position, heading and speed report on the Japanese ships and been cleared to attack by COMAIRSOLS We set up a bow-to-stern quartering run from 15 miles out, approaching from an east-southeast direction.

My bombardier, Vince Zdanzukas, was making corrections to his bombsight. Smitty was calling off positions from his radar every 30 seconds or so, as "Zuke" worked from his scope to set up the LAB attack. The radar "spinner" located in the ball turret position made one revolution every three seconds in its normal search mode but, once we locked onto a target, Smitty would switch it to sector scan, meaning it would only oscillate 30 degrees on each side of the aircraft's dead center. This gave us a stronger radar image and repeated a clean screen reading every second. Like almost all our LAB runs, we were at 1,200 feet throughout.

For my part as the pilot, the PDI [pilot's directional indicator] on my instrument panel made sure I kept a constant altitude and airspeed, and within five miles of the target, any corrections were made with the rudders. At this point, the only voice that was heard was Smitty still calling off the range. The bombs were normally dropped by the system right after he made the one-quarter mile call. That night we knew we had a big, fast-moving and important warship target and we released all six 500-pound bombs at 30 to 40-foot intervals on the first run, with a one-tenth-second delay set on both nose and tail fuses. I counted, "one thousand … to four thousand" and then banked the aircraft hard over to the left to watch the impact. All six bombs exploded in sequence, each walking closer to the starboard side of the ship, and the last detonated directly alongside, so we called it a "very near miss." The amazing thing was that this warship did not fire one shot at us, even after we near-missed her.

We continued to circle this task force, radio in position reports and I elected to make another LAB-guided close-aboard run, flying right up the phosphorescent wake of this or another large warship. Again, not one shot fired at us. Amazing. We stuck with this task force until it was met by our own U.S. Navy surface ships and then all hell broke loose below us. Early in that fight a warship was set afire and burned bright. We were apparently looking at the Japanese Navy light cruiser *Sendai*, which was sunk that night. But we would not learn the identity of the ship we had earlier hit—the heavy cruiser and task force flagship *Haguro*—until many years later. We had been out eight hours by the time COMAIRSOLS called us home and we landed back at Carney knowing we had run a great mission.

Ranging Farther From Munda

In our hunt for target vessels, which had become scarce in our normal patrol areas by December, we installed belly tanks in the front bomb bay position to give us an extra hour or two in the air. One mission that I recall was staging through Munda on 19 December. As was the routine on Munda, we were briefed by a U.S. Marine Colonel named Pitcher on possible Japanese convoy activity and we launched close to midnight and went out well beyond Rabaul. Here we found a nice eight-ship convoy that seemed to have departed Rabaul to head to Truk. We radioed in to COMAIRSOLS, reported our contact and asked for an okay to attack. We received no response. Our IFF was working and did not trigger a response from the ships below. A reasonable conclusion was that they were Japanese.

Not prepared to continue waiting for a COMAIRSOLS response, and not wanting to go home without attacking this target, we set up at 10 miles and made a LAB run on the largest target indicated by the radar, dropping three and getting two amazing hits. I had banked the aircraft over sharply after bomb release, almost standing it on its left wingtip, and flames from the exploding bombs seemed to come right through the open bomb bay doors. The ship continued to explode and burn and we went out to circle at 20 miles distance and could even see clearly from the flames on the water at 25 miles or more.

On radar we watched several of the other ships converge on the dead-in-water target, probably taking off crew or soldiers or whatever. After an hour or so, not wanting to waste our three remaining bombs on this sinking target, we went after what our radar told us was the second-largest target in the group, but only near-missed her, claiming no damage.

The problems began when we landed back at Munda. The good Colonel Pitcher was waiting for us, not to just debrief us but, as his first priority, to chew my ass, and chew on me he did. He yelled that we did not have permission to attack the convoy and as we were, "almost across the line and into MacArthur's Southwest Pacific Command area," and that convoy could well have been one of his task forces! But then he smiled broadly, shook my hand, held it firm and said "great mission guys."

Working with the Marines

We knew that Rabaul probably had dedicated night fighters, or at least was now putting fighters into the air to intercept us in our night attacks there. A Marine pilot who came up with the idea to mate his U.S. Navy PV-1 Ventura with my aircraft in a hunter-killer combination convinced me to work with him. Our plan was that I would fly at and over Rabaul at 10,000 feet or so, and he would keep station on my six o'clock about a mile or so back and a thousand feet below us. We would use our radar to seek Japanese fighters and when we detected the same activity around our aircraft, or even coming after us, we would alert him and guide him with our radar to his target for an interception. He had radar that he could use in a closing phase but needed us for the search and, I suspect, to act as bait. We practiced this with a Navy fighter over Munda as our target and then made an SB-24 plus PV-1 run to Rabaul. We could not draw out any Japanese fighters that night so we threw in the towel, no more bait-the-hook missions over Rabaul for Lieutenant Hershberger. But it seemed like a novel idea that just might work and, after all, we were at war.

<u>Almost Dead</u>
Sometimes it is not the fighters or the anti-aircraft or even blown-out engines on takeoff that kills you—it's your own crew. On a mission up the St. George's Channel in one of the other original Wright B-24Ds (our *Devil's Delight* was in for engine overhauls), we found a target, made a LAB run and missed and headed home. My co-pilot wanted left-seat time so we switched and I thought that I might catch a cat nap. I had trimmed the aircraft out and set it to autopilot and she was flying nicely. But even with the autopilot flying, minute adjustments had to be made from time to time. I knew that Thompson also had a habit of drifting off to catnap on the way back so I watched him from the right seat out of the corner of my eye. He would drop his chin and close his eyes but always seemed to catch himself at the five-second point and regain focus. I made the mistake of falling asleep but did not realize that our flight engineer, who normally was with us on the deck and could watch Thompson, was back on the rear deck transferring fuel from the bomb bay tanks, thus I had no backup eyes on Thompson.

The aircraft bumped and I glanced at Thompson. He had his chin buried deep into his chest, was sound asleep, but his hand was on that autopilot knob, making those adjustments as he snored. But at that point, Flight Engineer Pona yelled on the intercom that he had pump valve problems and fuel starvation. "NUMBER FOUR CUT OUT, NUMBER THREE CUTTING OUT!" With this loss of all power on the two starboard engines the two functioning engines overcame the autopilot and Thompson was still not fully awake and had not reacted. When I glanced at the instruments, I realized that we were almost on our back and we were down to 120 miles an hour and we had been cruising at 1,000 feet. I reached instinctively to feather number four prop to reduce drag on that right side, flicked off the autopilot, hit the fuel booster switches, grabbed the control wheel and hit the top rudder. All this time I was yelling at Thompson, "Could you give me some damn help!"

We got the ship back level and managed to get the nose down to pick up airspeed, got number four going and then number three and came into level flight somewhere between 30 and 50 feet off the surface of the water. We had just survived a near-death crash into the sea. Such a situation would typically see a B-24 stall out at this airspeed with the plane in this position—flaps up, 110 mile an hour and almost on our back. But this mission from hell was just starting. As we flew at 50 feet or so and I was checking all instruments my radarman Smitty yells, "TWO SHIPS DEAD AHEAD! LOOKS LIKE DESTROYERS! PULL UP, PULL UP!" I yelled back, "The hell with them, I have to get this plane flying again," as we passed just over the top of a destroyer's mast. Given the location, we assumed they were ours, and if they were, some U.S. destroyer got the closest buzzing that any B-24 delivered in the Pacific.

But more was to come. This particular aircraft was the known "gas hog" of the Wright Project aircraft. No matter how much we reduced power settings and leaned her engines out, she consumed so much that every mission with her was a close run. After clearing the ships, we did a quick calculation and realized we could not make it back to Munda. We had an emergency landing field on Treasury Island off the south coast of Bougainville so we called them and said we were headed in. They suspected Japanese aircraft so they had us do a turning exercise so they could watch us on radar, then check all the IFF signals, clear us as "friendly" and allow us to land. Finally, convinced that we were who we said we were, they turned on the landing lights. But we weren't down yet.

I climbed back to 1,000 feet, made my crosswind leg and had just turned on the downwind leg when my navigator, Alabama-born and bred Cecil Cothran, came on the intercom. Drawling, Cecil said, "Vince…there….is…a…two…thousand…foot …mountain…right…out…there." Now everyone on the crew was shaking as they thought that I was flying us into a mountain. But I turned on to the base leg hoping we had avoided it. It was raining very hard and when I turned on our landing lights my co-pilot went crazy and yanked the control column back. He was screaming, "PULL UP, PULL UP, WE'RE ON THE WATER!" I reached across and gave him a karate chop, pounded on him, yelled some very bad things at him and his hands dropped off the control column. He had been blinded by the combination of the pounding rain hitting the front glass and our landing lights coming on and he thought we were crashing into the sea.

I got it down and we taxied to a hard stand off to the side of the runway. The rain was still beating down on us as we sat in that airplane. Pona crawled up on top of the wing, opened the access panel to the wing tank and shined the flashlight. He could see the metal bottom. We had just made it. Our bombardier, "Zuke" Zdanzukas, came on the intercom, wanting to confirm the time of mission termination that he would enter into his bombing device log. He then asked, with total seriousness, "And just how much time should I log for Jesus Christ on this mission? Because you know, Vince, He was with us all the way!"

CHAPTER 11

Munda to Momote

April–June 1944

A mix of missions, relocations and respite

April 1944 was dominated by 868th missions to Truk, as noted in the chapter devoted to that target, when both the single-aircraft SB-24 midnight runs were made to harass the airfields and port facilities, and daylight missions that found one or more Snoopers serving in pathfinder or guide roles for larger formations of dispatched by the XIII Bomber Command. And while this pattern of visits to Truk would continue into May and June, additional targets did begin to receive the squadron's attention. Other targets in the Carolines that could have presented a problem to the Central Pacific drive were attended to, such as Satawan Island, some 150 miles southeast of Truk proper, which held a Japanese garrison and an airfield. On 17 April, Lieutenant Alsop in aircraft 486 led a formation of 307th Bomb Group Liberators on a daylight strike that cratered the runway and kept Japanese heads down.

Second to "Bastion Truk" as emerging priority targets were Palau and Woleai, both recently active Japanese bases with developed airfield facilities and long-established garrisons to defend them from seaborne attack. The Palau group of the Caroline Islands, part of the so-called "Spanish East Indies" since the 1800s, had been acquired by the Japanese from Germany during World War I. With its capital on the larger island of Koror, the island chain had been part of the Japanese Empire, based on a League of Nations mandate, for 30 years by the time the 868th was tasked with suppressing it. In one of the more controversial planning decisions of the Central Pacific drive, the Allies would invade the southern-most islands of Peleliu and Angaur in mid-September 1944, with the fighting on the former occasioning heavy U.S. Marine casualties in its taking. The U.S. First Marine Division, later joined by the elements of the U.S. Army's 81st Division, would experience heavy casualties as the 10,000 Japanese defenders fought to the death against the 28,000 Americans committed to secure the island. The six-mile by two-mile island delivered a 40 percent casualty rate of dead and wounded Americans and provided yet another foretaste of what was to come in the months ahead.

Woolly Woleai

Woleai Atoll in the eastern Caroline Island group had the island of Woleai at the center of another Allied bull's eye. This was mainly because it stood between the gathering momentum of the Central Pacific offensive and that thrust's main target for conquest, the Marianas. Strategic planners had settled on the occupation and planned airbase building on the Marianas for the basing of a massive fleet of B-29 bombers that would be soon available. The Superfortress fleet, based on Tinian and Saipan, would be able to strike at the Japanese homeland to devastate its factories and cities. As recently as 1943, recognizing that their Empire was collapsing around them and the Marianas were likely to be at the center of U.S. strategic planning, the Japanese had rushed to fortify Woleai in an attempt to block the Allied approach. Eleventh-hour improvements included an airbase, a seaplane facility and additional Army and Navy troops prepared to resist any invasion. In any event, that invasion did not come to Woleai, but the decision to bypass it guaranteed that waves of carrier and land-based air attacks would call on it to keep it neutralized.

The Thirteenth Air Force, including the 868th, were in range of that island by late April, based on the squadron's relocation to its new base at Momote, so Woleai gained importance. By mid-April, Woleai was an established 868th target, this after fast carrier attacks by Task Force 58 which began on April Fool's Day 1944. Two days after relocating to Momote, on 25 April, Art DeLand and crew launched on their first dedicated daylight mission to strike at Woleai, a planned nine-hour run to and from that target. An hour out, *Ready, Willing and Able*'s number three engine burned itself out and they aborted the mission, jettisoned their bomb load and returned safely to base. Three days later, old 396 was back in action, ready and able. On Mission 17 for this crew, they hit Woleai for the first of nine visits to that target over the May to July period.

On the 18th, the Thirteenth Air Force daylight B-24s began their own sustained effort against Woleai, with the bombers returning no fewer than a dozen times by the end of that month, a maximum effort that placed a total of 250 B-24s over the target. Snooper aircrews led by pilots Carlson, Colt, Splane and others frequently led the daylight B-24s, typically on missions employing 15 to 24 aircraft, to the target. Once the daylight lead aircraft locked on to the target optically, the SB-24 would relocate within the formation to bomb with the group at higher altitudes. These late April missions were opposed by the Japanese fighters still active on Woleai, with Dick Colt's mission report of 24 April noting that the island's "Tonys and Zekes met us at the target and stayed with our formation, attacking for a good 35 minutes." On that mission, XIII Bomber Command suffered no losses, apart from many shot-up aircraft, but this was a lucky day.

During May, even as the 868th shifted its attention to other higher priority targets, the island of Biak for one, the squadron was still dispatched to patrol the waters around Woleai at night to intercept any shipping attempting to run supplies into the island. It was also assumed that the Japanese would attempt to evacuate valuable flight and aircraft maintenance personnel for return to the Home Islands. On 16 May, the aircraft of Lieutenants Louis Beck and Fred Bryan conducted such a LAB search and, after a two-hour hunt around the island that found no vessels, lined up their radars and walked the length of the Woleai airstrip with their six 500-pound bombs. That month, the squadron placed 10 aircraft over Woleai on various escort and individual missions and was most fortunate to only collect a few flak holes in its aircraft, with no aircraft lost on this target and no casualties registered.

Punching Palau

The islands in the northern end of the Palau island chain, as noted above, would be bypassed, in part because the Central Pacific command judged that they did not need to occupy them if these more dangerous locations could be pounded down and neutralized. But because critical islands to the immediate south in this same island chain, namely Peleliu and Angaur, had been recently conquered and occupied by the Allies, there was no choice but to assign the larger islands in the same group to the north as priority targets.

Among other bomb groups, the 868th drew Palau as a nighttime target for its sea-search and harassment strikes. On 24 April, the SB-24s of Lieutenants Splane and Rauch notched up another first for the 868th when they and their crews struck Koror in the Palau Islands. This two-aircraft mission involved a 1,100-mile run to the target and back, consuming 14 hours in the air for the round-trip strike.

But Palau's bypassed islands would represent another "tough nut," as one of the crews who flew to it solemnly recalled, mainly due to its hardened character and heavy concentration of increasingly accurate anti-aircraft guns. On 5 May, Lieutenant Rauch and crew were assigned to return to Palau Island and, after completing a LAB search for shipping around the island and finding no targets, attacked the airfield from 2,000 feet. The gunners were waiting and shot out Rauch's number two engine, disabled his electrical system and knocked out the SCR-717-B, denying the airplane the ability to navigate home by radar. The aircraft then encountered severe tropical storms and was driven off course to the southeast.

Fuel exhaustion led to a water landing with 468 ditching in waters off Wewak, New Guinea. The survivors, including pilot Rauch, were picked up by a U.S. Navy Coronado seaplane patrol bomber. The big four-engine Coronado was nearby, heard the Rauch distress call as 468 headed toward the water and set down near the crash site to pull the survivors aboard. Three of the Rauch crew were declared missing in action, lost with the aircraft when it broke apart and sank soon after the landing.

The organization tightens

As the April mission tempo increased with the arrival of new crews and aircraft, Major Leo Foster remained in command of the 868th, with Major Joe Bricker as his second in command and Major Francis Carlson serving as the squadron Operations Officer. The three designated Flight Commanders were Captain Frank Reynolds (A Flight), Captain Kenneth Brown (B) and First Lieutenant Vince Splane (C). Other key members of the executive team included Captain Edward Ackley as the squadron Intelligence Officer and Captain Ernest Barriere as the squadron "Radio-Special" Officer. Barriere was in fact the squadron radar officer but, in accordance with squadron, 5th Bomb Group and XIII Bomber Command orders, mission reports and other documents were not allowed to use the term "radar" and instead were required to refer to all classified LAB systems as the "special equipment."[1]

In the case of the Boston-bred, Harvard-trained and highly refined Captain Ackley, he was the master of the pre-mission intelligence overview and the post-mission debriefing sessions to which he and his team subjected the crews upon their return. Most anticipated those Ackley after-action sessions by demanding a double shot of the standard-issue "Old Overholt" whiskey dispensed by the squadron flight surgeon, Captain Krug. Ackley was also the proud owner of the squadron mascot, "Snooper," a similarly refined terrier he had picked up in New Zealand while on leave there.[2]

Interestingly, although most of the 868th squadron personnel did not know it at the time, the unit's new Technical Support Officer, Second Lieutenant William R. Kenney, was the son of Fifth Air Force Commander Major General George Kenney, MacArthur's dynamic air commander extraordinaire. Bill Kenney was low-key, did his job and was well-regarded by the officers and men of the unit during his tour of duty there.

Prior to the loss of the Robbins and Arthur crews, the squadron could count 36 rated pilots and co-pilots on its roster and a full team of navigators, bombardiers, radar operators, flight engineers and gunners. Its ground support group was well-staffed for the first time, as were its maintenance crews, so critical to the operation of the aircraft that were lifting into the sky each night, and now often into the daylight. Finally, the mid-March 868th squadron roster included 10 "attached combat personnel" who were assigned to fly with the 868th as added crewmen, one or two per aircraft, on the LAB missions. The origins and squadron service of these "walk-on" Snoopers and their relationship with the 868th are dealt with below.[3]

Wracked by dysentery

As if Truk failed to deliver enough punishment to the 868th in April and May 1944, the primitive living conditions on Munda and at Momote ravaged the squadron from early April with a wave of dysentery. The outbreak stayed with the squadron as it moved to Momote later in the month, taking down half the 200-odd men assigned to the squadron, including pilots and crews as well as mechanics and support staff. The same outbreak saw several of the 5th Bomb Group squadrons similarly decimated as well as nearby U.S. Navy Seabee units. This emergency forced the group's medical staff to order the closing of all mess facilities and the officers and men were instructed to consume only K-rations. Daily doses of sulfadiazene and quinidine sulfate were the order of the day and eventually brought the infections under control.

While this camp-wide assault was overcome by mid-May at Momote, the damage to the bodies and mental state of the men had been significant. Sickness and weight loss would be the constant companion of all men who fought in the South Pacific and, while great measures were taken to prevent such outbreaks, they were an underlying threat. With many men, weight loss was extreme and the consequent loss of physical energy damaged the integrity of the squadron. The 868th would fall victim to intestinal attack again, and in some cases, it would inflict more damage than the Japanese that the squadron would fly against on a given day.

Rest and recreation leave

The miseries inflicted by the dysentery outbreak notwithstanding, the officers and men of the 868th were now availing themselves of rest and recreation (R&R) leave in Sydney. While leave in New Zealand had been great and its citizens welcoming hosts, the golden destination for all in the 868th, indeed for all in the Thirteenth Air Force, was Australia, and that meant one place—swinging Sydney. And although men headed for leave there had previously been compelled to shuttle to Australia via rear area hops that took them back through Guadalcanal and New Caledonia, a more pleasant route from their forward bases was now available via a C-87 flying directly to the land of nightlife, good food, welcoming bars and women. The C-87 was the transport version of the B-24D, in some cases having exited the factory configured as such. In other instances, the leave carrier was a worked-over product of squadron action, a war-weary B-24 saved from the "boneyard" and rehabilitated to perform cargo and passenger services.

A typical R&R flight from Munda or Momote to Sydney and return saw 10 to 20 men, usually one or two crews who had acquired the number of combat missions required for such leave, heading for Sydney on a single set of orders. They were allowed nine glorious days on the ground wherever those orders took them and could be away for as long as 15 days, depending on the availability of return flights, before willingly subjecting themselves to any late-return reprisals. A set of such "Temporary Duty" orders in early April sent eight Snooper officers and men to beautiful Sydney and authorized officers $2.50 per day in "per diem expenses," with the enlisted men, always getting the short end of the stick, garnering a measly $2.25 per diem allowance. The men on leave, most of whom ran together there as a crew, spent wildly and lived every day as if it was their last, but most remembered to use whatever funds they had left to cart home to their squadron as much booze as they could carry in their B-4 bags.[4]

But this R&R routine, however welcome and refreshing to the men of the squadron, would later have a downside as well. The 868th was not satisfied with the air service provided by XIII Bomber Command as C-87s were scarce and often committed to transporting wounded soldiers and airmen to the rear areas and hauling critical cargo on the return flights to the frontline airfield. Timing was unpredictable and many a scheduled squadron R&R activity would see flights canceled with orders revoked and the Sydney visit postponed indefinitely. The only solution was for the squadron to acquire and operate, with its own crews and for its own priority return-flight cargo-hauling purposes (plenty of booze and lots of good food), its very own aircraft. That opportunity would soon present itself.

From Munda to Momote

In late April, the 868th acquired a new home and address, Army Post Office (APO) 324, when it relocated from Munda in New Georgia to Momote Airfield on Los Negros in the Admiralty Islands. The move, during a period when the squadron was formally attached to the "Thirteenth Air Task Force," was timely in that it allowed the squadron SB-24s to range more deeply into the Central Pacific as the Allies moved westward. The move was accomplished late in the month, with most of the aircraft relocating to their new home on the 23rd. The flight from Munda to Momote was a six-hour-plus flight for the crews, some 700 miles to the northwest. At their new location, the men of the squadron assumed that, after the scant ship-hunting offered by Truk and other Munda-based strikes, the new territory would provide Japanese shipping and new land strike opportunities. There were, however, some complications in the Munda–Momote move.[5]

A brief visit to Nadzab

When the 868th was ordered to relocate to Momote on Los Negros Island in the Admiralties there was a particular sense of urgency. Two lines of the grand offensive in the Pacific were gathering momentum and twin invasions portended—one in the Central Pacific and one in the Southwestern Pacific Command area. Each arm of the two strategic pincers was moving inexorably toward the Home Islands of Japan. XIII Bomber Command had a role to play in each and therefore placed a priority in getting its LAB squadron to Momote to operate from there as quickly as possible. As a result, when the 868th began its move to Momote on 17 April it was realized that the engineers working there had not cleared sufficient space to accommodate the entire unit, and only 11 combat crews and their aircraft could be directly relocated.

However, the entire squadron was needed at the front line and, for this reason, the balance of seven aircraft and crews were sent on temporary assignment to Nadzab

Airbase on the New Guinea mainland. Here operated the Fifth Air Force and its most far forward B-24 units, including the 63rd Bombardment Squadron. The seven-plane 868th contingent would operate from Nadzab for two weeks and rejoin the others at Momote on 4 May. At that point, with combat and operational losses having dented the squadron, the 868th could report 13 crews and as many aircraft as "combat ready."

The advent of May, with the complete squadron now bedded down and operating from Momote, saw a change in emphasis with strikes directed at four targets. Although the airfield and support facilities on the various islands of Truk Atoll were still on the mission list, the airfield and beach fortifications on Biak Island would receive heavy attention, Woleai would come to the fore as a target and Manokwari airdrome, located on the northeastern tip of New Guinea, would be attended to as part of the Biak effort. Palau in the Central Pacific would also remain a target, missions there demonstrating the ability of the 868th SB-24s to reach out in multiple directions from Momote, supporting two theaters of combat at the same time. But each of these old and new targets would exact its toll on a squadron operating at maximum efficiency.

Busting Biak

In the case of Biak, General MacArthur's strategy remained fixated on his "I will return to" and recapture the Philippines commitment and obsession. Biak, located off the northwestern tip of New Guinea, was the next location to be taken on that path of personal redemption. Not coincidently, it was also on the route to the north towards Tokyo. Biak was an important base for the Japanese and had recently been reinforced by Imperial Army troops and aircraft. The Japanese correctly perceived that, by jumping to Biak, the Southwest Pacific Command planned to bypass the western portion of New Guinea proper and, in doing so, isolate the important Japanese Army garrisons still lodged along that coast.

The Japanese Navy agreed that it was critical to hold Biak and was prepared to dispatch a major surface fleet to engage the U.S.-led amphibious force and its covering surface fleet positioned at Biak. But the parallel advance by U.S. Central Pacific forces to invade the Marianas and capture Saipan and Tinian, and then to recapture Guam, seized the Japanese high command's attention. Instead of a major counterattack at Biak, Japan was forced to contest the U.S. invasion of the Marianas. These islands in the Northern Marianas, particularly Saipan, were regarded as sovereign territory of the empire and their potential loss to the Allies was regarded as both a tactical defeat as well as the portent of a national humiliation that threatened the stability of the government in Tokyo. Although these events did compel Japan to turn away from a forceful contest over Biak, its high command was still determined to do everything possible to deny its conquest by the Allies. In the run-up to the Allied invasion itself, over the May–June 1944 period, the Thirteenth Air Force was called upon to support General Kenney's Fifth Air Force in reducing the targets on and around that island; XIII Bomber Command answered that directive by committing all of its B-24 units to that fight.

On 4 May, an 868th Squadron SB-24 aircraft guided a XIII Bomber Command strike, led by its 394th Squadron against Mokmer Airdrome on Biak Island. This attack was delivered as MacArthur's amphibious convoys assembled to approach the island and as Fifth Air Force bombers and fighters attempted to secure dominance over the planned invasion beaches. The daylight bomber mission was opposed by 10 Japanese fighters over the target and one of the daylight B-24s was lost; the Snooper returned intact to Momote.

On 10 May, three SB-24s teamed up with four SB-24s of the 63rd Bombardment Squadron, "The SeaHawks," of the Fifth Air Force to strike at Biak. This was the first such combined action by the companion LAB squadrons of the two Air Forces, units that had been organized at and dispatched from Bid Dolan's radar bombing graduate school at Langley Field. Many of the pilots and crews of the 63rd had shared quarters and trained with the men of the Wright Project back in the May–August 1943 period at Langley. The 63rd had essentially been Dolan's "second wave" of well-schooled LAB crews when it was dispatched to join the Fifth Air Force in the Southwest Pacific Command a few months after seeing off the Wright Project's 10 crews in August.

On the 13th, Splane and the men of *Devil's Delight* drew Sorido Airfield on Biak for a bombing mission and laid fifteen 500-pound bombs across its runway and aircraft dispersal areas. On 20 May, the Wright Project veteran crew of Captain Frank Carlson struck Manokwari Airdrome and nearby Dore Bayon, New Guinea, installations which had been occupied since April 1942 by Japan and developed into a major staging area for operations to the west. During May, this same location would attract 17 more attacks by 868th aircraft, severely limiting its garrison's ability to interfere with the landing on nearby Biak.

Against Biak proper, the 868th scorecard for May would tally 34 individual missions, a typical one being a bombing of beach installations at Bosnek shortly before MacArthur's actual invasion on the 27th. On that mission, four squadron SB-24s teamed with eight near-identical LAB aircraft of the 63rd Squadron, all 12 flying from the Nadzab airbase complex. The squadron's end-of-month report also noted that only one LAB search turned up a shipping target during the entire month. That "rare find" had occurred on 22 May when Lieutenant Nicholas and crew found and attacked a three-ship convoy off Manokwari that appeared to be running supplies and infantry reinforcements to Biak. The convoy, dissuaded by the attacks and near-misses, turned away with whatever they carried denied to the Biak garrison.

This May 1944 strike tempo allowed the squadron to chalk-up a record 99 missions, including 67 radar-assisted and 32 visual bomb releases, by the end of that month. At that point, the squadron had a full complement of officers and men and was awaiting some additional aircraft. Only two had been lost during the month, that of Rauch and crew on the return from Palau and a second plane which had bellied in on take-off with no casualties and was thought to be salvageable.

Momote in June

The squadron history for May 1944 noted that the month had begun with three mission themes: anti-ship LAB-enabled sea-search missions that occurred normally at night; pathfinder missions leading fellow XIII Bomber Command B-24s on daylight missions; and nighttime heckling missions over Japanese bases. June would see some new targets but, for most of the 868th crews, it would be more of the same—Truk, Palau and Woleai—and a price for these assignments would be paid. In the earlier chapter devoted to Truk, the losses of four crews during June in missions involving Truk were noted: those of Dyer on 10–11 June, Wagner on 11–12 June and Booth and Haynes in the course of mid-June missions.

A more comprehensive view of the evolving situation in this period is provided by the publication *Air Campaigns of the Pacific War* developed in 1947 by the Military Analysis Division of the United States Strategic Bombing Survey. It records as follows:

> Southwest Pacific: Advance to Morotai. Rapid surface advances in the Southwest Pacific Area now became possible—because air domination had been won. Following the air–ground–amphibious pattern … the Southwest Pacific Forces, including the Fifth Air Force, advanced from Hollandia to Morotai in the Halmanheras by September 1944. In this operation, Biak, the Gelvink Bay area, and Noemfoor successively were neutralized and occupied. From Morotai, the range of land-based aircraft could now be extended to Mindanao (in the Philippines) and Borneo, and the waterways of the Netherlands East Indies.

Typical of that postwar publication's accounting, short or no shrift was given to the companion efforts of the Thirteenth Air Force, including its B-24 bomb groups. But no one was then paying any attention nor asking for any credit.[6]

June missions for the 868th, beyond those already noted above in the discussion of Truk (four squadron losses), were Palau (one loss), Woleai and Biak target groups, and included assorted atolls and islets. On the 1st, Lieutenant Hickson and crew struck Puluwat near Truk. The following day the crew of Lieutenant Bryan ranged to Mesegon Island, at the southern end of Truk Lagoon, where the Japanese were clearing land to build an airfield. Two days later, the Conrad crew hit Yawata Shima, one of the air defense islets protecting Truk Lagoon. That first week also saw the Conrad and Alsop crews return to Woleai while "Rocky" Rockwood, one of the still serving Wright Project crews, made the 868th's first attack on Yap Island in the eastern Carolines. Yap was an important base that would suffer carrier strikes and be bypassed on the march to Tokyo, but it was important that the Thirteenth Air Force could put one of its SB-24s over the island to hold it down.

And in June the Japanese served notice that they were not done with Biak and its environs. A surprise midnight attack on 6/7 June occurred when the squadron staged seven aircraft to Wakde. An 868th mission was flown to intercept Japanese shipping that was reported to be making a run to land reinforcements on Biak. The LAB search found no targets and shortly after the SB-24 strike group returned to Wakde, the

Japanese aircraft struck. The attack caught the seven Snoopers on the ground, as one man later said, "fat, dumb, refueled, being bombed up and thank GOD, empty of their crews." Squadron veteran *Long Distance* (410) was hit, temporarily written off as heavily damaged and fated for a trip to the local boneyard. The seven crews returned home in the six surviving aircraft, many of them holed by the Japanese bombs, to have them patched up for the next mission.[7] The squadron ended June with a solid tally of missions, some 40 strikes alone having been devoted to Truk, with almost as many to Woleai and other choice locations. At month's end, the 868th counted 18 crews and 13 aircraft as "mission ready" with more of both in the pipeline to arrive in July and August. While basing was still confused, and about to become more so, the overall attitude was upbeat despite the losses incurred over the past three months of combat.

Understudies—The 419th finds the 868th

In September 1943, the Thirteenth Air Force had welcomed to Guadalcanal its first AAF night fighter unit, the 419th Squadron. Its first element arrived with a combination of P-70 Nighthawks and P-38 Lightnings and operated there on a limited basis in cooperation with the Venturas of a U.S. Marine squadron, VMF(N)-531. The aircraft assigned to the 419th were far from optimal and the unit waited with growing impatience for the arrival of the AAF's first true night fighter aircraft, the Northrop P-61 Black Widow. Over the October–December period, this unit flew night intruder missions over many of the same targets being worked by the Snoopers of the 868th and took operational and combat losses as a consequence. Such losses included squadron aircraft shot down by over-eager U.S. anti-aircraft gunners and air combat with Zero fighters along the way.

The continued absence and the loss of some crews, including the squadron's commander, Captain John McCloskey on 22 November, when combined with the delayed arrival of the promised P-61s, understandably impacted squadron morale. One solution that worked well was for the unit's radar operators, for whom there were no stations in the P-38s that dominated the unit, was to fly with the 868th in both training and combat flights. The 868th welcomed these men into their ranks, with the first group of seven joining missions in January, serving as back-up or "relief" radar operators on the combat missions. In night harassment or "heckling" missions over Rabaul, the 419th operator worked the SCR-717-B scope and became the eleventh man in the normal SB-24D crew of 10 men. All attached operators flew 10 missions and were then replaced by a second group, seven joining in April to continue the program. As this program picked up momentum, the P-38 missions continued and the squadron maintained its combat edge in the pilot department.[8]

There were other advantages to the 419th beyond the valuable experience they were gaining on the "ride-alongs" in the SB-24s. The completion of 10 missions with the

868th qualified a radar operator to receive the Air Medal and, perhaps more importantly, to enjoy a 10-day R&R trip to New Zealand or Australia. On R&R leave, the 419th aircrews associated with their new combat-tested friends in the 868th and managed to return laden with "the good stuff" for their 419th compatriots and maintenance men, those supplies being mainly hard liquor and beer.

The 419th relocated to Munda soon after the 868th made that transition and continued to operate there. In one recent account of this squadron, *Night Hawks and Black Widows: 13th Air Force Night Fighters in the South and Southwest Pacific, 1943–1945*, author Terry M. Mays describes the arrival of the 419th and its association with the 868th on Guadalcanal and Munda.[9]

On a related note, it is pleasing to remark on the fine attention paid by the U.S. Navy personnel stationed on Green Island who supported the 419th when the unit staged there for night patrols. This support was similar to the treatment extended to the 868th crews that staged through there on their missions. A U.S. Navy Reserve Supply lieutenant, Richard M. Nixon, figured prominently in this welcoming role and was later remembered by one and all. Logistics officer "Nick" Nixon apparently operated "Nick's Hamburger Stand" to serve the best in grilled purloined beef patties with bottles of cold Australian beer to the visiting aircrews.[10]

The Far East Air Force

Mid-June brought another organizational change to the Thirteenth Air Force and, by extension, to the 868th. General MacArthur and his Fifth Air Force Chief, Lieutenant General George Kenney, had for many months advocated, to any and all who would listen at U.S. Army Air Force Headquarters in Washington, D.C., and within the Pacific Command, for the Thirteenth Air Force to be combined with Kenney's Fifth to create an amalgamated force.

At this point in the drive toward Japan, with the actions of the Central Pacific Command and the Southwest Pacific Command merging more completely, the need for a separate South Pacific Command, and its Thirteenth Air Force, evaporated. Recognizing this reality, as of 15 June 1944, the Thirteenth Air Force was subsumed by a new organization that the powers that be directed—the Far East Air Force of the Southwest Pacific Area (FEAF/SWPA).

Kenney was put in charge of the FEAF and the Thirteenth and Fifth Air Forces became sister organizations, each left with their original bomb groups and squadrons intact. More often than not, aircraft from the squadrons of the bomb groups subordinate to the two Air Forces became intermixed and mutually supporting on shared targets and missions. As a consequence, on this same date, the 13th Air Task Force was disestablished and all units were transferred back to the authority of the Thirteenth Air Force and, with that transfer, to the control of the newly created FEAF. The 868th's APO address was also changed from 324 to APO 719. For many in the squadron, these changes only meant confusion and the possible disruption for mail coming from home. Many simply did not care. There was a war going on and the fact that the 868th was now a member of the Kenney FEAF organization made absolutely no difference.[11]

Yet these organizational changes reflected the reality that the Allied buildup in aircraft and men in the greater South Pacific had reached the point where there were seemingly more squadrons of fighters and bombers than there were forward airfields capable of operating them. U.S. Army Air Force and U.S. Navy aircraft formations were moving forward to occupy the new airfields at an almost unsustainable tempo, with the result that groups were literally competing to occupy the new or reclaimed airfields. U.S. Army engineering battalions and U.S. Navy Seabees were carving these new airbases and logistics hubs out of the raw jungle or clearing and expanding former Japanese airfields, often as the dead combatants were still being buried and Japanese counterattacks arrived to threaten the newly won airstrips.

Squadrons that had a year before been under-equipped with aircraft, aircrews, maintenance crews and support crews were now fully or even over-staffed as the American genius for production and logistics doubled down on the equipment and supplies delivered to the front. More were stacked waiting in rear areas as the momentum reached its apex in the Pacific. The move of the 868th from Munda to Momote, completed in early May, was a prime example of this "move forward, but to where" mandate that saw aircraft and service crews temporarily separated.

This same challenge would repeat itself several times over by the time the 868th arrived on Okinawa's Yontan airfields a year later in the summer of 1945. The pace of the ever-forward Allied movement toward the Home Islands of Japan, and the consequent frequent changes in aircraft basing, was also a reflection of Japan's ongoing collapse as a military power. To the men of the 868th and their fellow bomber groups and squadrons, this was all good news as it suggested that the war was moving into its final stages.

Targets attacked and destroyed along the way to Tokyo meant that these lost ships, destroyed airplanes and bypassed or killed infantrymen would not reach Japan to participate in the final struggle when the Home Islands were invaded. Given the ferocity of the fighting in the Pacific to date, it was assumed at every level of the high command and with individuals in combat that the war would have to be brought to the beaches, fields and streets of Japan to be concluded. The officers and men of 868th assumed that, as the Allied forces fought their way toward Japan, from the South Pacific, from the Central Pacific and from the far west in the China–Burma–India Theater, that the war then had two or more years to run. History would later confirm that this would have been the case without the defining arrival and deployment of the ultimate weapon of war.

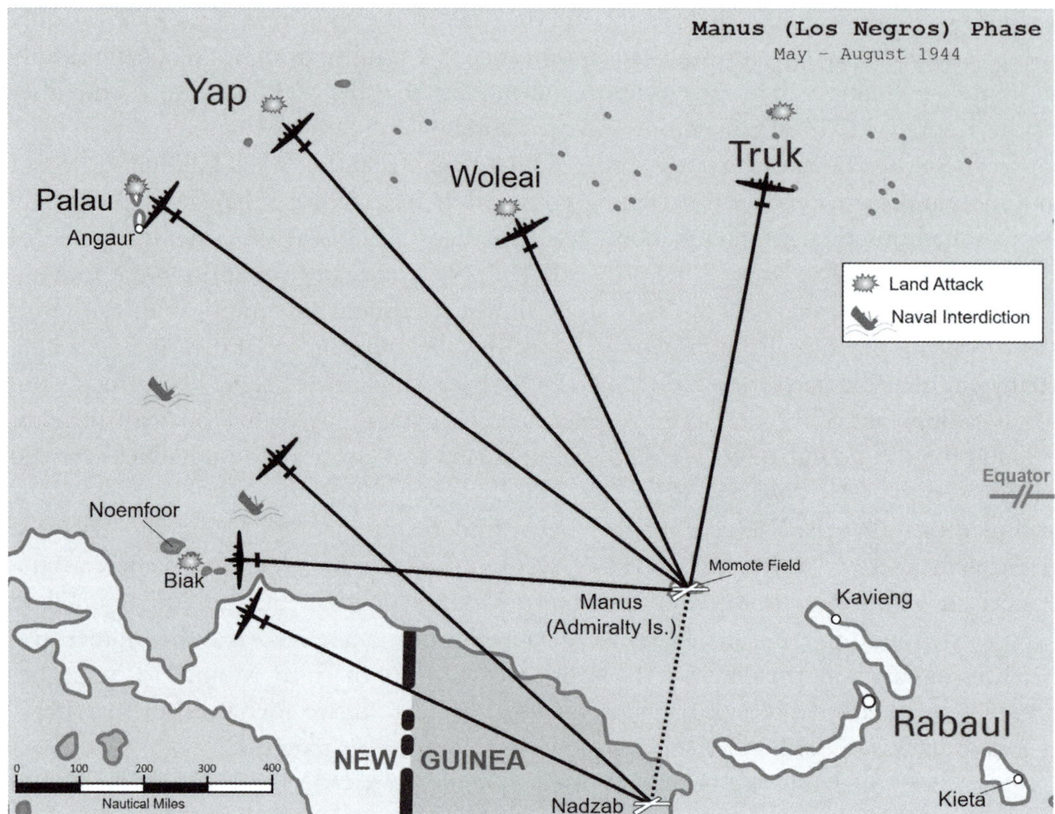

Manus (Los Negros) phase May–August 1944, indicating 868th Squadron sea-search and land target strikes to the north (Truk), northwest (Palau) and west (Biak and Dutch East Indies). (Chris Chen/Telemus)

CHAPTER 12

The Art DeLand Crew and 396

April–June 1944

Four decades after the events described in this book, one of the 868th Squadron command pilots reflected on the war, his crew, his airplane and the missions they flew in the Pacific against the empire of Japan in 1944. Arthur DeLand was a modest man of modest origins who joined the Army Air Corps before Pearl Harbor because he expected America would soon be in the fight. Assuming he would be called to the service of his country, Art elected to fly into combat as a bomber pilot with the U.S. Army Air Force. DeLand and his close-knit crew were one of the first replenishment crews to train for the LAB mission at Langley Field and be dispatched across America and into the Pacific to join the 868th. As Art DeLand recalled in an interview with the author in 1980, some 40 years after he went to war:

My crew
Even by the standards of the 868th, my crew was extremely close-knit from the outset of our training and throughout our combat deployment. We began to come together in April 1943 when I reported to Portello Army Air Base, fresh from three months of advanced pilot training at Smyrna Airfield where I flew B-24D and E-models and B-17Es. At Smyrna they culled out 10 crews to send to the China–Burma–India Theater where they would fly the cargo version of the B-24 [the C-87] on "over the Hump" missions. A further 10 pilots, myself included, were assigned to the 382nd Group at Portello for more training and crew building. Soon after my arrival they called all the officers to a hangar and separated the officers into four groups: command or "first pilots," co-pilots, navigators and bombardiers. The enlisted men were also collected into function groups: flight engineers, gunners, etc. The first pilots went to each officer group in sequence and had individual conversations, making the selection process an almost collaborative event.

My first selection was Gerard Westerland as my navigator, and I then choose Howard Blackwelder as my bombardier and, moving to the enlisted groups, Weldon Richards and Alan Rosenthal as my flight engineers, followed by Henry Johnson and John Hawkersmith as my aerial gunners. The man I had selected as my co-pilot soon checked out as a first pilot, was sent to Boise, Idaho, to collect his own crew and they went to England to fly against Germany. I checked out three candidate co-pilots and finally selected Edward Snead, who would remain in my right seat during the entire tour.

Once at Langley Field, Hawkersmith was released from our crew and we gained Jacob Jones as our radar operator. I also picked up George Manchester when we learned that we needed a nose turret gunner with the J-model aircraft we would receive. This was our crew.

<u>Portello</u>
At this location, we received a lot of time in the air and this was mostly enjoyable and allowed us to close up our team. I was 24 at the time, and the ages of my crew ranged from 19 to 30, but they all called me "Pop." The man who would fly as my co-pilot throughout our combat tour, Paul Snead, had just turned 20. The only negative event occurred when a senior officer—a group colonel—had scheduled us for back-to-back missions over several days in a row and I went to him to complain that, after three long flights in as many days, he had now scheduled us to climb back into the plane for a midnight to dawn flight. I insisted that we needed a one-day break and, when I learned from our Operations Officer that we had been selected for the additional flight because the good colonel was trying to set a record for the longest time in the air with our crew, I refused to fly. He walked away, did not report me for insubordination, we did not fly and we did not hear of this again.

<u>On to Langley Field</u>
Special Order Number 186 sent 15 B-24 crews to Herrington, Kansas, for further processing and onward crew assignments to different units and theaters. Five of the 15 crews would later be sent to Langley Field in Virginia for LAB-related training—me (DeLand), Thomson, Kaplan, Hoffman, Gay and Bryan—and four of those would later serve with the 868th in the Pacific after training on the LAB system at Langley. By 1 August we were settled into our new home, with Special Order Number 27 showing these five crews plus 10 additional crews as assigned to the 3rd Sea-Search Attack Squadron of the 1st Sea-Search Attack Group, all with "combat crew" status. Interestingly, these same orders show several members of that unit newly assigned to the Wright Project, those being Majors Carlson and Foster, Captains Lehti, Reynolds and Zinn, plus Lieutenants Brown, Easterling, Martus, Rockwood and Tillinghast. This suggests that the new arrivals for LAB training had a three-week overlap with the original Wright Project crews before they departed Langley for Guadalcanal.

<u>Langley operations and LAB Training</u>
Once assigned to the 3rd Sea-Search, we flew only four missions with the B-18Bs but soon moved on to the B-24D and E-models as they became available. At Langley, we flew only 165 hours and of that only five missions were rated as combat anti-submarine patrols. Our closest call was a near collision with a U.S. Navy blimp that was out of position and appeared directly in front of us at an altitude of 1,000 feet. Our B-24 cleared it by a few feet, but it was a close call with our good friends, the U.S. Navy. In company with another crew and plane, that of Phil Hoffman, we would be the second group to depart Langley Field as replacement crews and aircraft for the 868th. A group of three aircrews departed Langley to join the Wright Project in the Pacific in mid-November, beating us out the door by a few weeks.

<u>We get our forever plane—396</u>
We were introduced to our aircraft, a brand-new B-24J fresh off the assembly line at Consolidated Aircraft, not a Willow Run B-24. We thought her to be perfect in every way and I signed for her as I would any item of government-issued equipment. Aircraft 42-73396, which we flew for the first time on 17 January 1944, was our responsibility and over the next couple of weeks we prepared to take her to war.[1]

We calibrated the airspeed indicators, swung the compass and jammed her full of the replacement parts and equipment we assumed we would need to service her wherever we were headed. We flew

396 only five times before departing from Langley on 26 January 1944 for Mitchell Field on Long Island, New York, where we would process for overseas duty. The crew voted to name her *Ready, Willing and Able* as we believed that, as a crew, we were just so and we did have total confidence in our abilities. Several of the crew suggested that we name her *Millie's Angel* after my wife, as other command pilots had done, but I rejected that. The name we chose was just right and reflected our attitude and our desire to get into the war.

A painting of a beautiful girl was also applied above her name and she would be much admired by our colleagues in the 868th. We carried an improved version of the radar component in the LAB system and a full set of spares for that set just in case these had not yet reached the 868th in the field. Our 396 was the first B-24J to reach the 868th and Phil Hoffman and his crew, dispatched to the 868th on the same set of orders as us, would land with a second J-model a few days behind us.

The lemon

In stark contrast to our 396, Hoffman's plane was a real "lemon," not exactly a "hangar queen" but pretty bad. Its rear end was out of rig coming from the factory and there seemed to be nothing that could be done to correct this. When our crew flew the Hoffman plane it was always an issue, and when other crews became aware of "the monster's" faults they attempted to avoid being assigned to fly her. This B-24J (42-73410) looked sharp and the Hoffman crew named her *Long Distance* and hoped for the best with her. But no one at Munda believed this plane could go the distance and I recall that the squadron eventually gave up on her, towed her to our boneyard and cannibalized her for spare parts. When I asked another pilot who I respected as a real perfectionist, Don Thomson, what was wrong with 410, he paused a few seconds and said, "Well, just about everything. She is badly rigged, has three bad engines, lousy hydraulics and the fuel system leaks. And nobody can fix her!"

In combat over the next many months, we would fly our 396 every chance we could get—she was still "ours"—and, apart from some anti-aircraft damage along the way, we would end up signing her over to a new crew, that of Captain Earle Smith, when we departed after 40 strike missions at the end of our tour. For some reason, the new crew elected to rename her, and replaced *Ready, Willing and Able* with their own *Our Baby* nom de guerre. Our 396 was considered a well-performing and lucky airplane—we never lost a man on board her—and this new name may have been the Smith crew's way of claiming ownership of this ship.

But Smith's crew did manage to keep the girl as we had originally had her painted at Langley through the duration of the life of 396. She had taken us to war, brought us back from every mission and we said goodbye to *Ready, Willing and Able* when we went home. I flew the B-29 as a command pilot in the Korean War, had 20 missions over North Korea and the B-29 was a Lincoln Continental compared to the B-24J Chevy in every way. But the B-24J and our 396 will always be my favorite warplane, maybe like the first "true love" that you always pine about.

Deployment to the Pacific

Departing Mitchell Field on 28 January 1944, we staged through Memphis Municipal, Davis-Monthan Airfield in Tucson, Arizona, and onto Fairfield-Suisun in California. We departed Fairfield-Suisun late in the night on 5 February "heavy," weighing out at just over 72,000 pounds, and I pointed 396 into the night toward Hickam Field, Hawaii. We opened our orders, stamped "Secret," in the air as we headed west and these confirmed that our destination would be Carney Field, Guadalcanal, to report there to the Thirteenth Air Force's Thirteenth Bomber Command.

We arrived at Carney on 13 February after ferry stops in Canton Island, Nadi in the Fiji Islands and Espiritu Santos in the New Hebrides and went forward from Carney to join the 868th on Munda Airstrip on 15 February. Wasting no time, we flew our first combat mission three days later in a squadron B-24D, a solo shipping search and destroy mission up the St. George's Channel and into the Bismarck Sea. This involved a departure shortly before midnight, a 12-hour LAB mission "up The Slot" in which we found no targets worthy of our attention, and a mid-morning recovery to Munda with our bomb load intact.[2]

Combat missions from Munda

In the coming weeks, roughly February through the time we moved from Munda to Los Negros in late April, we flew 15 "strike" missions, as combat missions were then called. These were mostly 10 to 12-hour LAB search-and-destroy efforts that failed to find shipping targets and saw us divert to secondary targets to deliver our ordnance on Japanese airfields and bases. One mission that stands out was Strike Number 7 when we almost crashed on take-off from Munda on 9 March when we lifted off at midnight for a 10-hour run up The Slot. Shortly after take-off, at about 600 feet in altitude, fully loaded with five 1,000 [lb] bombs on board, we lost engines two and four.

Luckily our bombardier, Howard Blackwelder, had just moved to his working position in the nose from his take-off spot amidships and was where he needed to be. I yelled to order a salvo of all bombs, pulled the aircraft up just above the water, went around to land safely and turn the airplane over to the mechanics. The fully loaded take-off at 72,000 pounds plus was by far the most dangerous part of the mission, save for Japanese interceptor aircraft or well-directed flak over a defended airfield. We almost lost 396 that night but we saved her and ourselves for another mission. Others at max weight who lost engines on take-off would not be so lucky.

The loss of Lt. Gerald Westerland

Our first loss among our crew, and recall we had been together for over a year since we came together in Portello, hit us all hard. Gerard was probably the best-liked man in the crew and probably the best natural navigator I had in two wars. He had a calming demeanor and a beautiful singing voice. His finest was the "Whiffenpoof Song" and he would entertain us with it as we rode in an open vehicle or walked to our aircraft for the pre-flight check before aircraft take-off on a strike mission. The night he was lost over Truk with the Haynes crew, on 25 June 1944, he had volunteered to substitute for the Haynes navigator who had come down sick. It was an all-night mission and I recall that my bombardier, Howard Blackwelder, came into my tent in the middle of the night to wake me, telling me that he had a premonition that Haynes was down and Westerland was lost.[3]

Hours later, when the Haynes aircraft was declared overdue and missing and presumed down, we volunteered to search. We flew a long daylight mission, searched an arc that reached out to about 30 miles south of Truk and worked the route back to base that Haynes would have flown. No trace of the crew was spotted by us or the other searchers and we assumed that their plane had been shot down over the target.

The losses of other entire crews, when they went missing on a solo strike mission or crashed on take-off or landing, did not impact us as much as the loss of our own crewman. But when those who we knew well were lost, those with whom we had trained at Langley Field and served with in the 868th until their loss, it hit us hard. The crews of Fred Bryan, Don Thomson, Dick Gay, Pete Colt and Phil Hoffman were our "buddies" with whom we trained and went to war, and when the crew or any one man was lost it hit us because we knew them well and, in many cases, their families.

We hardly knew the King, Robbins, Arthur, Rauch, Booth and Wagner crews as they came into the squadron well after our arrival and we simply did not socialize with them. Looking back, the 868th lost a lot of crews, many of whom just went missing and were never accounted for. In the case of all men lost, sorting out the personal effects to be mailed home to the wife or parents was probably the most difficult undertaking, even where one was not a friend with the man who had gone "missing and was presumed dead."

<u>Missions to Rabaul</u>
Although Truk may have been our toughest target, we also found that Rabaul was a very dangerous night mission. As a major bypassed Japanese base, they were well-armed and always waiting for us, capable of putting up a high volume of anti-aircraft fire with dozens of searchlights dancing across the sky as we approached, trying to capture us in their beams for their guns. One night we counted over 60 searchlights and once they found us and fixed on us, we could read a book in the aircraft. The counter we developed was to de-synchronize our engines to confuse the acoustic detectors we knew they were operating, linked to the spotlights and the guns, and this seemed to work well.

On final approach to the target at the IP or "Initial Point." I tuned the Pratt and Whitneys to set a spread of 50–75 RPMs among the four engines, trying to establish the best "beat" for our friends listening below. We assumed, without knowing for sure if this tactic, which suggested four aircraft had arrived to harass them instead of our single plane, actually worked. We hoped that their searchlights, radars, anti-aircraft guns and whatever would be reacting accordingly and looking for four B-24s overhead instead of just one—ours.

But the Japanese night fighters were there as well and they were persistent, tracking us as the lights tried to grab and hold our plane. When a fighter lost us and then picked us up again a few minutes later, our radar operator, Sergeant Jacob Jones, managed to spot and track him and vectored me to dive away so we could set up for another bombing approach. One night over Rabaul, during our Strike 11 on 18 March 1944 in aircraft 396, we had a harassment mission that required us to make repeated passes over the target during a three-hour period. We played tag for over an hour with one fighter pilot. He was very good, determined to find us and shoot us down, but he never managed to close with us for a firing pass. Other missions of the 868th would not be so fortunate in this night fighter hide-and-seek department.

<u>First land-based attack on Truk</u>
This was a well-briefed and carefully planned two-plane night mission, with our crew paired up with that of Don Thomson. We both staged from Munda to Piva airstrip on Bougainville, launched from there, hit Truk and recovered directly to Munda. It was a 13-hour, 45-minute mission and our crew's 13th Strike. If one counted the set-up run from Munda to Piva that same day, our mission time was about 15½ hours in the air. On 28 March 1944, Thomson's plane attacked Truk about 10 minutes ahead of us and our plane lost our radar about 10 miles out from the target. But we had no problem with our bomb run on Moen. Thomson's attack had started several fires and we homed in on the largest one, hit it again with our full bomb load, dove left off the target and turned for home.

<u>Strike mission preparation and departure</u>
We checked the squadron bulletin board at about 11am each morning to see if our crew had been scheduled for a mission that night. It was frequently a single crew but often two or three aircraft would be scheduled, each for separate mission profiles. We had fallen into a three-day rotation by spring 1944 so a given crew pretty much knew when they would fly. After dinner and a mission briefing on the target specifics, we would load into a truck for a run from the camp to the hard stand in the revetment area, and offload at our aircraft with our gear. On the truck ride to the aircraft, we would try to keep our tension under control by singing bawdy songs and this routine would often end with Westerland singing his signature song.

Once at the aircraft, we would stow our gear aboard and begin our inspection routine, with the bombardier and navigators working through their checklists at their stations while the co-pilot and I did a complete walk-around. About 25 minutes before take-off, the entire crew would gather in front of the plane and run the engine props through by hand turning—this to clear the engines of any moisture or hydraulic locks. It would then be time to attempt one last relief of our bladders, but as anticipation was quite high, this was too often not successful. We would then don our Mae West life preservers, board the aircraft and settle in. Snead and I would go through our pilot's checklist with our flight engineer standing just behind and between us. Engines would be started in a sequence of 3-4-2-1 and after a short run-up of those engines, we would be ready to taxi.

Once the tower cleared us for take-off, we would complete our T.O. checklist, now at the end of the taxiway and I would tell the crew on the intercom that we were ready to fly. The J-model of the B-24 had a set of four dashpots for adjusting the superchargers and these were positioned on the right-hand corner of the control pedestal. I would run each engine in turn to full throttle and reach 2,700 RPM and screw the turbo-control until we reached 49 inches of mercury. At that point, I would call the tower and note we were ready for take-off. The tower would acknowledge using our code name for a given mission—we were often "Brunette One." When the tower released us, I would recheck for full brakes, run the engines to 2,700 RPM and 30 inches and tell my co-pilot to follow me through on the throttles and then release the brakes.

Because most of our takeoffs were in the dead of night, I would have my co-pilot call out the airspeed as we hit 80, then 100 and finally 120 mph as we rolled down the strip. I would be looking at the airstrip and not the instrument panel but I would chance fast glances to check manifold pressure, engine RPMs and airspeed. At about 90 mph I would ease back on the control column to take pressure off the nose wheel. The strip at Munda was 7,100 feet in length and, with our B-24D or J model at 72,000 pounds, we needed every inch of it.

As soon as we broke ground, normally abreast of the last runway light, I would call out "gear up" and flash Snead a thumbs-up to make sure he got it. At the same time, I would tap the nose-wheel brake for two reasons—to make sure the spinning wheel did not damage the wheel well and because a spinning nose wheel acted as a gyro to disrupt the balance of the plane. Also, within the same few seconds, I would shift my focus to the flight instruments: the artificial horizon, the rate of climb and the gyrocompass. With all the gear fully retracted I would have Snead milk up the flaps, but gently, because any dump of the flaps all at once would cause the aircraft to sink before it stabilized. Our routine was to pull them up five degrees at a time.

On take-off the radarman, the assistant engineer and tail gunner would be in the rear of the plane, the flight engineer would be between the two pilots and the radioman, nose gunner, bombardier and navigator on the flight deck or in the deck well just behind. At the take-off point, as gear was being retracted and the flaps coming up, the bombardier would scramble/crawl past the nose wheel and into the nose, positioning himself for an emergency salvo of our bomb load.

The pilots had an emergency bomb salvo lever on the face of the control pedestal near the bottom, but if we were having trouble during take-off, the co-pilot and I would be too busy flying the plane, feathering runaway engines, or whatever, to grab that salvo level and pull. Our practice of having the bombardier with his hand on his salvo control up front paid dividends and saved us from a certain crash on 9 March when our trusty 396 lost two engines on take-off. In that instance, our procedure worked, we dumped the bombs, did a quick 180 and put her back down in good shape. We flew a successful Strike Nine two days later once the mechanics gave us back 396 in good shape.

<u>The run to target and return to home</u>
Returning to our mission profile, on take-off, after we were "cleaned up" with the landing gear stowed and the plane gradually climbing, we would reduce our RPMs to 2,550 and set our manifold pressure at 45 inches. From this point on, it was a matter of maintaining a good climb altitude, holding the airspeed at 125 mph and checking the engine temperature to stay under the redline. Once at mission altitude, we would go above it, level off and pick up speed, drop about five degrees of flaps and soon come down to our cruise altitude. At this point, I would call for 32 inches and 2,200 RPMs on the engines and we would go over the remainder of the crew checklist. With the

autopilot now engaged I could sit back, relax a bit and enjoy my first cigarette. I would call the gunners on the intercom and have them test fire all guns.

On the bomb run, as we approached our IP, we would increase power to best stabilize our airspeed to the level to which the bombardier and I had agreed. Any deviation by the pilot on speed over the target would create a bomb "over or under" situation and a miss on the target. After bomb drop and diving away to the right or left, we would pick up good speed to exit the target area and then set the cruise for home. I would do an intercom roll call with each of the crew reporting in to determine if any had been injured by the anti-aircraft fire or saw damage on the aircraft.

Once we had cleared the target area, my bombardier would join me in the cockpit area to write our mission report. As we cruised and burned fuel, with our bomb load gone, we would be much lighter and run our return leg to base at 26 inches and 1,950 RPM. The flight had become monotonous at that point, but I found that, unlike others, including my snoring co-pilot, I could not sleep for the entire trip home to base. Once parked on the ramp we sat for a quick mission debriefing by the intelligence guys and enjoyed one good shot of "Old Overholt" whiskey provided by our squadron physician, "Doc" Krug. Mission over, it was time for some sleep.

Woleai and Palau

After Truk, as other Snoopers were still hitting that target, we were sent to Woleai and Palau. These comprised our Strikes 17 through 33, so about 17 missions in all. Most of the Woleai attacks were fairly easy and the Palau strikes tough. Our first mission to Woleai, on 1 May, was in one of the remaining Wright Project B-24D models, but most of the balance was in Js, namely our trusty 396. The only outlying mission, which was not credited as a strike, was when we joined the search for the missing Haynes crew that had been lost over Truk, as mentioned above. Regarding Woleai, these were mostly daylight runs of nine hours duration, all mounted from Momote and later from Mokerang Airfield on Los Negros. I cannot recall any active fighter opposition but the flak gunners there were good and always ready for us, and sometimes too accurate in their welcome barrages. On the eight missions to Palau, we hit Koror Island five times and Ngesebus Island three times, and in every run we flew over or near the two islands in the Palau group that our U.S. Marines had invaded and taken such high casualties—Peleliu and Anguar.

Combat tour concluded and headed home

By early December 1944, we had completed our required 40 strike missions, plus a dozen or so other flights, such as searches for missing crews, runs to Australia and qualification or "check out" flights for prospective pilots where I was responsible for approving new arrivals or co-pilot crossovers as command pilots. Final flights included my fourth R&R flight to Australia piloting the squadron RB-24D and a check-out flight at Noemfoor on 22 December in a B-24J coming out of maintenance.[4]

I would end my tour in the Pacific with 628 hours, most spent in the B-24J and the B-24D, plus some time in our C-47. I would return to CONUS [continental United States] about one year to the day that I had reached Guadalcanal, to qualify on and fly the B-29 before discharge in July 1945. I would close out my (first) Army Air Corps career with about 1,400 hours in various aircraft types. In 1952, I would be recalled to active duty and fly the B-29 from Japan on 18 combat missions over North Korea.

As I said, the B-29 was a Cadillac or Lincoln Continental compared to my B-24J, but our 396 *Ready, Willing and Able* was still my absolute favorite airplane of all time. She took us into combat, brought us back and, throughout that year in war in the Pacific we only lost one of my crew, he of the "The Whiffing Poo Song."

Several years later, after I returned from my Korean War tour, my wife and I visited another 868th Squadron veteran who had been close to Lt. Westerland. The latter's bride, Virginia or "Ginny" as she was known in the Sea-Search family at Langley, was a quiet lady who was also from Chicago. The colleague revealed that Westerland's widow, some 10 years after his death at Truk when he had flown with the Haynes crew, had then recently become nationally known in the media as the central figure in the so-called Bridey Murphy controversy. Gerald Westerland had met and married his wife, Virginia, about the same time that my wife and I married, during our stay at Langley Field in the months before our crew's deployment to the Pacific.

Bridey Murphy was the name by which this lady had subsequently become famous. She was the subject of a well-received and controversial book, *The Search for Bridey Murphy*, and numerous articles, not to mention a movie of the same name, all in the postwar 1952–1957 period. I was later able to confirm, at least to my satisfaction, that my lost navigator's former wife "Ginny" had indeed been the same lady who the public had come to know as Bridey Murphy. I honestly do not know if this is true with total certainty, but if so, it is yet another one of those incredible coincidences that only occur in war when young men randomly come together and bond for a lifetime.[5]

CHAPTER 13

Radar Reflections

1943–44

The LAB system was the capability around which the Wright Project, and indeed the entire program, was built and the Rad Lab-developed SCR-717 microwave radar was the heart of that system. The speed and efficiency with which this system was engineered, developed, prototyped and perfected were only matched by the pace at which it was deployed in combat and how it was sustained in the advanced bases as a dependable system.

Radar and LAB from Langley forward

Radar technician extraordinaire Floyd Hune, who had been with the Wright Project from before its birth as one of Dolan's men with the 1st Sea-Search Attack Group from early 1943, recalled his experiences with the introduction of the LAB system that would soon go to the Pacific with the first deployment of the project:

<u>First sets</u>
We received our first SCR-717 while I was working the test bench at the 3rd Sea-Search Attack Squadron at Langley. Up to that time, we were using the old British radar in the B-18s for sea search. I set up that first production SCR-717 on the bench and worked the bugs out of it with several modifications. Later on, we got our first B-24 which was to be called *The Lady Margaret*. We made our first installation in that plane along with some control modifications and it was sent to Wright Field where nine more planes were equipped exactly the same way. After all those units were tested out, they became the 10 Wright Project aircraft. When we departed for the South Pacific, we had with us a supply of spare units and spare parts which all our radar mechanics took along, and each plane had an assigned radar mechanic and a radar operator. My aircraft was the *The Lady Margaret*.

I recall one night at Langley with Colonel Wright, a week or so before we departed for the Pacific, discussing the performance of the system. He sat for several hours at the end of our radar bench asking me about each component of the system, and he noted that he would be happy if we could demonstrate an equipment availability rate of 75 percent. I recall that during the 27 months I was with the squadron we averaged a 94 percent operational rate for the equipment, that is, the equipment as installed and tested in aircraft before mission start. This was a testimony to the design of the system, particularly the radar, the ruggedness of the equipment and the incredible care taken by the radar section to constantly test, repair, re-install and test again every system in every aircraft before it was cleared to fly into combat.

Deployment

The Wright Project's radar section was probably the most unorthodox, innovative, creative and nothing-is-impossible group that existed at that time in the Pacific. Two civilians assisted us every step of the way—Horace Clark from Western Electric and Ed Sharkey from Bell Laboratories. Both left with us from the States in August 1943 and stayed with us for much of our time overseas. Sharkey was the "slide rule" type and Clark was the man who always seemed to have the practical answers and ideas for equipment and how it would be operated.

I recall that Sharkey came to me when we were going to hit Truk Atoll and asked if it was possible to change the maximum range from 100 miles to 200 miles. Because I had been working the "717 bench" and knew that radar, we worked together to "soup up" the equipment and modified the scopes to provide a 200-mile range. On the runs to Truk, the 868th, whether flying in single-mission night search-and-attack mode or in leading formations of daylight B-24s to the Atoll, the radars consistently ranged the islands at 100 miles or more, and sometimes at 150 miles.

Another interesting fact was that all the radar units and the "plumbing"—what we called the antenna lines—were plated with gold. Western Electric had to use gold due to a severe shortage of silver in wartime. The gold was very attractive but was softer than silver and, as a consequence, it burned through by arcing much faster than silver. This caused us to remove and replace each piece after every flight and polish it. So, one could say that we were installing and testing a new transmitter and plumbing for every aircraft after every flight. Also, after we were at the front for some time, we had to begin replacing our alternators on the equipment. The new alternators started throwing bearings almost immediately and we discovered that the so-called "greased for life" bearing with which we were supplied had never been greased. We created our own grease press and pumped grease into each alternator after every flight.

No spares and innovation

The fact is that we received no spares from the U.S. for 18 months and we had to scramble at times to keep all the LAB systems working to the level at which they had to perform. I built a transformer winding machine and kept all of our transformers in shape and built up a reserve supply so we could swap them out when they failed, as they so often did. When the radar shop, or "the shack," relocated with the squadron to a new island base, we were able to set up a new radar bench within a few hours and kept the systems running. There was a sign above the bench that pretty much said it all—"If the tubes are lit and the voltages are right, the damn thing will operate."

Another task was to train the new crews that were coming from the States. As the longer we were out in the Pacific, it seemed that the new crews were coming in with little LAB experience or even no radar training. We would work with the radar operators and brief the pilots and bombardiers to make sure that they all knew how the systems worked and we shared the experiences that the squadron had accumulated over the past months of deployment.

In the later months of the 868th in the Pacific, from perhaps mid-1944 forward, the new B-24s would come in with improved versions of the radar systems and the equipment would always arrive burned out. In one case of a brand-new aircraft with a burned system, the squadron commander came to our shack and asked us if we could get the systems repaired and operational for missions scheduled for the following night. Rudy Nelson, Bob Lambert and I removed the equipment and studied the new systems, speculating as to the function of each. For example, we had to measure the radar antenna to confirm what frequency it was operating at, all the basic stuff that a manual (and there were none) would normally have told you. We mastered the new components and rebuilt the system in time for the mission.

One night we found that a radar test bench existed on the island base in another camp and Lambert and I took off to find it. We were in a blinding rainstorm and dragged the equipment onto the bench, with six inches of water coursing through the tent below our feet. In our haste to power up and run the test, Lambert twice touched the water stream and was hit by 25,000 volts. He was knocked off his seat and landed off to the side in the water but lived to tell about it. We got the job done, installed the recalibrated and rebuilt systems and the first two of the new planes went off the next night on their missions.[1]

The Lady Margaret is identified as the first installation of a production SCR-717 and the first Wright Project aircraft to receive the LAB system. It is a testament to that aircraft and its maintainers that three years later, in April 1945, this same aircraft was still on the rolls of the 868th. She was, at that time, having accumulated 1,165 hours on her airframe, serving as the squadron's "Fat Cat," assigned to shuttle supplies and personnel among the rear areas and Australia. Aircraft B-24D 42-40639, *The Lady*, had been named back in July 1943 at Langley Field by its Wright Project crew, the crew of George Tillinghast, in honor of Tillinghast's wife. Consistent with his above recollections, Technical Sergeant Floyd Hune had apparently done an excellent job of keeping the electronic systems in "his airplane" finely tuned and in-commission for the next day's mission, day after day and month after month, as he had promised Colonel Wright he would endeavor to do.

Radar recognition from the highest levels

In April 1944, the 868th's then Commanding Officer, Major Leo Foster, was pleased to receive a formal letter of praise from the Commanding General of the Army Air Forces, General Hap Arnold. The classified telegram, dated 2 April 1944, reached Foster on Munda Field and Foster was justly proud to share it with his squadron. He also had memos of commendation placed in the personnel files of the unit's radar section as well as the lead drafter of the report that is mentioned in the Arnold commendation, Captain Charles Rockwood. A series of reports generated by the 868th had detailed the performance of the LAB system and recommended improvements in the support of those systems.[2]

TO: COMAF THIRTEEN
INFO: COMGENSOPAC
NR WAR 17463-SECOND
CONTAINED IN REPORTS OF 868TH BOMB SQUADRON COMMENTS REGARDING UNSATISFACTORY CONDITION OF SPECIAL RADAR EQUIPMENTS AND IMPROVEMENTS WHICH SHOULD BE MADE IN INSTALLATIONS HAVE BEEN FORWARDED TO MATERIAL COMMAND AND LANGLEY FIELD. HOWEVER, SUCH MATTERS SHOULD ALSO BE REPORTED ON STANDARD UR FORMS. ADVISE IF SUCH ACTION IS BEING TAKEN. ALL REPORTS RECEIVED BY AIR COMMUNICATIONS OFFICER TO DATE REGARDING MAINTENANCE, PERFORMANCE AND OPERATIONAL USE OF SPECIAL RADAR AND BEACON EQUIPMENT HAVE BEEN EXTREMELY VALUABLE AND HAVE RESULTED IN SIGNIFICANT IMPROVEMENTS IN EQUIPMENT DESIGN, AIRCRAFT INSTALLATIONS AND TRAINING PROGRESS. THE PERSONNEL RESPONSIBLE FOR PREPARATION OF THESE REPORTS DESERVE TO BE HIGHLY COMMENDED FOR AN EXCELLENT JOB. MCCLELLAN SIGNED ARNOLD.

Regular reporting in both the established and in unconventional direct-to-Wright Field Army Air Force Material Command channels by the 868th served three purposes. First, the unit was eager to record the success of the LAB system and its application to nighttime sea-search and attack missions, as well as daylight missions as pathfinders for larger formations, and its application to adverse weather navigation. Second, there were many improvements in the current generation system that suggested themselves, modifications that could only be identified and recommended in the course of the system's deployment in combat conditions. Third, as mentioned in the Floyd Hune comments above, by spring 1944, new B-24J aircraft were joining the squadron with defective or damaged systems and components, shortcomings that should have been identified and resolved before the aircraft were released from Wright Field or Langley Field to head overseas.

The reporting by the 868th prescriptively wove these latter issues into the narrative and prodded the Army Air Force, at the highest levels, to send the message down through its operational layers to drive needed changes. Arnold's right-hand man, General McClellan, took it from there and, within a few weeks, the new aircraft began arriving with their LAB systems in much better condition. Colonel Aldrin, then back at Wright Field as McClennan's overseer and problem solver, also weighed in to ensure tighter procedures were established for the testing and qualification of LAB aircraft and crews prior to their release for dispatch to the Pacific.

A radar operator remembers

From the point in the mission that an 868th aircraft lifted into the night, through to its landing 10 or more hours later, the lives of the crew were in the hands of the two pilots and the man who operated the B-24's advanced radar system. Others played their respective roles—the navigator, the bombardier, the flight engineers and gunners—but it was the man on the scope to whom all looked to for their safety, the crew member who had the "eyes" that peered into the dark.

Technical Sergeant Horace Sullivan joined the 868th in December 1943 as a member of the Don Thomson crew, one of the first dispatched from Langley Field to reinforce the Wright Project's original 10 crews. His combat mission recollections include the following:

> <u>Selected as a radar operator</u>
> I went to Army Air Corps radio school at Truax Field in Madison, Wisconsin, in the fall of 1942, graduated and tried to enter flight cadet training and was turned down. I then volunteered to fly gliders but was told my depth perception was bad, but all I knew was that I wanted to fly. At that point, a few of us who had done well in radio school were called into a meeting and asked if we would volunteer to "do something special and secret." My hand went up, as did those of the others in the room, and we all soon found ourselves on a slow train for Boca Raton, Florida. There we entered a special school that seemed to be more a prison than a military camp. Once there we were marched into a camp-within-a-camp, a further protected compound that featured armed guards to lock us in at the gate and a barbed wire-topped fence. We had no idea what was going on.

Civilian instructors nominated by Rad Lab managed the classrooms and laboratories and we soon began to appreciate what we had fallen into. The senior civilian introduced us to "RADAR" with a question, "Men, what if I told you that you could fly a plane in the dark of night and tell distance and direction, that is, see in the night electronically?" The guy next to me responded with "Bullshit" a bit too loud but the speaker ignored him and he had our full attention. They pushed us hard on the basics of the equipment, to the degree that we students had to be able to draw the entire circuitry of the different radars that we were to master.

When I graduated, I knew radar, at least as it was being installed in the B-24s that were waiting for us at Langley Field. We saw a beautiful new B-24 at the Boca Raton airfield that had stopped over, and it created a "rush" among us radar students, such a contrast to the B-18 we knew well by then. When we arrived at Langley, we were interviewed and selected by the crews that were already there flying the ASV-equipped B-18s and B-24s on test hops. I was fortunate and was selected to join a great crew, that of Don Thomson, and I would go to the Pacific with these fine folks.

Combat mission preparation

Prior to the mission, after receiving the target area briefing, we radar operators would delve into the geography of the mission flight route and the target area, cross-checking the outlines of the islands we would cross or fly near, the mountain elevations and any landmarks that one could imagine would register on our radar. We would also have worked during the day with our radar technicians to make sure the equipment was functioning at an optimal level.

Once at the aircraft, while the balance of the crew did its walk-around, the radar operator would do a final test run with his systems, to the degree this was possible on the ground, and pronounce to the command pilot that his radar system was up and mission ready. As with all critical systems, if I declared an issue, we probably would not fly that night. Our radar systems were almost always mission-ready, made so by the excellent technical services of the Rad Lab folks who were with us and our own squadron radar and electronics team. After I told the pilot that our radar was "ready to go" I would shut the system down and rejoin the crew outside the aircraft for the pull-through of the props. We would then gather as a crew at the front of the plane, say a prayer or have a small talk and climb on board.

Radar set-up and operation

The early B-24s, including the D-model that we encountered when we deployed as a crew to Carney, had the radar operator's station and all his equipment directly behind the pilot. From my seat I could turn to my right to look at the bomb bay and often did to watch the bomb release. Having both the radar and the radio on the flight deck made for a cramped and usually very warm situation, particularly at the low altitudes at which we flew—and it was the South Pacific after all. My regular combat garb consisted of a T-shirt, shorts and a pair of moccasins, hardly standard issue but about right for a 10-hour mission.

Once we were airborne, with the plane trimmed out and preparing to start our search, I turned on my set and warmed it up and then walked back to the radar antenna that was located in the position normally occupied by the ball turret in other B-24s. This trek took me through the bomb bay area and along the catwalk there. The antenna had to be lowered and raised by a hand crank. When I lowered it, a parabolic type housed in a fiberglass cover, I let the pilot know so he could trim the aircraft to account for the deployed antenna. The antenna rotated in place but also could be tilted to various angles in the vertical plane from the radar operator's position. This allowed me to scan for other aircraft, except for when the bombardier had the entire system locked up in the final minutes of the LAB bombing run to target. The radar was excellent at detecting enemy aircraft at a distance and tracking them as they tried to find us at night.

The eeriest time of the flight for me was when I crawled through the small door at the front of the bomb bay and stood up to head to the radar antenna. Alone on the catwalk, with the cold hard bombs resting around me, the wind coming in through the spaces in the bomb bay doors and the door at the back of the bay closed, I was all alone with my thoughts and our cargo of death. Would we make it this time, would we find the enemy, would he find us and could we get home to complete another mission?

On the models beyond the B-24D, the radar operators' position was shifted to a place near the bomb bay and here the radar operator sat alone for most of the mission. We often carried one or two auxiliary fuel tanks in the front bomb bay positions to allow longer duration search missions or long-range strike missions. On such occasions, the flight engineer would come to my area to operate the pumps that would transfer the fuel from these auxiliary tanks and into the wing tanks to flow fuel into the system. Andy would take his time in this process and would also use this space next to me to pray. He was a Catholic and was quite devoted, always praying with his rosary. He loved us all and we respected his deep religious beliefs. It was a tragedy for our crew when he was lost to us.

Radar as a navigational aid

Radar was a critical navigational aid in night flight as it allowed us to "see" landmasses and imagine them as they appeared on our relief maps, detecting and identifying them on our screen, with our aircraft at the center of my display. We had four range settings and used the first two as long-range navigational aids. This was essential given the inclement weather we constantly experienced in the Pacific, allowing us to identify the landmasses and guide the pilots around the worst of the weather. This advantage applied in both night and daylight missions as the weather issues applied to both. The navigator set the course but our radar got us to our target safely and brought us home once the bombs were dropped. Of course, the performance of the systems varied, and the flight or weather could vary as well, but the performance of our radar system was always good and sometimes it was outright amazing. The unmentioned fact was that our radar-equipped aircraft survived because of that radar system when others, without our SCR-717, did not.

I recall that on one daylight mission I identified a target blip on my screen some 12 miles away, called the bearing and range and the pilot went after it. As we approached, I dropped the radar to its most discriminating setting but the target was elusive, fading in and out. But when it was there, the signal was strong. When we reached the target area the pilots and crew declared it to be a "phantom" or false reading, with the intercom cracking jokes at my expense. I asked for another run on my target and coached the pilot around, pinpointed the contact, explaining that it could be the periscope or conning tower of a submarine. As we passed over my contact, we saw it clearly—a large coconut palm frond bobbing vertically in the waves. There were no more jokes about me or my radar.

A very close call

Sometimes our radar and our navigator simply got things wrong. As mentioned, we spent a lot of time around the islands of New Britain and New Ireland and we often encountered a lot of small enemy ships that mounted anti-aircraft guns and hugged the shorelines. We worked to identify our approach routes to Rabaul and other targets as well as escape routes after an attack that allowed us to avoid these types of ambushes by the small craft. Our navigator, Clayton Seaver, found one of these that crossed over New Ireland, and on a particularly stormy night we elected to use it. From the map and radar, it looked workable and we entered this cross-cutting valley with confidence.

About mid-way into our valley, the intercom suddenly crackled with, "SKIPPER, looks like a hill ahead, better pull up!" We gained altitude but then came, "Better pull up some more" with Don Thomson applying more power to climb faster. Finally, our flight engineer Andy Paladino, normally calm as a cucumber, yelled, "Pull up, Skipper ... FOR GOD'S SAKE, PULL UP NOW!" As our pilot poured on the power and, as he stood the plane on its tail, we started to stall out to the left. We cleared the mountain, and it sure as hell was not "a hill." Because we had a great pilot, we were simply damn lucky that night and we all knew that God was with us on that flight. We leveled out on the other side of New Ireland to fly home and after we landed, we collected foliage from the aircraft engine cowlings—it had been that close. We had a squadron staff officer with us that night, along as an "observer" to collect some hours in the air on a combat mission. When we landed, he was still shaking and swore he would never fly again. And he did not, either with ours or any other crew.

<u>Hitting land targets</u>
Although the main objective of the Wright Project and the 868th was to hunt for and sink Japanese ships, there were many missions when the Japanese Navy simply was not out there in our patrol area or where the weather was so bad we could not fly our mission profile, let alone detect any shipping. We discussed this back at Carney and Munda and decided that rather than just jettisoning our bombs after an unproductive mission (we were not given the option then to bring the bombs home due to the fragile construction of the airfield), we should plan in advance to attack selected land targets as secondary or default targets. We radar operators explained that since most Japanese airfields were easily discerned on our radars and located adjacent to or protruding into the sea, these were good targets for a LAB attack. This decision made, we soon found ourselves hitting the active airfields on a regular basis.

I recall one evening mission from Munda, in the dead of night, of course, the weather was atrocious with heavy turbulence throughout the flight. Our long Davis wings were flapping and St. Elmo's Light was dancing on our props and wings, building up then discharging and then building back up for another discharge. A driving rain penetrated our plane around the top gunner's turret which was above me and drained water on me as I sat at my radar. We opted to search up the coast of New Ireland and approached a secondary target, Kavieng Airdrome, located at the far tip of that island. We knew this target was well-defended as the daylight bombers who attacked Kavieng were usually intercepted by fighters and faced heavy anti-aircraft fire. But the storm was so bad we judged that they would not be able to put up fighters.

This may well have been the first time the squadron had diverted to strike a land target, and it certainly was our first time, so there was an intercom discussion among the crew about this action amid the storm. The Skipper actually took a poll on the intercom, and the decision to "go for it" was unanimous. We first made a dry run into and over the target to make sure we had it correctly identified on the radar and that the direction or bearing of our attack would carry us down the length of the airstrip. In retrospect, this may have been a bad decision—the Japanese were now alert to our presence—but this was for us a first-ever event and we wanted to get the attack right.

We went out about eight miles, did a 180-degree turn and began our attack run. When the bombardier took over on his scope, the weather was still very bad with heavy rain, but just as we were on final approach to the target, the weather broke wide open, with a bright moon illuminating the airfield. Shining down from above us, the moon guaranteed that we were clearly visible from the airfield. When we had picked the target, we had agreed to set the bomb release at maximum distribution so we could cover the entire length of the strip with a well-spaced bomb pattern. As I leaned over the bomb bay, I expected the bombs to release in sequence with concussions to match. Instead, without telling any of us, the bombardier elected at the last moment to reset the release to minimum distribution, and when he triggered the full load of 500-pounders we happened to catch a flak burst directly below the belly of the plane. The combination of bombs detonating almost together, the Japanese shell burst and the lift of the aircraft due to the sudden reduction in the weight of the bomb load, threw me out of my seat and partway across the plane. When still airborne

I managed to grab the footrest of the top turret above me and hung on for dear life. We cratered that runway, at least one part of it, and made it home without further incident.

<u>Most vulnerable time</u>
The last three miles or so of the run into the target were always very stressful to me as the radar operator because we were then very vulnerable to attack from fighter aircraft. With the radar antenna locked onto the target for this period, I could not place my system into scan mode to search for enemy aircraft. At Rabaul, Kavieng, Truk and other "hot target" locations, we knew there probably would be night fighters up on patrol looking for us, possibly being directed by Japanese radar or acoustic systems. Locked on to a steady course on the bomb run into a target for the last three to five miles at 1,500 feet placed our aircraft in a highly vulnerable situation. It was the only time I did not have the ability to scan defensively to alert our pilots to approaching night fighters and I sweated those minutes. The second the bombs were dropped, I regained control of my radar and went into full sweep mode. At this point, the pilot normally dove to the right to take evasive action but he would be looking to me to pronounce that our tail was clear.[3]

Radar teamwork

The men of the 868th counted themselves incredibly fortunate to have some of the best technicians the USAAF had to offer with the Wright Project from day one. Several of the men in the radar section that deployed to the Pacific with the original 10 aircraft and crews had been with the LAB program with Bid Dolan at Langley Field since mid-1942. They had worked hand-in-hand with the engineers of Rad Lab, Bell Laboratories and Western Electric as the prototype versions of the microwave radar sets were tested at Langley and improvements made. They had offered suggestions as the LAB components were mated to the early production versions of the SCR-717 and four elements of the LAB system brought together, tested in the air from Langley and at Wright Field and qualified as a combat system ready for deployment in combat. They also had the benefit of the two civilian technicians, Clark and Sharkey, who worked with the radarmen at Langley and volunteered to accompany the Wright Project when it flew into the Pacific.

Very importantly during the "proof of concept" phase of the LAB effort, the Rad Lab men, along with the engineers and technicians assigned to work at Langley by the involved private sector firms, interacted daily with the men selected to be radar operators on the mission aircraft. Once deployed at the forward-based airfields, radar operators often sat in the radar shack with the military technicians after each mission with the former debriefing the latter on the performance of the radar and LAB systems. These brain-storming sessions were designed to improve the performance of the systems and often resulted in mission-specific "fixes" to the equipment.

As one radarman noted, "There were no manuals, no instruction books. We were writing our own." Innovation at the squadron level was the order of the day, from the "radar cart" that was hand-crafted to roll up to the mission aircraft to perform one final check-out of the LAB system just prior to the plane's departure, to the stockpiling of rebuilt units that could be swapped out on a half-hour notice to qualify an aircraft to fly. An aircraft that failed to check-out would be swarmed over in an all-hands radar team effort and declared "mission ready" an hour later.

Radar leadership

Leadership of the unit's radar operation was critical and the Wright Project was fortunate to have Captain Ernest "Ray" Barriere as its initial "Radio Officer," as the unit roster carried him on its Movement Orders and in later Table of Organization listings. In making his report to USAAF leadership in October 1943 on the LAB program, and in subsequent debriefings with other senior officers (Colonel Edwin Aldrin at Wright Field for one), Colonel Wright singled out Barriere as the single most important officer in the squadron, ensuring that he had the performance and mission reliability of the LAB system.

Barriere was replaced on 26 June 1944 by Lieutenant Fred Howell, and again the squadron "lucked out," as one pilot put it, with the man now formally designated as the unit's Radar Officer. Howell had come to the 868th from the 31st Bombardment Squadron of the 5th Bomb Group and had been a radar devotee from the first time he sat with Barriere on Guadalcanal in September 1943. In October, he had been assigned by that bomb group's commander and LAB advocate, Colonel Unruh, to join the "Fifth Bomb Group Project." Howell had been selected by Unruh and Stud Wright as a second to Ray Barriere and a likely replacement as most assumed that Barriere would be called back to Wright Field to work on a new radar program.

Fred Howell was recognized by Brigadier General William Matheny of XIII Bomber Command with a special commendation on 17 June 1944 that commended him for "the splendid work in connection with the development and improvement of the special equipment and installations as used by an organization of this Command ... which resulted in the extremely valuable and significant improvements in equipment design, aircraft installations and training progress throughout the Army Air Forces." Howell was quick to pass most of the credit to his radar team, but the commendation had been well earned. He was promoted to captain in July 1944 and would continue to serve as the unofficial but prominent-everywhere "radar leader" of the Thirteenth Air Force through the summer of 1945.[4]

Captain Howell would be detailed in January 1945 for a special mission, selected by Lieutenant General Kenney who was then commanding the FEAF. Dispatched to Australia and later to forward airfields where Royal Australian Air Force squadrons were based, Howell schooled these units in the SCR-717 system and other electronics that were becoming standard equipment in the RAAF B-24 units being formed and rushed into combat. The Australians appreciated this assistance and gained a deep respect for Howell, who considered that he had been adopted to be one of them. He established relationships that would last for the balance of his life. The RAAF awarded Fred Howell a special commendation for his work with them and he was awarded the Bronze Star for his service to the Thirteenth Air Force from January 1944 to August 1945.[5]

To release Howell for his "special detachment" period with the Australians, he was replaced as the 868th Radar Officer by Lieutenant Don Oliver in January 1945. Trained in the U.S. before he arrived at the front, Oliver would serve ably in this position for the balance of the war.

CHAPTER 14

Ever Forward Toward Tokyo

July–September 1944

The summer of '44 in the Pacific

To the men of the 868th, positioned as they were so close to the equator, every month of the year was summer and the only change in the weather was the weekly deluge delivered by the stream of typhoons that ravaged their island bases. July began with a three-aircraft combat visit to Peleliu by the crews of Rockwood, Thomson and Rauch to beat down the island in anticipation of the U.S. Marines' invasion that was scheduled to occur six weeks later. At the southern end of the Palau group, Peleliu and Angaur were now on the list of islands to be seized and not bypassed, as was the atoll of Ulithi, the latter to be used as fleet anchorage. For the 868th, Peleliu's defense facilities and its 10,000-man Japanese garrison, including the airfield, were the designated targets. In the next few weeks, the crews of Lieutenants Nicholas, Bryan and Binford would revisit the same location and the Thirteenth Air Force daylight B-24 groups would also strike the islands.

But the main squadron attractions in July continued to be two other island bases judged to present a threat to the Allied advance across the Central Pacific—Woleai and Yap. In the case of the former, the aircrews of Beck, Conrad, DeLand, Hoffman, Nicholas, Binford and Colt, in nighttime and late afternoon raids, typically deposited nine 500-pound bombs on the airfield and its revetments to ensure that it remained inoperable. Daylight missions to the same destination usually involved delivery of thirty 100-pound bombs on or adjacent to the runway, designed to catch any visiting enemy aircraft or crews that had arrived overnight to prepare for onward missions. The anti-aircraft fire was predictably moderate to light and no intercepting fighters were encountered, leading many in the squadron to label Woleai a "milk run" mission. That month alone the 868th flew 69 missions against Woleai and, apart from a few minor flak hits and scratches, sustained no damage, reinforcing the appeal of this target. Every run to Woleai was counted as a combat "strike" and built points for rotation home and, more immediately, for a week's leave in Australia.

Yap was a similar situation, with the squadron flying against this base, visiting it every three days or so with single-aircraft missions to let the garrison there know it was being watched and suppressed. A Japanese naval mini stronghold in the western Carolines, the island held some 6,000 Army and Navy troops and offered an airfield for attacks that were being staged with mixed success against the flank of the Allied advance. Yap would be bypassed in the now tried-and-proven Allied strategy of island-hopping, but it still had to be "suppressed" and its airfield kept out of action. In July, the 868th flew 12 missions against it, some night patrols followed by strikes, and others in daylight missions accompanying other XIII Bomber Command B-24 formations.

Despite this relatively easy run of missions, the squadron continued to be plagued by operational losses. On 16 July, Lieutenant Bob Rauch and crew, lifting off from Mokerang Airfield in aircraft 806 at 2200 hours, experienced engine failures and crashed at the end of the runway. The heavily laden aircraft caught fire as it impacted the ground and exploded, blowing itself apart and tossing men around the broken and burning plane. Two crew members, Lieutenant Joseph Hackett and Technical Sergeant Harold Boggs, the plane's navigator and radio operator respectively, died in the crash. The balance of the crew, including pilot Rauch and co-pilot Michael Adamski, suffered third-degree burns, as did all of the other survivors.

Rauch's statement to the squadron's Accident Board told the tale:

> The plane checked okay for take-off, started down the runway and was doing between 120–130 mph when the plane became airborne. We were nearing the end of the runway so "gear up" was called, there was a slight mushing, a loud report and the plane lurched to one side. I tried to pull the plane into the air but it lost speed and mushed faster, until the ground was struck.

Commenting on the loss, a member of the accident investigation team found no cause other than engine failure and an inability to recover at that point in the take-off. Rauch and his crew, having experienced their second crash, were considered fortunate despite the lives lost. Of the eight survivors, six would go home to have their third-degree burns treated and two would stay to join other crews to fulfill their mission quotas.[1]

The following day, the two men who did die in the Rauch crash, Hackett and Boggs, were laid to rest with full military honors in the small but growing U.S. military cemetery near Momote Airfield, Los Negros Island. The squadron attendance was complete and when the ceremony closed, the men returned to their airplanes to prepare for the night's missions. One of Bob Rauch's best friends later remarked, "Bob was a very good pilot and a fine man but he was one of us who just should not have come to the War. He had two turns of bad luck, was lucky to go home with his burns. We would miss him, but at least he went home to his family."

July also featured an expanded training program for newly arrived crews, involving both night missions to familiarize crews with LAB procedures and daylight flying to practice formation flying, as the latter was increasingly becoming a regular feature with XIII Bomber Command. A priority was placed on improving the unit's uneven bombing skills. A favored target for the daylight flying was Manus Island, captured a few months before in late March 1944. Manus was adjacent to the Los Negros airbase at Momote and thus a few minutes flight time for the 868th and other squadrons stationed there, and it offered several areas for practice bombing sorties. LAB and daylight runs involved releasing 100-pound ordnance, some 500 being expended in 31 practice drops during the month, an "almost real" training program that allowed the squadron's newer crews to substantially improve their circular-error-probable, or CEP, bombing accuracy.

The transition within the squadron from the original Wright Project crews was ongoing and the overlap of the first replacement crews that had arrived in late 1943 and early 1944 had done much to bridge the experience gap. But the fact was that many of the summer 1944 arrivals did not have the LAB or other training required to be certified by the squadron as "mission capable." The veterans also realized that many of these crews had low levels of night-flying experience and, as a direct consequence, risked making basic mistakes in "instrument only" take-offs and landings. These deficiencies were simply a fact of where the war was and had to be mitigated as much as possible.

This shortcoming aside, the squadron continued to build its capacity during the month, with 265 officers and men assigned, including 17 combat crews. Of the latter, an average of 11 crews was available for strike missions on a given day. Apart from the crash of the Rauch crew and another (non-fatal) loss mid-month, there were no other casualties. The squadron was also encouraged by the realization that it was possible to survive if a crew went down at sea after coming off a target. The survivors of the Wagner crew and the account of their 19-day ordeal at sea when they returned to the squadron in early July, was a good testimony to that possibility.

Headed home

Vince Splane would have the distinction of being the first 868th command pilot to go home, based on a normal rotation and completion of 50-plus missions. He had served in B-17s from mid-July 1943, moved to daylight B-24s before the arrival of the Wright Project and was reassigned to fly with that "project" in late September. His orders taking him home were dated 5 July 1944 and he caught a flight on the 27th. Other men of the 868th Squadron who departed with him on the same set of orders included First Lieutenant Art Enger, Captains William Schuber and Ned Estes and Technical Sergeants Charlie Bespole, Robert Cunfer, Harold Dennis, Bill Prosser and John Young.

Of these men, Estes, Prosser, Dennis, Bespole and Cunfer were members of the original Wright Project, the Charles Rockwood crew, having arrived at Carney Field in *Madame Libby*. Bill Schuber had arrived as the bombardier on *Ramp Tramp* with the Ken Brown crew and John Young hailed from the *Coral Princess* crew of Frank Reynolds. All these men were original personalities within the squadron, the charter members of the "Snoopers old boys' club." Their departure signaled that most or all of the Wright Project men would be gone within a matter of weeks, their combat tours completed.

A second group of Wright Project officers and men received their orders in late August to "return to Continental U.S. via GAT or U.S. military aircraft." They signed their clearance sheet (equipment turn-in and debts paid), packed up their carry-on gear and headed home by air on the 25th. They flew the Nadzab–Guadalcanal–Canton Island–Hawaii–California route, gained a day somewhere along the way and started their rest leave on the 28th at Hamilton Field. For these men, it had been a year and a week since they had passed this location when they headed for Guadalcanal with Stud Wright, his 100 good men and 10 aircraft.[2]

The departure of Splane and the men who went home with him in late July, and the pending rotation home of others of the original Wright Project crews in the coming weeks, not to mention the departure of squadron commander Foster, resonated within the unit. Unavoidably there was speculation as to what the "real combat mission" count had to be for an individual or a crew to receive orders to rotate home. Many were aware that B-24 and B-17 crews in Europe and the Mediterranean Theaters had been allowed to complete their initial combat tours after only 25 missions. No one in the 868th begrudged those men their 25-missions-and-home as it was understood that the combat over Germany was inherently more challenging and dangerous, notwithstanding the 868th's recent run of losses.

There was also the minor issue, but certainly important to some who were eager to complete their tour and head home, as to what actually counted as a "combat mission" or made the grade as a credited "strike." Practice or training flights did not, check-out flights for repaired aircraft coming out of overhaul did not, of course, nor did pilot or crew qualification flights. These last-mentioned included night take-offs and landings, and LAB practice missions designed to address the inexperience of several of the new crews. Additionally, armed search missions to find crews that had become "overdue and missing," even when the search flights took aircraft within 20–30 minutes of a defended target (Truk), were not credited as combat missions. No one complained but there was always hope that a crew would catch an odd mission credit along the way. Crewmen, notably gunners, volunteered to join the crews of the daylight B-24s to gain credit for missions flown. There was also a desire to use their turret and waist guns against Japanese fighters that rose to attack the daylight formations. To all men, every mission counted.

At one point, the squadron was told that "30 was your lucky number" for rotation home, but this was soon modified to "40 or maybe more." By July 1944, the number was rumored to have crept up to "50 for sure will get you home." By that point, many aircrews simply became resigned to not knowing. Many understood that they would not even know what their magic number was until they held the orders in their hands. There was also the growing realization that the war with Japan had a long way to go. Among the pilots and aircrew, the assumption was that, even if one rotated home, it would be to train and return within a few months in the B-29 fleets then being assembled for the massive offensive against the Japanese Home Islands.

There was the companion conviction that it would probably be necessary to invade the Home Islands and fight on the ground all the way to Tokyo to bring the war to an end. This, of course, was the way the situation in Europe was playing out during the same summer of 1944. In July 1944, the Normandy invasion was but weeks behind the Allies, and German forces still had the Americans, British and Canadian Forces bottled up with resistance building. There were suggestions by American military leaders that Japan could be forced to accept surrender terms by some combination of Allied air and sea power, starving out the Japanese leadership. Still, the U.S. Marines and U.S. Army soldiers who had fought the Japanese in the islands in the Pacific knew better. The men of the 868th, then flying from Momote to clear the way for the invasion of the Philippines, which was slated to occur within a few months, were also convinced that it most probably would be a battle to the death on the ground.

No one then could have imagined the advent of the atomic bomb and its ability to force the war to a conclusion short of an actual invasion of Japan proper. The expectation was that the war would last for years, not months, and that the toll would be great for airmen as well as those on the ground. Thus, it was not unrealistic for a man going home to assume that he would be back in the Pacific, probably in less than a year, in a bigger bomber based on another island, doing battle over the cities and beaches of Japan.

The men of the 868th were not fatalistic but they were resigned to their fate and did not consider themselves to be in any way special or deserving of better treatment. In most cases, their brothers and closest friends were fighting in Normandy, Italy, Burma or China or, quite often, on other islands in the vast Pacific. Most of these men, including those of the 868th, were between the ages of 18 and 23, with "an old man" in an aircraft crew or an infantry platoon keeping pace at the age of 27 or even 30. In the 868th, some of the newly arrived pilots, navigators, bombardiers and flight crews were barely 20.

A squadron command change

On 20 August 1944, Major Leo Foster handed over command of the 868th Squadron, packed his bags and headed back across the Pacific, his tour of duty completed and a future assignment waiting. He had led the Wright Project from the day Colonel Wright handed him the baton in September 1943 and, over 11 months, had presided over the unit's transition from the 394th Squadron, to the "5th Bomb Group Project" and, finally, in January 1944, the creation of the 868th as an independent squadron within XIII Bomber Command. Foster had been with Dolan from the beginning—in Boston at MIT's Rad Lab and at Langley Field when the 1st Sea-Search Attack Group was formed. Foster had been selected by Wright as his lead pilot and the man he wanted to take command when he headed home to present his report to General Arnold. Foster piloted *Devil's Delight* across the Pacific to Guadalcanal and flew the first LAB strike missions against the Tokyo Express. His experience and leadership would be sorely missed.

During the September 1943 to August 1944 period, Foster had led the squadron through some of its darkest days, including the losses of crews and aircraft flying against Rabaul and later Truk. He had lobbied for the dispatch of replacement crews from Langley Field and the allocation of the aircraft, maintenance and support personnel needed to complete the unit as a self-sustaining squadron. One veteran 868th crewman, radarman Horace Sullivan, reflecting on Leo Foster's leadership over the critical first year in the Pacific was blunt in his praise:

> Many identify Colonels Bid Dolan and Stud Wright as the "fathers" of the Wright Project and LAB patrol bombing, but to many of us, the third leader who made it all happen was Leo Foster. He was low-key, effective and highly professional and he always got the job done. When a pilot was down sick or had been transferred and we were waiting for a replacement command pilot to join the unit, Leo Foster climbed into the left seat and took the mission. He never complained and was always there. We were deeply sorry to see him leave. But, like all of us who wanted to go home, it was his time to leave.

Foster's replacement was Major Jim Barlow, an experienced B-24 daylight command pilot who XIII Bomber Command thought was the right man for the LAB mission. Jim Barlow would face his own challenges and issues and, while he would master most of these and work diligently to keep the unit together, fate would intervene and he would be gone within five months.

Stud Wright's men depart for home

In July, the target assignments handed to the 868th by XIII Bomber Command represented a seamless transition from the previous month, given the pending invasion of the Palau Island chain's Pelileu and Angaur. The first week was all Woleai, striking to maintain maximum pressure there, and then shifting the missions for the balance of the month to hit Palau targets non-stop. The crews of Lieutenants Nicolas, Hoffman, Colt, Hickson, Thomson, Binford, Alsop, DeLand and Bryan flew every second or third day on daylight missions, interspersed with night sea-search and strike patrols, to pound Koror at the center of Palau proper, Utagal Island, Malakal and other islets that intelligence had identified as holding a Japanese presence that might be brought to bear on the invasion force approaching Peleliu and Angaur.

Reflecting the mission tempo for the above-mentioned nine crews, it was notable that, for the first time since the project's arrival a year earlier on Guadalcanal, no strike mission was flown by an original Wright Project crew during the month. As noted above, with only a couple of exceptions, these men had either departed or were standing down from combat missions to await their orders for home. The combat record of one such Wright Project pilot and crew is a useful point of reference. An "Analysis of Strike Record" memorandum for the crew of Captain Charles "Rocky" Rockwood, by the 868th Squadron for presentation to XIII Bomber Command, dated 22 July 1944 notes as follows:

Number of Strikes Scheduled	62
Number of Strikes Completed:	60
Number of Strikes Hitting Primary Target:	60
Number of Strike Turnbacks:	2
Number of Strikes Aircraft Unable to Take-off:	0

Note: The two turn-backs resulted from a failure of Special Equipment to operate.

While it is difficult to accept this exceptional level of mission performance, showing a mission completion rate of over 90 percent, it would appear that this was almost the base standard for those crews who arrived with the Wright Project, flew for the first year and survived. These men had a deep understanding of their systems, had flown hundreds of hours in the night and "under instruments" in the Dolan B-18s and Langley Field B-24s and were highly skilled coming into the program. Their aircraft maintenance crews were exceptional and were only dealing with a relatively small set of aircraft, sometimes as few as eight and never more than 12 or 14. Maintenance teams "owned" individual aircraft, at least up until the summer/fall of 1944 and crews often stuck with, and insisted on flying, "their airplanes."

The Rockwood crew's two strike "aborts," both assigned to underperforming radar or LAB equipment, is also an incredible statistic given the fact that the radar and the entire LAB system were true first-generation production versions. They were modified and repaired and constantly updated in the field, usually on an "instructions not included" basis. This analysis implies a LAB/radar readiness rate of over 95 percent as well. Given the attention that Rockwood was known to devote to the radarmen and the time he spent with them in their "radar shack" seated at the bench where work was being done, this availability rate should be expected. Still, these are impressive numbers.[3]

One of the Wright Project outliers who resisted his orders to rotate home for a rest leave and reassignment was Rocky Rockwood. He did not want to go home. Rather, he thought the war with Japan would be a long one, saw that many of the new pilots arriving were lacking experience and thought he should stay for another one-year tour with the command. He was told in no uncertain terms that, if he elected to volunteer for another tour, he would not be allowed to fly combat missions. The air taken out of his sails, Rocky accepted orders for a return to the U.S. and an onward assignment. The command rewarded his offer by allocating him the lowest priority for a return passage. Unlike his Wright Project comrades, he would travel by cargo ship and enjoy the hospitality of the newly commissioned USS *Morton*, spending 15 days on his homebound "cruise" before disembarking in San Francisco.

Aircrews and airplanes

In August, the squadron would mount a total of 53 strikes, with 38 directed at Palau-related targets and 15 assigned to Woleai. At the same time, the newer crews were receiving intensive training, mostly with practice bomb runs on nearby Kacheo Island. The goal of new commanding officer Jim Barlow was to achieve a minimum "combat qualified and available for mission assignment" goal of 15 crews. He also worked hard to secure as many of the J-model B-24s properly equipped with the latest generation of LAB gear as the system would allow. In August, the same 10 pilots and aircraft had carried the squadron baton and delivered, but it was past time to expand his team. Aircraft available to the squadron included 396, 651, 268, 271, 277, 272, 639, 819, 822, 957 and 979. These 11 aircraft would often go on a mission every other night, and properly maintaining them and declaring them "mission ready" was becoming more of a challenge.

Of the 11 aircraft regularly available to fly combat missions that month, only three—822 *Bums Away*, 651 *Ramp Tramp* and 639 *The Lady Margaret*—traced their lineage from the original stable of the 10 B-24Ds that had arrived with the Wright Project. The rest were J-models equipped with the factory-installed power turret in the nose and other structural improvements. The J-models were somewhat heavier than the D-models and consequently, many of the more seasoned pilots preferred to fly in the few Ds that were left, irrespective of the older model's vulnerability to head-on fighter attacks. But more crews were scheduled to arrive in the coming weeks with their J-models, so things were looking up in the aircraft and aircrew department at month's end. Also, to the positive, the squadron lost no aircrews or aircraft during August and managed to avoid serious illness with zero outbreaks of sickness.

On the road again—Noemfoor bound

In the last week of August, the FEAF of Lieutenant General George Kenney ordered XIII Bomber Command to move its forces forward and directed that the 868th relocate to a new operations base with all due dispatch. The new home was Noemfoor Island, located about 60 miles to the west of Biak. This small (10-mile diameter) island had been the site of a Japanese garrison that included three airfields, two of which were functioning and one still under construction when the island was assaulted by Allied forces on 2 July.

The thrust of MacArthur's forces through this area, moving ever closer to the immediate goal of an invasion to recapture the Philippines, Operation *Cyclone*, included the occupation, expansion and use of Noemfoor's airfields. With Biak secured, and Mokmer Airfield there operational by late June, it was essential that Noemfoor be seized and established as a forward airbase. The island had been defended by 2,000 Japanese Army troops and, although the island was declared "secured" on 7 July, resistance did not end on the ground until 31 August, two days after the arrival of the first 868th aircraft.

The 868th flew its last mission from Momote, Los Negros, on 28 August when the crews of Lieutenants Alsop and Bryan struck Koror in Palau, departing for their missions as the squadron scrambled to pack its gear and move out. The Thirteenth Air Force allocated no fewer than 62 C-47 flights to bring the unit to Noemfoor, beginning the lift on the 29th and completing it four days later. Within a day of the invasion, as the airfields were occupied and the Japanese pushed back, Australian and U.S. construction battalions arrived to repair and expand the air facilities, with Kornasoren featured as the primary airfield.

First to arrive on the island was an RAAF P-40 Kittyhawk squadron that flew in on the 7th as the fighting was still going on. Two weeks later, they were joined by several U.S. P-38 squadrons and the following week the 868th was told to expedite its relocation. Engineers moved quickly to build out two parallel 7,000-foot runways at Kornasoren, and these were being finished as the SB-24s touched down. The ground echelon with the squadron's heavy equipment followed within two weeks. The construction of a new base camp for the squadron seemed to occur at a blazing pace. Tents and other structures were set up, mess facilities established, the mechanics accommodated and the radar team allocated its special quarters. There was even a squadron outdoor movie area where the first movie was shown on the evening of 31 August. The speed with which this base camp was created was a testimony to the incredible progress the U.S. had made in organizing its logistics and base-building operations.[4]

Striking west from Noemfoor

The basing of FEAF units at Noemfoor allowed B-24 bomb groups and their squadrons to mount strikes deep into the Dutch East Indies. The important targets in this region were Japanese facilities and infrastructure that Tokyo considered critical to its ability to prosecute the war and ensure the survival of the empire. Japan's master strategy to create, by force of arms, its own Greater East Asia Co-Prosperity Sphere in Southeast Asia, involved a "strike south" move in December 1941 that seized the Dutch East Indies. Here the natural resources already being exploited by the colonial powers and Allies, including the extraction of oil, tin and rubber, were found in abundance. The provision of these resources to the Home Islands to feed Japan's war industries, and in particular the access allowed to the oil and petroleum needed for its ships and aircraft, was an overriding obsession for the empire. It had also provided a self-serving rationale to go to war against the United States.

Japan's battle fleet required access to oil and impressive collections of battleship groups and carrier forces still existed to challenge the Allied advance as the latter gathered ever more momentum. Many of the key fleet units had been temporarily relocated to the Borneo area for the sole reason that access to increasingly scarce fuel oil could be assured given the proximity of oil fields and refineries. A core component in the Allied strategy to take the war to the Japanese Home Islands was a determined offensive to starve Tokyo of the essential materials sourced in and shipped from Burma, Malaya, the Dutch East Indies, the Philippines and Formosa. The effort to sever this lifeline between the resource base and the Japanese homeland had been far advanced by the U.S. submarine fleet, with an all-out offensive that had ravaged Japan's merchant fleet over the 1943–44 period. But the killing blow that would deny this resource could best be struck at its base; that is, a systematic destruction of the oil facilities themselves by delivering bombs on targets.

Kenney's FEAF had developed plans to send its B-24 bomber squadrons against the oil facilities in the Dutch East Indies in a determined and sustained effort to destroy them in place. It was recognized that these facilities were heavily defended and were serviced by Japanese engineers and labor that could repair damage and resume production within a matter of weeks after being attacked. The solution was to bomb heavily and often. B-24s ranging from Noemfoor would begin this task in late September and the 868th would be at the proverbial tip of the bomber spear, as always.

September missions

With this move to Noemfoor, the 868th fell under the temporary control of the Fifth Air Force and was directed tactically by that entity's 309th Bomb Wing, in a further evolution of the FEAF. During the first two weeks of September, the 868th took a few days to settle into their new surroundings, maintain the aircraft, tune up the LAB systems and prepare for the next phase of the offensive. The invasion of Palau's two southern islands of Peleliu and Angaur was scheduled to begin on the 15th and all assumed the Japanese fleet might well sortie from its East Indies bases to challenge the Allied force there.

On 7 September, the squadron launched its first combat strike from Noemfoor, and for the next eight days pounded the Palau main islands to deny the Japanese any ability to base aircraft there that might disrupt the pending invasion. The 868th sent three aircraft to Palau over four straight nights, from 7 to 10 September, and doubled down on the 11th to put five crews overhead throughout the night to harass the defenders with loads of 100-pound bombs distributed over several hours. Hit were the Ngesebus and Peleliu airdromes, the seaplane base at Arakabasan and Palau proper. An atypical mission on the 9th had a three-bomber attack switch to 500-pound ordnance for the first target mentioned above. This "maximum squadron effort" involved the crews of Lieutenants Bryan, DeLand, Hoffman, Colt, Alsop, Thomson, Hickson, Nicholas and the new squadron commander Major Jim Barlow, with these crews collectively making 22 strikes. These men were now the squadron's new "first team" and as such, they were destined to carry the reputation of the Wright Project and the 868th into its next year of combat.

On the 15th, as the 1st Marine Division went ashore at Peleliu and Angaur under the protection provided by U.S. Navy carrier and surface forces, the 868th rested and refitted. With fighting underway in the Palaus, the mission pivoted to attack suspected Japanese airdromes and sea routes further to the west that might contest the ongoing island combat. The squadron began its "Celebes Campaign" on the 16th with the Nicholas and Bryan crews flying deep to the west to hit Manado in the Celebes. The airfield was the target and the LAB run into that airdrome placed a total of twelve 500-pound bombs down its runway and hangar area. Manado had been in Japanese hands since it was invaded in early 1942 and it had remained an active airbase and staging site for bombing runs against Biak during the fight for that island. The city itself, its two airports, a seaplane facility and its port were all valid targets for the squadron, and disruption of Japanese activity in this area was a tactical priority.

Over the next 10 days, continuing a near-maximum effort, the squadron sent 22 missions to the Celebes, with the same 10 crews committed, joined by the newly arrived crews of Lieutenants Muller, Wallace and Smith. On "another first" for the squadron, over three successive nights, the Smith, Wallace and Binford crews flew the length of the Makassar Strait, deploying the LAB systems to search for surface targets while gathering weather data needed by the 5th Bomb Group for its daylight missions. The Makassar Strait runs between the Dutch East Indies islands of Borneo and Sulawesi and connects the Celebes Sea in the north to the Java Sea to the south. This relatively narrow body of water was an important shipping route for the Japanese and was a planned route of transit for daylight B-24s preparing to attack targets further in the west, hence the requirement for real-time weather information.

Other targets in the Celebes mini-offensive included Gorontalo warehouse and shipment point, where two SB-24s struck the first blow on 16 September to disrupt Japanese military supplies. They utilized the tried-and-true mission plan that had the LAB system define the target and the route of approach, confirming the "IP" or initial point for the run into the point of bomb release, with the bomb toggle triggered automatically by the Norden bombsight. The aircraft came out of the night, achieving complete surprise, and returned unharmed.

Another typical mission to the Celebes was that of Lieutenants Muller and Hoffman in 899 and 900, arriving over Manado an hour apart in the early morning hours of 22 September. They struck the port area with a combination of general-purpose and incendiary bombs, smashing the jetty, warehouses and cargo handling facilities, triggering a series of secondary explosions and setting fires. The LAB system allowed a radar-assisted approach; no anti-aircraft or fighter opposition was encountered. A third SB-24 assigned to this mission, that of the crew of Lieutenant Hanff, failed to join the mission and the two attacking SB-24s only noted its absence after the attack runs.

Upon their safe return to Noemfoor, the Muller and Hoffman crews discovered that their wingman had gone down with all hands shortly after take-off from Noemfoor.[5]

Paying the price

The back-to-back campaigns took their toll and September was a month that claimed too many fine crews and their aircraft. The toll was particularly heavy among the crews who had most recently joined the squadron from the United States, some only in the previous two weeks.

On 9 September, Lieutenant Don Thomson took the crew of Lieutenant Dwight Barry into the night as part of a three-aircraft strike on Ngesebus Island. Thomson was piloting the veteran *Ramp Tramp* as a check pilot to qualify the recently arrived crew on its first combat mission. Also on board was veteran bombardier Lieutenant Robert Curnow in his role as an Instructor Bombardier to observe and qualify his fellow bombardier. This gave the aircraft a complement of 12 men that evening.

As the Liberator lifted off, an engine failed and the landing gear refused to retract. The pilot struggled to retain lift, establish control and jettison the bomb load to permit a safe recovery. The bomber failed to gain altitude, still carrying a maximum load of fuel and twelve 500-pound bombs. Seconds later, the crash terminated squadron mission 868-312 as the bomber slammed into the water and broke apart, killing five young men and injuring seven. To the relief of the crew and to the surprise of many on the ground, none of the bombs exploded as the plane impacted the water, allowing the rescue of the survivors.

Mission Report 868-312 contained the following statement from command pilot Thomson:

> On runup the right mag on Number Two engine dropped 50 RPMs. Take-off was normal and in sufficient time at 130 MPH. After plane was airborne, the landing gear could not be retracted because of a jammed solenoid block. At 100 feet in altitude, the plane began to mush when engine number two manifold pressure dropped to 40 inches. The plane continued to mush as the altimeter reached field elevation and more elevator tab was applied to keep the plane airborne. The plane struck the water with noted airspeed at 120 MPH.[6]

On take-off, six men were on the flight deck, three were in the flight deck well and the remaining crew were in the rear of the aircraft. The five men who died that night were the navigator Lieutenant Sterling Shipla, bombardier Robert Roehl, radar operator Thomas Milton and gunners Michael Rakiec and Edmund Russell. The other seven men were hospitalized at the local 71st Evacuation Hospital.

On the night of the Thomson/Barry crash, three SB-24s had been dispatched to strike in sequence the island airbase of Ngesebus in the Palaus—the Thomson/Barry crew in 651, the Art DeLand crew in their regular 396 and the Bryan crew in 654. The latter experienced fuel leaks in tanks three and four in the first minutes of its outbound leg and Bryan opted to return to base to swap his crew into another SB-24 to complete the mission. As they approached the airfield, they spotted the just-crashed Thomson/Barry aircraft in the water and were instructed by the tower to circle the wreckage to assist the rescue boats that had been dispatched. Bryan dropped flares, guided the boats in and coordinated searchlights that reached out from the field to illuminate the wrecked airplane. The DeLand crew reached their target, bombed well and returned to learn the fate of their fellow mission aircraft and crew.

On 21 September, Lieutenant Peter Colt, who had been designated one of four squadron "check pilots" in late August, sat alongside as First Lieutenant Isaac Hanff lifted off at an estimated "absolute maximum weight" of 72,000 pounds. Hanff's 277 was the third aircraft in the three-plane strike headed to Manado, with the Muller and Hoffman crews noted above. At some point shortly after take-off, they developed engine trouble, lost and regained altitude and reported to the tower that they had lost an engine, had a windmilling prop and would attempt to return to Kornasoren. Although the crew apparently did manage to jettison the bomb load, they were unable to maintain flight and crashed into the sea five miles southwest of the runway. All 12 men aboard 277 were lost. In this case, a Royal Australian Navy corvette happened to be in the area, patrolling for Japanese submarines, and was quickly on the scene. The airfield put up its spotter plane, but within minutes the SB-24J and its crew were gone. No bodies were recovered as the sea had them.[7]

At that point in their combat tour, Isaac Hanff and his crew had completed 20 missions, and Hanff was about to qualify as a senior or "command" pilot, as some veterans still referred to this elevated status. He had been designated a "check pilot" by squadron orders a week before. Colt's presence was apparently required to further qualify Hanff and his crew; Colt was eager to join Hanff, his co-pilot Damon Brown, bombardier Morris Zeiler, navigator Thomas Philbrick and the balance of the crew for this mission.[8]

On 22 September, the squadron appointed Lieutenant Clayton Seavers, a friend of both Colt and Hanff, to "inventory and dispose of the effects" of the 11 men who died in the crash, all officially declared "missing in action." Formal War Department notifications were then on their way to their families, and the squadron commander, Major Jim Barlow, had sat down to write personal letters of condolence to the families of each of his lost men.

Three days later, on 24 September, disaster struck again when the crew of Lieutenant Muller, returning from another successful mission to attack Manado, ditched two miles out, with the loss of three killed. Eight survivors were rescued but three were badly injured. Unlike the water crashes of the two other downed aircraft, which occurred on take-off and were related to equipment failure (combinations of lost engine power and landing gear that failed to retract), this crash appears to have resulted from a failure to properly set the radio altimeter. The plane was basically flown into the water on approach.

The squadron assessment stated, in part:

> … the pilot failed to call for field pressure, due to his having changed his altimeter on his bombing run, and although the plane was in the landing pattern preparing to land, no boosters were on and the landing gear remained up. The altimeter indicated a setting of 30.05 when actual field pressure was 29.8. When the pilot realized that his altitude was under 200 feet, he immediately pulled back on the controls to gain altitude, but the plane struck the water.

Seven men survived this crash and the three who died were declared "killed in action" based on the recovery of their remains from the aircraft. Lost were the bombardier, Lieutenant Vernon Landhuis, radar operator James Burnett and engineer Edwin Stevens. Inventories of their personal effects were made, letters were sent and the surviving crew members, most with minor injuries, checked out of the hospital and were back with the squadron within days.[9]

Notwithstanding the losses incurred by the squadron, the wholesale relocation of the unit from Momote to Noemfoor at the opening of the month, as well as the demands of the two "maximum effort" assignments, the 868th managed to turn in an impressive September. The official record details 20 missions that placed 45 aircraft over their targets, dropping a total of 84 tons of bombs on Manado (28 tons) and Gorontalo (3 tons) in the Celebes; and Ngesebus (36 tons), Peleliu (10 tons) and Arakabesan (7 tons) in the Palaus.[10]

The combination of these four aircrew and aircraft losses over the July–September period, and the fact that six aircrews in total were affected by the four crashes, with command pilots Colt and Thomson flying with the Hanff and Barry crews respectively as check pilots, was disruptive to the integrity and morale of the small unit. The squadron swallowed hard and went on, with many of the surviving and injured crewmen returning to duty and requalifying with different crews for combat missions.

Within the other B-24 squadrons of XIII Bomber Command, where losses on daylight missions were accepted as the norm, the 868th was perceived as a high-risk, high-loss outfit. The fact that almost all the 868th aircraft crashes occurred in the black of night, often on take-off as the other crews sat watching the nightly outdoor movie, or on an aircraft's return to base in the early morning hours when daylight crews still slept, only deepened the impression that the Snooper crews were different, true risk takers if not risk seekers. This image did not encourage personal relationships outside the social confines of the squadron and the men of the 868th, both officers and enlisted, tended to "keep to their own kind" on the base.

The run of losses and the turnover of the aircrews as replacements arrived also altered the unit's overall dynamic. Some of the pilots and their aircrews noticed that the squadron's aircraft mechanics and technicians, and the non-flying operational personnel, seemed more reluctant to befriend those who flew. This was a natural reaction to the reality that the men who did not go into the sky at night had seen too many of the aircrews that they had bonded with not come back. But as September closed out, the unit considered itself to be in relatively good shape and seemed prepared to go the distance as the Pacific War advanced.

Balikpapan and Makassar Strait

October 1944

Closing with the Home Islands

In October 1944, the parallel drives by Allied forces across the Pacific were beginning to converge on Japan's inner defense perimeter. In the Central Pacific, the U.S. Navy-led task forces had stormed the Marianas, capturing Saipan, Tinian and Guam. The fight over the Marianas had brought the Japanese carrier fleets out in force and the defeat delivered to them in the air had decimated that once-elite force, effectively terminating Japan's carrier threat for the balance of the war. U.S. Navy F6F Hellcat fighters dominated the battle and, in company with the gunners of well-screened U.S. Navy task groups, shot hundreds of aircraft out of the sky in engagements that were dramatically one-sided. Most of what had remained of the cadre of Japan's elite pilots and aircrew were lost in this exchange; such men were irreplaceable. The remnants would go home to prepare the last lines of defense for the air battles that all assumed would come to mainland Japan.

To the south, MacArthur's Southwest Pacific forces had rolled up the coast of New Guinea, bypassing stranded Japanese garrisons which were being systematically isolated and literally starved out of the war. With the invasions of Biak and beyond, these U.S. Army and Allied forces had penetrated the Dutch East Indies, all to prepare for the reconquest of the Philippines. The timing of that invasion had been advanced from the original plan by a month and would begin on the island of Leyte in October. In the weeks that followed, MacArthur's offensive would move to Luzon and eventually involve the battle of Manila. The Japanese would continue to contest the Philippines for the balance of the war by retreating into the mountains and jungles, but the islands would be declared liberated in late 1944.

The 868th was still with the Thirteenth Air Force which was one element of the now-integrated FEAF. The Thirteenth served in the good company of the Fifth and, eventually, the Seventh Air Forces. In this combined air armada, the 868th always seemed to be positioned at the front of MacArthur's advance, relocating to base themselves where the SB-24s could reach the deepest into the hostile territory of Japan. The U.S. approach to the Philippines both complimented the Central Pacific offensive and competed with that U.S. Navy-led drive in the war's advanced stages. Rivalries aside, the two columns of advance were inexorably converging to bring the war to Japan proper.

In October 1944, the Allied master plan to accomplish this was still being formulated and questions remained as to which islands or land areas would be invaded on the path to the Home Islands. The working assumption, a consensus estimate accepted as fact by all involved U.S. and Allied planners at every level, was that there would be no option but to invade the Home Islands to force the surrender, probably at the very gates of the Imperial Palace in Tokyo. The war was reasonably projected to last well into late 1946, if not the following year.

In this same timeframe of October 1944, the efficacy of the strategic air war that the USAAF planned to wage against Japan from the massive airbase complexes under construction in the Marianas was yet to be demonstrated. On 12 October, as the 868th was launching toward targets in the Makassar Strait and the Balikpapan oil refineries, the first B-29 Superfortress of XXI Bomber Command touched down at Isley Field on Saipan. The squadrons of the 73rd Bombardment Wing were joining the war from their training bases in Kansas and beginning the tune-up for operations against Japan that would begin three weeks later.[1]

Major General Haywood Hansell would initially lead XXI Bomber Command, an organization that was chartered to operate independent of both MacArthur and Central Pacific chief Admiral Nimitz. Hansell would have his ideas as to how best to employ his fleets of B-29s and other air commanders would have their own. Curtis LeMay was still waiting in the wings and the B-29 offensive would get off to an uneven start that would leave many leaders uncertain of the ability of the force to accelerate, let alone determine, the outcome of the war.

In October 1944, many of these issues were still in the future, as was their resolution. In the meantime, the SB-24s of the 868th and their daylight sister B-24s would grind out the war by hitting and wearing down the Japanese wherever they could find them. One less barrel of precious oil or aviation gas denied to the Home Islands, or one less ship to transport the same or bring home stranded Japanese infantrymen to fight on the beaches of Kyushu or Honshu, made a difference. While matters of strategic planning and invasion options were above the pay grades of the men who climbed into their aircraft on Noemfoor and other island airstrips, they all knew that they had their roles to play in this greater scheme of war in the Pacific.

Missions to Balikpapan

In the early morning hours, as September clicked into October, the B-24s of the Thirteenth and Fifth Air Forces were winging their way toward the oil fields and refineries of Balikpapan. Their attack would be the first of a dedicated campaign directed at the heart of Japan's petroleum resources in the Dutch East Indies. This first mission was timed to strike those facilities at daybreak on 1 October.

The previous three nights, to pave the way for the FEAF's initial effort, the 868th had sent SB-24s to patrol the route that the daylight squadrons would take, reporting any shipping that could give the alarm on the pending attack. The carefully probing Snoopers approached within 50 miles or so of the target, confirming land features and radar signal returns and scouting for new enemy airfields that the planners may have missed. However, the primary mission of the Snooper's three-night sweep was to report on the weather conditions the bomber formations would face on their way to the target.

The crews of Captains Earle Smith and Dave Wallace, both having just arrived and flying one of their first missions, and that of Charles "Chuck" Binford, provided this "weather service" reconnaissance for their daylight brethren. The SB-24s on these flights were configured as "unarmed" aircraft with their bomb load swapped out to accommodate extra fuel tanks in the bomb bays and reduced ammunition loads to further extend their range and flight duration. These flights established a pattern that would prevail in the months ahead, the 868th providing a pre-mission weather recon service and, in the strikes, a pathfinding or navigational escort role for formations of daylight B-24 squadrons tasked with assaulting unfamiliar targets at extreme ranges.

The SCR-717-B radar systems and LAB equipment that were standard features in the SB-24s, and not present in the daylight B-24s, allowed the 868th aircraft to navigate with confidence through the adverse weather to pinpoint the target, delivering the bomber groups to their IP for the bomb run. The XIII Bomber Command meteorologists anticipated that the weather fronts along the mission routes would challenge the larger formations and likely disrupt their approaches to the targets. These concerns over the issues related to weather would, unfortunately, be proven to be correct in the weeks ahead. But with Balikpapan considered for good reason to be the "Ploesti of the Pacific,"[2] there was every reason to attempt these missions.

On 1 October, the 5th and 307th Bomb Groups of the Thirteenth Air Force, joined by the 90th Bomb Group of the Fifth Air Force, attacked Balikpapan in three waves. The Bomber Barons, the Long Rangers and "Jolly Rogers" each sent 24 aircraft, beginning at 40 minutes after midnight, with a B-24 lifting off every 90 seconds from Kornasoren Airfield. This was a 1,243-mile moonlit mission, a nearly 2,500-mile round trip, and XIII Bomber Command would claim this as "the longest daylight formation ever flown by B-24s up to this point in the war." Leading this formation attack was 5th Bomb Group Commander Colonel Thomas Musgrave and this mission, and the series of attacks on Balikpapan that followed, would be regarded as one of the group's best efforts of the war.[3]

When the 5th Bomb Group's Liberators crossed over the Celebes, about two hours before the first wave of the attack reached its target, two Japanese fighters appeared to pace the leading aircraft, relaying information ahead to the defenders. When the B-24s entered the target area, there were 30-plus fighters in the air to greet them. The flak gunners were also well prepared and at their guns, throwing up fire that was heavy and accurate. The Japanese fighter pilots were graded as "experienced" by the bomber crews and they pressed their attacks on the Liberators, including head-on runs. The formation was bombing visually with the Norden bombsight and the group found that its primary target, the Pandansari refinery, was obscured by cumulus clouds. A quick transition to bomb the secondary target allowed the 23 aircraft of the group that reached the target to bomb from 12,000 feet with 60 percent of the bombs impacting the related facility. Anti-aircraft fire damaged 15 of the B-24s and the combination of this intense flak and the fighter passes claimed three of the Bomber Barons and their crews.

The Long Rangers arrived over the target five minutes later to find the entire area blanketed in cloud cover, forcing the aircraft to bomb by radar, bomb through the clouds or divert to hit the nearby paraffin plant. The Fifth Air Force's Jolly Rogers met even denser cloud cover, with some aircraft bombing based only on an "estimated time over target" basis. All aircraft came off the target with the fighters focused on hunting down bombers that had been damaged by ground fire encountered over the refinery complexes.

FEAF intelligence assessed that the Pandansari refinery alone supplied no less than 12 percent of Japan's entire supply of aviation fuel. Sinking tankers on their way to Japan was one way to cut off the supply reaching the Home Islands but taking out the plant that produced it was far better. Of the 66 planes that made it to the target, four were lost. The gunners claimed nine intercepting fighters shot down. Many aircraft came home damaged with wounded crew members; several of these aircraft were fortunate to recover at all, with fuel tanks dry and engines starved of fuel as they taxied to their hardstands at Kornasoren.

The mission was declared a success and while it is probable that claims of extensive refinery damage were inflated, the B-24 crews had proved their worth as a long-range threat to critical Japanese infrastructure. This strategic asset would, from this point forward, be exposed to disruption if not destruction, and the Japanese would be forced to divert front-line aircraft to defend these facilities. They would also be compelled to commit scarce resources for repair and restoration if they were to continue to depend on these facilities to provide the empire's petroleum lifeblood. In this case, they had no option but to do so.

On 5 October, as a follow-up to the initial strike, the B-24 bomb groups of the Thirteenth Air Force went back, again unescorted by U.S. fighters, with the squadrons of the 307th Bomb Group in the lead. The Liberators were met by over 40 interceptors over the target and these defenders stayed with and attacked the formation for over an hour. This time the Long Rangers lost five B-24s and claimed 40 fighters shot down. The 5th Bomb Group was close behind and placed 19 aircraft over the Edeleanu refinery, losing two of their number.

On this mission, Lieutenant Hickson and crew of the 868th accompanied the 307th in a lead role to provide radar-enhanced navigation to the target. Once arrived, with the targets in the optics of the Norden bombsights, Hickson and crew dropped to the side and fell into formation to deliver 897's load of ten 250-pound bombs onto the refinery.[4]

Two days later, Lieutenants Robert Alsop and Robert Thompson and their crews went back to bomb and harass the refineries with night missions, bombing by radar, and, on the 9th, it was the turn of Nicolas and Wallace. By this point, the 868th team of intelligence officers and photo interpreters were getting the full measure of the layouts of the various targets in and around Balikpapan, mapping the flak positions and calculating more precise landmarks that would assist the LAB radar operators to select and navigate to the choice targets. Targeting became a plant by plant, production line by line, storage tank by tank exercise, right down to identifying the barracks where the gunners would sleep and from which they would have to dash to their weapons.

On the third large group daylight mission on 10 October, respecting the severity of the Japanese fighter threat, 27 Morotai-based P-47 and P-38 fighters were sent along as escorts. These fighters had their "legs" extended with the provision of large drop tanks that allowed them the make the mission distance with some minutes to spare over the target. It was another instance of innovation driven by the acute need to protect the bombers over the target. On this occasion, the Fifth and Thirteenth Air Forces combined to send a "big show" attack with no fewer than 107 B-24s dispatched to the Balikpapan targets.

During this mission, the 868th was tasked with flying in front of the daylight formations with two SB-24s paving the way to distribute bundles of "window" to jam the Japanese radar systems.[5] Bomber command intelligence suspected that the first generation of such radar systems was installed and operating to alert and direct Japanese interceptors. At 60 miles from the target, each aircraft began pitching a thousand pounds of this material into the airstream from 10,000 feet to jam and confuse any radar systems attempting to track the incoming daylight formations. These missions were flown by the 868th crews of Dave Wallace and Robert Nicolas who then slid back into the formations to drop their reduced bomb loads.

The result of this attack was judged to be "exceptional" with great and lasting damage delivered to the primary target, the Pandansari refinery complex. Over and beyond the target, 90 Japanese interceptors rose to do battle with the escort fighters and a major air battle developed. More than 30 Japanese Army and Navy fighters were claimed as shot down by the Allied fighters and gunners. Four of the Fifth Air Force B-24s were lost to anti-aircraft fire and the Japanese interceptors, and once again, many of the Liberators limped home with damage and casualties.[6]

On the 12th, the recently arrived crew of Lieutenant Robert Cooke hit the Pandansari refinery with LAB precision, and on the 17th, Bob Thompson and crew struck the same target again, both arriving in the dark of night with LAB radar guiding them in. On the night of 13/14 October, Dave Wallace and crew came in at 1,000 feet to deliver a LAB attack on the main Pandansari plant to find fighters waiting for them. The radar allowed Wallace to avoid them and he put bombs into the still-smoldering works. His crew counted 20 searchlights reaching out to find their plane and when they captured it, they held 902 for its entire run. The lights allowed the ground gunners plenty of time to bracket and hit the Liberator with accurate fire and the crew came home to report that the flak men seemed to be getting a lot better at their trade. On 16 October, Lieutenant Cooke returned to keep the pressure on the Pandansari defenders with a radar-assisted bomb run. His mission put six bombs on the target which was still smoldering and sparking from the previous assaults.[7]

On 18 October, the Thirteenth Air Force sent 52 B-24s against the Balikpapan complexes but adverse weather forced the bombers to drop through the clouds based on estimates of time over target, with the result judged to be "highly uncertain." FEAF fighters again accompanied the B-24 squadrons, with 70 dispatched but only eight managing to find their way to the target area. Typhoon-quality weather tossed and disbursed bomber and fighter alike and turn backs were the order of the day, but there were no interceptions and no aircraft lost. The disappointing results of this mission brought home once again the frustrations of the radar-deficient daylight bombers on long-range missions where the weather made it a challenge to arrive over the target. Once arrived, after a six-hour plus flight to get there, too often cloud cover denied the formations the ability to release bombs visually with the Norden bombsight with any degree of accuracy or confidence. A huge effort for both the fighter and bomber commands was denied success by the elements encountered. LAB-quality radar was not the entire answer but in the cases of these exceptionally challenging missions, it would have helped significantly to increase the chance of success.

Two days later, another new arrival to the 868th Squadron, Lieutenant Green Wadsworth and his crew, found the lube oil plant at Balikpapan and deposited ten 250-pound bombs in its midst. His crew saw the fires they had started from 30 miles away as they made a clean escape for home. The objectives of these independent missions by the aircraft of the 868th, usually timed to arrive in the hours between midnight and before dawn, was both to disrupt those on the ground that were attempting to repair damaged facilities and to erode the defender's ability to oppose an incoming daylight formation strike. Photo intelligence gathered during the daylight missions also allowed operational planners to pinpoint higher value facilities that would be particularly vulnerable to LAB runs. In the case where the next morning brought no daylight strike, the SB-24 attack would have served to harass the defenders, upsetting their routine and wearing them down physically and mentally. The intensity of these strikes by the 868th and the damage delivered by the LAB pinpoint attacks seemed to do just that.[8]

The following day, on 21 October, some 98 B-24s from the Fifth and Thirteenth Air Force returned to strike the Edeleanu refinery and again enjoyed the escort of P-47s and P-38s from the former Air Force and more P-38s from the latter. The fighter battle was intense and the U.S. escorts lost five of their number in exchange for claiming 30 shootdowns of the opposition. Only one B-24 was lost. On this occasion, the 68th Fighter Squadron had sent its P-38s from an advance base at Middleburg Island on an escort mission of nearly 1,900 miles, an impressive achievement at this stage of the war.

On that same day, shortly after midnight, several hours before the daylight aircraft arrived, Lieutenant Dave Wallace struck alone with a LAB attack on the nearby Balikpapan lube oil plant. This was a return visit to the same facility that the Wadsworth crew had damaged; Wallace dropped bundles of "window" before and during the attack to confuse the defenders by simulating a much greater force. Searchlights stabbed into the night in an attempt to find the SB-24 but failed to do so until after the bomb run. They caught him as his bombs detonated and held him for two full minutes; anti-aircraft fire was heavy and close but damage to the Liberator was minimal. As Wallace left the blazing lube plant, an interceptor was detected by the SCR-717-B operator so, when the fighter closed to engage, Wallace dove away, pouring on the power to disappear into the night. The crew had lifted 897 off the airfield at 1600 hours, hit the target at midnight and recovered at home base as the sun rose at 0700, completing a 15-hour mission.

In these five raids over a three-week period, some 321 B-24 sorties had placed 433 tons of bombs on or near their Balikpapan targets, claiming the destruction of Edeleanu and the crippling of the larger Pandansari facilities. However, the cost of this mini-offensive against Balikpapan was significant, some 22 B-24s were lost in combat or operationally, in addition to nine of their escort fighters. And the human component was tangible, 200 crewmen had been shot down or crash-landed after the attack on the way home. While 60 were rescued by U.S. Navy PBYs or submarines tasked to search for downed crews, letters would go out to the families of over 140 men to explain that they were now officially declared to be "missing in action" and to acknowledge the sacrifice they had made for their nation.

The enemy in the air

In these battles over the targets against which the 868th and the sister B-24s of the Thirteenth Air Force flew in late 1944 and into the spring of 1945, particularly the strikes against shipping in the Makassar Strait and the oil facilities on Borneo, many of the fighters that rose to intercept the Snoopers likely belonged to the Japanese Navy's 381st *Kokutai*. While fighter units of the Japanese Army Air Force were also active in these areas, as witnessed during the many encounters with interceptors described by B-24 crews as Oscars, it appears the Japanese Navy took lead responsibility in the defense of critical sites in the more western Dutch East Indies. The 381st *Kokutai* was organized in Japan for dispatch to the Netherlands East Indies in late 1943 and began to populate airbases there a few weeks later. This deployment anticipated the approach to the Borneo–Celebes–Java region of the East Indies by Kenney's FEAF. The *Kokutai's* basing assumed that these valuable shipping and oil facilities would become vulnerable to Allied air attacks for the first time in the war by late 1944.

By mid-1944, the 381st *Kokutai* had on strength some 50 fighters, including 40-plus A6M Zeros and 10 of the latest generation naval fighter, the J2M *Raiden* (Thunderbolt), assigned the Allied code name "Jack." In addition, over the course of late 1944 and early 1945, no fewer than 10 J1N1-S *Gekkō* night fighters joined this *Kokutai*. This combination of interceptor aircraft was stationed throughout the islands including Laikan airdrome on Makassar, Kendari in the Celebes, Balikpapan on the coast of Borneo, Surabaya on Java and other locations. A typical deployment at a major base, such as Kendari, Balikpapan or Batavia, would include a dozen or more Zeros, several "Jacks" and a few of the night fighters. The outlying airfields would see the rotation of six or more aircraft, assigned to defend a target to which the FEAF had shifted its attention.

At the time of the 868th attacks on the Balikpapan oil facilities and other petroleum-related land targets and oil tankers, the Japanese Navy had almost 90 aircraft scattered among a dozen airfields available to contest the air over the squadron's targets. During the larger daylight B-24 formation attacks on Balikpapan, the defenders claimed to have shot down 80 B-24s (the actual B-24 loss was 17 to all causes over this period) in exchange for the loss of only eight defending aircraft. The actual attrition suffered by the 381st was much higher, particularly when the FEAF developed a plan to send U.S. fighter escorts all the way to the target with the B-24s. The defenders were also crippled by the shortage of spare parts and the absence of skilled maintenance crews, with more than half of the aircraft on hand unable to fly. This was also a consequence of the ongoing disruption to movement within the region delivered by the incessant Allied air attacks and by Japan's increasing inclination to send aircrews and skilled mechanics back to the homeland to prepare for combat there.

By early spring 1945, with its pilots and aircraft exhausted and increasingly cut off from the Home Islands, most of what was left of the 381st was called home. There the unit would reorganize and replenish itself to prepare for the forthcoming battle over Japan proper. Two other points of interest are worth mentioning. First, accounts of this Japanese Navy air unit noted that they deployed the so-called 3-GO airburst bomb against the B-24s and considered these unusual weapons to be successful, even though they were anything but. The Zeros typically approached the B-24s from several thousand feet above and released these parachute-retarded explosives to detonate as they passed through the bomber formations. Success was extremely rare, with the 868th aircrews almost dismissing the weapons as a nuisance. More ominously, the presence of the night fighters assigned to these units suggests that several of these may have been successful in attacking B-24 formations, not to mention the SB-24s prowling the Makassar Strait at night. If this did occur, it appears that the aircrews of the 868th were not even aware that their old foe, the "Irving," was hunting them at night.[9]

Sweet home Noemfoor

September had allowed the 868th to settle into their new camp on the sidelines of the growing Kornasoren airfield complex, and as October moved toward November, the logistics support delivered by the U.S. Army and Navy engineers and supply personnel became increasingly better. Living quarters were the best experienced to date in the year that the squadron had been at war. The tents were floored and orderly, latrines were plentiful, mess facilities were staffed and good food was available. While the eggs were still served "scrambled and green" from cans of unknown powdered substances, other servings were more palatable. The men now had assured access to medical services that contained real doctors and some nurses, and the latter were the only non-native females seen since leave in Sydney.

On the hygiene side, during the first weeks at the new base, the long-serving and respected squadron flight surgeon, Captain Dr. Alfred Krug, was allowed to impose his "Krug system of bathing" on all members of the unit. The line-up began at 1500 hours each day and participation was mandatory—at the head-of-line station one gallon of water was poured on the naked man for "soaping up purposes," and the man was then monitored as he moved along and soaped and scrubbed vigorously. At the second station, another bucket of cold water was dumped on him. The squadron history proudly noted that, by this procedure, "precious supplies of water were conserved … instances of itching stopped … and peace and harmony reigned throughout the camp." The historical narrative continues by reporting, "Idyllic as these somewhat primitive shower arrangements proved, our Squadron was not one to stand in the way of progress, and soon 'modern' plumbing facilities were installed of the very latest showerhead and suspended drum type."[10]

"Doc" Krug also lectured on "Ocean Survival," a topic dear to the men who had seen their friends disappear into the Pacific, most never to be seen again. In this same vein of survival, there were sessions on "Escape and Evasion" referencing the possibility of a shoot down or crash landing in an area still occupied by Japanese forces, either bypassed or under active contention. These briefings were now much more relevant to the mission profiles being flown as the routes to and from the targets carried aircraft and crews over large land areas occupied by Japanese forces. The degree to which the native populations in the varied islands of the Dutch East Indies were loyal to the occupiers or, alternatively, inclined to assist downed Allied airmen, was anyone's guess.

The hand-out to the aircrews of a Bahasa language single-page sheet that explained the identity of the bearer and requested assistance, prepared by the command's intelligence staff, were encouraging but hardly confidence-building. After all, the people of the Dutch East Indies were colonial subjects of the Dutch, the Dutch were members of the Allied forces and the Japanese had made some effort to bill themselves as the liberators of the oppressed. To the men of the 868th, it seemed that parachuting into or wading ashore from a ditched aircraft to seek shelter on one of the hundreds of islands would be a "crap-shoot" experience in terms of local reception and eventual recovery. This was not the Philippines where the Americans had years before pledged to grant the country independence in 1946. Rather, the locals of the Dutch East Indies probably assumed that the Dutch would come back to re-establish colonial control, and with that reasonable assumption would either be ambivalent or possibly hostile to downed American airmen.

For the first time that many could recall, there were also briefings to make the squadron aware of its place in the greater war. Lectures on "The World at War" were held where briefers from the Intelligence Section set up their maps and brought officers and men up to date on the progress of the global conflict. By that October, the Allied forces in Normandy had broken free of the beachhead and were penetrating into France; in Italy, the bloody drive up the peninsula against German forces continued; and in the China–Burma–India Theater, the Japanese offensive was stalling out. Closer to the squadron's home, and much more relevant to those sitting for a weekly update, just to the north in the recently captured Marianas, airfields were being prepared for the arrival of fleets of B-29s that would operate from Saipan and Tinian to carry the war to Tokyo and other Japanese cities.

The first edition of the *Snooper News* was circulated in early October, a simple four-page publication to be shared within the squadron and mailed home. It was well-organized with such features as "The World News," "Special Service Notes," "Side Line Chatter" and "The Flak Column." The latter focused on the quirks and antics of selected personnel. The "News" also contained editorials and further exhortations by the squadron leadership and was careful to highlight the accomplishments of all officers and men, including the ground crew.

This squadron publication complemented the other "newspaper" that circulated on the island, the *Jungle News* as it was known by its readers. Its more formal name was, *The 13th Jungle Air Force in the News* and, although it arrived irregularly, it did a nice job of packaging U.S. wire service news stories that featured the men and deeds of the Thirteenth, sometimes including missions flown by the 868th that made it through the cutting room of the censors.

Major Barlow also devoted energy to two other areas where attention had been lacking—the recognition of the efforts and sacrifices of the men who flew the missions and the formalization of better-defined leave policies that would allow more men to travel to Australia for rest and recreation. In the recognition area, individual strike missions were better documented and well prepared, and individuals and crews were properly cited for their performance in combat as well as combat support roles. Commendations were rewarded and higher-level award recommendations were sent "up the line" to XIII Bomber Command, the Thirteenth Air Force and often to the attention of the FEAF Commander, Lieutenant General Kenney. This feature had existed over the past year of combat, but the process was unavoidably uneven and often failed to catch up with a given officer or crewman until he had left the unit, either by death in combat or by rotation home.

On the leave side of the equation, the squadron had decided to convert one of its overused and abused B-24s, that was otherwise destined to occupy the "boneyard," to the elevated status of a "Fat Cat" by stripping out the weapons systems and installing crude seating. This would allow the squadron to own its own transportation, both to deliver supplies from the rear areas and to directly haul groups of 15 or so men to their leave destinations in Australia for a week of rest or rambunctious behavior, or some combination of both. The ability to have a "squadron-owned" aircraft-in-waiting in Sydney would also facilitate the ability of the leaders of a given liberty party to collect the men and bring them back, mostly on schedule, nine or so days later. In the coming weeks, a reclaimed "Snooper C-47" would join this service, rescued and bartered out of the boneyard after having been declared excess to the needs of the Thirteenth Air Force transport element. The squadron's Service Section delivered a spruced-up, re-engined aircraft that sported "Snooper Airlines" livery.

Also, in October, squadron briefing and command tents were set up and the unit's administrative staff organized itself and caught up with its paperwork for the first time in months. The aircraft maintenance group was fully staffed and capable of servicing 15 or more aircraft, even as the tempo of operations increased. Once the rear echelon group arrived by sea transport, the all-important radar shacks were again operating at full speed. There were now three, each with test benches anchored to flooring positioned above the local flood plain. Long-needed spare parts that had been requested months before began to arrive, but "just improvise" remained the solution to most LAB system issues, and while there were still no instruction manuals for the equipment, the work was getting done and the SB-24 LAB aircraft were always "mission ready."

Beyond instilling camp discipline, Barlow was determined to see that his officers and men were rewarded for their efforts with good living conditions, good food, a schedule of athletic events and programs and entertainment when it was available. Outdoor movies under the trees were now a nightly feature. Importantly, on the morale front, tented clubs for squadron officers and enlisted men went up and it was left to the members to construct and maintain these facilities in good order. The "868th Snoopers Officers Club" soon took shape and became the evening gathering spot for all unit officers and their guests. It was the venue for the swapping of stories about recent missions, hopes for the return of the men out that night and the speculation of those scheduled to fly the following night.

In the midst of all this activity in and around the squadron, there was little doubt that the new squadron commander was working non-stop to place his personal imprint on all activities. By overseeing, directing, inspecting, correcting and instructing all elements of the organization, the man had taken a firm hand on the helm. Major Barlow was a by-the-book taskmaster who demanded a clean camp, daily inspections of all facilities, morning roll calls for all hands and the display of proper military etiquette at all times. This was a change from the looser discipline of the previous months when crews and aircraft numbered in the single digits and the entire unit stood at 150 officers and men on a good day. With the squadron now counting nearly 250 on its rolls, and more aircraft and men on the way from the United States, it was time to tighten up the proverbial 868 ship. Major Barlow and his headquarters staff were the right men for this new phase in the life of what had been the Wright Project and was now the "regulation" 868th Bombardment Squadron (Heavy).

Makassar Strait moments

The second undertaking of the 868th during October, no less important than the Balikpapan missions and certainly more in line with the traditional role of the SB-24s, was the squadron's aggressive patrolling of the Makassar Strait. This body of water, as noted above, was an important route for merchant shipping carrying raw materials and other cargo to the Japanese Home Islands. It was also a route used by the Japanese Navy to move its warships and troop convoys from the Banda and Java Seas into the Celebes Sea, then onward to the Philippines and Formosa, and from there on to Japan proper.

As the passage between Borneo and the Celebes, the strait also provided access to the Balikpapan oil complex and other natural resource export facilities on Borneo's east coast. As such, it was the route oil-laden tankers would transit if they elected to steam north to reach Japan, rather than circling around the south of Borneo to transit the full length of the South China Sea. At this point in the war, either route presented a Hobson's choice for Japanese convoys but, in the waters of the latter, U.S. submarines owned the territory. Over the previous two years, U.S. Navy's fleet boats, assisted by excellent intelligence, had made an art of intercepting and torpedoing anything that moved under a Rising Sun flag. For good reason, the 868th deduced that "the strait" would offer good hunting and this guess was correct.

The action began on 5 October when Captain Earle Smith and crew made an amazing discovery in a dawn patrol up the Makassar Strait when they turned up a six-ship convoy at anchor in an isolated bay. A light cruiser, assessed to be of the single stack Agano-class, was accompanied by two destroyers and two medium-sized cargo ships. Smith's run by visual bombsight went astray when the bombs did not release properly. Flying in 396, the J-model which Art DeLand and crew had brought over from Langley, the Smith crew radioed in the contact and the squadron and the command scrambled to dispatch a daylight mission. Detected and now hunted, the enemy ships made haste and completed their escape. The failure of the bombing system received a lot of attention back at the home base and while the problem was mechanical and had nothing to do with the aircraft's electronics or the LAB system, the incident did bring home the fact that the B-24 was an imperfect creature, subject to failure no matter how well attended and maintained.

The Smith crew did not blame their plane, but it was showing its age. With its original DeLand crew about to rotate home, the Smith crew had stepped in to claim "ownership" of 396. It was now *Our Baby* and, until it came to grief some months later, would be known to the other crews by that name. But, as Art DeLand and his crew observed as they packed their bags to go home, the Smith crew kept the painted lady just as she was, outstretched in her glory next to her new name.[11]

On 8 October, the Nicolas crew staged through Sansapor to patrol the length of the strait, the mission bounded by Cape Karangan and Cape Santigi. They found a medium-sized tanker 10 miles off the Borneo coast at 1300 hours, heading south at eight knots toward the Balikpapan complex. In 902, they made Norden runs and placed three bombs alongside to claim "oil slick damage" on the ship. Two days later, the crew of Bob Alsop, back in 902, jumped a small convoy at high noon and made two attacks on a patrol boat escort at 150 feet off the deck. They followed with a third run that scored a direct hit, lifting the ship out of the water, and then made additional runs to strafe the sinking vessel. Recovery was direct to home base at Kornasoren, with enough time to debrief before dinner and grab a beer or two at the Officers Club.[12]

The following day, Bob Thompson and crew flew 897 to the same area, his mission profile becoming the routine, with a takeoff from Kornasoren at daybreak to fly direct along the equator to reach the strait at noon and patrol its length for three hours. A return route took the aircraft to Wama Airstrip on Morotai Island by 1930 in the evening, landing there to refuel and lifting off an hour later to reach home by 2300 hours.

On this mission, Thompson and crew found the same, or a related, convoy that Alsop had hit the previous day. The cargo ships this time were attended by two small escort vessels. Their anti-aircraft fire was moderate but the defense on this occasion was supplemented by a "Jake" seaplane that hovered overhead. The floatplane caught up with the Liberator and maneuvered above to attack Thompson with a brace of phosphorus bombs that sailed past and exploded harmlessly below. The attack was a first for the 868th and the unit took note. The SB-24 gunners drove the Jake away and Thompson attacked the escorts, near-missing both, but claiming the two ships as bomb-damaged and heavily strafed.

On 13 October, as other 868th crews were preparing for or already on their way to Balikpapan, Earle Smith's crew patrolled the strait and found a large subchaser scooting along to join a convoy somewhere. He took his plane to the deck, staying at 50 feet above the water, to bomb and strafe the target. His crew expended thousands of rounds of .50-caliber ammunition from all turrets and waist gunners, but 271 took a number of hits in return. One crewman was wounded and the airplane came home damaged, but it did come home. The following afternoon, Bob Hickson went back to this same area and found a small escort vessel shepherding what appeared to be a collection of landing craft and attacked them.

During the third week of the month, the Balikpapan offensive diverted most of the squadron's aircraft and gave the Japanese ships plying the strait a respite, but the Snoopers returned to attend to that body of water on 21 October. Bob Thompson undertook an armed ship search from Hog Point to Cape Sebatik and caught two small subchaser-type warships in the open. The crew rolled in to attack with bombs sinking one with a direct hit and damaging the second. This ship beached itself where it was strafed by the bomber, tearing it up from stem to stern.

On 25 October, the 868th sent Dave Wallace and his crew beyond the strait to scour Puerto Princesa Harbor on the eastern coast of Palawan Island in the Philippines. Here he found a new airstrip under construction and the garrison still half-asleep at 0700 hours. Wallace and his crew initially considered that they had "hit the jackpot" when they found three large coastal cargo vessels, tagged "Sugar Dogs" for identification purposes, at anchor in the harbor. Aboard 902, the Wallace crew bombed twice from 4,000 feet, then proceeded to hammer the port with four low-level strafing passes. On his third low pass, the crew spotted nine "Rufe" Imperial Navy seaplanes moored in a side cove and went after them.

The nose, top turret, two waist gunners and even the tail gunner poured on the firepower and tore up the sitting planes and nearby piers. On the last pass at 100 feet off the deck, the Japanese crews were on their guns and the return fire was intense, riddling the plane from nose to tail, tearing apart the nose turret. Sergeant Donald L. Harstad died as he expended the last rounds from his twin fifties. When the Wallace crew made its escape, his body was pulled from the mount and laid out on the bomb bay catwalk. The official claim for Mission 868-363 was straightforward: "One (1) Rufe destroyed, six (6) Rufes damaged and three (3) Sugar Dogs damaged."

On the night of 27 October, two SB-24s left Kornasoren at dusk and headed back to Puerto Princesa, arriving at two in the morning, with the Dave Wallace crew in 902 leading Bob Thompson and crew in 078. The first aircraft over the target had been briefed to crater the runway from 8,000 feet by Norden bombsight, but Wallace found the visibility too hazy. He opted to hold his bombs and go around, dropped to 2,000 feet for the second run and was still not satisfied. He then decided to get it right and made a third pass at a still lower altitude. After walking forty 100-pound HE bombs through the aircraft revetment, hangar area and the aviation gas storage tanks, Wallace returned to again strafe the burning aircraft and buildings.

As Wallace turned for home, the fires were raging and secondary explosions were lighting up the night sky. Bob Thompson came in minutes later and had no problem finding the target as the flames licked hundreds of feet into the air. He deposited his 100-pounders along the other side of the airfield, made a strafing pass, but with the ground gunners now energized and becoming uncomfortably accurate, he then elected to head for home. This was rated as another "highly successful" mission and the airfield and seaplane base, not to mention the pesky "Rufes" settling into the water, were out of the war, at least for some extended period of time.[13]

The Battle of Leyte Gulf

Meanwhile, the largest and most ambitious U.S. move of the Pacific War was about to occur—the invasion of the Philippines—an event that would, in turn, be the catalyst for the multiple sea battles of Leyte Gulf. As MacArthur's Sixth Army was being conveyed to the beaches of Leyte and U.S. Navy task forces were positioning themselves to defend that landing, the Japanese were preparing to move as well. Three groups of Imperial Navy surface ships had sortied from various locations under a *Sho* operation that directed them to converge on the beachhead to engage and destroy the U.S. naval forces guarding the transports. The objective was the destruction of the amphibious shipping and the isolation of the U.S. forces ashore. The latter would then be destroyed by Japanese Army troops that would pour onto the western side of the island from a reborn Tokyo Express.

At least one of these Japanese task forces would steam from southern waters, from the anchorages at Lingga Roads and from the naval base in Singapore which was just north of that fleet holding area. This powerful group of warships would lead the expected attack on the U.S. invasion fleet in Leyte Gulf. To do so, this surface force, including Japan's premier battleship and heavy cruiser divisions, would have to pass through the waters now patrolled by the 868th. The Snoopers were told to get into the air to find the Japanese fleet. The actual invasion at Leyte on the 17th, with U.S. Army troops splashing ashore and a massive fleet of 500 ships and landing craft offshore, convinced Japanese command to initiate the counterstrike. This was nothing less than an all-out effort mounted by all the warships that the embattled nation had to risk. On the 19th, the Japanese fleet lifted anchor at Lingga Roads and moved north.

In these hours, the night-stalking bombers of the 868th quietly made their own history. Interestingly, the details of that event are not widely known nor generally acknowledged. At eight in the morning on 20 October, Lieutenant Bob Thompson and crew, deep into a patrol recorded as squadron mission 868-357, discovered a Japanese task force comprising no fewer than 13 warships. The aircrew recorded these as three probable heavy cruisers and a possible battleship, escorted by a pack of destroyers. His crew fixed the position in the Sulu Sea at 04° 30' North with the task force moving at a respectable 15 knots.

Aircraft 899 flashed this important sighting to its home base and continued to shadow the task force as the ships maneuvered and headed toward their destiny at Leyte. When Thompson and crew landed at 1300 hours after 13 hours in the air, they were debriefed and all aspects of the sighting reports they had sent were reconfirmed. A Thirteenth Air Force assessment later allowed that the Thompson sighting and its stream of reporting was the first hard indication of a Japanese approach to contest the Leyte landings.[14]

Historian and author John Prados's recent book *Storm Over Leyte*[15] provides an exceptional accounting of what is broadly characterized as "the greatest sea battle of the Twentieth Century." In that examination of the grand naval engagement, the following commentary appears:

> At this critical time, Allied scouts detected the Imperial Navy task force. That morning a B-24 search plane saw what it identified as a battleship, three light cruisers, three destroyers and a half dozen other warships off the north coast of Borneo. This important sighting seems to have been lost in the

confusion. Though Pearl Harbor radio repeated the Seventh Fleet message, and someone denigrated it with an "open to doubt" notation, the sighting was real. The Japanese picked up the plane's signal. Admiral Ugaki noted that radio operators on the battleship *Yamato* overheard a nearby transmission that took the form of a sighting report. Destroyer Flotilla Ten recorded no less than nine sighting type messages from before noon until late in the day. Most likely on the basis of this sighting the Owada (Japanese radio intelligence) Group warned of a high probability the Kurita fleet had been discovered.

Irrespective of how well the U.S. Pacific Command and its subordinate task forces processed, relayed and employed the alert provided by Bob Thompson and his crew that morning, the 868th SB-24 on patrol had done its job and delivered the goods. The Japanese admiral commanding the strike force headed to Leyte knew this and assumed his enemy had been notified. The admiral's leadership in the Navy General Staff headquarters in Tokyo knew this as well, probably before the U.S. leadership of Leyte was informed. This was not unlike the night a year before when another SB-24 flown by Lieutenant Vince Splane and his crew found a Japanese flagship and sounded the alarm. In that case, it had been the opening round in the battle of Empress Augusta Bay, and fate had placed a Wright Project airplane exactly where it needed to be. That night, Splane and his crew in *Devil's Delight* discovered the enemy task force with radar, sent his sighting report and repeated that report twice to make sure the U.S. Navy task force that lay in wait knew the Japanese cruiser force was coming. He then dropped to a thousand feet and dashed in on a LAB approach to hit the heavy cruiser *Haguro* with a near miss that rattled the ship and disrupted the battle group it led.

The excellent accounting of this decisive battle provided by Kenneth I. Friedman in his 2009 book, *Afternoon of the Rising Sun—The Battle of Leyte Gulf*, which accurately reconstructs this chain of events:

> On the morning of October 20, 1944, (Seventh Fleet Intelligence Officer) McCollum's appraisal proved to be correct. Patrolling off the northern New Guinea coast, an American search plane observed a large fleet of Japanese ships, noting that it had at least one battleship, three light cruisers, three destroyers, and six other warships. The plane's pilot radioed a report to Pearl Harbor. However, the naval communications center essentially ignored the sighting since they knew that Kurita had many more ships than those seen by the plane's crew. McCollum was skeptical, too, about the sighting, and after the war he told an interviewer that planes in that area had never reported ships before. Nonetheless the search plane's crew was right: a large Japanese naval force had passed under their nose.[16]

In October 1944, when Bob Thompson and his crew sat in the 868th Squadron debriefing tent back on Kornasoren Airfield, they could hardly appreciate that they had just played a minor part of what was about to be the decisive naval battle of the Pacific War. Thirty years later, when they met and recalled the events of that day, retelling their discovery and the tracking of the Japanese task force, they found it difficult to appreciate what they had been a part of in those hours over the Sulu Sea. But they did remember that Doc Krug joined them with the intelligence team to pour each man an extra measure of "Old Overholt" whiskey to relax them after a mission well done.[17]

The various sea and air battles of Leyte raged for three days and in their wake, the scattered remnants of the Japanese fleet retired to lick their wounds, some fleeing to Manila, some to Japan and others seeking refuge to the south. On 26 October, the SB-24 of Lieutenant Chuck Binford was out hunting for these bloodied ships in 080. He found a group of two cruisers and a destroyer at 10° N 120° E, near Zamboanga Island, making 20 knots. Binford reported their position, tracked them and attacked without claiming damage. Other squadrons of the FEAF, U.S. Navy and carrier aircraft were on the hunt as well, attempting to track down the fleeing ships, but the Japanese Navy had been shattered and would never again challenge the Allied steamroller moving inexorably toward the Japanese homeland.

To cap off this extraordinary month, on Halloween night Lieutenant Green Wadsworth and crew flew to the Balabac Strait, located between the north coast of Borneo and the southern tip of Palawan Island. There he found another "trophy target" in an oil-laden tanker making a transit through this choke point. The vessel was well protected and the anti-aircraft fire of the escorts was intense, hitting the SB-24 on each of its three attack runs. The Liberator's bombs straddled the tanker, damaging it and bringing it to a stop. But the flak gunners were good and exacted a terrible toll on 079. Riddled end to end, both wings were heavily damaged, the hydraulic system shot out, the radio and radar systems destroyed and the right landing-gear wheel well blown clear of the wing by the flak hit.

The plane's bombardier, Lieutenant Matthew Ernser had an explosive shell detonate close along his side, severing his heel from his body and sending shrapnel through his legs. The crew administered first aid as best they could, managed to staunch the bleeding and he survived to go home. The Wadsworth crew made for Noemfoor but realized that the damage and fuel condition would not allow them to make it that distance. At 1700 hours on 1 November, Wadsworth put what was left of his Liberator down hard on Morotai airfield, crash landing and wiping out the plane.

October round out

The squadron finished the month in fairly good shape in terms of crews and aircraft available. On 30 October, before the Wadsworth mission that crashed B-24J 079 on Morotai, the unit counted 13 aircraft as mission capable or "under maintenance for mission capable" status. Eight of these were J-1s and four were J-3s, along with the single original Wright project B-24D still in the game. Two B-24Ds had departed the squadron rolls in October and one J-1 and four of the improved J-3 models had reported in for duty. On the aircrew side, all the Wright Project crews and some other early replacement crews had checked out for home and new men had arrived to fill out the roster. The active roster included the crews of Alsop, Barry, Binford, Cooke, DeLand, Hickson, Nicol, Nicholas, Smith, Thompson, Wadsworth and Wallace. Additional new crews had reported in but were not yet qualified as "combat qualified" for missions. Coming off the robust mission tempo of October, the squadron was determined to qualify every crew possible.

Another significant squadron statistic drew positive 5th Bomb Group and FEAF attention and praise: the 868th could claim to have dispatched 53 sorties during the month with only one turn back due to mechanical problems or issues. This "mission completion" rate was unmatched by other squadrons and testified to the results routinely delivered by the squadron's ground crews, including the engine mechanics, who consistently kept a high percentage of squadron aircraft mission ready. It was also a nod to the continuing superior performance of a radar section that rebuilt, bench-tested and field-tested every component of the LAB system before each mission.

Earle Smith, a command pilot who served during this time remarked, with some level of disbelief:

> I can recall only one time in 60 missions when we had an in-flight failure of a critical aircraft system. In that case, it was a radar component that shorted out on the way to our patrol area. We turned back, landed and swapped it out. And then we went back into the night to do the mission. This was an amazing record, not only in that time, but over my entire 25-year career in the United States Air Force.

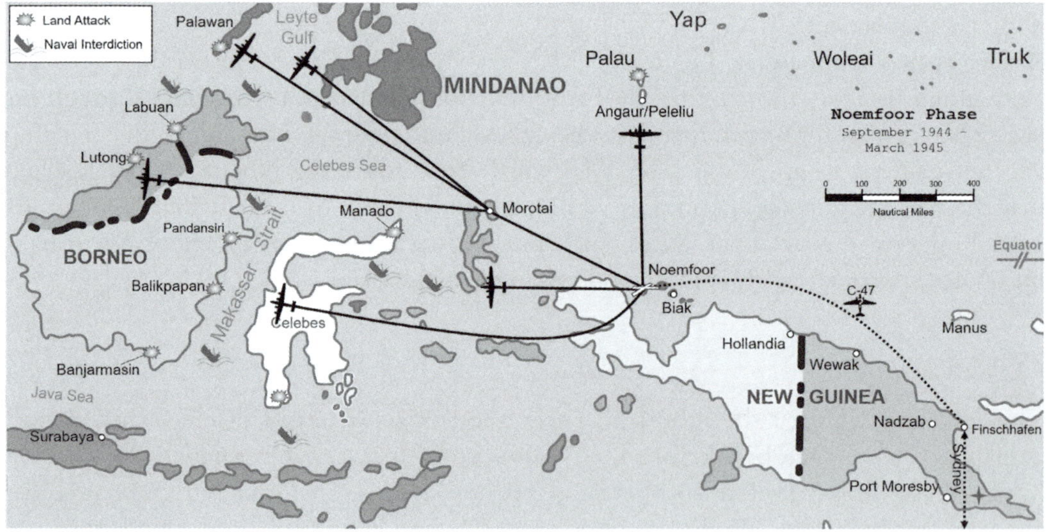

Noemfoor phase September 1944–March 1945, indicating 868th Squadron sea-search attacks and land target strikes to the north (Palau), northwest and west (Philippines and Dutch East Indies). (Chris Chen/Telemus)

CHAPTER 16

The Philippines

November–December 1944

The retaking of the Philippines

On 20 October 1944, the largest assembly of amphibious craft and warships in the Pacific War, at least up to this point, arrayed itself off the beaches of Leyte and prepared to disgorge an American assault force across an 18-mile beachhead. Days of bombardment by U.S. Navy surface forces and sustained air attacks that ranged over the island of Leyte, and indeed pummeled all of the Philippines, had prepared the way for the invasion. General MacArthur had insisted that the archipelago had to be retaken and liberated at this point in the march toward Tokyo and had also insisted that Leyte would be the strategic heart of that battle.

The MacArthur-supervised official history of the greater Pacific conflict, prepared in the months after the Japanese surrender, retrospectively blessed this assessment:

> The Leyte operation was to be the crucial battle of the war in the Pacific. On its outcome would depend the fate of the Philippines and the future course of the war against Japan. Located in the heart of the archipelago, Leyte was the focal point where the Southwest Pacific forces of General MacArthur were to converge with the Central Pacific forces of Admiral Nimitz in a mighty assault to wrest the Philippines from the hands of the enemy.
>
> …
>
> The Allies were now posed with their full power at the very threshold of (Japan's) inner structure and if they should break through, the Homeland itself would stand dangerously exposed—an inviting target for the next invasion.[1]

This narrative stressing the critical importance of the taking of the Philippines in the eventual defeat of Japan was composed in Tokyo by MacArthur's staff after the Japanese surrender in an effort that began a year or so after U.S. troops waded ashore at Leyte and consumed several years. This recounting, as ever MacArthur-centric, subordinated the importance of the bloody invasions of Okinawa and Iwo Jima and ignored the debate that had occurred over an invasion of Formosa as a reasonable alternative to the Philippines.

Also not mentioned was the hard reality that an operation many times the size of the Philippines would have occurred in Operation *Downfall*, the invasion of Japan proper, had the twin atomic detonations not forced Japan's surrender short of *Downfall*.

As U.S. planners assumed, with the Leyte invasion the Japanese came out in force, throwing every available ship and aircraft that they could muster against the Allies. More than a death ride, the Japanese were consciously pursuing their favored concept of a single "decisive battle" that would turn the tide of the war. Beyond Leyte itself, MacArthur's overall offensive—*Musketeer*—would move ever north to reclaim the key islands of the archipelago, importantly Mindoro in mid-December and then Luzon, invaded in January 1945, and the resulting battle for Manila. This latter investment destroyed Manila, in street-by-street combat which would not conclude until March 1945. But even this did not end the Japanese resistance on Luzon, nor in the Philippines. Two weeks after Tokyo surrendered on 15 August 1945, General Yamashita walked out of the mountains to surrender the remnants of his Fourteenth Area Army.[2]

The point here is that the fight in and around the Philippines was a prolonged struggle, literally consuming MacArthur and his forces for six months. Meanwhile, the Nimitz-led drive of the Central Pacific Forces rolled toward Tokyo on its own axis of advance. The two lines of Allied strategic approach would converge in the summer of 1945 in preparations for the invasion of the Home Islands, with *Downfall* scheduled to occur in stages, beginning with *Coronet* and the landings on Kyushu which were then scheduled to occur in late October or early November 1945. In a best-case scenario, assuming Kyushu would be conquered as planned, the main island of Honshu would be invaded sometime in early to mid-1946. Tokyo would presumably be taken some time in the summer or fall of that year, hopefully compelling an Imperial surrender. It would turn out that this schedule, absent the arrival of the atomic bomb, may have been too ambitious. The Japanese planning for a last-ditch resistance, modeled on the Okinawa experience, was extensive and prescient as to where the final Allied landings would occur. Given these preparations, Kyushu undoubtedly would have been a bloodbath.

The FEAF of Lieutenant General Kenney were in the thick of the extended battle over the Philippines, accepting the air battle baton to replace U.S. Navy fast carrier groups that had slammed the Japanese surface fleet and decimated the Navy and Army air elements that Tokyo had fed into the battle in its early weeks. However, in November 1944, with the troops ashore on Leyte and pressing their offense there, the U.S. Navy was collecting itself in the rear areas to replenish and prepare for its next offensive.

The battle in the air over and around the Philippines was mostly left to the Thirteenth and Fifth Air Forces, with squadrons flowing into new and crude airfields on Leyte and positioning themselves on nearby islands to support the fight. MacArthur had to deliver on his claim that his occupation of the Philippines would position the Allies to sever the connection between Southeast Asia and Japan, effectively strangling the Home Islands from its resource base. To accomplish this, he would depend heavily on the ability of Kenney's air forces to project themselves over and dominate the sea lanes that ran between the length of the Philippine archipelago and mainland China. This was no easy task, but the 868th, in the company of its sister daylight B-24 bomber squadrons, as well as medium bombers and fighters, would be at the center of that effort.

November missions

The 868th was tasked to "interdict" the sea routes that flanked the Philippines and the ports, airfields and other facilities to the immediate south, locations from which the Japanese were attempting to sustain contact with Japan or reinforce their armies in the Philippines. This assignment was in many ways a throwback to the early months of the Wright Project of August 1943 when the 10 original B-24Ds deployed to Guadalcanal with their LAB-enabled search-and-attack mandate. To the priority of ship hunting, the destruction of critical port and infrastructure facilities was now added. In these same weeks of November 1944, the squadron was also assigned to repeat strikes on Japanese-held oil facilities that had been damaged in the squadron's earlier attacks. The aircrews were also asked to seek out facilities that had not yet been "touched," and to these deliver the class of strikes at which the squadron had become proficient. A final task was to harass and heckle Japanese Army and Navy airdromes that had been previously put out of service to ensure they would not be reactivated to attack U.S. forces fighting on Leyte, or the Allied troops preparing to invade Mindoro.

On 3 and 4 November, the 868th sent night raids to Negros Island airdromes at Racalod, Alscante, Carolina and Fabrica and a few days later two Snooper aircraft visited Mapanget Airdrome in the Celebes. Some of these attacks were "secondary targets" to which an aircraft diverted itself when an armed shipping search along the northern coast of Borneo failed to turn up any decent targets. Other "primary targets" which were selected to disrupt possible enemy use of airstrips included Opon Island, Panay Island, Zamboanga, Puerto Princesa and Labuan Islands. Additional secondary targets visited when shipping searches proved negative included the radar station on Sibago Island and warehouse and supply points on Labuan and at Sandakan Point.

The search for shipping was slow to produce results in early November but LAB sorties became better in the late month. This partly reflected a temporary shutdown of the Japanese logistics system south of the Philippines in the wake of the Leyte invasion. But the action did pick up and when the seaborne targets came out, the SB-24s were all over them. An initial find by a three-aircraft search comprised of the Thompson, Binford and Cooke crews on 2 November allowed these Snoopers to press an attack on three subchaser-type warships off Palawan, with all three claimed damaged. On the 6th, Lieutenants Alsop and Hickson found some smaller shipping targets off Palawan that were hugging the coastline and attacked and damaged them. Brunei Bay was a warm spot and in the early hours of 18 November, two 868th Squadron aircraft discovered and scattered a loose assembly of vessels there, attacking two. The crews of Richardson and Morgan had one of their first tastes of LAB attacks and the disruptive impact of selected runs on an entire flotilla of ships. The crowd of an estimated two dozen ships ran hither and yon into the bay, and cargo barges trying to load them were left scattered.

On the night of 19/20 November, a 300-foot merchant vessel was discovered in Brunei Bay and attacked with a LAB run at 1,200 feet by Bob Thompson and crew on mission 868-409. Two hits were made on the ship, secondary explosions observed and the ship left burning and drifting. That same night, the radar sweep of a second 868th aircraft crewed by Binford in aircraft 025 found two medium-size cargo vessels in a nearby area and attacked, with results unobserved. Interestingly, an SB-24 of the 63rd Squadron of the Fifth Air Force was also out that night and hurried to the scene to join the 868th aircraft. Once over the target with its radar locked on, the SeaHawk crew made a LAB approach and dropped a brace of flares that lit up the night. The 63rd Snooper reported "either a Fox Tare Able or Baker already partially submerged and sinking" from the 868th attack. The Fifth Air Force Snooper also reported a probable destroyer hurrying to assist the sinking ship and went in for its own LAB attack.[3]

The following week, after another dozen fruitless sea-search missions, determined patrolling paid benefits when the radar operators of the Smith and Richardson crews found a 12-ship convoy off Brunei Bay, including a probable light cruiser and a destroyer or two. Several of the larger cargo vessels were attacked shortly after midnight and near-misses for damage were claimed.

In the last week of November, Cooke and Nicholas returned to the same area of the bay and found a warship and large cargo vessel mix of targets apparently forming into a convoy. The light cruiser-size target and an assessed naval auxiliary ship, steaming north off Miri, put up a spirited anti-aircraft defense to defend themselves and their merchant charges. The two aircrews claimed damage to both warships. Finally, on the last night of the month, Richardson and Wadsworth were back above the Miri area of Brunei Bay and found a large escort ship accompanying a medium-size cargo vessel. They worked both over with repeated bomb runs but made no claims of damage. In the debriefing tent back at base, the intelligence officers pored over maps and proposed a succession of follow-up missions to these same locations, judging that damaged ships would tuck into shore or even ground themselves to prevent sinking. Their hunch was right and in early December missions would arrive overhead to pick up where the November effort had ended.

Caught on Morotai

One incident of note that caused the squadron's only combat casualties for the month occurred on mission number 868-416 on 22 November and involved the crew and aircraft of Captain Dave Wallace. They had deployed in 902 from Kornasoren airfield to Morotai that evening to stage for a shipping search, had refueled and were taxiing for takeoff from Morotai when a Japanese air raid materialized. A "Condition Red" was flashed, shutting down the field. Engines were switched off and the crew sought cover.

The Japanese aircraft bombed and strafed the field and seemed to target the SB-24 parked in an exposed position. A bomb detonated near the aircraft and killed tail gunner Sergeant Louis Brenciani and seriously injured two men, co-pilot Paul Whitehead and Lieutenant E. S. Carp, putting both in the local medical facility. The aircraft received minor damage, was repaired in short order and Wallace and his remaining crew recovered to Kornasoren the following day.

New crew concerns and remedies

One significant development that posed new challenges to the 868th involved the arrival of new crews who had not been trained in LAB, and therefore had no knowledge of its mechanics or the operational approach to combat it offered. For the first time in the squadron's history, multiple crews were reporting in who had proceeded, some with new aircraft and most with none, directly to the Pacific without any advanced combat training, either at Langley Field or another base. This was a factor of the flow of available B-24 crews and aircraft and the increased demands on this same pool of crews and aircraft by units active in other theaters of the war. The U.S. war machine was generating these crews and aircraft in growing numbers, but raw demand simply outstripped the expanding flow of qualified men and machines and limited the time available to more fully prepare them for war.

Equally concerning was the fact that fewer of these new crews were "instrument proficient" and too often had only limited or almost no experience in night flying. Previous replacements had typically been more experienced, higher-hour B-24 pilots and crews who had been through the radar indoctrination program and LAB training at Langley Field. As a consequence, such "experienced crews" normally arrived at the squadron with confidence and at least a minimum level of LAB experience. Such crews could be brought up to "combat crew" status quickly, and often qualified to fly night missions within a week of arriving. With November's new arrivals, this was no longer the case, a reality of which both the squadron leadership and the existing crews were well aware. It was a serious problem.

Of the six new crews that reported to the squadron during November, only one was familiar with radar systems and none had any exposure to the SCR-717 system and the LAB equipment. To rectify this situation, the squadron established a training program to cover "all aspects of the SCR-717-B and the AN-APQ-5," including lectures and hands-on training on radar systems and use, and bench time with the radar technicians and their training equipment, with 15–20 hours spent on every facet of the radar's operational use. Pilots, co-pilots, radio operators and flight engineers were schooled and tested. The goal was to cram a given crew through an intensive training program that would have required six or more weeks back in the United States into two weeks in the field. By month's end, four of six new crews had passed all their exams, had been flight-tested and were declared to be fully combat mission capable. This would be the trend going forward and the squadron would evolve and refine its training program accordingly.[4]

November missions numbered 47 and involved 54 aircraft sorties. Of the 54 aircraft dispatched, all were considered to have reached their target, patrol missions completed as assigned and primary (31) or secondary (22) targets attacked. Combat casualties involved a single death, that of Louis Brenciani, and two men were wounded during the Japanese attack on Morotai airfield which caught an SB-24 in transit there. The mission available rate for all assigned strike aircraft was 90 percent and reflected the performance of the squadron's Engineering Section, sustaining that team's reputation as one of the best in the command.

Aircraft on strength at the month's end included five J-3 models, eight J-2 models and the single (original Wright Project) D-model. The latter was wearing out but was kept "mission ready" by its dedicated maintenance crew. It continued to be a favorite of squadron pilots, mostly the more experienced ones, for the simple reason that it was lighter and therefore a bit faster and more maneuverable. In addition, there was a psychological component in that *The Lady Margaret* was a survivor with an excellent service record and therefore considered to be a "lucky" plane to fly. The recommissioned C-47 was active on its shuttle flights to Australia and had received a new paint job, complete with a "Snooper Airlines" banner identity that ran the length of the fuselage, with a lightning bolt underlining the name. As the squadron prepared for December, everything was looking up and the unit was again at a high point in terms of personnel, aircraft, training and quality-of-life accommodations on Noemfoor.

A very rough December 1944

December 1944 would be a tough month for the 868th, maybe its toughest of the war. Much like November, many successful missions would be flown but, in a dramatic contrast to the past month, the squadron would experience considerable losses. Operationally, the 868th worked to deny the Japanese their vital shipping routes from Southeast Asia to the Home Islands, patrolling the waters around Borneo and the other island groups in the Dutch East Indies. At the same time, SB-24s were tasked to strike the petroleum facilities in the region to deny their product to the enemy, blocking exports at the refineries themselves as well as the pipelines that carried crude oil from the fields to the point of processing and export. A couple of tallies told the tale: the squadron began the month with a headcount of 573 officers and men and closed the month with 469, a net loss of more than 100 men, nearly all of whom were either dead or declared missing in action and presumed deceased. The aircraft count went from 15 to nine, inclusive of the loss of the Snooper Airlines C-47 which took 20 of the squadron's best to their death mid-month. This loss is detailed below and remarked upon in Chapter 17.[5]

Scouring the sea lanes

Although the squadron had many experienced crews to commit to these missions, men that had flown against most of these priority targets and knew the area, to bring coherence and credibility to the overall squadron, all crews designated as "combat qualified" would have to make their mark by completing take-it-to-the-enemy missions. Six new crews had been qualified on the LAB system by early December and these men now came into the mission mix, some to excel and others to die before they had a chance to prove their mettle.

Successful sea searches generated strikes. The LAB action began on the night of 1/2 December when the crews of Nicholas, Binford and Wallace tracked and attacked shipping found in the hot spot off Miri on Brunei Bay. Striking shortly after midnight, the three Snoopers found a Fox Tare Charlie cargo vessel beached hard, close by where the other squadron crews had hit it two days before. The ship was bombed anew, with Nicholas' four 1,000 pounders walking up to and through its stern to move this ship from the "possibly damaged" column to the "beached and probably destroyed" category.

On the 3rd, the threesome of the Hickson, Barry and Wallace crews went back to Miri on Brunei Bay and discovered, near daybreak, a very large merchant ship, believed to be a tanker laden with oil and headed to Japan. The ship was hit at least three times with LAB runs, multiple explosions followed and, while the aircraft circled their target, radar operators watched the ship break into two and disappear beneath the sea. This pattern of LAB sea-search patrolling continued through the balance of the month and surface ship contacts were made on 18, 23, 25 and 27 December with LAB strikes made on a variety of Sugar Charlies and their smaller cousins, Fox Tare Charlies, with a number of near-miss damage claims.

Crews active in the squadron during the balance of the month, additional to the six mentioned above, included those of Captain Smith and Lieutenants Richardson, Wadsworth, Barry, Greene, Thompson, Beaver, Upfield, Workman, Rogers and Plunkett. This rotation placed 17 crews in the mission mix during the month, temporarily bringing the squadron to its highest level of combat-certified crews in its existence. These crews shared access to 14 of the SB-24 LAB aircraft on strength during the month, and two and three-aircraft missions were therefore possible, at least through the mid-point of the month.[6]

The leveling of Lutong

Beyond the sea-search missions mentioned above, the squadron stepped up its game in December when it accepted the challenge of destroying the Lutong oil facilities in northwest Borneo. Second only to the Balikpapan complex in importance to the Japanese, the refinery, process plants and oil pipes at and near Lutong presented a high priority and high-profile target to the FEAF. To lift some detail from the squadron's history, the area included a refinery and tank farm in Lutong and oil fields at Miri and Seria. Fed by the nearby oil fields, the refinery produced some seven million barrels of petroleum products annually. The importance of the oil fields themselves lay in the fact that the black oils they produced were being used for bunker oil without the need for any refining. Bunker-quality fuel for the Japanese Navy and the cargo carriers was in short supply and the Balikpapan strikes had made the situation worse.

Although the Lutong target was technically within the range of daylight B-24 formations, issues of extended range, weather challenges and operational efficiency caused bomber command to look first to the 868th to take out these targets. Moreover, the squadron had been roaming the area for more than a month, hunting the tankers and coastal shipping off Miri, and its aircrews were familiar with the coast. The Lutong complex had not been taken under attack and in this sense was a "virgin target" for the Snoopers. The squadron Intelligence Section assembled a detailed mission brief which identified the key facilities and Captain Dave Wallace and crew were selected for the 868th "first in" mission.

The mission aircraft left Kornasoren on the afternoon of 7 December, staged through Morotai and came into the target area a few minutes before 0800 on the 8th. The defenders were not caught unaware and met the Wallace aircraft with a full-force anti-aircraft barrage.

Wallace and crew were instructed to "get the cracking plant" and this they did by laying fifteen 250-pound bombs across it. Wallace then descended to 100 feet to make six strafing runs on the oil storage tanks at the side of the refinery and added a small cargo ship standing off the refinery to his gunners. Spotting a "Betty" medium bomber parked on the Miri airstrip, he made strafing runs to set it alight. The cracking plant was devastated as fires jumped from the buildings and sent a column of black smoke to 15,000 feet, visible at 75 miles.

Back at base, the engineers counted 33 holes in the aircraft (080) and patched it up with strips of sheet metal riveted over the holes. But the strike had taken a toll—one 25-mm round penetrated the bomb bay bulkhead and exploded next to the radar spinner in the belly of the plane, wounding two crew members: radar operator Bill Keenan and engineer Ralph Trustham.

An extensive debriefing of mission 868-435 allowed the squadron to plan for a series of follow-up strikes against Lutong based on this same formula, using one or two bombers delivering a low-level attack at daybreak. Captain Earle Smith launched on the same route two days later on 10 December. Smith and his crew found Lutong still smoldering from the Wallace raid with repairs underway at the cracking plant. They came low and hit the cracking plant again, destroying its Trumble oil processing units and the boiler plant. The bomb drop was visual, with bombardier Ron Moyer lying prone in the nose of the aircraft and toggling a tight pattern of fifteen 250-pound bombs with long delay fusing, released at the point when the plane flew over a barracks structure. Repeating the earlier strike, Smith's crew strafed the oil storage tanks, making four passes at 100 feet and in return caught heavy and accurate fire from the flak gunners. The Smith plane was holed and an exploding heavy-caliber round wounded radar operator Jerry Pelat. Given the warm welcome the Smith crew received, including rifle fire from every window in the barracks, they counted themselves lucky to have made it home safely.

The missions to Lutong earned the Smith crew the Distinguished Flying Cross (DFC), one of the Air Force's most honored recognitions for bravery and accomplishment in combat. The citation, dated 7 February 1945, signed by Lieutenant General George C. Kenney, Commanding Officer of the FEAF, included the posthumous award of the DFC to Lieutenant Eugene Morgan, Smith's co-pilot on this mission. Morgan had died as a result of wounds suffered in the course of another combat mission a few days later.

The Citation read:

> For extraordinary achievement while participating in aerial flight over Miri, Borneo on 10 December 1944. These officers and enlisted men comprised the crew of a B-24 which took off on a 2000-mile round trip to bomb the heavily defended oil refinery at this enemy base. Approaching the target, a barrage of intense and accurate anti-aircraft fire holed the aircraft in thirty places. Nevertheless, a bomb run was made at an altitude of eighty feet over the cracking plant area, and the entire bomb load struck with telling effect. At the same altitude, and despite continuous anti-aircraft fire, the B-24 then made four strafing passes over the target, exploding and setting afire four storage tanks. The outstanding courage and devotion to duty displayed by this crew on this vitally important mission are worthy of the highest commendation.[7]

In a separate mission that same day, squadron veteran pilot Lt. Hickson led two newly arrived crews, those of Lieutenants Thompson and Greene, to a target that deserved special attention—a trestle bridge that carried a critical pipeline that moved oil directly from the fields to an export facility. Weaving their way up a river at tree-top height, the threesome found the target and Hickson and Thompson put five bombs into the trestle, dropping it in four jumbled pieces into the river. A month later the pipeline remained severed, the Japanese Navy thereby denied its bunker fuel oil.

With the pipeline in the water, Greene and crew were directed by Hickson to hit the export facility, and Greene found a small tanker in port waiting to take on oil. Greene bombed and strafed the tanker and the port facilities, and the three aircraft headed home, with Hickson nursing a shot-out engine. The three crews collected a DFC, with Hickson awarded the deserved Silver Star for leading the mission. (A more complete version of this mission is offered firsthand by Bob Thompson in Chapter 21.)

On 12 December, the squadron elected to send two SB-24s back to Lutong to finish the job, with Lieutenants Barry and Thompson and their crews making the runs. Barry and Thompson elected to mix things up a bit, with Barry arriving over the target at the crack of dawn, delivering nine 500-pound bombs at the Snooper standard rooftop height, manually releasing a bomb train of 480 feet. The Barry strike in 902 included several strafing runs and initiated new fires and dense smoke that blanketed the area. For his trouble, Barry's aircraft was holed in the bomb bay, wings and had his number three engine supercharger shot out. The Thompson crew in the ever-faithful 396 came in four hours later at 4,000 feet, bombing by Norden bombsight, and spread the wealth across the breadth of the facility with thirty 100-pound bombs deposited in a train of 840 feet.[8]

The combination of these multiple direct strikes on the Lutong facilities, plus the attacks on the other oil fields, pipelines and petroleum complexes, further crippled the entire production capacity of the Dutch East Indies. The success of the four initial squadron missions to Lutong would be favorably compared to the results of the earlier B-24 daylight formation raids on Balikpapan, which involved no fewer than 280 sorties over a two-week period, with significant operational and combat losses. The details of the Lutong strikes would receive considerable attention from higher command levels and FEAF public relations officers would provide briefings to an eager press corps who soon highlighted the events. A few months later *Air Force Magazine* would carry its own story—"What Four Snoopers Did to Lutong."[9]

On 13 December, Captain Smith and crew were out on a sea hunt along the east coast of Borneo that came up empty. They then elected to divert to their briefed secondary target—the oil storage and support installations of the Samarinda Louise oil fields at Sangga Sangga. Smith pressed home his attack, destroying several large oil storage tanks and a group of Sugar Baker class oil barges on a nearby river. The anti-aircraft fire was "intense and accurate" with a 25-mm shell exploding in the cockpit, seriously wounding the co-pilot, Lieutenant Eugene Morgan. The navigator, Lieutenant Leo Tuft, was also wounded by shrapnel and glass shards. The aircraft was well shot up but managed to make it home with a good landing. Morgan was kept alive by the crew but, as mentioned, died a few days later of his grievous wounds.

A tragedy over New Guinea

In early December, two 868th crews, a total of nine officers and 12 enlisted men, boarded the "Snooper Airlines" C-47 twin-engine cargo plane and headed for a week of rest and relaxation leave in Sydney. The two first pilots were George Thompson and Robert Cooke and most of the men with them on the flight were members of those two crews. The initial leg of the aircraft's route took them to the U.S. airbase at Finschhafen, located on the coast of New Guinea's Huon Peninsula, for a refueling stop. The standard Snooper Airlines route then took the aircraft to the south to cross Australia and arrive at Sydney.

Their orders allowed the men a 10-day stay in Sydney and the aircraft waited there for its return flight. One of the pilots, Lieutenant Cooke, missed the return leg out of Sydney due to a medical procedure on his eye and thus the squadron ship carried 20 men back to their unit on Noemfoor. When the C-47 failed to appear back on Kornasoren on 10 December, the squadron began to backtrack the flight and initially confirmed that the plane had been delayed in returning. It had apparently reached Finschhafen, had refueled there and taken off for home base. Several days elapsed and confusion came to dominate the squadron headquarters staff, with garbled messages and misunderstandings all along the plane's route. On 12 December, the aircraft with its 20 crew and passengers was declared missing and a more formal search began. Nothing was ever found of this aircraft or the 20 officers and men of the 868th that the gleaming silver Snooper Airlines C-47 carried into oblivion.[10]

A week or so later, Lieutenant Cooke was released from his stay in the Sydney medical facility, returned to Kornasoren to find his crew missing and recognized that he had cheated death one more time. One of the lost souls was Technical Sergeant Isadore La Mica, the hero who had pulled two of his fellow crewmen out of the wreckage of the Gay aircraft nine months before, holding them afloat in waters off Munda Point until they were rescued by a crash boat. Another was Ralph Misenheimer, a member of Phil Hoffman's original *Long Distance* crew. He was about to complete his combat tour and return home but had opted to take one last leave in Sydney. The loss of 20 good men—the equivalent of two combat crews—shook the squadron and damaged morale, piling on to the losses already suffered in recent weeks.

The Christmas dinner debacle

The single most disruptive event to impact the squadron in December, and one that would live forever in the minds and stomachs of the men impacted, occurred when a sumptuous Christmas dinner was prepared for the entire squadron. The supply and mess officers had procured (traded and bartered for) a quantity of turkey and it was set out with all the fixings of a home-cooked meal. The problem was the meat was rancid and the men had eaten heartily. All were struck with food poisoning within a matter of hours and the base medical team pronounced an outbreak of "gastroenteritis acute and severe, caused by the ingestion of contaminated meat." The entire squadron was shut down, with nearly 100 men admitted to the 361st Station Hospital and another 125 confined to quarters, so sick that most could not rise from their beds. Kneecapped by this mini pandemic, all operations ceased for several days.

One man died as a result— Flight Officer and bombardier Leo Feldman. The local base command ordered the squadron to abandon its camp area and relocate en masse to another area of the base and this was accomplished in short order. Given that the squadron counted some 400 men in its ranks at this point and 250 were taken down for a week or more, the disruption was significant. Several of those who lived through this "Christmas dinner experience" confided that, nearly four decades later, they still had to swallow hard before tucking into roast turkey when it appeared on the family table. Others claimed that they never ate turkey again for the balance of their lives.

It happened that one squadron aircraft lifted off for a mission shortly after its crew had consumed the dinner and was outbound for about two hours when the poisoning slammed the crew. All went down terribly ill and most became incapacitated. The co-pilot passed out and other crewmen were so sick that they could not extract him from his seat. The crew caught a break, however, as the pilot hated turkey and had devoured two peanut butter sandwiches, foregoing the bird feast. As chaos developed around him, he had an incoherent co-pilot alongside him, and all others stripped off their soiled clothing and were reduced to writhing in crab-like body positions in the waist of the plane.

The pilot had no choice but to calmly jettison the bomb load and turn the plane to make an emergency landing at a nearby friendly airstrip. The airplane was a mess, and his crew had to be dragged out and stretchered to the local medical facility. Shaken, but practical, the pilot went to a tented officers club to look for a cold beer. It may well be that this incomplete mission is accounted for in the monthly report that claimed only one turn-back for the month. Either way, turn back was what *Our Baby* did on that dreadful night.

Squadron management and movement

On the 29th, perhaps coincident with the Christmas turkey dinner disaster, the squadron commanding officer, Major James Barlow, was replaced by Lieutenant Colonel John R. Knight. Barlow had led the squadron well for six months and was eager to return to the states to join another program. Earlier that same month, several other members of the squadron leadership had been replaced as the tours of the incumbent officers ended or officers were transferred to other units in XIII Bomber Command. Major James Kendrick, formerly on the staff of XIII Bomber Command, took the Operations Officer position and brought his Langley Field LAB experience into the squadron. New Executive, Ordnance and other support division officers reported in to fully staff the squadron at all levels.

The food poisoning incident, when coupled with other issues, may have diverted the squadron from its intended future, at least for several months. On 9 December, a 50-man squadron advance team had departed for Leyte to establish a new camp there, as directed by XIII Bomber Command senior planning staff. These men were working under the assumption that the 868th would be relocated in January, in another first-in-command deployment to a new airfield that had become routine for the 868th. It did seem natural that the unit would be among the first to relocate when the Leyte airfields became available, given its mission of nighttime patrol and interdiction to seal off the shipping route that ran between the Philippines and the China coast. Back on Noemfoor, the support staff and ground crews began crating their equipment and spare parts, preparing to bid farewell to Kornasoren Airfield within a matter of weeks. For a combination of reasons, a relocation to Leyte would not be on the cards for the 868th and Noemfoor, for better or worse, would remain home for several months to come.

The squadron had 15 combat-qualified crews still on the roster at the end of the month, and the only component missing was aircraft. As noted, the mission available count was reduced to nine at that point, with the loss of three J-models which had been declared "salvaged." Two had been lost in "operational incidents" including a mangled landing that resulted from a broken nose gear on New Year's Eve. The engineering team declared another unrepairable and it was written off due to battle damage. These aircraft were towed to the local "boneyard" where they would be picked apart for badly needed spares to keep other B-24s flying. But the squadron was assured by higher command that more aircraft were on the way and aircrews would be adjusted to allow the squadron to reestablish itself at full capacity in the coming weeks. This rebuilding process would take longer than planned, mainly as a consequence of the hard fighting and the combat and operational losses incurred by the squadron during the October–December period. The "rough times" for the squadron, as many recalled it, had just begun.

The LAB system coming of age

In many of these missions to the west, into the islands of the Dutch East Indies, the cloud cover was dense and highly unpredictable and the absence of decent weather data compounded the situation. The detection of, and attack on, Japanese shipping was only possible because the SB-24 radar and LAB system allowed the aircraft to penetrate the night and the weather. In the case of daylight B-24 or medium bomber missions to these same areas, even in cases where intercepted and decoded intelligence informed planners that the targets were there, those targets would often not be detected. The daylight crews were also challenged to navigate with accuracy in the face of inclement weather, and mission aborts short of the target area were common. Thus, heavy cloud cover, which frequently hid enemy shipping, had become the Japanese Navy's first line of defense. The most efficient tactical checkmate was precision airborne surface search radar. In the instance where a radar system was fitted in a daylight aircraft, and that system was operative on mission day, neither the resolution offered by the system nor the level of confidence it was able to generate for a pilot, was adequate to the task. The USAAF was learning the hard way that it was far more efficient to send a single or small number of well-trained SB-24s against a target than a formation of daylight B-24s.

In a sense, the SB-24s of the 868th Squadron were the front-running protagonists of "stealth," as it would come to be defined 50-plus years later. Out in the night, they were able to complete a mission from take-off roll to touchdown recovery flying only "on instruments," navigate over long distances or on long-duration patrols with confidence in the night or in heavy weather and proceed with confidence during the attack phase of a mission. The SB-24s were never blind, usually knew exactly where they were and were always able to scan broad areas with a fine-tuned and well-operated radar. That radar also informed an onboard system with which the aircraft could strike with precision at low altitude, an attack enabled by a radar-informed, computer-aided calculated release of weapons. Some in the squadron's ranks wondered if the USAAF leadership knew the extent of the capability that had come into being. In fact, many did, and planners for the next generation of aircraft took note.

CHAPTER 17

Captain Earle Smith and Lieutenant Ron Moyer

August 1944

In the spring of 1944, three new crews arrived in the Pacific to join the 868th Squadron—those of Captains Earle Smith and David Wallace and Lieutenant William Beaver. Lieutenant Ron Moyer was the bombardier on the Smith crew and in the summer of 1978, the two men paused to reflect on certain events they had experienced in the Pacific in 1944 with the Snooper squadron.[1]

Before the 868th

Colonel Earle Smith, after his retirement:

> My path to join the 868th was a bit different than most but I considered myself fortunate to be able to finally get to the Pacific War, to fly in combat with my crew, to do so in the B-24 aircraft that I came to respect, and to serve with the 868th Squadron. I had reported for primary flight cadet training at Tuscaloosa, Alabama, in February 1941, went to Basic at Montgomery, Alabama, and then single-engine advanced at Selma, Alabama, Class 41G. I was tagged as an instructor and spent a year training pilots in basic at Cochran Field in Macon, Georgia, and then another year instructing at Greenwood, Mississippi. But most of us instructors wanted "out," desired a combat assignment and would do about anything to achieve that end.
>
> In my case, escape to a combat tour was pure happenstance. I was working in the orderly room over a weekend and a radiogram came in tasking the commanding officer to find and dispatch a qualified pilot who had 2,500 hours of training in four-engine bombers. This was my ticket and I raced to secure a signature on orders I had typed out that sent me to Smyrna for B-24 transition training. Make no mistake, the men who were instructors were critical to the production of good pilots and these men made a real contribution to the war effort. I did it with dedication and believe that I was instrumental in producing many top-quality pilots. One of my best friends and a 41G classmate, Edgar Wardell, was killed at Macon flying as an instructor, so there were real risks in that role. But for me, two years as an instructor was more than enough—it was time to get into the war.
>
> We all wanted "fighters," but I was ready to take the B-24, and I soon learned that I could master it, and I came to love flying that plane. Some of my best friends were obsessed with being a fighter pilot and, while I was as well for a time, I became accustomed to the "combat crew" concept and

knew that I had found my calling. After combat crew training at Blyth Field, we went to Langley for LAB training and after some weeks there we were declared ready for combat deployment. We took our brand-new LAB-equipped B-24J from Langley across the country to Hamilton Field in California, and from there across the Pacific to the Thirteenth Air Force, where we joined the 868th in mid-August 1944. On the way to the South Pacific, we had a refueling stop (no leave allowed) in Hawaii but as we neared our landing at Hickam Field our flight engineer reported that the aircraft's generator was "out of commission" and needed to be repaired. When we landed, I declared a layover to fix the troublesome generator, which our crew managed to accomplish on their own over a three-day/three-night period. Amazing work, and it only took three days!

When we arrived at Munda our aircraft carried its shiny natural metal finish. We were immediately "kicked out" and sent down to Townsville, Australia, to the maintenance center to have the 868th standard camouflage scheme applied. By the time we came back, the squadron was at Noemfoor, where we joined them to begin combat operations.[2]

Lieutenant Colonel Ron Moyer:

I had enlisted in the U.S. Army's infantry branch in California in early 1940 by claiming I was already 17 (I was not), went on to join the Air Cadet program and I soon found myself in Midland, Texas, learning to be a bombardier with a minor in navigation. After graduation, in December 1943, I was sent to Salt Lake City where I joined the Smith crew. We were together as a crew from that point forward, in company with the Wallace crew, and at Langley Field we picked up our LAB radar man.

The routing to the South Pacific took us to Hawaii, Canton Island and deposited us at Munda briefly. Regarding our forced stopover in Hawaii, I think "by the book" Smith knew that the generator problem was a ruse and just went along with it, in a "just don't get us in trouble" approach. The crew did notice that he came back from the beach with a nice sunburn, so nobody was the wiser when we set off from Hickam 11 happy young men. Once at Noemfoor as "the new guys" our two crews were "nobody newcomers," rank was not an issue and you got respect only when you earned it with several combat missions under your belt.[3]

Check pilot and squadron Operations Officer

Earle Smith:

The squadron allowed our crew a couple of warm-up missions with midnight strikes on a bomb-pocked airstrip that had been previously put out of action. We went there to deliver more 500 and 1,000-pound bombs to everything on the island to make sure it stayed that way, but this was a good introduction to the squadron routine and the formations of the XIII Bomber Command. Our first true combat missions were LAB outings to patrol the Makassar Strait and coastal areas of Borneo where the hunting was good.

In late September I was designated, along with Art DeLand, as "check pilot," which meant that I was responsible for accompanying new crews which were being qualified within the squadron for combat status, and either approving them for that status or mandating additional training. Three other squadron pilots had been so designated back in mid-August and one of those, Lieutenant Pete Colt, had died with the entire crew of recent arrival Lieutenant Isaac Hanff less than a month later on 21 September. The Hanff/Colt aircraft went down on take-off at Kornasoren with 11 men and Pete Colt was in that aircraft in his "check pilot" capacity. Don Thomson, on a check pilot flight a week earlier on 13 September with the crew of Lieutenant Dwight Barry, also went down on take-off when an engine failed. Don and the crew's pilot (Barry) and co-pilot survived to fly again but five men died in the crash. The aircraft that night carried 12 men, including Instructor Bombardier Bob Curnow, a regular member of Don Thomson's crew, who did survive with injuries. The man he was instructing, Lieutenant Robert Roehl, died in the plane as did radar operator Thomas Milton and three others who were brand new to the unit.

Several of us "old hand" pilots found the new arrival pilots to be well-qualified in the fundamentals and to be competent in flying the B-24 but almost all lacked flying-by-instrument experience, including night flying, with some having very little time in the air at night. Without hours in this environment, it was easy to become disoriented and the extreme weather we were encountering in the South Pacific only made instrument flying at night all the more challenging and sometimes deadly. Take-offs were real problems and over the coming months, we would lose more crews in the first minute or two after the plane left the ground when mechanical problems or disorientation took an aircraft into the water.

On 2 October, to my surprise, I was appointed squadron Operations Officer, effectively the number two position behind Major Barlow. In this role, I was not allowed to fly combat missions and thus I became temporarily detached from my crew. This position should have gone to Dave Wallace who technically outranked my captain rank by a few days, but he somehow, as he always did, talked his way out of it. As the only other captain in the unit, I was stuck with this assignment for a month or so, until we found someone else to step in and take the position (good for promotions in the future I guess) and I was able to pick up with my old crew and step back into the combat rotation.

The 5 October 1944 mission fail

Earle Smith:

On this day we missed the target of a lifetime, or at least a combat tour. We caught that group of warships and the two cargo vessels they were escorting "fat, dumb and happy" at anchor, perfect for a Norden run. They were alerted when we overflew them at 8,000 feet and I did a quick turn to set a bomb run. One of the destroyers had steam up and charged out of the bay, headed to open sea and then reversed course to return to the anchorage, guns blazing at us. All the ships were now alert and firing, and the anti-aircraft fire was intense and accurate, bursting all around us. I had never seen flak before and it jolted the plane as we held steady on the run. We had departed Kornasoren on the 4th, overnighted at Sansapor to stage from there and launched before dawn in aircraft 902 to fly west on the equator to the Makassar Strait. The Agano-class cruiser and its destroyers were sharp-looking and seemingly perfect targets.

Over the target, my bombardier, Ron Moyer, called out "Bombs Away" on the intercom but when I looked at the control panel, I saw the light that signaled that the bombs had not released, apparently hung up in the bomb bay. I salvoed the load and took evasive action, banking to the left and climbing. The four bombs hit open water 600 feet from the cruiser. But the flak followed us and I thought it was a miracle we were not hit. The ships we missed would have made a perfect nighttime LAB target. We would have detected them for sure, outlined by our radar as they sat off the shore. A LAB run in to such stationary ships would have made for a set-piece attack at 1,200 feet. Even a formation of daylight Liberators attacking from 10,000 feet would have had to try hard to miss that light cruiser and the cargo ships. This was the single most disappointing mission of my entire career, in the Pacific and in the many years beyond that I spent in a U.S. Air Force cockpit. I kept a copy of Mission report 868-333 in my personal file to remind me that anything could go wrong at any time, and it's not always your fault.

Ron Moyer:

Talking over this incident back at the mission debriefing, we realized that the bomb bay doors, always an issue in the B-24s, had simply jammed or hung up as they were being rolled up for the bomb run. The door mechanism was difficult to test on the ground because the bombs had to be in their racks and thereby stressing the plane's airframe to duplicate the bomb load and release sequence. It seems we had problems with several things in our aircraft, and with me, it was the Norden, when we used it, because it was simply not dependable in the rugged environment in which we operated. The guns could not be test-fired on the ground, so sometimes the gunners, no matter how many times they disassembled and cleaned them, found issues only when they test-fired them in flight on the way to our target. But the engines ran well, as they usually did, and when the radar and LAB systems functioned, as they almost always did, we were in good shape for the mission. We had a lot of very smart people in our crew and in our squadron and when we had to "improvise" we usually came up with a solution and managed to get it right.

Missions to Lutong and Labuan

Earle Smith:

We struck Lutong on 10 December, two days after Dave Wallace and his crew bombed and strafed the refinery. We were well briefed and the mission came off exactly as planned, right to the minute. We had a perfect bomb release into the side door of the refinery building and we followed up with strafing in an attempt to set fire to or blow up the large oil tanks. Sometimes they just smoldered as we strafed them and sometimes, they blew up. In the latter cases, the explosions could rock the plane or knock it to the side.

On the 13 December mission, we received heavy return fire and the Japanese gunners tore up the plane, seriously wounding my co-pilot Gene Morgan, one hell of a good guy. Hit in the head by an exploding shell that tore up my right arm badly as well, he was carefully lifted from his seat and dragged to the rear by Ron Moyer, our bombardier. I knew others were wounded as well but I had to do all I could to keep the plane in the air, "drive" her with my left arm and yell back and forth with my navigator, Leo Tuft, to keep the right heading for home. Frankly, because the plane was not in bad shape mechanically and seemed to be flying well, I was confident that we would make it back. On this mission, the Japanese had made us pay our dues.

Over Labuan, Borneo, on 29 January 1945 we delivered a successful attack but again paid a high price. In addition to the wounded, the plane was so badly shot up that I expected, and told the crew, that we probably would not make it back. The number three prop ran away when we were hit and I feathered it, and we were still fuel-heavy to the point that I could not gain altitude on three engines. The crew jettisoned everything, including the waist guns, ammo and flak vests, but she would not climb. All our instruments and radios and radar were shot up. We therefore had to navigate for hours by dead reckoning and I set the engine power by sound, trying to fine-tune each of the three remaining for maximum fuel efficiency.

I was almost resigned to accept that we had to ditch when I tried number three engine again and discovered that I could keep the prop from running away at low RPM and power settings. It was a minor miracle. This helped a lot and we were then able to slowly reach cruise altitude where I could set more normal power settings on the other three engines. The big issue was now fuel consumption—if I could nurse the engines for the remaining five hours or so we might be able to reach home. As we neared home, the engines began cutting out, fuel starvation was beginning and we were cross-feeding from various tanks to milk out all the fuel we could to keep the engines running.

We had been sighted by our own early warning radar and because we had no IFF, fighters had been scrambled to intercept us. They came up alongside for a close look, saw that we were badly shot up and escorted us in. We were closing with our field but even a slight turn to adjust our approach caused the high wing engines to cut out for lack of fuel. But with the field in sight and at a good altitude I did not start to descend until I thought we could make it power-off, if we ran out of fuel and the engines cut off completely. The manual gauges all showed empty and we were sputtering even in level flight. Our flight engineer Paley, sticking with normal procedure at this point in an approach, unlocked the landing gear and started to crank them down. The left main gear and the nose gear came down and locked into place but the right main gear hung up, due to flak damage over the target which had destroyed the unlocking mechanism. If we had known that the right gear would hang up, I would have elected to land gear up, bellying her in.

But it was too late, two of the three gears were down and we were out of fuel. Moyer was standing alongside as he always did on landing and I had him cut the electric switches as my right arm was unless. He placed his hand on the electric bar just as the left gear touched down normally and I struggled to keep the right wing up until it lost all lift, at which point it dropped ever slowly down then dragged in, spinning the now-sliding aircraft in a 180-degree half-circle. The ground loop threw us off the runway and carried us into the drainage ditch that ran along the runway. The emergency crews were racing along with us and were all over the plane in seconds and we were fortunate as somehow the plane did not catch fire. Except for the seriously wounded and Palley—who was trapped in the bomb bay, he never gave up trying to free that damn landing gear—most got out under their own power.

I honestly do not remember how I got out of that plane—probably was thrown through or climbed out the left windshield. I was dazed because the next thing I knew from the point of the crash and ground loop was that I was laying on the ground and I could see the rescue crew chopping at the right side of the cockpit to extricate my co-pilot, Don Nicol, who had been badly wounded over the target. They chopped Paley out as well—great work by those guys. The emergency crews chopped through the fuselage to remove the seriously wounded and the trapped Paley and rushed all of us to the base hospital. At the wreck site, the crash commander was shaking me, asking me for a count of the crew, and the more I tried the more I kept coming up one short. After counting the men several times, we realized that I had failed to count myself! At the hospital, they elected to leave one piece of shrapnel in my arm, about the size of a dime. Forty years later it's still there.

Ron Moyer:

On the 10 December Lutong strike we had perfect weather all the way—incredible for the area—were briefed extremely well on the target layout and flew all night to arrive shortly after daybreak. My bombsight was removed as we were to come in at an extremely low altitude, and I laid on the deck of the aircraft with a toggle switch in my hand to trigger the bomb release.

A brief explanation here. The Norden bombsight had two components—a servo-motor section that was permanently attached to the aircraft floor and a head section that snapped into place, not unlike a lens on a 35-mm camera. The latter section could be easily removed and, in the United States, was always removed for secure storage and was only attached at the beginning of the mission. In the Pacific, this component was never removed and always remained with the aircraft unless the aircraft was out of service. On this mission, and on that of Dave Wallace before us, the headend was left behind and allowed me to lean over the base unit, giving me a clear view of the target through the nose glass.

The toggle switch to release the bombs had two positions. The number one salvo position allowed the bombardier (as well as the pilot who had a similar switch) to release the entire bomb load at one time. This was used only in emergency situations (as on take-off when an engine quit and we had to lighten to remain airborne) or when we had an incredible target opportunity that deserved to receive a full load of ordnance in one release. The number two position allowed for the individual release of bombs, including a spacer or individual timer. By pre-setting airspeed and altitude, the bomb release could space them to strike 50 to 200 feet apart, with one push of the switch triggering the full train of release.

The final run in *Our Baby* had us aligned to fly in between two two-storey barracks and the release point was a small pond between them at the far end, near the side of the cracking plant. A tight 50-foot spread with the single release triggered in my hand allowed the bombs to tumble into the refinery structure, blowing it apart and finishing the job Wallace had started two days before. The strike was perfect, lifting the roof off and blowing out the sides. Our nose gunner opened fire as we passed between the buildings and we could see Japanese in their white sleeping gowns diving out the windows and into the pond below.

Intense fire of every type hit us hard, from medium-caliber flak to rifle fire and Pelat, our radar operator, was hit. He had no gun station and was standing at the waist gunner door with his camera, clicking away. A round hit him square in the helmet, knocking him across the waist area and out cold. We found him still holding his camera, alive but badly shaken. Our strafing runs drew a lot of fire and we were shot up pretty well, and with over 250 holes counted by the ground crew back on Noemfoor. On that day, we were very fortunate to not have anyone killed or the plane brought down.

The 13 December mission was a very bad one in that we were hit very hard over the target during our third strafing run. Earle Smith called me to the cockpit and I found our co-pilot, Gene Morgan, badly wounded by ground fire that had raked the cockpit. He was unconscious and a large part of the right side of his head was split open. With the help of one of our gunners, Sergeant Bednarsyk, we laid him out on the flight deck. I wrapped his head in a wound bandage and we tried to cushion his head with a flight pillow, taping him into a cradle to reduce his movements. The next step was to get blood plasma into him as he had lost a lot of blood. "Bed-check" as we called him, opened the plasma kit and mixed the solution and I tried to get the needle into Gene's arm. The needle would not hold as Gene was writhing all over and three of us could not hold him down. I finally got it into his ankle and we were able to get some blood into him.

Once on the ground, hours later, Gene was still alive and I rode with him to the hospital in the ambulance, holding the lantern over him as the doctor worked on him, shaved his head and prepared him for surgery. At the hospital, I waited for the doctor to finish the surgery and joined him in his room. He opened his safe and pulled out a bottle of real bourbon, told me that we had done a great job in maintaining Gene's life and he had just done the most complicated brain surgery of his life. We drank several shots and finally I asked him if he thought Gene would live and he said "no." This shocked me and I poured more bourbon and asked him why. He reached over with a small medical tong and removed a ball of gray matter from the top of my flight suit where it had lodged in the plane. He explained that this was part of Gene's brain and he did not think he had saved enough for him to remain alive. I left the field hospital but came back every day to visit Gene, who never fully regained consciousness. The squadron leadership thought we had been through a lot and sent those of us who could fly to Sydney on leave. While we were gone, on about Christmas Day 1944, Gene died and was buried.

On the 29 January mission, all hell broke loose on the airplane when we were hit on the strafing run. On the first bomb run over the ship, and we were very low, I set the intervalometer to space the bombs at 100-foot intervals. One of them skipped once and exploded directed over the ship, detonating fifty feet or so below us, blowing the plane straight up. But before that bomb took out the deckhouse and the deck gun of the ship, we had a real Dodge City shootout with the gunners atop that deckhouse. Our nose gunner Paul "Rags" Ramaglia faced off with them and chopped up the gun position and the deckhouse just as we released the bombs. Breaking to the side after the hit, we watched the entire crew jump ship and begin swimming to the shore.

We had used up our bombs on the shipping and elected to hit the runway and the revetments as several aircraft were visible and good targets. But as Rags blasted them with his twin .50s, the ground gunners off to the side of the runway hit us all over the aircraft. The impact was so strong that the explosions seemed to stop us in mid-air. One of the gunners hit Rags square in the nose, smashing the face of the turret, spraying him with a million shards of plexiglass. He was temporarily blinded and trapped in his turret—it had been skewed to the side by the hit. I got to him, cranked the turret to centerline and forced open the door to pull him out. His face was as purple as an eggplant but there was no blood. He was wounded in the shoulder and his foot was half shot away. I wrapped his foot as best I could and gave him a shot of morphine but heard others calling out for me from the rear.

When I got to the flight deck, I found chaos. With Russo wounded but conscious, I turned my attention to our new co-pilot Charles Nichol. He was a big man and try as I could, I could not budge him from his seat. His arm was almost completely severed, but whatever had sliced through him had sealed the blood vessels and he was not bleeding that badly for the size of the wound. We bandaged him well and he seemed to stabilize with morphine. I went back to Russo and he was yelling at me that his back was killing him. I saw no damage there and bandaged his arm and hand. He had a harness on that wrapped around his back and I could see no blood so I thought he was hallucinating. Far from it, because when we got him on his side and removed his harness, his entire back opened up, exposing his lungs from the rear. We placed the flight suit and his skin back on him and bound him tight, and stabilized him with a minimum of bleeding, for the long ride home. I went forward to check on Earle and found he had several smaller wounds in his right hand and arm and wrapped him up as best I could. He was in pain but he had to fly the plane.

The crew had joked with me after the earlier shoot-up of our plane and had begun to call me "Doc" because I had worked on all the wounded. I now flew with my flight suit stuffed with bandages, morphine injectors, the works. I even had a pair of surgical scissors tied on a rope around my neck. It was not a joke as I was the only one on the plane that, once the bombs were toggled, had no gun or backup gunner station. It made sense for me to be the "designated medic" on the aircraft and I felt this allowed me to make even more of a contribution to our crew. After patching up co-pilot Nichol, Russo and Earle Smith, I focused on the other crewmen who were wounded, most only moderately, bleeding a lot but nothing life-threatening. This took me an hour or so, and I then scrambled back up front.

Our navigator, Leo Tuft, sat unwounded at his table with his charts, yelling course corrections and time checks to Earle. Under the conditions, with no instruments and no radar, his navigation was incredible over those four-plus hours, and he delivered us to this speck in the ocean that was our airfield, on the money and at the exact minute he promised Earle we would arrive. Earle was struggling with the plane as he tried to set up the landing and he had me brace myself between the two pilot seats, told me to place both hands on the electric circuit bus bar and cut all power to the plane when he yelled "Cut it!"

When our gear hit the runway, I think I did cut all the circuits because minutes later, when Earle and I crawled toward each other in the dirt alongside the wrecked airplane, he yelled at me "Did you cut?" I looked down and realized that I was crawling with the bar in my right hand and raised it to show him. The plane did not catch fire. Earle was concerned that an electrical spark would ignite the fuel tanks that only held fumes and the wreckage would burst into fire on impact. No fire, we all got out, eventually, and I had my bus bar as a souvenir. Against all odds, we had made it back. And for this, I credit Earle Smith, absolutely the finest pilot I have ever flown with, and of course, GOD.

The mission as recorded in the 868th Squadron Notebook of Captain Earle M. Smith:

Date: 29 January 1945 Aircraft 42-73396 SB-24J LAB "Our Baby"
Captain E.M. Smith and Crew
Search Miri Bay to Labuan: Ship 200 foot long, appeared to be a salvage ship, salvaging another damaged ship, was bombed. Both vessels sunk. Then Sugar Charlie was bombed, strafed and made five runs at minimum altitude, scoring one direct hit which disintegrated the vessel, with smoke rising to 4,000 feet. Made strafing runs on runway at Labuan. Dropped two bombs in hangar area. Also strafed and destroyed one aircraft on the ground. Hit by medium AA fire, with following catastrophes:

> Sgt. Ramaglia, nose gunner, had left foot shot off. Turret was severely holed.
> Lt. Moyer, bombardier, helmet and flak suit shot off. Flak in hand.
> Lt. Nichol, co-pilot, hit in right leg, left shoulder and left eye, lost eye.
> Captain Smith, pilot, flak in right arm.
> Lt. Tuft, navigator, flak hits and burns.

Autopilot and engine instruments shot out. Radios shot out. Hydraulic system shot out. Hole in #3 gas tank. Six 20-mm holes from nose to flight deck. #1 engine damaged from ground fire. Threw out ammunition, waist guns, flak suits, and excess equipment. Came back through bad weather on six-hour remaining trip. Lost gas. Lost #2 engine twenty miles from base due to no gas. #3 engine out 4–5 miles from base. The left gear and nose had to be put down by cranking. No right gear. The entire crew was briefed prior to landing about cutting switches, etc. to avoid fires, etc. made left wheel landing. Engineer Palley, stayed in bomb bay trying to get wheel down even after landing. Pinned in bomb bay after cracking up. Palley devised a way of getting gas from the bomb bay tank to main fuel tank, which was necessary as the pump was shot away. Ramaglia held by Stoner in nose compartment during landing. Rest of crew banged up on landing. Ramaglia had cut head. Moyer sprained back. Pelat banged up side of his face. Stoner was bruised. Plane complete wreck. Bombardier Moyer and Engineer Palley gave excellent medical attention to wounded men.

The Christmas dinner massacre

Ron Moyer:

Earle Smith was the only one in our crew who declined the turkey dinner. Instead, he ate the terrible peanut butter sandwiches he always preferred. In the aircraft, about an hour after take-off and well on the way to a staging stop at Morotai before heading to our patrol area, the entire crew except for Earle was hit at about the same time. And we became so ill so quickly that we could barely move. Three of us attempted to pull our co-pilot out of his seat as he had passed out and was laying over the controls as Earle flew the plane. But we were all too weak by then to move him, so we just propped him to the side and strapped him in place.

I went back to the rear of the plane and found the entire crew naked or trying to get that way, horribly sick, several crabbed up on the floor or holding on the waist gunner straps. I think I passed out at some point but Earle flew the plane and set it down. Laying on the ground next to the plane I came to, and the medical people kept asking me my name. I could not remember, could not answer and passed out again. If Earle had eaten that damn turkey, we would have all died that night, gone straight into the water. It took a while to register, but that was the reality.

Earle Smith:

The inside of the airplane was a holy mess, but I had it pretty much under control. The crew were carried out by the ground crews, several unconscious, laid out next to the plane with doctors attending to them, firemen hosing them down and then carried naked and unconscious to a medical tent. I found the control tower and reported in to the squadron, and then went for beer. Back at the squadron camp, the entire unit was down so I don't even know if they missed us. It was a horrible experience, but I never liked turkey, not before and certainly not after. And I don't tell this story to a lot of folks around the Thanksgiving dinner table.

Captain Dave Wallace

Ron Moyer:

Dave Wallace was the best friend of our pilot, Earle Smith, and our crew was tight with the Wallace crew from Salt Lake City forward, back in spring 1944, before we went to Langley Field for LAB training. Wallace was a great pilot for sure, but we all thought he was an absolute "wild man" in every sense of the word. Risk prone and highly competitive, he was the polar opposite of our "by the book" Earle Smith, who our crew always joked "knew the book cover to cover and followed that book." Wallace told anybody and everybody who would listen that he "hated bombers" and wanted "out of bombers" and said he would do whatever he had to do to get to his true calling—the P-38 Lightning.

Wallace operated his B-24 like a fighter plane and scared the hell out of his crew. On that first raid to Lutong, after he bombed, he made so many strafing runs "on the deck" that the crew lost count, so don't believe the official mission report. No crew member other than his own would fly with him and when he did transfer into a fighter squadron no one complained, particularly his crew. But he did set the pace as the most aggressive pilot in the squadron for a good six months and we were glad that this daredevil was on our side.

Earle Smith:

Dave Wallace was an excellent pilot and he was absolutely obsessed with escaping from bombers and becoming a fighter pilot. I was as well but once I settled into the routine of a command pilot in the B-24 I realized that it was a great weapon of war and that a tight crew made it so. Wallace took crazy chances but was never reckless, as some suggested. One time we were flying in a loose formation with Dave on my wing. He dropped back and disappeared from view but didn't come up on the radio so I assumed all was well. A few minutes later he came soaring past my right wing, on three engines with the number 1 feathered, staring at us from his seat with a big smile. He wanted to show us that he could push his plane hard enough on three engines to leave us behind, and he did.

Dave was ready for every mission and had a great crew, and he had a solid co-pilot in Phil Whitehead that he managed to keep alive until he left the unit. When he made the jump to fighters, he asked me to go with him and I could have done so but declined. I had lost two co-pilots and was on my third when Dave left. Gene Morgan had been killed next to me and his replacement, Nichol, had almost died in the same seat, and had gone home for good. With a new co-pilot who was not qualified as a first pilot, and with uncertainty as to who would take over my crew as the command pilot, I simply could not leave.

Dave showed up a few weeks later, flew into Morotai, leading a junior wingman in his P-38. He found me, brought me to his plane and checked me out as we stood alongside the cockpit. My mouth watered and he was rubbing it in. I had never flown a P-38 before but Dave convinced me to go up with him for some "demonstration flying" off to the side of the field. In the air, I flew on his wing and stayed with him through every maneuver he took us through. My guess was that he was trying to show off for those on the ground, including his wingman whose plane I had, demonstrating what he could do in that P-38. I think he was disappointed that he could not lose me. Back over the field, we did a full-power buzzing of the bomber command headquarters, and the staff came outside to watch the two of us roar away, pitch up and turn back and buzz the field again.

When we landed, we pulled to a side hardstand and I jumped out and ran behind a building as a staff jeep rolled up to Dave to get his name. A formal complaint was filed by our Command's general, apparently citing Dave and his wingman for this reckless behavior over our airfield. I think his own fighter unit laughed it off as a bunch of bomber boys crying foul who failed to appreciate the élan of the P-38 pilot community. They probably assumed that the bomber general was just plain jealous of the fighter boys. Dave survived the war and I saw him over the years and played a lot of golf with him. He was forever Dave the wild man, untamed.

Into January 1945 I flew several more missions, including the long-distance attacks deep into the Dutch East Indies in the right seat with our new squadron commander, Baylis Harris. It was one hell of a tour with some incredible individuals, many of whom did not make it home, including a lot of good crews who simply disappeared into the night.

When our tour was up and we headed home I assumed that we would be retrained in B-29s to return to fight, because we all assumed that the war would continue well into 1946 and we would be needed in the final offensive over Japan. My plan was to petition for a fighter billet and take a P-38 or P-51 back to the Pacific. But the two atomic bombs ended the war and Victory Over Japan Day put an end to that plan. I stayed in the Air Force and had a great career, retiring as a full colonel and went to work with Lockheed. My B-24 crew in the 868th was the best ever and, as I said, I loved that Liberator as the plane that could take a beating and could almost always bring us home.

The disappearance of the 868th Snooper Airlines C-47

Earle Smith:

This tragic event really involved a series of misunderstandings and failures, an almost "Murphy's Law" situation where, over the two weeks or so that it played out, it seemed that everything that could go wrong, did. For a while, I thought myself somewhat responsible in that I had flown the aircraft on the most recent run down to Sydney and back, returning a week or so before Cooke and George Thompson, and the two rated co-pilots, took the aircraft for another R&R run to Sydney. I spoke with both Cooke and Thompson the day before they departed with the other 19 men and told them that I was concerned with the left engine. It had cut out on me a couple of times and while it seemed fine for the last three hours of my final leg back into Kornasoren, I was still a bit concerned. I suggested that the pilots have it checked out by the mechanics, maybe have the engine replaced or overhauled. They listened but apparently did not do so, and after taking it on a test hop, they declared the C-47 ready to go. They filed the flight plan, boarded the group and headed out to Sydney.

In the same conversation, I also warned them about Wewak on the New Guinea coast at Hansa Bay. This was a large Japanese Army garrison that MacArthur's forces had bypassed back in August 1944 when he had his forces leapfrog along the New Guinea coast to invade the Hollandia area. The Japanese airbases at Wewak had been destroyed beginning with a massive air attack in August 1943 and had been pounded down by the Fifth Air Force since that time. The ground garrison there was still untouched, had ten thousand or more troops and a lot of anti-aircraft gunners who had plenty of time on their hands to get very good at what they did. The two-leg C-47 route ran from Noemfoor to our airbase at Finschhafen on the New Guinea coast further to the east of Wewak, refueling there for the final leg, which ran almost due south to Sydney.

The first leg took the C-47 uncomfortably close to Wewak, basically a fly-by, with Wewak passing by 40 miles off the left side of the aircraft (on the flight down). I told the two pilots that Wewak is still "very hot and dangerous" and suggested they give it a wide berth on both the outbound and return flights. My point was that, on a flight of this distance, with Finschhafen ahead and Sydney beckoning after that stop, it would be too easy to drift mid-flight and fly over or pass too near Wewak. They said they understood and we parted company. The only man I ever saw again was Lieutenant Cooke who was not on the return C-47 flight.

There was another "screw up" when the plane did not arrive back on Noemfoor and concern developed that it had gone down somewhere. When our squadron began checking to see if the plane had departed Sydney on time, and if it had arrived at Finschhafen, had refueled there and departed, the response along the way was positive—the plane had departed Sydney and also Finschhafen on the scheduled date of its planned transit. From this, our squadron and the group assumed the plane was either lost or had made an emergency landing somewhere on the final leg, that is, somewhere between Finschhafen and Noemfoor. Our operations team started checking U.S.-held airfields in between, such as our huge complex at Hollandia. But when I insisted on a recheck, the folks in Finschhafen came back to say that they had made a mistake—the aircraft departure that they had referenced was my flight, the same aircraft and tail number, from three weeks before.[4]

So, 35 years later, my thought remains that one of two things happened to this plane and the 20 men of our squadron who disappeared. Either they had engine problems and went down, with that return flight fully or over-loaded, somewhere between Sydney and Finschhafen, possibly over the Coral Sea or more likely in the Owen Stanley Mountains of far eastern New Guinea. Or, the airplane may have struggled to make altitude over the range and if an engine gave out then it would have been very difficult to recover. Less likely, if they did make it to Finschhafen, refueled there and then flew too close to Wewak on the final leg home, they could have been shot down in that area. My guess is that they went down in the Owen Stanleys heading north on the first leg of their return, but we will never know until someone finds that airplane. It would be good to bring those 20 men home. They had all earned their Sydney leave in combat and they deserve to be found and returned to their families.[5]

B-24J Our Baby *with Smith Crew and Crash Landing*

B-24J Our Baby *crash landing on Morotai, January 1945. (Author's collection)*

B-24J Our Baby *with Smith crew, Noemfoor, late 1944. (Author's collection)*

Wagner crew rescued after shootdown over Truk. (Author's collection)

Smith crew in 868th Officers' Club, Noemfoor, early 1945. (Author's collection)

Squadron engine crew on Noemfoor, late 1944. (Author's collection)

Tough Times

January–February 1945

War in the Pacific—War in the world

With the advent of 1945, in the Pacific the two-pronged advance toward the Japanese Home Islands continued apace, with momentum building in both the South Pacific along the line of MacArthur's approach and from the east as the Central Pacific forces pressed forward. The latter, overseen by Admiral Nimitz in Hawaii, maintained an aggressive schedule to move beyond the battle of Leyte Gulf and seize Iwo Jima in mid-February. This allowed the creation of an airbase to provide fighter support for the B-29 raids that were then being launched by the Twentieth Air Force from the Marianas, as well as a place for an emergency field for those aircraft returning from Japan but unable to make Saipan and Tinian. A battle-damaged Superfortress landed there on 4 March, the first of many saved by that speck of land, validating the high price paid by the 5th Marine Division for this volcanic real estate.

The much more ambitious and immensely costly battle of Okinawa loomed, with landings scheduled to occur on 1 April 1945. A combined force of U.S. Marines and U.S. Army divisions were preparing to throw some 100,000 men against Japanese defenders who had altered their strategy to fight inland rather than on the beach. The battle on this piece of Japan proper would last until late June and inflict the highest casualty rates on the Americans thus far in the Pacific War. The U.S. Navy would attempt to protect the beachhead with the fleet offshore and with fast carrier raids against the Home Islands in March 1945 that preceded the Okinawa invasion. But the U.S. Navy would find its ships subjected to sustained suicide attacks by every manner of Japanese Navy and Army Air forces aircraft.[1] The devastation exacted on the U.S. ships and their crews at and near Okinawa was shocking and signaled what was to come in spades when the Allies turned to invade the Home Islands.[2]

In the Philippines, some 200,000 troops of the U.S. Sixth Army had come ashore on the main island of Luzon at Lingayen on 7 January to begin the push toward Manila, the "Pearl of the Orient," MacArthur's overriding obsession since being expelled by the Japanese almost three years before. His combat commander on Luzon, General Walter Krueger, disagreed with his superior's assessments of Japanese strength and strategy and delayed his advance on Manila until sufficient forces were available for the task at hand. Krueger was correct in all aspects, insisted that the always-condescending MacArthur inner circle had underestimated the enemy's strength, doubted that the Japanese would abandon Manila and assumed a brutal fight there would portend. MacArthur expected to celebrate his 65th birthday with a parade through Manila that his staff had scheduled to take place in late January, and he was deeply disappointed when the Japanese did not comply. Although General Yamashita did not envision a battle to the death in Manila, preferring to move his Japanese Army forces into the hills to wage a protracted war, the strong Japanese Navy contingent present in Manila did seek an urban conflict and took matters into their hands to ensure it happened.[3]

Manila would not fall until early March, in what one author has described as having all the elements of a "Greek Tragedy," and the war in Luzon would not be won until the Japanese formal surrender in early September. For this reason, as the Central Pacific offensive rolled forward, MacArthur was destined to continue the fight in the Philippines and the Japanese, in part to protect their access to the Dutch East Indies, were willing to accommodate him. The air offensive managed by Kenney's FEAF had no choice but to commit its fighter and bomber groups to support the fight in the Philippines while continuing to beat down the Japanese oil facilities and airfields to the south of the archipelago. An equal priority for the FEAF remained the interdiction of shipping that continued to move through these areas to connect with the Home Islands.

To the west of the South Pacific and Central Pacific offensives, action in the China–Burma–India Theater to pressure Japan from that direction was building. But the Japanese found ways to delay and stimy those Allied advances, including an all-out offensive operation Tokyo dubbed *Ichi-Go* that allowed them to expand their presence in eastern China. This lasted from April–December 1944 and was designed, at least to a large degree, to deny the U.S. and Allied air forces based there the ability to strike targets to the east in the South China Sea, not to mention Japan proper. The U.S. Tenth Air Force, established in February 1942 out of the remnants of the defeated Allied forces driven out of southeast Asia, and the Fourteenth Air Force, created in March 1943, had mounted punishing small formation raids but had struggled to create and sustain a heavy bomber force. But, by early 1945, these commands were beginning to receive the aircraft and aircrews they needed to build capacity to press the war from the west. During January and into February, however, the Japanese were still active with *Ichi-Go*, over-running airbases in China and keeping the Allied air efforts on the defensive.

In the European Theater of Operations, in the fight with Germany, combat continued in Italy a full 15 months after Rome elected to opt-out of the war by surrendering to the Allies. Hitler was determined to prevail there, and the German war machine grudgingly gave ground in blood as the Allies battled past Rome and up the peninsula. Two young U.S. Army lieutenants who would become United States Senators, Robert Dole of Russell, Kansas, and Daniel Inouye of Hawaii, led platoons that assaulted the German Gothic Line that stretched across the Apennine Mountains north of Bologna. Dole served with the 10th Mountain Division and Inouye with the famed all-Nisei 442nd Regimental Combat Team.[4]

In Western Europe, January 1945 found the Allies fighting to regain the initiative after a surprise German counteroffensive that had begun on 16 December and continued to rage in the Ardennes area of Belgium well into the New Year. American forces, surrounded at the crossroads town of Bastogne, had been relieved in late December but the "Battle of the Bulge," as history would know it, would remain a slugfest well into late January. The fight eventually pitted over 400,000 German troops against 600,000 Americans and was the largest and most costly battle for the U.S. during World War II. Nearly 90,000 U.S. soldiers would become casualties, of which 19,000 would die in the snow of the Ardennes Forest. The German offensive, although blunted and reversed by February, erased the hope that the war in Europe could be won quickly. Hard fighting lay ahead as the German armies fell back to defend their Siegfried Line and prepared to die for Germany proper.

The initial success of the German offensive in the Ardennes reflected failures at every level of U.S. and Allied intelligence and revealed overconfidence on the part of Allied leadership. One consequence of the delayed advance into Germany, and the recognition that the conclusion of the war in Europe would be delayed, was the planning for the repositioning of American divisions from the European Theater to the Pacific in preparation for the planned invasion of Japan.

The first phase of that vast undertaking to compel the surrender of Japan on the steps of the Imperial Palace in Tokyo, Operation *Olympic* and the landings on Kyushu, the southern-most island of the Home Islands, was still slated to occur in October 1945. However, some of the U.S. units being shifted from Germany would now have to hurry to re-cross the Atlantic, travel by rail across the United States and embark on the West Coast to arrive in the western Pacific staging areas in time to support the Kyushu assault and participate in the landings expected to follow six months later, directed at the main island of Honshu and Tokyo itself.

The combination of this and the "News of the World," as conveyed to the men of the 868th on Noemfoor in January, delivered a mixed message. Progress was being made in the greater endeavor, painful setbacks were being reversed, but the war obviously had a long way to go and the costs were mounting. For both those still fighting in Europe and the men climbing into their planes on Noemfoor, Japan was mobilized to repel the invasions it expected in the year ahead.

A squadron adrift

Coming off a difficult and uneven December, the 868th found itself, in January 1945, to be struggling on all fronts—hobbled by a shortage of combat crews, serviceable aircraft, functional on-board equipment and support facilities at the base. Perhaps most tellingly, morale remained a serious issue. The weekly report for the period ending 6 January identified one problem as the departure of experienced combat crews at their end-of-tour, and the temporary relocation of what remained of these men to forward bases where they would brief 868th mission crews who were staging from those airfields. The result was an expanded hollowing out of experience within the unit's aircrew capable of educating the new arrivals, be they pilots or bombardiers or radar operators, on the operating characteristics of the planes, the LAB equipment and the difficult "lessons learned" from combat.

The deficiencies in all types of support to the squadron at the current base (Noemfoor), in part due to the forward relocation of the Air Force Supply Command's unit that had previously supported the unit, is grimly noted in the monthly reporting. Evaporating support included basic ground transportation (trucks were now borrowed from other units for limited use each day as each remaining unit sought to protect its own inventory) and also included unrepaired aircraft engines that would henceforth have to be discarded to the engine yard. The squadron had to scramble to secure its own aircraft refueling services and spare parts were in short supply for the first time in months.

Still recovering from the massive outbreak of food poisoning that sidelined the squadron in December and continued into the New Year, the reporting noted that almost all the sick men returned to duty by mid-January. The relocation of the entire squadron, including its living quarters, mess halls, latrines, showers and all support facilities, was completed and the new camp was occupied by mid-month. In an atypical statement of fact, the unit history notes, "the morale of the personnel of this squadron was unusually low … but an encouraging uplift (was noticeable) with the relocation to a new and better campsite (which occasioned) an outburst of activity which ordinarily accompanies the erection and refinement of living quarters."[5]

On the radar side, the squadron seemed to have once again lost its "special relationship" with Wright Field, the Army Air Force Materiel Command and other sources of equipment. Appeals to the Thirteenth Air Force Service Command were not particularly useful and the departure of key radar personnel had left the squadron without the direct personal links to counterparts back home that the technicians had enjoyed since the Wright Project deployment in August 1943.

Replacement parts for both onboard LAB components and testing equipment were slow to arrive and backorders remained unfilled for weeks or even months. The only answer was to "improvise" by field repairing, and often completely rebuilding, the systems, an approach referred to as "patching up" over-used equipment, with a consequent reduction in aircraft and system "availability." New equipment that was arriving to ostensibly enhance the operations of the SB-24 unit, such as an improved LORAN device, promised to be of use, but again there was a disconnect. The LORAN installation team completed its work, and while the equipment now resided on each aircraft, and some training had occurred, instruction manuals were at a premium and, most importantly, no LORAN charts for the mission areas were available in the system.[6]

Reading between the lines, it is not difficult to discern that, in many ways, the squadron had been left behind on Noemfoor by the Thirteenth Air Force and its XIII Bomber Command. To a limited degree, it might have appeared that the radar folks back home had lost interest in the squadron and the servicing of its needs de-prioritized. Perhaps there was the presumption on the part of those back at Wright Field or at Langley Field, where LAB was no longer a priority, that since the Wright Project had always managed to take care of itself, no special support from home base was needed.

This occurred as the leading squadrons and command elements of XIII Bomber Command relocated north to Morotai and airfields in the Philippines. This "left behind" situation reversed the squadron norm where it was typically the first to relocate to the forward-most bases in a "tip of the spear" mode because of the need for its unique capabilities to be deployed as far forward as possible. In the past, when the squadron had found itself ordered to jump-deploy to a new base with its service units scrambling to follow by sealift, it would immediately enjoy such support as was available in that new location. Now, as a left-behind unit, the near-opposite situation was now the case.

Recall that, in early December, the squadron had been told to "crate its equipment" on a three-day timeline to prepare for a relocation to Leyte. XIII Bomber Command ordered a 50-man squadron advance party to Leyte to plan for the movement of the entire unit within two weeks. Presuming its transfer there, the advance group spent a week laying out the camp area and arranging for local base support for the squadron. In late December, this movement alert was canceled, with an explanation that the advancing Allied forces were unable to accommodate any aircraft types save for fighters and medium bombers. While this rang true for a time, by February it appeared that the 868th was no longer a desired front-line unit that should be brought forward to the Philippines.

A number of factors may have combined to see the 868th temporarily sidelined, beyond the combat and operational losses experienced in the previous three months. The latter of course included the two crews lost in the C-47 disappearance, overlaid by the wholesale take-down administered by the food poisoning incident. There also appeared to be elements of command friction and other personnel concerns. With all of the original Wright Project combat crews long gone, and many of the replacement crews that had arrived during late 1943 and early 1944 either departed or about to depart with tours completed, the squadron found itself with very few combat-tested crews. While there were a handful of "new veterans" among the mission-capable crews, many of the fresh crews coming into the squadron from late 1944 forward were not trained on the LAB system or even qualified for instrument-only night missions. The absence of the first and second groups of command pilots, navigators, bombardiers and radar operators, who would normally school the new arrivals based on their own experiences, was telling.

Early in January, the squadron commanding officer, Major James Barlow, returned from a two-week absence and found that the overall situation had deteriorated during his time away. His period of command, from August 1944 forward, had seen significant ups and downs and many accomplishments, particularly on the long-range strikes mounted against the petroleum facilities of the Dutch East Indies. Aircrew and aircraft readiness had been generally excellent over this six-month period and the series of negative events that had bedeviled the squadron and his command from December had seemed to overwhelm him. He was determined to prevail, though, and did his best to deal with the new situation that had been imposed on his squadron.

Missions in January

In the official sense, the squadron was still an active participant in the Dutch East Indies Campaign directed at supporting the fight to the north in the Philippines and severing the shipping lifeline that sustained Japan proper. In the first week of the month, only a few missions were flown. They were attacks mounted as LAB searches along the northern coast of Borneo, Labuan Island and the ship-building yards at Sandakan. Over these seven days, a grand total of nine 500-pound, nine 250-pound and thirty 100-pound napalm incendiary bombs were released over targets, for a claim of one Sugar Charlie destroyed.

The tempo did pick up during the balance of the month, in spite of severe shortages of available mission aircraft (see below) with diversions from sea hunting to attack land targets as secondary targets. A typical week saw three nighttime LAB searches and a half dozen daylight anti-shipping missions. All of these involved the greater Borneo target set, with attacks on Miri, Maura Island, Sandakan, Labuan Island and Sanga-Sanga, where small and medium-sized cargo vessels were found and attacked.

One of the most notable missions during the month was mounted by Lieutenant Alsop on 15 January. The radar of 081 found a large tanker sitting off Lutong at three in the morning; Alsop made four quartering and beam attacks with his load of four 1,000-pound bombs, watching the ship catch fire and separate on radar into two targets. Alsop reset his altimeter to ensure that he was at 200 feet and bore in to strafe the target. It glowed and slipped beneath the surface as he approached.[7]

But even in this reduced tempo of activity, there were losses. In a mission on 12 January, Lieutenant Bruns and his crew failed to return from a daylight search that took his aircraft from Hog Point to Sanga-Sanga, where he had elected to attack the oil export facilities. No further information on the fate of this crew or their aircraft reached the 868th, at least during the remainder of the unit's tour in the Pacific.

A second loss occurred two days later when Lieutenant Plunkett and his crew in 271 returned from an anti-shipping attack and crashed into the water just off the southern tip of Ngele Ngele Island. A crash boat was dispatched to the scene but only found the nose wheel and two Mae Wests floating on the surface. On this mission, the Plunkett crew had welcomed Flight Officer Otto Schick, the navigator of the newly arrived Olsen crew, on this mission for familiarization purposes; he was lost as well.

The month ended with the 29 January strike by the Earle Smith crew on Labuan which involved a violent shoot-out at the point of attack, extensive damage to the mission ship *Our Baby*, a rough ride back to base and a crash landing at home.[8]

The month concluded with the squadron attempting to dispatch as many aircraft to targets as its limited resources allowed. The aircraft service group was able to declare a 97 percent mission available rate for the four to six airplanes it managed to position on the flight line. By late January, the strikes included locations in Borneo, including five secondary target runs over the still-smoldering Balikpapan plants, attacks on the railroad yards at Jesselton and attacks on the still-functioning topping plant at Louis oil field on Borneo.

Serious aircraft issues

During this month the aircraft situation reached a true nadir in terms of aircraft availability and the condition of those still on the squadron rolls. The bad news actually began on 30 December when a squadron aircraft lost its nose wheel on landing at Morotai at the end of a mission. Although no crew members were seriously injured and all returned to duty, the aircraft was surveyed in early January, declared unrepairable and dragged off to the local boneyard.

Apart from the three combat losses noted, operational incidents continued to plague the 868th. A notation of 7 January in the 868th Squadron's Monthly History report confirmed that, after the return of 899 from the Far East Air Service Command's Depot 3 for the application there of anti-searchlight camouflage paint, the first mission of the plane saw it return to base with a failed number three engine: "The poppet valve in the prop governor stuck, not permitting the engine to be feathered, with consequent great damage done to the engine. The other three engines struggled and were damaged, requiring the complete replacement of all four engines and superchargers, resulting in a two-week downtime for the aircraft."[9]

The disappearance of the Bruns crew on 12 January took the squadron down to seven aircraft for operations and the subsequent loss of 271 (Plunkett) on 14 January further reduced the aircraft rated available for combat missions. The downward slide continued.

On 24 January, 358 returned from Morotai where it had been under repair since Christmas Day 1944 for damage to its landing gear incurred during a post-mission crash landing. The repairs were judged to be "very poor," resulting in the unit's maintenance team being required to reconstruct the landing gear. A formal protest was filed detailing the poor quality of this work but, as was usually the case, it was a war and nothing came of the incident. In this same week, smarting from top-down criticism, the unit's Engineering Section declared that two additional squadron aircraft, numbers 025 and 081, would be "grounded" for necessary engine changes, with uncertainty as to when such work might take place.

Finally, on 25 January, 899 sustained nose-wheel damage at Morotai upon returning from a mission; the local service team there estimated at least four weeks of repair would be required to return the aircraft to service. As if to endorse the Engineering Section's demand that more aircraft be listed as no longer "mission capable," Lieutenant Cooke took off on 26 January only to declare an emergency return to base with only two of his engines functioning.

The sum of all this was that, as of 29 January, the unit was down to four aircraft capable of undertaking missions. The gain of the non-LAB B-24 aircraft 464 secured from a sister XIII Bomber Command squadron, was offset by the loss of *Our Baby*, the faithful and former *Ready Willing and Able* of Art DeLand. As previously noted, the trusted ship had been flown by the crew of Earle Smith into a Japanese hailstorm of flak over the Labuan and limped home to crash land, breaking apart in the drainage ditch that paralleled the airstrip. Dear old 396 was cut up and carted away in pieces to the boneyard.

With only four aircraft combat-ready as the month ended, the squadron was not considered by higher authority to be a mission-ready unit. The norm for a B-24 squadron was a minimum of 12 assigned aircraft, ideally with two to six spares on the rolls, to provide a mission capable minimum of nine or 10, allowing for ships under maintenance or combat damage repair. The 868th had always operated below these minimum numbers in every category but, with only four SB-24s ready to fly, this was a new low. Noting these deficiencies, XIII Bomber Command in January promised "more planes soon" but when asked by Major Barlow when this would produce more airplanes on the squadron's ramp, higher authority was careful to not provide any details.

Radar, *LORAN* and Lady June II

On the electronics side, during January, the squadron scrambled to keep its radar and LAB systems in commission, as noted above, and trained the incoming bombardiers on these systems. New radar operators had arrived as well, and these men had to be qualified on the LAB systems and integrated into the crews that had arrived without operators. Without declaring as much, the squadron was slowly rebuilding itself by completing and training the new crews.

A real plus arrived when the 394th Squadron donated a slightly used B-24L-5 (44-41464) to the 868th. It arrived configured as a standard daylight Liberator and had no provisions for LAB equipment. A decision had been made to modify this aircraft as a "special mission" plane by installing radar countermeasures (RCM) equipment that had recently been made available to XIII Bomber Command. The belly turret of 464 was removed to make room for an SCR-517B radar set plus other radar signal receptors. The RCM ship was soon painted with a Vargas-like swimsuit-clad beauty stretched across its nose and was named *Lady June II*. "The Lady," or simply "464," would continue to serve the squadron throughout the balance of the war and fly the lead on a number of high-profile missions.

Other frustrations

Contributing to the sense that they had been abandoned by XIII Bomber Command were a host of minor irritants that the squadron took far too personally, particularly as aircraft and crew losses mounted and the overall capability of the unit continued to decline. Close behind the deficit noted in aircraft engines and radar spares, came trucks and typewriters. Experiencing "transportation as a serious problem," the squadron demanded more jeeps and trucks—it only had five jeeps and four 6x6 general cargo trucks on hand and several were down for repair. Higher command ignored the requests and seemingly disrespected the squadron by ignoring repeated requests for more trucks and, the important instruments of war, typewriters. The squadron's orderly room was apparently forced to operate with only two and this shortage placed a strain on its ability to deliver its reporting. Other complaints to higher command involved an urgent need for "official and unofficial publications" to entertain the troops.

February blues

The January challenges in mission-capable aircraft, personnel shortfalls and other operational issues persisted into February and dominated that month, despite Major Barlow's best efforts to correct the situation. In mid-February, the squadron received a new commanding officer, Major James B. Kendrick, who would serve in an interim capacity for several weeks until a new permanent replacement for Barlow arrived.

New pilots and aircrews arrived and were brought into the unit's routine, but the combination of inexperience in night and LAB flying, and the limited number of operational aircraft, hampered their ability to attain combat status. But the problems that now commanded the unit's attention and led to wider frustration included shortages of critical radar and LAB components, many of which had been on backorder for months and some of which had gone missing somewhere on the long transit from the United States. The unit's Radar Section had tracked the progress of these missing components and discovered that some were being held in other locations for unexplained reasons, with the since-departed XIII Bomber Command either unable or unwilling to share information.

For the first time since the deployment of the Wright Project, dispatched aircraft were aborting missions due to failures in their LAB or radar systems. In late February, Lieutenant Barry turned back mid-patrol over the Makassar Strait when his SCR-717 went "inoperable." The squadron's LAB equipment was getting tired and needed to be replaced or rebuilt but replacement components were not arriving as promised and entire systems for aircraft transferred from other units devoid of LAB systems were nowhere in sight.[10]

In February, two incoming non-LAB aircraft had to be equipped with LAB sets and, after failing to receive the required sets or parts, the Radar Section stripped its bench set to cobble together a complete LAB installation for an aircraft. A week later, two missing AN/APQ-5 sets were discovered at a rear area base and shipped to the 868th, allowing the bench set to be replaced and a second installation to be made in a newly arrived, but hardly new, aircraft. The first daylight aircraft, a B-24L-5 (44-40937), was declared to be mission-ready by the end of the month and a second was being reworked to accommodate the LAB system.

The Engineering Section also continued to rebuild engines and searched for replacements in the supply chain. At mid-month, C-47s flew in eight new R-1830-65As and 081 was quickly rolled into the service area to have its engines swapped out. Aircraft 025, stranded at Morotai, was serviced by a team of 868th engine specialists who were flown in to assist in the engine replacements, an initiative that the squadron thought might speed things along.

More significant incidents led the unit to complain officially in a memo to the commanding general of XIII Bomber Command on 10 February, citing continuing issues of missing spares, delayed responses from service units and outright safety violations related to the misuse of squadron aircraft by the command. That authority had apparently held them at Morotai and was dispatching them on missions without the concurrence of their parent squadron back on Noemfoor. Aircraft 358 had apparently been dragooned into flying three consecutive missions with only one daily inspection performed, a serious abuse of the system. Moreover, it appeared that the squadron had sent a standby crew to Morotai to recover the aircraft and this crew was sent packing back to Noemfoor after being told that their services were "not needed," effectively blocking the return of the aircraft to the squadron.[11]

This state of affairs signaled that the 868th, previously XIII Bomber Command's highflyers, was not only being disrespected but was now being abused by higher authority. Finally, as if the other problems were not enough, and to add insult to injury, it was discovered that a half dozen new jeeps dispatched to the squadron had been "diverted" at the point of arrival on Noemfoor by a rogue U.S. Army engineering unit, the 49th Ordnance Company. These opportunists had then absconded with the new jeeps to their next station or bartered them for other "supplies" along the way. Attempts to recover the "appropriated" vehicles were unsuccessful. Typewriters also failed to appear or disappeared along the way, and other items went missing.

Driving this situation home, in the third week of February, XIII Bomber Command instructed the squadron to send three of its four mission-capable LAB aircraft, those of Lieutenants Barry (081), Bartelemes (358) and Albert (937) for "detached duty" to Angaur airfield at the southern end of the Palau Island chain. The three SB-24s were tasked to perform LAB sea searches for Japanese submarines which were believed by intelligence to be operating in the approaches to the Palau main islands to the north of Angaur. The submarines were suspected of running supplies to those bypassed bases or perhaps retrieving high-value aircrew or engineers marooned on Palau for return to the Home Islands. The sub searches turned up no contacts but managed to deprive the squadron of these aircraft and crews for several days.

Combat missions

During February, night sea-search LAB patrols were run on 13 occasions, all to the established hunting grounds of the squadron, including the Makassar Strait, and the southern, eastern, northern and western coasts of Borneo, all with negative results in the hunt for shipping. All planes diverted to their secondary targets, namely the Balikpapan facilities, the Louise oil plants and the airdromes at Bintulu and Mangar. In addition, six daylight missions were flown during the month with no results other than diversions to secondary targets when no shipping was found. Two attacks in February of note included an 8 February LAB search that discovered a 300-foot target running up the Makassar Strait, identified as an escort carrier class warship. While two near misses may have damaged the ship, no claim was made. On the 26th, another SB-24 flying a LAB search found a 300-foot vessel, believed to be a tanker, anchored at Adang Bay an hour after midnight. The crew put two 500-pound bombs alongside it, claiming close-aboard near misses and damage inflicted.

But the Grim Reaper was still riding with the squadron. On 7 February, a newly arrived crew, that of Lieutenant Lee, crashed on take-off half a mile east of Kornasoren airstrip, killing Lee and his co-pilot, bombardier, assistant engineer and nose gunner. Aircraft 080 was scoured for usable spares and equipment but because the wreck was completely submerged at high tide, almost nothing of value was retrieved. Its departure had been delayed by a nose-wheel change, but the maintenance team thought it to be in excellent condition given that they had just done a complete engine work-over in January.

The men of the Lee crew were close to the crew of Lieutenant Binford, and the latter's co-pilot, Harlan Price, was struck by the Lee crash. Price recalled that evening and related those events:

> That night on Noemfoor, several of us were sitting on a coconut log watching a movie and a
> bomber command clerk came to us with an urgent request to launch an aircraft on a night mission
> toward the Philippines. The crew was to fly to Morotai, bomb up there, top off the fuel tanks and

get their orders. A senior officer was seated next to me and I volunteered to go down to the flight line to help the selected crew prepare its aircraft for launch.

Lee's crew included several men who had begun deployment with other crews, survived crashes and been collected into that rebuilt crew, as I recall. When we were loading their gear into the designated mission aircraft the flight engineer noticed that a large patch of rubber had come off the tire so I checked with the engineering section and we moved on to the second alert plane. In the engine run-up, Lieutenant Lee noticed that one engine was low on oil pressure by about ten pounds so he wisely elected to not take that plane. At that point, the aircraft that our crew (Price/Binford) normally used, number 053, came in from a patrol and was declared mission capable. For whatever reason Lee elected to change the tire on his original ship to go with that airplane and that took another hour or so.

During the two-hour or so delay, Lieutenant Lee and I sat in one of the engineering tents talking and he shared with me that a few hours before he had been handed a radiogram that gave him splendid news—his wife had delivered twins the day before!

He was very proud to be a brand-new father but, as we sat there, I saw that he was holding his head, and he told me that he had suffered a headache all day, couldn't get rid of it. I suggested that he could opt out of the mission that night—there were several replacement crews available. He insisted that he was okay and was determined to fly the mission.

As he taxied out, I walked over to the "tower" and climbed up to where I could see him and his crew take off. The "fans" were all purring as his plane went by the tower and lifted off, but when the plane was about 100 feet in the air, I sensed something had gone wrong. The running lights on the rudder went high and then disappeared and I knew that they were in the water. There had been no radio call since clearance for the take-off. I yelled for the searchlight to be turned on and its beam directed at the water where Lee had hit, and then called the engineering section to send out an amphibious DUWK to the crash site.

Of the 10 crew, Lee and four others were killed and the other six were uninjured. The sadness of this was made worse when the crash men worked all night to cut the radio operator out of the plane where he was trapped by the framework of the upper turret. Men took turns holding his head out of the water as a small crane tried to pull that mangled turret out the wreckage to free him. The combination of leaking fuel and saltwater overcame him and he died at daybreak shortly after they were able to pull him free.

The following morning, I went with Major Barlow, who was still assigned to the unit and awaiting his orders, to view and identify the bodies of Lee, his bombardier, his radio operator and two flight engineers. It was deeply saddening as I noted that all the dead were the same age as me—21. But I felt I was a lot older.[12]

Tough times for sure for the men of the 868th in the closing days of February 1945 but, as March approached, things were about to take a turn for the positive; overdue but welcomed.

CHAPTER 19

Turnaround and Baylis Harriss

March 1945

Watching from a distance

As March opened, the 868th continued to function in a semi-stranded condition on Noemfoor, while its XIII Bomber Command leadership and fellow daylight B-24 squadrons operated from Morotai to the north. One man in that bomber command leadership had paid close attention to the squadron as it continued to drift. Major Baylis E. Harriss, the Assistant A-3, was a decorated combat veteran who had begun the war well before Pearl Harbor, volunteering to fly with the bomber command of the RAF over Europe. He was eager and had sought a combat assignment in the FEAF for over a year. He came to the Pacific War determined to test the limits of the aircraft and the men he would command. In discussions with XIII Bomber Command leadership, he lobbied to assume responsibility for the 868th by emphasizing that he was confident that he was the man to turn the squadron around and take it forward. As the 868th leadership floundered in the first weeks of the year, as losses in crews and aircraft mounted and as morale reached new lows, it was obvious that something had to be done.

Missions in early March

Even before Harriss arrived on Noemfoor there was a surge of activity as the aircrews that had joined the squadron found their sea legs and turned up the tempo of aggressive patrolling and strikes. On 1 March, Lieutenant Barry and crew began the squadron's assault on Japanese radar stations by hitting the Sibago Island installation with thirty 100-pound fragmentation bombs (frags) and then went after the sister station at Donggala Point with a strafing attack. On the night of 6/7 March, Lieutenant Cooke went back to Donggala in the *Lady June II* "ferret" on a repeat run with double the bomb load of frags. Dropping by radar from 9,000 feet, Cooke placed 28 frags on and around the radar site. On the 15th, Cooke spent the midnight hours investigating the Japanese radar net and signs of night fighter activity that might be directed by the net in the Makassar Strait.

Squadron sea-search missions found Lieutenant Albert and crew dispatched from Noemfoor to patrol the Makassar Strait where they found two medium-size vessels. The IP was Cape Simitang in the Celebes where shipping was believed to be active. Attacking into medium anti-aircraft fire, the LAB runs at 900 feet struck both ships with direct hits and Albert's crew circled for an hour and watched by moonlight as the ships heeled over in shallow water to sink. Two nights later, Lieutenant Bob Thompson found a large merchant ship with a destroyer escort and had two alongside near-misses to claim damage. The following night, on 6 March, Lieutenant Upfield caught a 250-foot merchantman just after midnight and his LAB run near-missed the target to claim another damaged ship.

The single biggest action for the 868th for the entire month occurred on the night of 6 March when Lieutenant Bartelemes's radar patrol discovered a large target running the Strait at 21 knots on a course of 20 degrees shortly before midnight. The target was identified as a 600-foot escort carrier with six aircraft airborne to protect it. The airborne patrol attempted to intercept the SB-24 before and after the LAB attack, but the SCR-717 radar tracked each aircraft as they struggled to find the Snooper.

The LAB attack was made broadside to the target with two direct hits and two close-aboard near-misses registered. The target was observed to burn and go dead in the water as the Bartelemes crew circled it for over an hour. The fighters patrolled above the ship as it burned and their presence provided further verification that the subject of the attack was a carrier of some variety. Intelligence intercepts did not allow this target to be identified or confirmed, at least at the time, but when this claim of an escort carrier was challenged by others, the squadron continued to carry it on its rolls as a successful attack that badly damaged one light or escort carrier.[1]

On 10 March, Lieutenant Bartelemes and crew were out again and found a four-vessel convoy steaming north in the Makassar Strait. They delivered a LAB attack at 0300 hours and watched as two of the ships burst into flames, flashed secondary explosions and sank. During this period, hunting was good and the assumption was that small convoys slated to make their runs to the Home Islands, that had stood down or delayed movement during the Philippines invasion, were again being dispatched from various locations in the Dutch East Indies. By passing through the Makassar Strait, they were running a gauntlet of sorts, a punishing transit over which the 868th flew and struck with radar at night.

But 10 March, the day Major Harriss took over, was also marred by the loss of the crew of Lieutenant Dwight Barry who crashed on take-off at Morotai. Theirs was a special mission mounted in support of Allied landings that day on the Zamboanga Peninsula at the southwestern tip of Mindanao Island in the Philippines. The Zamboanga landing was important given its location astride the Basilan Strait, one of only two approaches to the Asian mainland from the southwest Pacific. This was the first invasion of Mindanao and the fight on the island would continue for several months, but with Zamboanga in Allied hands, the Sixth Army's encirclement of the Philippines was almost complete. Lieutenant Barry and crew were to support that amphibious operation by observing the beachhead during the pre-invasion surface fleet bombardment and directing the naval gunfire by interacting with the U.S. Navy ships to shift their fire as the invasion progressed. The only survivor of the 10-man Barry crew was the radar operator, Carl Daye, who was badly burned but recovered to fly again with a new crew. Aircraft 952, a recently arrived B-24J-1, was destroyed. It was the only squadron aircraft loss of the month.

The mission during which the Barry crew was lost (868-536) comprised two aircraft, with Lieutenant Cooke in 357 flying a duplicate profile with an embarked infantry observer who directed the fire support from above the U.S. Navy ships off the beachhead. Lieutenant Vogel used his perch in the SB-24 to fire flares that initiated the gunfire support mission and then interacted by voice communication with the command vessel to coordinate and reposition the gunfire. The Zamboanga landings were well-supported by the mission and for once all of the involved elements operated with excellent communication in the four hours that Cooke circled the beachhead.

The fact that the 868th was tasked with this "unique mission" by XIII Bomber Command seemed to underline a renewed confidence that senior management had in the squadron and may also have reflected the badgering of its new commanding officer that the squadron be entrusted with more demanding missions than had recently been the case.[2]

During the balance of the month, the squadron doubled down on its LAB shipping searches and put more planes in the air. On 17 March, Lieutenant Beaver, in the recently re-engined 081, found three smaller cargo vessels off Balikpapan attempting to take on oil. His LAB run smashed one ship so hard that the explosion tossed the aircraft several hundred feet into the air, causing the crew to retire to check for damage. They made it home to claim two ships damaged and one sunk for a good night's work. At sunset on 20 March, Lieutenants McDaniel and Whitehead departed Morotai and, working as a pair, discovered four "Sugar Dogs" in convoy just north of Balikpapan. The latter led a two-aircraft low-level attack to bomb and strafe all four vessels, leaving three sinking.

An hour later, Whitehead and crew, proceeding up the Strait, found two small oil luggers and made five strafing passes to leave both ablaze and sinking. And so, it continued, with the crews of Upfield and Olsen partnering for a 25 March mission that took them to Brunei Bay to jump oil barges and luggers as strafing targets. To finish the mission, the pair then proceeded to Labuan for Norden runs to crater the airfield.

On the last day of the month, Upfield and Olsen paired-up once more to make a daylight attack on Pare-Pare harbor in the Celebes. They found five small merchantmen or tankers at anchor and loading cargo. The two largest were singled out for attack and both were struck hard, with one belching a thick column of smoke that rose to 4,000 feet, still visible from 50 miles away as the two aircraft headed home. Olsen's crew also claimed as destroyed "one large military truck" which they had raced alongside and exchanged fire with when they strafed the shipyard at Pare-Pare. The defenders at the shipyard were active and fairly accurate, hitting both aircraft. On his fifth pass at very low level, Olsen had the turbo-supercharger on his number one engine shot out and his left elevator was damaged in a close call with the mast of one of the ships being attacked. Aircraft 357 and 939 recovered to Morotai but both went "not mission capable" into the repair area to be patched up.[3]

Improved squadron capabilities

In terms of combat qualified aircrews, the 868th could count on the crews of Lieutenants Albert, Barry, Bartelemes, Beaver, Cooke, McDaniel, Olsen, Putnam, Rogers, Thompson, Upfield, Whitehead and Workman for a total of 54 missions that put 66 aircraft on target. The single "failure to complete" was the loss of the Barry crew on take-off. During the month, the squadron managed to place 88 tons of bombs on Makassar shipping, a half-dozen radar sites and various active Japanese airfields on Mindanao, Zamboanga and Jolo.

During this period, the fighting in the Philippines continued apace with the land battle now focused on the retaking of Manila on Luzon. The squadron's role in choking off any Japanese fuel supplies to the islands remained critical by finding and sinking the smaller vessels to which the Japanese had turned to move valuable oil products to their fighting front. The squadron took some pride in an Associated Press story that was headlined, "Orchids to The Thirteenth Air Force" and continued, "Looks as Though Murderous Raids Paid Off—Japanese on Luzon Seem to be Fresh Out of Gasoline." The story is datelined, "With the U.S. Army's 14th Corps on the Road to Manila, note to the Boys in the 13th Air Force down in the Netherlands Indies for a job well done." Praise was lavished on the attacks on the "Balikpapan and other Borneo oil centers," crediting these with the drying up of all aviation supplies to Japanese fighters and bombers stranded on Luzon airfields with "bone dry" gas tanks.[4]

On the aircraft front, the beginning of the month saw reinforcements arrive that allowed the squadron to count no fewer than 16 B-24s on strength; they comprised two J-5s, seven J-1s, five M-1s and one L-5. These were complemented by the non-LAB *Lady June II* RCM aircraft, now re-designated as a B-24L-3. While the above-mentioned loss of the Barry crew and other aircraft placed into maintenance due to battle damage reduced the numbers somewhat, the squadron had the planes and the aircrews it needed to mount multiple missions each night. The "Fat Cat" B-24 639, would rejoin the squadron mid-month, fresh from a swap-out of its fuel cells, and in doing so would set some sort of a XIII Bomber Command record with 1,165 hours on its tired airframe.

The Fat Cat was the last of the original Wright Project B-24Ds and would serve as the utility aircraft to move supplies and men between the various airfields where squadron aircraft were being repaired or maintained. Some of the new aircraft had arrived without LAB systems but the logistics pipeline had finally become unstuck and was now supplying the systems to be installed in the new aircraft. Finally, a replacement C-47 had been acquired from the boneyard and would undergo a month-long rebuild to give the squadron its link to Australia for leave purposes, not to mention the return freighting of large quantities of Australian beer and whiskey. The latter would be bartered back at home base for better food for the squadron mess and other "basic necessities."

The big move—Noemfoor to Morotai

No event in March complemented the arrival of Major Harriss as well as the FEAF mid-month order to relocate from Noemfoor to Morotai, that is, APO 704 to 719. Although the 868th had been staging through Morotai for many weeks for its combat missions, its home had remained at Noemfoor. Many in the squadron believed that the only reason the unit had finally escaped Noemfoor was because of their new commander's efforts. One of the conditions he placed on XIII Bomber Command when accepting the assignment was that the squadron had to move forward. In any event, the "big move" started during the third week and moved as rapidly as the C-47s detailed to relocate the squadron would allow.

In the typical "wait, wait, go yesterday" mentality of the war, the promised fleet of C-47s (20 a day for a week) for the airlift of the squadron failed to materialize, with some days seeing only a handful arriving at Noemfoor. In these harried days, Harriss and his staff were all over the Air Transport Group for more aircraft and the job was done by month's end. The heavy lift of equipment and spare engines and the like by surface transport would take another month but the 868th would deem itself operational on Morotai by 1 April 1945. No one would miss Noemfoor all that much and many found it a relief to be sending and receiving mail from their new APO 719.

One 868th pilot recalled the relocation to the new base and new quarters with great satisfaction.

> We were finally at Morotai for good, and we set about helping the engineers build out our new tent city. At Morotai we had wood crate beams for flooring and new tents that were not grossly stained and did not stink. I should admit that most of those stains on the old tents that we had lived in at Noemfoor for six months were the result of the warm Aussie beer that we were allocated once a week, six or eight cans. When we opened them in the tent and they semi-exploded to drench the top and side of our tent, it was the price to be paid for the warm ration.
>
> Back on Noemfoor, when we were forced to build an entire new camp after the Christmas dinner disaster, we worked hard to handcraft a new "luxury latrine" for our officers' area, an eight-holer that was the rage of the other squadrons left on the base. Once commissioned, officers of the other B-24 squadrons strolled into our officers' country to admire our work, and several pronounced

it to be the best in the South Pacific. But by then on Morotai—near the front lines—the question was how long we would stay before moving further forward. Harriss had his eye on Okinawa and in April I would fly there with him to scout out a possible camp area. So, we thought we might not remain all that long on Morotai and did not put much into the camp area there.[5]

Harriss in charge and much hailed

Major Baylis Harriss took command of the 868th on 10 March and Major Barlow went home for a well-deserved and long overdue 30-day rest, to be followed by an assignment to a new unit. There is little doubt that, by the end of the month, Harriss was delivering what he had promised XIII Bomber Command was possible in rejuvenating the squadron. The arrival of new aircraft and crews, the maturing of the crews that had joined the unit in the early weeks of the New Year and the movement of the squadron from what many perceived to be a "backwater of the war" of Noemfoor to Morotai, all combined to lift the unit. The squadron's monthly report spared no prose to trumpet the impact of Harriss, with over-the-top hyperbole the order of the day for the squadron scribe, as the 868th Monthly Report chronicled:

> Morale as usual with this squadron operates like a fever thermometer. It reaches the depths, then grasps at a straw and boosts itself to the top. When news permeated the Organization of the assignment of Major B.E. Harriss as the new Commanding Officer, morale, in general, took a decided upward swing. Major Harriss in his first talk to the personnel, seemed to have "struck home." He knew their plight, their problems, and without glowing promises won their hearts and support for a new and better deal for the 868th. Shortly after Major Harriss assumed Command, the squadron was ordered to move their current base.
>
> Major Harriss was hailed with great promise. He appears to know what this organization requires and has set about—in a most unostentatious manner—to put this Squadron on its course. To this date, he has made a most commendable beginning. He is quiet, reserved, very democratic visits and talks to the men on their various jobs and listens with much understanding to their problems and suggestions. Major Harriss comes rather highly recommended, has an enviable record as a pilot and an Executive Officer and seems fair well to live up to the expectations the personnel hold of him.[6]

Reading this account of Harriss' first three weeks in command of the squadron one envisions nothing less than Julius Caesar entering Rome in a war chariot having slain the Huns, returning in glory to mount the throne. But the extravagance of the narrative notwithstanding, much of this early praise was justified as Baylis Harriss worked hard to rally the troops and infuse them with a renewed sense of mission and purpose, all while promising them, with great certainty, that the squadron was about to do some incredible things to help win the war.

It was also clear that, while he was not yet prepared to share his thoughts as to what might be possible in future missions, Harriss clearly was thinking of taking the unit and its aircraft beyond what they had come to see as their routine. Once he had the measure of the men and aircraft, he would shift into "planning mode" and he was eager to do so. The right man had indeed arrived to lead the 868th at a critical point in its history.

Morotai Missions

April 1945

A squadron combat surge

The relocation of most of the 868th to Morotai was completed in early April and aircrews and aircraft more permanently installed at this new base allowed the squadron to shift to an increased operational tempo. Major Harriss now had the full measure of his men and was determined to put as many aircraft into the sky as possible, pushing the aircrews, the ground maintenance sections, the radar team and the entire support staff to support a surge in combat activity. The month began with four aircraft sent off to hit targets on 1 April. The Harriss plan was to mix, whenever possible, three and four-plane daily missions to the sea routes his unit was mandated to cover with larger, more complex strikes by five to ten of his squadron aircraft on more distant targets. The latter would require the 868th to reach out further than it had to date in terms of mission distance and time of flight to hit high-value targets that had heretofore remained mostly untouched by the war. The concept was to test the operational limits of the aircraft and their crews while driving home to the Japanese that facilities which they may have considered out of range were now at risk. If that message was brought home by the 868th with its strikes, the enemy would be compelled to shift resources in fighter aircraft and ground defense units to protect these assets. Forcing the Japanese to make defensive adjustments would further strain the fast-depleting resources of the empire.

On 1 April, two hunting SB-24s were sent to the area where the Makassar Strait meets the Flores Sea and another two were sent to patrol the Strait itself to the north. On the following day, four Snoopers were dispatched to Pare-Pare Bay on South Sulawesi to scour for shipping; here the crews of Bob Thompson, Robert Upfield, Ralph Albert and Richard Workman had their time with a half-dozen Sugar Dogs that had collected there, sinking or damaging several. Thompson's aircraft attacked and sank a small patrol boat which managed to place a good deal of anti-aircraft fire into its attacker before it suffered a detached stern and sank. Thompson and crew came home safely on three engines with no battle casualties but with a lot of holes to be patched. A companion aircraft had its hydraulic system shot out and came home to land with a brace of parachutes deployed out the waist windows as the plane touched down to slow the Liberator to a safe landing. On this same day, Lieutenants Olsen and McDaniel were sent to strike Oelin Airdrome near Banjarmasin on Borneo in the third of a dozen raids against this target designed to exterminate activity on this airfield. Quite a kick-off for the month.

The day following this six-aircraft effort, Harriss sent three SB-24s to patrol the Makassar Strait and one to hit Sepinggan Airdrome near the Balikpapan oil complex. The former found 12 large schooners lugging cargo off Bira and sank four. On 4 April, two SB-24s performed a sea search down the Makassar Strait to find and sink a 150-foot Sugar Charlie while two sister aircraft attacked Mandai Airdrome on Sulawesi Island. On 5 April, one SB-24 was sent back to Mandai to beat it up again and three were sent to hunt for shipping off the east coast of Borneo.

The 6th was an all-airdrome effort for the squadron when five aircraft struck Kendari in the Celebes Islands, and the previously hit Oelin and Sepinggan airfields. The 7th saw three Snoopers destroy everything that moved, or did not move, on Bima Airfield on Sumbawa Island while a fourth searched for shipping off the Borneo coast.

This flood of offensive strikes from Morotai to the south in the Dutch East Indies was designed in part to target as many airfields as possible, many of which had originally been built by the Dutch colonial administration but upgraded by the Japanese after their conquest of the islands in 1942. In many cases, these secondary but capable airdromes were being used as dispersal sites for Japanese Army aircraft that had been moved from combat areas in an effort to husband what was left of the Japanese air fleet for later use. At this point in the war, the Japanese were also beginning a determined effort to flow as many aircraft as possible back home, where they would be disbursed and prepared to join the battle for the Home Islands. The Japanese expected this to happen in October 1945 with an Allied invasion of Kyushu, an assumption that just happened to be accurate. Finally, there was another method to the airfield-specific suppression as several of these airbases happened to be on the path of future missions that were then being planned by the new squadron commander.

The above April mini-offensive by Harriss, with no fewer than 32 strikes mounted by 12 different crews over seven days, caught the attention of XIII Bomber Command and the FEAF senior officers, as well it should have. This accomplishment signaled that the 868th was back and running at full speed, with Harriss in charge. He needed this demonstration to reclaim a leading role within the command for his squadron. He also wanted to position himself to secure higher-level approvals for the longer-range and more challenging missions he had been considering and would soon propose to undertake. While at XIII Bomber Command serving as the senior mission planning officer, Harriss had made a reputation for himself as an advocate for more aggressive and more complex missions on the part of the daylight B-24 bomber groups, as well as the medium bomber groups equipped with the B-25 Mitchell. In part, this reflected his experiences in the RAF as well as his confidence in his own capabilities. As one man who attended the earlier bomber command presentations noted, he was not arrogant but "he was usually very certain that he was right."

When pilots and aircrew from the 868th had overnighted at Morotai in the days the unit was still stationed at Noemfoor and had sat in the back rows to observe Harriss brief a mission, they were impressed. His command of the routes to target, the selection of the IP for the final bombing run, the calculations of fuel burn and power settings on ingress to and egress from the target area were almost masterful. This was the reputation that proceeded his arrival to command the 868th and there was no doubt in anyone's mind that, once he did secure command of the squadron, they would all be in for "one hell of a ride," as one pilot put it. The questions many had were, what missions was Harriss planning, and how dangerous would these turn out to be, or not. They would find out within a matter of a week.

Maintaining this mission tempo into the second week of April, sea-search actions in the Makassar Strait, the east coast of Borneo and the Celebes coast were complemented by strikes against Balikpapan and various airdromes. Sugar Dogs were discovered and attacked on four occasions over the next few days. In many cases, these smaller cargo vessels were escorted by patrol boat-size naval combatants which put up strong anti-aircraft fire. Larger warships were also about, and on 12 April the aircraft of Lieutenants McDaniel and Putnam discovered a large group of Sugar Dogs and Sugar Charlies in a convoy being escorted by a destroyer. LAB runs were made by McDaniel flying 131, a recently arrived B-24M sporting a buxom swimsuit-clad lass and inscribed as *Lady Luck II*. The four Snoopers came home this day claiming several Sugar Dogs and Sugar Ables sunk or damaged, along with one destroyer.

No fewer than 30 combat sorties were flown in this one-week period (8–14 April) by 14 different crews, underlining the squadron's program to get as many crews as possible into the combat mode. During the balance of the month, when not reaching out on longer-range strikes, the 868th maintained near-daily night and daylight patrols of the Makassar Strait/Celebes areas, combined with attacks on enemy airfields believed to be operating Japanese Army or Navy aircraft, and repeatedly found and struck small and medium-sized cargo vessels of the Sugar Charlie and Sugar Dog variety. Large barges accompanied by ocean-going tugboats had now been put into operation by the Japanese to shuttle cargo, reflecting the dearth of larger shipping. In many cases, patrol craft and gunboats were there to protect the shipping and these proved to be tough customers, quick to shoot with the twin and triple barrel 25-mm anti-aircraft mounts that were standard issue in the Japanese Navy.

On the 19th, two Snoopers caught a group of barges with tugs attached, protected by a gunboat, and smothered them with bombs and repeated gunfire attacks. On the same day, two companion SB-24s struck Perak Airdrome on Java, and this was followed the next day with four aircrews hitting Kendari Airdrome on Sulawesi Island. Sea-hunt missions to the Java Sea and the Makassar Strait consumed many sorties until the end of the month, with airfields at Haroekoe, Perak, Tabanio, Langoan, Manpanger, Manggar and Boeloedawnag struck repeatedly to ensure that they would not be hosting any aircraft. There were also a half-dozen missions to protect Allied convoys moving troops for landings in the Dutch East Indies, with the squadron becoming day and night submarine hunters for the first time in months.

Surabaya—Here they come

In the midst of this "routine" daylight and night patrol and attack activity, the squadron pressed on to ever-deeper targets. The main island of the Dutch East Indies was Java and it hosted several major naval and air bases, including the capital city of Batavia, the nearby port of Tanjung Perak and the city and port complex further east at Surabaya. Major Harriss was determined to bring Java under the squadron's offensive reach and in April he led combat missions to this destination three times.

On 19 April, he took a two-aircraft mission on a run to investigate the approaches to Surabaya, the harbor itself and the nearby military airfield. Accompanied by Lieutenant Bartelmes, the flight confirmed to Harriss' satisfaction that the 868th could target Surabaya and its immediate environs. Over the port area, heavily defended with a range of anti-aircraft guns and coordinated searchlights, the defenders' reaction was delayed but became intense once the enemy realized that a dark-of-night attack was being mounted. Neither SB-24 was hit but it was a close call operationally. Harriss returned to base with one engine feathered due to fuel starvation and the mechanics measured only 50 gallons of fuel remaining in the aircraft's tanks. The distance to the target and back, including time over target, was 2,900 statute miles and the flight time was over 17 hours. This was also believed by the FEAF to be the first time that land-based heavy bombers had struck Surabaya since the Japanese invasion of 1942.

Profiting from this effort to "break trail" on missions to Western Java, it was obvious that careful planning would be required to execute a larger squadron effort. Such was mounted on 24 April with three SB-24s, Harriss leading with the crews of Captain Townsend Rogers and Lieutenant Putnam making up the trio. On this mission, Harriss and Rogers came in first at a medium altitude, with the intention of attracting the searchlights and ground fire, disbursing napalm incendiaries over the naval base. It was planned that this combination of illumination and distraction would allow Putnam to roam in the harbor area to visually acquire and attack shipping anchored there.

Rogers flew *Lady June II*, the RCM aircraft, and Harriss an aircraft equipped with the H2X high-altitude radar-enabled "blind bombing" system. The mission was partially frustrating when the bombs of the lead aircraft hung up at the release point, the malfunction occasioned by a misalignment of the bomb racks. Rogers carried no bomb load but unloaded several hundred pounds of propaganda leaflets to let the local inhabitants know that the Americans had arrived and the Japanese occupiers were doomed.

Putnam's aircraft came in for his low-level run at the naval installations and shipping and bombed the dock area, starting fires visible for some distance as the Snoopers flew home. The Harriss plan to disrupt and distract the defenses to allow a low-level penetration to occur was judged to be successful in that Putnam's aircraft was not successfully targeted by the defensive systems until after it had completed its bombing run. The Liberators arrived back at Morotai undamaged and with sufficient fuel. Lessons learned, a new, larger and more ambitious strike was planned.[1]

On 29 April 1945, the 868th undertook its third Surabaya run in 10 days. Major Harriss led a seven-ship maximum-effort attack that employed a modified operational plan. On this occasion, Harris and Rogers flew lead as "flare ships" to arrive slightly ahead of the five other SB-24s, with each dispensing 10 M-26 "Recco" flares. These oversized pyrotechnics were designed to illuminate, blind and confuse the defenders while permitting photography from the two lead aircraft. Three aircraft, those of Lieutenants Whitehead, Bartelmes and Workman, each carried four 400-pound napalm bombs to hit harbor installations, while the remaining two aircraft of Lieutenants Upfield and Olsen carried six 500-pound general-purpose bombs. These last two aircraft were to descend to make low-level runs the length of the naval basin and the commercial harbor to find and attack shipping.

The seven aircraft departed Morotai at 1330 and proceeded individually to a rendezvous point above Satengar Island six hours later. Proceeding in a loose formation, Harriss set course for a second rendezvous point over Raja Island where the seven climbed to their respective attack altitudes. After the attack the entire flight recovered to Truscott Airbase in Australia, landing at 0600 the next day, a mission duration that approached 17 hours.

The effectiveness of the attack was mixed, mainly due to malfunctions with the flares intended to illuminate the targets for the five attack aircraft. As Standard Mission Report 868-626 states:

> The accuracy of the attack depended largely on the satisfactory employment of the M-26 Recco Flares. A/C 397 (Harriss) intended to go over the target first dropping the flares using the H2X equipment, but the H2X proved inoperative and A/C 464 (Rogers) went in first dropping five of ten flares on a pre-computed radar run. These flares were dropped southeast too far out to be of any value for the target area. The same aircraft made a second run and the flares burst at 10,000 to 12,000 feet (not lower as required) and the five bombing aircraft carrying bombs followed at one-minute intervals stepped down in trail. The H2X aircraft (Harriss) went over the target in the fourth position and dropped ten flares in an attempt to illuminate the target for the other bombing aircraft. The flares all burst 1000–3000 feet below the aircraft, doing nothing more than illuminating our own planes.

In other words, the attack was, in the GI lexicon of that war, a "FUBAR"[2] situation that was a confused mini-disaster, with the flare-illuminated bombers fortunate to not be shot down by the anti-aircraft fire that greeted the arrival of the seven aircraft. Apart from the excellent performance of Rogers's RCM aircraft, as detailed in the section below, and the execution of the flight to the target, there was disappointment in the air. When the crews came home to Morotai the following day, introspection was in the air and a morning-after hard critique followed. The flares were a disaster and represented the classic "single point of failure" for the mission. But there were other issues as well, including an over-dependence on the new (to the squadron) H2X radar system that flew with Harriss on the lead SB-24.

The employment of the H2X system installed in the Harriss aircraft was one of the first attempts by the unit to use this system. It was regarded by many in the broader AAF community as the single most decisive element of the daylight bombing campaign being mounted by the Eighth Air Force to destroy the German industrial base, allowing high-precision bombing through the heavy cloud cover that too often enveloped Europe. Developed on a "highest priority" basis by Rad Lab and the AAF's electronics warfare researchers, the earliest sets were headed for Langley Field and Bid Dolan for prototype testing when the Wright Project departed for Guadalcanal in August 1943. Dolan's last-minute pitch to several of his favored officers to remain behind to work with him on "another top-secret radar project" was a reference to this system.[3]

Twelve pre-production sets of the AN/APS-15, as it was officially designated, were installed in B-17 daylight bombers and flew to England in October 1943. In early November, nine wings of Eighth Air Force heavy bombers struck Wilhelmshaven and precision bombed through 10/10 cloud cover with bomb release triggered by H2X "pathfinder" aircraft. On 13 December, some 740 heavies hit Bremen and Kiel, again led by H2X-equipped aircraft. The entire H2X program was one of the most brilliantly conceived and executed American technological achievements in World War II, with U.S. lab development to deployment in the United Kingdom completed in three months from July to September 1943.

By early 1945, when Harriss and the 868th flew with the system, it was a standard feature on the B-29s then lifting off daily from the Marianas to strike Japan. That it failed to perform in the Harriss aircraft when it was by then a dependable component in other Pacific Theater heavy bombers was both a disappointment and an embarrassment. At that point, the squadron had several officers back in the States receiving H2X training, so it was not unexpected that system kinks would initially plague the unit's system.[4]

But back on Morotai, after analyzing the third mission to Surabaya, Harriss and his operations staff were undaunted and undeterred. They remained determined to strike at the Japanese presence on Java and had established the 868th within the command as the squadron that knew how to get there and back and drop ordnance on the targets. Planning began the next day for an even more ambitious follow-on mission against the BIG target, the Dutch East Indies capital city of Batavia and its harbor.

Radar ferrets and Lady June II

As noted earlier, XIII Bomber Command had allowed the 868th Squadron to be among the first in its bomber groups to adopt the radar countermeasures or "RCM" concept when it facilitated the transfer of a newly arrived "virgin" daylight B-24J to the squadron. This occurred back in January 1945 and many suspected that Major Harriss, then the command's lead mission planner with an eye on leading the 868th, had a hand in this decision. The squadron set to rework the aircraft, 44-41464, by converting its bomb bay into space for a brace of electronic equipment and the two or three technicians who would operate those systems.

The RCM concept had come about more than two years before when, in late 1942, it was discovered that the Japanese had installed a radar system on Kiska in the Aleutians Island chain. They had occupied some of these islands in June 1942 and the U.S. was in the process of retaking them. The commander of the Eleventh U.S. Army Air Force fighting that war in the north had asked for help in addressing this problem. He wanted the radars found and destroyed as quickly as possible. Two young lieutenants fresh out of an RCM course at the radar school at Boca Raton, Florida, answered the call with a proposed solution. A factory-new B-24D, later designated *Ferret I*, was taken in hand by the technical team at Patterson Air Force Base and within weeks delivered a reasonably equipped RCM radar hunter. By mid-January 1943, *Ferret I* delivered the goods by detecting the Japanese radar's signal, homing in on it, photographing the site, logging all of the enemy radar's parameters—frequency, power and pulse repetition frequency—and plotting the coverage provided by that system.[5]

The first Ferret aircraft was followed by others, including three B-17s configured as dedicated RCM aircraft which arrived in the Mediterranean Theater a few months later, flying missions along the enemy coast from Spain to Crete. This unit, provisionally designating itself as the 16th Reconnaissance Squadron, embarked on "investigational missions" to detect, plot and plan against each enemy radar emitter. Not unlike the Wright Project's early months on Guadalcanal, the unit was a self-starting organization that had to scramble to provide for itself. Flying at 500 feet to avoid detection, the B-17s found enemy radar sites "every thirty miles along the coast" and in finding and countering these sites, made a name for itself in that theater.

During 1944, the RCM program continued to grow in size and sophistication, with new equipment developed, tested and deployed on a "get it into combat yesterday" tempo. RCM officers designated to plan and manage the aircraft were complemented by aircrew trained on the systems and technicians who would be dispatched to service the equipment. Selected communications officers who graduated from the school at Yale University, Scott Field, or the more specialized course at Harvard and MIT's Rad Lab, were combined with operators who trained at Elgin Field and Boca Raton.[6]

In the Pacific, the first two U.S. custom-built Ferrets appear to have been assigned to the Fifth Air Force operating in MacArthur and Kenney's Southwest Pacific Area, soon to become the FEAF. These were B-24D models, equipped in the U.S. for the RCM mission and dispatched in early 1944 to be notionally assigned to the SB-24-equipped 63rd Bomber Squadron of the 43rd Bomb Group. These two aircraft were subsequently designated *Ferret VII* and *Ferret VIII*, flew from New Guinea, later from Australia, and by late 1944 were operating from Morotai to support the heavy and medium bomber units of the FEAF.

However, these aircraft, and future RCM B-24 Ferrets that would be dispatched into the theater, operated within the bomb groups, were "managed" and tasked by a higher authority—General MacArthur's SWPA Section 22. By the time the 868th secured its *Lady June II* and modified and declared it operational in a dedicated RCM role on behalf of the squadron, a dozen custom-built B-24 Ferrets were either operating in the Pacific or on the way there. B-24 Ferrets were also serving in the China–Burma–India Theater with the Fourteenth Air Force and in Alaska with the Eleventh Air Force.

By 13 April, veteran pilot Earle Smith was released from his assignment as the unit's Executive Officer and was no longer constrained from flying with his crew by the no-fly status of that position. On that day he flew what was probably the first combat mission of the squadron's B-24J-3 464, *Lady June II*, which had been modified over the past few weeks to serve in an RCM role. On 19 and 21 April, the same Smith crew and 464 went out again to search the coastline of French Indochina and the Celebes and Borneo areas to confirm Japanese radar operations and coordinates. These missions provided information for future route planning and for attacks that would be directed at the radar sites themselves. In the coming weeks, other 868th crews would fly this aircraft to either search for Japanese electronic emitters to catalog them for future attention or to plot them for attack and elimination. One such mission is treated from a first-person pilot's perspective in the following chapter.[7]

On the Surabaya raid of 24 April, Captain Rogers flew *Lady June II* and the mission report notes the RCM results with satisfaction:

> Aircraft #464 successfully jammed and confused searchlight, air warning and GLR [gun-laying radar] by dropping "ropes window" and actively jamming two radars, one in the Straits near Boen and at Surabaya. Both of these radar stations were DF'd [direction finding] as well as another radar located 300 miles west of Surabaya. Major Harriss stated that, through the use of the RCM equipment, the defenses of Surabaya were only half as effective as on his previous missions to the target.

Other comments related to air defense measures noted that the 868th aircraft desynchronized their engines during the attack to throw-off audio systems believed to be used by the ground defenders and it appeared that the "silver aircraft on the mission (397) was more easily picked-up and held by the searchlights over the target."

In the seven aircraft strike on Surabaya of 27 April, *Lady June II* with Captain Rogers and crew led the way, and the Mission Report 868-626 recorded its performance:

> Enroute to the target A/C 464, the RCM aircraft, DF'd all enemy signals but failed to locate any new stations [emitters]. Our formation was tracked by [Japanese] Early Warning Radar for 225 miles before reaching target. Searchlight and Gun Laying Radar was picked up 75 miles from the target and was jammed. Jamming was turned off (by A/C 464) during the first rendezvous and commenced again 20 miles out for the target and there was a second deployment of the radar-jamming Window which continued over the target area.

The onboard RCM operators claimed all enemy systems had been jammed.[8]

The determination of the 868th to have its own RCM capability and fly those missions reflected the coming of age of the entire Allied radar countermeasures program in all theaters of the war. Back in January 1942, when the National Defense Research Committee of Dr. Vannevar Bush authorized the creation of the Radio Research Laboratory (RRL) at MIT, this same Presidential Commission deemed it imperative that a dedicated counter-electronics group within the Microwave Section begin operations concurrently. This group, the Radar Countermeasures Laboratory of RRL, otherwise referenced as Rad Lab's RCM Lab, was soon up and running, developing systems and programs to identify and defeat the radar systems of Germany and Japan. The program was classified SECRET and, like the Rad Lab's ASV microwave team, it delivered quality products, straight from the research bench to the front line, at incredible speed.

A standard reference for this RCM effort is Alfred Price's *The History of U.S. Electronic Warfare*,[9] published in 1984 with the assistance of the men who worked in the Rad Lab facility to develop and perfect the systems that went to war, as well as the pilots and crews who flew the RCM missions. With regard to the effort of the 868th to field-build its own RCM aircraft, the book notes, in a chapter devoted to efforts to detect, categorize and defeat Japanese radar systems, that it was not until "a B-24 Ferret of the 868th Squadron positively established that a 200 MHz Japanese radar at Balikpapan was directing anti-aircraft searchlights" that this deployment could be confirmed.

Days later, as the landings at Leyte were pending, *Lady June II* intercepted signals from a Japanese search radar on Suluan Island, overlooking the entrance to Leyte Gulf, where the invasion troops were to go ashore. As a result of this discovery, a party of U.S. Rangers landed on Suluan before the main invasion and destroyed the set. Good work indeed.[10]

Combat losses still

Although the expanded mission tempo and the strikes against more distant and heavily defended targets were expected to generate an increase in combat losses and operational incidents, this did not occur. Probably plain good fortune combined with better operational planning and improved maintenance of aircraft created this month of best efforts and low losses, but there was one incident that took down a veteran aircrew and airplane and marked a turning point in the trend of the war, at least to the men who watched it and relived it back at Morotai.

On 21 April, the crews of Lieutenants Beaver and Cole mounted Mission 868-616 in 081 and 397 respectively, and headed to patrol the southern Makassar Strait, looking for shipping that had been reported active there. Shortly after noon, they found a small convoy and ran in to bomb and strafe these ships. Both aircraft were still bomb-laden and were maneuvering to make follow-up attacks when they were intercepted at 6,500 feet by three fighters. These fighters were believed to have been dispatched from the airdrome at Makassar and the three pressed attacks on the Liberators. Five firing passes on the Beaver aircraft were made, the closest passing within 200 yards in a head-on approach. The Japanese aircraft, described as one "Zeke" and two "Tojos," also dropped phosphorous bombs on the two SB-24s which were ineffective.

The Mission Report takes the narrative to its fateful conclusion:

> The third plane, a Tojo that had dropped its wing tanks, flew parallel and to the right of the wing Snooper (Beaver) 1000 feet above. The Tojo then went ahead and turned into the lead plane attacking from 1 o'clock high in a dive. The Tojo dove below the level of the SB-24 and the last phase of the attack was from below. The Snooper turned down and nosed into the path of the fighter bringing the attack to 12 o'clock low. Both the Snooper and the fighter were firing and neither aircraft veered from course.
>
> The fighter first struck the Beaver aircraft under the nose, chewing along the underside of the Snooper and ramming itself up into the bomb bay. The fighter appeared to disintegrate and the SB-24 burst into a ball of flame, nosing up and falling off on the left wing. The Beaver plane settled into a tail-down flat spin and crashed into the water six miles off Makassar Town. Approximately five seconds after the collision one chute partially opened and emerged on fire from the falling wreckage. It is the opinion of the (Cole crew) that this flaming chute was that of the fighter pilot.

The two surviving fighters flew with and continued to attack the surviving SB-24 for about 25 miles and then broke off and headed back to Makassar airdrome. The Cole aircraft completed its mission and landed at midnight, there telling the sad tale of the first squadron loss by "ramming." Some conjecture by squadron veterans ensued with many believing that this was not a suicide attack but rather a misjudgment on the part of the attacking Tojo who had not expected the Beaver aircraft to turn into his path of attack to bring the full firepower of the nose turret to bear. In any event, these 10 men of the William Beaver crew were recorded as "Killed in Action" as the only squadron casualties of the month.

The month in retrospect

The squadron's monthly report to higher command for April 1945 was impressive, recording 71 missions involving no fewer than 131 aircraft reaching assigned targets. Over 120 tons of bombs were dropped on targets and more than 70,000 rounds of machine-gun were fired while strafing. The squadron had done it all—missions to all the major water routes from Java north to Borneo, the Celebes, French Indochina, convoy overflight protection on the anti-submarine front, radar ferret missions to find and categorize enemy radar sites throughout the operational area and, finally, the extreme long-range strikes on Surabaya. Impressively, the Harriss operation saw 21 first or command pilots in action, including Harriss and his new Operations Officer, Captain Robert Townsend. The squadron manpower had nearly doubled as the operations staff was expanded and more aircraft and crews joined the squadron. The 868th was back.

With its usual unbridled enthusiasm, the squadron's monthly historical narrative heaped attention on all the new officers who had come into the expanding unit, profiling each and emphasizing that the new squadron commanding officer was staffing up with his hand-selected managers at all levels. Not unexpectedly, the man most lauded was Major Baylis E. Harriss:

He is but thirty years old and was born in Galveston, Texas, however he has maintained his residence in Clovis, New Mexico and Tucson, Arizona. He attended Columbia Military Academy, St Edwards University in Austin, Texas, and the University of California. He engaged in the business of livestock, soon became interested in flying and prior to entering service, he became a commercial pilot. With over 1000 hours to his credit in 1941, he joined the Royal Air Force as a combat pilot.

While in the RAF he received a wealth of experience under all combat conditions. Major Harriss has a total of 2460 hours of flight time with the RAF, 1300 hours of which were in combat, comprising 300 hours in fighters, 550 in medium bombers and the balance in Ferrying Command. In 52 bomber combat missions out of the United Kingdom, he flew against France, Germany, Italy and Czechoslovakia and was in the formation that smashed the famous Skoda Works. As a Squadron Leader of the RAF's 408 Squadron, he flew Lancasters, Halifax and Bostons, and in fighters flew Spitfires, Hurricanes and Beaufighters.

His daring achievements in the air and against the enemy targets soon distinguished him and he received many commendations and awards, including the Order of the British Empire, the British Distinguished Flying Cross, the English Star, the American Volunteer Commemorative Medallion and the Allied Service Medallion, among others. He joined the U.S. Army Eighth Air Force in Europe in July 1943 and returned to the United States and was sent to the Pacific in October 1944 for combat service.[11]

The above overwrought praise continues for another full page of closely spaced commentary. The one telling sentence that stands out, however, is the stark admission that when Harriss took command of the squadron, everything and everyone was on the ropes. Details are provided as to how Harriss basically "cleaned house" at the executive level, and proceeded to unite the "combat crews, the grease monkeys and pencil pushers," turning around the demoralized, undermanned and unattended squadron. In so doing, he "accomplished the seemingly impossible." Although it probably did not need to be said, our squadron scribe finished his monthly report with a commanding salute to the new sheriff in town: "Truly and deservedly, he has become the nucleus and motivating factor for all squadron activities." This complemented an opening observation that "His experiences and adventures would make for a first-rate thriller!" The monthly report goes on to profile the entire squadron executive team in equally effusive terms.

Getting into the Big Show—Japan

Much of the aggressiveness orchestrated by Harriss that month and beyond could be ascribed to his personal conviction that the squadron could be turned around in short order under his leadership. He realized that his men and aircraft would have to prove their worth if the 868th were to claim a prominent role in the upcoming invasion of Japan. Many knew that the first of a series of invasions of the Home Islands would begin in the final months of 1945, and a reasonable assumption was that the invasion would probably begin on the southern island of Kyushu in October. This was the plan and the fight over those islands, beyond the strategic bombing campaign of the Twenty-First Air

Force and its fleets of B-29s, had already begun. The U.S. Navy fast carrier fleets were striking mainland tactical targets and the fighter and bomber groups of the FEAF were jockeying for positions on the airfields on Okinawa.

Harriss was determined that the 868th would be there, up front to fly against Kyushu from Okinawa, to perform its own missions as the first invasion approached and as that fight played out. Much of what was to occur in the 868th as it continued to operate from Morotai in the coming weeks was designed to call attention to the squadron and reinforce its commander's effort to have the unit transferred to Okinawa. To be somewhat repetitive, almost all involved were not counting on an early or clean end to the war and assumed that Japan would only be broken when the main island of Honshu was conquered, Tokyo occupied, the emperor deposed and the empire shattered by the blood of American and Allied combat troops on the soil of Japan proper. Harriss was planning, as he should have, that he would lead the 868th through at least another year of war and that the squadron would not go home until sometime in 1946, if not even later.

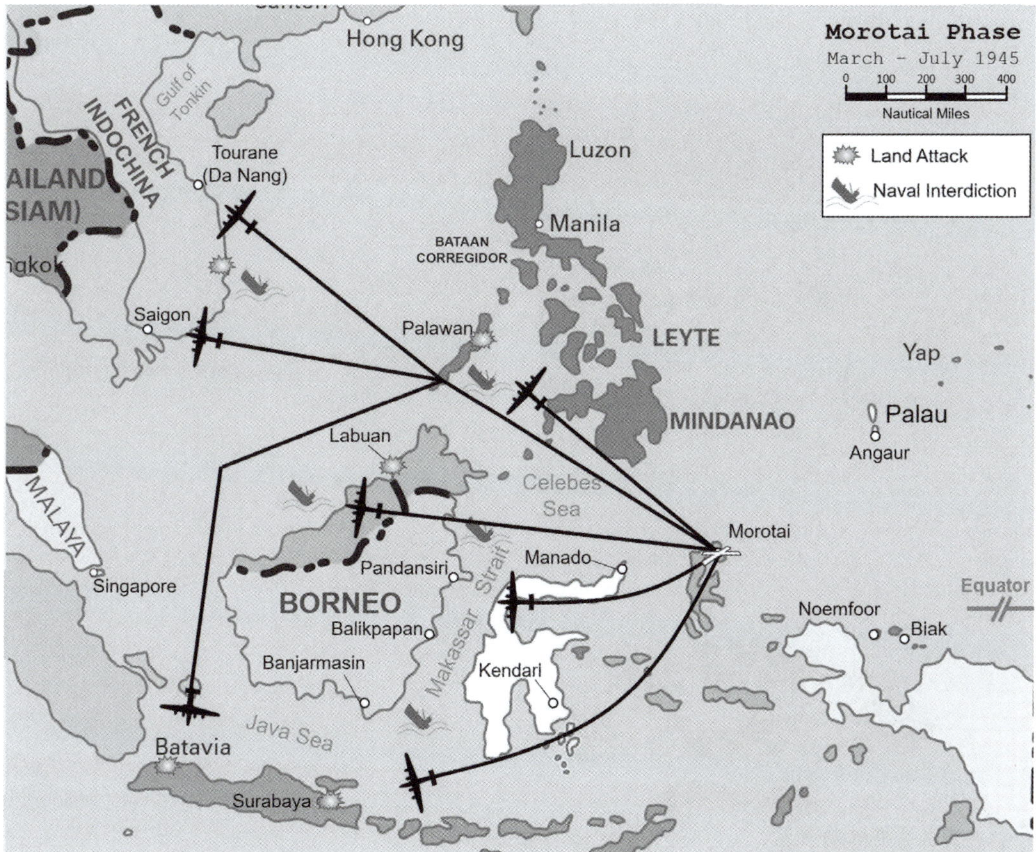

Morotai phase March–July 1945, indicating 868th Squadron sea-search attacks and land target strikes to the northwest (Philippines and French Indochina) and west and southwest (Dutch East Indies). (Chris Chen/Telemus)

868th Squadron Aircraft and Activity

Squadron group photo, Noemfoor early 1945. (Author's collection assembled/restored from 868th Squadron veterans and Colonel Werner)

Squadron "Snooper Airlines" C-47 transport. (Author's collection assembled/restored from 868th Squadron veterans and Colonel Werner)

Squadron "Snooper Express" B-25C transport. (Author's collection assembled/restored from 868th Squadron veterans and Colonel Werner)

Squadron signboard, Okinawa, August 1945. (Author's collection assembled/restored from 868th Squadron veterans and Colonel Werner)

Squadron attack on Serina oil field installations, Borneo, December 1944. (Author's collection assembled/restored from 868th Squadron veterans and Colonel Werner)

Squadron attack on Sanga Sanga oil installations, Borneo, December 1944. (Author's collection assembled/restored from 868th Squadron veterans and Colonel Werner)

Squadron attack on oil tanker, Basset River, French Indochina, July 1945. (Author's collection assembled/restored from 868th Squadron veterans and Colonel Werner)

Attack on oil pipeline bridge, Borneo, November 1944. (Author's collection assembled/restored from 868th Squadron veterans and Colonel Werner)

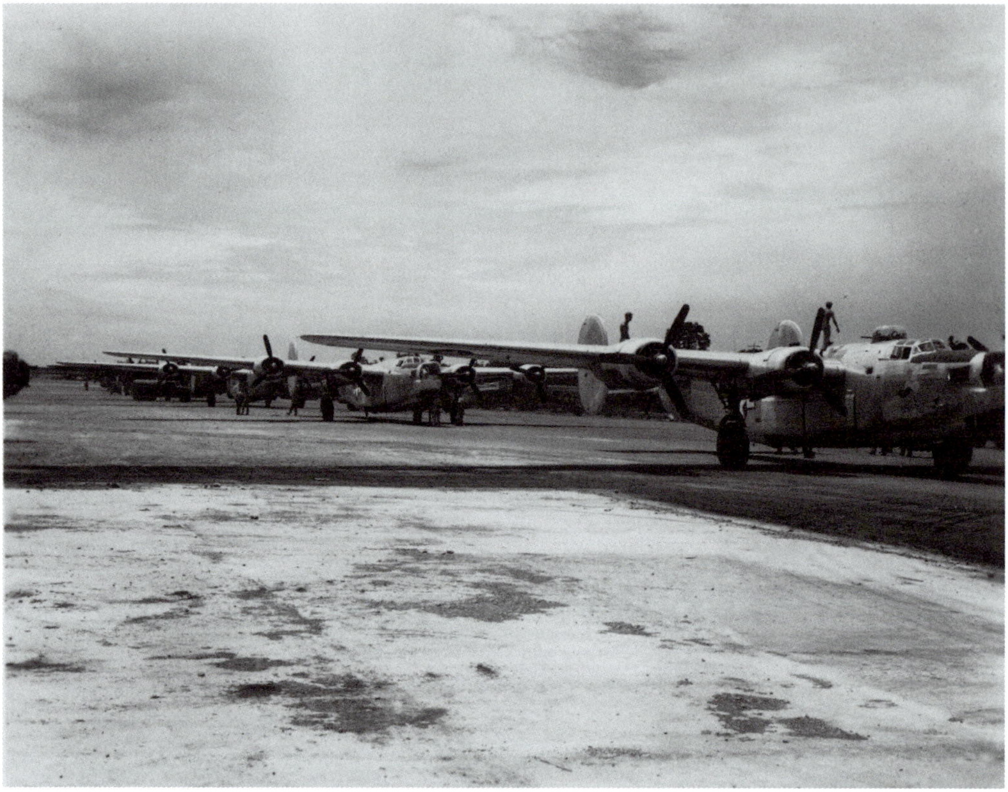

868th Squadron SB-24s depart for the Batavia mission.

Okinawa -
Dear Snooper — 8, Sept. '45
Words cannot express my feeling of gratitude for the spirit of cooperation, consideration, and loyalty you've given me - the cheerfulness and grim determination you've shown when things were tough, the way you have tackled impossible jobs and the way you've overcome all obstacles to make our outfit the best - is the greatest honor I'll ever have bestowed upon me. I shall always cherish our association and remember your friendship - Good hunting, and good luck to you always -

Most Sincerely

Bayles E. Harriss

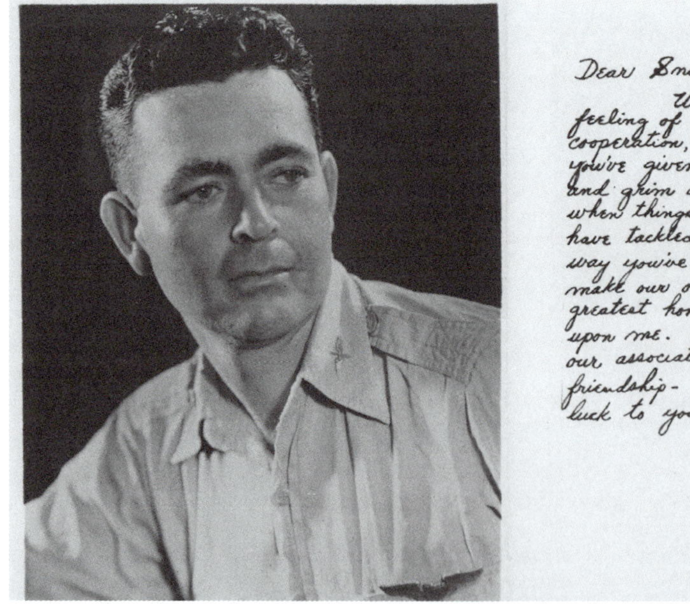

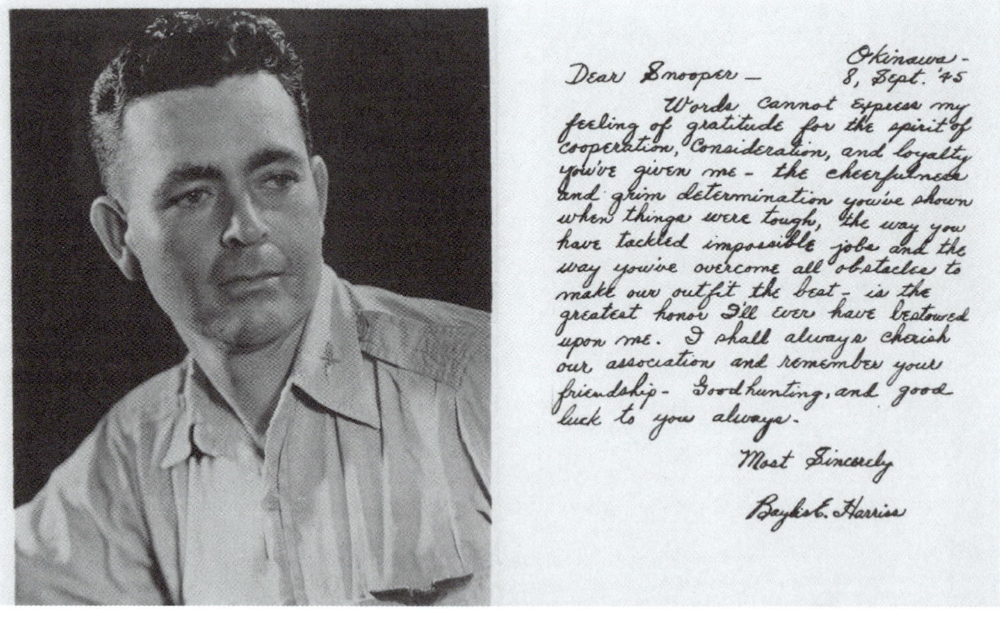

The message to the squadron from Harriss on 8 September 1945 as the unit is demobilized.

CHAPTER 21

Bob Thompson and Crew

November 1944–June 1945

Thirty-five years after his service in the Pacific, Robert "Bob" Thompson, an advertising executive with his own firm and part-time journalist living in Shreveport, Louisiana, recalled his days with the squadron and the events that shaped his future life. He did believe, in company with all of the 868th veterans, that the Snooper unit was truly unique, both because of the special mission profiles it flew and its relatively small size as a quasi-independent squadron within the expansive Thirteenth Air Force and the FEAF organizations. He considered that his was a "single ship business" with each plane out to hunt, not unlike the "quick fox in the hen house" where individual initiative and risk-taking were promoted and rewarded. Thompson related this service in the 868th to his coming of age "in the woods and marshes of South Louisiana, hunting in the light of dawn or at dusk, to strike a prey from an unexpected quarter, just doing it my way. Once inured, I would not have wanted to (go to war) any other way." As related to the author, in Bob Thompson's own words:

<u>Finding the 868th</u>
My crew and I flew with the 868th Squadron from mid-November 1944 through mid-June 1945 and while we had a good run and saw some combat, we had the feeling that we had missed the "heyday" of the unit when there were more shipping targets. We had trained as a regular daylight unit and had no experience as a LAB crew, learning this only once we were with the squadron for a few weeks. But my first impression when we arrived in the South Pacific was that somehow the higher command had lost track of the unit! When we arrived at the replacement depot at Nadzab, New Guinea, we were issued a non-LAB replacement airplane and were directed to join the squadron by an officer who "thought" the 868th was then based on Biak Island further up the New Guinea coast. So, we flew to Biak. There we were told that the 868th was not there but was "probably" at Morotai, so we flew there. No luck again. But they sent us down to Noemfoor and we finally located our squadron and signed in as a new crew. There was definitely a "backwater" mentality building there and, of course, the squadron was having a variety of issues—aircraft losses, memories of the poisoning at Christmas and support units had departed to bases further advanced. But those who were flying the missions were aggressive and impressive, especially for a crew like ours who were new to the war.

A DFC on our first mission

With almost no introduction or squadron-level training, we were selected as one of three crews to attack an oil installation just north of Balikpapan. We departed overloaded with fuel and bombs shortly after midnight, flew west to the Borneo coast and rendezvoused at dawn exactly on schedule at the mouth of a river. We went up the river in a train of three aircraft, ours the last of the three, flying at a level BELOW the treetops, maybe only 50 feet above the water. The plan was to "pop up" as we reached the target and once we were into that field, bomb and shoot up everything at the oil field, including a trestle bridge that carried a large pipeline across an expanse of water. One of the crew came on the intercom and noted, stating the all too obvious, that we had never trained for this back in the states and here we were at the treetop level going up a river with people shooting at us from both the banks!

Ours was one of two absolutely new crews, the other being that of a Lieutenant Greene, which occurred to me to be a very appropriate name in this situation. The mission lead was a crew captained by Bob Hickson, an experienced and very skillful pilot who took us up that river, a run of 10 miles or so. He broke us out of the tree line to begin the attack exactly as programmed. The oil field installations—pumping stations, wells and storage tanks—were suddenly right under us and all three planes were shooting everything up, all guns firing, racing along no higher than 100 feet above the derricks. The enemy gunners came alive and were shooting back, their fire defined by the tracers that seemed to reach out and hit all three planes as we flew right down the middle of the complex. At that point, I realized that I was falling behind the first two planes so I poured on the coal to gain speed and catch up. Straight ahead was the bridge with the pipeline and our mission leader Hickson toggled his load to have the delayed fuses explode his bombs alongside the target.

Greene was behind the leader and was next in line to hit the bridge. But I suddenly realized that I had made up too much distance and that I would probably arrive over the target at the exact time that Greene's bombs would likely be exploding—directly beneath our airplane! I cranked the B-24 hard over to the right to begin a 360-degree turn to go around to take a "safer" run to bomb the trestle bridge. In doing so I flew us directly over the oil field and its by now very active gunners. There were people running across the oil field and everyone was shooting at (by then only) us with anything they had. As I banked the aircraft as sharply as I dared at that incredible low altitude what crossed my mind was, "Damn, if all the missions are like this first one, there is no way I will survive this war."

As I started to come out of the turn and looked for Greene, we realized that he had not released his bombs, apparently due to some malfunction, and that he was making a mirror image go-around, having overflown and turned off the target to loop around to the left. He was circling to line up for another run. I was determined to hit the bridge and as we approached, I saw that flight leader Hickson had hit it square with two sections dropped into the water. Our bombs struck it as well and blew it apart, dropping more of it into the water.

At this point, as Greene made his new approach, it was clear that his bombs might be better placed elsewhere. Our leader announced that Greene should take his aircraft back to the harbor area where there might be a "target of opportunity" for Greene and his bombs and Hickson was right. With Greene in the lead and the two of us following at distance to provide "fire support," we went back across the oilfield, only to be greeted on our third transit by the AA crews. Greene found a small tanker sitting at a dock taking on oil and bombed it squarely, sinking it in place. Hickson and our plane strafed the entire mess and we collected together and departed.

As we left the target area, Hickson realized that he had lost an engine to the anti-aircraft (AA) fire and had to feather it. We had all taken a lot of fire but incredibly, not one man was wounded or killed. As we departed the scene and headed home, having nothing to compare this experience with as it was our first mission, I thought the future of our crew with the 868th would be quite short.

Back at base, the intelligence people and after-action assessments noted the great damage we had done with this low-level mission, in contrast to the daylight higher-altitude B-24 formation attacks which had failed to deliver. XIII Bomber Command leadership opted to award the Distinguished Flying Cross to all three of the crews, and our flight leader received the Silver Star. He deserved it.

On this mission, Hickson and crew flew aircraft 899, Greene flew 025 and we flew *Our Baby* 396. The "Official Mission Report" strangely has it all wrong as to who did what with these aircraft. Greene's bombs hung up and it was Hickson in 899 who had the engine shot out. I recall discussing the mission with my co-pilot and remarking, to his full agreement, that if one of the three of us had to take an engine hit and get the plane home on three fans, it was best that it happened to the most experienced pilot, not two crews who were on their first mission. Another item missed in the Report was the fact that our three planes carried a total of 27 five hundred-pound bombs. Greene put his on the dock area and the tanker, and Hickson and I put the balance on the trestle, with "eight direct hits observed," and the Report then leaves it at that. Beyond the bombs that exploded when dropped, several of ours had deployed with fuses delayed for detonation at the 24 or 48-hour points. The intent was to take out any rebuild or the crews that might still be doing the repair work a day or two later. A month after our attack that oil pipeline trestle was still in the water in a half-dozen pieces and the pipeline was not providing oil to the export terminal or refinery.

On the second mission to this oil complex, to Lutong/Miri/Seria on 12 December, we were pleased to be able to bomb at 4,000 feet altitude and we probably should credit this as more of a "piece of cake photo run" than a full low-level strike. Earlier that day Lieutenant Barry did complete another bombing and strafing attack at 100 feet so we all thought that he should get the award for derring-do. We all had to compare ourselves, one way or the other, to Captain Wallace who had established the profile for low-level repeat attacks over a defended area with his Lutong strike. We knew that on the 8 December single-plane mission he made no fewer than 16 on-the-deck strafing runs over the oil facility, not the lower number reflected in some reports. This guy had the personality of a fighter pilot and I do not think that he had the right psychological profile to take a crew to war in the B-24. When he transferred out to join a P-38 squadron it was the right thing for him, his crew and the 868th. He was our "ace" for sure and exhibited real courage, but he scared a lot of people with his aggressiveness, including me.

<u>Two mission close calls</u>
What memories one carries sometimes include the pleasant but also the most terrifying. After that first attack on the oil field, the missions settled into a routine, with night missions on radar patrols, daylight strikes and RCM searches and attacks on radar sites. But one black-of-night engagement stands out for me. In the Makassar Strait, we detected a small convoy, maybe three ships, and as we closed on them, they detected us and started taking evasive actions and throwing the AA at us, eight miles out and with heavy fire with tracers. There was good direction in the firing and we knew that these were NOT merchant ships. We closed several times, but the combination of their wild maneuvering and the heavy pyrotechnic AA fire caused my bombardier to fail to get a fix on a target at the three-mile-out point. We would turn away, line up with radar and come in again.

Finally, we got a good LAB run and pressed in to attack, closing with the ship that was throwing a lot at us. I noticed that my knees and legs were shaking uncontrollably and I could not regain my composure. Fortunately, our bombardier then had control of the airplane and held it through bomb release at 1,500 feet. We flew directly over the ship and, as we did so, the primary and secondary explosions lifted us and tossed us high and to the side. I stuck the nose down, piled on the speed and we rolled off and got out of there.

And there were events on the "just plain dumb" side of the equation when you make tactical decisions that you should have avoided and get punished for it. In one daylight patrol, we found what we thought was an easy target in the Makassar Strait, made a run on it from 6,500 feet and we took him far too lightly. On our run he hit us four times with his 25-mm mount, Japan's version of our multiple-barrel "Chicago Piano" mount, once just under the flight deck (our seat), once in the bomb bay, once in the waist area and once on the forward edge of the left horizontal stabilizer, peeling back the metal like a giant flower blooming. This last hit effectively blanked out 50 percent of the vertical control surfaces and it became impossible to hold the plane straight and level. The B-24 had to be man-handled and both the co-pilot and I had a physical struggle on our hands.

The shell that exploded in the bomb bay sent fragments into the fuel tanks and gasoline was pouring and spraying everywhere. The hydraulics were also hit and we lost all fluid. We cut the electrical systems—all radios, lights, everything—to reduce the fire hazard and I put the plane on autopilot. The plane bucked and jumped around in the sky as that autopilot struggled to control it but it settled down to keep us on an even keel. Meanwhile, I had dumped the remaining bombs and I pointed us to the nearest land, enemy-held or not, assuming that we would have to put it down in the water. When we approached that island, we discussed it and agreed that we might be able to make it back to Morotai, about five hours away. That would make our ETA about nine at night and necessitate all the dangers of a night landing with a plane that was only controllable on autopilot. With hydraulics out, we would have to hand-crank the landing gear down, pump down the flaps by hand and rig parachutes out the waist doors to brake the plane once it touched down. There would only be one chance in this landing, no go-around.

An hour or so after being hit, we joined up with another 868th ship that had just completed its mission and communicated with it by Aldis lamp, explaining our situation, and they radioed ahead to the field to prepare for our return. When we reached the base, we "talked" to the tower by Aldis lamp and they gave us the green light for our one try. We went out a bit and I asked the crew if they wanted to bail out or ride in with the co-pilot and me. They all voted to stay with the plane. We made a slow turn and headed in, still on auto, the plane now bucking and vibrating from the buffing on the tail surface, like it was refusing to try to land. When the engineers cranked the gear down and my co-pilot George started pumping down the flaps, I yelled at the guys in the waist to complete the rigging of the two parachutes on each side tied to the gun supports and prepare to pop them when the wheels hit.

We came in over the beach at 300 feet, too high, and I reached up and cut the autopilot, chopping back on the engines, causing the nose to drop quickly. George and I braced hard on the rudder pedals and hauled back on the control wheels, still trying to get the nose up. At that second, she "porpoised" up and the wheels hit the coral surface, we "crabbed in" on one wheel and the first two 'chutes were popped and immediately were torn away by the speed of the plane. The second two held and slowed us and we rolled to a stop at the very end of the runway. We all climbed out, got down on our knees alongside the plane and literally kissed the ground. It had been one terrifying flight home. We had taken that single ship for granted and it hit us hard for that arrogance, almost killing us. This was a lesson learned for our tour and for our lives. The service section counted over 200 fragment holes in the plane and it was a real miracle that none of the crew had been hit or killed.

<u>Managing fear or not</u>
Looking back objectively I can say that we probably feared our initial missions because we were not sure of what we were doing but, somewhere around the fifth mission the brain stepped in and gave us the ability to cope. In my case, I split into two personalities. The "inner me" was quiet and sublimated by what I saw around me, but with an intense desire to live and a nagging fear that I would not. The outer me was sullen and deadened to the inner feelings, indifferent with an "I don't give a damn" attitude toward risks. A "what difference does it make, we all have to die sometime, over Borneo or in bed." The outer me dominated and this sustained me throughout the majority of

our missions, even as our mission numbers piled up. But around mission 35, when we had only five to ten to complete before rotation back to the States, a change occurred in me and the old dreads returned. Suddenly we *did* give a damn again and the last weeks were as bad as the first in terms of fear of death. The squadron must have sensed this issue and typically assigned "milk runs" for our last three missions.

That last mission was an operational challenge but did not involve any combat. It was the most extended B-24 flight I had ever made—a long-range weather recon that was scheduled for 21 hours but which we completed in 19. We carried four bomb bay tanks and no bombs, stripped the plane of all armor, with guns removed and flew only a seven-man crew. It was an easy mission and when I brought that big black bird back to Morotai, I greased it in for a decent landing, taxied into a revetment, switched it off, got out and walked away from the war.

But I did have to contend with what I would call "uncontrollable fear" with one of my crew. He had a paralyzing concern on take-offs but once we were in the air, he was fully functional and fine. Toward the end of our tour, he would position himself close to our navigator and hold his face in his hands, press his head into the navigator's stomach, in a childlike clinging to Phelps insisting that his friend hold him. Once we were airborne, this crewman would rise and go to his position and function well for the rest of the mission. On our thirty-eighth mission, though, he broke mentally and suddenly jumped up from his kneeling position as we rumbled down the airstrip. Racing back into the waist of the plane he attempted to jump through the partially open bomb bay doors. Our navigator and bombardier ran him down and grabbed him, holding him on the deck as we lifted off at 120 miles an hour, undoubtedly saving his life. On the next mission, now number 39, I had both the bombardier and the navigator hold him physically on take-off to prevent a repeat performance.

On the last mission, the 19-hour run, I asked our squadron physician to ride along in case we had any problems. I was determined that this crewman would complete this last mission with the rest of the crew so that we could all go home together. Many years later, he and his wife visited me in Shreveport and nothing of this incident was mentioned except for the fact that he told me quietly that, after his return to the States from the Pacific, he had never flown again in an airplane and would never do so for the balance of his life. I quipped that his comment seemed to be one hell of a recommendation for my reputation as a pilot. He only smiled and said nothing, but it was obvious that the fear he had developed over the Pacific in our B-24 was still very much with him.

All of this made me realize that the baptism of fear we had all received in those missions had served me well and that in the face of subsequent travails in my life, nothing that came my way could ever match the fear that I had already experienced and learned to overcome.

RCM missions in *Lady June II*

I flew this aircraft on several missions and I think this was one of the first such dedicated aircraft in the entire South Pacific, or perhaps in the XIII Bomber Command. My recollection is that the RCM plane had two roles: first as a search and destroy aircraft that would go out to locate, plot and ideally destroy enemy radar stations and, second, to lead on group missions where we would identify the early-warning radar and then attempt to jam the enemy radar defenses as the other aircraft came in with us.

This first exercise was a cat-and-mouse situation where we knew the approximate location of [a] Japanese radar installation but did not know, and therefore could not attack, the exact structure. We would "fly a box" in our designated search area, search for the radar's signal and once found then use our directional receiver to get a relative bearing on the radar's location. Our navigator then used the equipment to draw several "lines of position" [LOP] that gave us different vectors that intersected on his plotting board. This work provided us the exact location of the target. With this plot we would go back out 20 miles and then run in to visually identify and attack the radar installation.

But the enemy radar operators were clever and if we saw them, they saw us and knew that we were looking for them. Typically, after we entered the second leg of our box to get a 90-degree fix, or on the third leg for sure, his radar would go from sweep scan to vector scan, an indication that we were out there looking for him. He would then shut down and wait. Often, we would proceed to what we thought the location might be, and when we found him, we would attack his "hut" and his bedsprings antenna. If we failed to find him, we would go back out and fly just above the wave tops for a while to hide our plane from his radar. After an hour or so, we would pop back up, try to catch his radar signal anew and plot him with a new LOP or two.

If we did find him and attack, there was usually very light anti-aircraft fire as the locations were remote. We found that we could put a radar out of action fairly easily and that, even if we did not destroy the unit, the enemy would disassemble it and move it, shutting it down for several days— mission accomplished. On these missions, we carried 11 men, our normal 10 and an RCM specialist and the RCM equipment was located in the waist area just behind the bomb bay and before the waist gunners' area. The *Lady June II* was painted flat black and was basically indistinguishable from other SB-24s in the squadron. I recalled her as a good ship to fly.

<u>Australia and the Aussies</u>

We had incredible respect for the people of Australia who seemed to welcome us on our leave there. By the time my crew visited Sydney for 10 days of "rest and recreation" at the halfway point in our service, perhaps after 20 missions or so, the country had seen a lot of Americans and I was pleasantly surprised that the common people had not seen too much of us. In fact, on the streets, it was my experience that older Aussies would approach us and extend a hand to thank us for our service. But there was a special kinship here, almost a refresh of the spirit of the American Old West, as these were a rugged bunch who were just taking on the trappings of the 20th century, with frontiers yet to be tamed. By kinship I mean they seemed to identify with us that we had traveled a similar road to independence and they expected us to have a rebellious spirit like them as we were Americans.

What a great group of people. I recall a briefing that we were given before our trip to Sydney which went something like this: The Australians were friendly but we Americans were not to take advantage of this friendship to "push our weight around." Their beer was twice as strong as ours and an Aussie male, if provoked to action, would not hesitate to put some knots on your head. Australian girls were a good deal more open about sex but if an Aussie family did invite a U.S. serviceman to spend a night in their home, as was often the case, this was not an invitation to "romp beneath the sheets with their daughters."

The plain fact is that I fell in love in Sydney with a girl named Anne. It happened quickly and was unexpected by both of us. Once our crew was on the ground in Sydney, we all scattered to the wind and I paired up with my navigator Phelps. After a few nights on the town, we ended up at Luna Park, an amusement center in Sydney Harbor. There I met a beautiful quiet girl, no "Sheila" this one, and we talked. She lived with her parents in a small town on Botany Bay south of the city. She invited me to spend time with her parents there and while she told me what train to take in the morning, I was uncertain that she would be there to meet me. But I took the chance that she would be at the train station and there she was as my train pulled in, waiting for me on the platform, dressed in a chiffon frock, a picture-perfect hat, with a small dog on a leash and a shopping basket on her arm. She was to me a vision—and the war, the flying, the islands, the enemy and the mud and the rain were all far away.

I spent the rest of my leave there with her and her family. Mom and Bill were wonderful people as well and over that week or so we became a family of sorts. Their son was in the Atlantic in the Royal Australian Navy, and I wore his work clothes to mend fences and such. I knew my crew probably wondered where I was, but I had simply disappeared. I was confident that none of them would have believed me if I had tried to find them and explain. Finally, after a welcome five days of delay, the ATC told us that they had a plane back to base and we collected to go back to war.

Anne came with me to the airport to see me off. We wrote for months, her letters arriving in beautiful longhand on tissue-thin pages. She sent a photo of her and the parents, and a stuffed koala bear that finally went to pieces on Morotai. Her letters stopped about the time I went home to the States and to this day, almost 40 years later, I have her letters. I tell this because it was part of the story of the war. I will never forget her name, her letters, the love I felt for her ... and the way she looked in that chiffon dress that morning when I first got off the train to meet in her hometown station.

<u>My crew</u>
I was blessed to go overseas with and keep company throughout our combat tour with a solid crew. I say "solid" because they were a real mix of individuals:

Co-pilot—George Lewellen. A Portland, Oregon, boy who was the oldest man in the plane at age 27, married with no children, who had begun a career in the heavy trucking industry. He had no experience in the B-24 when he joined us as he had trained to fly in the B-17. He was a "good old boy" in every sense of the word, maybe not a great pilot, but solid on the mechanics of everything, always able to figure out the system and fix it. He was not a genius—none of us were—but he never broke under stress. George had a desperate desire to live and get home to his "Ruby" and get on with life. This was a great attitude.

Navigator—Richard G. Phelps. From Rhode Island and the "baby" of the officers at age 19. He was very intelligent and witty and a precise navigator, made not one mistake in the year we were flying together. He had a high school sweetheart, I believe her name was "Thelma," who he wrote to each day. I found out that he came home and married her. We all kidded him about his lack of sexual experience and he took that good-naturedly. Just a good man all around who was still growing up and doing so very fast, as were we all.

Bombardier—David Peavler. A Fort Worth-born and bred real Texan in his mid-20s. A wiry smallish man, at least then, with taciturn disposition who had been married but who was now overseas in the war and divorced. He maintained a certain aloofness, but that was fine by all and he was probably the most fatalistic man in the crew. He showed little emotion one way or the other and elected to stay in the Air Force after the war and make a career of it.

Flight Engineer—Jack Smith. In his early 20s from somewhere in Kansas. He was a "likable lug" from a small town who was a real eager beaver type, with a let's get into the airplane and do our job attitude. He was impressed by the responsibility he had with our plane, and our crew was impressed by him. We depended on him in so many ways. He had no formal education beyond high school but knew what he was doing in that plane. He returned to Kansas and married and I have thought about him a lot and stayed in touch over the years.

Radioman—Clarence Beaver. From Oklahoma originally and very focused and serious about his duties. He was quiet by nature but sought out other crewmen to partner with and would depend on them to help him to face the dangers of flying and combat. He was 18 or 19 at the time and came from a rural background, went back home after the war and married there.

The other crewmen—they were a cross-section of America. None gave me any problems and we all respected one another for who we were and where we came from.

Pilot—Robert Thompson. I was all of 25 when in command of that B-24, had grown up on a small farm in South Louisiana as the only child of an insurance man. He died when I was 11 and while we were not "dirt poor" we had to struggle. Public high school and then a graduate of LSU in 1940, I became a radio and print journalist before the war and I returned to that career after the war and created my own small company. As I write this, I am 60 and am remarried after losing my first wife of 24 years of marriage.

When we went to war, we were hyped, eager and willing to serve and do so proudly. To most of us, it seemed like we were participating in a great adventure that was blessed by God, in the Army Air Corps and wearing those silver wings. In the space of a few months, I went from the wheel of a '37 Ford 60 horsepower coupe to the control of a 4,800 horsepower B-24 heavy bomber, from a "jock" manning a 250-watt radio station to an "officer and gentleman" wearing his "50 mission crush" cap. It was quite an ego trip. We were unknowing and unsophisticated, believed everything we were told and we did not question authority. That is how things have to be when you go to war.

We knew absolutely that some of us would die but we believed that our nation was invincible. Our beliefs were simple—Rita Hayworth, War Bonds, Mom's apple pie and the girl that was waiting for us, some of us, back home. Simple and sentimental. And I did not have any burning hatred for the Japanese. They were just the "enemy" when we met them in the sky, to be defeated so that we could just get the war done and come home to the "way it was supposed to be." I was never disillusioned because we were simply doing what had to be done. And we did it and came home.

I never wanted to be a bomber pilot, and not because I considered myself to be a candidate "hot rock" fighter pilot. Rather, I simply did not want the responsibility, as a command pilot, for the lives of 10 other people. Being an only child and growing up remotely on a farm I was something of a loner as a youngster and had never been "in charge" of other men. In a way, with the 868th, I had the best of both worlds. While I accepted and came to enjoy the responsibility of the lives of 10 other men, we flew our missions as a single plane and made our own decisions on how we approached a mission and any attack and had that degree of control over our fate. In a way, in that B-24 over the South Pacific in command of that plane on a combat mission, I was back in the marshes of South Louisiana stalking geese in the rice fields of my childhood.[1]

The Barksdale B-24 rebuild

In the spring of 1979, I signed on to participate in the rebuild of a B-24 by a group of World War II veterans, ably assisted by a group of younger folks and "civilians" at the museum hosted by the nearby Barksdale Air Force Base. The aircraft, which we have provisionally named the *Ramp Tramp*, was in sorry shape when she was claimed by the organization, badly in need of replacement parts and a lot of hard work. Left to decay on an airfield in Arkansas, the hulk was lifted by helicopter into Barksdale early that year to begin the restoration work. One night we worked until almost midnight getting two new tires on the old girl, allowing the plane to be towed into a hangar and protected for work there.

As of July 1979, when the article "Ramp Tramp" appeared in the *Shreveport Journal*, we had located four engines, the wing tips, cowling assemblies plus had leads to acquire four turrets. In return for my volunteer work, I demanded my rights to be a "taxi test pilot" when she is finished. Interestingly, although this B-24 was built in 1944 and did not see combat overseas, she did serve at Langley Field as a training aircraft! In that role, she could have been a LAB ship but more likely an H2X bombing trainer, or maybe both.[2]

CHAPTER 22

Strangling the Empire, Morotai Operations

May–June 1945

Slugging it out in the Dutch East Indies

Sometime in May, Baylis Harriss and his superiors at XIII Bomber Command on Morotai began to fix their sights on the Home Islands and a projected movement of the squadron forward to base their bombers on Okinawa once it was secure. But until they could make that move, the current mission focus had to remain on the south and west—the Dutch East Indies. The Japanese were anticipating the inevitable invasion of their Home Islands and were scrambling to move as much war material and oil north to shore up war stocks on the four main islands. The Japanese expected to make an extended defense of the Home Islands and hoped to wear down the Allies over a year or more of prolonged and bloody ground combat to best position Japan to negotiate an acceptable peace treaty. An important component of this plan was the relocation of troops and aircraft which were now scattered throughout the empire back to Japan to reinforce units being reorganized for the last-ditch fight.

Once the Philippines were deemed to be lost and the defense of those islands left to the Japanese Army that had retired to the hills, the focus once again became the withdrawal of critical personnel from all points to the south, embarked for Japan on anything that could float and steam north. From Singapore and a dozen other ports, warships and merchantmen crammed thousands of military personnel and some civilians into their hulls and on their decks, making desperate runs for the home ports. The interception and destruction of the ships fleeing north was an immediate end in and of itself designed to reduce the available Japanese merchant or warship tonnage. But it was also an effort to deny the return of war-critical supplies, men and aircraft to Japan that, once home and re-provisioned, would be thrown against the Allied invasions to come. A plane, a ship, or a soldier trapped and bypassed in Southeast Asia would be one less to be faced by an American soldier or Marine wading ashore on Kyushu. A sailor fighting off a kamikaze strike on his ship could be spared one less diving aircraft. Thus, the active interdiction of these would-be "returnees" had become an obvious priority for the aircraft positioned to block them from returning home.

In one "dash for home" example known to this author, a collection of 500 aircrew and flight mechanics who had been assigned to Japanese Army Air Force training units scattered throughout Malaya were brought together in Singapore in late 1944. There they boarded the battleship *Haruna*. The ship embarked more than 1,000 Japanese troops and made a full-speed run to Sasebo, arriving safely six days later. The squadron's 20-odd aircraft, basic trainers of the Mansyū Ki-79 variety, had been based near Kwantan on Malaya's southeast coast. They were flown back to Japan that same month, where they were incorporated into a newly formed "special attack" or suicide unit for use at the time of the Allied invasion of Kyushu. The aircrew who made it back to Japan on the *Haruna* assumed that they had been brought home to fly their own one-way death missions, either in the battle for Kyushu or in the follow-up invasion of the main island of Honshū.[1]

Victory in Europe, War in the Pacific

On Morotai there was a brief pause when, on 9 May, the squadron personnel and the entire Pacific Theater learned that Germany had surrendered and the war in Europe was over. Victory in Europe Day (VE Day) meant that additional forces would soon flow to the Pacific as the invasion of Japan loomed. These forces were additional to those already training and moving across the United States to West Coast embarkation ports. It also meant that those at home waiting for the "world war" to be over would now turn their full attention to the Pacific with unrealistic expectations that the war there could somehow be won faster. But there was no expectation among the men on Morotai preparing to launch on their next mission against the enemy that the war against Japan was anywhere near being over. A "Victory Europe" celebration that evening with an extra beer ration was in order, and the 307th Bomb Group would re-show their latest outdoor movie—*A Tree Grows in Brooklyn*. Another man's diary would recall a celebration of sorts the following day when a group of P-40s flew low over the airfield in a "V E" formation, and he would write "impressive" to record the day. But that same night of 9 May and at daybreak the next morning, SB-24s rolled down the airstrip and lifted into the sky. It was business as usual.[2]

May missions

In the first week of May, the squadron sustained the expanded mission pace that the increase in available aircraft and crews allowed Major Harriss to direct. In this seven-day period, no fewer than 34 aircraft patrolled the Makassar Strait, searching along the south and eastern coasts of Borneo and the coast of the southern Celebes. Many of these shipping searches turned up no activity but, when ships were found, they were aggressively attacked, resulting in Sugar Charlies left sunk or sinking. This period was also "airdrome week" with attacks mounted on enemy airdromes at Manggar (seven aircraft sortied), Langoan (six), Mandai (five), Boeloedowang (four) and Mapanget (two).

A new mission was added in these weeks: the protection of the sea lanes on which Allied convoys were now moving. Squadron aircrews undertook anti-submarine patrolling by day and night, resulting in 10 aircraft sent aloft. A single RCM or "ferret" mission was flown by *Lady June II* against a newly established radar site near Surabaya. Only one aircraft was badly damaged when a Snooper came home shot-up and was compelled to deploy parachutes for its landing. The plane had been holed by ground fire in the left stabilizer, the waist area and the bomb bay. (This incident was recounted by Bob Thompson in the previous chapter.) Aircraft 107 was towed away for a one-month stay in the hands of the repairmen of the 40th Service Squadron. One measure of the squadron's effort was the hour count for the week—a collective 1,700 hours in the air—more than doubling the previous week's 720 hours. Topping off a great week, the 868th combat enlisted men's basketball team defeated the ranking roundball team put on the court by XIII Bomber Command, 30 to 20! An extra ration of warm Australian beer was authorized.

The second week of May saw a return to the long-distance strike favored by squadron commander Harriss and with this mission the squadron would claim a record. On 7 May, the 868th sent a 10-aircraft strike against the Surabaya naval and commercial shipping basins on the island of Java. Four of the SB-24s carried a belly-load of 55-gallon napalm tanks which were deposited on the shipping found in the two harbors, while six aircraft made LAB runs against the ships anchored or maneuvering near the port in the Madura Strait. The harbor targets were hit and fires raged from the berthed shipping and dockyards that were still visible when the crews looked back from 50 miles away. Five choice shipping targets, ranging from 200 to 350 feet in length, were radar-detected and LAB-attacked outside the basin areas, with all claimed sunk or badly damaged. The RCM aircraft (464) flown by Lieutenant Olsen and crew performed its radar jamming mission in fine fashion and the strike was rated a solid success.[3]

Captain Earle Smith recalled this mission in a subsequent interview:

> This was my last mission before heading home to train with a B-29 squadron. Because I had served as the squadron's Operations Officer for several weeks my standard crew was one mission ahead of me in the mission count to rotate home. Baylis Harriss tapped me to sit in the command pilot's left seat in the RCM ship and it was a very long but almost routine flight. Great preparation had gone into this effort and fuel management was critical. We staged through Palawan and there topped off our tanks, even refilling AFTER our engine run-up by having the crew and locals sit in the tail to pull her end to the ground so we could literally "top-off" the wing tanks to the point of overflow, all to gain the extra miles.
>
> On the approach to target, our *Lady June II* confirmed that the local radars were asleep at the switch and we would be achieving total surprise. Over the target, shortly after midnight, the lights

> were all on in the harbor and the low-level aircraft had clear runs at the anchored and berthed shipping and the dock areas. The enemy below did not wake up until after our bombs were away and our aircraft were clearing the target area. On the flight back home, it was all about precise fuel management. When I landed and parked old 464 she had almost a half-hour of fuel left in her tanks. Two or three of the strike aircraft went dry as they taxied in and their starved engines began to quit, and they were towed into the pads. All in all, it was a good mission for the squadron and I went home about a week later with my crew.[4]

The squadron had put up 10 of its 14 available Liberators and each one performed as advertised with no turn backs or fouled equipment over the target. More impressively, the route flown by the 10 aircraft comprised 2,660 statute miles and the average mission time was 17 hours and five minutes. Indeed, during the first two weeks of the month, with 31 missions flown and 73 aircraft launched to accomplish them, there had only been two turn backs due to equipment issues. In the Pacific War at this point, given the conditions under which the unit was forced to work, including the chronic shortage of parts, a mission completion rate of over 90 percent was among the best that was put on the board by any unit in the command.

Other missions during the month included the almost-routine single-aircraft "ferret" patrols featuring the specially configured *Lady June II*. On these missions, 12-man crews either continued looking for new or relocated Japanese radar emitters or flew against radar sites that were known to exist but had eluded destruction, at least until the date of a given mission. Radar sites near Surabaya and Lemo in the Celebes were probed and a known site on Wowoni with two operating radars was struck to damage its towers, antennas and support buildings.

The RCM ship also looked to the east, back over the squadron's shoulder in the Pacific, with a three-mission return to "Fortress Rabaul" and its vicinity. The search here was for radar systems that had been reported as being active again in this bypassed area. Over a three-day period at mid-month, *Lady June II* searched the Rabaul, New Ireland, Buka and Tanga Island areas and discovered a new radar system up and running at Muliama. After "DF'ing" and plotting this installation for a follow-up attack by a daylight unit, the crew struck Rabaul proper with twenty-seven 250-pound bombs over three missions, just to remind the occupants that the 868th was still out there watching them.

Squadron operations

During May there were issues good and bad on the electronics front. Mid-month, a new H2X aircraft joined the squadron, a replacement for 081 which had been lost a few weeks before. The H2X ship appeared to function as advertised and it was put to use immediately. On the negative side, the squadron found itself begging for parts that its LAB systems required and borrowing test equipment that it had not yet acquired. The radar techs found that they had no equipment to bench test the AN/APS-15A and were allowed to use the test sets of other bomber units but could only do so between midnight and daybreak. This naturally resulted in a good degree of grumbling.

The little irritants were there as well, typical in a war zone where every unit was fending for itself. The radar shack's brand new 4x4 one-quarter ton vehicle, its pride and joy as its very own "jeep," had been stolen in late April and, over the following weeks, a determined scouring by squadron investigators failed to recover the purloined vehicle. Suspicion fell on the same U.S. Army ordnance company that had absconded with the squadron's six brand new jeeps back on Noemfoor, a loud-mouthed gang tented across the airfield. Another investigative effort was being made to determine which unit had pilfered the effects shipped by sea from the squadron's previous base at Noemfoor to the new digs at Morotai. U.S. Navy Seabees were the suspected parties, but the missing generators and equipment were all long gone.

The bureaucracy of "forms" had now arrived at the front to vex the 868th. No survey or report on the missing equipment could be filed in the absence of "WD AGO Form 15," none of which were available on Morotai. No forms, no claim, no path to ask for replacement equipment that was still on the inventory of the squadron but by now serving some other unit. Was it possible that the same U.S. Navy crewmen who sidetracked and bartered off the squadron's equipment for beer and steaks also had the forethought to steal the boxes of WD AGO Form 15s en route to Morotai? Anything was possible.

In the scramble to find and secure replacement parts for its growing fleet of SB-24s, the 868th could now employ two full-time utility aircraft. The venerated B-24D "Fat Cat" had recently departed the scene for the scrapyard, but a boneyard-fresh and now salvaged C-47 had been found to replace the "Snooper Airlines" C-47 that had disappeared somewhere between Sydney and Noemfoor back in December. This loss remained a mystery to the unit but the squadron needed its own passenger/cargo-liner and soon found a replacement. Bartering had acquired a rehabilitated B-25D Mitchell (43-3378) medium bomber from another unit on Noemfoor, shortly before the squadron had departed (worn aircraft were left behind by other units). By early May, the squadron's maintenance shop had it in hand, subjecting it to an engine change and a comprehensive overhaul, ready to fly and serve.

This sleek aircraft made its initial supply run for the squadron mid-month, heading to the large FEAF depot at Biak to collect critical parts that had kept two of the SB-24s grounded for several weeks. The B-25's Morotai–Biak connection demonstrated the aircraft's capacity at an "on-call" basis to range throughout the South Pacific to collect parts and equipment, which it proceeded to do on a regular basis. The all-cargo express B-25 was stripped of everything not required to fly the plane and had its bomb bay rigged to jettison its cargo in an emergency. The squadron's rehabilitated C-47 was configured as a passenger aircraft for R&R and "critical supply" runs to Australia. In May, the aircraft had a galley installed, complete with an electric stove and cabinets.

The 868th was stepping up in the world and regaining much of the independence it had lost during its previous "rough period."

On the combat side of the effort, testing and re-validating each of the squadron aircraft's LAB systems was again the order of the day. So too was a program that compelled crews to relearn some of the lessons which the Wright Project had brought to the Pacific almost two years before, many of which had been "unlearned" in the bad months of late 1944. There was also the issue of crew experience and continuity—crews rotating home at the 40 or 45 mission point had not been required to sit down with replacement crews and talk them through the systems. It continued that many of the crews arriving from the States had little training on the LAB systems that had been, and would be in the future, the core capability of the SB-24s.

For example, the computer unit of the LAB system, the AN/APQ-5B, was found to be vulnerable to mis-calibration with the result that LAB runs on a target would see bomb release delays and "overs" where none should have happened. This was particularly the case when an incorrect altimeter input was allowed or the pilot failed to hold a steady altitude throughout the full run to bomb release. These were errors of inexperience or overconfidence and had to be overcome.

Again, the early months of 1945 saw each of these deficiencies identified in the new crews and made right by the ever-vigilant Harriss team before any crew was declared as LAB-mission qualified. Higher command needed to be convinced that the squadron had regained its edge and could again work the dark-of-night LAB-abetted anti-shipping missions that it had brought to the Pacific War. Harriss was equally determined that his squadron would be able to claim this role as the war moved ever closer to Japan proper.

In the area of maximizing the utility of existing weapons systems, the 868th experimented with, and perfected the use of, the SB-24's radio or radar altimeter, the SCR-718. This piece of electronics had been a key component of the LAB system since day one but would now be employed for "radar pilotage" in inclement weather when other navigational systems failed or were not available. The SCR-718 was employed to navigate when weather denied celestial fixes, the AN/APS-15A system was inoperative, or proper LORAN charts were not available to allow that relatively new system to be used.

In this application, the aircraft was set on a heading and the SCR-718 was used to detect height-above-return when the aircraft passed over land and when it returned to the sea. By noting the altitudes registered from the radar altimeter, and referencing navigation maps, a reliable ground track was available for the navigator and allowed him and the pilots to continue a mission to target and then bring the plane home. It was not a perfect solution, but the aircrews proved they could make this work in a crunch as it allowed missions to be completed that otherwise might be aborted.

During May, in the missions/completion rate mentioned above, Harriss and his engineering section achieved an impressive 85 percent "in commission" rate for all available aircraft, bettering the previous month's 75 percent. The squadron's aircraft were in the air for a total of 1,977 hours, again setting a new level for the unit, particularly when compared to the March figure of a mere 700 hours. This achievement on the part of the engine mechanics, the hydraulic specialists, the "metal benders" and other repairers and maintainers was significant. All of this was accomplished despite shortages in replacement engines and parts. In many cases, a plane would be mechanically cleared to fly combat missions but kept offline due to issues with electronics, such as a failed radar or a mis-calibrated radar altimeter. But the radar and electronics shop was itself regaining high levels of performance as well, both with the existing LAB, radio and navigation systems as well as new systems that were being introduced into the aircraft.

Now based on Morotai, the squadron enjoyed access to FEAF and XIII Bomber Command subordinate service units, such as the 29th Mobile Training Unit. This team temporarily joined the 868th to retrain the crews on everything from engine and fuel systems and electronic supercharger controls to improvements in autopilot and bombsight revisions. The 868th's co-location with its bomber command and the two B-24 daylight bomb groups allowed the squadron to participate in regular command-level updates to which it had not had access to when it was "marooned" on Noemfoor. For example, the 307th Bomb Group Communications Division held radio operator classes daily and other group-level instruction was available on the flight line.

The core squadron accomplishment in May 1945 was that the 868th was demonstrating that it could absorb and maintain a larger number of aircraft—now in the fifteenth month of its presence in the Pacific—and offer them to higher command as combat-crewed and mission-ready. The squadron was considered to be "all up" with no fewer than 25 combat crews available for missions, or arrived and in the process of qualifying as such, with 15 SB-24s on the squadron rolls, inclusive of the single RCM ship.

Overall squadron personnel now numbered over 600 officers and men and all of the critical mission support divisions and teams were fully staffed. As one of the conditions set by Harriss in taking over the squadron, he had insisted that XIII Bomber Command deliver such support in aircraft, aircrews, maintenance personnel and equipment if the squadron performed as he promised it could. The command, with the squadron established on Morotai and demanding attention from across the airfield rather than from Noemfoor, was delivering on all fronts.

In the monthly narrative for May, the squadron's Deputy S-2 exceeded his previous emotive chronicling of the unit's progress, with this month's report to higher headquarters conveying his and the unit's increased enthusiasm:

> Indeed, with a spirit of daring, pride and achievement the Snoopers carry on: keeping alive the traditions and memories of their comrades, who gave their lives in a cause that shall forever immortalize their deeds. In the bright light of day and in the black of night, they seek out the enemy, destroying his weapons and carriers of destruction. No task or mission has yet been beyond their abilities and eagerness to accomplish.

The report continues:

> It was with this self-same spirit that Major Baylis E. Harriss, their Commanding Officer, led a formation of ten Snoopers against Surabaya, Java—one of the most heavily-fortified bases in the Dutch East Indies. The attack was carried out with such daring that before the enemy were aware of the Snoopers' presence, they had already completed their mission of destruction, leaving the naval and commercial basins in a shamble of ruins and fire and explosions that were visible for thirty minutes after our aircraft left the target area. In order to accomplish this mission, every possible precaution was taken in its preparation and planning. As this was one of the longest missions ever flown by B-24s, it was necessary that the crews be thoroughly and expeditiously briefed for every possible emergency. The outstanding feature in their pre-mission briefing was contributed by Major Harriss, who was to lead the formation. A very dramatic touch was added when Major Harriss, at the end of the briefing, told the men who were to take up this formation, that no plane would leave the target area until all had dropped all their ordnance on the assigned mission targets.[5]

The squadron narrative continues for another half-dozen paragraphs relating more details of the Surabaya mission in this vein, all centered on the leadership, planning competence and deft operational execution of Major Harriss. While this type of reporting may seem, in retrospect, a bit over-the-top and excessively personal, the point here is that Harriss, in planning and leading these types of missions, drove the entire squadron to realize its maximum potential as a combat unit.

His leadership talent was obvious as was his ability to motivate all the members of the squadron. When the mission briefing was completed, word spread throughout the squadron, down to the most junior engine maintenance mechanic rebuilding an engine, a recently arrived radar technician, or a mess cook, that the squadron commander was taking 10 aircraft to Surabaya to attack the Japanese there. This attitude instilled pride in the unit, provided squadron members bragging rights on the island base and allowed each of the men to be a party to the briefing and the mission about to be launched. Harriss justly deserved credit for his hands-on leadership and his "lead-from-the-cockpit" approach.

Okinawa on fire

In the last days of March 1945, the Allied offensive in the Pacific rolled toward Japan and mounted a massive invasion of Okinawa, the largest island of the Ryukyu chain, a territory which Japan had long considered to be part of its Home Islands. The island was critically positioned a mere 360 miles southwest of Kyushu. As such, it had been judged by Allied planners as the key organizational, basing and launch point for the pending invasion of the four main islands. The fight on Okinawa was extremely bitter and costly, approaching the intensity of Saipan, with a heavy toll taken on the Japanese garrison and Okinawa civilians, many of whom had been willingly or unwillingly conscripted into combat service by the Japanese. Equally distressing was the human toll in dead, wounded and missing of the U.S. Army and U.S. Marines committed to the battle, not to mention the sailors offshore.

In the rugged terrain of Okinawa, the Japanese fought a cave-by-cave extended battle that continued to rage through all of April and into May. More alarming than the ground fight was the damage done to U.S. Navy and Allied warships and their crews by the attacking waves of Japanese suicide aircraft. The air assault was horrific and came as a shock to sailors who thought they had seen the worst of sea combat but were now facing a different class of determined enemy. Every Allied planner understood that all of this, on land with the phased resistance and at sea as the kamikazes slammed into U.S. ships, was but a foretaste of the combat expected when the first of the Home Islands was invaded.

But the taking of Okinawa was unavoidable and there would be no "bypassing" this fortress, as had been the case with Rabaul and a dozen other smaller but well-staffed Japanese island bases over the past year. As a contemporary official history of the events of the day noted:

> Okinawa … had long been regarded by the Joint Chiefs of Staff as a military objective of the greatest strategic importance. Allied control of this outpost in the Japanese home waters would provide bases from which to launch overwhelming air and naval forces against the main enemy islands and their sea approaches. Such bases would support further operations in the regions bordering the East China Sea and would cut enemy communications between the Japanese Empire and Formosa, the mainland of Asia and the Netherlands East Indies. Allied surface vessels would have access to the coasts of China and Korea and … amphibious invasions could be mounted against the Japanese archipelago … and the island's proximity of the island to Japan (allow) the use of medium bombers and land-based fighters against Kyushu and Korea.[6]

During the fighting on Okinawa, in mid-April, General MacArthur assumed command of a new organization—the Army Forces, Pacific or AFPAC—whose purpose was the planning and execution of Operations *Olympic* and *Coronet*. These would be the invasions of the main islands of Kyushu and Honshu, slated to occur in early November 1945 and sometime in spring 1946, respectively. On Okinawa, as the coastal land was cleared and the fighting moved into the hills and valleys where the Japanese sustained a fight-to-the-death resistance, U.S. Army Engineers swarmed onto the island to build airfields. Some 31,400 combat engineers would be on-island by May, with no less than nine separate airfields planned for reconstruction or new building.

Yontan Airdrome, fast by the East China Sea on the island's southeastern coast, was a hub of activity and it was to this location that Baylis Harriss was determined to relocate his squadron. Yet the May–June 1945 period was still the time for Harriss and the 868th to send more missions to the south and west. This continuing battle rhythm was designed to take the war to the enemy wherever he could be found while improving the proficiency of the unit. It also served to increase the squadron's ability to claim a first-among-equals position within XIII Bomber Command. Harriss and his staff were quietly planning the best approach to relocate the squadron to Okinawa as quickly as the AFPAC and FEAF overall force relocation programs would allow. But from Morotai, for the time being, the fight would continue.

A solid June 1945

As May spilled into June, the sea-search and attack missions were sustained, with strikes on Dutch East Indies and French Indochina airdromes, warehouse facilities and supply centers, shipyards and radar sites. Most of these attacks on shore targets were diversions to secondary pre-designated targets when anti-shipping searches turned up nothing worthy of an attack. The Allied push through the Philippines, the ongoing carrier aircraft strikes on Japan proper and U.S. Navy positioning around Okinawa, plus the devastation delivered by the Snoopers and other Fifth and Thirteenth Air Force aircraft over the past several weeks, had combined to effectively clear the seas around the Dutch East Indies of Japanese shipping.

A typical week in June had 30 to 40 aircraft involved in combat strikes, allowing the monthly total to exceed 100 sorties, thereby maintaining the dispatch rate of the previous best-ever month for the squadron. On 9 June, in the featured anti-shipping mission of the month, a patrolling SB-24 caught a collection of medium-sized coastal cargo vessels off the east coast of Borneo. In a dedicated attack, the aircrew scored direct hits with bombs on two Sugar Dogs and a large lugger and continued with strafing attacks at 100 feet on three other ships to sink all of them. Moving to patrol further down the coast at Banjarmasin, another group of large barges was discovered and strafing attacks pressed home, for a claim of five ships sunk and two damaged. These attacks were important as they disrupted and discouraged the Japanese attempts to shuttle cargo along the coast for cross-loading to the larger ships which were still trying to make for the Home Islands.

On one such mission, the enemy returned the favor. The airplane, a B-24M-6 (44-50306), was relatively new to the squadron and in its baptism of fire was badly shot up. Out of a sense of caution and far from home base, the pilot elected to divert to an emergency landing at the airstrip at Sanga-Sanga on the island of Tawi-Tawi in the far southern reaches of the Philippines. The former Japanese airfield on Tawi-Tawi had been captured just weeks before and U.S. Army Engineers had repaired it for limited use when the wounded 868th aircraft dropped in as its first bomber customer. None of the crew was wounded but 306's tires were shot out and hydraulics damaged. The 868th immediately dispatched its B-25 with a seven-man repair crew to Tawi-Tawi. They had the Liberator sufficiently patched up for a local test hop and a return home in 10 days.

On the RCM front, the "ferret" missions continued, mostly to locate and categorize enemy radars by type and function, but, mid-month, an all-out attack was sent against one site in the Koatai River Delta on Borneo's east coast. The RCM aircraft located the radar site and made three bombing runs, following up with six strafing attacks. In addition to knocking down the radar antennas, the radar shack was hit by the gunners and left riddled and smoking. The claim was one large radar station heavily damaged and put out of action, at least temporarily. With these radars, the assumption was that, having been located and attacked, the Japanese would simply pack it up, patch it up and relocate what was left to a new location. So, the "cat-and-mouse" RCM game would continue.

The longest mission

Even as the squadron leadership was exploring options for increasing the range of its B-24s, a mission was undertaken that truly pressed the limit. On the night of 3/4 June 1945, the 868th sent seven aircraft against the Japanese naval seaplane base located in Tanjung Priok, the harbor of Batavia, the capital city of the Dutch East Indies. Staging through the airstrip at Palawan in the Philippines again, the aircraft finished refueling and departed just after noon, flew at 500 feet and arrived over the target at 2300 hours. They found the harbor well-lit and the gunners sleeping. Repeating the three-element attack employed in the most recent Surabaya strike, a single SB-24 ran slightly ahead of the main group, dropping "window" to counter gun-laying radar, and bombing with incendiaries, a mix of five M-46 photo flash bombs and ten 100-pound M-47s, to light up the night and create general confusion.

A second wave of three Snoopers then entered the harbor area at a medium altitude to bomb facilities there, in part to draw attention and anti-aircraft fire to that altitude. A third group of aircraft followed and entered at low level to strike individual ships and any aircraft moored in the naval area of the harbor. Lieutenant Olsen and crew were among the third wave water-skimmers and found a destroyer hurrying to escape the harbor. It held a true course north and 808 dropped 10 bombs, with several hits and near-misses, allowing this crew to claim a damaged destroyer.[7]

The mission covered a range of over 3,000 statute miles and air time averaged 18 hours and 15 minutes for each crew. The mission report stated its case: "This represents the longest mission ever flown by a strike formation of B-24 aircraft since the development of the B-24 bomber." The author has not seen a challenge to this statement but assumes that somewhere out there such a challenge awaits.

At the time the 868th and its parent XIII Bomber Command made this claim, and Kenney's staff repeated it within the FEAF, they faced the Twentieth Air Force public relations machine that was in high gear. The latter heralded the "strategic capabilities" and performance of its B-29 Superfortress bomber fleets striking Japan from the Marianas. The B-29s had become the darlings of the Pacific air campaign and their ostensible contribution to the war effort, at least at that point, was considered by many to be overrated. The tried-and-true Liberator was simply not getting the center-ring attention and respect it had once held and the FEAF thought the men flying this veteran aircraft deserved better. The Batavia strike was a start.

Training and more training

The May–June period included the introduction of more training at every level of squadron activity, much more so than had been experienced over the past year. The gunners, for example, were presented with actual nose and tail turrets fabricated as ground-based trainers, allowing the operators to simulate air engagements by tracking and firing at targets, while waist gunners worked their free-swinging .50 caliber weapons in their own mock-up positions. Post–mission critiques were held where strafing attacks were recreated and reviewed by larger groups, lessons learned shared and combat actions graded.

Flight engineers were run through in-flight fuel pump problems to be solved and hydraulic lines to be rerouted and repaired in flight. Navigators were put through the paces with mandatory training flights where radars were disabled and celestial fixes were performed and graded; and so it ran with all radio operators retrained and graded, and radar operators placed "into the shed and under the hood" for new equipment familiarization and requalification, and only then graded as "combat mission qualified." In part, this intensity was due to the recent embed of the above-mentioned 29th Mobile Training Unit, but once that unit departed the squadron for its next assignment, the 868th leadership made these training programs the routine rather than the exception.

"Give me more range"

In the wake of the successful long-range attacks on Java's port city of Surabaya, the quest that provoked Baylis Harriss to further action was "How do we strike deeper to reach all the important targets in the entire Dutch East Indies from Morotai, with staging through Palawan or some other field?" Range was the issue as the 2,600-mile missions to Surabaya had strained the limits of the B-24s available to the squadron and the soon-to-be executed Batavia mission even more so. In April, the squadron commander had ordered his Maintenance Division to "go find and fabricate a range extension solution, give me more range."

The "metal benders" set about doing that and by late May were hand-crafting options. The installation of wing tanks for the SB-24s, one 164-gallon tank secured under each wing, increasing the gross take-off weight of each aircraft by 2,386 pounds, was calculated to extend the range of the plane by at least one and one-half hours, assuming best fuel management and transfer among the tanks in flight. This required racks to be installed on the wings and the sheet metal team set about to get the job done.

By early June, the first tank had been fabricated and the second was nearing completion, with 395 nominated as the test ship. The wing tanks would be "droppable," that is, manually jettisoned from the flight deck. The flight engineer would be responsible for fuel supply management as revised pumping controls were manipulated in flight to transfer the fuel among the various tanks. The first twin-tank flight occurred on 7 June with "excellent results" reported, the fuel flowing and both tanks jettisoned in flight with no trajectory issues. Aircraft speed when flying with the tanks was reduced by only 3 mph, and total aircraft tankage among the wing, main and auxiliary tanks rose to 3,124 gallons.

The first combat mission by 395, equipped with twin wing tanks, occurred on 9 June and was undertaken with a senior engineer of Consolidated Vultee Aircraft Corporation, the manufacturer of the B-24, observing. This installation was the subject of a special report by XIII Bomber Command and the FEAF operations group and a photo team was on hand to chronicle the mission. All involved third parties recorded that this was an 868th Squadron initiative that took only five weeks to move from concept to deployment in combat.

In a parallel effort, in a "belt and suspenders" approach to hedge bets in the case of a failure with the wing tank concept, three extra bomb bay tanks were installed and tested in 810. Here again, the issue was the trade-off between increased fuel capacity and the price to be paid with the increased weight of the aircraft from the fuel tanks themselves, the supporting structure within the plane and the re-rigging of the fuel transfer system. An initial squadron calculation was that an aircraft departing on a combat mission would carry 3,994 gallons of fuel, and its weight would increase by 2,800 pounds.

Squadron aircraft roster

In mid-June, the squadron completed an inventory of its assigned aircraft based on combat missions flown, with the following results:

Aircraft	Number of Missions	Author's Comments
939	64	Grounded in May due to lack of replacement engines
025	57	
899	53	
357	52	
358	43	
464	35	Grounding refused by XIII Command; RCM missions critical
937	33	
129	27	
810	26	Used as test aircraft for additional bomb bay tanks
024	25	
803	23	
107	19	Badly damaged on 4 May mission, returned to duty
397	12	H2X system plus linked camera system installed in June
131	16	Tree strike on 15 May, trunk embedded in wing, repaired
395	10	Shot-up on 12 May mission, repaired and returned to duty H2X system plus linked camera system installed in June
308	6	Damaged on 9 June mission, diverted to Tawi Tawi, recovered H2X system with linked camera system installed in June

Not listed on this 868th roster of "currently available aircraft by missions completed" were 972 (which did not enter the squadron inventory until late June) as well as the two squadron utility aircraft, the C-47 and the B-25. Thus, with the loss of the crew and aircraft of Lieutenant Harter on 20 June, the squadron could count 16 SB-24J and M models as "in service and combat available" at the end of June 1945. As mentioned in the text, some 25 aircrews were assigned to the squadron and available to man these aircraft at month's end. Allowing for about five crews who would reach the 40-mission point in early July and thereby qualify for the "end of combat tour" rotation home, the squadron would enter July with 20 or so qualified combat crews. This may have been the highest aircraft and crew count of the entire Pacific War for the 868th.

June losses

The month did not see any diminution of Japanese resistance in the air, even though the Japanese Navy and Army air units were sending some of their aircraft to Japan to prepare for the defense of the Home Islands. Helping the calculation was the fact that operational losses were nil for this period, although some mishaps did occur, but, unlike previous months, such non-combat crashes had almost been eliminated. Better airfields, better maintenance, better-trained aircrews and luck all played a part, and while the combat losses incurred by the squadron were minimal in terms of missions flown and the damage inflicted, they still hurt and served to remind the aircrews that they faced a determined enemy.

On 19 June, in a two-aircraft mission by the crews of Lieutenants Ober and Mills against Mandai Airdrome, fighters, believed to be Japanese Army Oscars, pressed home their attack on both Liberators. On the third firing pass on the Ober aircraft, the Oscar drew blood when its cannon and machine-gun fire chewed up the waist section of the B-24, killing the radar operator instantly and seriously wounding the radio operator. Both bombers were holed throughout the fight and the damage inflicted on the Ober machine, plus the dead and wounded on the aircraft, caused it to return directly to base. Mills completed the rest of his sea-search mission and returned to Morotai after a 12-hour mission. The deceased radar operator was buried with full military honors the following day in Morotai's FEAF cemetery.

The following day, two 868th aircraft set out to attack Tabanio Airdrome and conduct a photo reconnaissance of other airfields in the Celebes. On this squadron Mission 868-751, Lieutenants Ellingson and Harter completed their attack on the Limboeng airfield at high noon and, as the two aircraft headed to Mandai for their photo mission, Harter was seen to pull away from the Ellingson SB-24 as if to turn in the direction of Mandai. The Harter aircraft did not respond to a radio call and disappeared into the clouds as its sister plane made for its assigned target.

Over his target, Ellingson was intercepted and fought off a lone, but very aggressive, Tojo fighter that pressed an attack from one o'clock high and passed within 30 feet of the nose. Ellingson "headed for the deck" and opened up the throttles; after making a third firing pass, the fighter pulled up and away and headed home to Mandai. The Harter aircrew and 358 disappeared, did not make radio contact and was declared missing and presumed down. No trace of the plane or crew was ever found.[8]

That month of June 1945 involved a total of 28 missions with 40 combat sorties. Higher authorities also assigned two long-distance weather recon missions to inform their planning for scheduled daylight formation B-24 strikes, and also sent 12 SB-24s to perform anti-submarine patrols over west and east-bound Allied convoys. Only one RCM ferret mission was flown, that to strike a radar set known to be active in the Samarinda area. In fact, after the mission-surge month of May, the squadron was now pacing itself, building additional aircrew capacity and qualifying more crews for daylight and night missions. The seven-plane mission to Batavia in early June had established the unit as more than ready for heavier action up north and Harriss and his executive team knew that they were about to get the nod.

Movement alert

In the last week of June, the FEAF and Thirteenth Air Force alerted the 868th to "prepare for movement" to the north, and the assumption was that the much-anticipated relocation to Okinawa was at hand. XIII Bomber Command stepped in to coordinate the delivery of lumber to build crates and package equipment for movement, and the squadron operations and service components scrambled to organize its equipment, spares and other essentials. The hope was that they would be able to complete the move without the pilfered loss of their more valuable supplies.[9]

The relocation to Okinawa would present the 868th with a different kind of war, that facing the Japanese main islands and the seas connecting and surrounding them. This would include the Sea of Japan with its connection to the southern coast of Japan's colony Korea, and westward to China. The assumption was that this would be a "big move," perhaps a permanent basing for the balance of the Pacific War, for as long as that would last. The consensus was that the squadron would be in the thick of the fight for Kyushu which was expected to begin with Operation *Olympic* as early as October. It was already July; the clock was ticking.

CHAPTER 23

Morotai to Okinawa via Leyte

July 1945

On Morotai, headed north

July 1945 was a month that had the 868th Squadron continuing to fly its combat missions while moving itself toward Japan in a two-hop advance, a jump to a new base on Okinawa that forced it to pause briefly on Leyte in the Philippines. The record of movement is confusing and reflects the FEAF's determination to get its premier night-attack squadron onto Okinawa as quickly as possible, even if the new base there was not quite ready to accommodate it. The FEAF's Thirteenth Air Force had alerted squadron commander Major Baylis Harriss and his executive staff back in mid-June that the 868th would probably be one of the first B-24 units to relocate to Okinawa, with the expectation that most of the daylight B-24 squadrons would follow sometime in August or even September. It was planned that the FEAF build-up would see most of its fighter, medium bomber, heavy bomber and support units eventually populate several of the new airfields under construction on Okinawa in time to support the invasion of Japan's southernmost island of Kyushu, with that massive undertaking now slightly delayed and scheduled to occur in the first week in November.

The FEAF and the squadron's parent XIII Bomber Command had it busy packing its equipment for the big move by the last week of June. Some legacy complications on movement had already impacted the squadron's ability to relocate, issues that dated back to October 1944. At that time, it appeared that the 868th would move immediately from Noemfoor to Morotai, and thence to Leyte in the Philippines. As a result, the squadron's heavy equipment had been loaded to move by ship to Leyte and, a few weeks later, to facilitate this planned move, a squadron advance party had been dispatched to Leyte to prepare a new base camp there. All that became moot when it was decided to halt all squadron movement and instead retain the unit on Noemfoor, a situation that prevailed during its "dark period" of late 1944 through to late March 1945. As the squadron struggled in the early weeks of the New Year and XIII Bomber Command considered its options for dealing with the semi-independent and too-often problematic 868th, the higher authority basically elected to leave it right where it was—on Noemfoor—until its issues could be resolved.

Although not stated in the official record, serious consideration was apparently given by FEAF and XIII Bomber Command to simply disband the unit and reassign the depleted squadron's aircraft, aircrews and support elements to the two daylight B-24 heavy bomb groups. Another option would have been to simply combine what was left of the 868th with its sister LAB-equipped B-24 squadron, the 63rd SeaHawks. This unit had been in the Southwest Pacific since late 1943 and had been assigned since its arrival to the Fifth Air Force. As mentioned in previous chapters, and as further described in a later chapter devoted to the other LAB Nightstalker squadrons sent to war from Langley, the 868th had occasionally mingled with the 63rd and flown combat missions with that unit. Thus, the option of combining these two squadrons, both now resident within the FEAF, seemed a reasonable, if not obvious, path as the entire FEAF re-postured itself as it prepared to relocate to Okinawa.

The fact that the 868th did maintain its independent status and was the first to move to Okinawa was apparently related to two hardly coincidental factors: the FEAF's desire to maintain the 868th special night interdiction capabilities for the months of combat it assumed were ahead as multiple invasions in Japan portended; and the appearance of Baylis Harriss who stepped forward to take the unit in charge and rebuild it to its former role. As we have seen, during that April–June 1945 period, the squadron essentially reinvented itself with a reinvigorated attitude, the assignment of more aircrews and aircraft, the adoption of more aggressive missions and better tactics, more training and a complete leadership transition.

In any event, by June 1945 that rebuilding had occurred and the squadron was at peak performance and operational capacity. It was nominated to move, as expeditiously as possible, to base itself on Okinawa to begin operations against Japan proper by mid-July. This would entail a fan-shaped mission set that would lie nearly due north from Okinawa to patrol the waters around the main islands of Japan and the all-important waters connecting Japan with Korea. The focus on the shipping routes between Korea and Japan was critical to the isolation of the Home Islands, and this enforced sea lane blockade looked hard at the southern and eastern coasts of the Korean peninsula from which the Japanese were still drawing reinforcements and war supplies from Manchuria, China and Korea proper. But missions to the Home Islands and Korea were still in the future in early July 1945 as the squadron continued to fly from Morotai, hitting its assigned targets to the west and south as it prepared to move north.

Morotai missions in July

The month began as a continuation of the previous, with a night-bombing run to the oil processing facilities at the now-familiar target of Balikpapan, Borneo. The crews of Lieutenants Ober and Toole hit with forty 100-pound bombs, scattered across the complex over two hours in the dark of night. The following day, Smitherman and Cole struck Oelin Airdrome, with Gilman and Olsen running anti-shipping patrols off Borneo's northern coast on the 5th, and the Cooper and Jenson crews striking Banjarmasin on 7 July. This tempo of two-aircraft missions continued for the first three weeks of the month with 40-plus sorties flown against established Dutch East Indies oil, airfield, warehousing and shipping targets.

But the shipping was gone, the facilities and airfields fully suppressed, and these one-time bustling islands dear to the Japanese war machine were cut-off and isolated. Importantly, the 868th aircrews flying these missions were mostly new, the names of the more experienced Rogers, Ober, Smitherman, Reidy, Mills and Ellingson were intermixed with Marcotte, Vermilya and a half-dozen others. Squadron Commander Harriss was building his capacity with the additional crews he would need in the August–December campaign during the fight for Kyushu. A typical two-aircraft mission would have a more experienced aircrew accompany a new crew to show the latter the operational "ropes" and oversee the performance of the new men on the block.

On the 21st, the Mills and Sheely crews went out to search for a Japanese destroyer that was reported to be at sea, failed to find it, and hit their secondary or diversion target, the seaplane base at Saoebi. And there were the RCM ferret missions as well, with MacKenzie and McClintick out on 19 July to hit a known radar site that had been reported as being back up and running, at least for a while.[1]

Although these missions were considered "routine," they were not without pain. On 17 July, the crews of Ober and Marcotte set out to search the Makassar Strait and, after finding no target worthy of bomb runs and strafing attacks, turned for home. This was the second combat mission for the Marcotte crew and occurred three days after they had flown one of the month's most productive missions when the two discovered and struck a pack of Sugar Charlies in the Marakam River area of Borneo, bombing and then mounting mast-high strafing attacks. But on this day luck turned against the new crew. As the Marcotte aircraft, 397, approached the field, it lost its way and slammed into a mountain, killing 10. Incredibly, one man was thrown free of the aircraft and survived, walking out of the jungle days later.

But the last week of the month included some new targets not previously visited by the 868th, namely those of Japanese-occupied French Indochina. Launching to search this coastline was deemed to be a major event and the squadron sent four aircraft that way on 21 July, those of Lieutenants Low, Jenson, Sprawls and Koonsman. Mission 868-794 staged through Palawan to arrive in the mid-afternoon in a search along that coast, flying a search from Saigon to the north, to hunt for a small convoy with a destroyer escort.

The convoy was not found but the aircraft separated to continue the hunt. One found several large coastal cargo ships anchored in the harbor of Ha-Tien and took these under attack, while two aircraft elected to hit railroad bridges. Ground fire was moderate and the group was attacked by four fighters near Ha-Tien. Lieutenant Jensen, flying 131, *Lady Luck II*, was hit and holed by fighter gunfire but came home with no casualties. This was considered a good first outing to French Indochina and the squadron elected to go back for more.

On 23 July, a three-aircraft mission consisting of Lieutenants Low, Sprawls and Koonsman returned to the French Indochina coast for more action and this time they got more than they bargained for. Staging from Palawan and flying 15-hour missions, the three aircraft found a range of shipping targets in the late afternoon. They struck coastal shipping, river ferries, oil barges and other commercial and military vessels. Lieutenant Low bore in on a large oil barge being towed by a tug and dropped low to bomb it, his bombs set for delayed detonation. Unfortunately, the oil barge was filled to capacity and primed to explode; it proceeded to do so as 808 pulled off the target. The detonation blew out the aircraft's waist windows, damaged the engines and wings and threw Low out of his seat. The number two engine caught fire and had to be feathered and the damaged aircraft struggled to make altitude.[2]

A crew bail-out was unavoidable and Low contacted Lieutenant Koonsman and his crew who were nearby, waiting to escort the wounded plane home. Koonsman in turn contacted a nearby U.S. submarine and was given coordinates for a rendezvous with that rescue vessel. The Low crew spilled out in a sequence of three-five-two as the plane made three passes over the designated bail-out location. The Koonsman crew observed all 10 parachutes open and land within a relatively tight radius in the water. Three men, including Low, were rescued but the other seven were not recovered and therefore declared Missing in Action.

As the squadron began its relocation from Morotai, technically relocating to Leyte for a few days on the way to Okinawa, it continued to mount its combat missions from its soon-to-be-former base, often staging through smaller airfields to extend the range. On 24 July, the aircrew of Lieutenant Callison headed to southeast Borneo to strike the airdromes of Tabanio and Oelin where enemy aircraft activity had been reported. On return from the target, a little after nine at night, the crew sent a FLASH message reporting that the primary airfield targets had been hit successfully and the plane had turned for home. Six hours later another radio message was received in the form of an "SOS" with the report that the Liberator would "LAND AT MAJOE ISLAND." No further communication was received. At first light, the plane was declared "overdue and presumed down due to fuel exhaustion" based on a calculation of mission mileage and the fuel aboard the aircraft.

In fact, the Callison crew and aircraft had made a forced water landing due to fuel exhaustion and the entire crew was in the water. Five of the 10 men on board, including Callison, and the co-pilot, radar observer and two gunners, would be rescued by a destroyer that had been directed to the scene by an Australian fighter. The latter had been attracted by a flashing mirror used by the floating survivors, radioed the U.S. Navy warship and led it to the stranded airmen. This was the fifth combat mission of the Callison crew and fuel management issues probably played a role in the loss of this aircraft on a near 14-hour mission.[3]

Relocation to Okinawa completed

The multi-stage movement of the squadron from Morotai to Okinawa proceeded according to plan with the initial staging to Leyte on 3 July and the final hop to Okinawa's Yontan Airfield on the 29th. The squadron's "advance echelon" had been sitting in Leyte since November and the stop there allowed the unit to re-consolidate itself for the more permanent move to Okinawa. As previously noted, it was assumed by XIII Bomber Command and FEAF planners that the squadron would remain there for several months to support the multiple invasions of Japan, probably relocating on-island to be based at one of the new airfields under construction, at least through the summer of 1946.

In this relocation to Leyte and beyond to Okinawa, some 128 missions were flown by FEAF C-47 transports, hauling slightly more than one million pounds of material and people. The heavy equipment followed by ship but, by 1 August, the 868th was on Okinawa to stay, its aircraft having flown in by that date as well. The 868th would be the first and only Thirteenth Air Force B-24 unit to be stationed on Okinawa when the war ended, one measure of the importance assigned to its early transfer there.

The Detroit News *finds the 868th*

It happened that in mid-July a war correspondent from *The Detroit News* arrived on Morotai with a temporary press pass to report on the war from there. XIII Bomber Command arranged for Jack Carlisle to be assigned to the 868th squadron for a one-month stay, basically in a role that later wars would describe as an "embedded" journalist. The initial story ran on 5 August and reported on the disappearance of Lieutenant Marcotte and his crew in the course of his sea-search mission to Marakam on Borneo, in company with the aircraft of Lieutenant Ober. The article picked up an emotional exchange between Lieutenant Francis "Frank" Reidy and squadron Operations Officer Captain Townsend Rogers, with the former demanding to be sent out to search for the missing crew.

Carlisle had been with the squadron for nine days at this point and was beginning to come into the rhythm and the personalities of the unit. Rogers accedes to the request and Reidy and a pick-up crew launched into the drizzle, with Carlisle on board for the 12-hour mission. Carlisle describes the quickly collected crew organized by Reidy, the 24-year-old with white streaks in his hair. The pick-up crew hailed from a collection of hometowns, including Boston, Cincinnati, Peoria, Brooklyn and Red Wing among others, all "eager beavers" to join the search.

Searches by this and other aircraft failed to turn up any results and the fate of the Marcotte crew was unknown until several days later when a single survivor walked out of the jungle, as related above. The loss of the Marcotte crew impacted Carlisle because a member of the missing crew had become close to the reporter and because it was the first loss of life he had observed firsthand. Carlisle would fly with the Reidy crew again and report on these and other missions, including a PBY patrol plane search for the missing Marcotte crew. These stories would continue to appear daily in *The Detroit News* over a three-week period during the 5–23 August 1945 period, for a total of 23 articles in all. Stories continued to appear after the Japanese surrender on 15 August to finish out Carlisle's stint with the 868th.

He would also report on a mission he flew with Captain Rogers in *Foul Weather Fie Fie* on a 9 August strike to Banjarmasin. The story ran with an impressive photo of that aircraft and its crew on the departure ramp, with Carlisle standing proud as the eleventh man in the crew. Although the newspaper series was "all-Snoopers all-the-time" and devoted considerable time to the Detroit and Michigan natives in the squadron, he found space to highlight men from hometowns across the nation. In his twelfth article, appearing on 16 August, one day after VJ Day, he profiles the loss of another Detroit native, Lieutenant William Grieves, a co-pilot who had been lost when another 868th aircraft had gone missing when it crashed into a jungle mountain on its return to base after a successful raid over French Indochina.

When the *Detroit News* series began in early August, that city had just passed the 18,000 mark in war casualties. The paper had that same day published a new list of 21 families in that city who had been notified the day before that their sons were either missing in action or had been killed in action. Detroit would experience nearly 20,000 dead, wounded and missing before the war was over, a not unusual toll for a city of Detroit's size. Several "Detroiters" and more "Michiganders" would be declared killed in action or go missing before the war was over and when Carlisle filed his story from Morotai, the expectation was that the forthcoming invasions of Japan would see many more deaths for the city.

Within the 868th, Carlisle was watching these losses play out before him and reporting on them for the readers at home. Most of his reporting was upbeat, emphasizing the courage and determination of the young men he encountered. In one story, he described a night sortie on a PT boat in which he rode into a hunt for the Japanese in the company of squadron pilot Lieutenant Fred Olsen of Lombard, Illinois, a risk-seeking man who reveled in the name his squadron mates had given him, that of "Olie the Hot Rock." Their PT boat patrol was mostly uneventful but "Hot Rock" sat at the bow, positioned behind the gunner manning the forward 37-mm gun, ready to share any action. The roar of Packard diesels, built in that company's immense plant right in Detroit, pushed the plywood boat across the Pacific at 40 knots and along the shore of the Japanese-held island. Carlisle found Detroit boys on that boat and bonded with them. He presented them to his readers as he described the PT's guns unleashing a barrage into the jungle to hit a suspected Japanese strongpoint.[4]

The squadron's July summary

During July 1945, despite the disruptions of movement to Okinawa through Leyte, and the requirement to absorb, train and qualify the new crews for combat missions, the squadron managed to fly 32 missions and sent 60 aircraft against the enemy. The "campaigns" of the Pacific War in which the unit officially was registered to have participated were "The Netherlands East Indies" 1–31 July, "The Battle of Borneo" 1–31 July and the "China Campaign" 21–24 July, the last-mentioned a product of the strikes against French Indochina. Three aircraft were lost and 22 airmen had been declared Missing in Action, one of whom survived to walk out of the jungle to come home to the squadron. The 868th monthly report did solemnly note that "Despite the fact that there were but fifty-nine sorties during this period compared with 130 and 132 during the preceding two months, casualties were extremely heavy."[5]

Importantly, for the purposes of the unit's overall warfighting capabilities as it prepared to move to Okinawa, the squadron could now count 23 combat-qualified crews, net of the losses of the Low, Marcotte and Callison crews, as available for relocating forward. The addition of more aircraft, many of which were now configured with improved LAB systems and some with the H2X blind-bombing radar, meant that the 868th would arrive on Okinawa well-equipped and fully prepared to fly against the Home Islands of Japan.

Once based on Okinawa, the 868th Squadron would be expected to throw its full weight in missions and men against the four Home Islands and, in this effort, they would be expected to play a key role in severing the link between Japan and the Korean peninsula. The air campaign over and around Kyushu would of necessity be based on Okinawa and prepare the way for MacArthur's early November invasion of that southern island. Japanese opposition to this interdiction campaign would be intense and no doubt at a level not yet experienced in the Pacific by the squadron.

Postwar assessment of the Japanese preparations for the invasion of Kyushu confirmed that the defenders were exceptionally well prepared for the ground fight and had correctly anticipated the Allied plans for the invasion locations. During that extended period of combat on Kyushu, which was expected to last at least four if not six months, Kenney's FEAF would seek to isolate the island to disrupt the flow of any reinforcements from the main of island of Honshu. As had been the case in other Pacific War campaigns, the U.S. Navy carrier task forces would position themselves for sustained air operations over Kyushu to support the Allied ground forces there. But these naval forces would face massive suicide attacks from the air and sea and war planners held reasonable concerns as to their staying power.

In this situation, any sustained air presence over the battlefield would have to come from the Okinawa-based FEAF fighter, medium and heavy bomber forces that were being assembled on the dozen or more airfields on the island. The 868th would therefore be in the thick of this struggle from the day it arrived on Okinawa and it was assumed that the demands for night and day missions would only increase as the date of invasion approached. Baylis Harriss knew this and was doing his best to prepare his men for this undertaking.

CHAPTER 24

Okinawa and Japan

August 1945

Move to Okinawa

As noted in the previous chapter, the move from Morotai, from where combat missions were being flown, and from Leyte in the Philippines, where most elements of the squadron had relocated in July, to Yontan Field on Okinawa, dominated the first week of August. In completing the move to Okinawa, the 868th had reached its closest point of approach to the Home Islands of Japan. All expected that Yontan Airfield, or another of the many airfields under construction on the island, would remain the squadron home base for the next 12 months, if not beyond. With the invasion of Kyushu set for early November, followed by an invasion of Honshu at some point in the spring or summer of 1946, the squadron set about building a semi-permanent camp. These would best any accommodations experienced to date in the unit's march across the Pacific.

On 1 August, the squadron disembarked from U.S. Navy transport ships that had picked up the assembled 868th ground elements on Leyte, personnel and equipment and supplies—essentially the entirety of the squadron that did not fly. The monthly squadron narrative, still created with a dash of irony, caught the moment:

> In true form and consistent with every move this squadron has made—it was raining—and our selected campsite was a mass of mud. The area was laid out and the tents were set up while the boat was being unloaded. However, during the midst of the unloading, a typhoon was reported heading for this area and all shipping in the harbor was put out to sea. For the next few days, a raging typhoon swept the entire area, the unleashed winds and rain upset most of the tents and shelters that had been erected. However, the Snoopers were by this time well accustomed to such "helpful gestures" and this typhoon was taken in the usual stride. When the storm subsided, the unloading resumed, but the campsite was inundated with mud and water.

In this challenging situation, the squadron prevailed but the situation on the recently conquered island was grim. One day the squadron found itself well-fed ("the best ever") and the next its personnel were given no choice but to revert to field rations, a "lowest ebb" situation that would exist for the entire month of August. Potable water was at a premium, with an allocation of 800 gallons a day for the squadron's 500 men. Necessity being the mother of innovation, the squadron found a way to dig its own well and, anticipating a water liberation of sorts, also built a set of first-class showers. Hopes were dashed when no pump for the well could be found to bring water to the surface. At month's end, the pristine showers would stand unused "to mock all efforts expended in their erection."[1]

Invasion planning and concerns

Yet the 868th was settling in for a long-term stay on Okinawa and the squadron took its time to complete the shift of its aircraft and crews from Morotai. The established targets to the south in the Dutch East Indies were still being worked from that base early in the month as space for the aircraft on Okinawa was still being arranged. The new basing on Okinawa would permit the squadron to range targets to the west and northwest, namely the Home Islands of Japan and Korea. The FEAF and its components, the Fifth and Thirteenth, now joined by the Seventh Air Force which had operated in the Central Pacific, were all repositioning and sorting themselves out to prepare for the slugfest they expected would come.

XIII Bomber Command, now located at Clark Field in the Philippines, remained the administrative command under which the squadron served, but temporary operational command of the 868th had moved to V Bomber Command of the Fifth Air Force. The latter had established itself on Okinawa and had assumed tactical control of all FEAF bomber units, including the 868th. There was confusion in this evolving mix of air units, but a mighty war machine was moving inextricably toward Japan and forming itself for a massive effort. And as all the heavy bomber, medium bomber, fighter, reconnaissance and transport squadrons of the three Pacific Theater air forces began to come together in August, it was clear that MacArthur's air strength would number in the thousands of aircraft and aircrews. He and his planners knew they would need every plane they could put over the beachhead, and beyond, to mitigate the Japanese onslaught that would be occasioned by the initial invasion.

With the FEAF moving its premier night-bombing squadron, the 868th, to Okinawa to begin operations against Japan and Korea. The assumption was that the second LAB squadron—the 63rd—would join the 868th late in the month. It was also possible that SB-24s from the Hopson Project in China might be tasked to join the LAB squadrons on Okinawa. The Hopson Project aircraft had been consolidated into a single unit as the 373rd Bomb Squadron of the Fourteenth Air Force's 308th Bomb Group. Would that melding have occurred, the FEAF could have fielded as many as 50 LAB-equipped SB-24s and 80-plus crews on Okinawa by late September. So positioned with combat missions centrally coordinated, this night-hunting radar-equipped force would have been able to blanket the main islands of Japan and the coasts of Korea and northeastern China. This would have further countered Japanese attempts to bring forces back from the Asian mainland to reinforce their Army and air assets for the coming battles.

Much has been written about Operation *Downfall*, the overall plan for the invasion of Japan and the fight ashore that would be pursued to eliminate Japanese resistance and force a surrender. The twin sequenced invasions of Kyushu in early November 1945, Operation *Olympic* and the later Operation *Coronet*—the invasion of the larger island of Honshu sometime in mid-1946—had been in the planning stage for months. Over the first six months of 1945, as America and its Allies digested the costs of the taking of Saipan and experienced the massive bloodshed of the Okinawa invasion and grinding fight there, it became increasingly apparent that both invasions of Japan proper would be extremely costly in blood and national treasure. Expected were heavy losses of the infantrymen who would wade ashore and press combat on the ground, the aircraft and aircrew who would support the ground forces and fight above them and the ships and sailors who would land the men and attempt to sustain and support the actual invasions.

In those cases where the Japanese elected to resist—and all-out resistance to the death was the norm—there would be no quarter spared and no surrender in the ground fight. As a consequence, trapped civilians had died en masse on Saipan and Okinawa and many more would be exposed to the conflict and die on the Home Islands. At the recently concluded battle of Okinawa, waves of "Divine Wind" kamikaze aircraft had been remarkably effective against the U.S. Navy ships against which they flew and, in the fall of 1945 in Japan, another 10,000 were prepared to throw themselves at the ships. Okinawa showed the way and Japanese planning was straight-forward: make the price to be paid by the invading Allies on the ground of the Home Islands so high that, even in defeat, Japan would avoid an "unconditional surrender" and thereby be able to secure favorable terms. The latter would presumably preserve the emperor, the military leadership and avoid any foreign occupation of Japan. This was the reality of the Japanese mindset and the extended war for which the FEAF and its squadrons were preparing.

In more recent discussions of the use of the twin atomic bombs to force an end of the war short of the actual invasion of Japan and an extended fight there, it has become fashionable to denigrate wartime estimates of the casualties that the Allies would have experienced in the invasion. Thankfully, balanced scholarship and detailed research now inform any objective reader that, if anything, the Allied leadership under-estimated the Japanese capacity to resist. In so doing, the estimates of Allied casualties, in the hundreds of thousands dead and missing and in the millions of wounded, not to mention millions of Japanese, soldiers and civilians alike, were far short of what would have been the reality of the event. In this area, no better explanation can be found than D. M. Giangreco's comprehensive *Hell to Pay*.[2] A more recent publication, Richard B. Frank's *Downfall: The End of The Imperial Japanese Empire*, takes the former book one step further to lay this controversy to rest. This is a truly seminal work of research, detailed analysis and writing and it carries its arguments in unemotional and convincing terms. In any approach to better understand the situation faced by all parties involved in the Pacific War in the summer of 1945, this book is an essential read.[3]

August combat missions

For the aircrews of the 868th, the month began with a two-aircraft strike from Morotai against Kendari Airdrome in the Celebes of the Dutch East Indies by the crews of Lieutenants Sheely and Mills. The following day, Lieutenants Frahm and Ellingson struck the Saoebi seaplane base in the same general area, these being the two final missions in that campaign. After a five-day hiatus as the aircraft and crews moved up to Okinawa, the Ellingson and Mills crews went north to Korea, there to search the southern coastline where Japanese ships were moving to deliver troops and supplies to the Home Islands. One crew failed to return and we shall return to this loss a bit later.

On the 8th, Lieutenant Sheely and crew flew a night LAB search within the so-called "blind bombing zone" off the China coast. Finding no shipping target within the authorized attack zone, the crew diverted to its assigned secondary target at Shanghai, hitting the Texaco oil storage facility at two in the morning. This was an eight-hour mission and mounting it from Okinawa allowed a full search within the zone, plus a strike on the secondary target, emphasizing the range-to-target allowed by the new base.

On the same day, Lieutenant Sprawls performed a weather recon mission and plowed through some incredibly foul weather, encountering "severe thunderstorms with 10/10 cumulus nimbus from the deck to 25,000 feet." He hit the oil storage tanks at Tsingtao on China's coast and came home to Yontan. On 9 August, there occurred something of a special event for the 868th when the squadron delivered a two-aircraft attack on the main island of Kyushu. This was the unit's first direct strike on the Home Islands. It was assumed that this was the opening round of hundreds of such missions to come over the next many months. Lieutenants Smitherman and Sheely spread 61 100-pound bombs over the major Japanese Navy airfield at Kanoya on Kyushu over four hours from 2300 to 0300 hours. The two Snooper visitors drew plenty of anti-aircraft fire over the target area as searchlights reached out in an unsuccessful attempt to find the attackers.

Also, on the night of the 9th, Lieutenants Cole and Maggioncalda performed a weather recon and harassing mission to Genzan (now Wonsan) on the Korean Peninsula, a major city and base. There they deposited three 1,000-pound bombs each on factories deemed war targets. This was the second mission to Korea and, in this instance, the Snoopers found a ship that pumped anti-aircraft fire into the night sky. The fire was inaccurate but came from a fair size ocean-going merchant ship, a sure sign of the presence of the shipping that the 868th knew was there somewhere. On the 10th, the LAB search area was the southern Korean coast again, with a focus on the large southern port of Fusan (Pusan). No shipping was found so Lieutenant Sprawls and crew moved to hit their assigned secondary target near Makurasaki on Kyushu Island. For the first time over Japan, the SB-24's LAB radar detected a night fighter up and searching for them at midnight. It closed to within a mile, but the SB-24 pilot swung away and used his radar to avoid the fighter.

The following night, Lieutenants McClintick and Makenzie and their crews went to Genzan (Wonsan) in Korea for another strike, with an H2X-enabled bombing of the docks in that port, dropping their ordnance at three in the morning. This flight did meet with an issue when the Makenzie crew, near the end of its return flight to home base, apparently became confused when a fuel management problem seemed to signal that the aircraft was going dry and might have to ditch. As the crew prepared to do so, one crewman did not wait for the execution command and jumped. The fuel issue was resolved and the plane came home safely, minus one Corporal T. A. McMurran who was left floating in his Mae West about 30 minutes from base. A PBY Catalina, alerted by the SB-24 crew, took up the search and spotted him, landed alongside the swimmer and recovered him at first light. It was later explained to the recovered airman that "prepare to jump" did not mean "jump now."[4]

On 11 August, Lieutenants Sheely and Ellingson and crews attacked the harbor installations of Genzan once more, this time at daybreak. That night's mission had apparently been delayed for several hours by "demonstrations" at Yontan, celebrations occasioned by rumors on Okinawa that the Japanese had surrendered or were about to. This was not yet the case—no such decision in Tokyo had been arrived at and certainly had not been conveyed to the squadrons on Okinawa. But something was clearly in the air.

The first atomic bomb had been dropped on Hiroshima by a Tinian-based B-29 a few days before, on 6 August, when the "Little Boy" enriched uranium device tumbled out of Colonel Paul Tibbets' *Enola Gay* at 0915 that clear morning. Word spread fast, internationally and of course within the FEAF and all personnel on Okinawa. Four days later, on 9 August, the plutonium-based "Fat Man" device detonated above Nagasaki, delivered by the crew of Major Charles Sweeney in *Bockscar*. The primary target that day had been the arsenal city of Kokura, but it was shrouded in cloud. Specific instructions told the crews that they could not bomb through the clouds and that a clear target was required for any release of the weapon. As a consequence, the city of Nagasaki, where the clouds parted, got the second weapon.

A third bomb assembly, another Fat Man, was on the way to Tinian should it be needed and the components of more atomic bombs were being assembled Stateside. But the twin atomic bombings suggested that the Japanese might want to strongly consider capitulating and, for this reason, the Yontan airfield complex was buzzing with wild anticipation. Only a few weeks earlier, a far gloomier suggestion was making the rounds, a theme that recognized the hard fight ahead on the soil of Japan. An earlier hopeful refrain had changed from "Home Alive in '45" to "The Golden Gate in '48." Suddenly, the former now seemed, with the twin atomic detonations and the certainty of more to come if the Japanese declined to surrender, to again be possible.[5]

Final combat missions

On 12 August the squadron sent Lieutenant Cole and crew back to Korea to search the area around the port of Fusan, where shipping targets had been reported. Cole's SB-24 found his prey a few minutes after midnight and made a LAB attack from 3,000 feet, bombs falling close aboard but no confirmation of a sinking. On the same night, the squadron commander, Major Harriss, led a two-aircraft mission with Lieutenant Maggioncalda on his wing to Genzan port. The latter reached his target and delivered a nine-bomb attack on the dock installations there. The aircraft of Major Harriss, and here his frustration is almost palpable, developed engine trouble five hours into the flight and was forced to salvo its bomb load and turn back. Meanwhile, Maggioncalda identified four ships lying off Genzan harbor after he delivered his bombs on the docks and, in doing so, confirmed reports that Japanese ships were still collecting at Genzan to attempt a run to Japan.

On the following night, Lieutenant Sprawls went back to the southern coast of Korea in a LAB shipping-search mission. He found five contacts moving together and attacked the two largest targets on offer, bombing each from 2,000 feet. The return fire from the ships was heavy but inaccurate and the Sprawls crew claimed one solid hit on its first target that knocked out all counter fire and stopped the ship dead in the water. The crew was jumped by three enemy aircraft that attempted to find the Snooper and closed to within one mile. Radar guided the pilot to avoid the fighters and the crew made it home safely. Given the events of the following night, these two attacks on Mission 868-815 on 12 August 1945 may have been the last LAB attacks of the Pacific War.

On 12 August, two 868th Squadron SB-24s lifted off from Yontan Airfield to make a weather recon to Genzan and bomb the airfield there. Lieutenants Gustavus "Gus" Smitherman and McClintick and their crews were six hours into their mission and approaching their target when a radio message instructed them to terminate the mission, drop their bombs "without fuses and safe-in-water" and return directly to base. On the way home, a Japanese anti-aircraft crew on Shimono Shima opened fire with no effect and the two planes came home safely. Smitherman landed a few minutes after seven in the morning in his favorite airplane, *Carolina Carol*. He made a reasonable claim that he had completed what justifiably could be called the last combat mission of the Pacific War, at least for the 868th Squadron. Others accepted that claim and so it stands. His partner aircraft, that of McClintick, landed an hour or so later. Mission 868-816 was indeed the squadron's last mission to the enemy. Smitherman and crew flew 107 and McClintick 780.[6]

The last combat loss

Recall that on the night of 6 August two SB-24s lifted off from Yontan Airfield and headed to Korea, those of Lieutenants Ed Mills and Bob Ellingson. This mission, 868-804, would be the first for the squadron to Korea. Intelligence had confirmed that there was heavy ship traffic between various ports on Korea's southern coast and the Home Islands and that Japanese military units from Manchuria and Korea were being shuttled into Kyushu and Honshu from these ports. The two Liberators were to fly to the southeastern coast and then part company to enter their respective hunting areas. Ellingson and crew in 780 flew slightly to the north, up the coast from the major port of Fusan, and then turned back to the south to search the waters in the approach to Fusan.

The Ellingson crew scoured that area for two hours, approaching the Japanese naval base at Chinhae slightly to the west of Fusan. At 0320 on the morning of 7 August, he found his target, a 200-foot cargo vessel steaming due north at 10 knots, probably returning from Japan to collect another cargo of men and supplies in Fusan. Ellingson attacked from 1,800 feet using his LAB, making three runs on his target with his load of nine 500-pound bombs. He claimed a direct hit that stopped the ship cold, with other bombs placed alongside in a classic radar-assisted low-altitude ship strike. After the attack, at around 0400 hours, Ellingson flew south to the rendezvous point over Gyu Island to meet up with Mills.

The wait was in vain as the Mills crew failed to arrive. Repeated radio calls from 708 to 131 went unanswered. Ellingson circled for over two hours, then headed home to Yontan as his deteriorating fuel situation demanded. He landed at 0900 after some 11 hours in the air. Squadron records indicate that the two aircraft maintained VHF radio contact until almost 0200, after which time there was no contact between the two. Squadron and V Bomber Command ground stations failed in attempts to establish contact with Mills once it was determined that there was a problem. Ed Mills and crew were declared missing in action and presumed down by hostile action the following day.

Early that following morning, Lieutenant Ellingson sought and received permission to search for the Mills crew. He launched into the dark at five in the morning with an all-volunteer crew and reached the Gyu Island rendezvous point three hours later to begin his search. The Fifth Air Force had promised the 868th a fighter escort as the area was known to be infested with Japanese interceptors during daylight hours, but that escort failed to materialize. Ellingson and his crew were not permitted to extend their search in the absence of these escorts and terminated their search to return to Yontan.

Bob Ellingson and his men felt the loss of Mills and his men deeply as the two crews had been together since Langley and had flown to the 868th together to begin their combat tours in June. A reconstruction of the Mills sortie on that night shows that, once the crew, flying *Lady Luck II*, parted company with Ellingson, they headed to the assigned LAB search area to the west of Fusan. In this instance, they were to range across the southern coast, maneuvering among the hundreds of islands that sat off that coast.

Japanese shipping moving from ports farther to the west, namely Mokpo in the southwest to Yŏsu at the mid-point, tended to use these islands to hide during the day for nighttime runs to Japan. The port of Yŏsu was of particular concern as it harbored a military port, munitions-related factories and a Japanese Army Air Force airdrome at nearby Sacheon.

At about the time that Ellingson was making his LAB run on the shipping off Fusan, Mills and crew found their way into Yŏsu Bay, where a number of ships were anchored to take on cargo. The anti-aircraft gunners came alive and, while there were no fighters up that night from nearby Sacheon airfield, the bay was alive with fire as *Lady Luck II* maneuvered to line up on a target. At that point, the aircraft simply disappeared. That night, and for the balance of the war, back at the 868th operations tent on Okinawa there was not even a hint that Yŏsu had claimed the Mills crew.

Such disappearances had been all too common among the 868th over the past two years of war, the price paid for single-ship missions to a target where there were no other aircraft to see a plane go down or explode in mid-air and file a report. Mills and his 10-man crew was down somewhere, and soon presumed killed in action, the last combat loss of the 868th Squadron's long war in the Pacific. When the last of the unit went home in October, the Mills crew, not unlike so many others, was simply "lost" and none of their squadron mates assumed that they would ever be found. They were wrong, but it would take the men of the 868th a full 33 years to "find" their comrades in arms.

Lieutenant Edward B. Mills Jr. and his crew had been in combat since June and had experienced their share of rough missions. As recounted in Chapter 22, on 19 June, the Mills crew had flown with that of Lieutenant Ober when the two struck Mandai Airdrome in the Celebes. They were met by eager and skilled Japanese Oscars over the target which pressed their attacks, riddling Mills' aircraft in its wings, fuselage and destroying the radar equipment. The Ober aircraft was hit harder, with the intercepting fighters punching holes throughout the plane, killing the radar operator and wounding the radio operator.

On 18 July, the Mills crew had been part of the three-aircraft daylight armed shipping search of the Java Sea that failed to find any shipping worthy of attack. The threesome then struck their secondary target, the Japanese Navy floatplane base at Saoebi, destroying support facilities and going low to strafe coastal shipping offshore. On 1 August, the Mills crew flew with that of Lieutenant Bob Sheely to strike the Kendari Airdrome in the Celebes in the unit's last mission in the Dutch East Indies before relocating to Okinawa. That mission occurred only six days before the disappearance of the 11-man crew over Yŏsu Bay in Korea.

Rumors of a Japanese surrender

By mid-month, the news—or at first only a rumor—that Japan was preparing to surrender caught the squadron in the midst of its camp construction program. The anticipation that peace was at hand became a major distraction, a disruption with which the squadron leadership had to contend and would find itself at pains to resolve. There were conflicting stories of a possible early war termination, suggestions rampant that the squadron would be moved back to the Philippines and, by mid-month, according to official squadron records, a "general state of lethargy had set in" as combat operations were suspended. Major Harriss had a complex situation on his hands and he and his core executive team worked hard to motivate the men and keep them focused on their mission. As news of a pending surrender by Japan continued to circulate and strengthen, many hands imagined that an overnight discharge and return to home might be possible. The squadron history relates that "a pandemonium of celebration swept the camp and all construction activities ceased during this period of excitement."

The actual surrender of Japan did not occur until 3 September 1945 when the military and government leadership of the two sides gathered on the deck of the USS *Missouri* at anchor in Tokyo Bay to sign the official war termination documents. Until that time, there was a high level of distrust in the intentions of the enemy, a disbelief that Japan had in fact decided at the highest levels to surrender and accept occupation. There was an even stronger concern that, even if the emperor and the government had so decided, rogue elements of the Japanese military would not accept this fate and the war would continue. It would turn out that such concerns were fully warranted. Thus, while the Japanese signaled their intention to surrender mid-month and proceeded from that point to go through all the motions of laying down their arms, the distrust prevailed.

As Harriss and others in the squadron leadership insisted the unit hope for the best but assume the worst—that the war would continue—unit morale and cohesion were maintained. When a flight of Betty bombers, painted all over in white with green crosses splashed on their sides, arrived on Okinawa to bring surrender negotiators for meetings, the mood changed but the attitude remained one of disbelief and doubt.

In this uncertain environment, Major Harriss and his command team, along with the entire leadership of the forward-based FEAF air elements on Okinawa, struggled to continue to plan for war and the invasion of Japan. The second half of August had the squadron catching up on personnel records and administrative matters to place all in order should the surrender prove to be real. The work to build out the 868th camp continued, aircraft were maintained, aircrews were made proficient and softball games proliferated. As selected AAF and U.S. Army ground units on Okinawa were told to prepare for a relocation to occupy installations in a defeated Japan, becoming part of the occupation force, pressure rose among those not tagged for occupation duties. If they were not part of the occupation force, the men wanted to go home and expected to be allowed to do so yesterday.

But the U.S. military system simply could not do this, and, in fact, in that mid-August of 1945, troop ships were still spread across the Pacific and headed west toward Okinawa and Japan, bringing troops and supplies in preparation for the planned invasion of Japan.

There was also the consideration of which men would constitute the first wave of those rotating home and, even once this was decided, how these men returning for discharge from service might get there. The working assumption was that the officers and men of the squadron would depart in groups, probably beginning in mid-September, and that this flow would be based on the points-for-service system.

But, as the month closed and the world embraced the Japanese surrender as a done deal, it was not yet "done" for the men and machines poised to invade Japan. The Japanese government had yet to finalize the surrender by signing the document that defined the specifics, and occupation forces that would enforce the defeat and make it real had not yet landed in Japan. The men of the squadron were told to prepare for a resumption of hostilities or random hostile acts such as raids on the Okinawa airfields. Nobody was going home yet and while the volleyball and softball fields were full of activity, the Liberators still stood "mission capable" in their revetments on Yontan. In a sense, uncertainty was a companion of hope on Okinawa.

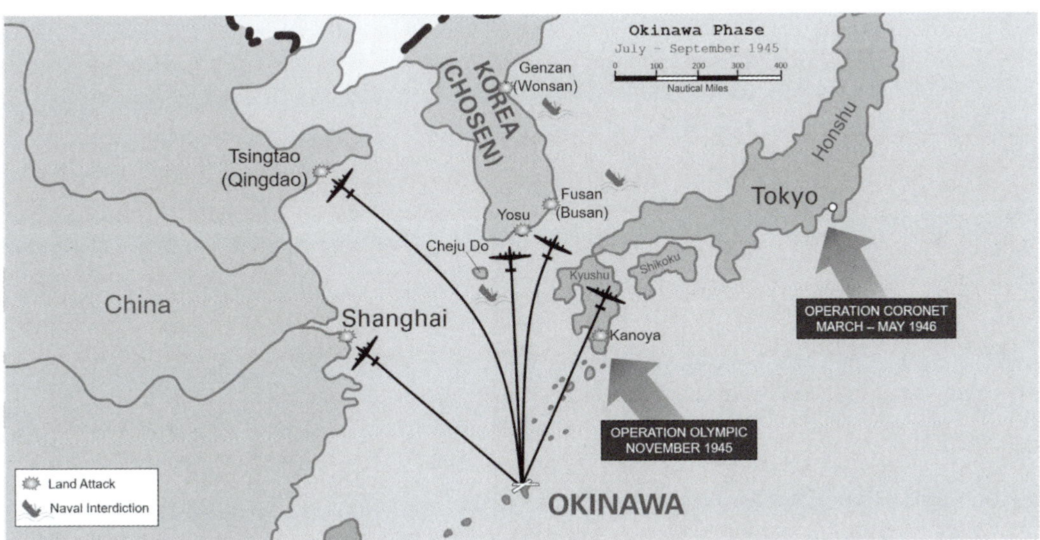

Okinawa phase July–September 1945, indicating 868th Squadron sea search attacks and land target strikes to the north (Japan and Korea) and northwest (China). (Chris Chen/Telemus)

Lady Luck II *with Mills Crew and Namhae Island*

B-24M Lady Luck II *with Mills Crew, July 1945. (Author's collection)*

Crew of Lieutenant Binford and SB-24M Sunsetter. *(Author's collection)*

B-24M Carolina Carol *flew last mission of war, 13 August 1945, here with Lieutenant Scott Smitherman. (Author's collection)*

Namhae village first grave marker for Mills crew, mountaintop, September 1945. (Author's collection)

Namhae village pharmacist Kim solicits donations for Mills crew memorial, 1956. (Author's collection)

Namhae village memorial to Mills crew dedicated in 1956. (Author's collection)

Namhae village ceremony at Middle School, 1956. (Author's collection)

868th Squadron Association appreciation delivered to Namhae Village, 1979. (Author's collection)

CHAPTER 25

Coming Home

September–October 1945

September–October events

Throughout the world, but especially on Okinawa, a great cloud of uncertainty lifted with the completion of the 3 September surrender ceremony in Tokyo Bay. The departure of occupation personnel, aircraft and ships destined for various locations in Japan from the island base brought home the reality that Japan had indeed surrendered and that there would be no invasion. The formal end of the war also highlighted all the issues of return and there was the consideration of which men would constitute the first wave of those rotating home.

Even as this was decided at the squadron and Bomber Command levels, the larger issue arose as to how these men selected to return to the "States" for discharge from service might get there. The working assumption was that the officers and men of the squadron would depart in groups, probably beginning in mid-September, and that this flow would be based on the points-for-service system. In fact, this is how it developed, and on 22 September the first group of 50 men departed the squadron. This group comprised those men who had accumulated 85 points as of 12 May 1945. This was a somewhat arbitrary date, but someone had somehow set it in stone.

Things got more complicated and some tempers short as the "but what about those who had 85 points after 12 May" question came to the fore. A week or so later, XIII Bomber Command weighed in with an instruction that all men with 80 or more points were to report to the 22nd Replacement Depot in Manila for processing to return to the United States. This instruction shifted the onus to the rear-area managers in Manila to sort it all out and find ways to get the men moving towards home. By 24 September, 117 men from the 868th were gone, headed home via a processing stay in Manila. This activity would take a couple of months to run its course but, once the flow home started, the tension within the squadron dissipated. It was now a given that they would all go home, and "home by Christmas" seemed a strong possibility.

As the squadron phased down its manpower, with the most experienced of all ranks and occupations the first to depart, the remaining men of the unit found a looser organization that was attempting to adjust from a war to peacetime tempo. A certain slackness did set in, despite their commander's determination to enforce discipline and control. The entire unit—pilots and aircrew, service crews and technicians, and the operations staff—pitched in to build the "finest mess hall in the history of 868th Squadron." This great structure was commissioned mid-month and a special ration beer party greeted opening day. Again, the still-serving squadron historian noted that "with the aid of our cooks in preparing a special feast, an enjoyable time was had by all." The living quarters were also prime, with wooden floors all around, great latrines and, finally, those world-class showers that now ran with abundant water.[1]

But as that same squadron history also noted, with something of an understatement, "this feeling of security was short-lived." On 17 September, a massive typhoon struck Okinawa and for two days raging winds and monsoon-quality rains slammed the camp. The Orderly Room, the Post Exchange and many tents were destroyed, the camp scattered and debauched. This was Typhoon *Ida* and, once beyond Okinawa, it roared north to hit the Japanese island of Kyushu, devasting Hiroshima Prefecture and killing over 2,000 people.[2]

Reconstruction of the squadron camp took a week, but the war was over and restoring the camp became a shared objective. The beach was opened for swimming and life went on. Baylis Harriss made several runs to Manila to meet with XIII Bomber Command to make sure the men of his squadron were receiving equal attention on the rotation home front. Upon his return to Okinawa, he always held a briefing that updated the squadron and, as his explanations noted, everything about "going home" was changing fast.

The fact that the 868th had been the first Thirteenth Air Force bomber unit to forward deploy to Okinawa now placed the squadron at a disadvantage in arranging for the men to depart for home as all administrative decisions impacting the squadron were occurring in Manila. By the end of September, it was established that the 8th Service Unit in Manila was to accelerate the complete relocation of all squadron personnel and aircraft and that the entire unit was slated to be deactivated in October.

Yet, beyond the typhoons and demobilization complexities, other events injected themselves. On 24 September, the squadron was tasked to participate in the ferrying of Allied prisoners of war (POWs) who had been liberated from work camps in Japan to Clark Field near Manila for onward movement to their home nations. Six 868th Squadron SB-24s were to fly that day, typhoons to the south notwithstanding, and carry 90 former POWs on the first leg of their return. The first aircraft lifted off with 15 passengers but the second crashed when its nose wheel snapped as it was about to lift off from Yontan Airfield. Many on board were injured and four were killed, including a squadron crewman, Corporal James M. Kraschel. The loss of the three British POWs, who had endured years in Japanese labor camps, made the crash doubly tragic. The wreckage of the broken Liberator blocked the runway and reports of inclement weather—another typhoon on the way—caused the remaining four aircraft to forgo their flights. Two days later, the squadron resumed its ferrying of POWs, carrying 60 to Clark Field in four aircraft, this time without incident.[3]

Another tragedy struck when September turned to October and the squadron's C-47, the so-called "Snooper Airlines" second souped-up transport aircraft, went down on a test hop. Killed were Lieutenants Vermilya (the pilot), Byron (navigator) and McDaniel (also a pilot). The cause was thought to be an engine fire that ate through the structure of the airplane before it could be landed, but the destruction of the war-weary aircraft did not permit any definitive answers.

Several squadron veterans recalled in later years that the plane had been damaged during the 17 September typhoon. The squadron had elected to secure it by strapping a Caterpillar tractor to one wing and a heavy 6x6 truck to the other, but, as one man recalled, "she still got away from us," and the C-47 was dragged by the wind across the airstrip, pulling the twin anchors with her. The aircraft went in for major repairs, some engine work and had to be test flown. Three good men volunteered to take that test hop, all of whom had served in combat. When the plane came apart in midair, they were gone, just as the rest of the squadron was packing its bags to go home and return to their civilian lives.

The squadron roster at month's end stood at 457 officers and men—flying and ground personnel—down from over 600 at the beginning of the month. The aircraft count was down as well, comprising four B-24M-1s and seven B-24M-6s. Lost or discarded were one B-24M-6 (the POW crash), the C-47A (lost at end of month) and the squadron "hot rod" B-25D (discarded to the local boneyard). On the combat crew side, squadron Special Orders Number 45 of mid-October 1945 identified 22 combat crews for return to the States, to be transferred to XIII Bomber Command at Clark Field, Philippines, under the "Sunset Project."

During October, departures from the squadron accelerated and it appears that, from incomplete records, there were only 50 or so men left when the squadron was declared deactivated in the Pacific Theater. By late October, all had shipped out or flown away. The Wright Project, the 394th Squadron, the 5th Bomb Group Special Project and the 868th Bombardment Squadron (Heavy) had been at war for 26 months and it was time to close up shop.[4]

Fate of the aircraft

Sometime in mid-October, the squadron flew home a handful of aircraft, mostly nearly new arrivals and all B-24M models. Eight-man crews traveled on a routing Okinawa–Guam–Kwajalein–Hawaii to their destination at Mather Army Air Field near Sacramento, California. The crews parked their planes, "switches off," and signed them over to units that would survey them and retire the combat aircraft from active service to a variety of fates. Some would go to reserve units, some would be sold as war surplus for five cents on the taxpayer dollar and many would be flown to remote desert locations for storage and eventual scrapping.

While records at this point are unclear and may be non-existent given the frantic pace of demobilization that was occurring, it seems that at least six, and as many as eight, B-24Ms were flown home by reduced crews. Photos exist of the all-black SB-24s sitting on Mather Field in November 1945, but it was not clear how many of the 868th aircraft collected there for onward flights into infamy. Among those was 107, a real veteran of an airplane that flew its last combat mission on 9 August 1945 with the crew of Lieutenant Smitherman against the Japanese airfield at Kanoya, Kyushu.

Many of the squadron aircraft that did not go home were retired "in theater," as war-worn combatants ready to be laid to rest. Most of these were flown to aircraft assembly locations in the rear areas of the theater and simply dumped in their state of repair or disrepair, left under the sun or in the jungle. One 868th Squadron veteran who had returned to the States several months before the end of the war when his combat tour was completed made a surprise discovery half a year later in February 1946.

Crowell "Butch" Moyer, who flew 46 combat missions as the navigator on the original Wright Project crew of Bob Lehti in *Bums Away*, stayed in the U.S. Army Air Force/U.S. Air Force for a career of more than 20 years. In January 1946, as a recent graduate of the Air Force's Technology Institute and a protégé of Colonel Edwin Aldrin from their days together with Bid Dolan at Langley Field, Moyer was selected to be the group navigator for the Tropical Science Mission. That group flew a 50,000-mile around-the-world route to map navigation instrumentation and collect weather data. In February of that year, his flight touched down for a day at the former Fifth Air Force base at Nadzab, New Guinea.

Captain Moyer found himself wandering around a sea of broken aircraft that had been collected almost randomly and dumped next to the airfield. Nadzab had been a major airbase complex from mid-1944 and a rear-area maintenance and supply center for both the Fifth and Thirteenth Air Forces. Later in the war, it served as a supply center for the entire FEAF when that organization was formed. At one point in his stroll down memory lane, Moyer found himself standing in the graveyard of a large collection of B-24 Liberators, mostly daylight aircraft from the Fifth Air Force. But also in that mix was a number of broken Thirteenth Air Force B-24s. At the center sat two of the 10 Wright Project B-24D models. Moyer had flown in both with the original Lehti crew, and then with the squadron's commander, Foster, and with pilots Carlson and Reynolds when Lehti left the squadron.

The plane Moyer had taken from Langley Field to Guadalcanal in August 1943, *Bums Away*, sat stripped of its outer wing panels and all four engines. Yet, its forward cockpit area and fuselage were largely intact. Moyer climbed into the aircraft and emerged from the cockpit to have his photo taken by another member of the Tropical Mission. He then took a hack saw to the aluminum skin of the aircraft to cut out the nose art of *Bums Away*, and that of sister B-24D *The Lady Margaret*. Carefully wrapping them in his flight jacket, he brought several nose art panels with their figures home. Thirty years later they still held a place of honor on the wall of his den in Albuquerque, New Mexico.[5]

And the men came home

Walking away from these aircraft on U.S. soil, the final collection of 868th Squadron pilots, co-pilots, navigators, bombardiers, flight engineers, radio operators, radarmen and gunners would be discharged as quickly as the system allowed. It was not uncommon for one of the officers or enlisted men who flew these handful of aircraft home to leave Okinawa on a Sunday in October and be a civilian on the streets of his hometown two short weeks later. Others arrived by ship, the voyages either direct and fast on U.S. Navy combatants or more often on slow-poke cargo vessels that steamed home from the Pacific.

When the men came home from Okinawa in October 1945, their country was eager to see them discharged and returned to their homes to resume their former lives. Apart from the few who elected to remain on active duty and make a career in the Air Force, all were gone from active service by November. They were eager to pick up their lives, many electing to attend universities under the G.I. Bill. Each man built his own career, began families, but over time the men of the 868th drifted apart. The 1946 movie, *The Best Years of Our Lives*, which won several Academy Awards that year, captured these highly personal coming-home transitions in all their varied complexities and did so completely.

Yet many considered their time in the service of their country in war to be the finest moments of their life, and their greatest experiences shared with the men they had met, trained with, flew with and survived with to come home.

One man's fate was exceptionally sad. Major Baylis Harriss, respected by all who served with him in the 868th, returned home and attempted to adjust to civilian life, successful to a degree and for a while. Harriss was, by upbringing and inclination, a rancher and, shortly after mustering out, he and his wife Mildred bought a ranch in the Avra Valley near Tucson, Arizona. He also had a flying service and offered crop dusting over a wide range of the western states. But he was a man that was made for war, and the war in the Pacific had almost been made for him. Before Pearl Harbor, with experience as a commercial pilot, he had found a place for himself as a combat leader, first serving with the RAF and then across the Pacific with the Thirteenth Air Force and the 868th Squadron.

Baylis Harriss apparently attempted to resume active duty during the Korean War but was unable to do so. In November 1959, outside Madras, Oregon, flying his crop-dusting Stearman biplane, he crashed into the ground from a high altitude and died instantly.[6]

Reunited and reinforced

In the early 1970s, at the point when many of the squadron veterans were in their mid-to-late fifties and some in their early sixties, and as several were considering retirement, they found that they had more time to relax and reflect. Looking back over three decades, the men of the 868th began to seek one another out, first searching for their individual crews or men with whom they were close with in support units, then reaching beyond their own crews to find other men of the squadron. Former Captain Vince Splane, who had joined the Wright Project on Guadalcanal in September 1943 as a replacement command pilot, began his hunt in earnest.

Over a five-year period, Dr. Splane found many of the men of the squadron. As he built his list, he created the 868th Snooper Veterans Association, and with that effort organized and staged reunions that brought many of these men and their wives together over a 20-year period. This author was privileged to attend their fourth reunion in November 1978 as a guest of the Association. As of November 1982, the Association counted 148 active members and it would continue to correspond and meet for many years thereafter.

Importantly for all, including this author, Vince Splane wrote and circulated the *Snooper News*, a home-grown publication that reported on the reunions, conveyed information from fellow "Snoopers" who wrote to him to share recalled events and passed along selected mission reports. Others helped Vince and his wife Joanie organize their information, all to the end of locating more 868th veterans and bringing them into the fold. Liberator historian and author Al Blue provided mission reports that he had accessed at the National Archives and other data storage centers and these became part of the Splane 868th project.

Dr. Vince Splane passed from this life in October 1989 at the age of 70. All of the other 868th Squadron veterans with whom this author established a relationship in the 1978–82 period have also passed as of 2022. But over a 20-year period, Vince Splane and his wife maintained their special project as their "mission" that benefited all the squadron members and their families, honoring a special collection of men who had earned the sobriquet of "the greatest generation." It was an honor to meet Vince and share his passion, and it was to Vince Splane and a score of other 868th Snoopers to whom the author pledged to research and write their story.

CHAPTER 26

The "Other Snoopers": The Scott and Hopson SB-24 Projects

1943–45

No account of the Dolan 1st Sea-Search Attack Group, the Wright Project and the 868th Squadron would be complete without reference to the two sister LAB projects, those being the slightly younger Scott Project and the follow-on Hopson Project. The former would serve with the Fifth Air Force in the Southwest Pacific Theater and the latter in the Fourteenth Air Force in the China–Burma–India Theater. In this mention, the story of each unit is incomplete and perhaps yet to be written in a more comprehensive form. But these men in their LAB B-24s were out there in the war along with the Wright Project and the 868th Squadron. It is therefore appropriate to pass along what is known, respecting again that other sources offer much more detailed elements of the history of each of these two organizations.

The LAB concept validated

One of the reasons that Bid Dolan was not allowed to follow his dream of leading the first LAB crews to war in the Pacific and was compelled instead to watch as Stud Wright did so, was that General Arnold and his staff had become sold on the low-altitude bombing concept. By early 1943, as the initial 10 crews who would form the Wright Project were coming together and perfecting their skills in newly arrived B-24s at Langley Field, Dolan had been ordered to build out two additional B-24 LAB projects for deployment to combat in the Pacific. One would be dispatched to the Fifth Air Force in General MacArthur's Southwest Pacific Command and arrive there a few months after the Wright Project began to fly its combat missions from Carney Field on Guadalcanal. A second LAB unit would be assigned to fly with the Fourteenth Air Force in the China–Burma–India Theater and would depart Langley for that part of the war in early 1944.

After the departure of the 10 Wright Project crews for the Pacific in August 1943, the two sister groups dedicated to the LAB mission continued to train at Langley. Like the Wright crews, these men served with Dolan's 1st Sea-Search Attack Group, initially flying with the ASV-equipped B-18B fleet to gain experience and later converting to their own B-24s as those aircraft became available. By September 1943, as the Wright Project was doing battle in The Slot, the two follow-on LAB projects were staffing up, expanding their training and preparing to depart Langley Field.

During this same period at Langley, other LAB crews were training alongside the two new groups, men who were preparing to join the Wright Project. These crews would begin to flow forward from November 1943 and join the Wright Project, and later the 868th Squadron, over the next many months. These additional Wright crews would replace lost crews and aircraft and augment the inventory beyond the first 10 crews and airplanes. In this situation at Langley, the crews that would be assigned to the three discrete projects and their respective air forces, each with their distinct operating areas, were often intermixed until a final selection was made as to which crews would be assigned to the different projects. In the case of the Wright Project, some of the initial crews would be dispatched without aircraft, the intent being to fully staff up the Wright contingent as it adjusted its crew strength to match existing and incoming aircraft. For the two additional projects, most crews received their aircraft at Langley, were dedicated to their respective "Project" squadrons and took their aircraft overseas to join their new commands.

The Scott Project and General Kenney's Air Force

At the time the men of the Wright Project were separated within the 1st Sea-Search Attack Group in May 1943 by the creation of the 3rd Squadron, a collection of experienced ASV aircrews remained with the 2nd Squadron to form what would become the Scott Project. The designated leader of this second LAB B-24 unit would be Lieutenant Colonel Edward W. Scott, a proven combat leader nominated by Lieutenant General Kenney to travel to Langley to work up this squadron and bring it back to his Fifth Air Force.

Scott had been with Kenney before there was a Fifth Air Force, commanding a beat-down B-17 unit during the summer of 1942 as Kenney and MacArthur struggled to rebuild the ground, air and naval components of the Southwest Pacific Forces. Kenney writes of then Captain Scott in his memoir, *General Kenney Reports*,[1] and compliments Scott for his resolve to attack the Japanese when the squadron had only three serviceable B-17s available, and war-weary ones at that. Scott took command of the 63rd Squadron in November 1942, within the 43rd Bomb Group of V Bomber Command of the Fifth Air Force, when Kenney elevated the squadron's storied leader, Major William Benn, to be his chief-of-staff. Scott led the 63rd from the front of the formation and, as the B-24s began to arrive in the Fifth Air Force, the B-17s of Scott's squadron continued to serve. Equipping with newly arrived B-17Es, Scott drove his aircrew to attack at low-level, based on the tactical approach that had been aggressively advocated and proven in combat by former squadron commander Benn.[2]

Scott was in the air in March 1943 during the battle of the Bismarck Sea when the Fifth Air Force eviscerated a Japanese convoy carrying reinforcements to New Guinea from Rabaul. In a three-day engagement subsequently labeled by commentators as the "Sea of Blood," the Fifth Air Force threw every plane it had against this convoy. By then a major, Ed Scott was flying his B-17E *Tuffy*, struck a destroyer to stop it dead in the water, and then went to wave-top height to deliver repeated strafing attacks on the convoy. The engagement saw all seven transports destroyed, three of the eight destroyers sunk and an entire Japanese Army regiment wiped out. The Japanese would never again expose a convoy of this size in the range of the growing fleet of B-25s, A-20s, B-17s, Beaufighters and fighter formations.[3]

When General Arnold at AAF Headquarters offered Kenney a LAB-equipped B-24 squadron in the spring of 1943, Kenney eagerly accepted and dispatched the recently promoted Lieutenant Colonel Scott to Langley to take charge of what would become the "Scott Project." As mentioned, Dolan worked with Scott to blend several of Langley's more experienced ASV and LAB crews into the new unit. The 12 aircraft of the Scott Project, designated as classified "Project Number 96189—Restricted," departed Langley in late September and arrived by air in the Southwest Pacific a few weeks later, followed by the ground element that arrived by sea. The unit was in place by late October to begin missions soon thereafter. This positioned the Scott Project to operate from New Guinea bases with the Fifth Air Force about eight weeks after the Wright Project began its missions from Guadalcanal in service with the Thirteenth Air Force.[4]

The Scott Project movement and operational orders provide a fairly complete reconstruction of the unit by crew, aircraft serial number and other movement-related details. It is also possible to assign many of the names associated with the individual aircraft and crews through contemporary sources, but this process is less certain. This author's best presentation of the original 12 Scott Project crew members and their assigned aircraft, and the names which may have been associated with them is as follows:

Crew Number	Aircraft Number	Command Pilot	Name Associated
FK-600-AB 1	42-40904	Capt. Robert Coleman	*Queen of Hearts*
FK-600-AB 2	42-41051	Lt. George Biddison	*Pitti-Sing*
FK-600-AB 3	42-40896	Lt. Arthur Millard	*Art's Cart*
FK-600-AB 4	42-41058	Capt. William Hamill	*Lady Luck*
FK-600-AB 5	42-41049	1st Lt. Charles Quinette	*Who's Next*
FK-600-AB 6	42-40955	1st Lt. Grover Hallman	*At Ease*
FK-600-AB 7	42-41050	1st Lt. William L. Burghoff	*Mallet Head*
FK-600-AB 8	42-41053	1st Lt. Stephen Ring	*Kentucky Virgin*
FK-600-AB 9	42-41041	1st Lt. Alvin McGehee	unknown
FK-600-AB 10	42-40972	1st Lt. William Hafner	unknown
FK-600-AB 11	42-41043	1st Lt. James Harris	unknown
FK-600-AB 12	42-40475	Capt. Craig Mcintosh	*The Swan*

The Provisional Flight Leader for this 12-aircraft movement, designated Project Number 96189-Restricted, Lieutenant Colonel Edward W. Scott, would fly with FK-600-AB 2, the aircraft and crew of Lieutenant George Biddison. The assigned Technical Officer, Lieutenant John Brewster, would fly with FK-600-AB-10, the aircraft and crew of First Lieutenant William Hafner. All other project personnel would "proceed by rail to San Francisco as the Port of Embarkation, thence to overseas destination by water." Movement Order Number 3 for this "permanent change of station" also authorized the "two civilian technical representatives to travel as passengers in the tactical aircraft of this movement."[5]

When the Scott Project reached the Fifth Air Force in the Southwest Pacific Theater in mid–October 1943 fresh from LAB training at Langley Field, it found that the Fifth Air Force comprised no fewer than four heavy bomb groups. The 43rd Bomb Group, a daylight B-24 unit that called itself "Ken's Men," included the 63rd Bomber Squadron (Heavy). After some discussion, the men and aircraft of the Scott Project were assigned to this existing unit and it became an all-SB-24 or LAB-equipped B-24 squadron. Thus, with these changes, the SB-24s of the Scott Project would serve as the 63rd Squadron under the 43rd Bomb Group and the Fifth Air Force for the balance of the war in the Pacific.[6]

Lieutenant Colonel Scott led the 63rd into its first combat missions but soon gained a promotion to full colonel and turned over the unit to another commander. Within the B-24 heavy bomber groups of the Fifth Air Force, the "SeaHawks," as they came to be known, claimed more than their share of tough missions. Like the 868th Squadron, the 63rd flew both night LAB patrol missions and, more than was the case with the 868th, often flew with their parent 43rd Bomb Group as part of larger daylight B-24 formations. But at the bottom line, the 63rd was a true Snooper unit as well, and it regularly maintained itself as such with new special mission capabilities, as those became available, to enhance the performance of its radar and LAB systems. Project leader Scott was soon moved up again, this time to lead the squadron's parent, the 43rd Bomb Group. He was further elevated in March 1945 to become a member of Kenney's immediate staff as the Assistant A-3 in the FEAF.[7]

During its time in combat, the 63rd Squadron was covered by *RADAR*, the bi-monthly classified publication assembled at Rad Lab and published by the Army Air Forces Air Communications Office beginning in early 1944. Although the first articles in issue number one focused on the Wright Project's LAB experiences, subsequent issues covered radar and LAB developments more generally, and several focused on the RCM or Ferret missions in the South Pacific. Notably, the 63rd was one of the first in the Pacific Theater to acquire and fly the H2X blind-bombing system. In the planning exercise for FEAF support before and during the twin invasions of the Home Islands, it was assumed that the 63rd would join with the 868th to fly from Okinawa on LAB and Ferret missions designed to isolate those islands from China and Korea. The Japanese surrender set these plans aside and the 63rd was demobilized; the squadron crews turned in their aircraft and went home over the next two months, along with most of the men of the other B-24 formations of the FEAF.

A book which focuses heavily on the 63rd Squadron, *World War II B-24 "Snoopers": Low Level Bombing Targets Manila Bay Shipping; The Story of WWII's Secret Anti-Shipping Night War Against the Japanese*, by Stephen M. Perrone,[8] provides a focused account of the experiences of selected crews of the SeaHawk squadron. This 2001 publication covers both the 63rd and the 868th and draws heavily from the 868th Squadron's veteran organization publication *The Snooper News*. As such, this book highlights selected contributions to that publication made by 63rd Squadron veterans. Injected as well are accounts of the 868th veterans, some of which parallel those found in this book.[9]

Different command structures

The different operational command situations experienced by the Wright and Scott Projects, the former remaining independent of any bomb group subordination and the latter being an integrated squadron serving as part of a heavy bomb group, had two consequences. In the case of the 868th Squadron, the original Wright Project would retain its independent relationship and all mission planning would occur at the level of the Thirteenth Air Force's XIII Bomber Command. In the case of the 63rd Squadron, mission planning and control would emanate at the level of the 43rd Bomb Group. This made little difference at the tactical level of daily mission assignments but did constrain somewhat the ability of the unit to resist being drawn into group-level daylight formation missions.

The second consequence of the 63rd Squadron's subordination to the group, important for military historians, was that World War II air power narratives most often reference and draw from the operational histories at the bomb group level. It was typical that detailed records were maintained and postwar unit histories of those groups were created at this bomb group level. In this situation, the Wright Project and its successor 868th were disadvantaged somewhat, remaining an outlier with no affiliation with a bomb group, a historical quasi-orphan as it were. This has also led to some confusion among those attempting to reconstruct the Pacific campaigns of the Wright Project in that it is often assumed that, once designated the 394th Squadron, it remained as such under the Thirteenth Air Force's 5th Bomb Group. This would not be the case. Once free of the SB-24's contingent, the 394th Squadron would serve proudly as the 5th Bomb Group's fourth B-24 squadron for daylight missions.

In missions later in the war, 868th LAB aircraft would infrequently support and fly with their daylight B-24 brethren of the 5th and 307th Bomb Groups, taking part in large-scale missions against industrial facilities. Some retellings of these combined missions would inject further confusion into otherwise accurate historical accounts.

This was particularly the case when aircraft of the 868th flew with 5th or 307th Bomb Group formations in "pathfinder" roles and were recorded as part of a given formation on the mission reporting of the daylight B-24 unit.

As mentioned in earlier chapters, there were occasions when the 868th teamed up with the 63rd to fly combined missions, both daylight and night strikes. In late April 1944, the two joined forces to place 17 aircraft over Mokmer Airdrome on Biak when the command ordered all Fifth and Thirteenth Air Force units to make a maximum effort against that island. The following month, each squadron contributed three aircraft and crews for a joint sea-search mission to find a convoy that had been reported and, failing to find that, together hit the secondary target—Mokmer Airdrome. In late May, the two squadrons put a combined 12 aircraft in the air to fly from Los Negros to strike enemy defenses at Bosnek on Biak Island.

The two units drifted apart physically when the 868th found itself stranded on Noemfoor in late 1944 but became reacquainted when the 868th moved up to Morotai in May (the 63rd was then at Leyte). It was planned that the 63rd would catch up with the 868th on Okinawa in August 1945 for coordinated FEAF attacks on Japan proper but, in the event of the Japanese surrender on 15 August, this did not occur.

Another coincidence related to the Wright and Scott Projects is the fact that four men who were intimately involved in bringing the SB-24 LAB capability to the Pacific War and sustaining it in combat there were classmates in the Army Air Force "Class of 40-A." These men graduated in March 1940. Stud Wright, the leader of the first LAB unit to deploy to war; Edward Scott, the leader of the second deployed LAB unit; Leo Foster, an original Wright Project command pilot who replaced Wright as the project commanding officer in September 1943 when the latter went to Washington, D.C., to present his report; and James Barlow, who replaced Foster when the latter rotated at the end of his tour back to the United States. Barlow turned over command of the 868th in early 1945 as Baylis Harriss arrived to command the unit.[10]

The Hopson Project in the China–Burma–India Theater

Also, as earlier noted, the third and final contingent of Bid Dolan's Langley Field LAB program, that of the Hopson Project, saw that SB-24 unit formed after the Scott Project and assigned to the Fourteenth Air Force in the China–Burma–India Theater. The unit trained under Lieutenant Colonel William D. Hopson with Dolan's 1st Sea-Search Attack Group and left Langley in March 1944, arriving in China in early May. The Fourteenth Air Force operated under the leadership of Brigadier General Claire Chennault, of "Flying Tigers" fame, who had insisted to AAF Commander Hap Arnold that he needed a numbered air force and a mix of fighter, medium and heavy bomber and transport groups to support the Chinese Army that was battling the Japanese in central China. The Fourteenth was established in March 1943 as a successor to Chennault's

China Air Task Force and received a full complement of new squadrons over the ensuing months, each of which brought with them new crews and aircraft.

Among the forces committed to the Fourteenth was the 308th Bomb Group (Heavy), a unit that had been activated in April 1942 with four daylight B-24 squadrons assigned, those being the 373rd, the 374th, the 375th and the 425th Bomb Squadrons. These squadrons arrived in the China–Burma–India Theater of Operations in February 1943 and were initially based in northeastern India. The units then "flew the Hump" the following month to relocate to forward bases in China proper, with the 308th command unit and the 425th Squadron basing at Kunming, the 374th and 375th locating to Chengkung and the 373rd to Yangkai. These locations placed the B-24s within the aircraft's striking range to attack many Japanese targets that had previously received only limited attention from the other Allied units operating in this theater.

In positioning the fighters and bombers of this air force in these locations, General Chennault and his staff were betting that the Japanese would not be able to extend their existing area of occupation in China to challenge these operating airfields, either by air attack or land offensives. This was a risk that Chennault was willing to accept as a trade-off for the capability to attack the targets he wanted his B-24s to strike. The gamble paid off, albeit at a heavy price in operational and combat losses. The Fourteenth did fly aggressively to strike the southeastern coast of China, hitting a variety of high-profile targets from Hong Kong to Formosa to Hainan Island.

But the initial positioning of these aircraft at the forward airfields in China was highly problematic as a considerable effort had to be devoted to supplying the squadrons with the fuel, bombs and other supplies required to sustain combat operations. All these provisions had to be air-lifted from rear area bases in India. It was estimated that three to five supply flights over the Hump were required to accumulate enough fuel and bombs sufficient to launch a single long-distance mission from a forward base in China. In this shuttling process, many valuable aircrews and aircraft were claimed by the Himalayas all too frequently. The hauling of supplies to provision a strike situation took a heavy toll on the aircrews and aircraft that survived the Hump to fly the strike missions, with one account noting that a typical 308th B-24, one *Cocky Bobby*, would finish its tour with 39 combat missions and at least 50 missions "over the Hump" on supply runs to the forward airfields.

This was the situation when the Hopson Project arrived in India in mid-May 1944 to begin its familiarization and prepare for onward staging into China. At this point in the history of SB-24 LAB operations, the Wright Project had become the 868th and was entering its tenth month of combat, and the Scott Project, operating as the 63rd Squadron of the Fifth Air Force, and had been flying its missions in the Southwest Pacific for about seven months. The 20 aircraft of the Hopson SB-24 contingent, all factory-new J-models, had flown to India on a routing that was the opposite of that traveled by the Wright and Scott aircrews, launching to fly east across the Atlantic rather than winging west across the Pacific.

Upon their arrival in the China–Burma–India Theater, the aircraft and crews of the Hopson Project were distributed, or parceled-out, to the four individual daylight B-24 squadrons of the 308th Group. The Hopson Project SB-24s flew their first mission on 24 May and experienced their first loss a day later when a crew failed to return from a mission. An excellent account of the SB-24 contribution to the Fourteenth Air Force can be found in Edward Young's *B-24 Liberator Units of the CBI*.[11] As Young's book records, a posthumous Congressional (sic) Medal of Honor was awarded to Major Horace Carswell for his actions on 26 October 1944 in attacking a convoy and attempting to nurse his crippled SB-24 back to base. Carswell was the only airman in the China–Burma–India Theater to be so honored.

In this disbursed arrangement among four daylight B-24 squadrons, the Hopson crews performed with distinction. They managed to answer the call and mixed their missions between participation in daylight formations and single-aircraft anti-shipping patrols off the coast of China and Indochina. However, the allocation of aircraft to the four daylight B-24 squadrons denied the Hopson aircrews the distinction of a squadron identity and tended to reduce the efficiency of logistics support and aircraft servicing that was the norm for the 868th and the 63rd Squadrons. This arrangement also complicated the tasking of coordinated LAB search missions originating from different squadrons based at a variety of locations and tended, at least initially, to make the night-hunting capabilities a secondary consideration to the 308th Bomb Group's operational planning.

This situation reversed itself when the SB-24s began to establish their reputation as highly effective ship hunters once let off the leash. A second echelon of the Hopson Project B-24s departed Langley on a Movement Order dated 8 July 1944 and its route of travel was Bangor, Maine, to Gander, Newfoundland, then to the Azores in the mid-Atlantic, and from there a long march from Marrakech in North Africa, through Tunis, Cairo, Abadan, Karachi and Agra to its destination in northeast India. This contingent joined its sister SB-24s in August 1944 and together these aircraft, in commission and ready for dispatch into the night, frequently numbered 20 or more SB-24s. An interesting first-person account of the experiences of a Hopson Project pilot, Elmer "Bud" Haynes, is provided in the book *General Chennault's Secret Weapon: The B-24 in China* by A. B. Feuer.[12] This book transcribes the diary maintained by Haynes during the period July 1944 through May 1945 and contains a foreword by Colonel William D. Hopson, USAF (Retired).[13]

The hardships experienced by the B-24s of the Fourteenth Air Force in just being able to position themselves to launch against the Japanese cannot be overstated. The aircrews and aircraft of the 308th Bomb Group essentially had to fend for themselves, working an air transport route between its logistical bases in India and the forward operational bases beyond the mountains to secure and transport in their own bomber aircraft everything that was required to sustain their presence in China. There was no land route from India to the bases in China nor was there any U.S. Navy shipping to deliver the tons of supplies needed for the missions as was the case in the Pacific. Some months later, the Japanese mounted a major ground offensive that drove these U.S. squadrons out of China and overran the airfields. This sent the 308th Bomb Group, in company with fighter and medium bomber units, back to bases in northeastern India.

Later in the war, as the Japanese lost ground and abandoned their gains, the Fourteenth Air Force and its heavy bomber units returned to bases in China and redoubled their offensive against what remained of the Japanese shipping that was still attempting to shuttle through the South China Sea. When the shipping targets dried up, as they had for the two sister LAB squadrons operating to the east, the SB-24s of the 308th focused their attention on other precision bombing targets, busting bridges and hitting railroad service yards to deny the Japanese the ability to transfer troops and supplies within China.

In February–March 1945, as the war rolled forward in China and the China-based B-29 fleet moved to the Marianas, the 308th assigned three of its B-24 squadrons to occupy the airbases made available by that departure at Chengdu. The SB-24 crews and their aircraft were consolidated into a single squadron, the 373rd, bringing that unit the aircrew and aircraft cohesion that it had lacked since its arrival in the China–Burma–India Theater. Soon joined by the 308th Bomb Group's RCM aircraft, the SB-24s would fly as an integrated unit for the balance of the war. The expectation was that, much like the planning ongoing in the 868th and 63rd Squadrons of the FEAF, the SB-24s of the Fourteenth would be repositioned in August 1945, probably assigned to a new airbase in Okinawa, to fly against the Home Islands in preparation for the planned November invasion of Kyushu.

The LAB missions of the Hopson Project were well covered in *Radar* magazine. The sixth edition of November 1944 included a multi-page article entitled "LAB Versus Japanese Shipping." This presentation began with the claim that, "In fourteen months a handful of LAB planes have sunk more than 500,000 tons and, with the invasion of the Philippine Islands, the record in the months to come may be even more impressive." The article acknowledges the hardships of operating against the Japanese in the East China Sea from remote bases in China and posits that the Japanese counter-offensive in China may soon deprive the LAB aircrews of the forward bases necessary for them to launch missions into that sea. This setback had in fact already occurred by the time the magazine reached its readers.[14]

The article claims that the performance of the Hopson squadron, at least as of year-end 1944, far outdistanced that of the sister 868th and the 63rd squadrons hard at work in the FEAF to the east. This assertion was based on a calculation that the LAB newcomers had racked up the impressive total of 1,700 tons of Japanese shipping sunk on an average mission. The claim was grounded in a statistic generated somewhere in the AAF that in September 1944 alone the Fourteenth Air Force LAB crews had sunk no less than 110,000 tons of enemy shipping. At this time, there was doubt that the merchant shipping running the gantlet of the South China Sea in the stretch between

Formosa and the Chinese coast was there in great numbers. All things considered, these claims seem exaggerated, but the fact was the Hopson crews were out there patrolling and hitting targets in the night and choking the sea routes to Japan from their bases in China.

The *RADAR* article is impressive in that it describes the substantial advantages the LAB system imparted to the SB-24 aircrews well, particularly when compared with the uneven performance of the daylight heavy and medium bombers employed against Japanese shipping. The emphasis here is on the efficiency of radar-based anti-shipping bombing and the lower aircraft loss ratio when searches and attacks by individual aircraft were compared to formation attacks against moving or even anchored (protected) targets. The point is made, no doubt accurately, that LAB attacks accounted for nearly half of all Japanese shipping sunk by the entire XIV Bomber Command over a four-month period. To achieve its daylight balance of 50 percent, XIV Bomber Command employed four times the number of B-24 sorties, personnel and bombs as did the "handful" of LAB aircrews. The article states with great pride of accomplishment that, in the Hopson Project's first three months in the war, it flew 134 combat sorties, sank 113,000 tons of cargo shipping and damaged an additional 53,000 tons. This total included seven warships, with a light cruiser claimed as sunk off Hainan Island.

U.S. Navy and U.S. Marine B-24s

Lastly, but with no less importance, no real history of the 868th Squadron would be complete without some mention of the U.S. Navy and U.S. Marine patrol bomber and reconnaissance squadrons that flew into combat in the Pacific. The aircraft initially operated were the B-24 as the PB4Y-1 and its variant, the PB4Y-1P. An improved version based on the B-24 airframe and its Davis wing, the single-tail PB4Y-2 Privateer, joined the war in late 1944 and brought the B-24 series to final perfection.

Although these were not dedicated LAB aircraft per se and the U.S. Navy and U.S. Marine squadrons typically flew daylight patrol-strike missions against land and sea targets, the operational profile was similar to that of the three USAAF B-24 squadrons. These were typically high-risk "lone wolf" squadrons that sent single or small groups of aircraft against heavily defended targets to destroy and harass the enemy. These heavily decorated squadrons each have their own unit histories and racked up an impressive combat record as they made their way across the Pacific. The U.S. Navy and Marine aircraft were often in the same sky as the SB-24s of the 868th and the 63rd Squadrons and frequently found themselves stationed at the same airfields.

The first units to deploy to the Pacific were equipped with B-24Ds, configured much like the original 10 B-24Ds of the Wright Project and those of the Scott Project. Dissatisfied with their glassed-in noses, these aircraft were frequently modified in the field to carry a nose turret, useful given the proclivity to take on targets in daylight with down-the-throat direct approach attacks. A parallel program operating dedicated reconnaissance (photographic) squadrons, based on the B-24D and future variants of that airplane, were fielded and became a major resource for assessing invasion candidates and keeping track of the Japanese movement of air and fleet assets.

It appears that late-war variants, mainly those of the PB4Y-2, did carry some form of a LAB system and occasionally operated these in night missions, but this author cannot confirm the degree to which this was the case equipment-wise, and the extent to which it may have been used is not known, at least for the purposes of this narrative. A large number of excellent books are devoted to the PB4Y-1 and its impressive younger sibling, the PB4Y-2. The books not only describe the aircraft themselves, but also the combat record of the squadrons that flew them.[15]

1945–80

To continue the story of Namhae Island and its intrepid villagers from the prologue, we must return to the morning hours of 8 August 1945. The Japanese, ever alert to signs that the local populace was disloyal to the emperor, soon learned of the irreverent activity by Mr. Kim and his fellow villagers who had trekked up the mountain hours before. The Japanese Army unit dispatched from the nearby base made their way up the mountain to the crash site only to discover the still-smoldering wreckage and that the bodies of the American airmen had been buried in shallow graves, covered by rocks with a make-shift wooden cross planted at the site. Descending to the village at midday, they rounded up the villagers they were able to identify as having buried the Americans. Kim's home was searched and he was arrested. American airpower now dominated the daylight hours and word, or rather rumor, of the atomic bombing spread as did the certainty that the end of the war might be a reality.

The other Namhae villagers were soon released but, as the suspected ringleader of an anti-Japanese clique, Kim was tortured for three days at the nearby Japanese airbase. He was confronted, as evidence of his anti-state activity, with a picture of Abraham Lincoln which the military police had found tacked to the wall in his two-room home. Kim was later released and, during the two days it took him to walk and boat his way back to Namhae, the second American atomic bomb found its mark on Nagasaki. The Japanese emperor was compelled to accept the Allies' terms of "unconditional surrender" a few days later.

Weeks later, after the official surrender of Japan on 3 September 1945, the Japanese colonial masters were replaced by American forces who arrived in the lower half of the peninsula. The U.S. forces occupied that part of Korea to disarm the Japanese and to enforce a political decision to grant Korea self-rule. At that point, Kim called a village meeting. The suffering of the villagers who had lived under Japanese colonial rule, and died opposing it, as well as the young Americans who gave their lives in the last week of the war, could not be forgotten. A village commitment was made to create the "Korean–American Air Force Memorial Association of Namhae Island." A cardboard charter which, 40 years later, still hung on the wall of Kim's drug store, was drafted. It was agreed that the mountain-top site of *Lady Luck II*'s violent death would be an appropriate place to hold memorial services and construct a permanent shrine that would endure long after the death of the villagers who had attended the scene.

The people of this isolated island were poor in 1946. As the summer rains ended and the rice harvest began in September, the graves were carefully tended, a small area cleared and the first annual memorial service held. The same year also saw the arrival of an American war graves registration group which, with the assistance of Kim and the village elders, located and recovered the remains of the 11 men. This same registration team was also able to confirm the identity of the men to the village so that their names could be permanently recorded. The village gave up their American airmen with great dignity. In an official ceremony in the village square, officials turned over the remains of the men they had buried and protected to fellow Americans who promised that the dead would be properly cared for.

The village's dedication to the men of *Lady Luck II*, however, was only beginning. The Korea–United States Air Force Memorial Association held its first formal mountain-top service in September 1947 and every September thereafter witnessed the trek up Man Gun San by the villagers. The activities of the memorial association, now firmly established, complete with a signboard as an adjunct to Kim's small drug store sign, moved forward as donations were accepted for a formal monument, and services continued to be held each September. But as Namhae Island sought to rebuild itself in peace, outside forces seemed determined to destroy all that was decent. In 1948, communist infiltrators from Soviet-occupied North Korea came ashore and systematically assassinated several islanders who supported a free government. This included one man who had returned as a doctor, after 20 years in the United States, to help his native country develop.

In June 1950, the North Korean communists attacked the young nation. In overrunning the length of the new country, Namhae Island was occupied by the North Koreans a few weeks later. The new occupiers consulted their carefully arranged blacklists to seek out for torture and execution those villagers identified as pro-American. At the top of the North Korean list was Kim and the men of the memorial association. Kim was tortured—his eardrum broken, his fingers smashed—and he was left to die in a rice field as a blood-covered example to any on the island who would oppose Communism and embrace American ideals.

Near the peak of Man Gun San, overlooking placid Yŏsu Bay, the communists found a simple wooden marker containing 11 vertical Korean language characters. The sign, the first erected by the association, read simply: "That which has been paid for in blood shall be repaid in peace by the next generation." That simple signboard was destroyed. But Pharmacist Kim considered himself fortunate. As the Communists approached, he buried his association materials, including the cardboard sign which hung above his drug store door. Throughout his interrogation, he refused to acknowledge himself or any of his villagers as "American agents." He refused a self-demeaning confession and explained that he was a simple man who only felt that the 11 young Americans of the *Lady Luck II* deserved a decent burial as liberators of the nation. Kim also noted, more out of disrespect for the Communists' intelligence than for the record, that as he did not speak or understand a word of English, he would be hard put to politically conspire with the Americans.

Kim's detention by the North Koreans was interrupted by the counterattacking drive of U.N. forces across Korea. For the second time in five years, Kim escaped death when American troops moved through Namhae to liberate the village. The Man Gun San memorial service of 1952 was thus doubly significant and drew many villagers and farmers from the surrounding area. Kim's group dedicated a small part of their lives to the memorial. A self-imposed island-wide commodity tax campaign slowly but surely amassed the funds registered to replace Kim's original wooden shrine on the mountain with a more dignified memorial. By 1956, through the force of Kim's organization and willpower and the generosity of the village, the association was prepared for its crowning achievement.

On 30 November 1956, more than sixteen thousand people gathered on the grounds of Namhae Agricultural High School. Amid banners, elementary school choruses and local high school bands, a dedication ceremony was conducted. U.S. military and Republic of Korea military and civilian government representatives were invited by Kim and the association to share the rostrum. Kim had also attempted to write to all of the families of the crew to explain the island's memorial program and invite them to the dedication.

The official ceremony, complete with individual photographs of the 11 Americans, was held under a clear fall sky on the local high school field. Speaker after speaker proclaimed, in English and Korean, the mutual friendship of both peoples and the responsibilities of all generations to the memory of fallen soldiers. The assembled group then began their one-hour climb up Man Gun San where a granite memorial bearing the names of the 11 airmen was formally unveiled. Atop this monument rose a second 11-foot granite memorial stone donated by then President of South Korea, Dr. Syngman Rhee. This second memorial stone contained President Rhee's personal message to the Namhae Memorial Association. American representatives included not only local U.S. Army and Air Force general-grade officers but also a special representative of President Dwight D. Eisenhower.

The eleventh anniversary ceremony, however successful and fulfilling to Kim and the other surviving founding members of his group, did not complete the process. Rather, it provided added incentive to continue and expand their association. In 1957, Kim began his second 11-year campaign which he hoped would build a memorial hall in Namhae village for use as a community center and a functional memorial structure that Koreans and Americans could point to as a symbol of bilateral friendship. The collections and annual ceremonies continued into and through the 1960s and he had hopes of beginning the construction of the hall by 1970. But Kim's plan for a memorial hall was not to be—the entire memorial association treasury was embezzled by a villager who escaped to Japan with the funds.

As the years progressed, Kim's small business prospered and the village grew to become a town. The island, sharing fully in the "economic miracle" of Korea which advanced the nation's standard of living at an almost unbelievable pace, developed its homes and explored its past. A graceful suspension bridge was built in 1973 to link, for the first time in the nation's history, the island with the Korean mainland. Today, Namhae, with all of its still unspoiled cultural and historic beauty, can be reached by car not far off an expressway that runs across Korea's south coast. Visitors coming from the nation's capital of Seoul have finally discovered Namhae. In the warm summer months, they crowd its few resort hotels to enjoy clean beaches and visit local historic shrines such as that recently erected to honor Admiral Yi Sun-shin, Korea's greatest national hero. Yi, not unlike the crew of *Lady Luck II*, achieved his martyrdom in a series of naval battles which defeated Japanese attempts to invade and occupy Korea in the 16th century.

The author's involvement in the story of the Wright Project, the 868th Squadron and the crew of Lieutenant Ed Mills is worthy of a brief recounting. My connection with the events and personalities of World War II related in this book began in September 1977. At that time, I was serving as a Foreign Service Officer at the U.S. Embassy in Seoul with responsibilities in the Commercial Section. This included the monitoring of large-scale industrial projects in South Korea to which the United States was contributing funding. This involvement typically featured loans arranged by the U.S. Export-Import Bank designed to accelerate South Korea's economic development. In this role, I oversaw energy matters and heavy industrial projects, such as steel mills, nuclear power plants and shipyards, many of which were being constructed at remote locations across Korea's southern coast.

In the course of one of my site trips to these projects, after visiting a new shipyard under construction on nearby Koje (Geoje) Island, I elected to return to Seoul on a secondary road. This took a path that ran along the country's southern coast. Although not on my formal schedule, I wanted to view the bridge that had been erected a few years before to link Namhae Island to the mainland of Korea. U.S. aid had financed that bridge and it was something of a minor success story within the Embassy.

When we crossed the bridge and descended into the island's village shortly after noon, we discovered it to be nearly void of activity, not really a ghost town but certainly shuttered. Stopping one of the few people on the street we were told that the people of the village were "up on the mountain with the Americans." Puzzled by this odd explanation we asked further and learned that many in the small town were involved in an annual ceremony that celebrated Korea's liberation from Japan, a gathering that required a trek up to the top of Man Gun San. But this day was not the day on which the nation of Korea formally celebrated its independence, that day being 15 August.

On 15 August, the day of Japan's capitulation in 1945, the entire nation of Korea had been an oppressed colony for 45 years. The people celebrate the "The Day of the Lifting of Darkness," as it continues to be honored to this day, but the people of Namhae had instead apparently elected to honor the liberation of their nation on the very day we had by chance stopped there. We would soon learn that, to the people of Namhae, their liberation occurred when "the Americans came and died" to free them from Japanese colonial rule. We were told that much of the village, under the leadership of the local pharmacist, Mr. Kim Duk-Hyung, would soon return to reopen their stores and resume their routine as the mountain top ceremony, complete with a Christian religious service, typically concluded in the early afternoon.

I elected to wait for the return from the mountain of Pharmacist Kim. In the company of a score of villagers, he appeared a few hours later, tired from his trek, but very willing to sit in his home for a long conversation about that night 32 years before. Over barley tea, he recounted all that had occurred to him and his village during those August weeks of 1945 and related other events over the subsequent years related to "the men on the mountain." That evening, as I closed my notebook and bid him a sincere thank you for all that he and his friends had done, he mentioned that although he knew very little of the American crew, no more than the names that had been provided by the war graves team, he had saved one item that might help us identify where and with whom they had served. He explained that, as he and the villagers moved about the crash site on the second day to reinter the Americans, he had discovered and carefully pocketed a photograph which he had subsequently managed to conceal from the Japanese.

He had protected this single item over the many years since. Charred by fire on one side, Kim had removed this photo from the shirt pocket of one of the deceased young Americans. He retrieved this small photo from under a floorboard in his home. He handed it to me with hope and a request. "Maybe you can find their friends in America. Please tell those men, the men with whom they flew, what happened here on that August night in 1945. Tell them also what the people of this small village have done over the years to honor their sacrifice." Parting company with Kim, I promised that I would do my best and I bid him thank you and farewell. That journey, once undertaken on an fall evening in 1977, has as its result this book.

Back at our Embassy in Seoul, I wrote to one man who I thought might be able to help me learn about the 11 young American airmen who had died that early morning on Man Gun San—Steve Birdsall. The small photo handed to me by Kim depicted an 11-man crew positioned in front of the nose of an all-black B-24 bomber, the nose adorned with a painted likeness of a swimsuit-clad Vargas-like girl along with the aircraft name *LADY LUCK II*. A respected Australian aviation historian and author, Steve had written *Log of the Liberators* a few years before and was an obvious contact for my outreach. I wrote to him and he responded within a fortnight, saying that, while he had no idea as to the identity of the crew, he had set in motion some contacts back in the United States who might prove useful, and provided to these fellow historians my name and contact information.

A few weeks later, I was awakened by a phone call at three in the morning. I happened to be the Embassy duty officer that week and assumed this was just another early morning call about an errant American tourist who had wandered into trouble in some remote location in the Korean countryside. As I cleared my head, three gentlemen engaged me with a barrage of questions. The conversation began, "We think you may have found our last missing crew. Is it the Ed Mills crew?" The call lasted for more than an hour as I related the Namhae story. They tried to explain their connection to the men and the aircraft that had come to a tragic end three decades before. From this initial phone call, and a flurry of exchanges over the next several months, I came to know the men of the 868th Squadron, engaged by a veteran's group that been established by one of the squadron pilots, Dr. Vincent Splane.

As explained in the previous chapter, these men had found one another in the early 1970s and organized themselves to reference their service in this squadron during World War II. They also sought to honor their comrades who had died in the Pacific War, their brothers who did not come home. The immediate issue for these 868th veterans in 1977 was that I recount as much as possible about their squadron's last lost crew. Among other lost crews, these were men whose fate had remained a mystery when the squadron was sent home and disbanded in the fall of 1945. The missing men were those with whom they had trained, lived and flown and, when they died or disappeared, their squadron mates had mourned them. These deeply personal losses had remained unresolved, to these men, over the 32 years that had since elapsed. It seemed that I was now capable of helping them close that knowledge gap and, with this knowledge, allow them to "bring home to the squadron" its last missing crew.

I was invited to attend the 868th squadron reunion in 1978 and eagerly did so, making a presentation which provided the veterans and their families, who were gathered in San Francisco that weekend, all that we then knew of the fate of the Ed Mills crew. I summarized the experiences of Pharmacist Kim and the villagers of Namhae Island related to the Mills crew and together we agreed that, now that the 868th had found its last crew, the organization should express its appreciation to the people of Namhae. The men with whom I met had organized themselves as the 868th Squadron Veterans Association and this group committed to complete a memorial plaque. I arranged for this to be crafted in Korea and conveyed to Pharmacist Kim and the villagers the following year by a senior representative from the U.S. Embassy in Seoul. The American Ambassador sent along his own greetings in a letter that thanked the village for its dedication.

The plaque presented to Pharmacist Kim and the village of Namhae was inscribed in English and Korean as follows:

IN REVERENT MEMORY OF LT EDWARD B MILLS AND THE CREW OF THE LADY
LUCK II AND TO MR KIM DUK HYUNG AND THE PEOPLE OF NAMHAE AND THE
REPUBLIC OF KOREA FOR THE SACRIFICE AND UNSELFISH DEVOTION AND
REMEMBRANCE OF ELEVEN OF OUR AIRMEN LOST ON SEVEN AUGUST 1945
PRESENTED BY THE MEMBERS OF
THE 868 BOMB SQUADRON "SNOOPERS" OF WORLD WAR TWO
JULY 1979

During the 1978 reunion, I was approached by Vince Splane and several of the attendees and asked if I would undertake to write a history of the unit. Ideally, this would cover the squadron from its inception as a highly classified "special project" in early 1942 at Rad Lab MIT in Boston, through the formation of the 1st Sea-Search Attack Group at Langley Field later that year and to the creation of the Wright Project and its dispatch to the war in the Pacific in mid-1943. Such an undertaking would include the project's transition to becoming the 868th Squadron and its move to fight at the front of the Allied advance westward across the Pacific during 1944 and 1945, complete with its basing on Okinawa at the conclusion of the war. I soon found that these men who engaged and encouraged me held a discrete piece of the history, but none had even half a complete picture of what had evolved over the three and half years that America was at war in the Pacific.

I agreed to take this mission on, but explained that I would not be able to work full-time or even make a sustained effort given the demands of my Foreign Service career. What I could not explain was that I was a career officer in another service and had willingly accepted the burden of two careers, one atop the other, and that this situation often placed incredible demands on my time. But it was a worthy challenge and I was honored to be asked to do this by the men of my father's generation.

Over the next several years I corresponded with many of the 868th veterans, conducted in-person and phone interviews and assembled information from many sources, some of which I reached out to find, others who came to me almost by happenstance. In the latter case, it occurred that when I was assigned to Washington, D.C., on a tour of duty, a co-worker who was "the old boy guru on electronic systems" had retired and left behind a safe full of publications dating from World War II, all of them subsequently declassified. Amid this bundle of detail was a fine collection of material on the MIT Radiation Laboratory's development of radar systems. This find was, at least for me, a mini-gold mine as it related directly to the work at Rad Lab in Boston and led to the Bid Dolan group, the Wright Project and its successor, the 868th Squadron.

All this work, including an initial partial draft of the 868th manuscript, went into storage along the way as I moved from overseas location to location in my government assignments. In the late 1980s, I lost track of my draft and the great quantity of materials

I had assembled to inform the book. Stored in various locations along the way, I simply did not have time to collect what I needed and indeed feared that some materials were lost to me. In recent years, I recovered this information and reassembled it all to complete my draft of this book.

I recognize that the completion of this work is one part an obligation—the fulfillment of a commitment I made to these men when we first met in San Francisco more than four decades ago. It is also one part sheer pleasure in that this has been a personally fulfilling effort to put this story together for others to enjoy. One realizes as well that the men who flew these missions into the night in World War II, most in their early twenties and some even younger, have now passed from this life. There is embarrassment that I have failed to deliver this book during their lifetime and for this I am deeply regretful.

To partially atone for this delay, this work is appropriately dedicated to the sacrifice of the men who went to war and returned home to America to build their lives as part of the "Greatest Generation." More deeply, this history also honors those young airmen who flew into the night and sacrificed their lives so that their comrades could enjoy the benefits of the country for which they were willing to serve and risk all.

I hope that this work delivers the recognition so richly deserved by the American scientists and technicians at Rad Lab, the pilots and crews of Bid Dolan's 1st Sea-Search Attack Group and the 100 men who went with Stud Wright and his LAB project to the South Pacific. Leo Foster's year of leadership was critical to guiding the provisional unit that would become the 868th Squadron. This was followed by the dynamic personality of Baylis Harriss in the closing months of the war as he prepared the 868th Snoopers for what all assumed would be a long struggle over the months if not years ahead. These leaders, and the men they led, each made their individual contributions. All were humble in that sacrifice, to the very end. The fate of Ed Mills and his crew personifies that sacrifice and this incredible spirit of young Americans who went to war—our nation asked and we have answered.

"Radar Middleman," *Radar Magazine*, Volume 9, April 1945

If Col. William C. Dolan ever gave radar a serious thought before February 1942 nobody knew it. Yet by February 1945, when he was lost flying the second of the new APQ-7 installations to the ETO, he had helped to ready a whole string of microwave airborne radars for combat. He came in with the first U.S. microwave ASV and went out with high-resolution Eagle. In between he left his stamp on all of these: 517A, 517C, 717A, 717B, LAB and APS-15.

Col. Dolan was a sort of radar middleman, bridging the gap between production and theater use. He flight-tested the equipment, developed tactics and techniques for getting the most out of it and trained crews to use it.

Most people who knew sandy-haired, fiery Bid Dolan wondered what kept him glued to U.S. chores when battles were being fought elsewhere. He did it for radar. But he was forever scouting ways and means of battle-testing the equipment himself, and occasionally, as in the anti-sub campaign, he succeeded.

Chance threw him face to face with microwave radar. What he saw made him fall for it. On the basis of background, a hundred thousand other men would have seemed likelier apostles. He was no operational analyst. He was far from being a scientist. And he was short on formal education. But he was a good instrument pilot – one of the best – with a keen instinct for the tools that upped an aircraft's fighting value. To significance as a machine gun or a compass. He expounded on that steadily.

With respect to radar, he was the crash product of the crash period. The Army needed some instrument pilots to test the first microwave ASV's, fresh from the Laboratory, against the U-boats which in 1942 were sinking 16,000 tons of shipping daily. Colonel (then Lieutenant Colonel) Dolan was rooted loose from his B-26 squadron command under secret orders and shortly found himself at Cambridge, Mass., looking at his first radar installation. He did plenty of looking during February and March 1942 while being initiated into the new art. He ran ASV tests against friendly subs off New London, detecting and homing. Once he homed too well, for when he brought his unarmed plan in close over the target, he found a U-boat and tender shooting at him. "I sure got the hell away from there," he said.

By the time the 1st Sea-Search Attack Group was activated on 17 June 1942 with Col. Dolan in charge, he had already led radar hunts from Boston, New York and Key West (later from Trinidad, too) and was building up a reputation as an anti-sub tactician. The "killer" techniques he developed went a long way toward defeating the U-boat, although the credit goes jointly to the RAF, Antisub Command and others. Day in, day out, Col. Dolan's group worked at testing and improving radar and associated devices.

When U-boat warfare shifted to the other side of the Atlantic, there was plenty of activity on radar bombing to take its place. Col. Dolan trained and equipped the Wright, Scott and Hopson Projects, which brought LAB to the 13th, 5th and 14th AFs, delegating some of his best sub-fighters as the nucleus. After the Sea-Search Group was inactivated in April 1944, Col. Dolan, by now Deputy Base Commander at Langley, gave birth to a 4-day radar indoctrination course for AAF officers from Generals to Lieutenants, and pitched in on the instruction. After his transfer to the 8th AF in August 1944, the school moved to Orlando.

In the ETO he dug in on the knotty problems of high altitude radar bombing. He felt handicapped because he hadn't flown combat over Germany, so he wrangled and wheedled until permission was forthcoming. By unofficial count he had 16 missions.

He had followed APQ-7 during his days at Langley and early in 1945 he flew to Florida to hurry the installations. He was taking one back when he ran into storms over Newfoundland and disappeared.

Today Bid Dolan's interest in radar is commonplace. But a few years back it was truly unique. That makes him one of radar's operational pioneers; his students are at work the world over.

Notes on Colonel William C. Dolan

Briefing document by the Headquarters Staff of U.S. Army Air Force in late February 1945 shortly after Colonel Dolan's disappearance over the Atlantic Ocean during his return flight to the rejoin the Eighth Air Force in the United Kingdom.

1. Colonel Dolan or "Bid" Dolan, as he was more widely known, was a pioneer insofar as radar and the Army Air Forces is concerned. His association with radar development started late in 1941, when he took ten B-18's to Boston where the Radiation Laboratory at M.I.T. installed the first of the ASV Radars.

2. In March or April of 1942 Colonel Dolan brought these ten B-18's to Langley Field for use in combating Axis submarine attacks in the Atlantic. These aircraft operated at various times from Boston, New York, Key West and Trinidad, using sea-search tactics developed by the Colonel. Their successful efforts contributed measurably to easing the Atlantic submarine menace.

3. In June 1942 Colonel Dolan was directed to activate the First Sea-Search Attack Group and was appointed Commanding Officer of the Group. The primary function of the Group was the testing and development of radar and associate devices. The Group, during its existence assisted with the development of the MAD for detecting submerged submarines, the Forward Firing Rocket for illuminating areas of water at night, the Airborne Searchlight also for illuminating water areas, the Corner Reflector, the Echo-Box, the Edgerton Camera, the Odograph, various bomb fuses, the SCR-517 and 717, LAB, and the AN/APS-15. Much of the initial work on radar bombing was accomplished under the direction of Colonel Dolan.

4. During its existence, the Group trained and equipped the first two LAB Projects—the Wright Project and Scott Project. Replacements for these two projects were also trained by the Group. When interest switched to high altitude bombing and

H2X, the early crews for the Eighth and Fifteenth Air Forces were trained by the Group.

5. In April 1944 the First Sea-Search Attack Group was inactivated and Colonel Dolan then carried on at Langley Field in the dual capacity of Deputy Base Commander and Director of Training and Operations. His greatest contribution to radar, however, was not in its technical nor operational development, but in convincing the skeptical minds within the Army Air Force itself of the worth of radar. His experience with radar in its many phases had thoroughly convinced him of its essential value and he was determined that others should see the light. It was his contention that radar would never attain full stature in the Air Forces until its officers at the top were convinced and enthused. To this end, he started radar training at Langley Field for high ranking staff officers of the Army Air Forces. This training was given at Langley Field from June to September 1944. The Colonel not only gave birth to the idea but in his enthusiasm served also as an instructor. It is interesting to note that the same course is today being continued at AAFSAT, Orlando, Florida.

6. In August of 1944 Colonel Dolan was sent to the Eighth Air Force as Assistant A-3 in charge of training. At the time of his arrival, the future of radar high altitude bombing was doubtful. It required a personality of vast energy and enthusiasm, as well as knowledge and experience to overcome the skepticism and doubt concerning H2X. The Colonel was equal to the task, however, and he sold radar in the ETO as successfully as he had previously sold it at Langley Field.

7. While still at Langley Field, Colonel Dolan had followed the development of the AN/APQ-7 with extreme interest. He left for the ETO before the equipment reached the production stage, but when it did become available, he urged its use by the Eighth Air Force. As a result, he was returned to the United States on temporary duty to bring the first of the APQ-7's back to the ETO. It was on his return trip to England with his equipment that his plane and crew encountered bad weather and were reported missing.

8. The contributions of Colonel Dolan to radar development were of interest and value, but of even greater interest was the man himself. He approached his work with intelligence, youthful enthusiasm, vigorous vitality and above all, a keen sense of humor. He enjoyed life and he liked people. These characteristics were reflected in the high morale and genuine respect of his officers and enlisted men. He was also possessed of the characteristic sensitivity of the Irish, which would become quite apparent on those occasions when he lost one of "his boys." On such occasions he would break the news to the family personally and when this was not possible, we would personally correspond. He had a great love of athletic activity and while at Langley he was a familiar figure on the baseball diamond, football field and bowling alley. The Colonel, above all, was possessed of a thoroughly Democratic spirit which tempered his every thought and action.

Wright Project officers and enlisted men as assigned from the 3rd Sea-Search Attack Squadron (H)

HEADQUARTERS
FIRST SEA SEARCH ATTACK GROUP (M)
LANGLEY FIELD, VIRGINIA

2 June 1943

General Orders Number 2

1.   The following named officers and enlisted men, 3rd Sea Search Attack Sq. (H), are relieved from their present duty and assigned to duty with the <u>Wright Project</u>. Colonel Stuart P. Wright, AC, will be responsible for the training. The 3rd Sea Search Attack Sq. (H) will be responsible for maintenance of aircraft and furnishing all operational facilities for this project. Personnel indicated below will arrange their affairs immediately for movement outside the continental limits of the United States.

PILOTS

Major FRANCIS B. CARLSON, 0-22876	Major LEO J. FOSTER, Jr., 0-388659
Capt. ROBERT W. LEHTI, 0-431229	Capt. FRANKLIN T.E. REYNOLDS, 0-424676
Capt. JOHN F. ZINN, Jr., 0-424017	1st Lt. KENNETH E. BROWN, 0-791268
1st Lt. ROBERT E. EASTERLING, 0-790813	1st Lt. FREDERICK A. MARTUS, 0-790688
1st Lt. CHARLES L. ROCKWOOD, 0-412817	1st Lt. GEO. A. TILLINGHAST, Jr. 0-791254

NAVIGATORS

Capt. WILLIAM P. SCHUBER, 0-360507

1st Lt. JAMES E. POPE, 0-431763

1st Lt. CROWELL B. WERNER, 0-433150

2nd Lt. JOHN C. BURT, 0-789199

2nd Lt. EARL COX, 0-790116

1st Lt. CLARENCE L. HARMON, Jr., 0-435534

1st Lt. FRANK N. SYLVESTER, Jr., 0-416458

2nd Lt. JOHN R. BULL, 0-789448

2nd Lt. CECIL D. COTHRAN, Jr., 0-790115

2nd Lt. GEORGE (NMI) DESCO, 0-790120

BOMBARDIERS

1st Lt. JUNIOR M. BARNEY, 0-434647

1st Lt. VINCENT R. ZDANZUKAS, 0-417388

2nd Lt. WILLIAM A. S. FURLOW, Jr. 0-660984

2nd Lt. SAMUEL l. FELIEGRINI, 0-744498

2nd Lt. HENRY B. WISE, 0-661059

1st Lt. NED B. ESTES, 0-434611

2nd Lt. CHARLES F. AMES, Jr. 0-662233

2nd Lt. ROBERT L. McLEOD, 0-745824

2nd Lt. FRED A. WHEATLEY, 0-661053

2nd Lt. ROBERT E. TRESSEL, 0-661046

AERIAL ENGINEERS

T/Sgt. GLENN M. CHANDLER, 35119025

T/Sgt. SAMUEL C. PONA, 12038524

T/Sgt. RAYMOND W. TRIMBLE, 1604826

S/Sgt. ALBERT G. LEBLANC, 34155215

S/Sgt. CURTIS A. POND, 14069204

T/Sgt. GROVER R. McDONALD, 35203879

T/Sgt. WALTER A. ROSE, 34155468

S/Sgt. CHARLES R. BESPOLE, 16036632

S/Sgt. JOSEPH (NMI) OUIMETTE, 11032680

S/Sgt. JOHN H. TERPSTRA, 12031295

ASSISTANT AERIAL ENGINEERS

S/Sgt. James D. Justus, 17032188

S/Sgt. FREDERICK E. PREYE, 12038503

S/Sgt. CHARLES J. SOTTONG, 15086859

Sgt. EDMUND PARADIS, Jr., 11029743

Sgt. JACK V. RANSON, 14067289

S/Sgt. JOHN A. PLOCEK, 15085220

S/Sgt. ELMER F. RUFF, 15087234

Sgt. PETER T. COST, 13085393

Sgt. DONALD C. PETERSON, 11037373

Sgt. JACOB A. STIEF, 13047733

RADIO OPERATORS

S/Sgt. LAWRENCE DE ST CROIX, 17036481

Sgt. HERMAN C. GOLDTRAP, 34189788

Sgt. CHRISTOFF G. KILZER, 35275450

Sgt. ANDREW J. MOORE, 39088662

Sgt. THOMAS W. OWEN, 34198634

S/Sgt. CLARENCE W. PATTERSON, 11047341

Sgt. EUGENE J. GOSSEN, 36234316

Sgt. JOSEPH A. McCALMONT, 35273532

Sgt. BERNARD B. NACHBE, 13043281

Sgt. DEWAINE J. WIEDERMAN, 36221364

AIRCRAFT ARMORERS

S/Sgt. MICHAEL (NMI) BIENDY, 33201343

Sgt. DALE (NMI) BURCH, 34450235

Sgt. JOHN (NMI) DOHAN, Jr., 11101176

Sgt. AUGUSTUS J. SAYKO, 33171402

Sgt. JOHN E. YOUNG, 34241145

S/Sgt. ANTHONY A. PELIEGRINI, 31043383

Sgt. ROBERT W. CUNFER, 13068465

Sgt. CHARLES G. REDHEAD, 32251389

Sgt. JOHN S. WILCOX, 32284618

Cpl. SIDNEY (NMI) SCHWARTZ, 12057139

RADAR OPERATORS

T/Sgt. RAY F. DAVIS, 39680061

T/Sgt. ALBERT R. SMITH, 7031313

S/Sgt. LOUIS V. GUERRA, 14064273

Sgt. GENTILE W. CESPINO, 32199491

Sgt. KENNETH T. EVANS, 15099399

T/Sgt. WILLIAM J. PROSSER, 15082519

T/Sgt. DAVID (NMI) WHITE, 36301045

S/Sgt. LEROY (NMI) RUBIN, 13032962

Sgt. GEORGE A. CUBBAGE, 3525867

Sgt. SYLVESTER P. HARMON, 15074404

RADAR MECHANICS

T/Sgt. LEON L. ARMSTRONG, 19016690

T/Sgt. THOMAS W. MILTON, 32184884

S/Sgt. FLOYD E. HUNE, 35267285

Sgt. RUDOLPH F. NELSON, 37271883

Sgt. ROBERT F. SANDRECZKI, 32189009

Sgt. HAROLD W. SHIREY, 35259241

Sgt. JOHN A. STANFORD, 38209030

Sgt. ANSTESS H. WEIR, 36501571

Cpl. ROBERT L. LAMBERT, 23651334

Cpl. JEROME (NMI) SOSIN, 32400536

By order of Colonel DOLAN:

(signed)
BOBBIE W. SADLER
Major, Army Air Corps
Executive

Distribution:
50- CO, 2nd SSA Sq.
100- CO, 3rd SSA Sq.
1-Col. Wright
1-each officer
1-Base S-1
1-File

Original Wright Project crews and significant personnel

R-E-S-T-R-I-C-T-E-D

HEADQUARTERS
FIRST SEA SEARCH ATTACK GROUP (H)
LANGLEY FIELD, VIRGINIA

3 August 1943

Special Orders Number 155

EXTRACT

The following named O's and EM, 3rd Sea Search Attack Squadron (H), are assigned to Movement Order Number 1, this Headquarters, dated 3 August 1943. Colonel STUART P. WRIGHT, 0-17920, FP-617-AD 1, 42-40832, is Provisional Flight Leader and is designated Provisional Flight Commander. Capt. ERNEST R. BARRIERE, 0-431828 (0145), FP-617-BD 5, 42-40822, Technical Officer.

Crew No. FP-617-AD 1 42-40832 "Devil's Delight"★
Major LEO J. FOSTER, JR. 0-388659 (1024)
★2nd Lt. JOHN A THOMPSON, JR., 0-802954 (1024)
2nd Lt. CECIL D. COTHRAN, JR., 0-790115 (1034)
1st Lt. VINCENT R. ZDANZUKAS, 0-417388 (1035)
T/Sgt. Samuel C. Pona, 12038524 (748)
T/Sgt. Howard L. Eastabrooks, 15088258
T/Sgt. Bernard B. Nachbe, 13043281 (755)
T/Sgt. Albert R. Smith, 7031313 (884)
S/Sgt. John (NMI) Dohan, Jr., 11101176

Crew No. FP-617-AD 2 42-40836 "Miss Cuddles"
Major FRANCIS B. CARLSON, 0-22876 (1024)
2nd Lt. WILMER B. HAYNES, 0-801330 (1024)
1st Lt. CLARENCE L. HARMON, JR., 0-435534 (1034)
1st Lt. JUNIOR M. BARNEY, 0-434647 (1035)
T/Sgt. Glenn M. Chandler, 35119025 (748)
S/Sgt. James D. Justus, 17032188 (748)
T/Sgt. Lawrence E. De St Croix, 17036481 (755)
T/Sgt. Ray F. Davis, 39680061 (884)
S/Sgt. Michael (NMI) Blendy, 33201343 (612)
M/Sgt. Thomas W. Milton, 32184884 (887)

Crew No. FP-617-AD 3 42-40854 "Uncle's Fury"
Capt. JOHN F. ZINN, JR., 0-424017
★2nd Lt. CHARLES V. CONRAD, JR., 0-801671 (1024)
1st Lt. JAMES E. POPE, 0-431763 (1034)
2nd Lt. SAMUEL L. PELLEGRINI, 0-744498 (1035)
T/Sgt. Raymond W. Trimble, 16048626 (748)
S/Sgt. Jacob A. Steif, 13047733 (748)
T/Sgt. Clarence W. Patterson, 11047341 (755)
S/Sgt. Sylvester P. Harmon, 15074404 (884)
S/Sgt. Dale (NMI) Burch, 34450235 (612)
Cpl. Jerome (NMI) Sosin, 32400536

Crew No. FP-617-AD 4 42-40833 "Coral Princess"
Capt. FRANKLIN T. E. REYNOLDS, 0-424676 (1024)
★2nd Lt. VINCENT D. BROOKS, 0-801826 (1024)
2nd Lt. GEORGE (NMI) DESKO, 0-790120 (1034)
2nd Lt. FRED A. WHEATLEY, 0-661053 (1035)
T/Sgt. Albert G. LeBlanc, 34155215 (748)
S/Sgt. Elmer F. Ruff, 15087234 (748)
T/Sgt. Herman C. Goldtrap, 34189788
T/Sgt. Kenneth T. Evans, 15099399 (884)
S/Sgt. John E. Young, 34241145 (612)
Sgt. Robert L. Lambert, 36251334

Crew No. FP-617-AD 42-40822 "Bums Away"
Capt. ROBERT W. LEHTI, 0-431229 (1024)
★2nd Lt. JOSEPH L. SULLIVAN, 0-803061 (1026)
1st Lt. CROWELL B. WERNER, 0-433150 (1034)

2nd Lt. CHARLES E. AMES, JR., 0-662233(1035)
T/Sgt. Walter A. Rose, 34155468 (748)
S/Sgt. Jack V. Ranson, 14067289 (748)
T/Sgt. Joseph A. McCalmont, 35273532 (755)
S/Sgt. George A. Cubbage, 35258567 (884)
S/Sgt. John S. Wilcox, 32284618 (612) S/Sgt. John A. G. Stanford, 38209030 (887)

Crew No. FP-617-AD 6 42-40839 "Princess Slip"
1st Lt. ROBERT E. EASTERLING, 0-790813 (1024)
*2nd Lt. EUGENE H. WHITE, 0-802371 (1024)
2nd Lt. JOHN R. BULL, 0-789448 (1034)
2nd Lt. WILLIAM A. S. FURLOW, JR., 0-660984 (1035)
T/Sgt. Grover R. McDonald, 35203879 (748)
S/Sgt. Charles J. Sottong, 15086859 (748)
T/Sgt. Eugene J. Gossen, 36234316 (755)
T/Sgt. Gentile W. Cespino, 32199491 (884)
S/Sgt. Anthony A. Pollogrini, 31043383
Sgt. Anstess H. Weir, 36501571 (887)

Crew No. FP-617-AD 7 42-40838 "Madame Libby the Sea Ducer"
1st Lt. CHARLES L. ROCKWOOD, 0-412817 (1024)
*2nd Lt. CHARLES R. BOWDEN, 0-801823 (1024)
1st Lt. FRANK M. SYLVESTER, JR., 0-416458 (1034)
1st Lt. NED B. ESTES, 0-434611 (1035)
T/Sgt. Charles R. Bespole, 16036632 (748)
S/Sgt. John A. Plocek, 15085220 (748)
T/Sgt. Harold A. Dennis, Jr., 12045451 (755)
T/Sgt. William J. Prosser, 15082519 (884)
T/Sgt. Robert W. Cunfer, 13068465 (612)
Sgt. Robert F. Sandreczki, 32139009 (887)

Crew No. FP-617-AD 8 42-40651 "Ramp Tramp"
1st Lt. KENNETH E. BROWN, 0-791268 (1024)
*2nd Lt. HARVEY E. CURRAN, 0-801837 (1024)
Capt. WILLIAM P. SCHUBER, 0-360507 (1034)
2nd Lt. HENRY B. WISE, 0-661059 (1035)
T/Sgt. John H. Torpstra, 12031295 (748)
S/Sgt. Frederick E. Preye, 12038503, 748)
T/Sgt. Christoff G. Kilzer, 35275450 (755)
T/Sgt. David (NMI) White,36301045 (884)

S/Sgt. Sidney (NMI) Schwartz, 12057139 (612)
S/Sgt. Rudolph F. Nelson, 37271833 (887)

Crew No. FP-617-AD 9 42-40653 "Gremlins' Haven"
1st Lt. FREDERICK A. MARTUS, 0-790688 (1024)
*2nd Lt. FOSTER M. HILL, 0-801696 (1024)
2nd Lt. JOHN C. BURT, 0-789199 (1034)
2nd Lt. ROBERT L. McLEOD, 0-745824 (1035)
T/Sgt. Joseph (NMI) Ouimette, 11032680 (748)
S/Sgt. Donald C. Peterson, 11037373 (748)
T/Sgt. Thomas W. Owen, 34198634 (755)
T/Sgt. Leroy (NMI) Rubin, 13032962 (884)
S/Sgt. Augustus J. Sayko, 33171402 (612)
S/Sgt. Harold W. Shirey, 35259241 (887)

Crew No. FP-617-AD 10 42-40639 "Lady Margaret"
1st Lt. GEORGE A. TILLINGHAST, JR., 0-791254 (1024)
*2nd Lt. LOUIS J. BECK, 0-802232 (1024)
2nd Lt. EARL (NMI) COX, 0-790116 (1034)
2nd Lt. ROBERT E. TRESSEL, 0-661046 (1035)
T/Sgt. Curtis A. Pond, 14069204 (748)
S/Sgt. Edmund (NMI) Paradis, Jr., 11029743 (748)
T/Sgt. Andrew J. Moore, 39088662 (755)
T/Sgt. Louis A. Guerra, 14064273 (884)
S/Sgt. Charles G. Redhead, 32251389 (612)
T/Sgt. Floyd E. Hune, 35267285 (887)

Sgt. John J. Purvis, 16064087 (891) and Cpl. Vincent P. Hoover, 32281062 (894) will proceed by rail and water to overseas destination.

BY ORDER OF COLONEL DOLAN

(signed)
BOBBIE W. SADLER
Major, Air Corps
Executive

*Author's Note: The names assigned by the crews to the individual aircraft have been added based on the personal records of Wright Project members, as provided to the author in 1978–80 exchanges and in photography provided by these veterans.

A companion Wright Project document, "Movement Order Number 1" of 3 August 1943, classified RESTRICTED, provided details of the actual transportation arrangements for all aspects and components of the Project, including all personnel and aircraft. Also included was a listing of "Additional Equipment" to be embarked or shipped separately (with Project personnel escorts), including spare components for the SCR-717-B, RC-217, SCR-729 and all Project test equipment. Also identified are the BPS beacon systems (a Rad Lab designed and developed prototype system that Colonel Wright elected, at the last moment, to bring to Guadalcanal for operational testing. It was a terminal beacon homing system that would assist in night landings on the mission return landing approach. It was subject to failure and there was no inclination to make it work as other systems were being refined.) and the Waukersha systems (also in prototype form but its exact function is not known).

This document also includes a warning notice that "All cases of leakage of information regarding troop movements will be investigated immediately and the facts in connection therewith reported to the War Department." This was a fairly routine component of all Movement Orders of the day, but in the case of the Wright project this warning was emphasized repeatedly as the unit prepared to depart Langley Field by air (the ten aircraft) and by rail.

Finally, the instructions for the Wright Project's movement to Guadalcanal also included Air Transport Command's "OPERATIONS ORDER NUMBER 13" of 9 August 1943, classified SECRET, which referenced Special Orders Number 155 (above) to further define the destination of the Wright Project. This order covered the movement "from Fairfield-Suisan Army Air Field, Fairfield California to Espiritu Santo, reporting upon arrival thereat to the Commanding General, 13th Air Force Service Command, for further orders."

Appointment of Summary Court Officers to inventory and dispose of the effects of the Haynes crew

868th BOMBARDMENT SQUADRON (H)
APO 324

26 June 1944

Squadron Orders Number 73

1. 1st Lieutenant CROWELL B WERNER, 0-433150, and 2nd Lt MILTON MISHKIN, 0360662, are aptd Summary Court Officers to inventory and dispose of the effects of the following named officers and enlisted men, of the 868th Bomb Sq (H), missing in action on 25 June 1944.

1st Lt WILMER B HAYNES	0-801330
1st Lt CHARLES R BOWDEN	0-801823
1st Lt GERALD R WESTERLAND	0-801047
1st Lt CHARLES F AMES, JR.	0-662233
T/Sgt John H Terpstra	12031295
S/Sgt Frederick E Preye	12038503
T/Sgt Yale A Earock	37330389
S/Sgt Robert L Beatty	33205925
S/Sgt Thomas J Peden Jr.	32435216
S/Sgt Rudolph H Wittachack	32310402

The Court will be governed by the instructions contained in AW 112, MCM 1928, AR 600-550, dated 14 May 1943, and WD Cir #195, dated 1 September 1943. Auth: AW 112 MCM 1928.

2.   Effective this date, 1st Lt FRED S HOWELL, 0-466881, is aptd Radar Officer vice Captain ERNRST R BARRIERE, 0-431828, reld.

FRANCIS B CARLSON
Major, Air Corps,
Commanding

Author's Note: Lieutenant Wilmer Haynes and crew were lost on the night of 25/26 June 1944 in a mission to Truk Atoll. As mentioned in the text, the Haynes aircraft, Wright Project B-24D Madame Libby The Sea Ducer, *was seen on radar that night from a distance, by another 868th Squadron aircraft, to pass over Truk to complete its strike mission. Departing the target area, radar contact by the trailing SB-24 was lost and the Haynes aircraft was assumed to have been brought down by anti-aircraft fire or night fighters or a combination of both. The lost crew comprised eight men of the original Haynes crew with 1st Lieutenant Westerland of the Art DeLand crew volunteering to substitute for Haynes's navigator who had been hospitalized that evening. Radar operator Thomas Penden was also lost on this aircraft, having joined for a familiarization flight on this, his first mission. He had just joined the 868th as a member of the Binford crew.*

"Disappeared—The loss of 20 officers and men of the 868th Bombardment Squadron of the Thirteenth Air Force in December 1944 in the South Pacific Theater of Operations"

In early December 1944, 21 officers and men of the 868th "Snooper" Squadron of the Thirteenth Air Force departed their forward operating base on Noemfoor Island for a 10-day R&R visit to Sydney, Australia. These men flew in the squadron's C-47A transport aircraft, dubbed the "Snooper Airlines Special." The established Noemfoor–Sydney routing used by the 868th Squadron and all aircraft of XIII Bomber Command on air cargo and R&R leave transits to Australia passed through the U.S. Army Air Force base at Finschhafen on the northeastern coast of New Guinea. On about 10 December, the 20 men of the 868th slated to return gathered at Sydney Airport and boarded the C-47A for the return trip to rejoin their squadron on Noemfoor.

The C-47 did not arrive at Noemfoor and the 20 men on board were declared "Missing" by the squadron on 14 December 1944. When the squadron began its search for the lost aircraft, there was miscommunication among the squadron operations staff, the Thirteenth Air Force operations staff on Morotai, the airport controllers at Sydney and, most importantly in terms of the confusion injected, the operations staff at Finschhafen airfield in New Guinea.

Lieutenant Robert Cooke was one of the two pilots and two co-pilots among the 21 officers and men, essentially two SB-24 combat crews, who flew the aircraft on its early December run to Australia. He developed a medical condition during the leave period in Sydney and was hospitalized there for surgery. He therefore missed the flight back to the squadron and as a consequence lost all nine members of his original crew. Once returned to the squadron some weeks later, Cooke formed a new crew and completed his tour of duty with distinction, returning to the United States in mid-1945.

A complete list of the 20 missing men of the 868th Squadron is as follows, listed by date of rank, serial number and crew position:

2nd Lt. JOHN E. MEISENHELDER	0-703078	Navigator
2nd Lt. WILLIAM K. TAYLOR	0-805218	Navigator
2nd Lt. WILLIAM T. WILKENSON	0-699883	Co-Pilot
F/O ROBERT W. DICKENSON	T-123314	Bombardier
T/Sgt. Isadore G. La Mica	32490262	Engineer
S/Sgt. Samuel L. Kinzer	33553493	Asst. Engineer
S/Sgt. Samuel A. Klock	32374435	Radar Operator
S/Sgt. Merel J. Lynch	3644906	Radio Operator
S/Sgt. Edward J. Rozycki	16143029	Gunner
Sgt. David A. Hensley	37498412	Gunner
2nd Lt. ANTHONY J. CANGELOSI	0-752313	Bombardier
2nd Lt. WENDELL F. SEAS	0-699866	Co-Pilot
2nd Lt. GEORGE E. THOMPSON	0-693576	Pilot
2nd Lt. THOMAS G. TOUCHSTONE	0-712950	Navigator
S/Sgt. Lloyd W. Burchett	39278177	Asst. Engineer
S/Sgt. Theodore W. Deck	13029749	Gunner
S/Sgt. Edward L. Gorae	33503201	Engineer
S/Sgt. Harold C. McConnell	37305438	Radio Operator
Sgt. Robert D. Fitzgerald	14155906	Gunner
Sgt. Douglas C. Geib	32713443	Radar Operator

Considerable speculation as to the fate of the Snooper Airlines aircraft and the missing men emerged over the following days and weeks as the squadron absorbed its loss of the combat crews who were part of this group. As noted, the contingent that disappeared included one command pilot, two co-pilots, three navigators, two bombardiers, two flight engineers, two radar operators, two radio operators, two assistant engineer/gunners and four gunners.

The book mentions that many theories and much speculation attended this loss at the time it occurred back at the squadron, running the gamut of a shootdown over Wewak to an engine-out spiraling loss into the Coral Sea. Some 35 years later, in discussions with several of the squadron veterans who were present on Noemfoor at the time of the loss, this author was exposed to several firmly held, mostly conflicting, scenarios.

The most prevalent and convincing explanation was that the C-47, heavily burdened with personnel and cargo, lost engine power as it attempted to cross over the Owen Stanley range and crashed into a remote mountain valley there. It is also possible that the wreck of this aircraft has been subsequently discovered and the remains of those on board recovered. But this author can find no record of such a discovery or recovery. Perhaps someday this mystery will be solved, possibly by the discovery of the aircraft wreckage and the remains of those on the aircraft.

The above compiled by the author. Sources include: "868th Bomb Squadron Historical Data for Month of December 1944, SECRET," dated 10 February 1945, and interviews with 868th Squadron veterans with firsthand knowledge of this loss during 1978–81.

"It was All Done by Four 'Snoopers',"
Impact magazine, March 1945

HEADQUARTERS
XIII BOMBER COMMAND
INTELLIGENCE SECTION
APO #719-2

23 December 1944

WHAT FOUR SNOOPERS DID TO LUTONG

The Lutong Oil Installation, located in Sarawak Province, Northwest Borneo, is the second most important in Borneo, ranking next to Balikpapan. The area includes a refinery and tank farm at Lutong; the oil fields at Miri, and Seria. The refinery produced nearly 7,000,000 barrels of petroleum products per year in peacetime. Despite fairly complete destruction by evacuating Dutch, the Japanese have repaired this refinery completely and have put the Seria and Miri fields lies in the fact that the black oils which they produce can be used as bunker oil without complicated refining, and the Japs are notoriously low on black oils.

The priority target in this area is the refinery and tank farm at Lutong, concentrated in a compact area about 5/6 of a mile long and 1/6 of a mile wide. The refinery area is 1160' × 840', consisting of two Trumble units which contain fractionating columns, shell stills, condensers and batteries of small receiving tanks. A boiler house, two pump houses and agitators are located within the refinery area. Welding and repair shops adjoin the area. A rundown tank farm located east of and adjacent to the refinery consists of one 15', twenty-six 30', five 35', three 45' cylindrical tanks and three 40' × 8' blimp type tanks.

The tank farm occupies an area 3320' × 840'. Evacuating forces destroyed ten 110' and three 70' tanks so at time of attack there remained three 140', five 110', and three 70' tanks.

Although not as large as any of the Balikpapan refineries the Lutong installation has taken on added importance as the production at Balikpapan and the shipping in the Makassar Strait has decreased. The Japanese were shoved further to the West and Luton is on their new shipping route. Although Luton is within range of B-24 formations, other requirements prevented a large strike. However, our mission included shipping searches along the northeastern and western coasts of Borneo. With the decrease in shipping, secondary land targets were often hit as unloading grounds. Lutong refinery area was one of the best of these targets. Up to 8 December, however, it had not been touched.

At 0750 hours on 8 December, as the sun was just coming up, a lone Liberator of the 868th Bombardment Squadron (H) dropped down to 100 feet, made a bombing run across the refinery, dropped his 15 × 250 pound bombs on the cracking plant then proceeded to make six strafing runs on the oil storage north of the refinery. A Betty on Miri Airdrome to the south and a lugger in the bay were also strafed. 1600 rounds of .50 caliber machine gun ammunition were expended. The cracking plan was left in flames with smoke rising to 15,000 feet and the fire could be seen for 75 miles. Oblique photos showed six oil storage tanks on fire. At 1353 hours another Liberator passed the refinery and took photos which showed one 125', five 110', and two 70' oil tanks to be on fire. The Japs didn't take this damage quietly. The anti-aircraft was medium and light, intense and accurate putting twenty 7.7mm and 13.2mm machine gun holes in the aircraft. A 20mm shell entered the plane through the bulkhead at the back of the bomb bay and exploded, slightly injuring two of the crew.

Those fires were still burning when another blow was struck on 10 December. At 0730 hours another lone Snooper came I over the refinery at 80 feet, dropped his bombs through the cracking plant scoring hits on one of the Trumble units and the boiler house. Large fires were started which added to the smoke already coming from the previously set fires. Expending approximately 1500 rounds of .50 caliber ammunition, four strafing runs were made against the storage tanks. It was reported that one large oil tank exploded, and two large oil tanks were set afire. Although other tanks were hit, they did not fire. Anti-aircraft was again medium and light, intense and accurate resulting in 30 machine gun holes in the aircraft together with two 20mm hits in the wing and under the waist window. One 20mm shell entered the ship through the bomb bay, ricocheted of the mount of the hand fuel pump, entered the waist and burst when it struck the Radar Operator's flak helmet injuring him in arm and face. Every window in the barracks was emitting small arms fire. Hazy photographs showed two large fires, but no accurate interpretation could be made.

Two days later 12 December, another lone Snooper attacked at 0717 hours. He came in on the deck at 100 ft, dropped 9 × 500 pound incendiary bombs and strafed on the run. The bombs fell in the rundown tanks and refinery area starting two fires, a large one in the refinery and as small one in the tank area. One tank was fired by strafing, two were hit but did not burn. Again, the anti-aircraft fire was accurate and left the aircraft with 6 holes and a 3 supercharger shot out.

On the same day a special mission was flown by the 868th Squadron to photography the Lutong area. At 1115 hours photos were taken and 30 × 100 pound bombs dropped from 4000 feet through the rundown tanks east of the refinery. 3 small tanks were hit but no fires were visible.

The cumulative damage interpretation from the photos shows that in Trumble Unit 2 50' × 45' section of the 115' × 45' building containing the furnaces was destroyed. One 30' × 25', one 20' × 15' and one 10' × 10' building were destroyed, and one 25' × 25' ground reservoir damaged. Although there are visible bomb craters in the area occupied by the unit there is no visible damage to the fractionating column, rundown tanks and coolers.

In Trumble Unit 3 the 90' × 45' building housing the furnaces was damaged and 2 of the 3 smoke stacks were destroyed. The adjacent fractioning column appears to have been badly damaged. One 25' × 2' pumphouse was damaged. The main boiler house and an adjacent 70' × 20' building were damaged. One 15' × 10' building adjacent to the rundown tank farm pumphouse was destroyed and one 60' × 60' shop building was damaged. The fire pumphouse was damaged and one of the four adjacent 20' water tanks was badly damaged. The steam and oil lines within the refinery area have been badly damaged, and in some places destroyed. Besides the ten 110' and three 70' cylindrical storage tanks that were destroyed by evacuating forces, three 110' and one 70' storage tanks were destroyed. One 140', two 110' and one 70' storage tanks were damaged. One 40' storage tank in the rundown tank farm was damaged.

Not all of the damage can be picked up by photo interpretation, especially in the refinery area, and although oblique photos allowed fires in storage tanks, damage is not apparent from later coverage. This damage is not included in the above.

It is impossible to compare the results of the bombing and strafing of these four B-24s with any other mission, however, a recapitulation of the Balikpapan damage may be interesting. A total of 280 D-24s hit Balikpapan concentrating on the three refineries of Pandansari, paraffin and Lube Oil and Edeleanu. The Edeleanu plant was destroyed by demolishing Unit 1 and adjacent boiler house, and damaging Unit 2 and the Sulpher Dioxide plant. This effectively put the plant out of action until it can be rebuilt.

The Pandansari refinery was put out of action, but is capable of repair. Although most of the installations were destroyed, the two vital installations, the boiler and fractionating towers, were not destroyed (the boiler is possibly damaged and one tower may have been slightly damaged). Three of the four storage tanks were destroyed. The paraffin and Lube Oil Refinery was damaged, not seriously, and is capable of fairly quick repair. The ends of the cooling installation were destroyed and the central portion damaged along with the boiler house, powerhouse, pumphouse and grease plant. The bulk of the refinery, including the tanks, agitators, wax presses, high vacuum units, and distilling units, is damaged. Temporary stoppage may have been caused by broken lines and fires, but the refinery must be regarded as still capable of operation after minor repairs. The oil storage facilities have not been lessened by destruction of 3 storage tanks and damage to 3 others in the Pantjoer tank farm.

It is also interesting to note that, based upon the results obtained at Balikpapan, the Lutong Refinery and Tank farm was analyzed by Operational Analysts who stated "A strike made up of 48 aircraft, each with 9×500 pound general purpose bombs with .025 second tail fuzing has an even chance of causing at least the following damage: A. Hitting 5-6 tanks in the storage area. B. Destroying some 09% of the installations in the refinery area, including 2-3 rundown tanks. C. Doing an undetermined amount of damage to installations not visible in vertical photos (such as pipe lines and valve junctions) and to areas surrounding the target area."

a/Robert Totten
t/Robert Totten
Colonel, Air Corps
AC of S, A-2

A TRUE COPY

(signed)
STUART BALDWIN
1st Lt, Air Corps
Intelligence Officer
Impact magazine, March 1945

It was All Done by Four "Snoopers"

The widespread damage caused by four 13th AF B-21 "Snoopers" at the Lutong oil refinery and tank farm in Borneo, when they flew in one at a time during three days in December, shows how a few single sorties, skillfully planned and executed, can in some instances be as devastating as one big attack. Lutong, second only to Balikpapan as a Borneo oil center, was particularly valuable to the Japs for its much-needed black oils.

Attacks were on 8, 10, and 12 December at minimum altitude with GP and incendiary bombs followed by strafing. On 8 December the cracking plant and six tanks were fired. On 10 and 12 December the cracking plant, Trumble units, boiler house and more tanks were hit.

The picture below shows principal Lutong area after four strikes. Two Trumble units and a fractionating column were severely damaged. Steam and oil lines were shattered. Thirteen oil tanks had been demolished long before by the evacuating Dutch; the

Snoopers destroyed four more and damaged five. Smokestacks, boilers, pump houses and shop buildings also suffered. Operational analysis estimated the four Libs smashed Lutong more effectively than average expectancy from 48 planes each dropping nine 500-lb. GPs.

Author's Note: The Impact *magazine article with its accompanying photographs was developed from the December 1944 XIII Bomber Command intelligence report, with photos provided by the 868th Squadron. It was published four months later when FEAF cleared this abbreviated article for circulation.*

"Snoopers," *Air Force Magazine*, January 1945

By Air Force Overseas Staff Correspondents

A crew of the B-24 "Snoopers" is being briefed. Weather and other factors pertinent to a long over-water flight and covers in detail. Then comes the payoff—target and mission for tonight.

"We believe," says the intelligence officer, "that the Japs must be staging their raids on our Leyte forces through airfields on Cebu Island. That is your target—every airfield you can find on Cebu. And your mission: to heckle the hell out of them all night long. That will be all, gentleman."

With that laconic instruction, the Snooper crew is on its own. The real briefing takes place within the B-24 as it gains altitude over the Celebes Sea; the mission is planned, decisions made, tactics evolved by the crew itself. Pilot, navigator, bombardier, electronics operator, all make their contributions to the plan of operations that will be translated into action by the superhuman Snooper devices, equipment that enables their plane to navigate unerringly across a thousand miles of open sea and weather, through the blanket of night, to spot a blacked-out, invisible target with the sureness of a thoroughbred pointer.

The Snoopers of the 13th Air Force in the Southwest Pacific are individualists, whether their mission is sea search, shipping attack, or the blasting of enemy airfields. They are wolves of the night, hunting alone, as against the pack tactics of their daylight brothers who fly formation.

This type of operation was born as a project of Lieutenant General George C. Kenney back in the days of the Bismarck Sea.

The Snoopers, one of these units now operating with the FEAF, did not attain the maturity of a permanent status until early 1944. Since then, like bats out of hell, their nocturnal B-24s and those of a similar outfit with the 5th Air Force have haunted the Japs from New Ireland to the Netherland East Indies, from Palau to the Philippines, have tormented Truk, bedeviled Borneo, walloped Woleai, struck shipping from battleships to barges.

Like huge, purring cats in the night, they pounce upon their prey without warning. Their eyes are a low altitude bombsight that sees in the dark far better than human eyes have ever seen in the daytime, enabling the Snoopers to come in undetected by the enemy and strike at an altitude of 1,500 feet or less, an altitude that makes the daylight boys shudder.

Snooping is hard work. Missions of the 13th Air Force Snoopers (who claim the global copyright to the name) are 2,000 miles and more over open water, without fighter escort; duration of missions varies from 10 to 18 hours in the air, is limited only by their gas supply. With their special electronic detecting, navigating and bombing devices, heavy bomb loads and maximum gas load, B-24 Snoopers carry more than 10,000 pounds in excess of the plane's designed load capacity.

Major James D. Barlow, of Oakland, Calif., former B-25 pilot and commanding officer of the Snoopers, explains that the outfit has had to adapt itself and its technique to fit the tactical situation, sometimes almost overnight. They have switched from shipping to land targets and back to shipping to land targets and back to shipping. A similar method of locating the invisible targets is used for attacking both shipping and land targets. The latter, however, does not permit as great accuracy in bombing, is more often of the "keep the Jap awake and alerted" variety.

By choice, shipping attacks are the favorite Snooper vocation. There is a definite satisfaction, they say, in being out there in the night, all on your own, sighting the target from 30 or more miles away, figuring out for yourself the best method of approach and attack, the challenge of closing in undetected on the victim, making the kill unassisted.

Every mission presents a new and different problem to be solved. Their target is an unknown quantity and may vary from a Sugar Charlie to large transports, cruisers, destroyers or battleships; each one requires a different technique. The ship may be alone or in convoy, it may be capable of sudden evasive action, possess an unexpected potential of firepower. As each mission is performed by an individual plane, it calls for extraordinary initiative on the part of each crew, the closest cooperation. Within each Snooper crew must exist the essence of teamwork.

Considerable research and practice went into the development of the Snooper—which has been referred to by the Japs as "the plane with a thousand eyes." Credit for much of the pioneering must go to Col. Stuart O. Wright, who in 1942 rounded up some veterans from the old First Sea Search Attack group and formed the first Snooper squadron.

First, they tried out the new equipment while hunting enemy subs. Then came months of additional testing at Eglin Field. Finally in the summer of 1943 they decided they were ready. In August of that year, the first squadron of Snoopers arrived in the Pacific and joined the 13th Bomber Command.

In those days the Japs were convinced they could hold the Solomons for a long time. We had fairly good control of the sky in daylight but at night Jap surface vessels could shift men and supplies from one island to another with little chance of detection.

But on the night of August 23, 1943, we gave the enemy one more indication that this war was going to be fought according to our time table and under our conditions.

Two Jap destroyers slipped out of their hidden harbors and moved into the slot that runs all the way up the Solomons between Santa Isabel and New Georgia. They were going to evacuate some troops from Kolombangara and Vella Lavella.

We knew they were coming. They had been doing this regularly for it had been almost impossible to intercept them due to treacherous waters and the darkness of night.

Confident that nothing could stop them, the men on those Jap destroyers probably didn't pay much attention to the drone of an airplane in the black skies above them. If they thought about it at all they probably figured that the Americans must be desperate to waste gasoline and airplanes in such darkness.

Suddenly several bombs rocketed down as if they were released along an invisible line connecting the plane with the ships. As they hit squarely on the destroyers, they tore the night apart. The airplane made two bomb runs and each time scored direct hits.

This was the first Snooper mission and a highly successful one. But the Japs evidently thought that precision bombing after sundown was purely a matter of luck. They continued to send shipping down the slot at night.

This refusal to face realities proved costly for the Japs on the night of September 29, 1943. In Snooper annals, this date is known as "the night of the Tokyo Express." On that night 11 enemy ships steamed down the slot to evacuate their men from Kolombangara.

The Snoopers were expecting them. They had six planes up and every entrance and exit in the slot was covered.

There is little twilight in the tropics and the darkness closes in quickly. It was just a few minutes before the last faint rays of the setting sun had vanished from the western horizon that the Snoopers caught the Jap convoy in Bougainville Strait.

By the time the battle was joined, it was completely dark but the Snooper crews could see their hits. Five distinct fires flared up from five of their targets. One ship blazed like a candle in a closet before capsizing.

In the early morning the action finally was broken off. The Jap information turned —what was left of it—and retreated back to its base. The enemy had used every means available to break through the aerial blockade. Their anti-aircraft fire was heavy and one of the Snoopers went down. But the Snoopers again had proved themselves.

As time went on, the Snoopers expanded the radius of their patrols alert for anything that moved below.

Perhaps the largest single victory for a Snooper plane occurred when one of them spotted a Jap aircraft carrier attempting to ferry fighter plane reinforcements to one of the battlefronts. This Snooper caught the flat top just off Buka passage and scored three direct hits. The next day there was little fighter opposition when our bombers came over Kahili and Bonis airdromes. The carrier later was detected in Simpson Harbor of Rabaul being patched up.

A Snooper mission generally will cover well over 2,000 miles and nothing is too small to escape attention. Admiral Halsey, the Commander of the South Pacific, said he was gratified with "the manner in which your searchers and Snoopers put the hot foot to shacks, barges and even canoes."

One day a Snooper caught a Jap submarine between Bougainville and New Britain. The sub went down—or so the Snooper reported. But the next day a search plane found it on the surface in exactly the same spot where the Snooper reported bombing it. The sub didn't move. It just dove whenever one of our planes appeared. And judging from the frantic work going on aboard, it was apparent that the Snooper had wrecked everything on the sub but its ability to surface and submerge. For the next three days "Bob and Joe," as the sub was affectionately called, was the delight of every plane that passed. All tried to catch it on the surface, but a destroyer finally sank it.

Then there is the story of one of our own subs that had been stalking a merchant vessel. Just as it was moving into position to let go a torpedo a string of bombs came out of the sky and the Jap merchantman went up in flames. The sub commander complained bitterly when he put into port and learned that a Snooper had beaten him to his prey.

One of the most important factors in the success of a mission is weather. Due to the length of Snooper missions, which makes every drop of gas count, they cannot afford to fly around weather but must go through it.

Lt. Clayton F. Seavers, of Cleveland, Ohio, a veteran Snooper navigator, tells of a new navigator he was breaking in on the electronic navigating equipment during a practice mission. When a bunch of weather was sighted ahead, Seavers let the neophyte solve the problem his own way, which was simply to go some 100 miles off course to skirt the turbulence.

The new navigator was quite proud of himself until Seavers explained that if it had been a combat mission, that extra 100 miles would have exhausted their gas supply many miles short of home base. He left it to the other navigator's imagination to figure out the fate of a heavily overloaded B-24 and its crew in a crash landing. It is possible to get out, but there are easier ways to complete the tour of duty.

The new navigator listened, but was not convinced that the electronic navigating device could have done any better, could have taken them safely through the weather. Seavers bided his time; it came on the next combat mission. A few hours out, bad weather was indicated some time before it actually was visible in the sky. Seavers saw that it was bad and so did the new navigator.

"We've got to go around it," said the new navigator.

"We can't afford the gas," countered Seavers.

"Then we'll have to turn back," said the new navigator.

"Snoopers don't turn back because of rough weather," said Lt. S.

"Then what do Snoopers do?"

"Find the safety zones on the equipment and weave their way through the weather. Go ahead, try it."

"All right," said the new navigator dubiously, but settling down to work. He became engrossed and fascinated as he picked his way along, shouting instructions to the pilot. Then the blackest and biggest front he had ever seen in the sky or textbooks loomed up ahead, and he hesitated.

"Go ahead, you're doing fine," encouraged Seavers.

When the B-24 pushed along and squeezed through a narrow space between two perilous fronts to emerge into a clear sky, no one drew a deeper sigh of relief than Seavers. He didn't tell the new navigator that it was a miracle that there had been that opening and more so that they had found their way through it. He did know that the new navigator had been sold on Snooper ways and was one of them.

Selling Snooper ways to new crews is an old story to the veterans. New crews listen to lectures, are exposed to practical demonstrations, read reports of successful employment of the special technique. More often than not they are decidedly suspicious of the low 1,500-foot bombing altitude, consider the electronic devices so many fancy gadgets, insist that navigation is navigation and not a mysterious interpretation of lights and shadows on a screen. So, they do it their own way. Their bombs splash harmlessly wide of the target they "had in the bag." Then they start wondering if they know it all. And that is what the veterans have been waiting for.

"Look here," they say. "You've tried it your way and washed out. Now why not try it the Snooper way?"

"That's all right for you to say," is the retort. "You've completed your missions, sunk your ships and waiting to go home."

"Well, isn't that proof enough that it works?"

That usually hits home. "OK, we'll give it a try your way."

Once is enough. To paraphrase an automobile manufacturer's sales slogan, the evidence of the effectiveness of Snooper tactics is to "ask a crew that has tried it." It gets in the blood. The hunting instinct is aroused. To get a ship becomes an obsession.

Time after time, bombardiers who have an enviable record of bombing land targets behind them seek out Capt. Fred S. Howell, of Jerseyville, Ill., in charge of Snooper electronic equipment and development, to ask for help.

"I've almost finished my missions," pleaded one, "and I haven't gotten a ship yet. You know, captain, I'd be one hell of a Snooper to go back home without at least one Jap ship to my credit."

The captain, a dyed-in-the-wool Snooper, understands. He coaches the bombardiers in all the fine points and tricks of the plane's special equipment. In fact, there are those who say that Captain Howell deserves a share of the credit for every ship the outfit sinks.

This passion for going after Jap ships, small and large, in any number, sometimes backfires. Take the case of the Snooper plane on which Lt. Charles W. Binford, of Michaux, Va., was pilot, and Lt. James L. Lockwood, of Hampton, Va., navigator.

"We were out over the Sulu Sea on a sea search," began Lieutenant Lockwood. "That means we weren't carrying bombs, just a pile of gas."

"Our Job," cut in Lieutenant Binford, "was to report something the brass hats call the 'trend of Jap shipping,' whatever that is."

"Well, anyhow," continued Lockwood, "it was the night after that big naval battle in Leyte Gulf. We'd searched and searched all night long without spotting so much as a canoe. We stayed up there as long as we could, until our engineer said we'd better hit for home unless someone know of a filling station in the middle of the Sulu Sea."

"And he wasn't kidding, either" said Binford. "I asked Lockwood to give me a heading home. That was off the coast of Palawan."

"Around dawn," added Lockwood. "And that was about when we first picked up the Japs on instruments, just about the same time one of the crew spotted them visually. There was a destroyer and two cruisers. We all had the same thought, 'What a snap for a Snooper…duck soup'."

"We didn't have any bombs, remember," broke in Binford. "But that didn't bother us; we were big operators. We'd go in at our usual 1,500 feet, take some photographs and scare the hell out of the Nips and make them change their course."

"Only 1,500 feet wasn't low enough for us," said Lockwood. "No, we wanted real close-up pictures, so we came down to about 700 feet."

"That's right," said Binford with a grin. "And then we had those Jap ships just where they wanted us… Sure they let us have it, like a 4th of July out of hell. We got out of there quick. I guess the laugh was on us that time."

"Might as well tell the whole store," said Lockwood.

"OK… Well, we were on our way back home, tail between legs, when we spotted a lone Jap destroyer. A chance for us to save face by scaring the living daylights out of him. That's what we thought. Before we could even turn into him, do you know what the son did? He chased us right out of there."

"That's what you call adding insult to injury," commented Lockwood, adding wistfully, "but if we'd only had a couple of 1,000-pounders…"

To celebrate Pearl Harbor day, the Snoopers inaugurated their lone wolf dawn patrols. Capt. Robert D. Wallace, Limerick, Maine, piloted his B-24 through the night to Lutong oil refinery, the next most important to Balikpapan in Borneo. He came in at dawn and made his run on the cracking plant at 100 feet, almost as if coming in for a landing. Then he came back, spotted some storage tanks and strafed them, got eight. Captain Wallace headed for home and sent a brief flash to the commanding general of Bomber Command. "Have some cold beer ready for our return to base." The general had beer ready, a whole case packed in ice.

On the other side of Borneo, there was a dock area at Labuan Town. The tense is correct, for Lieutenant Binford's crew came in, also at dawn, undetected, and made their run at 300 feet, placing a string of gasoline incendiaries the length of the waterfront, with every bomb in the target area. His flash report: "The daylight boys can scratch the target off their schedule. Labuan dock area doesn't exist anymore."

Bomber Command admitted that the demolishing job done by these two lone Snoopers could have been approached only by large formations of daylight heavy bombing from high altitude.

The epitome of Snooper individualism, their zeal to do any job on their own, unassisted, is the case of the B-24 piloted by Lt. Jack L. Wagner, of Ventura, California.

This Snooper was shot down after a night attack on Truk. All but two of the crew got safely into a life raft after a water landing. The navigator got his position; they headed for their home base, then in the Admiralites, some 650 miles away. As they paddled and sailed, several Jap Bettys flew overhead, but the crew managed to camouflage itself by holding up the blue side of a tarpaulin. They were evidently well camouflaged anyway, for almost daily friendly daylight heavies on the Truk run passed overhead without sighting them. They were doing all right on the 19th day when a Navy Cat spotted them.

The Cat swooped down low and gave them the once over. Their thin, worn faces and short cropped hair must have given them that hungry Nip look, for an observer on the Cat's wing called his pilot that they were Japs. A side gun was swung toward them, but couldn't quite make it. Meanwhile, Lieutenant Wagner was jumping frantically up and down, shaking his fist and shouting, "If you shoot, damn your eyes, I'll kill you!"

That convinced the Cat, and the rescue was made. When the Navy pilot asked about their experiences, Lieutenant Wagner's only comment was, "If we'd just been left alone down there another six days, we'd have made the Admiralities by ourselves."

The Snoopers have quite a few tall stories in their repertoire, including the time tey spotted what looked like a ship on the detector and made a bomb run on a waterspout; or the time their plane "jumped" over a mountain in New Ireland.

Tall but true are the stories of their first long overwater missions to Palau and Truk as guinea pigs to see if it could be done. The Snoopers made it, and only then did the daylight boys take over. When enemy fighter opposition took a heavy toll of our heavies on the first Balikpapan raid, Bomber Command decided something should be done about it. That something was for a Snooper, acting as bait, to go within range of Jap detecting devices an hour before the attack to jam them and to draw up enemy fighters.

No, it's no snap to be a Snooper—but if you ask one of them, he wouldn't be anything else.

The Detroit News, list of 23 articles, 5–27 August 1945

Beginning on 5 August 1945 *The Detroit News* ran a series of 23 articles written from the Pacific by its veteran war correspondent John M. "Jack" Carlisle. The series focused almost exclusively on the 868th "Snoopers" and reflected combat and other events within the squadron beginning on about 17 July through to late July 1945. The following is a compilation of those articles, which usually appeared on the newspaper's "War Page" or its "Around the World Page."

The articles available are listed below by the story number, the date of a given article's appearance, the lead headline of the article, the second headline and, in three instances, "Editor's Notes" which were positioned above the article. Also injected by the author in bold type are the dates of key events in the Pacific War which were coincident with the appearance of these articles as they appeared in print.

1. 5 August 1945, "Liberator Roars Out on Hunt for Lost Pals," "Among the Missing Is a Gallant Detroiter on Night Mission 12 Hours Overdue," by Carlisle and Black Snoopers, Editor's Note: "This is the first of a series about the Black Snoopers of the Pacific, of the Liberators of the 868th Bomb Squadron of the 13th Air Force, and their sensational missions against the Japs—and the vastness of the Pacific."

2. 6 August 1945, "A Lonely Search for a Missing Liberator," Editor's Note: "This is the second in a series about the Black Snoopers of the Pacific, the Liberators which fly alone, without fighter protection, to bomb enemy targets."
    B-29 *Enola Gay* drops "Little Boy" atomic bomb on Hiroshima, Japan

3. 7 August 1945, "A 13-Hour Flight Fails to Find Detroiter in Jungle," Editor's Note: "This is the third of a series about the Black Snoopers of the Pacific— about the gallant Liberators of the 13th Air Force, which fly alone, anytime and in all kinds of weather, through fog and thunderstorms, to bomb, strafe and harass the Japanese anywhere in their jungle lairs."

4. 8 August 1945, "Ebony B-24's Make Japanese Life Miserable," "Night-Flying Raiders Go After Shipping, Airdromes, Oil Fields, Gun Installations."

5. 9 August 1945, "A Bomber Crew is Briefed for 2,000 Mile Raid on the Japanese." **B-29 _Bockscar_ drops "Fat Man" atomic bomb on Nagasaki, Japan**

6. 10 August 1945, "Black Snoopers Defy Thunderstorms on Borneo Mission." **Soviet Union declares war on Japan**

7. 11 August 1945, "B-24 Crew Sweats and Jokes on Mission."

8. 12 August 1945, "Detroiters Sweat It Out in Rain Over Pacific." "Crew of the Black Snooper Just Before Taking Off on a Mission" (Group photo of 11-man crew of Captain Townsend Rogers assembled in front of B-24M _Foul Weather Fie Fie_. War Correspondent Carlisle, eleventh man third from left in photo, accompanied crew on this mission.)

9. 13 August 1945, "Gunner Scared Only in Waits."

10. 14 August 1945, "Bomber Crew Chats on Way to Hit Enemy," "Previous Raids Are Recalled in Long Flights Over Japanese Areas."

11. 15 August 1945, "Sun Shines Bright—and Borneo Below," "Gunners Go Away Mad—All Because There Was No Shooting on This Trip." **Japan surrenders on this date—Victory Over Japan Day or "VJ Day"**

12. 16 August 1945, "Adventurous Flight Over Borneo Jungle," "Plane Virtually Scrapes Treetops but Finds No Prey on Way to Tandjoeng," "Carlisle's Detroiter-Pilot Missing."

13. 17 August 1945, "Over Target at Last: and It's 'Bombs Away'," "Smooth Teamwork of Michigan Crewmen Hands Japanese a Punch Right on the Button."

14. 18 August 1945, "Foul Weather Fie Fie Rides Storm to Home," "Greatest Test of Stamina Came After Bombs Had Hit Target."

15. 19 August 1945, "Raider at 9,500 Feet Lays Four Bombs on Ship."

16. 20 August 1945, "First Bomb Mission Makes Nerves Dance," "Sweating It Out on 2000 Mile Trip Chases Sleep When Home Is Reached."

17. 21 August 1945, "Hardly a Shot Fired, and Still It's Exciting," "Eager Beaver—Also Called Hot Rock—Happy Even When Adventure Misfires."

18. 22 August 1945, "A Sole Survivor Story."

19. 23 August 1945, "Pals Comb Jungles for Missing Co-Pilot," "B-24 Fliers Won't Give Up Hope for Detroiter Who Crashed on Mission."

20. 24 August 1945, "Bantam Bombardier Made Mark in Pacific," "Now It's Home to Detroit for Lieutenant Who Raided Batavia and Soerabaja."

21. 25 August 1945, "Bomber Gil Is Gone—but Not Forgotten," "He Was a High-Strung Guy With a Big Heart and the Men Miss Him."

22. 26 August 1945, "Michigan Men Eager for Takeoff to Japan."

23. 27 August 1945, "Ocean Hell Survived by Detroit Castaway," "Life Raft Buffeted by 12-Foot Swells for 68 Hours, The 'Cat' Saves Eddie." **Japanese formal surrender on deck of USS _Missouri_ in Tokyo Bay—3 September 1945**

The complete texts of 22 of the Carlisle *Detroit News* articles can be found as they appeared in August 1945 on the "Nightstalkers" website at www.nightstalkers868.com.

Of note, a recent book, *The War Beat, Pacific—The America Media At War Against Japan*, by Steven Casey (New York, NY: Oxford University Press, 2021), captures the lives, frustrations and the challenges of reporting accurately from the front lines of battle in the Pacific. It was fairly reviewed in the *Wall Street Journal*'s "Bookshelf" column by Jonathan W. Jordan on 20 May 2021.

Radar magazine, volume Six 15 November 1944, Hopson Project Articles

–CONFIDENTIAL–

TO SQUADRONS BY DIRECTION OF THE AIR COMMUNICATIONS OFFICER

TABLE OF CONTENTS:

RADAR is issued with the technical assistance of the Office of Scientific Research and Development through Radiation Laboratory of the Massachusetts Institute of Technology, under the official direction of

The Air Communications Officer
Brig. Gen. H. M. McClelland

Report from Tokyo

The Japanese Home and Empire Service of Tokyo last month broke all security regulations affecting radar with a broadcast telling all to the Japanese homefront. Since the secret is now out, we quote:

"On the night of June 15, enemy B-29s took off from Chengtu and flew directly eastward. It is 2,560 kilometers to Yawata. What enabled them to fly this long distance and successfully reach north Kyushu was electrical waves. 'Guiding waves' are to a plane lost in the great skies what a stick is to the blind.

Next, among the crew members of the B-29, there is one in charge of the instrument which is a short wave finder known as radar, and the B-29 is equipped with this topographical instrument. It is possible to know the topography of the land, whether water, land, mountain or (city) with this (shortwave).

Next, its use in enemy night raids on ships. Enemy B-24s and B-29s are bombing our ships sailing in the South China Seas and waters off Formosa with the goal of smashing our supply lines. In such cases, enemy planes do not detect our ships with their naked eye, but utilize an electronic wave instrument which locates them. We can't imagine what that missing wave could be!"

LAB vs. Japanese Shipping

In 14 months, a handful of LAB planes have sunk more than 500,000 tons; with the invasion of the Philippine Islands the record in months to come may be even more impressive.

LAB has been pecking away at Japanese shipping for over a year now. Three projects operating under as many different air forces have in this period sunk 500,000 tons of cargo craft, damaged another 200,000, besides accounting for some carriers, cruisers and destroyers. Off Formosa in October a lone LAB bomber out on a sea sweep lent a little help to Admiral Halsey by sinking a cruiser.

For the Japs, LAB has been hard to get at. But lately they've had success in their drives on Kweilin and Liuchow, forward bases in China. Kweilin has been abandoned and Lab bombers may be forced to withdraw from Liuchow. Until the base problem is solved LAB aircraft are going to have a hard time hitting the bustling China Sea traffic.

The solution may not be far off. With the invasion of Leyte, bases near Jap shipping lanes and a way to bring in quantity supplies—essentials of large scale activity—seem to be coming up.

China Seas targets have kept LAB aircraft busy all through the summer. The territory has been patrolled since May 1941 by a special LAB force under Lt. Col. William D. Hopson, attached to the 14th AF. A year earlier, the 13th AF pioneered LAB in the Solomons area with Col. Stuart P. Wright in charge (RADAR, April 1944). Late in 1943 the 5th AF extended it (under Lt. Col. Edward W. Scott) westward into the Bismarck Sea, then upward and westward all the way to Mindanao.

The record of LAB in the 13th and 5th AF's is good, but it's better in the 14th. The first two averaged one sighting, 350 tons of sinkings per sortie. The latter, "fishing" where the fishing is best, has been clicking with 3 sightings and a 1,200 ton average from May through September. LAB results can be pretty well predicted if traffic is known. Thus, an 850 ton average per sortie for China Seas operations had been foreseen and this figure was on the nose for the first 2 months. Statisticians lost out when the enemy's drive to neutralize East China bases kindled the crews. During September 110,000 tons of shipping were sunk—1,700 tons per sortie.

Of late LAB crews of the 13th AF have been outside the big target zone, but they've kept their hand in with frequent practice. The 5th AF has better hunting, though hardly to be compared with what they expect before long.

Big LAB doings are looked for in the 7th AF, which will be able to throw well over 100 equipped B-24's against the Japs by the first of the year. The 11th AF has a few LAB bombers, hasn't used them much yet.

As a method, LAB today is no different than reported 6 months ago. Crews come better trained, learn more from the veterans; maintenance is better; refinements have come in. While it can't do everything that LAB planes in combat zones are called on to do, it does everything that it was built for. The following pages tell what and how.

All the Damage to Date Has Been Done by a Handful of Planes

As an anti-shipping weapon, LAB combines high precision with low combat loss. Besides the efficiency of the bombing attachment for its special job and a definite last-second knack that some LAB bombardiers seem to acquire, the high precision stems from the inability of targets to take effective evasive action against the low altitude bombing. Low combat loss results in the main from the protection of nighttime operations.

The whole works out to this sort of record: one LAB squadron accounted for 47% of all tonnage sunk during 4 months by one bomber command. The rest of the command used 4 times as many aircraft, bombs and personnel in strikes against shipping.

The Wright Project in the 13th AF opened plenty of eyes with its results. The Scott Project and its 5th AF successors, in 233 missions over a 6-month period, sank 122,050 tons and damaged 65,650. The Hopson Project, with the best hunting of all, in its first 3 months (134 sorties) sank 113,400 tons of cargo sipping, damaged 54,300 and, additionally, bagged 7 warships. Then, the month of September, it downed 110,000 tons.★

The combined sinkings by LAB actions to date can hardly be called a major Jap disaster. But all the damage had been done by a handful of planes. One bombardier has sunk 75,000 tons. Two out of every 3 legitimate targets located in the China sweeps had to go untouched because there was just more work than a lone B-24 could do. One out of every four ships attacked in Chinese waters goes down.

The LAB technique calls for bombing moving targets at low altitude and the equipment was designed with that in mind. Improved versions of the APQ-5 have been suggested providing accuracy at low, medium and high altitudes, particularly in combination with the better resolution of X-band APS-15, which is already going into some replacement aircraft. But at its favorite low altitudes APA-5 performs so expertly that it seems destined for quite a long and useful life.

Where heavy bombers are scarce, and that includes China, LAB aircraft are sometimes integrated into general-purpose squadrons and called on for a variety of odd-jobs. As Pathfinders in group operations, they haven't worked as well; their SCR-717-B radars lack the necessary discrimination. With APS-15 and APQ-13 this drawback may vanish. Other sweeps haven't been very fruitful for the same reason. Buoys, lighthouses islands look like logical targets.

LAB sorties are night missions. In much of their surprise and provides safety. Prior to the arrival of the LAB aircraft in the 14th AF, most attacks were done in force and during daylight hours. Just a few days before the Hopson Project began functioning one such operation lost four bombers in combat with an escorted 10-ship convoy. But in 4 months of LAB night sorties there hasn't been a single traceable combat loss; losses from other causes (weather, navigational errors, running out of gas, etc.) come to about 5/5. Today most sorties are carried out by a single B-24, although sometimes they take off in pairs and maintain fairly close support, if necessary, during separate hunts throughout the night. A lone B-24 usually carries twelve 500 pound bombs, enough for 4 runs. With the heavy amount of China Seas traffic lately, it takes pretty keen selectivity to pick the best targets.

Though target opportunities improve as we close in on Japan, the cost goes up, too. LAB successes in China have been achieved against tough obstacles that are getting tougher. Some of what it costs to keep LAB going in China is told on the following pages.

Every Undertaking Must Be Measured in Pints of Gasoline and Ounces of Bombs

The history of LAB in the 14th AF from May to September 1944 provides a working sample of the kind of problems AAF units are likely to encounter as they make the adjustment from other theaters to the Far East scene.

Chinese operations and tough supply problems go hand in hand—especially when you're dealing with heavy bombers, which drink gas almost faster than it can be brought in. "Get that gas-hog out of her," cried a base Commander in China when the first

LAB B-24 came in. First LAB results changed his mind. But, as Lt. Col. Hopson (LAB project officer) observed, it is still true that "every undertaking must be measured in pints of gasoline and ounces of bombs." In 4 months, LAB sorties, excluding other activity, swallowed up 100,000 gallons of gas and 800,000 pounds of bombs, all of which had been flown in over the Hump.

Lack of fuel prevented practice flights and for several weeks stopped regular missions altogether until LAB bombers, serving as air tankers, could haul gas from West China to the forward base at Liuchow. They'd haul fuel 2 trips and do LAB work the third. It was a good investment. One ton of Jap shipping was sunk for about each 1.7 gallons of gas expended.

All types of equipment, sorely needed, were on the do-without list. The forward detachment at Liuchow, representing one Bombardment Group, was the envy of all airmen in East China for its 6×6 truck. "There is nothing here but what we bring," wrote the Radar Officer. "We are grateful for many of the simple things we insisted on carrying out, saws, hammers, etc."

Right now, the problem of bases is the biggest headache. Kweilin is gone, Liuchow is far from secure. And even these big forward bases, providing nearest entry to the China Seas, have meant a minimum sortie of 1,500 miles, 65 per cent over land. Westward bases are used today, but the overland percentage is even higher, some of the best hunting ground is inaccessible, gas usage is heavier, flights are longer at night over mountainous terrain in areas of practically no alternate bases.

This last means a greater operational risk. Even from East China the high terrain, lack of emergency fields, weather hazards and navigational problems combined to destroy one LAB bomber and damage another every 20 missions. One crew was lost every 40.

LAB crews, forming at Langley Field, VA, are trained as a unit, with the navigator-bombardier-radar operator performing as a closely integrated team. So tightly do their jobs dovetail that spot replacements are out of the question. Three teams were out of action simultaneously not long ago because in each case one of the radar team was missing.

LAB men in China have the advantage of lessons learned by the 5th and 13th AF and better training by the LAB Training Squadron at Langley, whose officers are veterans of many LAB sorties themselves. Maintenance is improved, through the Jap land offensive means relocated setups and even heavier strain on equipment.

All sorts of odd jobs cut into LAB operations. That's one of the laments of LAB crews, who develop a downright affection for their basic work. But they recognize the necessity for pitching in on Group operations in a land where heavy bombers are scarce and multi-purposed. But the consequence is further diminishment of the anti-shipping assignment and that helps to explain why 4 months of operations in China showed less than 200 LAB strikes.

Crews talk of the day when they can work exclusively on LAB, can stop worrying about getting hold of gas for the next mission and can operate from bases that aren't under enemy assault and 500 miles from the scene of action as well That seems to point to the Philippine Islands, smack in the middle of Jap shipping lanes. When they get there the lanes will be contracting northward, but not so fast that the crews won't be able to get their fill of hunting.

For all the troubles, things might have been much worse. Forewarned, the 14th AF's LAB unit came well stocked with essentials and joined a veteran bomb group whose morale was high.

Target off Formosa: A Typical Sortie

It is 14 September 1944. Plane No. 715, brought up that day to a forward base new Liuchow, lifts heavily into the early evening dusk and heads for the South China coast.

In its wing are 2,750 gallons of gas. It carries twelve 500 pound bombs, good for 4 runs against Jap shipping. Its IAS is 165 miles. If all goes well it will be out some 9 hours and cover about the same mileage as from Washington, DC to Denver.

This is familiar territory, mountains and all. The navigator reads his PPI scope like a memorized map as No. 715 leaves the Jap-held coast and flies eastward into the hunting zone. The pilot heads down, way down, to check the pressure altimeter against the radar altimeter. Then up he climbs to search altitude and the radar operator starts looking. On other sorties the operator has spotted shipping as far off as 70 miles, but usually it's closer to 30 miles.

Not far off Formosa the radar operator calls, "Looks like something!" and focuses on it with this sector scan. He gives direction to the pilot, range and direction to the bombardier. But 15 miles away he says, disgustedly. "Sorry, gents, it's just an island."

It's like deep sea fishing, waiting for something to hit the bait. At 34 miles the scope shows something. "This is it, sure," says the operator, and quickly furnishes the data. He calls off the miles as they move up through the night, and 8 miles. This is for the bombardier, who meanwhile has been tracking in range and hearing. The plane belongs to the bombardier as they hit the 8-mile mark and the bombing run starts. He flies it with automatic controls and he leads directly toward the blip. On his LAB scope the target area ½-mile to each side is magnified 8 times over the search position. Altitude is set in the LAB equipment; a predetermined air speed is maintained and everything is synchronized for bombing.

Three miles from the target the operator reports, "It's a big boy." The crew gets grimmer and more eager at the same time. The bombardier is glued to his screen, making his adjustments to keep the target centered and motionless on the crosshairs. The APQ-5 does all the computing as course and range corrections are cranked in.

With the blackness and the overcast there's nothing to see visually. Now they're only seconds off. Then: "Bombs away," sings the bombardier, though the actual release is automatic. The crew is quiet as three 500 pounders plunge seaward, one after the other. They can't see a thing, but several seconds later they hear the explosion and see a burst of light. That means a strike. They can't see a thing, but several seconds later they hear the explosion and see a burst of light. That means a strike. They don't strafe and they use a flame-dampener so their own position won't be revealed. Now comes a tremendous secondary explosion that fills the sea and sky. They duck out, while the tail gunner yells over the intercom, "I saw her. She's big and fat, and she's going down sure."

Training and Practice Get the Results

Under the strain and split-second timing of LAB operations the most effective crews are invariably those with most training and seasoning: lucky strikes by green crews are few and far between. LAB squadrons get their training both at home and in the field, as the pictures here show. They get their seasoning from flying many a sortie like the one described on the opposite page. And then the interrogation officers get reports like those excerpted below (from 14th Air Force records, May–September 1944):

Three Sunk, One Damaged
Four targets picked up 10 to 12 miles apart east of Hong Kong. The biggest was bombed first and sustained a direct hit. The blip disappeared in about 6 minutes. Thirty minutes later a run was made on the second largest for another direct hit. There was a secondary explosion, seen by rear gunner. The blip left the screen. The third ship was attacked and sustained a direct hit. The blip disappeared. New targets were seen, but these were identified as an island and 2 reefs during bombing run. Four ship convoy located. Salvo straddled lead ship about 30 feet astern. Target stopped while convoy continued.

One Sunk
Object appeared on the screen at 20 miles. Aircraft approached through overcast: indication was identified as a large vessel. Following LAB run crew observed 2 bomb flashes and heard an explosion. After 3 ½ minutes the blip faded out.

Sunk: Two Ships, One Junk
One hundred miles east of Kowloon made run on indication and discovered it was a 50 foot junk too late to hold release. Junk sunk. No damage claimed on second target. Third target took direct hit. Exploded and sunk. Fourth got direct hit. Crew saw lifeboats in water, then ship go down.

Cruiser Sunk
Blip near Hainan was light cruiser. Direct hit on first run but didn't sink. Another bullseye on second run. Third run against heavy AA fire: third direct hit. Cruiser sank while aircraft was climbing to bomb again from higher up.

Ship Sunk
Dropped 3 bombs on 250 footer west of Liuchow Peninsula and confirmed sinking when blip disappeared from the target screen.

Sunk: One Cruiser, One Transport
Picked up convoy at 30 miles. Biggest blip in center bombed. Secondary explosion, sunk. Identified by rear gunner as 600 foot transport. Twenty minutes later made run on outside target (second biggest). Two bombs hit amidships. In light of secondary explosion seen as light cruiser. AA fire heavy.

Where Did They Come From?

A snapshot of the origins of the men of the 868th and its parent Thirteenth Air Force may be discerned from a Headquarters Thirteenth Air Force awards document, General Orders Number 228 of 9 December 1944, designating the recipients of the U.S. Army Air Forces Air Medal (Oak Leaf Cluster). The document identifies each man by name, rank and serial number and lists the next-of-kin, street address and the hometown of each man. These brief descriptions suggest the diverse origins of the young men who found themselves together in the South Pacific serving with the 868th Squadron at year's end 1944. The hometowns with names on this list included:

Longmeadow, Massachusetts	Junior Barney
Brocton, Massachusetts	William Bryant
Stonington, Connecticut	Charles Conrad
Platteville, Wisconsin	Robert Curnow
Indianapolis, Indiana	Harvey Curran
Pioche, Nevada	Ray Davis
Endicott, New York	George Desko
New York, New York	Henry Granowski
Lamar, Colorado	Eldon Hallmark
Church Point, Louisiana	Clarence Harmon
Knoxville, Pennsylvania	Phillip Hoffman
Youngstown, Ohio	Joseph McCalmont
Simsbury, Connecticut	Walter Bednarcyk
Cambridge, Massachusetts	Louis Fillios
Alhambra, California	Ronald Moyer
Brooklyn, New York	Sidney Palley
St. Louis, Missouri	Jerry Pelat
Bronx, New York	Paul Ramaglia

Philadelphia, Pennsylvania	Leonard Tuft
Fort Payne, Alabama	Gordon Stoner
Lockport, New York	Earle Smith
New York, New York	Arthur Russo
Portland, Oregon	Walter Gango
Flint, Michigan	Donald Gilman
Buffalo, New York	Townsend Rogers
Oakland, California	Eugene Morgan
Teague, Texas	Wyatt Norris
Chicago, Illinois	Ray Czerwonko
Douglas, Nebraska	John Kissinger
Pittsburg, Pennsylvania	Alex Wolititch
Pendleton, Indiana	William Ritz
Beaver Meadows, Pennsylvania	Peter Demanovich

A Wright Project Declaration

"Don't tell me it didn't happen! I was there! But I didn't do it!"
By Lieutenant James E. Pope

I know that I was the only sane person in the entire organization, from the first day I linked up with Bid Dolan at McChord Field in February 1942, through the day I climbed on an airplane and headed home from the 868th in the South Pacific in July 1944.

- I did argue non-stop with Bid Dolan, told him to his face that he was terrible flyer, could not fly a kite, let alone a B-18 Bolo, and certainly not a B-24 Liberator!
- It was Leo Foster and Frank Reynolds at Boston that dumped the B-18 into the harbor, not me, and Foster and Frank Carlson who plowed down the Logan airfield when they retracted the Bolo's landing gear too soon on their failed take-off and scooped up half a ton of cinders off the surface of the airfield, not me.
- It was Werner who loaded up the airplane with cases of booze on our leave in Sydney and had Reynolds fly under the great harbor bridge there. I was on the plane but it wasn't me that did it!
- At Langley when Reynolds and the gang got roaring drunk and went on an all-night spree, I was there, but it wasn't me. I did roll them all into Reynolds's car and brought them back to base.
- It wasn't me that cleared the .50 caliber machine gun as Pellegrini slept next to it, and I told him that it wasn't my fault when he jumped me and we fought it out.
- It wasn't me who kept getting to fist fights with Reynolds and Zane and a couple of others back at Langley and at Guadalcanal, because it was a wild bunch of guys. And while we worked great in the airplane in combat, back on the ground there was always something to fight about.

- It wasn't me that got us all thrown out of the Norfork Naval Air Station Officers Club for getting drunk and starting a fight. I think it was Wheatly, but it wasn't me!

- It was me who said that I would fly in those first edition B-26 hot ships that were crashing and killing crews, until they grounded them. No sane man would have stayed with that aircraft and seen two of his pilots, Mortanson at McChord, and my first pilot, a guy named Daugherty, who went down when my original B-26 unit, the 72nd Squadron combat deployed to Alaska.

- And right after Pearl Harbor, when they put us in A-29's that had been sold to the English and then appropriated by the U.S. Army Air Corps, I was the navigator that Dolan selected with the flip of a coin to go with him to Boston. We had a two week stop in San Antonio to pick up our B-18 Bolo and I met Dolan's wife, a great woman. She treated me like a son from that point on and tolerated my constant arguing with her husband by telling us to "knock it off and behave like two adults." But none of us then, including Dolan, had any idea what we had been selected for or where we would end up.

- It wasn't me that had two girlfriends at the same time, one at McChord that I said goodbye to when Dolan and I took the train to Sacramento to pick up our B-18, and the one that was standing alongside my mother at the train station to greet us when we pulled in. Dolan figured it all out, gave me smile, and invited my mother to dinner. Off I went with my old girlfriend. I owed Dolan a big one, and he collected on it many times over and even told me "Son, you went and married the wrong girl." Maybe he was right.

- It wasn't me that beached the Bolo off Langley Field when three of us who were up on ASV missions that night and ran into that incredible storm. One plane found its way to land at Newark, one somehow got back to Langley (mine) to land and another bouncing in on the sand. Not me.

- It wasn't me that hammed it up when we made that slap-stick training movie with the Hollywood director, with Foster partying all night and doing whatever. Okay, so I was there, but it wasn't me that caused the incident that got us thrown out of that director's fancy party!

- It wasn't me that egged Dolan on, when we polished off the U-boat that we had hunted for five days straight off Cuba, to get the First Sea Search Attack Group full recognition for the kill. He didn't need too much stimulation but some of our crew, maybe it was our pilot Lehti or maybe it was our bombardier Thiele, who harassed Dolan to ask for (and get) a formal review that eventually delivered the commendation. It wasn't me, but I was there and I sure egged them on!

- When Zinn, Rockwood and I ferried that Brit LB-30 to Westover Field and crashed it on landing, it wasn't me that did the crashing but I was there, I survived and had to explain to a lot of very upset people what happened.

- I didn't pick the fight with Dolan when he called me into his office in the Spring of 1943, when I was the squadron's navigation officer, confronting me with the paperwork I had put in to transfer out of his unit for pilot training. Dolan said, "I say you are too young, and too ambitious to become a good pilot" and I said that he was dead wrong and anyway, how would he know. The only response he could come up with was to yell "Get your damn trunks on and meet me in the gym. We're gonna settle this." In the gym I stood a full head taller than him and before we started, I said "What the hell does this fight have to do with my request to be a pilot?" He hit me first and we fought, and he blocked the request. He had real heart and showed to us in all kinds of ways.

- Some thought that it might have been me who Dolan called into his office the week before the Wright Project crews were scheduled to depart for Guadalcanal to suggest that I defect from my crew and remain at Langley to work with him on a new project, which I later discovered was the H2X high-altitude bombing system. I told him "Colonel, it's too damn late, and I'm going with Wright." He didn't argue but he was very disappointed that I turned him down flat. That WAS me. You needed to know how to look Bid Dolan in eye, disregard his rank, and just say "No, Sir!" He respected that.

James E. Pope
First Lieutenant
U.S. Army Air Corps 1941–1945
0431763
Third Sea Search Attack Squadron, First Sea Search Attack Group, January–August 1943
Project Number 96131—Restricted on 9 August 1943, Operations Order 13 (SECRET)
Navigator Wright Project Crew Number FP-617-AD 3 August 1943 (Captain John F. Zinn)
868th Bombardment Squadron (Heavy) Squadron Navigator as of 19 July 1944

A Liberator Bibliography

Alcorn, John S. *The Jolly Rogers—History of the 90th Bomb Group During World War II.* Temple City, CA: Historical Aviation Album Publication, 1981.

Birdsall, Steve. *The B-24D—Air Combat Special Number 3.* Rockaway, NJ: Eagle Aviation Enterprises, 1972.

Birdsall, Steve. *B-24 Liberator in Action, Number 21.* Warren, MI: Squadron/Signal Publications, 1975.

Birdsall, Steve. *Flying Buccaneers—The Illustrated Story of Kenney's Fifth Air Force.* Garden City, NY: Doubleday & Company, 1977.

Blue, Allan G. *The B-24 Liberator: A Pictoral History.* New York, NY: Charles Scribner, 1975.

Boeman, John. *Morotai: A Memoir of War.* Garden City, NY: Doubleday and Company, 1981.

Bowman, Martin W. *B-24 Liberator 1939–45.* Wellingborough: Patrick Stephens Ltd, 1995.

Bowman, Martin W. *B-24 Combat Missions: First-Hand Accounts of Liberator Operations Over Nazi Europe.* New York, NY: Metro Books, 2010.

Bowman, Martin W. *Bombers Fly East: WWII RAF Operations in the Middle and Far East.* Barnsley: Pen and Sword Aviation, 2017.

Carey, Alan C. *The Reluctant Raiders: The Story of the United States Navy Bombing Squadron; VB/VPB-109 in WWII.* Atglen, PA: Schiffer Military History, 1999.

Carey, Alan C. *We Flew Alone: United States Navy B-24 Squadrons in the Pacific, February 1943–September 1944.* Atglen, PA: Schiffer Military History, 2000.

Carey, Alan C. *Above an Angry Sea: United States Navy B-24 Liberator and PB4Y Privateer Operations in the Pacific October 1944–August 1945.* Atglen, PA: Schiffer Publishing Ltd., 2001.

Clive, John. *The Last Liberator.* Feltham: Hamlyn Books, 1981.

Cundiff, Michael J. *Ten Knights in a Bar Room: Missing in Action in the Southwest Pacific 1943.* Ames, IA: Iowa State University Press, 1990.

Davidson, Budd. "B-24 Liberator—Bombs Away," *Flight Journal Special* (Fall 2005).

Davis, James M. *In Hostile Skies: An American B-24 Pilot in World War II.* Denton, TX: University of North Texas Press, 2006.

Dorr, Robert F. *B-24 Liberator Units of the Pacific War.* Oxford: Osprey Publishing, 1999.

Dorr, Robert F. and Jon Lake. "Consolidated B-24 Liberator, Part One, Development and Allied Operations 1939–1943," *International Air Power Review*, Volume 4 (2002): 128–63.

Douglas, Graeme. *Consolidated B-24 Liberator: 1939 Onwards (all marks): Owner's Workshop Manual: An Insight into Owning, Servicing and Flying the American Second WW Heavy Bomber.* Sparkford: Haynes Publishing, 2013.

Doyle, David. *Consolidated B-24 Volume One, XB-24 to B-24E Liberators in World War II.* Atglen, PA: Schiffer Publishing Ltd., 2018.

Feuer, A. B. *General Chennault's Secret Weapon: The B-24 in China.* Westport, CT: Praeger, 1992.

Fisher, David E. *A Race on the Edge of Time: Radar—The Decisive Weapon of WWII.* New York, NY: McGraw-Hill Companies, 1988.

Forman, Wallace R. *B-24 Nose Art Directory.* North Branch, MN: Special Press, 1996.

Freeman, Roger. *B-24 Liberator of War.* London: Ian Allan, 1983.

Gaylor, Walter, Don L. Evans, Harry A. Nelson and Lawrence J. Hickey. *Revenge of the Red Raiders: The Illustrated History of the 22nd Bombardment Group During the WWII.* Boulder, CO: International Research and Publishing Corporation, 2006.

Ginter, Steve. *Consolidated PB4Y-1/1P Liberator.* Simi Valley, CA: Ginter Books, 2017.

Griffin, Alan. *Consolidated Mess: The Illustrated Guide to Nose-Turreted B-24 Production Variants in USAAF Combat Service*, White Series 9115. Sandomierz: MMP Books, 2012.

Harley, James. "The Fighter Pilot Podcast, Episode 129, The B-24 Liberator," 24 December 2021, available at http://www.fighterpilotpodcast.com.

Heiman, Judith M. *The Airmen and the Headhunters: The True Story of Lost Soldiers, Heroic Tribesmen and the Unlikeliest Rescue of World War II.* Orlando, FL: Harcourt, 2007.

Howard, Clive and Joe Whitley. *One Damned Island After Another: The Saga of the Seventh.* Chapel Hill, NC: The University of North Carolina Press, 2018.

Howell, Fred Stanley. *The Snoopers.* New York, NY: Vantage Press, Inc., 1991.

Hutton, Stephen M. *Squadron of Deception: The 36th Bomb Squadron in World War II.* Atglen, PA: Schiffer Military History, 1999.

Hylton, Wils. *Vanished: The Sixty-Year Search for the Missing Men of World War II.* New York, NY: Riverhead Books, 2013.

Johnsen, Frederick A. *The Bomber Barons: The History of the 5th Bomb Group in the Pacific During World War II, Volume One—A Pictorial History.* Tacoma, WA: Bomber Books, 1982.

Johnsen, Frederick A. *B-24 Liberator—Warbird History; Combat and Development History of the Liberator and Privateer.* Osceola, WI: Motorbooks International, 1993.

Johnsen, Frederick A. *B-24 Liberator: Rugged but Right.* New York, NY: McGraw Hill, 1999.

Johnsen, Frederick A. *Consolidated B-24 Liberator Warbird Tech Series.* North Branch, MN: Specialty Press, 2001.

Kirkness, Bill and Matt Poole. *RAF Liberators over Burma: Flying with 159 Squadron.* Oxford: Fonthill Media, 2017.

Kittrell, Ed. *Solo into the Rising Sun: The Dangerous Missions of a U.S. Navy Bomber Squadron in World War II.* Guilford, CT: Stackpole Books, 2020.

Lake, Jon. "RAF Liberators at War—Part One, UK-Based Operations," *International Air Power Review,* Volume 15 (2005): 158–73.

Lake, Jon. "RAF Liberators at War —Part Two, Service Abroad Variants and Operators," *International Air Power Review,* Volume 16 (2005): 156–73.

Lance, John F. *B-24 Co-Pilot,* as dictated in April 1991, transcribed and edited by his daughter, Kathryn Lance, 2016, self-published by Kathryn Lance.

Livingstone, Bob. *Under the Southern Cross: The B-24 Liberator in the South Pacific.* Paducah, KY: Turner Publishing, 1998.

Lloyd, Alwyn T. *Liberator: America's Global Bomber.* Missoula, MT: Pictorial Histories Publishing Company, 1993.

Murphy, Brian. *81 Days Below Zero: The Incredible Survival Story of a World War II Pilot in Alaska's Frozen Wilderness.* Boston, MA: Da Capo Press, 2015.

Norton, Bill. *American Bomber Aircraft Development in World War II.* Hersham: Midland Publishing, 2012.

Oakley, David G. with George D. Oakley, Jr. *On the Fiery Breath of Dragons.* Carroll, IA: Stone Printing, 2008.

Okerstrom, Dennis R. *The Final Mission of Bottoms Up: A World War II Pilot's Story.* Columbia, MO: University of Missouri Press, 2011.

O'Leary, Michael. *Consolidated B-24 Liberator* (Osprey Publishing Production Line to Frontline 4). Oxford: Osprey Publishing, 2002.

Perkins, Paul and Michelle Crean. *The Soldier: Consolidated B-24 Liberator.* Charlottesville, VA: Howell Press, 1993.

Perrone, Stephen M. *World War II B-24 "Snoopers": Low Level Bombing Targets Manila Bay Shipping; The Story of WWII's Secret Anti-Shipping Night War Against the Japanese.* Somerdale, NJ: New Jersey Sportsman's Guide, 2001.

Price, Dr. Alfred. *Patrol Aircraft vs. Submarine.* Charlottesville, VA: Howell Press, 1989.

Scearce, Phil. *Finish Forty and Home: The Untold WWII Story of B-24s in the Pacific.* Denton, TX: University of North Texas Press, 2011.

Scranton, Dennis. *Crew One: A World War II Memoir of VP-108.* Bennington, VT: Merriam Press, 2008.

Segal, Jules F. *The Jolly Rogers: The 90th Bomb Group in the Southwest Pacific, 1942–1945.* Atglen, PA: Schiffer Publishing Ltd., 1997.

Shacklady, Edward. *Consolidated B-24 Liberator: Classic WWII Aviation, Volume 3.* Bristol: Cerberus, 2002.

Simons, Graham M. *Consolidated B-24 Liberator.* Barnsley: Pen and Sword Aviation, 2012.

Stekel, Peter. *Beneath Haunted Waters: The Tragic Tale of Two B-24's Lost in the Sierra Nevada Mountains During World War II.* Guilford, CT: Lyons Press, 2017.

Watts, Perry. *The Famous "Witchcraft": The Enchanted Liberator: A Unique U.S. Bomber's Experience During World War II.* Atglen, PA: Schiffer Publishing Ltd., 2015.

Young, Edward M. *B-24 Liberator Units of the CBI.* Oxford: Osprey Publishing, 2011.

Young, Edward M. *B-24 Liberators vs. KI-43 Oscar: China and Burma.* Oxford: Osprey Publishing, 2012.

Young, Edward M. *Death from Above: The 7th Bombardment Group in World War II.* Atglen, PA: Schiffer Publishing Ltd., 2014.

Young, Edward M. *The Tenth Air Force in World War II: Strategy, Command, and Operations 1942–1943.* Atglen, PA: Schiffer Publishing Ltd., 2020.

A General Bibliography

AAF Historical Narratives. *Army Air Forces in the War Against Japan 1941–1942.* Washington, D.C.: Headquarters, Army Air Forces, 1945.

Appleman, Roy E., James M. Burns, Russel A. Gugeler and John Stevens. *Okinawa: The Last Battle.* New York, NY: Skyhorse Publishing, 2011.

Baggott, Jim. *Atomic: The First War of Physics and the Secret History of Atom Bomb, 1939–49.* Crows Nest, New South Wales: Allen & Unwin, 2009.

Baxter III, James P. *Scientists Against Time.* Boston, MA: Little, Brown and Company, 1947.

Bernstein, Morey. *The Search for Bridey Murphy.* Garden City, NY: Doubleday & Company, 1956.

Birdsall, Steve. *Flying Buccaneers: The Illustrated Story of Kenney's Fifth Air Force.* Garden City, NY: Doubleday & Company, 1977.

Blair, Clay. *Hitler's U-Boat War: The Hunters, 1939–1942.* New York, NY: Modern Library, 1998.

Borneman, Walter R. *Macarthur at War: World War II in the Pacific.* New York, NY: Back Bay Books, Little, Brown and Company, 2016.

Bowman, Martin W. and Tom Cushing. *Confounding the Reich: The RAF's Secret War of Electronic Countermeasures in WWII.* Barnsley: Pen and Sword Aviation, 2004.

Brown, Ken. *The U-Boat Assault on America: Why the U.S. was Unprepared for War in the Atlantic.* Barnsley: Seaforth Publishing, 2017.

Brown, Louis. *A Radar History at World War II: Technical and Military Imperatives.* Bristol: Institute of Physics Publishing, 1999.

Buderi, Robert. *The Invention that Changed the World: How a Small Group of Radar Pioneers Won the Second World War and Launched a Technical Revolution.* New York, NY: Simon and Schuster, 1996.

Burchard, John. *Q.E.D: M.I.T. in World War II.* New York, NY: J. Wiley, 1948.

Carey, Alan C. *Sighted Sub Sank Same: The United States Navy's Air Campaign Against the U-Boat.* Havertown, PA: Casemate Publishers, 2019.

Casey, Major General Hugh J., *Engineers in Theater Operations: Engineers of the Southwest Pacific 1941–1945; Vol. 1.* General Headquarters Army Forces Pacific, Tokyo, Japan: U.S. Army, 1947.

Clausen, M. P. *The Development of Radio and Radar Equipment for Air Operations, 1939–1944.* Booklet prepared for MIT, 1944.

Cleaver, Thomas McKelvey. *Under the Southern Cross: The South Pacific Air Campaign Against Rabaul.* Oxford: Osprey Publishing, 2021.

Conant, Jennet. *Tuxedo Park: A Wall Street Tycoon and the Secret Palace of Science that Changed the Course of WWII.* New York, NY and London: Simon and Schuster, 2002.

Connaughton, Richard, John Pimlott and Duncan Anderson. *The Battle for Manila: The Most Devastating Untold Story of World War II.* London: Bloomsbury Publishing Plc, 1995.

Cortesi, Lawrence. *The Grim Reapers: History of the 3rd Bomb Group 1918–1965.* Temple City, CA: Historical Aviation Album, 1985.

Duffy, James P. *War at the End of the World: Douglas MacArthur and the Forgotten Fight for New Guinea 1942–1945.* New York, NY: NAL Caliber, 2016.

Edgerton, David. *Britain's War Machine: Weapons, Resources, and Experts in the Second World War.* Oxford and New York, NY: Oxford University Press, 2011.

Fagan, M. D. (ed.). *A History of Engineering and Science in the Bell System: National Service in War and Peace 1925–1975.* New York, NY: Bell Telephone Laboratories, Inc., 1978.

Farrell, Don A. *Atomic Bomb Island: Tinian, the Last Stage of the Manhattan Project, and the Dropping of the Atomic Bombs on Japan in World War II.* Guilford, CT: Stackpole Books, 2020.

Feiffer, George. *Tennozan: The Battle of Okinawa and the Atomic Bomb.* New York, NY: Ticknor & Fields, 1992.

Fine, Norman. *Blind Bombing: How Microwave Radar Brought the Allies to D-Day and Victory in World War II.* Lincoln, NE: Potomac Books, 2019.

Fisher, David E. *A Race on the Edge of Time. Radar—The Decisive Weapon of World War II.* New York, NY: McGraw-Hill, 1988.

Forman, Wallace R. *B-24 Nose Art Name Directory—Includes Group, Squadron and Aircraft Serial Numbers and Photo Availability.* North Branch, MN: Specialty Press, 1996.

Francillon, Rene J. *Japanese Aircraft of the Pacific War.* London: Putnam & Company, 1979.

Frank, Richard B. *Downfall: The End of the Imperial Japanese Empire.* New York, NY: Random House, 1999.

Gailley, Harry A. *Bouganville 1943–1945: The Forgotten Campaign.* Lexington, KY: The University Press of Kentucky, 1991.

Gallagher, James P. *With the Fifth Army Air Force: Photos from the Pacific Theater.* Baltimore, MD: Johns Hopkins University Press, 2001.

Gamble, Bruce. *Fortress Rabaul: The Battle for the Southwest Pacific, January 1942.* Minneapolis, MN: Zenith Press, 2010.

Gamble, Bruce. *Target: Rabaul: The Allied Siege of Japan's Most Infamous Stronghold, March 1943–August 1945.* Minneapolis, MN: Zenith Press, 2013.

Gannon, Michael. *Operation Drumbeat: The Dramatic True Story of Germany's First U-Boat Attacks Along the American Coast in World War II.* New York, NY: Harper Collins Publishers, 1991.

General Staff of the General Headquarters (GHQ) Tokyo, Japan, *Reports of General MacArthur: The Campaigns of MacArthur in the Pacific, Volume I, as Prepared by His General Staff.* First published in 1950 in Tokyo, reprinted 1966 by the United States Army, Washington, D.C., 1966.

Giangreco, D. M. *Hell to Pay: Operation Downfall and the Invasion of Japan, 1945–47.* Annapolis, MD: Naval Institute Press, 2009.

Graff, Cory. *Shot to Hell: The Stories and Photos of Ravaged WWII Warbirds.* St. Paul, MN: MBI Publishing Company, 2003.

Hammel, Eric. *Munda Trail: The New Georgia Campaign.* New York, NY: Orion Books, 1989.

Hartcup, Guy. *The Challenge of War: Britain's Scientific and Engineering Contributions to World War II.* New York, NY: Taplinger Publishing, 1970.

Hata, Ikuhiko, Yasuho Isawa and Christopher Shores. *Japanese Naval Air Force Fighter Units and Their Aces, 1932–1945.* London: Grub Street, 2011.

Holt, Thaddeus. *The Deceivers: Allied Military Deception in the Second World War.* New York, NY: Simon and Schuster, 2004.

Hornfischer, James D. *The Fleet at Flood Tide: America at Total War in the Pacific 1944–1945.* New York, NY: Bantam Books, 2016.

Hough, Lt. Col Frank O. and Major John A. Crown. U.S. Marine Corps. *The Campaign on New Britain.* Washington, D.C.: U.S. Government Printing Office, 1952.

Huber, Dr. T. M., *Okinawa 1945.* Havertown, PA: Casemate Publishers, 2001.

Hutton, Stephen. *Squadron of Deception: The 36th Bomb Squadron in World War II.* Atglen, PA: Schiffer Publishing Ltd., 1999.

Hylton, Wil S. *Vanished: The Sixty Year Search for the Missing Men of WWII.* New York, NY: Riverhead Books, 2013.

Johnson, Brian. *The Secret War.* New York, NY: Methuen, 1978.

Kenney, George C. *General Kenney Reports, USAF Warrior Studies.* New York: Duell, Sloan, 1949.

Lambert, John W. *Low Level Attack: The Pacific.* North Branch, MN: Specialty Press, 1997.

Lindemann, Klaus. *Hailstorm over Truk Lagoon: Operations Against Truk by Carrier Task Force 58, 17–18 February 1944 (Second Expanded Edition).* Belleville, MI: Pacific Press Publications, 1991.

Marsh, Don and Peter Starkings. *Imperial Japanese Army Flying Schools 1912–1945*. Atglen, PA: Schiffer Publishing Ltd., 2011.

Mays, Terry M. *Night Hawks and Black Widows: 13th Air Force Night Fighters in the South and Southwest Pacific 1943–1945*. Atglen, PA: Schiffer Publishing Ltd., 2009.

McFarland, Stephen L. *Conquering the Night: Army Air Forces Night Fighters at War*. Washington, D.C.: Air Force History and Museums Program, 1998.

Mikesh, Robert C. and Osamu Tagaya. *Moonlight Interceptor: Japan's "Irving" Night Fighter*. Washington, D.C.: Smithsonian Institution Press, 1985.

Military Analysis Division, The United States Strategic Bombing Survey. *Air Campaigns of the Pacific War*. Washington, D.C.: U.S. Government Printing Office, 1947.

Moore, Stephen L. *Presumed Lost: The Incredible Ordeal of America's Submarine POWs During the Pacific War*. Annapolis, MD: Naval Institute Press, 2009.

Ness, Leland. *Rikugun—Guide to Japanese Ground Forces 1937–1945, Volume 2*. Solihull: Helion & Company, 2015.

Office of the Chief Engineer, General Headquarters Army Forces, Pacific. *Engineers in Theater Operations—Engineers of the Southwest Pacific 1941–1945, Volume I*. General Headquarters Army Forces Pacific, Tokyo, Japan: U.S. Army, 1947.

Parillo, Mark P. *The Japanese Merchant Marine in World War II*. Annapolis, MD: Naval Institute Press, 1993.

Parnell, Ben. *Carpet Baggers: America's Secret War in Europe*. Austin, TX: Eakin Press, 1987.

Perrett, Geoffrey. *Winged Victory: The Army Air Forces in World War II*. New York, NY: Random House, 1993.

Prados, John. *Combined Fleet Decoded: The Secret History of American Intelligence and the Japanese Navy in World War II*. New York, NY: Random House, 1995.

Prados, John. *Islands of Destiny: The Solomons Campaign and the Eclipse of the Rising Sun*. New York, NY: NAL Caliber, 2012.

Prados, John. *Storm Over Leyte: The Philippine Invasion and the Destruction of the Japanese Navy*. New York, NY: NAL Caliber, 2016.

Price, Alfred. *The History of U.S. Electronic Warfare: The Years of Innovation Beginning to 1946; Vol. 1*. Arlington, VA: The Association of Old Crows, 1981.

Price, Dr. Alfred. *Patrol Aircraft vs. Submarine*. Charlottesville, VA: Howell Press, 1991.

Reilly, Robin L. *Kamikazes, Corsairs, and Picket Ships: Okinawa, 1945*. Havertown, PA: Casemate Publishers, 2008.

Satterfield, George. *The History of Langley Field Virginia to September 1947*. Langley Air Force Base, VA: Langley Air Force Base Publication, 1957.

Schoenfeld, Max. *Stalking the U-Boat: USAAF Offensive Antisubmarine Operations in WWII*. Washington, D.C.: Smithsonian Institution Press, 1995.

Scott, James M. *Rampage: MacArthur, Yamashita, and the Battle of Manila*. New York, NY: W.W. Norton & Company, 2018.

Scranton, Dennis. *Crew One: A World War II Memoir of VPB-108*. Bennington, VT: Merriam Press, 2001.

Scutts, Jerry. *PBJ Mitchell Units of the Pacific War*. Osprey Combat Aircraft, 40. Oxford: Osprey Publishing, 2003.

Segal, Jules. *The Jolly Rogers: The 90th Bombardment Group in the Southwest Pacific 1942–1944*. Atglen, PA: Schiffer Publishing Ltd., 1997.

Stewart, William. *Ghost Fleet of the Truk Lagoon: Japanese Mandated Islands; An Account of "Operation Hailstone" February 1944*. Missoula, MT: Pictorial Histories Publishing, 1985.

Stille, Mark. *The Imperial Japanese Navy in the Pacific War*. London: Osprey Publishing, 2013.

Tarrant, V. E. *The U-Boat Offensive 1941–1945*. Annapolis, MD: Naval Institute Press, 1989.

The Massachusetts Institute of Technology. *Five Years: At the Radiation Laboratory*. Andover, MA: The Andover Press, Ltd., 1946.

Toll, Ian W., *Twilight of the Gods: War in the Western Pacific, 1944–1945*. New York, NY: W. W. Norton, 2020.

U.S. Navy Analysis Division, *Interrogations of Japanes Officials: Volume I*. Washington, D.C.: U.S. Government Printing Office, 1946.

U.S. Navy Analysis Division, *Interrogations of Japanes Officials: Volume II*. Washington, D.C.: U.S. Government Printing Office, 1946.

U.S. Navy Analysis Division, *The United States Strategic Bombing Survey (Pacific), The Campaigns of the Pacific War*. Washington, D.C.: U.S. Government Printing Office, 1946.

Werneth, Ron. *Beyond Pearl Harbor: The Untold Stories of Japan's Naval Airmen*. Atglen, PA: Schiffer Publishing Ltd., 2008.

Wheelan, Joseph. *Midnight in the Pacific: Guadalcanal—The World War II Battle that Turned the Tide of War*. Boston, MA: Da Capo Press, 2017.

Willmott, H. P. *The Second World War in the Far East*. London: Cassell & Co., 1999.

Willmott, H. P. *The Battle of Leyte Gulf—The Last Fleet Action*. Bloomington, IN: Indiana University Press, 2005.

Wolf, William. *Conquest of the Sky: Seeking Range, Endurance, and the Intercontinental Bomber*. Atglen, PA: Schiffer Publishing Ltd., 2017.

Yenne, Bill. *Hap Arnold: The General Who Invented the U.S. Air Force*. Washington, D.C.: Regnery History, 2013.

Yenne, Bill. *MacArthur's Air Force: American Airpower Over the Pacific and the Far East, 1941–1951*. Oxford: Osprey Publishing, 2019.

Zachary, G. Pascal. *Endless Frontier: Vannevar Bush, Engineer of the American Century*. New York, NY: The Free Press, 1997.

Endnotes

Chapter 1: World War Comes to America and to "Bid" Dolan, January–May 1942

1   The United States Army Air Corps was replaced by the United States Army Air Forces as the U.S. Army's air warfare component on 20 June 1941. While the USAAC continued as an element of the USAAF, mainly in the training and supply realms, to avoid confusion, USAAF will be used when referring to the Army's air arm after 20 June 1941.

2   Headquarters 42nd Bombardment Group, Air Force Combat Command Special Orders Number 22 of 16 February 1942 directs Lieutenant Colonel Dolan (O-17921) and six other officers and men to proceed by rail to Sacramento and "pick up one B-18A airplane from the 6th Reconnaissance Squadron and … proceed to San Antonio Air Depot for necessary alterations … thence to Municipal Airport, Boston … reporting to Liaison Officer, Radiation Laboratory at MIT."

3   As reflected in Operations Order Number 16, Headquarters 30th Bombardment Group, March Field, California, 17 February 1942, the seven members of the William Foley crew (Foley, Lehti, Werner, Illig, Bishop, Ring and Bradford), most of whom were then serving with the 38th Bomb Squadron at Muroc Field, were directed to proceed to Bakersfield to "pick up one B-18A airplane from the 41st Bombardment Group and proceed to … San Antonio Air Depot Duncanfield, Texas to arrive on or before February 21, 1942." These orders also directed that, after "alterations" to their aircraft, they were to proceed to Municipal Airport, Boston, Massachusetts, reporting there to the Liaison Officer, Radiation Laboratory, MIT, Boston.

4   An interesting anecdote in the broader tale of the Wright Project and the 868th Squadron is that the three men who would ensure the birth and the combat success of this project were contemporaries. William C. "Bid" Dolan, Edwin E. Aldrin and Stuart P. "Stud" Wright joined the Air Corps during World War I and, after traveling various routes in the lean years between the two world wars, found themselves together in the early weeks of 1942. In fact, Dolan's Air Corps commissioning identification, or ranking number, was 0-17920 and Wright's was 0-17921. Aldrin, a major when World War I ended in 1918, found himself still at that rank 10 years later. He resigned his commission, attended MIT to secure an engineering PhD, and joined Standard Oil of New Jersey where he excelled as a technical and marketing representative working in Europe throughout the 1930s. At General Arnold's request, Aldrin reclaimed his commission in 1939, albeit as a reserve officer (0-259547), and served during the war as a core member of Arnold's brain trust, applying

new technologies and tactics to the air war. In this mission, Aldrin moved constantly from his official perch at Wright Field to meetings in Boston (Rad Lab), Air Corps and later Army Air Force Headquarters in Washington, D.C., and Langley Field where new systems were field tested. Aldrin was a "details man" and followed these capabilities into front-line combat bases in Europe and the Pacific to validate their performance and define improvements he could bring home and advocate. As one Wright Project officer observed, "Aldrin was everywhere, all the time. He even showed up unannounced in the South Pacific to check on his and Dolan's boys." Colonel Edwin Aldrin passed away in December 1984 and was honored in several obituaries, including *Time* magazine. His son, Edwin "Buzz" Aldrin, graduated from high school during his father's interactions with Dolan, Wright, Giles and Arnold and attended West Point. He also became a U.S. Air Force pilot, flew 66 air combat missions in the storied F-86 Sabre during the Korean War and exited that conflict with two MiG-15s to his credit. Buzz secured an aeronautical engineering degree from MIT and became a NASA astronaut. A member of the *Apollo 11* crew, Colonel Buzz Aldrin was the second man to walk on the moon in 1969, stepping off the ladder of the moon lander moments behind Neil Armstrong.

5 Regarding B-18 nomenclature, *Model Designations of Army Aircraft* (11th Edition, January 1945), prepared by the Air Technical Service Command, indicates the designation "RB-18B" was applied to 10 B-18A aircraft equipped with "special radio equipment SCR-517-T4 (ASV)" as of that date. The "R" prefix indicated this was a "restricted" class of aircraft. The date of this restriction was 22 October 1942. This January 1945 document appears to clarify the earlier designation, in broad use in 1942 and into 1943, of B-18B that appears in AAC/AAF "Special Orders" during the first three years of the war. The original B-18 had transitioned into the slightly improved B-18A version by 1941 and the latter, as selected for modification, would be further transitioned into B-18B variants with the installation of the ASV equipment.

6 The B-18 in its various models has not been treated well by aircraft historians over the years since its birth in 1935. Its combat role in World War II was miniscule when compared to its heavier successors, namely the B-17, the B-24 and the B-29, not to mention the A-20, B-25 and B-26 medium bombers. This oversight was recently corrected by the publication of Dan Hagedorn's *The Douglas B-18 and B-23: America's Forsaken Warriors* (Manchester: Crécy Publishing, 2015). Also, a fine article on the B-18 can be found in *Wings* (Volume Three, Number 4, August 1973). One interesting event reflecting the Douglas inclination for the structural integrity in its design approach involved a B-18 that ditched in the Pacific off Los Angeles. The downed Bolo spent several days afloat and was then towed home to Biscayne Bay by a Pan Am Clipper flying boat. It was pulled on to dry land, repaired and flew again. American taxpayers got quite a lot for the $58,500 they paid in 1937 for each factory fresh B-18.

A second publication that gave the "Bolo" due respect is William Wolf's *Douglas B-18 Bolo—The Ultimate Look: From Drawing Board to U-Boat Hunter* (Atglen, PA: Schiffer Publishing Ltd., 2007). Wolf devotes a major portion of the book to the B-18's critical role in the 1942–1944 anti-submarine fight, noting in some detail the creation of Bid Dolan's 1st Sea-Search Attack Group.

7 The basic history of the B-18, including mention of the ASV B-18B, can be found on two websites: The Aviation History Online Museum (http://aviation-history.com/douglas/b18.html) and the Douglas B-18 Bolo page on Wikipedia (http://en.wikipedia.org/wiki/Douglas_B-18_Bolo). Mentioned are the two preserved B-18s on display as of 2021, a very early production B-18A in the collection of the National Museum of the United States Air Force at Wright-Patterson Air Force Base in Dayton, Ohio, and B-18B 37-505 restored and displayed at McChord Air Museum, McChord Air Force Base, Washington. It is only fitting that, among the five surviving B-18 aircraft,

one B-18B model resides at McChord, the same airfield from which many of the original Dolan aircrews departed for San Antonio with B-18As in February 1942 for the conversion of those aircraft to B-18B configuration.

8   Regarding the B-18 Digby in service with No. 10 Squadron under the RCAF's Eastern Air Command, a quality video rendering of this version in flight can be found at https://youtube/kp1VgbFUiI4. Another seemingly random coincidence is the fact that Colonel Bid Dolan would pass from this world into history near this same location—RCAF Station Gander. The account of his loss appears in a subsequent chapter.

Chapter 2: Rad Lab and Microwave Radar, 1940–43

1   The Rad Lab internal document "B-18-A Report February 13 to July 22, 1941," dated 5 August 1941, prepared by E. K. McMillian and classified "Restricted," describes in detail the progress of Rad Lab engineers in creating a functional microwave system, relocating a working system from a rooftop test site to the installation and testing of that system in an aircraft. Each pulser, magnetron, synchronizer, receiver, spinner, indicator/scope, RF circuit, klystron and power source is described in detail. Demonstrations of the system at Wright Field, Ohio, are summarized as is the conclusion that the system should (then) be capable of detecting targets at eight miles. At this point, as discussed in the text, the Rad Lab airborne microwave radar effort was focused on the detection of aircraft targets for the purpose of airborne interception.

2   James P. Baxter III, *Scientists Against Time* (Boston, MA: Little, Brown and Company, 1947), chapters 2–4.

3   See also Henry E. Guerlac, *History of Radiation Laboratory*, booklet prepared for MIT, 1946; M. P. Clausen, *The Development of Radio and Radar Equipment for Air Operations, 1939–1944*, booklet prepared for MIT, August 1944; John E. Burchard, *Q.E.D—M.I.T. in World War II* (New York, NY: J. Wiley, 1948); and Lincoln. R. Thiesmeyer and John E. Burchard, *Combat Scientists* (Boston, MA: Little, Brown and Company, 1947).

4   *Five Years: At the Radiation Laboratory*, as presented to the members of the Radiation Laboratory by the Massachusetts Institute of Technology, Cambridge, 1946, with part one drawing from the then unfinished manuscript of Dr. Henry E. Guerlac, *History of the Radiation Laboratory*, and part two comprising interviews with Rad Lab division heads and leading technicians. Appended documents include MIT's *Rad Lab Yearbook*, undated but presented under cover of a letter from MIT President Killian dated 2 October 1947.

5   A concise history of radar as the technology that won the war is presented in Robert Buderi's *The Invention That Changed The World: How a Small Group of Radar Pioneers Won the Second World War and Launched a Technical Revolution* (New York, NY: Simon and Schuster, 1996). This book is widely and correctly regarded as the seminal presentation of the political and technical history of radar. Decades after its publication, this book remains the standard reference for all World War II historians attempting to place radar in the context of engagements, campaigns and planning.

6   Interviews and correspondence with Lieutenant Crowell Werner, 1979–82.

7   Chapter one, Sea Search Attack Group Command History, Historical Officer, I Bomber Command, undated but assumed to be mid-1944, as found at www.uboatarchive.net/AAF/SSAGHistoryCH1.htm. This extensive document covers the period June 1942 through April 1944 in a three-chapter, 167-page presentation. As such, it fully captures, on a near real-time basis, the operational and technical achievements of the 1st Sea-Search Attack Group. The command history provides a particular focus on the 64 development "projects" with which the group was tasked, notably new electronics systems under evaluation for possible deployment in various combat commands.

Chapter 3: Langley Field and the 1st Sea-Search Attack Group, June–December 1942

1   Headquarters 4th Air Force Special Order Number 96 of 13 April 1942, as directed by Major General Kenney, provides a list of 42 officers and men reassigned from their West Coast bomber and recon units to Langley Field, Virginia; and Special Order Number 51, of 4 May 1942, which directed these same men to assignment with the 20th Bombardment Squadron based there.

2   The history of Langley Field and the role it played during World War II related to the events described in this book, as well as its contribution to the development of American aircraft technology over the preceding decades, are a matter of history. The inception of the facility begins with the birth of an organization—which would become known as the National Advisory Committee for Aeronautics— in 1915 by an Act of Congress, including an executive group that pressed for the creation of a permanent national aeronautic laboratory. The selection of a site a few miles north of the Newport News Naval Facility allowed funding under the Naval Act of 1917, with the small research center named after Samuel P. Langley, the former Secretary of the Smithsonian Institution. The result of these efforts was the establishment of the Langley Memorial Aeronautical Laboratory in 1924, a facility that would grow from its initial complement of 27 engineers and mechanics to nearly 6,000 employees in 1947. The history of Langley Field is captured well in several publications. Among them are *Langley Field: The Early Years, 1916–1946* (Langley Air Force Base, VA: Office of History, 4500th Air Base Wing, 1977); *The Aircraft of Langley Air Force Base 1917–1977* (Langley Air Force Base, VA: Office of TAC History, 1977), prepared by Tactical Air Command; George Satterfield, *The History of Langley Field Virginia to September 1947* (Langley Air Force Base, VA: Langley Air Force Base Publication, 1957); *A Brief History of Langley Air Force Base 1917–1956* by the USAF Historical Division Research Studies Institute (May 1957); and a recent article in the *Journal of the American Aviation Historical Society* entitled "The National Advisory Committee for Aeronautics— The Formative Years, 1915–1927" by Martin Maisel (Fall 2020). The first publication provides a brief history of the Dolan-era activity and the development at Langley of the LAB programs, while the second profiles the variety of aircraft the field hosted over the years. The third focuses heavily on the World War II years of system development and anti-submarine missions, while the fourth highlights the pre-war years, including the creation of the Army Air Corps in 1926 and the establishment of its General Headquarters Air Force at Langley Field in March 1936. Taken together, these provide a comprehensive account of this important facility as it evolved in the run up to the war years and its accomplishments during that demanding period of America's aviation history. One final publication is worth a brief mention: "Report on Langley Field," drafted by the Army Air Corps Assistant Chief of Staff (A-4), dated May 12, 1943 (CONFIDENTIAL). This memorandum provided a comprehensive survey of the varied activity underway at Langley, but it had as its main purpose the justification for Antisubmarine Command, located in New York City, to assume jurisdiction and operational control over Langley Field and its sub-bases. This reassignment of jurisdiction action would remove Langley from the First Air Force, under whose I Bomber Command it then resided, and all subordinate activity there, including Dolan's ASV unit, and reassign it to the direct control of Antisubmarine Command. As anticipated by this survey, all elements of that New York-based staff endorsed this report with the Headquarters Antisubmarine Command Assistant Chief of Staff (A-3) weighing in with a notation that "the Antisubmarine Command should attempt to absorb the Sea Search Attack Group" at Langley. What is also interesting is the same report and its many attached endorsements uniformly discouraged the suggestion that the Headquarters of the command should itself relocate from New York City to a new home in the semi-remote environs of Langley and the Tidewater area. The report and the commentary found a host of good and suspect reasons why Antisubmarine Command should remain in the "Big Apple" and so it did. The politics of this maneuver aside, the

memo provides a detailed snapshot of Langley Field at the very time the Wright Project aircrews were fine-tuning their LAB skills as they prepared to depart for the Pacific in the weeks ahead.

3   All available records indicate the 1st Sea-Search Attack Group initially contained only one operational squadron, the 2nd Sea-Search Attack Squadron, from the date of its inception until December 1942. This squadron operated between six and 12 B-18B aircraft and, for short periods, tested a wide variety of other radar-equipped aircraft types, including B-25s, B-24s, B-30s and B-17s. In January 1943, the 3rd Sea-Search Attack Squadron was added to the group. This new unit included more than half of the men assigned to the original 2nd Squadron and was apparently formed to provide an independent cadre, at least on paper, for the combat unit being formed for overseas duty in the Pacific, namely the Wright Project.

4   I Bomber Command Special Order 134 of 22 May 1942 instructs Dolan's 20th Bombardment Squadron to relocate 10 B-18 aircraft for anti-submarine combat patrols into the Atlantic and Gulf areas.

5   Correspondence with navigator Crowell B. Werner by author, 1978–80.

6   Special Order Number 249 of 19 September 1942 orders 10 aircraft and crews and a service component—a total of 78 officers and men—to temporarily deploy to Trinidad to provide anti-submarine coverage for the Operation *Torch* convoy. Special Order Number 57, 13 March 1943, awards those men the campaign medal for the American Theater of Operations on the occasion of the Dolan unit's only deployment outside of the continental United States. On this occasion, Dolan apparently elected to take nine B-18s to Trinidad, eight fully capable B-18Bs and one B-18 packed with spare components and engineers, to ensure his unit maintained a high-serviceability rate.

7   The sugar cane field event received a lot of attention from the local newspaper of San Francisco De Macoris, a town located some 90 miles northeast of the nation's capital city of Ciudad Trujillo, including photos of the marooned crew. One of the stranded officers, Lieutenant C. W. "Butch" Werner, a Texas native who spoke "railroad Spanish," stepped in to act as the interpreter. He was also designated as the paymaster for the sugar cane workers, the latter having negotiated a wage of 25 cents per 12-hour day. The payment was provided by the U.S. Embassy in the nation's capital and handed over there to Werner in the local currency. Werner then hand-lugged bags of the coins to the site to pay off the airfield crew. He also found himself responsible for liaison with the local military garrison commander, a bemedaled, portly gentleman who was delighted to arrange for the crew to dine "free of charge" at a local restaurant. More than two years after Bolo 7507 set itself down for a week of rest in the sugar cane field, Werner, who had just returned from a year of combat in the Pacific, found himself called on the carpet at his new assignment at Wright Field. He faced a thickly documented report recommending disciplinary action be initiated against him for alleged fraudulent activity. Apparently, back in October 1942, the Pohan B-18 crew had partied hard at the invitation of their hosts, failed to pay a bar bill at that local eatery and stood accused of having skipped out on a tab of $14.25. The bureaucracy of the U.S. government had caught up with the now Captain Werner who had signed the chit, and government bureaucrats had worked hard to validate the accusation and track down the culprit. Werner was forced to pay the bill plus interest. His career remained undamaged, but his respect for the hard-working diplomats of the wartime State Department deepened.

8   Taped interview with Captain (then Lieutenant) Rockwood in August 1978.

9   *Airview*, Douglas Aircraft Corporation (October 1942): 8–12.

10   Interview with pilot Frank T. E. Reynolds in August 1978.

11   Sea Search Attack Group Command History, I Bomber Command of the First Air Force, undated but believed to be drafted in late 1944.

12   An excellent profile of this aircraft in its service with RAF Coastal Command is found in Dr. Alfred Price's article "Sub Hunter Supreme—The Saga of Liberator AM929" in the fall 2005 edition of the *Flight Journal Special: The B-24 Liberator*. This aircraft was the last of the original batch of 25 Liberators

purchased by the British in 1940 for RAF Coastal Command anti-submarine patrols. In late 1941 and into 1942, several of the Dolan crews had ferried the first aircraft from the consolidated plant in San Diego to Canada for onward movement to the United Kingdom.

13   Interviews and correspondence with several of Colonel Dolan's original Rad Lab and 1st Sea-Search Attack Group members, including James E. Pope, Crowell Werner and others.

14   The crash of the Dolan B-24M has been heavily researched and portions of these air-crash postmortems appear in various print and electronic locations. One after-action report informs that, with the airfield socked in and the weather worsening, the control tower advised Colonel Dolan to avoid a landing attempt and divert to another airfield. This would have meant a backtrack for and likely a delay in the journey to the United Kingdom. The formal report noted that the missing aircraft "… was attempting an instrument approach to this field despite warnings to turn back …" Other accounts noted the airfield Approach Control "strongly advised inbound aircraft to divert to their alternate airfields but, for this Liberator … this was not an option." The crash site was discovered weeks later near Home Pond by a local rabbit trapper and this resulted in a recovery mission. Possibly due to the intensity of the search activity mounted by the USAAF at Gander (the latest version of the highly classified Eagle system was on board), rumors spread for a time that the plane carried a large amount of cash; this tale endured for years.

Three reference points on the Dolan crash are the Gander Airport Historical Society's "The Home Pond B-24" article, available at http://www.ganderairporthistoricalsociety.org/_html_war/ Home.Pond.B24.htm, the Geocaching site writeup of the incident and a CBC newsletter article "The '45 Gander Crash: Left Behind on the Home Front" describing a research project that examined the fate of the families, fiancées and girlfriends of the 10 men who died in the crash.

During World War II, Gander Field was the location of a major transit operation serving the air bridge between the U.S. and the U.K., hosting at times dozens of aircraft shuttling combat units and aircrews forward into the war zone as well as crews meeting there to pick up new aircraft, with B-24 and B-17 bombers prominent among them. Gander's location also facilitated anti-submarine patrols into the Atlantic by the RCAF units stationed there. In addition to the Dolan crash, two other losses were prominent. A Douglas Digby, "742," crashed on 24 July 1941, with no survivors among its crew of six as it returned from convoy patrol, and Liberator AL591, operated by RAF Ferry Command, crashed on 7 February 1943, with 21 crew and passengers on board, 19 of whom perished. The latter aircraft was inbound from Prestwick in England with ferry crews apparently headed to Gander to pick up B-24s for RAF Coastal Command service. This crash involved the largest loss of life at Gander during World War II.

15   "Radar Middleman—Colonel Dolan Knew What Microwave Could Do and Proved It," *Radar* magazine, Volume 9, (30 April 1945), 27. This summary of Dolan's commitment to radar notes that, as he worked to familiarize himself with the demands of the European Theater, he managed to fly 16 combat missions with the Eighth Air Force by the date of his death. It is possible that, at the time this edition of *Radar* went to print in April 1945, the fact that the remains of the B-24 and its 10-man crew had been located was not widely shared. It is also possible Dolan's death and the loss of the latest version of the APQ-7 were then considered restricted information and the details of his death were intentionally left vague.

Chapter 4: Low Altitude Bombing, January–July 1943

1   Command History, First Sea Search Attack Group, Special Project Report Number 13.

2   Special Order Number 285 of 27 October 1942 ordered "minimum crews" to begin flying B-24Ds from Wright Field to Langley Field for assignment with the 1st Sea-Search Attack Group. The Foley crash of one of the first B-24s allocated to the group was a considerable shock to the unit as Foley

was regarded as one of its best pilots, not to mention a close friend of the members of the original collection of "Dolan Boys" from their first days at Boston and Langley.

3   The command history credits Lieutenant Ned B. Estes as having made the original proposal for a radar bombsight on 10 May 1942, which Rad Lab then advanced with the fabrication of a crude, first edition "bread-box" model for further refinement.

4   Command History, Special Project Numbers 20 (LAB) and 52 (IFF Ship to Plane).

5   A magnificent account of all Bell Labs' work is contained in M. D. Fagan (ed.), *A History of Engineering and Science in the Bell System: National Service in War and Peace 1925–1975*, prepared by the Members of the Technical Staff, Bell Telephone Laboratories (New York, NY: Bell Telephone Laboratories, Inc., 1978). In this impressive work, chapter two "RADAR" consumes no less than 114 of the 700 pages.

Chapter 5: The Wright Project, July–August 1943

1   General Orders Number Two, Headquarters First Sea Search Attack Group (H), 2 June 1943. As noted, these orders did not assign or detach from the group to the Wright Project any co-pilot, radar operator, or (two each) aerial gunners. These additional crew members were later assigned by Dolan and Wright after discussions with the command pilots. In the case of the radar operators, Wright insisted on selecting the best 10 in the group. See Appendix C.

2   The B-24 Liberator is one of the most heavily documented and described combat aircraft of World War II, with literally hundreds of books and articles describing its design, evolution, its many variants and its combat history in all theaters of war. Books such as Steve Birdsall's *Log of the Liberators—An Illustrated History of the B-24: The Illustrated Combat Record of the B-24 Liberator and of the Men and Units that Flew in Them in the Second World War* (Garden City, NY: Doubleday & Company, 1973) provide profiles of individual units and aircraft. An earlier Birdsall work, *Famous Aircraft: The B-24 Liberator* (New York, NY: Arco Publishing Co, 1968), was the first book dedicated to this aircraft consumed by this author. Numerous books authored by pre-eminent B-24 historian Allen Blue define every aspect of the aircraft and its many applications in the livery of the U.S. Army Air Forces and U.S. Navy, as well as its impressive service in the hands of the RAF and the Royal Canadian and Australian Air Forces. Many authors have built entire narratives around the aircraft, with personal accounts of the men who went to war in this incredible airplane.

    I have included two bibliographies: "A Liberator Bibliography," focused on the B-24 as an aircraft and the units which operated these machines; and a companion "A General Bibliography." The latter is more comprehensive and recommends publications, most of which address the war in the Pacific and specific events related to the 868th as it moved forward toward Tokyo. Neither list is exhaustive, but each has its own nuggets of useful background information providing context on the aircraft, the men and the campaigns they waged.

3   Headquarters First Sea Search Attack Group (H), Langley Field Virginia, Movement Order Number One, 3 August 1943, includes an attached roster of all Wright Project officers and enlisted men, a comprehensive list of all spare electronic equipment, test sets, beacons and all related equipment "made necessary due to the specialized nature of the basic equipment installed." The shipment of the project's BPS and BGS Beacons, also perfected by Rad Lab, is also reflected in this Movement Order. Special Orders Number 155 of 3 August 1943, as noted in the narrative, complements Movement Order One with a list of all aircraft and aircrews, and is included as Appendix D.

4   The entirety of the Special Orders Number 155, listing each of the 10 aircraft and their 10 entire crew by name and AAF occupation designator, is provided as Appendix D.

5   Several publications cover the evolution and combat history of the Thirteenth Air Force; prominent among them is Kenn C. Rust and Dana Bell, *Thirteenth Air Force Story … in World War II* (Temple City, CA: Historical Aviation Album, 1981). This is nicely supplemented by the 13th Air Force

Veterans Newsletter. A nice photo summary is available in Frederick A. Johnsen, *The Bomber Barons: The History of the 5th Bomb Group in the Pacific During World War II, Volume One—A Pictorial History* (Tacoma, WA: Bomber Books, 1982), while Robert F. Dorr's *B-24 Liberator Units of the Pacific War* (Oxford: Osprey Publishing, 1999) captures the Fifth, Seventh and Thirteenth Air Forces with balanced attention devoted to the exploits of the U.S. Navy Liberators and Privateers at war in the Pacific.

6   A period document authored by Air Force Intelligence Officer Stuart Baldwin in late January 1945, entitled "Short History of the Thirteenth Air Force, January 1943–January 1945," provides an interesting view of the history which Air Force leadership desired to convey to its newly arrived officers and enlisted men when they reported to the Thirteenth Air Force for duty in the Pacific. Distributed to 868th Squadron members on its own letterhead, this account is of course incomplete, based as it was on information available to the drafting officer at that time. The war still had seven months to run and there was more history to be made but, by this point, the Thirteenth had a history to tell.

Chapter 6: Guadalcanal, August–September 1943

1   Report of Mission No. 73, 5th Bomb Group, 13th Air Force. Other mission reports as cited.

2   During the period 1 October–31 December 1943, the surviving eight aircraft, aircrews, and ground elements of the Wright Project had at least two designations. In official orders they were the "5th Bomb Group Provisional Squadron (Heavy)" and in 5th Bomb Group Mission Reports, they were often referenced as the "5th Group Project Group." One instance of the latter is the 5th Bomb Group Consolidated Mission Report (189) of 4 November 1943 which cites one SB-24 as accompanying and guiding aircraft from two of that group's squadrons in a daylight attack on a convoy. Other accounts of the 5th Bomb Group refer to Wright Project aircraft as assigned to the 394th Squadron through December 1943, even though all Wright Project aircraft and crews were disassociated from this daylight squadron as of 1 October 1943.

3   Interesting accounts of the effectiveness of radar-guided night attacks are presented from the Japanese perspective by Imperial Japanese Navy (IJN) Captain Tameichi Hara in his book, *Japanese Destroyer Captain* (New York, NY: Ballantine Books, 1961), and IJN Captain Jenji Orita in his book, *I-Boat Captain* (Chatsworth, CA: Major Books, 1977). Captain Hara, on pages 208–211, describes the Rabaul to Tuluva transport run by his destroyer *Shigure* under the cover of darkness and foul weather. He notes the horror he experienced on the bridge of his ship as a radar bomber struck out of the night, seemingly at mast height, to deliver a low-level attack. The *Shigure* survived this attack but other Japanese ships on other nights in these same waters were not so fortunate. Captain Orita makes frequent reference to nighttime attacks on his submarines and details several instances when patrolling aircraft used radar to detect surfaced submarines at great distances and then "swoop in like eagles to attack them." Not unlike their U-boat brethren, the ASV radar and the LAB Liberators had stripped away the cloak of night that had protected surfaced Japanese submarines for the first year and a half of the war. Radar attack had come to the war in the Pacific and it would increase in its intensity.

Chapter 7: Battles in The Slot, October–December 1943

1   One of Colonel Wright's interviews appeared in the April 1944 edition of the (CONFIDENTIAL) Rad Lab publication *Radar*, entitled "Low Altitude, High Precision" with a subtitle "Radar Bombing Blends Them to Strike Dispersed Jap Shipping." In a question-and-answer format with *Radar*, Wright provided the basics of the LAB program, lauds the technology and the technicians and profiles a

couple of missions. The article notes the critical roles played by lead radar officer Captain E. E. Barriere and civilian technicians E. H. Sharkey and H. L. Clark.

A photo of the Rockwood crew appears in front of their aircraft, with the antennas blanked over and the aircraft's name truncated to *Madame Libby*, the censors omitting, for obvious reasons, the balance of the aircraft's name, *the Sea Ducer*. The APQ-5 is pictured and Wright's comments are drawn from his report covering the 27 August–2 October 1943 period. Of interest, the *Radar* story only appeared some seven months after Wright's return from Guadalcanal. This delay was an obvious by-product of the U.S. Army Air Force's reluctance to share radar-related operational information, even in the restricted distribution and classified *Radar* publication.

2 Special Orders Number 111, 5th Bombardment Group, 19 October 1943, confirms Lieutenants Charles Conrad and Vince Splane as "Principal Pilots B-24D type airplane by order of Colonel Unruh, Commanding." Splane and Sumner were both well known to Unruh and personally selected by him to replenish the Wright Project's lead pilot shortfall in September 1943.

3 Official records and technical reports list several variations in the name used by the Wright Project during the period 1 October–30 December 1943, including the "Fifth Bomb Group Project" and the "Fifth AAF Bombardment Group Provisional Squadron (H)." These two names appear on various records, but it seems the former was in wider use. In any case, the unit retained a high degree of independence under XIII Bomber Command and was not mission-subordinate to the 5th Bomb Group as it waited for the balance of 1943 to be confirmed as an independent squadron with a numbered identity.

4 The IFF triggering problem was the source of continuing concern and technical investigation by the electronic specialists of the Wright Project. A 20 November 1943 technical report by civilian technician E. H. Sharkey discussed this issue but reached no conclusions other than the random IFF triggering remained a problem and as such presented a danger to the aircraft.

5 "Guadalcanal: APQ-5 Created for Work on the Line," *Radar*, no. 1 (April 1944): 25.

6 Sumner's initial contact was made at position 40°40'S 152°37'E. Sumner and Splane's attacks, particularly the latter on *Haguro*, are related in Hara's *Japanese Destroyer Captain*, 230–240. More complete accounts of the battle of Empress Augusta Bay can be found in John Prados's *Islands of Destiny: The Solomons Campaign and the Eclipse of the Rising Sun* (New York, NY: NAL Caliber, 2012) and Paul S. Dull's *A Battle History of the Imperial Japanese Navy (1941–1945)* (Annapolis, MD: Naval Institute Press, 1978). The Japanese refer to these two battles as the battle of Gazelle Bay and the battle of Cape St. George, respectively. Vince Splane's personal account of the events of that night are provided in Chapter 10 of this book.

7 Later in the war, *Haguro* participated in the battle of the Philippine Sea and the battle of Leyte Gulf. During the latter, from 22–26 October 1944, *Haguro* was part of the First Mobile Striking Force that was turned away from the U.S. invasion fleet in the battle off Samar and, in retreating from that surface action, was hit by airstrikes from AAF B-24s and U.S. Navy carrier aircraft. By February 1945, only two of the original 18 Class A heavy cruisers with which Japan began the war remained in fighting condition and *Haguro* was one of these "lucky survivors." Based in Singapore, the cruiser was dispatched into the Indian Ocean to resupply a Japanese garrison marooned on the Andaman Islands. As the most powerful Japanese Navy warship remaining in the southeast Asia area, *Haguro* was much hunted by the British fleet that had by then returned to the region, to the degree that Operation *Dukedom*, or the "Hunt for the *Haguro*," became that fleet's focus. In the dash to the Andamans, *Haguro* was tracked by both British carrier aircraft and an RAF B-24 scout, and later ambushed by five destroyers of the Royal Navy's 26th Flotilla. Raked by gunfire and hit by no fewer than four torpedoes, *Haguro* sank in the dark of night to a watery grave. Sitting upright 200 feet down on the ocean floor, the wreck is just 50 miles southwest of Penang, Malaysia. An exceptionally detailed account of the Japanese Class A cruisers appeared in *Warship International* (*WI*) in a seven-part series

by Dr. E. Lacroix. See in particular *WI*, no. 31984, Part IV. See also the *Haguro* entry at https://www.combinedfleet.com which provides the Tabular Record of Movement (TROM) for this ship. For all its detail, this TROM fails to include mention of the SB-24 attack on *Haguro*, during the cruiser's approach to the battle of Empress Augusta Bay, and the impact of the Liberator's attack on the course of the battle.

8   Various accounts of Admiral Kurita's ill-fated run between Truk and Rabaul credit a night encounter off New Ireland with a patrol bomber and a possible attack, but it is not clear such a sighting or even attack was made by a Wright Project SB-24. Three SB-24s were up that night and one was assigned the sector northwest of New Ireland in the very area through which Kurita's cruisers and destroyers were steaming at that hour.

9   As mentioned, on Mission 154, Rockwood carried as his observer Colonel Edwin E. Aldrin, then temporarily designated Air Corps Inspector General of the Thirteenth Air Force. We have met Colonel Aldrin before, at MIT's Rad Lab, at Wright Field, at Langley Field and at AAC/AAF Headquarters in Washington, D.C. In a sense, Aldrin was the Wright Project's "Godfather," the man who had supported Bid Dolan and nominated Stud Wright to take the project to the Pacific. Aldrin's son, USAF Colonel Edwin Eugene Aldrin Jr, was the second man to walk on the moon. The men of the Wright Project who were befriended by Colonel Aldrin and dined at the family table in 1943, knew young "Buzz" as a high school junior and standout athlete, but none could have expected this young man would walk on the moon as part of the *Apollo 11* crew 26 years later.

10   Imperial Japanese Navy submarine RO-100 was lost on about 25 November in the general area of Bougainville. Six additional submarines—I-182, I-25, RO-38, I-21, I-39 and I-40—were lost without a trace in this theater during the period September–November 1943. Four of these disappeared in late November. Brown's 27/28 November attack at 40°30'S 154°00'E probably claimed one of these submarines and it is possible other Wright Project attacks damaged or sank the other missing submarines. The loss of these boats is discussed in Orita and Harrington's *I-Boat Captain* (Chatsworth, CA: Major Books, 1976), 173–201.

11   The extent to which the United States was able to break the Japanese Navy and Army coded and encrypted messages during the period 1942–45 is only recently, with the use of declassified material, being fully appreciated and documented for the lay historian. An excellent and highly detailed overview of the U.S. success in this area and its contribution to the Allied victory in the Pacific is provided in John Prados's *Combined Fleet Decoded: The Secret History of American Intelligence and the Japanese Navy in World War II* (New York, NY: Random House, 1995).

    Two additional publications, Ronald Lewin's *The American Magic: Codes, Ciphers and the Defeat of Japan* (Harmondsworth: Penguin, 1983) and W. J. Holmes's *Doubled Edged Secrets: U.S. Naval Intelligence Operations in the Pacific during World War II* (Annapolis, MD: Naval Institute Press, 2012), are highly recommended. In many instances, code breaking not only allowed U.S. military planners an inside view of Japanese plans, but also provided tactical commanders with the timely, highly detailed information they required to direct Allied aircraft, submarines and surface ships to arrive at a given point to engage enemy ships and aircraft. The downing of Fleet Admiral Isoroko Yamamoto in April 1943 by a Thirteenth Air Force interception flight led by Major John Mitchell is but one example of the tactical and strategic advantage provided by the code-breaking effort. In sum, the combination of the forewarning provided by broken codes and the tactical advantage provided throughout the war by air and surface radar systems proved decisive.

12   Fifth Bomb Group Consolidated Mission Report Number 159 includes a very detailed description of this SB-24-led attack on the convoy, including the loss of one B-24 shot down and a second which crashed upon landing at Munda. The latter event is described in considerable detail as are the sustained attacks by the Japanese fighters on the 22 B-24s that made bomb runs over the convoy.

13 Splane's attack (Mission 213) was made at position 3°25'S 131°E. After its first attack, the SB-24 was able to retire out of anti-aircraft fire range and watch on the SCR-717 scope as the other vessels in the convoy converged on the stationary damaged target to take off personnel. The second vessel attacked by Splane also burned "like a Roman candle."

14 Unknown at the time and, for the duration of the war, to the men of the Thirteenth Air Force, Colonel Unruh's flak-damaged aircraft crash-landed just south of Rabaul near the shore of a Japanese-occupied island. Unruh and the other surviving crew members were captured by the Japanese Army and barged to Rabaul. Unruh was flown to Tokyo for enhanced interrogation and survived the war to be released after VJ Day. The rest of the survivors were held on Rabaul for the duration of the war and were summarily executed shortly before the Japanese surrender in August 1945. Unruh continued his Air Force career after the war, serving in one posting, at his request, as the Air Force Attaché in the American Embassy in Tokyo. One of the Wright Project command pilots, Frank Reynolds, visited Colonel Unruh in the latter's retirement years in his hometown of Pretty Prairie, Kansas. Reynolds found him at work building his own small airplane. Unruh had retired from the USAF as a colonel and prospered in retirement. He harbored no resentment toward the Japanese he had fought over Rabaul and in the Solomons. As Wright Project command pilot "Rocky" Rockwood said in an interview with this author, "Colonel Unruh was a great pilot, a born leader and a best friend. I was honored and pleased to sit alongside him in those B-24 missions up the Saint Georges Channel [*sic*] to Rabaul, or to wherever he led his 5th Bomb Group."

Chapter 8: Munda and Rabaul, December 1943–March 1944

1 Rabaul did not come by the title "Fortress Rabaul" lightly. It is worth noting the Japanese saw this extensive base, with its five airfields complementing one of the finest harbors in the South Pacific, as their single most important outer island facility after Truk. From Rabaul, the Japanese fleet could project power to the south into New Guinea and beyond to Australia proper, and to the southwest to invade the New Hebrides and New Caledonia to sever the sea route that linked America with Australia. In early 1944, Rabaul, although worn down by the relentless attacks of the Thirteenth and Fifth Air Forces and the slashing U.S. carrier strikes, remained a powerhouse of military capability and a fortress-in-being should Japan elect to reinforce it. John Prados's excellent recounting of this period of the Pacific War, *Islands of Destiny*, places the importance of Rabaul in the context of the overall struggle. He also notes that determination with which Japan sought to make Rabaul impregnable over the two years they had occupied it. Bruce Gamble's *Rabaul Trilogy* devotes three full volumes to Rabaul alone, building his five-year narrative around this formidable Japanese base and the role it played in the Pacific War. It is also not an understatement to comment that, as much as General MacArthur and his Southwest Pacific Command, including his Fifth Air Force Commander George Kenney, would have liked to destroy and capture this one-time critical outpost of Imperial Japan, any such attempt would have been extremely costly in men and material. Beyond that cost, such an effort likely would have disrupted the overall timeline of the Pacific War and delayed the arrival of the Allies at Japan's doorstep. MacArthur's service counterparts in the Pacific, including Admiral Chester Nimitz and his superior in Washington D.C., U.S. Army Chief General Marshall, recognized this and convinced their Southwest Pacific commander the war's end would be best served by a strategy that neutralized, bypassed and isolated the Japanese outpost. Prados notes that "The reduction of Rabaul by means of aerial attack … became the main function of AIRSOLS and the Thirteenth Air Force …", 65, with that tempo of attack measured in sorties over Rabaul increasing from 41 in November 1943, to 394 in December 1943, to 2,865 in January 1944. The pounding and "hold-down" of Rabaul would continue at this pace for months, peaking in the April–June 1944 period.

2   Unit History of the 868th Bombardment Squadron (Heavy)—Activation, on 1 January 1944, by authority contained in General Order 496, 16 December 1943, and by General Order 67, Thirteenth Air Force, 26 December 1943, with Major Leo J. Foster designated Squadron Commander. The station of activation was Munda, New Georgia Island, Solomon Islands. Also, Special Orders Number 10, Thirteenth Air Force, 12 January 1944, permanently reassigned various officers and men from the 5th Bomb Group to the 868th Squadron to complete the latter's transition to an independent unit under XIII Bomber Command. Special Orders Number 2 of 1 January 1944 directed the following appointments for the newly formed squadron: Major Francis B. Carlson (Executive Officer), Captain Ned B. Estes (Squadron Bombardier), Captain Franklin T. E. Reynolds (Operations Officer S-3), Captain Charles L. Rockwood (Assistant Operations Officer), Captain William P. Schuber (Squadron Navigator), 1st Lt. Edward W. Ackley (Intelligence Officer), 1st Lt. Fred S. Howell (Radio (V) Officer) and Captain Ernest R. Barriere (Radio (S) Officer noted as serving attached from XIII Bomber Command).

3   This attack is described from the perspective of the crew's radar operator in Chapter 13.

4   The roster of all combat crews and operations officers of the 868th Bombardment Squadron presented on 21 March 1944 in Special Orders Number 33 provides a comprehensive account of the 17 crews and officer assignments as of that date. Notably, eight of the original Wright Project crews remain on this roster, despite some changes to their composition.

5   The full text of the instruction reads: "Headquarters Army Air Base Langley Field Virginia (Classification: Restricted) Special Order 23 of 23 January 1944 directs the movement of two aircrew and aircraft of Project Number 96289-Restricted, then assigned to the 3rd Search Attack Squadron (Heavy) to the Pacific Theater, as follows: Crew Number FK-413-AM-1, 2nd LT PHILLIP HOFFMAN, 1024 (pilot) and Crew Number FK-413-AM-2, 1st LT ARTHUR DELAND, 1024 (pilot)." Individual crews were subsequently directed to proceed from the West Coast to their forward stations, in this case based on Headquarters, Station Number 10, Pacific Wing, Air Transport Command, Fairfield-Suisun Army Air Field, Operations Order Number 28 (SECRET) of 2 February 1944, which further directs the DeLand aircrew and aircraft to proceed to Carney Field, Guadalcanal, for a "permanent change of station" with assignment to the Thirteenth Air Force:

B-24J #42-73396 Crew #FK-413-AM-2

1st LT ARTHUR A. DELAND	0-796332	P
2nd LT EDWARD P. SNEAD	0-680523	CP
2nd LT GERARD R. WESTERLAND	0-801047	N
2nd LT HOWARD T. BLACKWELDER	0-676408	B
T/SGT WILLARD A. BRYANT	31139412	RADIO OPERATOR
SGT JACOB L. JONES	11114314	RADAR OPERATOR
S/SGT ALAN S. ROSENTHAL	34355122	AE
SGT HENRY C. JOHNSON	18045753	G
SGT GEORGE L. MANCHESTER	3226065	G
T/SGT WELDON W. RICHARDS	18126823	E

6   Multiple discussions, taped interviews and correspondence with 868th command pilots Don Thomson, Earle Smith, Vince Splane, Charles Rockwood and Art DeLand during the 1978–82 period.

Chapter 9: Mighty Truk, Deadly Truk, March–June 1944

1   These decisions related to the Central Pacific offensive are extremely well covered in Ian W. Toll's *The Conquering Tide: War in the Pacific Islands, 1942–1944* (New York, NY: W. W. Norton & Company, 2015) and are also vividly related in the late, great James D. Hornfischer's *The Fleet at Flood Tide: America at Total War in the Pacific, 1944–1945* (New York, NY: Bantam Books, 2016).

2   The Associated Press story on the Thomson–DeLand strike on Truk, datelined "Advanced South Pacific Bomber Base, Thirteenth Air Force, March 29 (Delayed)," quoted Don Thompson (*sic*) as saying, "We caught them with their pants down!" The story did provide a full listing of the entire Thomson crew, including crew positions and hometowns, and identified Art DeLand as the pilot that attacked second. The week before, a MacArthur command publication generated in Australia, *Guinea Gold*, provided, in its 19 February 1944 edition, intense coverage of the TF 58 attack by Mitscher's fast carriers on Truk. Headlined "Great Japanese Naval Base of Truk Attacked by Large U.S. Task Force—'Landing Made' Says Japan High Command," the story quoted a *New York Times* article praising Pacific Fleet Admiral Chester Nimitz as "a bold, courageous leader and a master of surprise tactics." The same *Guinea Gold* edition (Vol 2, No 93) noted a recent successful attack on a six-ship convoy bound for Rabaul, which had been located and struck some 130 miles northwest of New Ireland by a "Liberator on night reconnaissance." The dark-of-night attack damaged a tanker and destroyer, leaving the daylight "waves of B-24 Liberators and B-25 Mitchells" to polish off the convoy. A reasonable assumption is that this release related the previously described February LAB strikes by the Bryan and Rockwood crews as they patrolled the areas north of Kavieng.

3   Report—Historical Data—868th Bomb Squadron (Heavy) of 10 July 1944.

4   *Dumbo*, of course named after Disney's flying elephant, was also the code name for air–sea rescue (ASR) missions, initially by land-based aircraft carrying lifeboats. The term was eventually applied to all ASR operations, but also became a nickname for the Consolidated PBY Catalina, which was used extensively as an ASR aircraft.

5   Report—Historical Data—868th Bomb Squadron (Heavy), 10 July 1944. The Haynes crew included radar operator Staff Sergeant Thomas Peden, a member of the newly arrived Binford crew. Tom Peden was on his first mission, riding alongside Haynes's regular radar operator, Robert Beatty, in a familiarization mission. Navigator and First Lieutenant Gerald Westerland, a veteran member of the Art DeLand crew, was also with the Haynes crew that night. He had volunteered to replace the crew's usual navigator who had fallen ill that day. He would be the only member of the DeLand crew lost in action during that crew's combat tour in the Pacific.

6   Squadron Orders Number 73, 26 June 1944, appointment of Summary Court Officers to inventory and dispose of personal effects of the Haynes crew, with all crew listed. Appendix F provides the text of this document.

7   As further testament to the ruggedness of the Wagner crew that survived this ordeal at sea, some 30 years later seven of the eight men were still alive and active members of the 868th Bombardment Squadron Association, a vibrant veterans' group operating under the leadership of Dr. Vince Splane. Sadly, the Wagner crew bombardier, then Captain Charles R. Goerke, had died in July 1945 during an operational crash at Langley Field, Virginia, while acting as an instructor on B-29 systems.

8   Interviews and correspondence with Charles Whitmore and Vince Splane during 1979–80.

9   The formal designation of the later production version of the night fighter that would have operated in the South and Central Pacific from the summer of 1944 was the Nakajima J1N1-S Gekkō Model 11, referenced in Rene J. Francillon's exceptional work, *Japanese Aircraft of the Pacific War* (London: Putnam & Company, 1979). Another reference is Ikuhiko Hata and Yasuho Izawa's *Japanese Naval Aces and Fighter Units in World War II* (Shrewsbury: Airlife, 1990). In the latter publication, it is unclear which air group, 251, 351, or another, would have flown against the 868th Squadron's SB-24s in various locations, including Truk, during that February–July 1944 period when the squadron lost so many aircraft and crews. It is clear Gekkō pilots found the B-24 to be a vulnerable target given the Liberator's relatively slow speed and the medium and lower altitudes at which its formations normally operated. In the spring and summer of 1945, the Gekkō would find the faster, more rugged, better armed and higher-flying B-29s a much more difficult opponent. This occurred even as Gekkōs were equipped with the first sets of AI radar and attempted to blunt the U.S. Army Air Force attacks over the Japanese homeland with better tactics. The world's only surviving Gekkō, painstakingly restored

by the Smithsonian's National Air and Space Museum (NASM), can be viewed at the museum's Annex, the Steven F. Udvar-Hazy Center in Chantilly, Virginia, located near Dulles International Airport. The full history of this unusual type, including the details of the NASM aircraft's postwar recovery from Japan and movement to the United States for evaluation and its later restoration, is related in Robert C. Mikesh and Osamu Tagaya's *Moonlight Interceptor: Japan's "Irving" Night Fighter* (Washington, D.C.: Smithsonian Institution Press, 1985). Robert Mikesh was the Senior Curator at the NASM and Osamu Tagaya is a Japanese aerospace historian.

10 The loss related to Palau is covered in Chapter 11.

Chapter 10: Vince Splane and Devil's Delight, September 1943–March 1944

1 Special Orders Number 32 (RESTRICTED), Headquarters 11th Ferrying Group, Hamilton Field, 20 May 1943, detailing Shipment AH-707-AA for movement of 25 AAF officers from Fort Worth Army Airfield to Hamilton Field for overseas assignment.

2 Espiritu Santo, or "Buttons" to the warriors at Guadalcanal, was the fictionalized locale for James Michener's *Tales of the South Pacific*, which later became a stage play, and the Hammerstein musical, *South Pacific*. As a major rear-area base for the U.S. Navy, the Marines and the U.S. Army throughout the Pacific War, remaining so even as the war moved to the western Pacific, the area accumulated vast stockpiles of supplies and equipment. When Japan surrendered, the U.S. military closed up shop, said farewell to the locals and headed home. They also dumped most of their military and naval equipment, much of it brand new, into the ocean at a location now dubbed "Million Dollar Point." The former American President Lines passenger vessel, converted to wartime use as a troopship, SS *President Coolidge*, sank here in October 1942 after steaming into a friendly minefield. Like the Million Dollar Point collection of disposed of wartime equipment, this ship remains one of Vanuatu's most popular diving spots and tourist attractions.

3 Lieutenant Colonel Robert Westbrook was the leading fighter pilot of the Thirteenth Air Force's XIII Fighter Command, with a dozen confirmed victories when Vince Splane met him on leave in New Zealand. He flew with the 44th Fighter Squadron, the leading squadron of that Air Force, and was later credited with 16 victories during the war. Westbrook was killed in action on 22 November 1944 off Makassar in the Philippines while attacking a convoy at low level in his P-38 Lightning.

Chapter 11: Munda to Momote, April–June 1944

1 The survivors of the Rauch crew were rescued by a Consolidated Aircraft PB2Y-3 Coronado, most likely one operating with U.S. Navy Patrol Squadron VPB-13. This unit was then based in the area of the Marshall Islands, typically patrolling 600–900 miles from their base areas. Rauch's crew losses included bombardier Flight Officer John Perino, radio operator Warren Wolter and gunner Cecil Brown.

2 Many of the officers and enlisted men completed their tours with the 868th under the impression the good and proper Captain Ackley, with his barely intelligible heavy Boston accent, was English. This presumption was reinforced when the captain frequently admonished "Snooper," when the mascot relieved himself outside the intelligence tent, with a firm, "Snoooooooper, one does not squat to peeeee." It was noted that Snooper also apparently did not understand his master's voice as he continued to wander, squat and pee randomly throughout the squadron bivouac area. Snooper would move along with the squadron for a year or more, only to disappear somewhere between Morotai and Okinawa. Unkind squadron wags suggested the terrier may have ended up roasting on someone's spit.

3   Special Orders Number 33, 868th Bombardment Squadron (Heavy), roster of officers and enlisted men with combat crews indicated, 21 March 1944.

4   Headquarters Thirteenth Air Force Special Orders Number 99, 8 April 1944, directed "TD Trip Number 69" from APO 719 (Munda) to APO 715 (Sydney) and return via C-87 airplane, at "Priority 1" status. The orders covered 18 officers and men of the 868th and the 106th Reconnaissance Squadrons. On these same orders, 12 airmen of the 12th and 63rd Troop Carrier Squadrons were authorized similar temporary duty travel, but instead of C-87 transport were sent "GAT-Priority 1." Given these men were assigned to C-47 squadrons, one might assume they had already arranged their own transport and did not suffer any delays in either getting to Sydney or returning home, and probably arrived on day 14 at their APO 708 (New Hebrides) station.

5   Momote, located on Los Negros Island, was the site of a Japanese airfield constructed during their advance into the New Guinea area, on the aborted march to cut Australia out of the war. The Japanese called both the island and the airfield "Hayne Airdrome." It was invaded on 2 March 1944 by the U.S. Army's 1st Cavalry Division in one evolution of MacArthur's Admiralty Island offensive. The U.S. Navy 40th Naval Construction Battalion (Seabees) moved in to build out the facility and converted the primitive airstrip to a bomber-capable 7,800-foot runway with revetments and fuel depots, expanding it to a major aircraft repair and overhaul facility. The latter provided basing for U.S. Army Air Force, U.S. Navy and Royal Australian Air Force air groups for offensive operations throughout the region, and later served as a major basing complex for operations to the west and north, including the invasion of the Philippines.

6   *The United States Strategic Bombing Survey (Pacific), The Campaigns of the Pacific War*, July 1946, was drafted pursuant to a Presidential Directive and was compiled in Japan, based on U.S. war records and interviews with former Japanese officers. The MacArthur-led General Headquarters in Tokyo heavily influenced the content and conclusions of this study with obvious implications for its main themes and the conclusions reached.

7   Report—Historical Data, 868th Bomb Squadron (H), 10 July 1944.

8   The assignment of the men of the 419th, on an "Attached Combat Personnel" basis, is reflected in the Special Order 33 of 21 March 1944 combat roster document, which includes 10 non–868th men assigned as of that date.

9   Terry M. Mays, *Night Hawks and Black Widows: 13th Air Force Night Fighters in the South and Southwest Pacific, 1943–1945* (Atglen, PA: Schiffer Publishing Ltd., 2009). Complementing this excellent book, a relevant account of U.S. night fighter operations in World War II is provided in a monograph, Stephen L. McFarland's *Conquering the Night: Army Air Forces Night Fighters at War* (Washington, D.C.: Air Force History and Museums Program, 1998) accessible on the Hyper War website at http://www.ibiblio.org/hyperwar/AAF/AAF-Night/index.html. This narrative discusses the delayed deployment of the P-61 Black Window aircraft to the Pacific and, with its arrival in mid-1944, the improved performance offered by that aircraft's SCR-720 airborne radar system. The earlier night fighter efforts on Guadalcanal and subsequent locations with the P-38s and P-70s with far less optimal radar solutions, including that of the 419th, are related as well.

10 Logistics officer "Nick" Nixon apparently operated "Nick's Hamburger Stand." The aforementioned Mays notes that former 419th Squadron pilot Dick Stewart, in his postwar career as a commercial pilot, coincidentally flew for the Nixon Presidential campaign in 1968, piloting the aircraft of vice president candidate Spiro Agnew. He was invited to President Nixon's inauguration and relived their encounters a quarter of a century before in the Bougainville combat area and the informal hamburger stand on Green Island.

11 As mentioned, the consolidation of the Fifth and Thirteenth Air Forces under the FEAF banner on 15 June 1944 had been a long-time objective of the charismatic and nonstop self-promoter, Fifth Air Force Commander Lieutenant General Kenney. A cursory reading of Kenney's autobiographical and

congratulatory *General Kenney Reports, USAF Warrior Studies*, originally published in 1949, leaves no doubt MacArthur could not have won the Pacific War without Kenney at his right shoulder, advising "Mac" of his every decision and correcting most of his deficits in the nick of time. *General Kenney Reports* may well be the most egotistical book ever written, even by the standards set by MacArthur and his staff during and after the war. The Pacific War was, the Kenney account says, basically a "George and Doug" show all the way to Tokyo.

In the decades after the war, as some Thirteenth Air Force veterans read and reread official accounts of the conflict, they drew the unhappy conclusion that their "Jungle Air Force" had pretty much been written out of the conflict by Kenney, MacArthur and U.S. Air Force historians. Fair or not, the Kenney approach to publicly promote his Air Force and his own persona throughout the conflict, went a long way to forming this impression.

Chapter 12: The Art DeLand Crew and 396, April–June 1944

1   Headquarters Army Air Base Langley Field, Virginia, instruction ("Roster") dated 23 January 1943, related to Special Order 23, Headquarters movement instruction, for 3rd Search Attack Squadron (H) Project Number 96289R listing Crew Number FK-413-AM-1 (Philip A. Hoffman and 10-man crew) and Crew Number FK-413-AM-2 (Arthur A. DeLand and 10-man crew).

2   Headquarters, Station Number 10, Pacific Wing, Air Transport Command, Fairfield-Suisun Army Air Field, Fairfield, California, Operations Order Number 28, 2 February 1944, in connection with Project 96289-Restricted, directing the DeLand crew to proceed to Carney Field, Guadalcanal, for assignment to the Thirteenth Air Force.

3   This generation's adoption of the "Whiffenpoof Song," a tune that had been around in one form or another since the turn of the century, related to the popularity of a 1937 version sung by legendary crooner Rudy Vallée. The song was carried into the many fronts of the war by young men sent overseas to fight. It was reborn by singer Bing Crosby in 1947 and in subsequent years was broadly associated with World War II. It provides solemn background music in the 1949 movie *12 O'clock High* in which Gregory Peck starred as an Eighth Air Force bomber commander over Europe. It surfaced again in 1975 as the opening theme for the TV series *Baa Baa Black Sheep* which depicted the exploits of U.S. Marine Squadron VMF-214 flying F4U Corsairs in the South Pacific. At Yale University, "The Whiffenpoof Song" has traditionally been the closing number of the resident choral group, the Yale Whiffenpoofs.

4   Headquarters Far Eastern Air Forces Special Orders Number 181 of 12 December 1944 listed DeLand in company with 43 other Fifth and Thirteenth Air Force officers departing the Southwest Pacific Area of Operations.

5   In the book and in public discussions by its author, this lady's name was presented as Ruth Mills Simmons, a pseudonym employed at her request. The compelling claim was that Virginia Tighe (her real name) had a vivid recollection of a past life in Ireland some 150 years before. Under hypnosis she could recall, often in incredible detail, the life that had been lived by that long-passed County Cork personality, one Bridey Murphy. This particular instance of a "past life experience" on the part of Virginia Tighe was judged by many experts to be a case of cryptomnesia. The controversy and the mystery that surrounded Bridey Murphy, Ruth Mills Simmons and Virginia Tighe is well presented at http://en.wikipedia.org/wiki/Bridey.Murphy.

Chapter 13: Radar Reflections, 1943–44

1   *Snooper News*, Volume 14, March 1981, and correspondence with Floyd Hune, 1979–81.

2   MCCLENNAN SIGNED ARNOLD Radiogram, CONFIDENTIAL, 2 April 1944, and Letter of Commendation to Captain Charles Rockwood, 10 April 1944, referencing the Arnold radiogram, among other such Letters of Commendation to 868th Squadron radar personnel.

3   Interview and correspondence with Horace Sullivan, 1978–80.

4   Orders 21.22 Commendation, Headquarters Thirteenth Bomber Command, 17 June 1944.

5   Special Orders Number 2, 868th Bomb Squadron (Heavy) of 1 January 1944; Squadron Orders Number 73 of 26 June 1944; Special Orders Number 110 of 14 October 1944; Special Orders Number 217 of 7 August 1944; and Special Orders Number 278 of 22 January 1945.

Chapter 14: Ever Forward Toward Tokyo, July–September 1944

1   Historical Data, 868th Bomb Squadron (Heavy), 8 August 1944.

2   Headquarters Thirteenth Air Force, Special Orders Number 232, 19 August 1944, return to continental U.S. by Government Air Transportation or military aircraft of 20 officers and men, including Curran, Pope, Werner and others.

3   Analysis of Strike Record for Captain Charles Rockwood of the 868th Squadron prepared for Commanding General, XIII Bomber Command, APO 719 on 22 July 1944.

4   Office of the Chief Engineer, General Headquarters, Army Forces, Pacific, *Engineers in Theater Operations—Engineers of the Southwest Pacific 1941–1945, Volume I* (General Headquarters Army Forces Pacific, Tokyo, Japan: U.S. Army, 1947), provides detailed information on the planning and execution of engineering work at Noemfoor, as well as efforts in the Admiralities (Los Negros/Momote) and subsequent activity at Morotai and the Philippines.

5   Standard Mission Report 868-323/322 of the 868th Bomb Squadron, 22 September 1944, three SB-24 aircraft to Menado in the Celebes Group.

6   Annex to Mission Report 868-312, 868th Squadron Officer of Intelligence Officer, 13 September 1944.

7   Annex to Mission Report 868-323, 868th Squadron Officer of Intelligence Officer, 24 September 1944.

8   "The Last Flight of Lt. Thomas Philbrick—868th Bomber Squadron, Robert W. Philbrook," accessed 2001, http://www.philbrick-genealogy.org.

9   Annex to Mission Report 868-325, 868th Squadron Intelligence Officer, 1 October 1944.

10 868th Bomb Squadron Historical Data for September Missions, 8 October 1944.

Chapter 15: Balikpapan and Makassar Strait, October 1944

1   Hornfischer, *The Fleet at Flood Tide* and Ian W. Toll, *Twilight of the Gods: War in the Western Pacific, 1944–1945* (New York, NY: W. W. Norton & Company, 2020), each offer fine detail and great perspective on the Pacific War from mid-1944 to its conclusion.

2   Referring to the series of raids on the oil refineries around Ploeşti, Romania (now Ploieşti), the most famous and costly of which was Operation *Tidal Wave* on 1 August 1943.

3   Rust and Bell, *Thirteenth Air Force Story … in World War II*, 37–43.

4   Historical Data for September 1944, 868th Bombardment Squadron (Heavy) (SECRET), missions of 27, 28 and 29 September 1944.

5   "Window" was thin pieces of aluminum-backed paper that would reflect radar signals, hopefully swamping and confusing radar screens and their operators with thousands of returns and effectively shielding the true nature of the incoming formation.

6 Balikpapan had been struck before by B-24 Liberators in August 1943 in a series of raids by the newly formed 380th Bomb Group of the Fifth Air Force. Beginning on 13 August, it sent 12 "Flying Circus" aircraft from Darwin, Australia, due west on a 17-hour mission, each with six 500-pound bombs tucked in its belly. Eight of the planes made it to the target to hit ships in the harbor and damage oil facilities. A two-aircraft reconnaissance followed on the 16th and this set up a final nine-airplane mission on the 18th. These three runs at Balikpapan by the daylight groups encountered heavy fighter resistance, and while several of the planes were badly shot up, all recovered to home base. The Japanese threw themselves into repairing the refinery complex, buttressing their defenses, and prepared for the next attacks. These would come a full year later from the combined bomb groups of FEAF and this time the 868th would have its place in the forefront of the renewed and expanded bomber offensive. Steve Birdsall's *Flying Buccaneers: The Illustrated Story of Kenney's Fifth Air Force* (Garden City, NY: Doubleday, 1977) provides a good narrative of the August 1943 missions.

7 Standard Mission Report 868-346 of 868th Bombardment Squadron, of 14 October 1944 (SECRET).

8 Standard Mission Report 868-374 of 868th Bombardment Squadron, of 1 November 1944 (SECRET).

9 Hata Ikuhiko, Izawa Yasuho and Christopher Shores, *Japanese Naval Air Force Fighter Units and Their Aces, 1932–1945* (London: Grub Street, 2011).

10 Historical Data for September 1944. The author of this prose cannot confirm, but is believed to have been the hand of the then recently arrived assistant S-2 for Intelligence, one Lieutenant Milton Mishkin, who regarded himself to be something of a novelist.

11 Smith provides more detail on this event and several others in Chapter 17.

12 The Sansapor Airfield area, located on the Vogelkop Peninsula at the northwestern tip of New Guinea, was taken in a U.S. Army amphibious operation on 31 July 1944. Also known as Mar Airstrip, Sansapor was carved out of the jungle and beach area by battalions of U.S. Army Engineers. It was declared open for business for fighter aircraft in mid-August and for bomber staging on 3 September. A better airfield site was identified and developed on nearby Middleburg Island and the Sansapor/Mar airfield was left to host Fifth Air Force fighter and medium bomber squadrons as a "forward operational facility" rather than a base. But it did serve its purpose for the 868th and other B-24 units as it provided a staging point to extend mission range and a recovery point for damaged aircraft that could not make it to their home base.

13 Standard Mission Report 868-363, 868th Bombardment Squadron, 25 October 1944 (SECRET). The Allied code name "Rufe" was assigned to the Imperial Navy's Nakajima A6M2-N, a monoplane single-float fighter derived from the Mitsubishi A6M2 Zero that served on the front lines of Japanese naval aviation throughout the war. "Rufes" flew in the Solomons and the Aleutians and, at the end of the war, over the Home Islands. Given that the 868th aircrew were reporting "biplane single-float aircraft" as active in the area, it is likely the seaplanes the squadron SB-24s encountered over Balikpapan and strafed in Puerto Princesa harbor were not "Rufes," but "Petes." In the Japanese lexicon, these were Mitsubishi F1M reconnaissance aircraft, or the "Type Zero Observation Seaplane." Nearly a thousand "Petes" were built during the war and many were active in the Dutch East Indies as convoy escorts during the 1944–45 period.

14 Standard Mission Report 868-357, 868th Bomb Squadron (Heavy) of 21 October 1944 and Historical Data for the Month of October 1944, 868th Bomb Squadron (H) of 30 November 1944.

15 John Prados, *Storm Over Leyte: The Philippines Invasion and the Destruction of the Japanese Navy* (New York, NY: NAL Caliber, 2016).

16 Kenneth I. Friedman, *Afternoon of the Rising Sun—The Battle of Leyte Gulf* (Novato, CA: Presidio Press, 2009).

17 Discussions with 868th Squadron veterans in person and in correspondence, August 1978 through July 1982, as well as discussions with John Prados.

Chapter 16: The Philippines, November–December 1944

1   *Reports of General MacArthur: The Campaigns of MacArthur in the Pacific, Volume I,* chapters VII and VIII, prepared by the General Staff of the General Headquarters, 1950, as further published in 1966, with a foreword by Harold K. Johnson, General of the United States Army, Chief of Staff, Washington D.C., 1966.

2   In the months that followed the formal Japanese surrender on 3 September 1945, some 100,000 Japanese Army and Navy personnel were repatriated home from the Philippines, amid the massive flow of Japanese military and civilians returning home from all over the theater. MacArthur would soon have his personal revenge for the Japanese-organized resistance in the Philippines by stage-managing, from his perch at General Headquarters in Tokyo, a "war crimes" show trial in Manila that would convict General Yamashita of high crimes and hang him.

3   Squadron Operations Diary for Month of November 1944, 868th Bomb Squadron, a report to Commanding General, Thirteenth Air Force, 30 November 1944. At this point in the war, with the devastation delivered on the Japanese merchant fleet, the empire was forced to enlist a larger number of smaller merchant vessels to move its cargo and troops, including coastal shipping. The FEAF instituted a recognition program to classify these ships by size and configuration. The "Fox Tare Able or Baker" series of guides were used in defining these ships and reporting mission results.

4   Squadron Operations Diary for Month of November 1944 and interviews and correspondence with two 868th command pilots, Earle Smith and Art DeLand, during 1979–81.

5   Squadron Historical Data for Month of December 1944, 868th Bomb Squadron, 10 February 1945.

6   Squadron Historical Data for Month of December 1944 and 868th Squadron Mission reports 868-435 and 868-437.

7   General Orders Number 227, Headquarters Far East Air Force, 7 February 1945, of interest to the crew of Earle Smith in later years was the fact that this DFC Citation reflected a second navigator on this flight, Lieutenant Louis Fillios, making the crew that day 11 in all. As noted in the text, Lieutenant Gene Morgan, a member of the Smith crew since its formation in the spring of 1944, was severely wounded three days later and died of his injuries on Christmas Day 1944.

8   Standard Mission Report 868-440, 868th Bombardment Squadron, 12 December 1944.

9   "What Four Snoopers Did to Lutong," Intelligence Section of XIII Bomber Command, 23 December 1944, drafted as a "special report" by Captain Stewart Baldwin, the 868th Squadron intelligence officer. This was released by the authority of Colonel Robert Totten, the A-2 of XIII Bomber Command, and was a five-page document that combined the Squadron Historical Data narrative, individual mission reports and interviews with the crews involved, later released in a slightly edited version to *Air Force Magazine* and other publications.

10 A formal roster of the men lost in the disappearance of the 868th C-47 can be found in Appendix F of this book. In the months and years that followed, considerable speculation occurred as to what could have happened in the course of this fairly routine flight over mostly friendly territory. The possibility of mechanical failure (loss of one or both engines), navigational error, or a random shoot-down have been suggested. On this fateful flight, the first pilot (George Thompson), his two co-pilots (William Wilkenson and Wendell Seas), as well as the three navigators on the aircraft (John Meisenhelder, William Taylor and Thomas Touchstone) were all experienced airmen, and this fact deepened the mystery. To many of the men of the 868th who would pilot future "Fat Cat" or C-47 flights to Australia, this loss of two full crews came as a wake-up call, notifying one and all that no flight in the South Pacific, whether combat or operational, could ever be considered "routine." At the end of the war, in September 1945, as the squadron was preparing to return home for demobilization, there were rumors, all apparently unfounded, that one or more of the missing airmen, had "walked out of the jungle," had been recovered and had gone home. Records do not support this revelation, but

far stranger things have happened. If any clarity on the missing aircraft and its occupants had been subsequently made a matter of record along the way, it had not been communicated to those to whom it would have mattered, namely their fellow airmen of the squadron. A further commentary on the loss of this aircraft and the embarked 20 men of the 868th Squadron is contained in Chapter 17 and is further addressed in the cited Appendix F.

Chapter 17: Captain Earle Smith and Lieutenant Ron Moyer, August 1944

1   Operations Order Number 5, Headquarters 1504th Air Base Unit, Pacific Division, Air Transport Command, Fairfield-Suisun Army Air Base, Fairfield, California, 5 August 1944, directed three crews and their aircraft to report to the Far East Air Force Combat and Training Center at Port Moresby, New Guinea, for onward assignment. The three crews, by pilot/co-pilot names and aircraft numbers, were those of Earl Smith/Eugene Morgan (44-40897), Robert Wallace/Philip Whitehead (44-40902) and James Fredrickson/William Beaver (44-40898).

2   Interviews and correspondence with Colonel (retired) Earle Smith during 1978–82, plus his personnel records for 1943–45.

3   Interviews and correspondence with Lieutenant Colonel (retired) Ronald Moyer during 1978–81, plus his personnel records for 1943–45.

4   The author has been unable to determine if this aircraft has been found or any remains recovered. Although the interviews with Smith and other 868th veterans provided much more information than was available in any of the squadron records accessed, there remain important gaps involved in reconstructing this event. The loss of the C-47 remained an enduring mystery, at least with the men of the 868th, through 2000 and beyond. Wewak remained a bypassed stronghold through to the end of the war, one of the largest Japanese garrisons isolated by the Allied drive across the Pacific. As such, it posed a latent threat, much like other bypassed garrisons at Rabaul and Truk. VJ Day saw the 6th Division of the Australian Army pressing in on the enclave but the Japanese still offering determined resistance. MacArthur's *Reports of General MacArthur: The Campaigns of MacArthur in the Pacific, Volume I*, notes some 136,000 Japanese Army and Navy personnel were active in eastern New Guinea at war's end and did not surrender until 6 September 1945. Because the "Wewak Garrison" area extended far beyond the coastal area and airfields of Wewak proper, it is possible any deviation to the north by the C-47 from its intended flight path would have brought it within range of the anti-aircraft guns there.

5   Coinciding with the preparation of this book, in October 2017 the remains of a B-24D Liberator were discovered in the waters of Hansa Bay off Wewak, New Guinea. The aircraft, *Heaven Can Wait*, flew with the 320th Bombardment Squadron of the 90th Bombardment Group of the Fifth Air Force. It had gone down on 11 March 1944 during the above-mentioned Fifth Air Force offensive directed against the greater Wewak airfield complex and port facilities. The aircraft was brought down by the anti-aircraft batteries that continued to defend Wewak and carried 11 men to their deaths. The B-24 was discovered by "Project Recover," a not-for-profit collection of American businessmen, scientists and archaeologists who banded together to form a research team as part of a broader effort to recover the remains of U.S. airmen lost in the Pacific War. As of the date of this publication, it is believed human remains at the site have not yet been recovered by the U.S. Department of Defense entities responsible for such work.

Chapter 18: Tough Times, January–February 1945

1   Britain's Royal Navy, having returned to the Pacific, also contributed to the beachhead's defense by repeatedly attacking the airfields of the Sakashima Gunto, a string of islands used as stepping stones by Japanese aircraft heading to Okinawa from Formosa. The British Pacific Fleet was also subjected to suicide attacks.

2   Two recent volumes that capture in great detail the Allied march across the Central Pacific during the final 18 months of the war are Hornfischer's *The Fleet at Flood Tide* and Toll's *Twilight of the Gods*.

3   Two contemporary books providing an objective overview of the Luzon Campaign and the battle for Manila, are Richard Connaughton, John Pimlott and Duncan Anderson, *The Battle for Manila: The Most Devastating Untold Story of World War II* (London: Bloomsbury Publishing Plc, 1995) and James M. Scott, *Rampage: MacArthur, Yamashita, and the Battle of Manila* (New York, NY: W. W. Norton & Company, 2018).

4   "Nisei" refers to the "second-generation" Americans of Japanese ancestry that made up the majority of personnel of the 442nd Infantry Regimental Combat Team. In April 1945, both Dole and Inouye would be critically wounded and require years of hospitalization and recovery. Both maimed for life, Dole would be the Republican Presidential candidate in 1996 and Inouye would continue to serve in the U.S. Senate until his death, receiving the Medal of Honor from President Bill Clinton in 2000.

5   The suspected author of this uplifting narrative is Lieutenant Mishkin, the squadron's deputy S-2.

6   LORAN, long range navigation enabled by calculating the delay between two simultaneous signals (blips on a screen) transmitted by ground stations. If the time taken for the signal of one station to reach the other station is known, then the distance from both stations can be worked out. As there could be several possible locations based on the time delays, the operator then had to refine the calculation with further measurements, before applying "traditional" navigation practices to work out an exact position.

7   868th Squadron Weekly Activity Report for Period Ending 20 January 1945.

8   Per Chapter 17. The landing itself, including the photos of the broken aircraft from which the Smith crew was ejected, or extracted by the crash responders, has received attention in several publications, some of which misidentify the aircraft and its unit.

9   868th Squadron Monthly History Report, 7 January 1945.

10 Conversations and correspondence during 1978–81 with 868th Squadron veterans on the various issues faced by the unit in early 1945.

11 Weekly Activity Report for Period Ending 10 February 1945.

12 Interview and correspondence with Harlan Price, 1979.

Chapter 19: Turnaround and Baylis Harriss, March 1945

1   868th Bombardment Squadron Standard Mission Report 868-526 of 7 March 1945. The author could find no reference to this attack in the Japanese-informed TROM databases for any of the Japanese aircraft carriers still in operation on the date of this attack (6 March 1945), recorded as 00°29'N and 117°48'E. Because the available TROM information is often incomplete, or does not cover aircraft transport ships operated by the Japanese Army, it is possible that this ship was an escort carrier and was successfully attacked but only damaged. In such a case, if this same vessel was damaged, only to be later attacked and sunk by other Allied aircraft or submarines, there would be no credit assigned post-war to the 868th. TROM information may be found on the valuable website "Nihon Kaigun—Imperial Japanese Navy Page" at www.combinedfleet.com. Given the detail included in the after-action account, Mission Report (868-526/6), including precise radar images, the course and speed of the ship, the fact that eight airborne aircraft were detected operating above the vessel, the low altitude of the LAB attack (1100 feet) and the bomb damage observed, it is difficult to discount the probability of a successful attack. It is also possible that the ship attacked on this date was a large merchantman or tanker which was misidentified as an escort carrier.

2   The 868th Bombardment Squadron Weekly Activity Report, 13 March 1945. Barry and crew had struck the San Roque Airdrome on Zamboanga Island three days before the 10 March crash in a pre-invasion surge that targeted Japanese airfields on that island and nearby. The Zamboanga invasion

went off without a hitch as the U.S. Army's 41st Division waded ashore and pushed the Japanese back into Mindanao proper.

3 868th Bombardment Squadron Standard Mission Reports 868-552, 868-557 and 868-563 of 20 March, 25 March and 31 March 1945.

4 The Associated Press story "Orchids to the 13th Air Force" is undated but believed to have been filed in late February 1945.

5 Interview and correspondence with 868th Squadron veteran Harlan Price, co-pilot with the Charles Binford crew, 1979–80.

6 The 868th Bombardment Squadron Historical Data for the Month of March 1945. It is very obvious from this declaration of adulation that the previously identified 868th Squadron Assistant S-2, with the squadron's typewriter supply fully replenished and operating in new quarters on Morotai, was allowed to attain ever-higher levels of creative composition in the monthly reporting.

Chapter 20: Morotai Missions, April 1945

1 868th Squadron Standard Mission Report 868-623, 24 April 1945. On this mission, the Harriss–Rogers–Putnam threesome flew aircraft 397, 464 and 129 respectively, with Harris and Rogers crossing the harbor at 13,000 feet and Putnam arriving one minute later at 300 feet but crossing the target on a different heading.

2 F—d/Fouled Up Beyond All Repair/Recognition.

3 Although Colonel Dolan would play a key role in the prototype testing and qualification of the H2X system, his death in a B-24 in Newfoundland would, as stated earlier, be in connection with the development of a related follow-on airborne radar system, the APQ-7.

4 "Twelve Radar Bombers Keep Skies Open for the Eighth," *Radar* magazine, Issue One. The H2X or AN/APS-15, or more typically the "APS-15," was also referred to as "Mickey" and was the standard "BTO" or Bombing Through Overcast radar system. A recent publication, Norman Fine's *Blind Bombing: How Microwave Radar Brought the Allies to D-Day and Victory in World War II* (Lincoln, NE: Potomac Books, 2019) is useful but, as the subtitle suggests, somewhat overstates the importance of the H2X in the winning of the war in Europe. Its description of the process that took the British-supplied cavity magnetron to the ASV systems installed on Dolan's B-18s to the H2X development and deployment is adequate, as is the discussion of the "Mickey" in combat over Germany.

5 "The Work of the Ferrets," *Radar* magazine, Issue Four, August 1944, CONFIDENTIAL, 21–27; "The Search for Japanese Radar," *Radar* magazine, Issue Ten, June 1945, 9–11; "B-24 Bomber Out Looking for Ships Does 3-in-1 Job on Japanese Radar Instead," *Radar* magazine, Issue Eight, February 1945, 33; and "The Japanese Radar Net," *Radar* magazine, Issue 8, 1945, 29–33.

6 William Cahill, "Ferret: Evolution," *Air Power History*, Winter 2015, and "Far East Air Forces RCM Operations on the Final Push on Japan," *Air Power History*, Spring 2018. These two articles collectively provide an exceptionally detailed account of the deployment and operations of RCM aircraft in the Pacific Theater during World War II. These articles include mention of the 868th Squadron's *Lady June II* and suggest it was probably a "theater-built" RCM aircraft; that is, it arrived in the Pacific as a standard B-24J. This assessment by Cahill, as borne out in the text, is accurate. As the Cahill articles note, at least until early 1945, the RCM aircraft in the South Pacific Theater were "owned" and controlled by the Southwest Pacific Area's Chief Signal Officer Section 22, as opposed to the Fifth or Thirteenth Air Forces' bomb groups. It is likely that incoming squadron commander Harriss, noting this lack of control, arranged for an incoming B-24J to be transferred into the squadron to be converted to an RCM aircraft with the assistance of the local FEAF Section 22 personnel. Nevertheless, *Lady June II*/464 played the RCM role well and remained a dependable member of the squadron's team for the balance of the war.

Another William Cahill article, "Thirteenth Air Force Radio Countermeasures Operations, 1944–45," *Air Power History* (Summer 2017), 9–28, discusses both the "custom-built" RCM aircraft that arrived in theater already fully built-out for their RCM role, as well as the "ad-hoc" or theater-built RCM Ferrets such as *Lady June II*. The article includes a detailed description of the equipment installed and the critical role of Field Unit 13 of the Section 22 group mentioned in the text.

7   Interviews and correspondence with Earle Smith in 1978–81.

8   868th Squadron Historical Data for the Month of April 1945.

9   Alfred Price, *The History of U.S. Electronic Warfare: The Years of Innovation Beginning to 1946; Vol. 1* (Arlington, VA: The Association of Old Crows, 1984).

10 While several chapters in Price's book reference developments directly or indirectly related to the 868th, the two most relevant are chapter 14 "Countermeasures Aide the Island Hoppers" and chapter 15 "Climax in the Pacific." The book was published by the Association of Old Crows, with contributions from Rad Lab ECM researchers, systems builders and airmen, complete with forewords by General Curtis LeMay and Senator Barry Goldwater. The full text of the memo creating the RCM Laboratory is provided, as is a subsequent memo chartering the overall RCM effort as a national wartime priority and recognizing this as an entirely new form of warfare.

11 868th Squadron Historical Data for the Month of April 1945.

Chapter 21: Bob Thompson and Crew, November 1944–June 1945

1   This chapter developed from 11 exchanges of letters between the author and Bob Thompson during 1979–80.

2   Steve Smith, "Ramp Tramp Revived," *Shreveport Journal*, 13 July 1979. This museum, also known at one time as the Eighth Air Force Museum, subsequently evolved to become the Barksdale Global Power Museum and is located on Barksdale Air Force Base near Bossier City, Louisiana. This facility was established in 1979 by World War II Army Air Force veterans and the B-24 was the second aircraft to be acquired for restoration, the first being a B-17 Flying Fortress. As of 2021, some 20 aircraft are on display, including a B-29 Superfortress, a B-58 Hustler and an SR-71 Blackbird. The restoration of the Ford-manufactured B-24J (44-48781) is a continuing project. More can be learned at www.barksdaleglobalpowermuseum.com.

Chapter 22: Strangling the Empire, Morotai Operations, May–June 1945

1   The Mansyū Ki-79, or the Japanese Army Type 2 advanced trainer, was manufactured by the Manchuria Airplane Manufacturing Company (*Manshūkoku Hikōki Seizo KK*) located in Harbin, Manchukuo (the Japanese puppet state). Its attraction for an expeditious return to the Home Islands rested in large part on the fact that it was a metal-framed, wood-clad aircraft. As such, as the Japanese had discovered, the aircraft was almost invisible to U.S. air-search radar systems. Its low radar return made it a prime candidate for suicide missions. The Mansyū factory produced nearly 2,200 aircraft, almost all being Ki-79 trainers. The vignette on the travel of the Kuantan-based Ki-79 aircrew was developed in discussions between the author and former Japanese Army Air Force First Lieutenant Kim Doo-Bang in Seoul, Korea, in 1978. Postwar, Kim returned to his native Korea and served as a career Ministry of Transportation official, retiring in 1975 as the Director of the Civil Aviation Bureau of the Republic of Korea. For a profile of the Ki-79, see Rene Francillon, *Japanese Aircraft of the Pacific War* (London: Putnam & Company, 1979), a comprehensive presentation of all Japanese aircraft in service during World War II.

2   David G. Oakley with George D. Oakley, Jr. *On the Fiery Breath of Dragons* (Carroll, IA: Stone Printing, 2008). A very personal story informed by the wartime diary of George Oakley, a young man from Iowa who served with 307th Bomb Group from September 1944 to May 1945.

3   868th Squadron Historical Summary for May 1945. The 10 868th crews that attacked Surabaya on 9 May included those of Harriss (397), Olsen (464), McDaniel (395), Reidy (808), Workman (131), Sheely (358), Smitherman (357), Sprawls (899), Thompson (129) and Bartelemes (810).

4   Interview and correspondence with Earle Smith during 1978–81. After the war, Smith remained in the U.S. Air Force, secured his graduate degree from the University of Southern California and served as an Air Force "acceptance test pilot" for the P-80, the T-33 and the F-94 Starfire at the Lockheed Aircraft facility. During his tour in Europe, he flew British Hawker Hunters and was later assigned to the U.S. Air Force Academy as an instructor, retiring in 1968. His second career was with Lockheed Corporation as a program monitor.

5   868th Bombardment Squadron Weekly Activity Reports for 8, 14, 21 and 28 May 1945.

6   Major General Hugh J. Casey, *Engineers in Theater Operations: Engineers of the Southwest Pacific 1941–1945; Vol. 1.* (General Headquarters Army Forces Pacific, Tokyo, Japan: U.S. Army, 1947).

7   868th Squadron Standard Mission Report 868-709, 3–4 June 1945. The seven 868th crews and aircraft that attacked Batavia's Tanjung Priok seaplane base were that of Harriss (397), Reidy (308), McDaniel (395), Albert (464), Putnam (131), Bartelmes (107) and Olsen (808).

8   868th Squadron Standard Mission Report 868-748 and 868-751 of 19 and 20 June, respectively.

9   The forms required to report the previous theft that had occurred during the move from Noemfoor to Morotai had still not arrived. Lesson learned, the equipment shipped by boat to Okinawa would be accompanied and guarded by squadron personnel at all times.

Chapter 23: Morotai to Okinawa via Leyte, July 1945

1   868th Bomb Squadron Standard Mission Reports of 1–21 July 1945.

2   868th Bomb Squadron Standard Mission Reports 868-794 and 868-799 of 22 and 24 July 1945.

3   868th Bomb Squadron Standard Mission Report 868-791 of 26 July 1945.

4   In a second story that did not feature the 868th itself, the intrepid correspondent introduced himself to a group of Michigan men who were training on Okinawa for the occupation of Japan. The article was dated 25 August, 10 days after the Japanese surrender and a few days before the actual occupation was to begin. The article appeared in the Sunday 26 August 1945 edition and was entitled "Michigan Men Eager for Takeoff to Japan." A second headline read "Sergeant Expects Some 'Small Wars' but Nothing Like Any Serious Trouble." Carlisle wrote that the men had been told they were going into Japan, to land at Atsugi Airbase as General MacArthur's elite escort, on the following Tuesday, 28 August 1945. A quote from these veterans of the Philippines campaign is notable, describing the men to be restless and eager to get their boots on the ground in Tokyo. The war correspondent noted the men were busy "oiling and cleaning their Garands and Browning Automatic Rifles in the meantime, with that cool efficiency of top-notch fighting men." The article goes on to list by name, hometown in Michigan and street address, some 93 men serving with this unit. He seeks out Sergeant Robert E. Long, a 23-year-old squad leader from Detroit, decorated with the Silver and Bronze Stars for combat leadership in earlier Pacific campaigns, for a man's take on the upcoming occupation duty. Carlisle reports a quiet confidence that Long's men can "handle anything that happens" in Japan. The list of names is impressive for the range of nationalities present, seeming to represent almost every American ethnicity, from Halliday to Morenci, Broda, Kozlowski and Eschiliman. Catching this front-page story back home in Detroit or Flint or Paw Paw, Michigan, on a quiet Sunday morning, it is likely the reader would have then realized these same airborne infantrymen, without the Japanese capitulation on 15 August, would have been among the first to parachute into Kyūshū two months later. In that engagement on the soil of Japan, the U.S. General Staff expected casualty rates to reach 50 percent

or more of the invading U.S. force. Just how many of these young Michigan men's lives were saved by the twin atomic bombings that forced Japan's surrender is impossible to know. A reasonable guess is that 50 of the men listed would be dead or wounded within weeks of their opposed landing had the war not ended when it did. Instead, they were destined for a peaceful occupation duty with a compliant Japan before heading home a few months later to demobilization and onward movement to their families in Michigan. Appendix M provides a listing of the 23 stories filed by war correspondent Carlisle as they appeared in *The Detroit News* over the period 5–27 August 1945.

5   868th Bomb Squadron Historical Data for July 1945, dated 20 August 1945.

Chapter 24: Okinawa and Japan, August 1945

1   868th Bomb Squadron (Heavy) Historical Data for August 1945.

2   D. M. Giangreco, *Hell to Pay: Operation Downfall and the Invasion of Japan, 1945–47* (Annapolis, MD: Naval Institute Press, 2009). This book was originally published in 2009 and was substantially updated in 2017 with more recently secured research. The foreword was authored by military and political historian Stanley Weintraub. Three sentences in that foreword suffice to capture the essence of the Giangreco book: "The Japanese military culture had, historically, long rejected surrender. Okinawa was not a worst-case scenario, it was a reality. The far more extensive killing ground of Japan was waiting to happen," ix.

3   Richard B. Frank's *Downfall: The End of The Imperial Japanese Empire* (New York, NY: Random House, 1999). Frank's book was published to much attention and acclaim, so much so that he managed to outdo his previous *Guadalcanal: The Definitive Account of the Landmark Campaign* (New York, NY: Penguin, 1990). One of the more interesting aspects of Frank's account is the reference to U.S. active considerations of the use of nuclear weapons in tactical or battlefield scenarios during Operation *Coronet*, the fight on Kyūshū.

4   These mission-specific details were derived from 868th Squadron Standard Mission Reports Number 868-804 through 868-811 over the period 8–10 August 1945.

5   The atomic bomb missions to Hiroshima and Nagasaki (Kokura) are extremely well detailed in Don A. Farrell's *Atomic Bomb Island: Tinian, the Last Stage of the Manhattan Project, and the Dropping of the Atomic Bombs on Japan in World War II* (Guilford, CT: Stackpole Books, 2020).

6   Details from 868th Squadron Standard Mission Reports Number 868-814 through 868-816 over the period 11–13 August 1945.

Chapter 25: Coming Home, September–October 1945

1   868th Bomb Squadron (Heavy) Historical Data for the Month of September 1945.

2   The typhoon that struck Okinawa on 17 September, Typhoon Ida or the "Makurazaki Typhoon" to the Japanese, was and remains the strongest to ever strike the island, as measured in minimum sea level pressure and wind intensity. A few days before, Typhoon Ursula, tracking a similar course toward Japan as Ida but bypassing Okinawa, destroyed six U.S. aircraft ferrying just-liberated Allied prisoners of war between Okinawa and Manila, killing over 120 personnel. This was the greatest loss of life in an aviation disaster in peacetime recorded up to that point. The 1945 Western Pacific typhoon season was one of the most violent on record then or since. Earlier that same month, when the 868th arrived on Okinawa on 1 August and began offloading from transport ships, the island and the squadron were threatened by Typhoon Helen, a relatively weak sister with winds of "only" 120 miles per hour. It missed a direct strike on Okinawa but badly beat up Formosa and then slammed into the coast of China.

3   868th Bomb Squadron Historical Data for the Month of September 1945.

4   Incomplete records suggest that at the time the redeployment of the squadron began in September 1945 some 24 combat crews were on orders dated October 1945 to return home. The last six crews remaining on Okinawa included those of Lieutenants George Grupe, Jack Shattuck, Wallace Palmer, Warren Hoover, Richard Elston and Donald Sark. The source of this information is Dr. Vince Splane, writing in *Snooper News* No. 2.

5   Author's interview and correspondence with Butch Moyer during the period 1978–82. See photos taken by Moyer at the Nadzab boneyard during his 1946 encounter with the remains of the SB-24s in which he had flown.

6   Many authors have had a turn at defining and describing the phenomenon of men who hate war but love the experience of it. A recent publication by Nolan Peterson, *Why Soldiers Miss War: The Journey Home* (Havertown, PA: Casemate Publishers, 2019), does a reasonably good job of discussing this issue. To many of the men of the 868th who knew Baylis Harriss and watched him in his element, meticulously planning, organizing and leading combat missions, his death and the manner in which he passed came as no surprise. As Captain Earle Smith commented to the author in an interview in 1981, "Baylis Harriss was the finest combat leader I ever met, and the finest individual I had the pleasure of knowing in that war." Enough said.

Chapter 26: The "Other Snoopers": The Scott and Hopson SB-24 Projects, 1943–45

1   George C. Kenney, *General Kenney Reports, USAF Warrior Studies.* (New York: Duell, Sloan, 1949).

2   Interestingly, while Edward Scott is mentioned in the early chapters of Kenney's autobiography, he does not reappear until relatively late in the war, on page 402, with Kenney noting that in June 1944 "ten B-24s of Lieutenant Ed Scott's 63rd Squadron, using the new radar bomb-sight made contact east of the Halmaheras and went to work." At this point, the Scott Project, operating as the 63rd Bomb Squadron, had been in action for nine months.

3   Birdsall, *Flying Buccaneers.*

4   Movement Order Number 3, Headquarters First Sea Search Attack Group (Restricted) of 25 September 1943, provides details of the dispatch from Langley Field of the Scott Project, comprising "twelve B-24 replacement combat crews, forty-eight officers, seventy-two enlisted men plus a Provisional Flight Leader and one Technical Officer and two technical enlisted men," for a total Scott Project group of 124 officers and men. The accompanying Special Orders Number 195 of the same date listed the aircrews and aircraft involved.

5   The partial listing of the aircraft that served with the 63rd Squadron during the 22 months of combat with the Fifth Air Force is found at the "Ken's Men" website http://kensmen.com/birds. This listing appears to assign names to nine of the 12 Scott Project B-24D models when compared to the original Movement and Operations Orders. Other Liberator listings, including Wallace R. Forman's *B-24 Nose Art Name Directory—Includes Group, Squadron and Aircraft Serial Numbers and Photo Availability* (North Branch, MN: Specialty Press, 1996), have been compiled by dedicated B-24 enthusiasts over many decades of research, but this effort is far from complete. In the case of this publication, some of the 868th Squadron aircraft are listed with the two B-24 bomb groups of XIII Bomber Command, that is the 5th and 307th Bomb Groups and there is no separate entry for the 868th. It appears the only 868th aircraft and crew whose photograph appears in this compilation is that of *Lady Luck II*, posed with the crew of Lieutenant Upfield. In the case of the 63rd Squadron, such aircraft that are listed in the B-24 Nose Art Directory fall appropriately within the parent Fifth Air Force 43rd Bomb Group. Other websites have taken up the challenge of matching the aircraft names, their "nose art," with the serial numbers and the units in which they flew. All of these efforts are commendable but there is considerable speculation involved in all these efforts.

6   Colonel Scott is well-profiled in John S. Alcorn's book *The Jolly Rogers—History of the 90th Bomb Group During World War II* (Temple City, CA: Historical Aviation Album Publication, 1981). The "Jolly Rogers" was the 90th Bomb Group of the Fifth Air Force and Scott became the commanding officer of that group in June 1944. In the 63rd Squadron, he had served with the Fifth's sister B-24 group, the 43rd Bomb Group, or "Ken's Men" as that unit was known. This excellent unit history also includes a brief mention of "Radar Raiders" describing the SeaHawks crossing group lines to operate with the Jolly Rogers in the early weeks of 1945. Brigadier General Scott would subsequently command Strategic Air Command Wings, those of the 95th Bomb Wing (B-36) and the 22nd Bomb Wing (B-47), both nuclear weapons alert forces during the hottest days of the Cold War. He later commanded the U.S. Air Force's Air Command and Staff College. He died in a civilian aircraft incident in October 1968 while on active duty in Germany.

7   A ready reference for the three major U.S. Army Air Forces flying B-24s in the Pacific Theater, at least from the east toward Japan, namely the Fifth, Thirteenth and Seventh, is provided in Dorr's *B-24 Liberator Units of the Pacific War*. A fine photograph of the 868th SB-24 *Munda Belle* (144) appears, in company with excellent drawings of the 63rd Squadron's *Out of the Night II*, and what is purported to be the 868th's first *Lady June*. The book also includes a pristine photograph of a B-24J named *Our Baby*. This is not the aircraft of the same name flown by the 868th. This *Our Baby* flew with the 30th Bomb Group of the Seventh Air Force and was lost with its entire crew in December 1943.

8   Stephen M. Perrone, *World War II B-24 "Snoopers": Low Level Bombing Targets Manila Bay Shipping; The Story of WWII's Secret Anti-Shipping Night War Against the Japanese* (Somerdale, NJ: New Jersey Sportsmen's Guides, 2001).

9   Perone's book is also useful in defining the Scott Project's initial 12 crews by crew number, crew identities and aircraft serial numbers, as dispatched from Langley by a Movement Order dated 25 September 1943. The aircrews of the Wright Project are also listed. The balance of the book, that is, those chapters not adapted from the 868th *Snooper News* newsletters, highlight the missions of the 63rd and narrate the experiences of individual crew members on those missions. Of particular value are the verbatim diary entries of a member of Scott Project Crew Three, command pilot Arthur H. Millard. The author, Steven Perone, arrived in Dobodura in March 1944 as a member of one of the 12 replacement crews sent to reinforce the 63rd and thus offers firsthand knowledge of the SeaHawks from that point forward. In his preface he makes an interesting observation—that records relating to the operations of the Scott Project and the 63rd Squadron from the time of its arrival to serve with the Fifth Air Force, through most of 1944, are sketchy to non-existent.

10   Correspondence between the author and Colonel R. Frank Schirmer, USAF (Retired) during October–December 1983. Schirmer was then the historian of the U.S. Air Force (Army Air Force) Flying School Class of 40-A Association. An interesting aspect of this exchange was the fact that Schirmer served with his 40-A classmate, Lieutenant Colonel Wright, when both were assigned to the 9th Bomb Group in the Panama and Trinidad areas. Schirmer recalled his squadron commanding officer (Wright) taking a group of pilots with him to Boston to "take delivery of LB-30s with Yagi radar antennas and there to receive his initial briefings on LAB prototype equipment." It appears that Wright was then officially transferred to Boston's Rad Lab as the Army Air Corps' technical representative at Rad Lab sometime in early 1943.

11   Edward Young, *B-24 Liberator Units of the CBI* (Oxford: Osprey Publishing, 2011).

12   A. B. Feuer, *General Chennault's Secret Weapon: The B-24 in China* (Westport, CT: Praeger, 1992).

13   A. B. Feuer's book, as mentioned in the text, mostly relates the experiences of a single crew but does contain interesting details of that crew, its aircraft, movement orders and transit to the war front. Individual missions are described as are vignettes of successful attacks, frustrations encountered and survival when aircraft were shot down.

14 *Radar*, Volume Six, 15 November 1944, classified "Secret," 3–9, with articles subtitled "All the Damage to Date Has Been Done by a Handful of Planes," "Every Undertaking Must Be Measured in Pints of Gasoline and Ounces of Bombs," "Target off Formosa: A Typical Sortie," and "Training and Practice Get the Results." Of the publication's coverage of the 868th, the 63rd and Hopson Project aircrews, this series of articles is the most extensive and probably the most hyped. The full text of the *RADAR* article is provided in Appendix J.

15 In the category of aircraft detail, including excellent photography of the interior of the first generation of U.S. Navy Liberators, Steve Ginter's *Consolidated PB4Y-1/1P Liberator* (Simi Valley, CA: Ginter Books, 2017) has no equal. On the operational front, two books are recommended that provide the experience of combat in the Pacific, Alan C. Carey's *Above an Angry Sea: United States Navy B-24 Liberator and PB4Y Privateer Operations in the Pacific October 1944–August 1945* (Atglen, PA: Schiffer Publishing Ltd., 2001) and Ed Kittrell's *Solo into the Rising Sun: The Dangerous Missions of a U.S. Navy Bomber Squadron in World War II* (Guildford, CT: Stackpole Books, 2020).